Family in Transition

ELEVENTH EDITION

Arlene S. Skolnick

New York University

Jerome H. Skolnick

New York University

Allyn and Bacon

Boston • London • Toronto • Sydney • Tokyo • Singapore

Series Editor: *Jeff Lasser*
Editorial Assistant: *Susan Hutchinson*
Marketing Manager: *Judeth Hall*
Editorial-Production Service: *Omegatype Typography, Inc.*
Composition and Prepress Buyer: *Linda Cox*
Manufacturing Buyer: *Suzanne Lareau*
Cover Administrator: *Linda Knowles*
Electronic Composition: *Omegatype Typography, Inc.*

Library of Congress Cataloging-in-Publication Data

Family in transition / [edited by] Arlene S. Skolnick, Jerome H. Skolnick.—11th ed.
    p. cm.
  Includes bibliographical references and index.
  ISBN 0-205-32526-2 (alk. paper)
  1. Family. I. Skolnick, Arlene S. II. Skolnick, Jerome H.

HQ518 .F336 2001
306.85—dc21   00-040585

Contents

Preface

As in previous editions, we have had three aims in this version. First, we have tried to describe current trends in family life and place them in historical context. Second, we have tried to include articles representing the cutting edge of family scholarship and yet balance them with excellent older ones. Third, we have tried to select articles that are scholarly and yet understandable to an audience of undergraduates.

Among the new readings are the following:

- Anthony Giddens's exploration of how globalization and the information age are linked to a worldwide revolution in personal and family life.
- Robert M. Jackson's analysis of why modern societies are moving inexorably toward gender equality.
- Kathleen Gerson's study of how Generation X views changes in family life and gender roles.
- Kathryn Edin's study of why, for poor women, a good man is so hard to find.
- Barry Glassner's look at how the media distort the realities of U.S. family life through stories on "monster moms" and other supposed threats to the social fabric.
- Two articles on diversity *within* ethnic groups.

Again, we would like to thank all the people over the years who have helped us with suggestions for this book. Thanks also to Rifat Salam of the NYU Sociology department, whose literature searches, valuable suggestions, and general helpfulness made this edition possible.

Last but not least, thanks to the following reviewers who offered many good ideas for this edition:

Barbara Dobling	Kirkwood Community College
DeAnn D. Judge	North Carolina State University
Lynn Magdol	State University of New York, Buffalo
Scott M. Myers	Iowa State University
Louise Marie Roth	New York University
Barbara Ryan	Widener University
Rosalie Stone	University of Connecticut
Linda Wilcox	Southern Nazarene University
Diane Zablotsky	University of North Carolina, Charlotte

Introduction: Family in Transition

Cloning. Cyberspace. Dot.coms. Genetic engineering. The global economy. It is clear that in the opening decade of the twenty-first century, the world has entered into a period of profound transformation. "Every once in a while," states the introduction to *Business Week*'s issue on the twenty-first century, "the established order is overthrown. Within a span of decades, technological advances, organizational innovations, and new ways of thinking transform economies."

Although the state of the American family has been the subject of great public attention in recent years, the discussion of family has been strangely disconnected from talk of the other transformations we are living through. Instead, family talk is suffused with nostalgia and confusion—what happened, we wonder, to the fifties family of Ozzie and Harriet? Or as one prominent politician put it, "Why do we have all these problems we didn't have in 1955?"

The readings in this book show why this nostalgic approach to understanding the American family is seriously flawed. Of course family life has changed massively since the 1950s, and too many children and families are beset by serious stresses and troubles. But we can't understand these changes and problems without understanding the impact of large-scale changes in society on the small worlds of everyday family life. All the industrialized nations, and many of the emerging ones, have experienced the same changes the United States has—a transformation in women's roles, rising divorce rates, lower marriage and birth rates, and an increase in single-parent families. In no other country, however, has family change been so traumatic and divisive as in the United States.

Today most people live in ways that do not conform to the cultural ideal that prevailed in the 1950s. The traditional breadwinner/housewife family with minor children today represents only a small minority of families. The "typical" U.S. family is now likely to be one of four other kinds: the two-wage-earner family, the single-parent family, the "blended" family of remarriage, or the "empty nest" couple whose children have grown up and moved out. Apart from these variations, large numbers of people will spend part of their lives living apart from their families—as single young adults, as divorced singles, as older people who have lost a spouse. Furthermore, social and sexual rules that once seemed carved in stone have crumbled away. Unmarried couples now live together openly. Unmarried mothers keep their babies. Abortion has become legal. Remaining single and remaining childless, once thought to be highly deviant (though not illegal), have both become acceptable lifestyle options.

The changes of recent decades have affected more than the forms of family life; they have been psychological as well. A major study of U.S. attitudes over two decades

1

revealed a profound shift in how people think about family life, work, and themselves (Veroff, Douvan, and Kulka, 1981). In 1957 four-fifths of respondents thought that a man or woman who did not want to marry was sick, immoral, and selfish. By 1976 only one-fourth of respondents thought that choice was bad. Summing up many complex findings, the authors conclude that the United States underwent a "psychological revolution" in the two decades between surveys. Twenty years earlier, people defined their satisfaction and problems—and indeed themselves—in terms of how well they lived up to traditional breadwinner/housewife and mother roles. More recently, people have become more introspective, more attentive to inner experience. Fulfillment has come to mean finding intimacy, meaning, and self-definition.

Ever since the 1970s, the mass media have been serving up stories and statistics seemingly showing that the family is disintegrating, falling apart, or on the verge of disappearing. In the 1990s, the public discussion of family issues turned into a polarized, often angry political debate. In the 1992 election, then–Vice President Dan Quayle set off a firestorm by attacking the fictional television character Murphy Brown for having a child without being married. The show, according to Quayle, made a mockery of "the importance of fathers" and revealed "a poverty of values." The public clearly preferred candidate Clinton's definition of "family values" as "valuing families"—no matter what their form—traditional, two parent, one parent, or extended.

Yet less than a year after the election, "Dan Quayle was right" became the new national consensus. A sudden blizzard of newspaper columns, magazine articles, and talk show "experts" warned that divorce and single parenthood are inflicting serious damage on children and on society in general. This family structure, they argued, is the single biggest problem facing the country, because it is the root cause of all the rest—poverty, crime, drugs, school failure, youth violence, and other social ills.

The proposed solution? Restore the "traditional" family. Make divorce and single parenthood socially unacceptable once again. Do away with welfare and make divorces more difficult to obtain. These arguments flooded the media as welfare reform was being debated in Congress: both sides of the debate cited social science evidence to bolster their case. But putting social science into the middle of the "argument culture" (Tannen, 1998) that dominates our media and politics these days is not an effective way to deal with the complexities of either the research or family life itself.

Deborah Tannen points out that in the United States there is currently a pervasive warlike mentality that portrays any issue as a battle between two—and only two—opposing sides (1998). Popular political talk shows such as *Crossfire* and *Hardball*, which often amount to little more than shouting matches, are the most extreme examples. Such shows typically feature the most assertive advocates from each side. In general, arguments are regarded as newsworthy, while calm discussions of an issue are not. None of the media is immune, including newspapers and magazines. Howard Kurtz, a media critic, observes that "the middle ground, the sensible center, is dismissed as too squishy, too dull, too likely to send the audience channel-surfing" (1996, p. 4).

It's not surprising then that public debate about the family often sinks to the level of a "food fight" as it lurches from one hot topic to another—single mothers, divorce, gay marriage, nannies, and working mothers. Each issue has only two sides: Are you for or against the two-parent family? Is divorce bad for children? Should mothers of young children work or not? Is the family "in decline" or not?

The "two-sides" approach makes it difficult to realistically discuss the issues and problems facing the country. It doesn't describe the range of views among family scholars, and it doesn't fit the research evidence. For example, if someone takes the position that "divorce is damaging to children," the argument culture leads us to assume that there are people on the other "side" who will argue just the opposite—in other words, that divorce is "good," or at least not harmful. But as researcher Paul Amato suggests, the right question to ask is "Under what circumstances is divorce harmful or beneficial to children?" (1994). In most public debates about divorce, however, that question is never asked, and the public never hears the useful information they should. Moreover, the public never gets to hear what researchers have found out about what helps and what hurts children in divorced and single-parent families.

Still another problem with popular discourse about the family is that it exaggerates the extent of change. For example, we sometimes hear that the traditional nuclear family no longer exists, or has shrunk to a tiny percentage of the population. But that statement depends on a very narrow definition of family—two biological parents, in their first marriage, with a full-time breadwinner husband and a full-time homemaker wife, and two or three children under the age of 18. Of course that kind of family has declined for the simple reason that most wives and mothers now work outside the home. It has also declined because there are more married couples with grown children than there used to be.

Similarly, we hear that divorce rates have shot up since the 1950s, but we are not told that the trend toward higher divorce rates started in the nineteenth century, with more marital breakups in each succeeding generation. Nor do we hear that despite the current high divorce rates (actually down from 1979), the United States has the highest marriage rates in the industrial world. About 90 percent of Americans marry at some point in their lives, and virtually all who do either have, or want to have, children. Further, surveys repeatedly show that family is central to the lives of most Americans. They find family ties their deepest source of satisfaction and meaning, as well as the source of their greatest worries (Mellman, Lazarus, and Rivlin, 1990). In sum, family life in the United States is a complex mixture of both continuity and change.

While the transformations of the past three decades do not mean the end of family life, they have brought a number of new difficulties. For example, most families now depend on the earnings of wives and mothers, but the rest of society has not caught up to the new realities. There is still an earnings gap between men and women. Employed wives and mothers still bear most of workload in the home. For both men and women, the demands of the job are often at odds with family needs.

UNDERSTANDING THE CHANGING FAMILY

During the same years in which the family was becoming the object of public anxiety and political debate, a torrent of new research on the family was pouring forth. The study of the family had come to excite the interest of scholars in a range of disciplines—history, demography, economics, law, psychology. As a result of this research, we now have much more information available about the family than ever before. Ironically, much of the new scholarship is at odds with the widespread assumption that the family had a long, stable history until hit by the social "earthquake" of the 1960s and 1970s. We have learned from historians that the "lost" golden age of family happiness and stability we yearn for never actually existed.

Because of the continuing stream of new family scholarship, as well as shifts in public attitudes toward the family, each edition of *Family in Transition* has been different from the one before it. When we put together the first edition of this book in the early 1970s, the first rumblings of change were beginning to be felt. The youth movements of the 1960s and the emerging women's movement were challenging many of the assumptions on which conventional marriage and family patterns had been based. The mass media were regularly presenting stories that also challenged in one way or another traditional views on sex, marriage, and family. There was talk, for example, of "the population explosion" and of the desirability of "zero population growth." There was a growing perception that the ideal of the three-, four-, or five-child family of the 1950s was not necessarily good for the country as a whole, or for every couple.

Meanwhile, Hollywood movies were presenting a new and cynical view of marriage. It was almost taken for granted that marriages were unhappy, particularly if the spouses were middle class, middle aged, or affluent. Many people were defying conventional standards of behavior: College girls were beginning to live openly with young men, unwed movie actresses were publicizing rather than hiding their pregnancies, and homosexuals were beginning openly to protest persecution and discrimination.

It seemed as if something was happening to family life in the United States, even if there were no sharp changes in the major statistical indicators. People seemed to be looking at sex, marriage, parenthood, and family life in new ways, even if behavior on a mass scale was not changing very noticeably.

In putting together the readings for that first edition of *Family in Transition*, we found that the professional literature of the time seemed to deny that change was possible. An extreme version of this view was the statement by an anthropologist that the nuclear family (mother, father, and children) "is a biological phenomenon . . . as rooted in organs and physiological structures as insect societies" (LaBarre, 1954, p. 104). Any changes in the basic structure of family roles or in child rearing were assumed to be unworkable, if not unthinkable.

The family in modern society was portrayed as a streamlined, more highly evolved version of a universal family. According to the sociological theorist Talcott Parsons and his followers (1951, 1954), the modern family, with sharply contrasting male and female roles, had become more specialized. It transferred work and educational roles to other agencies and specialized in child rearing and emotional support. No less important for having relinquished certain tasks, the modern family was now the only part of society to carry out such functions.

The family theories of the postwar era were descriptively correct insofar as they portrayed the ideal middle-class family patterns of a particular society at a particular historical period. But they went astray in elevating the status quo to the level of a timeless necessity. In addition, the theories did not acknowledge the great diversity among families that has always existed in the United States.

Still another flaw in the dominant view was its neglect of internal strains within the family, even when it was presumably functioning as it was supposed to. Paradoxically, these strains were vividly described by the very theorists who idealized the role of the family in modern society. Parsons, for example, observed that when home no longer functioned as an economic unit, women, children, and old people were placed in an ambiguous position. They became dependent on the male breadwinner and were cut off from society's major source of achievement and status.

Parsons saw women's roles as particularly difficult: even at the height of the June Cleaver era, being a housewife was not seen as a real occupation; it was vaguely defined, highly demanding, yet not considered real work in a society that measures achievement by the size of one's paycheck. The combination of existing strains and the demystifying effects of the challenges to the family status quo seems to have provided, as Judith Blake (1978, p. 11) pointed out, a classic set of conditions for social change.

Part of the confusion surrounding the current status of the family arises from the fact that the family is a surprisingly problematic area of study; there are few if any self-evident facts, even statistical ones. Researchers have found, for example, that when the statistics of family life are plotted for the entire twentieth century, or back into the nineteenth century, a surprising finding emerges: Today's young people—with their low marriage, high divorce, and low fertility rates—appear to be behaving in ways consistent with long-term historical trends (Cherlin, 1981; Masnick and Bane, 1980). The recent changes in family life only appear deviant when compared to what people were doing in the 1940s and 1950s. But it was the postwar generation that married young, moved to the suburbs, and had three, four, or more children that departed from twentieth-century trends. As one study put it, "Had the 1940s and 1950s not happened, today's young adults would appear to be behaving normally" (Masnick and Bane, 1980, p. 2).

Thus, the meaning of change as a particular indicator of family life depends on the time frame in which it is placed. If we look at trends over too short a period of time— say ten or twenty years—we may think we are seeing a marked change, when, in fact, an older pattern may be reemerging. For some issues, even discerning what the trends are can be a problem.

For example, whether we conclude that there is an "epidemic" of teenage pregnancy depends on how we define adolescence and what measure of illegitimacy we use. Contrary to the popular notion of skyrocketing teenage pregnancy, teenaged childbearing has actually been on the decline during the past two decades (Luker, this volume). It is possible for the *ratio* of illegitimate births to all births to go up at the same time as there are declines in the *absolute number* of births and in the likelihood that an individual will bear an illegitimate child. This is not to say that concern about teenage pregnancy is unwarranted; but the reality is much more complex than the simple and scary notion an "epidemic" implies. Given the complexities of interpreting data on the family, it is little wonder that, as Joseph Featherstone observes (1979, p. 37), the family is a "great intellectual Rorschach blot."

1. *The Myth of the Universal Nuclear Family*

To say that the family is the same everywhere is in some sense true. Yet families vary in organization, membership, life cycles, emotional environments, ideologies, social and kinship networks, and economic and other functions. Although anthropologists have tried to come up with a single definition of family that would hold across time and place, they generally have concluded that doing so is not useful (Geertz, 1965; Stephens, 1963).

Biologically, of course, a woman and a man must unite sexually to produce a child—even if only sperm and egg meet in a test tube. But no social kinship ties or living arrangements flow inevitably from biological union. Indeed, the definition of marriage is not the same across cultures. Although some cultures have weddings and notions of monogamy and permanence, many cultures lack one or more of these attributes. In some cultures, the majority of people mate and have children without legal marriage and often without living together. In other societies, husbands, wives, and children do not live together under the same roof.

In our own society, the assumption of universality has usually defined what is normal and natural both for research and therapy and has subtly influenced our thinking to regard deviations from the nuclear family as sick or perverse or immoral. As Suzanne Keller (1971) once observed:

> The fallacy of universality has done students of behavior a great disservice. By leading us to seek and hence to find a single pattern, it has blinded us to historical precedents for multiple legitimate family arrangements.

2. The Myth of Family Harmony

To question the idea of the happy family is not to say that love and joy are not found in family life or that many people do not find their deepest satisfactions in their families. Rather, the happy-family assumption omits important, if unpleasant, aspects of family life. Intimate relations inevitably involve antagonism as well as love. This mixture of strong positive and negative feelings sets close relationships apart from less intimate ones.

Western society has not always assumed such a sentimental model of the family. From the Bible to the fairy tale, from Sophocles to Shakespeare, from Eugene O'Neill to the soap opera, there is a tragic tradition of portraying the family as a high-voltage emotional setting, charged with love and hate, tenderness and spite, even incest and murder.

There is also a low-comedy tradition. George Orwell once pointed out that the world of henpecked husbands and tyrannical mothers-in-law is as much a part of the Western cultural heritage as is Greek drama. Although the comic tradition tends to portray men's discontents rather than women's, it scarcely views the family as a setting for ideal happiness.

In recent years, family scholars have been studying family violence such as child abuse and wife beating to better understand the normal strains of family life. Long-known facts about family violence have recently been incorporated into a general analysis of the family. More police officers are killed and injured dealing with family fights than in dealing with any other kind of situation; of all the relationships between murderers and their victims, the family relationship is most common. Studies of family violence reveal that it is much more widespread than had been assumed, cannot easily be attributed to mental illness, and is not confined to the lower classes. Family violence seems to be a product of psychological tensions and external stresses that can affect all families at all social levels.

The study of family interaction has also undermined the traditional image of the happy, harmonious family. About three decades ago, researchers and therapists began to bring mental patients and their families together to watch how they behaved with one another. Oddly, whole family groups had not been systematically studied before.

At first the family interactions were interpreted as pathogenic: a parent expressing affection in words but showing nonverbal hostility; alliances being made between different family members; families having secrets; one family member being singled out as a scapegoat to be blamed for the family's troubles. As more and more families were studied, such patterns were found in many families, not just in those families with a schizophrenic child. Although this line of research did not uncover the cause of schizophrenia, it made an important discovery about family life: So-called normal families can often seem dysfunctional, or, in the words of one study, "difficult environments for interaction."

3. *The Myth of Parental Determinism*

The kind of family a child grows up in leaves a profound, lifelong impact. But a large body of recent research shows that early family experience is not the all-powerful, irreversible influence it has sometimes been thought to be. An unfortunate childhood does not doom a person to an unhappy adulthood. Nor does a happy childhood guarantee a similarly blessed future (Emde and Harmon, 1984; Macfarlane, 1964; Rubin, 1996).

First, children come into this world with their own temperamental and other individual characteristics. As parents have long known, child rearing is not like molding clay or writing on a blank slate. Rather, although parents are far more powerful, it's a two-way process in which both parent and child try to shape each other. Further, children are active perceivers and interpreters of the world. Finally, parents and children do not live in a social vacuum; children are also influenced by the world around them and the people in it—the kin group, the neighborhood, other children, the school, and the media.

4. *The Myth of a Stable, Harmonious Past*

Laments about the current state of decay of the family imply some earlier era when the family was more stable and harmonious. But unless we can agree what earlier time should be chosen as a baseline and what characteristics of the family should be specified, it makes little sense to speak of family decline. Historians have not, in fact, located a golden age of the family.

Indeed, they have found that premarital sexuality, illegitimacy, generational conflict, and even infanticide can best be studied as a part of family life itself rather than as separate categories of deviation. For example, William Kessen (1965), in his history of the field of child study, observes:

> Perhaps the most persistent single note in the history of the child is the reluctance of mothers to suckle their babies. The running war between the mother, who does not want to nurse, and the philosopher–psychologists, who insist she must, stretches over two thousand years. (pp. 1–2)

The most shocking finding of recent years is the prevalence of infanticide throughout European history. Infanticide has long been attributed to primitive peoples or assumed to be the desperate act of an unwed mother. It now appears that infanticide provided a major means of population control in all societies lacking reliable contraception, Europe included, and that it was practiced by families on legitimate children (Hrdy, 1999).

Rather than being a simple instinctive trait, having tender feelings toward infants—regarding a baby as a precious individual—seems to emerge only when infants have a decent chance of surviving and adults experience enough security to avoid feeling that children are competing with them in a struggle for survival. Throughout many centuries of European history, both of these conditions were lacking.

Another myth about the family is that of changelessness—the belief that the family has been essentially the same over the centuries, until recently, when it began to come apart. Family life has always been in flux; when the world around them changes, families change in response. At periods when a whole society undergoes some major transformation, family change may be especially rapid and dislocating.

In many ways, the era we are living through today resembles two earlier periods of family crisis and transformation in U.S. history (see Skolnick, 1991). The first occurred in the early nineteenth century, when the growth of industry and commerce moved work out of the home. Briefly, the separation of home and work disrupted existing patterns of daily family life, opening a gap between the way people actually lived and the cultural blueprints for proper gender and generational roles (Ryan, 1981). In the older pattern, when most people worked on farms, a father was not just the head of the household, but also boss of the family enterprise. Mother and children and hired hands worked under his supervision. But when work moved out, father—along with older sons and daughters—went with it, leaving behind mother and the younger children. These dislocations in the functions and meaning of family life unleashed an era of personal stress and cultural confusion.

Eventually, a new model of family emerged that not only reflected the new separation of work and family, but also glorified it. No longer a workplace, the household now became idealized as "home sweet home," an emotional and spiritual shelter from the heartless world outside. Although father remained the head of the family, mother was now the central figure in the home. The new model celebrated the "true woman's" purity, virtue, and selflessness. Many of our culture's most basic ideas about the family in U.S. culture, such as "a woman's place is in the home," were formed at this time. In short, the family pattern we now think of as traditional was in fact the first version of the modern family.

Historians label this model of the family "Victorian" because it became influential in England and Western Europe as well as in the United States during the reign of Queen Victoria. It reflected, in idealized form, the nineteenth-century middle-class family. However, the Victorian model became the prevailing cultural definition of family. Few families could live up to the ideal in all its particulars; working-class, black, and ethnic families, for example, could not get by without the economic contributions of wives, mothers, and daughters. And even for middle-class families, the Victorian ideal prescribed a standard of perfection that was virtually impossible to fulfill (Demos, 1986).

Eventually, however, social change overtook the Victorian model. Beginning around the 1880s, another period of rapid economic, social, and cultural change unsettled Victorian family patterns, especially their gender arrangements. Several generations of so-called new women challenged Victorian notions of femininity. They became educated, pursued careers, became involved in political causes—including their own—and created the first wave of feminism. This ferment culminated in the victory of the women's suffrage movement. It was followed by the 1920s' jazz-age era of flappers and flaming youth—the first, and probably the major, sexual revolution of the twentieth century.

To many observers at the time, it appeared that the family and morality had broken down. Another cultural crisis ensued, until a new cultural blueprint emerged—the companionate model of marriage and the family. The new model was a revised, more relaxed version of the Victorian family; companionship and sexual intimacy were now defined as central to marriage.

This highly abbreviated history of family and cultural change forms the necessary backdrop for understanding the family upheavals of the late twentieth and early twenty-first centuries. As in earlier times, major changes in the economy and society have destabilized an existing model of family life and the everyday patterns and practices that have sustained it.

We have experienced a triple revolution: first, the move toward a postindustrial service and information economy; second, a life course revolution brought about by the reductions in mortality and fertility; and third, a psychological transformation rooted mainly in rising educational levels.

Although these shifts have profound implications for everyone in contemporary society, women have been the pacesetters of change. Most women's lives and expectations over the past three decades, inside and outside the family, have departed drastically from those of their own mothers. Men's lives today also are different from their fathers' generation, but to a much lesser extent.

THE TRIPLE REVOLUTION

The Postindustrial Family

The most obvious way the new economy affects the family is in its drawing women, especially married women, into the workplace. A service and information economy produces large numbers of jobs that, unlike factory work, seem suitable for women. Yet as Jessie Bernard (1982) once observed, the transformation of a housewife into a paid worker outside the home sends tremors through every family relationship. It creates a more "symmetrical" family, undoing the sharp contrast between men's and women's roles that marks the breadwinner/housewife pattern. It also reduces women's economic dependence on men, thereby making it easier for women to leave unhappy marriages.

Beyond drawing women into the workplace, shifts in the nature of work and a rapidly changing globalized economy have unsettled the lives of individuals and families at all class levels. The well-paying industrial jobs that once enabled a blue-collar worker to own a home and support a family are no longer available. The once secure jobs that sustained the "organization men" and their families in the 1950s and 1960s have been made shaky by downsizing, an unstable economy, corporate takeovers, and a rapid pace of technological change.

The new economic climate has also made the transition to adulthood increasingly problematic. The uncertainties of work is in part responsible for young adults' lower fertility rates and for women flooding the workplace. Further, the family formation patterns of the 1950s are out of step with the increased educational demands of today's postindustrial society. In the postwar years, particularly in the United States, young people entered adulthood in one giant step—going to work, marrying young and moving to a separate household from their parents, and having children quickly. Today, few young adults can afford to marry and have children in their late teens or early twenties. In an economy where a college degree is necessary to earn a living wage, early marriage impedes education for both men and women.

Those who do not go on to college have little access to jobs that can sustain a family. Particularly in the inner cities of the United States, growing numbers of young people have come to see no future for themselves at all in the ordinary world of work. In middle-class families, a narrowing opportunity structure has increased anxieties about downward mobility for offspring, and parents as well. The "incompletely launched young adult syndrome" has become common: Many young adults deviate from their parents' expectations by failing to launch careers and become successfully independent adults, and many even come home to crowd their parents' empty nest (Schnaiberg and Goldenberg, 1989).

The Life Course Revolution

The demographic transformations of the twentieth century were no less significant than the economic ones. We cannot hope to understand current predicaments of family life without understanding how radically the demographic and social circumstances of U.S. culture has changed. In earlier times, mortality rates were highest among infants, and the possibility of death from tuberculosis, pneumonia, or other infectious diseases was an ever-present threat to young and middle-aged adults. Before the turn of the twentieth century, only 40 percent of women lived through all the stages of a normal life course—growing up, marrying, having children, and surviving with a spouse to the age of 50 (Uhlenberg, 1980).

Demographic and economic change has had a profound effect on women's lives. Women today are living longer and having fewer children. When infant and child mortality rates fall, women no longer have to have five or seven or nine children to make sure that two or three will survive to adulthood. After rearing children, the average woman can look forward to three or four decades without maternal responsibilities. Because traditional assumptions about women are based on the notion that they are constantly involved with pregnancy, child rearing, and related domestic concerns, the current ferment about women's roles may be seen as a way of bringing cultural attitudes in line with existing social realities.

As people live longer, they can stay married longer. Actually, the biggest change in contemporary marriage is not the proportion of marriages disrupted through divorce, but the potential length of marriage and the number of years spent without children in the home. By the 1970s the statistically average couple spent only 18 percent of their married lives raising young children, compared with 54 percent a century ago (Bane, 1976). As a result, marriage is becoming defined less as a union between parents raising a brood of children and more as a personal relationship between two individuals.

A Psychological Revolution

The third major transformation is a set of psychocultural changes that might be described as "psychological gentrification" (Skolnick, 1991). That is, cultural advantages once enjoyed only by the upper classes—in particular, education—have been extended to those lower down on the socioeconomic scale. Psychological gentrification also involves greater leisure time, travel, and exposure to information, as well as a general rise in the standard of living. Despite the persistence of poverty, unemployment, and economic insecurity in the industrialized world, far less of the population than in the historical past is living at the level of sheer subsistence.

Throughout Western society, rising levels of education and related changes have been linked to a complex set of shifts in personal and political attitudes. One of these is a more psychological approach to life—greater introspectiveness and a yearning for warmth and intimacy in family and other relationships (Veroff, Douvan, and Kulka, 1981). There is also evidence of an increasing preference on the part of both men and women for a more companionate ideal of marriage and a more democratic family. More broadly, these changes in attitude have been described as a shift to "postmaterialist values," emphasizing self-expression, tolerance, equality, and a concern for the quality of life (Inglehart, 1990).

The multiple social transformations of our era have brought both costs and benefits: Family relations have become both more fragile and more emotionally rich; mass longevity has brought us a host of problems as well as the gift of extended life. Although change has brought greater opportunities for women, persisting gender inequality means women have borne a large share of the costs of these gains. But we cannot turn the clock back to the family models of the past.

Paradoxically, after all the upheavals of recent decades, the emotional and cultural significance of the family persists. Family remains the center of most people's lives and, as numerous surveys show, a cherished value. Although marriage has become more fragile, the parent–child relationship—especially the mother–child relationship—remains a core attachment across the life course (Rossi and Rossi, 1990). The family, however, can be both "here to stay" and beset with difficulties. There is widespread recognition that the massive social and economic changes we have lived through call for public and private-sector policies in support of families. Most European countries have recognized for some time that governments must play a role in supplying an array of supports to families—health care, children's allowances, housing subsidies, support for working parents and children (such as child care, parental leave, and shorter work days for parents), as well as an array of services for the elderly.

Each country's response to these changes, as we've noted earlier, has been shaped by its own political and cultural traditions. The United States remains embroiled in a cultural war over the family; many social commentators and political leaders have promised to reverse the recent trends and restore the "traditional" family. In contrast, other Western nations, including Canada and the other English-speaking countries, have responded to family change by establishing policies aimed at mitigating the problems brought about by economic and social transformations. As a result of these policies, these countries have been spared much of the poverty and other social ills that have plagued the United States in recent decades.

Looking Ahead

The world at the beginning of the twenty-first century is vastly different from what it was at the beginning, or even the middle, of the twentieth century. Families are struggling to adapt to new realities. The countries that have been at the leading edge of family change still find themselves caught between yesterday's norms, today's new realities, and an uncertain future. As we have seen, changes in women's lives have been a pivotal factor in recent family trends. In many countries there is a considerable difference between men's and women's attitudes and expectations of one another. Even where both partners accept a more equal division of labor in the home, there is often a gap between beliefs and behavior. In no country have employers, the government, or men fully caught up to the changes in women's lives.

But a knowledge of family history reveals that the solution to contemporary problems will not be found in some lost golden age. Families have always struggled with outside circumstances and inner conflict. Our current troubles inside and outside the family are genuine, but we should never forget that many of the most vexing issues confronting us derive from benefits of modernization few of us would be willing to give up—for example, longer, healthier lives, and the ability to choose how many children to have and when to have them. There was no problem of the aged in the past, because most people never aged; they died before they got old. Nor was adolescence a difficult stage of the life cycle when children worked, education was a privilege of the rich, and a person's place in society was determined by heredity rather than choice. And when most people were hungry illiterates, only aristocrats could worry about sexual satisfaction and self-fulfillment.

In short, there is no point in giving in to the lure of nostalgia. There is no golden age of the family to long for, nor even some past pattern of behavior and belief that would guarantee us harmony and stability if only we had the will to return to it. Family life is bound up with the social, economic, and ideological circumstances of particular times and places. We are no longer peasants, Puritans, pioneers, or even suburbanites circa 1955. We face conditions unknown to our ancestors, and we must find new ways to cope with them.

A Note on "the Family"

Some family scholars have suggested that we drop the term *the family* and replace it with *families* or *family life*. The problem with *the family* is that it calls to mind the stereotyped image of the Ozzie and Harriet kind of family—two parents and their two or three minor children. But those other terms don't always work. In our own writing we use the term *the family* in much the same way we use *the economy*—as an abstract term that refers to a mosaic of forms and practices in the real world.

References

Amato, P. R., Life span adjustment of children to their parents' divorce. *The Future of Children* 4, no 1. (Spring, 1994)

Bane, M. J. 1976. *Here to Stay.* New York: Basic Books.

Bernard, J. 1982. *The Future of Marriage.* New York: Bantam.

Blake, J. 1978. Structural differentiation and the family: A quiet revolution. Presented at American Sociology Association, San Francisco.

Cherlin, A. J. 1981. *Marriage, Divorce, Remarriage.* Cambridge, Mass.: Harvard University Press.

Demos, John. 1986. *Past, Present, and Personal.* New York: Oxford University Press.

Emde, R. N., and R. J. Harmon, eds. 1984. *Continuities and Discontinuities in Development.* New York: Plenum Press.

Featherstone, J. 1979. Family matters. *Harvard Educational Review* 49, no. 1: 20–52.

Geertz, G. 1965. The impact of the concept of culture on the concept of man. In *New Views of the Nature of Man,* edited by J. R. Platt. Chicago: University of Chicago Press.

Hrdy, Sarah B. 1999. *Mother Nature.* New York: Pantheon Books.

Inglehart, Ronald. 1990. *Culture Shift.* New Jersey: Princeton University Press.

Keller, S. 1971. Does the family have a future? *Journal of Comparative Studies,* Spring.

Kessen, W. 1965. *The Child.* New York: John Wiley.

Kurtz, H. 1996. *Hot Air: All Talk All the Time.* New York: Times Books.

LaBarre, W. 1954. *The Human Animal.* Chicago: University of Chicago Press.

Macfarlane, J. W. 1964. Perspectives on personality consistency and change from the guidance study. *Vita Humana* 7: 115–126.

Masnick, G., and M. J. Bane. 1980. *The Nation's Families: 1960–1990.* Boston: Auburn House.

Mellman, A., E. Lazarus, and A. Rivlin. 1990. Family time, family values. In *Rebuilding the Nest,* edited by D. Blankenhorn, S. Bayme, and J. Elshtain. Milwaukee: Family Service America.

Parsons, T. 1951. *The Social System.* Glencoe, Ill.: Free Press.

Parsons, T. 1954. The kinship system of the contemporary United States. In *Essays in Sociological Theory.* Glencoe, Ill.: Free Press.

Rossi, A. S., and P. H. Rossi. 1990. *Of Human Bonding: Parent-Child Relations Across the Life Course.* Hawthorne, New York: Aldine de Gruyter.

Rubin, L. 1996. *The Transcendent Child.* New York: Basic Books.

Ryan, M. 1981. *The Cradle of the Middle Class.* New York: Cambridge University Press.

Schnaiberg, A., and S. Goldenberg. 1989. From empty nest to crowded nest: The dynamics of incompletely launched young adults. *Social Problems* 36, no. 3 (June): 251–269.

Skolnick, A. 1991. *Embattled Paradise: The American Family in an Age of Uncertainty.* New York: Basic Books.

Stephens, W. N. 1963. *The Family in Cross-Cultural Perspective.* New York: World.

Tannen, D. 1998. *The Argument Culture.*

Uhlenberg, P. 1980. Death and the family. *Journal of Family History* 5, no. 3: 313–320.

Veroff, J., E. Douvan, and R. A. Kulka. 1981. *The Inner American: A Self-Portrait from 1957 to 1976.* New York: Basic Books.

I   *The Changing Family*

The study of the family does not belong to any single scholarly field; genetics, physiology, archaeology, history, anthropology, sociology, psychology, and economics all touch on it. Religious and ethical authorities claim a stake in the family, and troubled individuals and families generate therapeutic demands on family scholarship. In short, the study of the family is interdisciplinary, controversial, and necessary for the formulation of social policy and practices.

Interdisciplinary subjects present characteristic problems. Each discipline has its own assumptions and views of the world, which may not directly transfer into another field. Some biologists and physically oriented anthropologists, for example, analyze human affairs in terms of individual motives and instincts; for them, society is a shadowy presence, serving mainly as the setting for biologically motivated individual action. Many sociologists and cultural anthropologists, in contrast, perceive the individual as an actor playing a role written by culture and society. One important school of psychology sees people neither as passive recipients of social pressures nor as creatures driven by powerful lusts, but as information processors trying to make sense of their environment. There is no easy way to reconcile such perspectives. Scientific paradigms—characteristic ways of looking at the world—determine not only what answers will be found, but also what questions will be asked. This fact has perhaps created special confusion in the study of the family.

"We speak of families," R. D. Laing has observed, "as though we know what families are. We identify, as families, networks of people who live together over time, who have ties of marriage or kinship to one another" (Laing, 1971, p. 3).

There is the assumption that family life, so familiar a part of everyday experience, is easily understood. But familiarity may breed a sense of destiny—what we experience is transformed into the "natural":

> One difficulty in the psychological sciences lies in the familiarity of the phenomena with which they deal. A certain intellectual effort is required to see how such phenomena can pose serious problems or call for intricate explanatory theories. One is inclined to take them for granted as necessary or somehow "natural." (Chomsky, 1968, p. 21)

Another obstacle to understanding family life is that it is hard to see the links between the larger world outside the home and the individuals and families inside. The selections in Part One aim to show us these links. For example, Anthony Giddens argues that there is a global revolution going on in sexuality, in marriage and the family, and in

15

how people think of themselves and their relationships. He argues that we are living through another wave of technological and economic modernization that is having a profound impact on personal life. Further, he sees a strong parallel between the ideals of a democratic society and the emerging new ideals of family relationships. For example, a good marriage is coming to be seen as a relationship between equals. Giddens recognizes that many of the changes in family life are worrisome, but we can't go back to the family patterns of an earlier time. Nor would most of us really want to. Nostalgic images of the family in earlier times typically omit the high mortality rates that prevailed before the twentieth century. Death could strike at any age, and was a constant threat to family stability. Arlene Skolnick's article reveals the profound impact of high mortality on family relationships, and how new problems arose from the lengthening of the life span over the course of the twentieth century.

Stephanie Coontz points to flaws in our nostalgic assumptions about the families of a more recent era—the 1950s—the era that Americans are most likely to think of as a golden age of family. People living at the time did not see it that way. Yet, Coontz argues, in many ways, because of a strong economy and governmental policies such as the GI Bill of Rights, the country really was a better place for families than it is today.

The readings in Chapter 2 are concerned with the meaning of family in modern society. As women increasingly participate in the paid workforce, argues Sharon Hays, they find themselves caught up in a web of cultural contradictions that remain unresolved and indeed have deepened. There is no way, she further maintains, for contemporary women to get it "just right." Both stay-at-home and working mothers maintain an intensive commitment to motherhood, although they work it out in different ways. Women who stay at home no longer feel comfortable and fulfilled being defined by themselves and others as "mere housewives." Correspondingly, working women are frequently anxious about the time away from children and the complexities of balancing parental duties with the demands of serious employment.

The cultural contradictions that trouble motherhood can be seen as a part of the larger "cultural war" over the family. But there are more than two sides in the family wars. Janet Z. Giele carefully diagrams *three* positions on the family: the conservative, the liberal, and the feminist. The latter, for Giele, is the most promising for developing public policies that would combine conservative and liberal perspectives. The feminist vision, she argues, appreciates the both the "premodern nature of the family" with the inevitable interdependence of family with a modern, fast-changing economy. Consequently, she claims, the feminist approach affords both a policy challenge and a policy synthesis to the culture wars that bedevil the institution of the family.

References

Chomsky, N. 1968. *Language and Mind.* New York: Harcourt, Brace and World.
Laing, R. D. 1971. *The Politics of the Family.* New York: Random House.

1 Families Past and Present

■READING 1

The Global Revolution in Family and Personal Life

Anthony Giddens

Among all the changes going on today, none are more important than those happening in our personal lives—in sexuality, emotional life, marriage and the family. There is a global revolution going on in how we think of ourselves and how we form ties and connections with others. It is a revolution advancing unevenly in different regions and cultures, with many resistances.

As with other aspects of the runaway world, we don't know what the ratio of advantages and anxieties will turn out to be. In some ways, these are the most difficult and disturbing transformations of all. Most of us can tune out from larger problems for much of the time. We can't opt out, however, from the swirl of change reaching right into the heart of our emotional lives.

There are few countries in the world where there isn't intense discussion about sexual equality, the regulation of sexuality and the future of the family. And where there isn't open debate, this is mostly because it is actively repressed by authoritarian governments or fundamentalist groups. In many cases, these controversies are national or local—as are the social and political reactions to them. Politicians and pressure groups will suggest that if only family policy were modified, if only divorce were made harder or easier to get in their particular country, solutions to our problems could readily be found.

But the changes affecting the personal and emotional spheres go far beyond the borders of any particular country, even one as large as the United States. We find the same issues almost everywhere, differing only in degree and according to the cultural context in which they take place.

In China, for example, the state is considering making divorce more difficult. In the aftermath of the Cultural Revolution, very liberal marriage laws were passed. Marriage is a working contract, that can be dissolved, I quote: "when husband and wife both desire it."

Even if one partner objects, divorce can be granted when "mutual affection" has gone from the marriage. Only a two week wait is required, after which the two pay $4 and are henceforth independent. The Chinese divorce rate is still low as compared with Western countries, but it is rising rapidly—as is true in the other developing Asian societies. In Chinese cities, not only divorce, but cohabitation is becoming more frequent.

In the vast Chinese countryside, by contrast, everything is different. Marriage and the family are much more traditional—in spite of the official policy of limiting childbirth through a mixture of incentives and punishment. Marriage is an arrangement between two families, fixed by the parents rather than the individuals concerned.

A recent study in the province of Gansu, which has only a low level of economic development, found that 60% of marriages are still arranged by parents. As a Chinese saying has it: "meet once, nod your head and marry." There is a twist in the tail in modernising China. Many of those currently divorcing in the urban centres were married in the traditional manner in the country.

In China there is much talk of protecting the family. In many Western countries the debate is even more shrill. The family is a site for the struggles between tradition and modernity, but also a metaphor for them. There is perhaps more nostalgia surrounding the lost haven of the family than for any other institution with its roots in the past. Politicians and activists routinely diagnose the breakdown of family life and call for a return to the traditional family.

Now the "traditional family" is very much a catch-all category. There have been many different types of family and kinship systems in different societies and cultures. The Chinese family, for instance, was always distinct from family forms in the West. Arranged marriage was never as common in most European countries, as in China, or India. Yet the family in non-modern cultures did, and does, have some features found more or less everywhere.

The traditional family was above all an economic unit. Agricultural production normally involved the whole family group, while among the gentry and aristocracy, transmission of property was the main basis of marriage. In mediaeval Europe, marriage was not contracted on the basis of sexual love, nor was it regarded as a place where such love should flourish. As the French historian, Georges Duby, puts it, marriage in the middle ages was not to involve "frivolity, passion, or fantasy."

The inequality of men and women was intrinsic to the traditional family. I don't think one could overstate the importance of this. In Europe, women were the property of their husbands or fathers—chattels as defined in law.

In the traditional family, it wasn't only women who lacked rights—children did too. The idea of enshrining children's rights in law is in historical terms relatively recent. In premodern periods, as in traditional cultures today, children weren't reared for their own sake, or for the satisfaction of the parents. One could almost say that children weren't recognised as individuals.

It wasn't that parents didn't love their children, but they cared about them more for the contribution they made to the common economic task than for themselves. Moreover, the death rate of children was frightening. In Colonial America nearly one in four infants died in their first year. Almost 50% didn't live to age 10.

Except for certain courtly or elite groups, in the traditional family sexuality was always dominated by reproduction. This was a matter of tradition and nature combined.

The absence of effective contraception meant that for most women sexuality was inevitably closely connected with childbirth. In many traditional cultures, including in Western Europe up to the threshold of the 20th Century, a woman might have 10 or more pregnancies during the course of her life.

Sexuality was regulated by the idea of female virtue. The sexual double standard is often thought of as a creation of the Victorian period. In fact, in one version or another it was central to almost all non-modern societies. It involved a dualistic view of female sexuality—a clear cut division between the virtuous woman on the one hand and the libertine on the other. Double Standard *

Sexual promiscuity in many cultures has been taken as a positive defining feature of masculinity. James Bond is, or was, admired for his sexual as well as his physical heroism. Sexually adventurous women, by contrast, have nearly always been beyond the pale, no matter how much influence the mistresses of some prominent figures might have achieved.

Attitudes towards homosexuality were also governed by a mix of tradition and nature. Anthropological surveys show that homosexuality—or male homosexuality at any rate—has been tolerated, or openly approved of, in more cultures than it has been outlawed.

Those societies that have been hostile to homosexuality have usually condemned it as specifically unnatural. Western attitudes have been more extreme than most; less than half a century ago homosexuality was still widely regarded as a perversion and written up as such in manuals of psychiatry.

Antagonism towards homosexuality is still widespread and the dualistic view of women continues to be held by many—of both sexes. But over the past few decades the main elements of people's sexual lives in the West have changed in an absolutely basic way. The separation of sexuality from reproduction is in principle complete. Sexuality is for the first time something to be discovered, moulded, altered. Sexuality, which used to be defined so strictly in relation to marriage and legitimacy, now has little connection to them at all. We should see the increasing acceptance of homosexuality not just as a tribute to liberal tolerance. It is a logical outcome of the severance of sexuality from reproduction. Sexuality which has no content is by definition no longer dominated by heterosexuality. *

What most of its defenders in Western countries call the traditional family was in fact a late, transitional phase in family development in the 1950's. This was a time at which the proportion of women out at work was still relatively low and when it was still difficult, especially for women, to obtain divorce without stigma. On the other hand, men and women by this time were more equal than they had been previously, both in fact and in law. The family had ceased to be an economic entity and the idea of romantic love as basis for marriage had replaced marriage as an economic contract.

Since then, the family has changed much further. The details vary from society to society, but the same trends are visible almost everywhere in the industrialised world. Only a minority of people now live in what might be called the standard 1950's family—both parents living together with their children of the marriage, where the mother is a full time housewife, and the father the breadwinner. In some countries, more than a third of all births happen outside wedlock, while the proportion of people living alone has gone up steeply and looks likely to rise even more.

In most societies, like the U.S., marriage remains popular—the U.S. has aptly been called a high divorce, high marriage society. In Scandinavia, on the other hand, a large proportion of people living together, including where children are involved, remain unmarried. Moreover, up to a quarter of women aged between 18 and 35 in the U.S. and Europe say they do not intend to have children—and they appear to mean it.

Of course in all countries older family forms continue to exist. In the U.S., many people, recent immigrants particularly, still live according to traditional values. Most family life, however, has been transformed by the rise of the couple and coupledom. Marriage and the family have become what I termed in an earlier lecture shell institutions. They are still called the same, but inside their basic character has changed.

In the traditional family, the married couple was only one part, and often not the main part, of the family system. Ties with children and other relatives tended to be equally or even more important in the day to day conduct of social life. Today the couple, married or unmarried, is at the core of what the family is. The couple came to be at the centre of family life as the economic role of the family dwindled and love, or love plus sexual attraction, became the basis of forming marriage ties.

A couple once constituted has its own exclusive history, its own biography. It is a unit based upon emotional communication or intimacy. The idea of intimacy, like so many other familiar notions I've discussed in these lectures, sounds old but in fact is very new. Marriage was never in the past based upon intimacy—emotional communication. No doubt this was important to a good marriage but it was not the foundation of it. For the couple, it is. Communication is the means of establishing the tie in the first place and it is the chief rationale for its continuation.

We should recognise what a major transition this is. "Coupling" and "uncoupling" provide a more accurate description of the arena of personal life now than do "marriage and the family." A more important question for us than "are you married?" is "how good is your relationship?"

The idea of a relationship is also surprisingly recent. Only 30 or so years ago, no one spoke of "relationships." They didn't need to, nor did they need to speak in terms of intimacy and commitment. Marriage at that time was the commitment, as the existence of shotgun marriages bore witness. While statistically marriage is still the normal condition, for most people its meaning has more or less completely changed. Marriage signifies that a couple is in a stable relationship, and may indeed promote that stability, since it makes a public declaration of commitment. However, marriage is no longer the chief defining basis of coupledom.

The position of children in all this is interesting and somewhat paradoxical. Our attitudes towards children and their protection have altered radically over the past several generations. We prize children so much partly because they have become so much rarer, and partly because the decision to have a child is very different from what it was for previous generations. In the traditional family, children were an economic benefit. Today in Western countries a child, on the contrary, puts a large financial burden on the parents. Having a child is more of a distinct and specific decision than it used to be, and it is a decision guided by psychological and emotional needs. The worries we have about the effects of divorce upon children, and the existence of many fatherless families, have to be understood against the background of our much higher expectations about how children should be cared for and protected.

There are three main areas in which emotional communication, and therefore intimacy, are replacing the old ties that used to bind together people's personal lives—in sexual and love relations, parent-child relations and in friendship.

To analyse these, I want to use the idea of what I call the "pure relationship." I mean by this a relationship based upon emotional communication, where the rewards derived from such communication are the main basis for the relationship to continue.

I don't mean a sexually pure relationship. Also I don't mean anything that exists in reality. I'm talking of an abstract idea that helps us understand changes going on in the world. Each of the three areas just mentioned—sexual relationships, parent-child relations and friendship—is tending to approximate to this model. Emotional communication or intimacy, in other words, are becoming the key to what they are all about.

The pure relationship has quite different dynamics from more traditional social ties. It depends upon processes of active trust—opening oneself up to the other. Self-disclosure is the basic condition of intimacy.

The pure relationship is also implicitly democratic. When I was originally working on the study of intimate relationships, I read a great deal of therapeutic and self-help literature on the subject. I was struck by something I don't believe has been widely noticed or remarked upon. If one looks at how a therapist sees a good relationship—in any of the three spheres just mentioned—it is striking how direct a parallel there is with public democracy.

A good relationship, of course, is an ideal—most ordinary relationships don't come even close. I'm not suggesting that our relations with spouses, lovers, children or friends aren't often messy, conflictful and unsatisfying. But the principles of public democracy are ideals too, that also often stand at some large distance from reality.

A good relationship is a relationship of equals, where each party has equal rights and obligations. In such a relationship, each person has respect, and wants the best, for the other. The pure relationship is based upon communication, so that understanding the other person's point of view is essential.

Talk, or dialogue, are the basis of making the relationship work. Relationships function best if people don't hide too much from each other—there has to be mutual trust. And trust has to be worked at, it can't just be taken for granted.

Finally, a good relationship is one free from arbitrary power, coercion or violence.

Every one of these qualities conforms to the values of democratic politics. In a democracy, all are in principle equal, and with equality of rights and responsibilities comes mutual respect. Open dialogue is a core property of democracy. Democratic systems substitute open discussion of issues—a public space of dialogue—for authoritarian power, or for the sedimented power of tradition. No democracy can work without trust. And democracy is undermined if it gives way to authoritarianism or violence.

When we apply these principles—as ideals, I would stress again—to relationships, we are talking of something very important—the possible emergence of what I shall call, a democracy of the emotions in everyday life. A democracy of the emotions, it seems to me, is as important as public democracy in improving the quality of our lives.

This holds as much in parent-child relations as in other areas. These can't, and shouldn't, be materially equal. Parents must have authority over children, in everyone's interests. Yet they should presume an in-principle equality. In a democratic family, the authority of parents should be based upon an implicit contract. The parent in effect says to the child: "If you were an adult, and knew what I know, you would agree that what I ask you to do is legitimate."

Children in traditional families were—and are—supposed to be seen and not heard. Many parents, perhaps despairing of their children's rebelliousness, would dearly like to resurrect that rule. But there isn't any going back to it, nor should there be. In a democracy of the emotions, children can and should be able to answer back.

An emotional democracy doesn't imply lack of discipline, or absence of authority. It simply seeks to put them on a different footing.

Something very similar happened in the public sphere, when democracy began to replace arbitrary government and the rule of force. And like public democracy the democratic family must be anchored in a stable, yet open, civil society. If I may coin a phrase—"It takes a village."

A democracy of the emotions would draw no distinctions of principle between heterosexual and same-sex relationships. Gays, rather than heterosexuals, have actually been pioneers in discovering the new world of relationships and exploring its possibilities. They have had to be, because when homosexuality came out of the closet, gays weren't able to depend upon the normal supports of traditional marriage. They have had to be innovators, often in a hostile environment.

To speak of fostering an emotional democracy doesn't mean being weak about family duties, or about public policy towards the family. Democracy, after all, means the acceptance of obligations, as well as rights sanctioned in law. The protection of children has to be the primary feature of legislation and public policy. Parents should be legally obliged to provide for their children until adulthood, no matter what living arrangements they enter into. Marriage is no longer an economic institution, yet as a ritual commitment it can help stabilise otherwise fragile relationships. If this applies to heterosexual relationships, I don't see why it shouldn't apply to homosexual ones too.

There are many questions to be asked of all this—too many to answer in a short lecture. I have concentrated mainly upon trends affecting the family in Western countries. What about areas where the traditional family remains largely intact, as in the example of China with which I began? Will the changes observed in the West become more and more global?

I think they will—indeed that they are. It isn't a question of whether existing forms of the traditional family will become modified, but when and how. I would venture even further. What I have described as an emerging democracy of the emotions is on the front line in the struggle between cosmopolitanism and fundamentalism that I described in the last lecture. Equality of the sexes, and the sexual freedom of women, which are incompatible with the traditional family, are anathema to fundamentalist groups. Opposition to them, indeed, is one of the defining features of religious fundamentalism across the world.

There is plenty to be worried about in the state of the family, in Western countries and elsewhere. It is just as mistaken to say that every family form is as good as any other, as to argue that the decline of the traditional family is a disaster.

I would turn the argument of the political and fundamentalist right on its head. The persistence of the traditional family—or aspects of it—in many parts of the world is more worrisome than its decline. For what are the most important forces promoting democracy and economic development in poorer countries? Well, they are the equality and education of women. And what must be changed to make these possible? Most importantly, what must be changed is the traditional family.

In conclusion, I should emphasise that sexual equality is not just a core principle of democracy. It is also relevant to happiness and fulfilment.

Many of the changes happening to the family are problematic and difficult. But surveys in the U.S. and Europe show that few want to go back to traditional male and female roles, much less to legally defined inequality.

If ever I were tempted to think that the traditional family might be best after all, I remember what my great aunt said. She must have had one of the longest marriages of anyone. She married young, and was with her husband for over 60 years. She once confided to me that she had been deeply unhappy with him the whole of that time. In her day there was no escape.

■ READING 2

The Life Course Revolution

Arlene Skolnick

Many of us, in moments of nostalgia, imagine the past as a kind of Disneyland—a quaint setting we might step back into with our sense of ourselves intact, yet free of the stresses of modern life. But in yearning for the golden past we imagine we have lost, we are unaware of what we have escaped.

In our time, for example, dying before reaching old age has become a rare event; about three-quarters of all people die after their sixty-fifth birthday. It is hard for us to appreciate what a novelty this is in human experience. In 1850, only 2 percent of the population lived past sixty-five. "We place dying in what we take to be its logical position," observes the social historian Ronald Blythe, "which is at the close of a long life, whereas our ancestors accepted the futility of placing it in any position at all. In the midst of life we are in death, they said, and they meant it. To them it was a fact; to us it is a metaphor."

This longevity revolution is largely a twentieth-century phenomenon. Astonishingly, two-thirds of the total increase in human longevity since prehistoric times has taken place since 1900—and a good deal of that increase has occurred in recent decades. Mortality rates in previous centuries were several times higher than today, and death commonly struck at any age. Infancy was particularly hazardous; "it took two babies to make one adult," as one demographer put it. A white baby girl today has a greater chance of living to be sixty than her counterpart born in 1870 would have had of reaching her first birthday. And after infancy, death still hovered as an ever-present possibility. It was not unusual for young and middle-aged adults to die of tuberculosis, pneumonia, or other infectious diseases. (Keats died at twenty-five, Schubert at thirty-one, Mozart at thirty-five.)

These simple changes in mortality have had profound, yet little-appreciated effects on family life; they have encouraged stronger emotional bonds between parents and children, lengthened the duration of marriage and parent-child relationships, made grandparenthood an expectable stage of the life course, and increased the number of grandparents whom children actually know. More and more families have four or even five generations alive at the same time. And for the first time in history, the average couple has more parents living than it has children. It is also the first era when most of the parent-child relationship takes place after the child becomes an adult.

In a paper entitled "Death and the Family," the demographer Peter Uhlenberg has examined some of these repercussions by contrasting conditions in 1900 with those in 1976. In 1900, for example, half of all parents would have experienced the death of a child; by 1976 only 6 percent would. And more than half of all children who lived to the age of fifteen in 1900 would have experienced the death of a parent or sibling, compared with less than 9 percent in 1976. Another outcome of the lower death rates was a decline in the number of orphans and orphanages. Current discussions of divorce rarely take into account the almost constant family disruption children experienced in "the good old days." In 1900, 1 out of 4 children under the age of fifteen lost a parent; 1 out of 62 lost both. The corresponding figures for 1976 are, respectively, 1 out of 20 and 1 out of 1,800.

Because being orphaned used to be so common, the chances of a child's not living with either parent was much greater at the turn of the century than it is now. Indeed, some of the current growth in single-parent families is offset by a decline in the number of children raised in institutions, in foster homes, or by relatives. This fact does not diminish the stresses of divorce and other serious family problems of today, but it does help correct the tendency to contrast the terrible Present with an idealized Past.

Today's children rarely experience the death of a close relative, except for elderly grandparents. And it is possible to grow into adulthood without experiencing even that loss. "We never had any deaths in my family," a friend recently told me, explaining that none of her relatives had died until she was in her twenties. In earlier times, children were made aware of the constant possibility of death, attended deathbed scenes, and were even encouraged to examine the decaying corpses of family members.

One psychological result of our escape from the daily presence of death is that we are ill prepared for it when it comes. For most of us, the first time we feel a heightened concern with our own mortality is in our thirties and forties when we realize that the years we have already lived outnumber those we have left.

Another result is that the death of a child is no longer a sad but normal hazard of parenthood. Rather, it has become a devastating, life-shattering loss from which a parent may never fully recover. The intense emotional bonding between parents and infants that we see as a sociobiological given did not become the norm until the eighteenth and nineteenth centuries. The privileged classes created the concept of the "emotionally priceless" child, a powerful ideal that gradually filtered down through the rest of society.

The high infant mortality rates of premodern times were partly due to neglect, and often to lethal child-rearing practices such as sending infants off to a wet nurse* or, worse, infanticide. It now appears that in all societies lacking reliable contraception, the careless treatment and neglect of unwanted children acted as a major form of birth control. This does not necessarily imply that parents were uncaring toward all their children; rather, they seem to have practiced "selective neglect" of sickly infants in favor of sturdy ones, or of later children in favor of earlier ones.† In 1801 a writer observed of Bavarian peasants:

> The peasant has joy when his wife brings forth the first fruit of their love, he has joy with the second and third as well, but not with the fourth. . . . He sees all children coming thereafter as hostile creatures, which take the bread from his mouth and the mouths of his family. Even the heart of the most gentle mother becomes cold with the birth of the fifth child, and the sixth, she unashamedly wishes death, that the child should pass to heaven.

Declining fertility rates are another major result of falling death rates. Until the baby boom of the 1940s and 1950s, fertility rates had been dropping continuously since the eighteenth century. By taking away parents' fear that some of their children would not survive to adulthood, lowered early-childhood mortality rates encouraged careful planning of births and smaller families. The combination of longer lives and fewer, more closely spaced children created a still-lengthening empty-nest stage in the family. This in turn has encouraged the companionate style of marriage, since husband and wife can expect to live together for many years after their children have moved out.

Many demographers have suggested that falling mortality rates are directly linked to rising divorce rates. In 1891 W. F. Willcox of Cornell University made one of the most accurate social science predictions ever. Looking at the high and steadily rising divorce rates of the time, along with falling mortality rates, he predicted that around 1980, the two curves would cross and the number of marriages ended by divorce would equal those ended by death. In the late 1970s, it all happened as Willcox had predicted. Then divorce rates continued to increase before leveling off in the 1980s, while mortality rates continued to decline. As a result, a couple marrying today is more likely to celebrate a fortieth wedding anniversary than were couples around the turn of the century.

In statistical terms, then, it looks as if divorce has restored a level of instability to marriage that had existed earlier due to the high mortality rate. But as Lawrence Stone

---

*Wet-nursing—the breastfeeding of an infant by a woman other than the mother—was widely practiced in premodern Europe and colonial America. Writing of a two-thousand-year-old "war of the breast," the developmental psychologist William Kessen notes that the most persistent theme in the history of childhood is the reluctance of mothers to suckle their babies, and the urgings of philosophers and physicians that they do so. Infants were typically sent away from home for a year and a half or two years to be raised by poor country women, in squalid conditions. When they took in more babies than they had milk enough to suckle, the babies would die of malnutrition.

The reluctance to breast-feed may not have reflected maternal indifference so much as other demands in premodern, precontraceptive times—the need to take part in the family economy, the unwillingness of husbands to abstain from sex for a year and a half or two. (Her milk would dry up if a mother became pregnant.) Although in France and elsewhere the custom persisted into the twentieth century, large-scale wet-nursing symbolizes the gulf between modern and premodern sensibilities about infants and their care.

†The anthropologist Nancy Scheper-Hughes describes how impoverished mothers in northeastern Brazil select which infants to nurture.

observes, "it would be rash to claim that the psychological effects of the termination of marriage by divorce, that is by an act of will, bear a close resemblance to its termination by the inexorable accident of death."

THE NEW STAGES OF LIFE

In recent years it has become clear that the stages of life we usually think of as built into human development are, to a large degree, social and cultural inventions. Although people everywhere may pass through infancy, childhood, adulthood, and old age, the facts of nature are "doctored," as Ruth Benedict once put it, in different ways by different cultures.

The Favorite Age

In 1962 Phillipe Ariès made the startling claim that "in medieval society, the idea of childhood did not exist." Ariès argued not that parents then neglected their children, but that they did not think of children as having a special nature that required special treatment; after the age of around five to seven, children simply joined the adult world of work and play. This "small adult" conception of childhood has been observed by many anthropologists in preindustrial societies. In Europe, according to Ariès and others, childhood was discovered, or invented, in the seventeenth and nineteenth centuries, with the emergence of the private, domestic, companionate family and formal schooling. These institutions created distinct roles for children, enabling childhood to emerge as a distinct stage of life.

Despite challenges to Ariès's work, the bulk of historical and cross-cultural evidence supports the contention that childhood as we know it today is a relatively recent cultural invention; our ideas about children, child-rearing practices, and the conditions of children's lives are dramatically different from those of earlier centuries. The same is true of adolescence. Teenagers, such a conspicuous and noisy presence in modern life, and their stage of life, known for its turmoil and soul searching, are not universal features of life in other times and places.

Of course, the physical changes of puberty—sexual maturation and spurt in growth—happen to everyone everywhere. Yet, even here, there is cultural and historical variation. In the past hundred years, the age of first menstruation has declined from the mid-teens to twelve, and the age young men reach their full height has declined from twenty-five to under twenty. Both changes are believed to be due to improvements in nutrition and health care, and these average ages are not expected to continue dropping.

Some societies have puberty rites, but they bring about a transition from childhood not to adolescence but to adulthood. Other societies take no note at all of the changes, and the transition from childhood to adulthood takes place simply and without social recognition. Adolescence as we know it today appears to have evolved late in the nineteenth century; there is virtual consensus among social scientists that it is "a creature of the industrial revolution and it continues to be shaped by the forces which defined that revolution: industrialization, specialization, urbanization . . . and bureaucratization of human organizations and institutions, and continuing technological development."

In America before the second half of the nineteenth century, youth was an ill-defined category. Puberty did not mark any new status or life experience. For the majority of young people who lived on farms, work life began early, at seven or eight years old or even younger. As they grew older, their responsibility would increase, and they would gradually move toward maturity. Adults were not ignorant of the differences between children and adults, but distinctions of age meant relatively little. As had been the practice in Europe, young people could be sent away to become apprentices or servants in other households. As late as the early years of this century, working-class children went to work at the age of ten or twelve.

A second condition leading to a distinct stage of adolescence was the founding of mass education systems, particularly the large public high school. Compulsory education helped define adolescence by setting a precise age for it; high schools brought large numbers of teenagers together to create their own society for a good part of their daily lives. So the complete set of conditions for adolescence on a mass scale did not exist until the end of the nineteenth century.

The changed family situations of late-nineteenth- and early-twentieth-century youth also helped make this life stage more psychologically problematic. Along with the increasing array of options to choose from, rapid social change was making one generation's experience increasingly different from that of the next. Among the immigrants who were flooding into the country at around the time adolescence was emerging, the generation gap was particularly acute. But no parents were immune to the rapid shifts in society and culture that were transforming America in the decades around the turn of the century.

Further, the structure and emotional atmosphere of middle-class family life was changing also, creating a more intimate and emotionally intense family life. Contrary to the view that industrialization had weakened parent-child relations, the evidence is that family ties between parents and adolescents intensified at this time: adolescents lived at home until they married, and depended more completely, and for a longer time, on their parents than in the past. Demographic change had cut family size in half over the course of the century. Mothers were encouraged to devote themselves to the careful nurturing of fewer children.

This more intensive family life seems likely to have increased the emotional strain of adolescence. Smaller households and a more nurturing style of child rearing, combined with the increased contact between parents, especially mothers, and adolescent children, may have created a kind of " 'Oedipal family' in middle class America."

The young person's awakening sexuality, particularly the young male's, is likely to have been more disturbing to both himself and his parents than during the era when young men commonly lived away from home. . . . There is evidence that during the Victorian era, fears of adolescent male sexuality, and of masturbation in particular, were remarkably intense and widespread.

Family conflict in general may have been intensified by the peculiar combination of teenagers' increased dependence on parents and increased autonomy in making their own life choices. Despite its tensions, the new emotionally intense middle-class home made it more difficult than ever for adolescents to leave home for the heartless, indifferent world outside.

By the end of the nineteenth century, conceptions of adolescence took on modern form, and by the first decades of the twentieth century, *adolescence* had become a household word. As articulated forcefully by the psychologist G. Stanley Hall in his 1904 treatise, adolescence was a biological process—not simply the onset of sexual maturity but a turbulent, transitional stage in the evolution of the human species: "some ancient period of storm and stress when old moorings were broken and a higher level attained."

Hall seemed to provide the answers to questions people were asking about the troublesome young. His public influence eventually faded, but his conception of adolescence as a time of storm and stress lived on. Adolescence continued to be seen as a period of both great promise and great peril: "every step of the upward way is strewn with the wreckage of body, mind and morals." The youth problem—whether the lower-class problem of delinquency, or the identity crises and other psychological problems of middle-class youth—has continued to haunt America, and other modern societies, ever since.

Ironically, then, the institutions that had developed to organize and control a problematic age ended by heightening adolescent self-awareness, isolating youth from the rest of society, and creating a youth culture, making the transition to adulthood still more problematic and risky. Institutional recognition in turn made adolescents a more distinct part of the population, and being adolescent a more distinct and self-conscious experience. As it became part of the social structure of modern society, adolescence also became an important stage of the individual's biography—an indeterminate period of being neither child nor adult that created its own problems. Any society that excludes youth from adult work, and offers them what Erikson calls a "moratorium"—time and space to try out identities and lifestyles—and at the same time demands extended schooling as the route to success is likely to turn adolescence into a "struggle for self." It is also likely to run the risk of increasing numbers of mixed-up, rebellious youth.

But, in fact, the classic picture of adolescent storm and stress is not universal. Studies of adolescents in America and other industrialized societies suggest that extreme rebellion and rejection of parents, flamboyant behavior, and psychological turmoil do not describe most adolescents, even today. Media images of the youth of the 1980s and 1990s as a deeply troubled, lost generation beset by crime, drug abuse, and teenage pregnancy are also largely mistaken.

Although sexual activity and experimenting with drugs and alcohol have become common among middle-class young people, drug use has actually declined in recent years. Disturbing as these practices are for parents and other adults, they apparently do not interfere with normal development for most adolescents. Nevertheless, for a significant minority, sex and drugs add complications to a period of development during which a young person's life can easily go awry—temporarily or for good.

More typically, for most young people, the teen years are marked by mild rebelliousness and moodiness—enough to make it a difficult period for parents but not one of a profound parent-child generation gap or of deep alienation from conventional values. These ordinary tensions of family living through adolescence are exacerbated in times of rapid social change, when the world adolescents confront is vastly different from the one in which their parents came of age. Always at the forefront of social change, adolescents in industrial societies inevitably bring discomfort to their elders, who "wish to see their children's adolescence as an enactment of the retrospectively distorted memory of their own. . . . But such intergenerational continuity can occur only in the rapidly disappearing isolation of the desert or the rain forest."

If adolescence is a creation of modern culture, that culture has also been shaped by adolescence. Adolescents, with their music, fads, fashions, and conflicts, not only are conspicuous, but reflect a state of mind that often extends beyond the years designated for them. The adolescent mode of experience—accessible to people of any age—is marked by "exploration, becoming, growth, and pain."

Since the nineteenth century, for example, the coming-of-age novel has become a familiar literary genre. Patricia Spacks observes that while Victorian authors looked back at adolescence from the perspective of adulthood, twentieth-century novelists since James Joyce and D. H. Lawrence have become more intensely identified with their young heroes, writing not from a distance but from "deep inside the adolescence experience." The novelist's use of the adolescent to symbolize the artist as romantic outsider mirrors a more general cultural tendency. As Phillipe Ariès observes, "Our society has passed from a period which was ignorant of adolescence to a period in which adolescence is the favorite age. We now want to come to it early and linger in it as long as possible."

The Discovery of Adulthood

Middle age is the latest life stage to be discovered, and the notion of mid-life crisis recapitulates the storm-and-stress conception of adolescence. Over the course of the twentieth century, especially during the years after World War II, a developmental conception of childhood became institutionalized in public thought. Parents took it for granted that children passed through ages, stages, and phases: the terrible twos, the teenage rebel. In recent years the idea of development has been increasingly applied to adults, as new stages of adult life are discovered. Indeed much of the psychological revolution of recent years—the tendency to look at life through psychological lenses—can be understood in part as the extension of the developmental approach to adulthood.

In 1976 Gail Sheehy's best-selling *Passages* popularized the concept of mid-life crisis. Sheehy argued that every individual must pass through such a watershed, a time when we reevaluate our sense of self, undergo a crisis, and emerge with a new identity. Failure to do so, she warned, can have dire consequences. The book was the most influential popular attempt to apply to adults the ages-and-stages approach to development that had long been applied to children. Ironically, this came about just as historians were raising questions about the universality of those stages.

Despite its popularity, Sheehy's book, and the research she reported in it, have come under increasing criticism. "Is the mid-life crisis, if it exists, more than a warmed-over identity crisis?" asked one review of the research literature on mid-life. In fact, there is little or no evidence for the notion that adults pass through a series of sharply defined stages, or a series of crises that must be resolved before passing from one stage to the next.

Nevertheless, the notion of a mid-life crisis caught on because it reflected shifts in adult experience across the life course. Most people's decisions about marriage and work are no longer irrevocably made at one fateful turning point on the brink of adulthood. The choices made at twenty-one may no longer fit at forty or fifty—the world has changed; parents, children, and spouses have changed; working life has changed. The kind of issue that makes adolescence problematic—the array of choices and the need to fashion a coherent, continuous sense of self in the midst of all this change—recurs throughout adulthood. As a Jules Feiffer cartoon concludes, "Maturity is a phase, but adolescence is forever."

Like the identity crisis of adolescence, the concept of mid-life crisis appears to reflect the experience of the more educated and advantaged. Those with more options in life are more likely to engage in the kind of introspection and reappraisal of previous choices that make up the core of the mid-life crisis. Such people realize that they will never fulfill their earlier dreams, or that they have gotten what they wanted and find they are still not happy. But as the Berkeley longitudinal data show, even in that segment of the population, mid-life crisis is far from the norm. People who have experienced fewer choices in the past, and have fewer options for charting new directions in the future, are less likely to encounter a mid-life crisis. Among middle Americans, life is dominated by making ends meet, coping with everyday events, and managing unexpected crises.

While there may be no fixed series of stages or crises adults must pass through, middle age or mid-life in our time does have some unique features that make it an unsettled time, different from other periods in the life course as well as from mid-life in earlier eras. First, as we saw earlier, middle age is the first period in which most people today confront death, illness, and physical decline. It is also an uneasy age because of the increased importance of sexuality in modern life. Sexuality has come to be seen as the core of our sense of self, and sexual fulfillment as the center of the couple relationship. In mid-life, people confront the decline of their physical attractiveness, if not of their sexuality.

There is more than a passing resemblance between the identity problems of adolescence and the issues that fall under the rubric of "mid-life crisis." In a list of themes recurring in the literature on the experience of identity crisis, particularly in adolescence, the psychologist Roy Baumeister includes: feelings of emptiness, feelings of vagueness, generalized malaise, anxiety, self-consciousness. These symptoms describe not only adolescent and mid-life crises but what Erikson has labeled identity problems—or what has, of late, been considered narcissism.

Consider, for example, Heinz Kohut's description of patients suffering from what he calls narcissistic personality disorders. They come to the analyst with vague symptoms, but eventually focus on feelings about the self—emptiness, vague depression, being drained of energy, having no "zest" for work or anything else, shifts in self-esteem, heightened sensitivity to the opinions and reactions of others, feeling unfulfilled, a sense of uncertainty and purposelessness. "It seems on the face of it," observes the literary critic Steven Marcus, "as if these people are actually suffering from what was once called unhappiness."

The New Aging

Because of the extraordinary revolution in longevity, the proportion of elderly people in modern industrial societies is higher than it has ever been. This little-noticed but profound transformation affects not just the old but families, an individual's life course, and society as a whole. We have no cultural precedents for the mass of the population reaching old age. Further, the meaning of *old age* has changed—indeed, it is a life stage still in process, its boundaries unclear. When he came into office at the age of sixty-four, George Bush did not seem like an old man. Yet when Franklin Roosevelt died at the same age, he did seem to be "old."

President Bush illustrates why gerontologists in recent years have had to revise the meaning of "old." He is a good example of what they have termed the "young old" or the "new elders"; the social historian Peter Laslett uses the term "the third age." Whatever it is called, it represents a new stage of life created by the extension of the life course in industrialized countries. Recent decades have witnessed the first generations of people who live past sixty-five and remain healthy, vigorous, alert, and, mostly due to retirement plans, financially independent. These people are "pioneers on the frontier of age," observed the journalist Frances Fitzgerald, in her study of Sun City, a retirement community near Tampa, Florida, "people for whom society had as yet no set of expectations and no vision."

The meaning of the later stages of life remains unsettled. Just after gerontologists had marked off the "young old"—people who seemed more middle-aged than old—they had to devise a third category, the "oldest old," to describe the fastest-growing group in the population, people over eighty-five. Many if not most of these people are like Tithonus, the mythical figure who asked the gods for eternal life but forgot to ask for eternal youth as well. For them, the gift of long life has come at the cost of chronic disease and disability.

The psychological impact of this unheralded longevity revolution has largely been ignored, except when misconstrued. The fear of age, according to Christopher Lasch, is one of the chief symptoms of this culture's alleged narcissism. But when people expected to die in their forties or fifties, they didn't have to face the problem of aging. Alzheimer's disease, for example, now approaching epidemic proportions, is an ironic by-product of the extension of the average life span. When living to seventy or eighty is a realistic prospect, it makes sense to diet and exercise, to eat healthy foods, and to make other "narcissistic" investments in the self.

Further, "the gift of mass longevity," the anthropologist David Plath argues, has been so recent, dramatic, and rapid that it has become profoundly unsettling in all post-industrial societies: "If the essential cultural nightmare of the nineteenth century was to be in poverty, perhaps ours is to be old and alone or afflicted with terminal disease."

Many people thus find themselves in life stages for which cultural scripts have not yet been written; family members face one another in relationships for which tradition provides little guidance. "We are stuck with awkward-sounding terms like 'adult children' and . . . 'grandson-in-law.' " And when cultural rules are ambiguous, emotional relationships can become tense or at least ambivalent.

A study of five-generation families in Germany reveals the confusion and strain that result when children and parents are both in advanced old age—for example, a great-great-grandmother and her daughter, who is herself a great-grandmother. Who has the right to be old? Who should take care of whom? Similarly, Plath, who has studied the problems of mass longevity in Japan, finds that even in that familistic society the traditional meaning of family roles has been put into question by the stretching out of the life span. In the United States, some observers note that people moving into retirement communities sometimes bring their parents to live with them. Said one disappointed retiree: "I want to enjoy my grandchildren; I never expected that when I was a grandparent I'd have to look after my parents."

■ READING 3

What We Really Miss about the 1950s

Stephanie Coontz

In a 1996 poll by the Knight-Ridder news agency, more Americans chose the 1950s than any other single decade as the best time for children to grow up. And despite the research I've done on the underside of 1950s families, I don't think it's crazy for people to feel nostalgic about the period. For one thing, it's easy to see why people might look back fondly to a decade when real wages grew more in any single year than in the entire ten years of the 1980s combined, a time when the average 30-year-old man could buy a median-priced home on only 15–18 percent of his salary.

But it's more than just a financial issue. When I talk with modern parents, even ones who grew up in unhappy families, they associate the 1950s with a yearning they feel for a time when there were fewer complicated choices for kids or parents to grapple with, when there was more predictability in how people formed and maintained families, and when there was a coherent "moral order" in their community to serve as a reference point for family norms. Even people who found that moral order grossly unfair or repressive often say that its presence provided them with something concrete to push against.

I can sympathize entirely. One of my most empowering moments occurred the summer I turned 12, when my mother marched down to the library with me to confront a librarian who'd curtly refused to let me check out a book that was "not appropriate" for my age. "Don't you *ever* tell my daughter what she can and can't read," fumed my mom. "She's a mature young lady and she can make her own choices." In recent years I've often thought back to the gratitude I felt toward my mother for that act of trust in me. I wish I had some way of earning similar points from my own son. But much as I've always respected his values, I certainly wouldn't have walked into my local video store when he was 12 and demanded that he be allowed to check out absolutely anything he wanted!

Still, I have no illusions that I'd actually like to go back to the 1950s, and neither do most people who express such occasional nostalgia. For example, although the 1950s got more votes than any other decade in the Knight-Ridder poll, it did not win an outright majority: 38 percent of respondents picked the 1950s; 27 percent picked the 1960s or the 1970s. Voters between the ages of 50 and 64 were most likely to choose the 1950s, the decade in which they themselves came of age, as the best time for kids; voters under 30 were more likely to choose the 1970s. African Americans differed over whether the 1960s, 1970s, or 1980s were best, but all age groups of blacks agreed that later decades were definitely preferable to the 1950s.

Nostalgia for the 1950s is real and deserves to be taken seriously, but it usually shouldn't be taken literally. Even people who *do* pick the 1950s as the best decade generally end up saying, once they start discussing their feelings in depth, that it's not the family arrangements in and of themselves that they want to revive. They don't miss the way women used to be treated, they sure wouldn't want to live with most of the fathers they knew in their neighborhoods, and "come to think of it"—I don't know how many times I've recorded these exact words—"I communicate with my kids *much* better than my parents or grandparents did." When Judith Wallerstein recently interviewed 100 spouses in "happy" marriages, she found that only five "wanted a marriage like their parents'." The husbands "consciously rejected the role models provided by their fathers. The women said they could never be happy living as their mothers did."

People today understandably feel that their lives are out of balance, but they yearn for something totally *new*—a more equal distribution of work, family, and community time for both men and women, children and adults. If the 1990s are lopsided in one direction, the 1950s were equally lopsided in the opposite direction.

What most people really feel nostalgic about has little to do with the internal structure of 1950s families. It is the belief that the 1950s provided a more family-friendly economic and social environment, an easier climate in which to keep kids on the straight and narrow, and above all, a greater feeling of hope for a family's long-term future, especially for its young. The contrast between the perceived hopefulness of the fifties and our own misgivings about the future is key to contemporary nostalgia for the period. Greater optimism *did* exist then, even among many individuals and groups who were in terrible circumstances. But if we are to take people's sense of loss seriously, rather than merely to capitalize on it for a hidden political agenda, we need to develop a historical perspective on where that hope came from.

Part of it came from families comparing their prospects in the 1950s to their unstable, often grindingly uncomfortable pasts, especially the two horrible decades just before. In the 1920s after two centuries of child labor and income insecurity, and for the first time in American history, a bare majority of children had come to live in a family with a male breadwinner, a female homemaker, and a chance at a high school education. Yet no sooner did the ideals associated with such a family begin to blossom than they were buried by the stock market crash of 1929 and the Great Depression of the 1930s. During the 1930s domestic violence soared; divorce rates fell, but informal separations jumped; fertility plummeted. Murder rates were higher in 1933 than they were in the 1980s. Families were uprooted or torn apart. Thousands of young people left home to seek work, often riding the rails across the country.

World War II brought the beginning of economic recovery, and people's renewed interest in forming families resulted in a marriage and childbearing boom, but stability was still beyond most people's grasp. Postwar communities were rocked by racial tensions, labor strife, and a right-wing backlash against the radical union movement of the 1930s. Many women resented being fired from wartime jobs they had grown to enjoy. Veterans often came home to find that they had to elbow their way back into their families, with wives and children resisting their attempts to reassert domestic authority. In one recent study of fathers who returned from the war, four times as many reported painful, even traumatic, reunions as remembered happy ones.

By 1946 one in every three marriages was ending in divorce. Even couples who stayed together went through rough times, as an acute housing shortage forced families to double up with relatives or friends. Tempers frayed and generational relations grew strained. "No home is big enough to house two families, particularly two of different generations, with opposite theories on child training," warned a 1948 film on the problems of modern marriage.

So after the widespread domestic strife, family disruptions, and violence of the 1930s and the instability of the World War II period, people were ready to try something new. The postwar economic boom gave them the chance.

The 1950s was the first time that a majority of Americans could even *dream* of creating a secure oasis in their immediate nuclear families. There they could focus their emotional and financial investments, reduce obligations to others that might keep them from seizing their own chance at a new start, and escape the interference of an older generation of neighbors or relatives who tried to tell them how to run their lives and raise their kids. Oral histories of the postwar period resound with the theme of escaping from in-laws, maiden aunts, older parents, even needy siblings.

The private family also provided a refuge from the anxieties of the new nuclear age and the cold war, as well as a place to get away from the political witch-hunts led by

Senator Joe McCarthy and his allies. When having the wrong friends at the wrong time or belonging to any "suspicious" organization could ruin your career and reputation, it was safer to pull out of groups you might have joined earlier and to focus on your family. On a more positive note, the nuclear family was where people could try to satisfy their long-pent-up desires for a more stable marriage, a decent home, and the chance to really enjoy their children.

THE 1950s FAMILY EXPERIMENT

The key to understanding the successes, failures, and comparatively short life of 1950s family forms and values is to understand the period as one of *experimentation* with the possibilities of a new kind of family, not as the expression of some longstanding tradition. At the end of the 1940s, the divorce rate, which had been rising steadily since the 1890s, dropped sharply; the age of marriage fell to a 100-year low; and the birth rate soared. Women who had worked during the depression or World War II quit their jobs as soon as they became pregnant, which meant quite a few women were specializing in child raising; fewer women remained childless during the 1950s than in any decade since the late nineteenth century. The timing and spacing of childbearing became far more compressed, so that young mothers were likely to have two or more children in diapers at once, with no older sibling to help in their care. At the same time, again for the first time in 100 years, the educational gap between young middle-class women and men increased, while job segregation for working men and women seems to have peaked. These demographic changes increased the dependence of women on marriage, in contrast to gradual trends in the opposite direction since the early twentieth century.

The result was that family life and gender roles became much more predictable, orderly, and settled in the 1950s than they were either twenty years earlier or would be twenty years later. Only slightly more than one in four marriages ended in divorce during the 1950s. Very few young people spent any extended period of time in a nonfamily setting: They moved from their parent's family into their own family, after just a brief experience with independent living, and they started having children soon after marriage. Whereas two-thirds of women aged 20–24 were not yet married in 1990, only 28 percent of women this age were still single in 1960.

Ninety percent of all the households in the country were families in the 1950s, in comparison with only 71 percent by 1990. Eighty-six percent of all children lived in two-parent homes in 1950, as opposed to just 72 percent in 1990. And the percentage living with both biological parents—rather than, say, a parent and stepparent—was dramatically higher than it had been at the turn of the century or is today: 70 percent in 1950, compared with only 50 percent in 1990. Nearly 60 percent of kids—an all-time high—were born into male breadwinner-female homemaker families; only a minority of the rest had mothers who worked in the paid labor force.

If the organization and uniformity of family life in the 1950s were new, so were the values, especially the emphasis on putting all one's emotional and financial eggs in the small basket of the immediate nuclear family. Right up through the 1940s, ties of work, friendship, neighborhood, ethnicity, extended kin, and voluntary organizations were as important a source of identity for most Americans, and sometimes a *more* important source of obligation, than marriage and the nuclear family. All this changed in the post-war era. The spread of suburbs and automobiles, combined with the destruction of older ethnic neighborhoods in many cities, led to the decline of the neighborhood social club. Young couples moved away from parents and kin, cutting ties with traditional extra-familial networks that might compete for their attention. A critical factor in this trend was the emergence of a group of family sociologists and marriage counselors who followed Talcott Parsons in claiming that the nuclear family, built on a sharp division of labor between husband and wife, was the cornerstone of modern society.

The new family experts tended to advocate views such as those first raised in a 1946 book, *Their Mothers' Sons*, by psychiatrist Edward Strecker. Strecker and his followers argued that American boys were infantilized and emasculated by women who were old-fashioned "moms" instead of modern "mothers." One sign that might be that dreaded "mom," Strecker warned women, was if you felt you should take your aging parents into your own home, rather than putting them in "a good institution . . . where they will receive adequate care and comfort." Modern "mothers" placed their parents in nursing homes and poured all their energies into their nuclear family. They were discouraged from diluting their wifely and maternal commitments by maintaining "competing" interests in friends, jobs, or extended family networks, yet they were also supposed to cheerfully grant early independence to their (male) children—an emotional double bind that may explain why so many women who took this advice to heart ended up abusing alcohol or tranquilizers over the course of the decade.

The call for young couples to break from their parents and youthful friends was a consistent theme in 1950s popular culture. In *Marty*, one of the most highly praised TV plays and movies of the 1950s, the hero almost loses his chance at love by listening to the carping of his mother and aunt and letting himself be influenced by old friends who resent the time he spends with his new girlfriend. In the end, he turns his back on mother, aunt, and friends to get his new marriage and a little business of his own off to a good start. Other movies, novels, and popular psychology tracts portrayed the dreadful things that happened when women became more interested in careers than marriage or men resisted domestic conformity.

Yet many people felt guilty about moving away from older parents and relatives; "modern mothers" worried that fostering independence in their kids could lead to defiance or even juvenile delinquency (the recurring nightmare of the age); there was considerable confusion about how men and women could maintain clear breadwinner-homemaker distinctions in a period of expanding education, job openings, and consumer aspirations. People clamored for advice. They got it from the new family education specialists and marriage counselors, from columns in women's magazines, from government pamphlets, and above all from television. While 1950s TV melodramas warned against letting anything dilute the commitment to getting married and having kids, the new family sitcoms gave people nightly lessons on how to make their marriage or rapidly expanding family work—or, in the case of *I Love Lucy*, probably the most popular show of the era, how *not* to make their marriage and family work. Lucy and Ricky gave weekly comic reminders of how much trouble a woman could get into by wanting a career or hatching some hare-brained scheme behind her husband's back.

At the time, everyone knew that shows such as *Donna Reed, Ozzie and Harriet, Leave It to Beaver,* and *Father Knows Best* were not the way families really were. People didn't watch those shows to see their own lives reflected back at them. They watched them to see how families were *supposed* to live—and also to get a little reassurance that they were headed in the right direction. The sitcoms were simultaneously advertisements, etiquette manuals, and how-to lessons for a new way of organizing marriage and child raising. I have studied the scripts of these shows for years, since I often use them in my classes on family history, but it wasn't until I became a parent that I felt their extraordinary pull. The secret of their appeal, I suddenly realized, was that they offered 1950s viewers, wracked with the same feelings of parental inadequacy as was I, the promise that there were easy answers and surefire techniques for raising kids.

Ever since, I have found it useful to think of the sitcoms as the 1950s equivalent of today's beer ads. As most people know, beer ads are consciously aimed at men who *aren't* as strong and sexy as the models in the commercials, guys who are uneasily aware of the gap between the ideal masculine pursuits and their own achievements. The promise is that if the viewers on the couch will just drink brand X, they too will be able to run 10 miles without gasping for breath. Their bodies will firm up, their complexions will clear up, and maybe the Swedish bikini team will come over and hang out at their place.

Similarly, the 1950s sitcoms were aimed at young couples who had married in haste, women who had tasted new freedoms during World War II and given up their jobs with regret, veterans whose children resented their attempts to reassert paternal authority, and individuals disturbed by the changing racial and ethnic mix of postwar America. The message was clear: Buy these ranch houses, Hotpoint appliances, and child-raising ideals; relate to your spouse like this; get a new car to wash with your kids on Sunday afternoons; organize your dinners like that—and you too can escape from the conflicts of race, class, and political witch-hunts into harmonious families where father knows best, mothers are never bored or irritated, and teenagers rush to the dinner table each night, eager to get their latest dose of parental wisdom.

Many families found it possible to put together a good imitation of this way of living during the 1950s and 1960s. Couples were often able to construct marriages that were much more harmonious than those in which they had grown up, and to devote far more time to their children. Even when marriages were deeply unhappy, as many were, the new stability, economic security, and educational advantages parents were able to offer their kids counted for a lot in people's assessment of their life satisfaction. And in some matters, ignorance could be bliss: The lack of media coverage of problems such as abuse or incest was terribly hard on the casualties, but it protected more fortunate families from knowledge and fear of many social ills.

There was tremendous hostility to people who could be defined as "others": Jews, African Americans, Puerto Ricans, the poor, gays or lesbians, and "the red menace." Yet on a day-to-day basis, the civility that prevailed in homogeneous neighborhoods allowed people to ignore larger patterns of racial and political repression. Racial clashes were ever-present in the 1950s, sometimes escalating into full-scale antiblack riots, but individual homicide rates fell to almost half the levels of the 1930s. As nuclear families moved into the suburbs, they retreated from social activism but entered voluntary relationships with people who had children the same age; they became involved in PTAs together, joined bridge clubs, went bowling. There does seem to have been a stronger sense of neighborly commonalities than many of us feel today. Even though this local community was often the product of exclusion or repression, it sometimes looks attractive to modern Americans whose commutes are getting longer and whose family or work patterns give them little in common with their neighbors.

The optimism that allowed many families to rise above their internal difficulties and to put limits on their individualistic values during the 1950s came from the sense that America was on a dramatically different trajectory than it had been in the past, an upward and expansionary path that had already taken people to better places than they had ever seen before and would certainly take their children even farther. This confidence that almost everyone could look forward to a better future stands in sharp contrast to how most contemporary Americans feel, and it explains why a period in which many people were much worse off than today sometimes still looks like a better period for families than our own.

Throughout the 1950s, poverty was higher than it is today, but it was less concentrated in pockets of blight existing side-by-side with extremes of wealth, and, unlike today, it was falling rather than rising. At the end of the 1930s, almost two-thirds of the population had incomes below the poverty standards of the day, while only one in eight had a middle-class income (defined as two to five times the poverty line). By 1960, a majority of the population had climbed into the middle-income range.

Unmarried people were hardly sexually abstinent in the 1950s, but the age of first intercourse was somewhat higher than it is now, and despite a tripling of nonmarital birth rates between 1940 and 1958, more than 70 percent of nonmarital pregnancies led to weddings before the child was born. Teenage birth rates were almost twice as high in 1957 as in the 1990s, but most teen births were to married couples, and the effect of teen pregnancy in reducing further schooling for young people did not hurt their life prospects the way it does today. High school graduation rates were lower in the 1950s than they are today, and minority students had far worse test scores, but there were jobs for people who dropped out of high school or graduated without good reading skills—jobs that actually had a future. People entering the job market in the 1950s had no way of knowing that they would be the last generation to have a good shot at reaching middle-class status without the benefit of postsecondary schooling.

Millions of men from impoverished, rural, unemployed, or poorly educated family backgrounds found steady jobs in the steel, auto, appliance, construction, and shipping industries. Lower middle-class men went further on in college during the 1950s than they would have been able to expect in earlier decades, enabling them to make the transition to secure white-collar work. The experience of shared sacrifices in the depression and war, reinforced by a New Deal–inspired belief in the ability of government to make life better, gave people a sense of hope for the future. Confidence in government, business, education, and other institutions was on the rise. This general optimism affected people's experience and assessment of family life. It is no wonder modern Americans yearn for a similar sense of hope.

But before we sign on to any attempts to turn the family clock back to the 1950s, we should note that the family successes and community solidarities of the 1950s rested on a totally different set of political and economic conditions than we have today. Contrary to widespread belief, the 1950s was not an age of laissez-faire government and free market competition. A major cause of the social mobility of young families in the 1950s was that federal assistance programs were much more generous and widespread than they are today.

In the most ambitious and successful affirmative action program ever adopted in America, 40 percent of young men were eligible for veterans' benefits, and these benefits were far more extensive than those available to Vietnam-era vets. Financed in part by a federal income tax on the rich that went up to 87 percent and a corporate tax rate of 52 percent, such benefits provided quite a jump start for a generation of young families. The GI bill paid most tuition costs for vets who attended college, doubling the percentage of college students from prewar levels. At the other end of the life span, Social Security began to build up a significant safety net for the elderly, formerly the poorest segment of the population. Starting in 1950, the federal government regularly mandated raises in the minimum wage to keep pace with inflation. The minimum wage may have been only $1.40 as late as 1968, but a person who worked for that amount full-time, year-round, earned 118 percent of the poverty figure for a family of three. By 1995, a full-time minimum-wage worker could earn only 72 percent of the poverty level.

An important source of the economic expansion of the 1950s was that public works spending at all levels of government comprised nearly 20 percent of total expenditures in 1950s as compared to less than 7 percent in 1984. Between 1950 and 1960, nonmilitary, nonresidential public construction rose by 58 percent. Construction expenditures for new schools (in dollar amounts adjusted for inflation) rose by 72 percent; funding on sewers and waterworks rose by 46 percent. Government paid 90 percent of the costs of building the new Interstate Highway system. These programs opened up suburbia to growing numbers of middle-class Americans and created secure, well-paying jobs for blue-collar workers.

Government also reorganized home financing, underwriting low down payments and long-term mortgages that had been rejected as bad business by private industry. To do this, government put public assets behind housing lending programs, created two new national financial institutions to facilitate home loans, allowed veterans to put down payments as low as a dollar on a house, and offered tax breaks to people who bought homes. The National Education Defense Act funded the socioeconomic mobility of thousands of young men who trained themselves for well-paying jobs in such fields as engineering.

Unlike contemporary welfare programs, government investment in 1950s families was not just for immediate subsistence but encouraged long-term asset development, rewarding people for increasing their investment in homes and education. Thus it was far less likely that such families or individuals would ever fall back to where they started, even after a string of bad luck. Subsidies for higher education were greater the longer people stayed in school and the more expensive the school they selected. Mortgage deductions got bigger as people traded up to better houses.

These social and political support systems magnified the impact of the postwar economic boom. "In the years between 1947 and 1973," reports economist Robert Kuttner, "the median paycheck more than doubled, and the bottom 20 percent enjoyed the greatest gains." High rates of unionization meant that blue-collar workers were making much more financial progress than most of their counterparts today. In 1952, when eager home buyers flocked to the opening of Levittown, Pennsylvania, the largest planned community yet constructed, "it took a factory worker one day to earn enough money to pay the closing costs on a new Levittown house, then selling for $10,000." By 1991, such a home was selling for $100,000 or more, and it took a factory worker *eighteen weeks* to earn enough money for just the closing costs.

The legacy of the union struggle of the 1930s and 1950s, combined with government support for raising people's living standards, set limits on corporations that have disappeared in recent decades. Corporations paid 23 percent of federal income taxes in the 1950s as compared to just 9.2 percent in 1991. Big companies earned higher profit margins than smaller firms, partly due to their dominance of the market, partly to America's postwar economic advantage. They chose (or were forced) to share these extra earnings, which economists call "rents," with employees. Economists at the Brookings Institution and Harvard University estimate that 70 percent of such corporate rents were passed on to workers at all levels of the firm, benefiting secretaries and janitors as well as CEOs. Corporations routinely retained workers even in slack periods, as a way of ensuring workplace stability. Although they often received more generous tax breaks from communities than they gave back in investment, at least they kept their plants and employment offices in the same place. AT&T, for example, received much of the technology it used to finance its postwar expansion from publicly funded communications research conducted as part of the war effort, and, as current AT&T chairman Robert Allen puts it, there "used to be a lifelong commitment on the employee's part and on our part." Today, however, he admits, "the contract doesn't exist anymore."

Television trivia experts still argue over exactly what the fathers in many 1950s sitcoms did for a living. Whatever it was, though, they obviously didn't have to worry about downsizing. If most married people stayed in long-term relationships during the 1950s, so did most corporations, sticking with the communities they grew up in and the employees they originally hired. Corporations were not constantly relocating in search of cheap labor during the 1950s; unlike today, increases in worker productivity usually led to increases in wages. The number of workers covered by corporate pension plans and health benefits increased steadily. So did limits on the work week. There is good reason that people look back to the 1950s as a less hurried age: The average American was working a shorter workday in the 1950s than his or her counterpart today, when a quarter of the work-force puts in 49 or more hours a week.

So politicians are practicing quite a double standard when they tell us to return to the family forms of the 1950s, while they do nothing to resolve the job programs and family subsidies of that era, the limits on corporate relocation and financial wheeling-dealing, the much higher share of taxes paid by corporations then, the availability of union jobs for noncollege youth, and the subsidies for higher education such as the National Defense Education Act loans. Furthermore, they're not telling the whole story when they claim that the 1950s was the most prosperous time for families and the most secure decade for children. Instead, playing to our understandable nostalgia for a time when things seemed to be getting better, not worse, they engage in a tricky chronological shell game with their figures, diverting our attention from two important points. First, many individuals, families, and groups were excluded from the economic prosperity, family optimism, and social civility of the 1950s. Second, the all-time high point of child well-being and family economic security came not during the 1950s but *at the end of the 1960s.*

2 Public Debates and Private Lives

The Mommy Wars: Ambivalence, Ideological Work, and the Cultural Contradictions of Motherhood

Sharon Hays

I have argued that all mothers ultimately share a recognition of the ideology of intensive mothering. At the same time, all mothers live in a society where child rearing is generally devalued and the primary emphasis is placed on profit, efficiency, and "getting ahead." If you are a mother, both logics operate in your daily life.

But the story is even more complicated. Over half of American mothers participate directly in the labor market on a regular basis; the rest remain at least somewhat distant from that world as they spend most of their days in the home. One might therefore expect paid working mothers to be more committed to the ideology of competitively maximizing personal profit and stay-at-home mothers to be more committed to the ideology of intensive mothering. As it turns out, however, this is not precisely the way it works.

Modern-day mothers are facing two socially constructed cultural images of what a good mother looks like. Neither, however, includes the vision of a cold, calculating businesswoman—that title is reserved for childless career women. If you are a good mother, you *must* be an intensive one. The only "choice" involved is whether you *add* the role of paid working woman. The options, then, are as follows. On the one side there is the portrait of the "traditional mother" who stays at home with the kids and dedicates her energy to the happiness of her family. This mother cheerfully studies the latest issue of *Family Circle*, places flowers in every room, and has dinner waiting when her husband comes home. This mother, when she's not cleaning, cooking, sewing, shopping, doing the laundry, or comforting her mate, is focused on attending to the children and ensuring their proper development. On the other side is the image of the successful "supermom." Effortlessly juggling home and work, this mother can push a stroller with one hand and carry a briefcase in the other. She is always properly coiffed, her nylons have no runs, her suits are freshly pressed, and her home has seen the white tornado. Her children are immaculate and well mannered but not passive, with a strong spirit and high self-esteem.

Although both the traditional mom and the supermom are generally considered socially acceptable, their coexistence represents a serious cultural ambivalence about how mothers should behave. This ambivalence comes out in the widely available indictments of the failings of both groups of women. Note, for instance, the way Mecca, a welfare mother, describes these two choices and their culturally provided critiques:

> The way my family was brought up was, like, you marry a man, he's the head of the house, he's the provider, and you're the wife, you're the provider in the house. Now these days it's not that way. Now the people that stay home are classified, quote, "lazy people," we don't "like" to work.
>
> I've seen a lot of things on TV about working mothers and nonworking mothers. People who stay home attack the other mothers 'cause they're, like, bad mothers because they left the kids behind and go to work. And, the other ones aren't working because we're lazy. But it's not lazy. It's the lifestyle in the 1990s it's, like, too much. It's a demanding world for mothers with kids.

The picture Mecca has seen on television, a picture of these two images attacking each other with ideological swords, is not an uncommon one.

It is this cultural ambivalence and the so-called choice between these paths that is the basis for what Darnton (1990) has dubbed the "mommy wars." Both stay-at-home and paid working mothers, it is argued, are angry and defensive; neither group respects the other. Both make use of available cultural indictments to condemn the opposing group. Supermoms, according to this portrait, regularly describe stay-at-home mothers as lazy and boring, while traditional moms regularly accuse employed mothers of selfishly neglecting their children.

My interviews suggest, however, that this portrait of the mommy wars is both exaggerated and superficial. In fact, the majority of mothers I spoke with expressed respect for one another's need or right to choose whether to go out to work or stay at home with the kids. And, as I have argued, they also share a whole set of similar concerns regarding appropriate child rearing. These mothers have not formally enlisted in this war. Yet the rhetoric of the mommy wars draws them in as it persists in mainstream American culture, a culture that is unwilling, for various significant reasons, to unequivocally embrace either vision of motherhood, just as it remains unwilling to embrace wholeheartedly the childless career woman. Thus, the charges of being lazy and bored, on the one hand, or selfish and money-grubbing, on the other, are made available for use by individual mothers and others should the need arise.

What this creates is a no-win situation for women of child-bearing years. If a woman voluntarily remains childless, some will say that she is cold, heartless, and unfulfilled as a woman. If she is a mother who works too hard at her job or career, some will accuse her of neglecting the kids. If she does not work hard enough, some will surely place her on the "mommy track" and her career advancement will be permanently slowed by the claim that her commitment to her children interferes with her workplace efficiency (Schwartz 1989). And if she stays at home with her children, some will call her unproductive and useless. A woman, in other words, can never fully do it right.

At the same time that these cultural images portray all women as somehow less than adequate, they also lead many mothers to feel somehow less than adequate in their daily lives. The stay-at-home mother is supposed to be happy and fulfilled, but how can she be when she hears so often that she is mindless and bored? The supermom is supposed to be able to juggle her two roles without missing a beat, but how can she do either job as well as she is expected if she is told she must dedicate her all in both directions? In these circumstances, it is not surprising that many supermoms feel guilty about their inability to carry out both roles to their fullest, while many traditional moms feel isolated and invisible to the larger world.

Given this scenario, both stay-at-home and employed mothers end up spending a good deal of time attempting to make sense of their current positions. Paid working mothers, for instance, are likely to argue that there are lots of good reasons for mothers to work in the paid labor force; stay-at-home mothers are likely to argue that there are lots of good reasons for mothers to stay at home with their children. These arguments are best understood not as (mere) rationalizations or (absolute) truths but rather as socially necessary "ideological work." Berger (1981a) uses this notion to describe the way that all people make use of available ideologies in their "attempt to cope with the relationship between the ideas they bring to a social context and the practical pressures of day-to-day living in it" (15). People, in other words, select among the cultural logics at their disposal in order to develop some correspondence between what they believe and what they actually do. For mothers, just like others, ideological work is simply a means of maintaining their sanity.

The ideological work of mothers, as I will show, follows neither a simple nor a straightforward course. First, as I have pointed out, both groups face two contradictory cultural images of appropriate mothering. Their ideological work, then, includes a recognition and response to both portraits. This duality is evident in the fact that the logic the traditional mother uses to affirm her position matches the logic that the supermom uses to express ambivalence about her situation, and the logic that the employed mother uses to affirm her position is the same logic that the stay-at-home mother uses to express ambivalence about hers. Their strategies, in other words, are mirror images, but they are also incomplete—both groups are left with some ambivalence. Thus, although the two culturally provided images of mothering help mothers to make sense of their own positions, they simultaneously sap the strength of mothers by making them feel inadequate in one way or the other. It is in coping with these feelings of inadequacy that their respective ideological strategies take an interesting turn. Rather than taking divergent paths, as one might expect, both groups attempt to resolve their feelings of inadequacy by returning to the logic of the ideology of intensive mothering.

THE FRUMPY HOUSEWIFE AND THE PUSH TOWARD THE OUTSIDE WORLD

Some employed mothers say that they go out to work for pay because they need the income. But the overwhelming majority also say that they *want* to work outside the home. First, there's the problem of staying inside all day: "I decided once I started working that I need that. I need to work. Because I'll become like this big huge hermit frumpy person if I stay home." Turning into a "big huge hermit frumpy person" is connected to the feeling of being confined to the home. Many women have had that experience at one time or another and do not want to repeat it:

> When I did stay home with him, up until the time when he was ten months old, I wouldn't go out of the house for three days at a time. Ya know, I get to where I don't want to get dressed, I don't care if I take a shower. It's like, what for? I'm not going anywhere.

Not getting dressed and not going anywhere are also tied to the problem of not having a chance to interact with other adults:

> I remember thinking, "I don't even get out of my robe. And I've gotta stay home and breast-feed and the only adult I hear is on *Good Morning America*—and he's not even live!" And that was just for a couple of months. I don't even know what it would be like for a couple of years. I think it would be really difficult.

Interacting with adults, for many paid working mothers, means getting a break from the world of children and having an opportunity to use their minds:

> When I first started looking for a job, I thought we needed a second income. But then when I started working it was like, this is great! I do have a mind that's not *Sesame Street!* And I just love talking with people. It's just fun, and it's a break. It's tough, but I enjoyed it; it was a break from being with the kids.

If you don't get a break from the kids, if you don't get out of the house, if you don't interact with adults, and if you don't have a chance to use your mind beyond the *Sesame Street* level, you might end up lacking the motivation to do much at all. This argument is implied by many mothers:

> If I was stuck at home all day, and I did do that 'cause I was waiting for day care, I stayed home for four months, and I went crazy, I couldn't stand it. I mean not because I didn't want to spend any time with her, but because we'd just sit here and she'd just cry all day and I couldn't get anything done. I was at the end of the day exhausted, and feeling like shit.

Of course, it is exhausting to spend the day meeting the demands of children. But there's also a not too deeply buried sense in all these arguments that getting outside the home and using one's mind fulfill a longing to be part of the larger world and to be recognized by it. One mother made this point explicitly:

> [When you're working outside the home] you're doing something. You're using your mind a little bit differently than just trying to figure out how to make your day work with your kid. It's just challenging in a different way. So there's part of me that wants to be, like, *recognized*. I think maybe that's what work does, it gives you a little bit of a sense of recognition, that you don't feel like you get [when you stay home].

Most employed mothers, then, say that if they stay at home they'll go stir-crazy, they'll get bored, the demands of the kids will drive them nuts, they won't have an opportunity to use their brains or interact with other adults, they'll feel like they're going nowhere, and they'll lose their sense of identity in the larger world. And, for many of these mothers, all these points are connected:

> Well, I think [working outside is] positive, because I feel good about being able to do the things that I went to school for, and keep up with that, and use my brain. As they grow older, [the children are] going to get into things that they want to get into, they're going to be out with their friends and stuff, and I don't want to be in a situation where my whole life has been wrapped around the kids. That's it. Just some outside interests so that I'm not so wrapped up in how shiny my floor is. [She laughs.] Just to kind of be out and be stimulated. Gosh, I don't want this to get taken wrong, but I think I'd be a little bit bored. And the other thing I think of is, I kind of need a break, and when you're staying at home it's constant. It's a lot harder when you don't have family close by, [because] you don't get a break.

In short, paid working mothers feel a strong pull toward the outside world. They hear the world accusing stay-at-home moms of being mindless and unproductive and of lacking an identity apart from their kids, and they experience this as at least partially true.

Stay-at-home mothers also worry that the world will perceive them as lazy and bored and watching television all day as children scream in their ears and tug at their sleeves. And sometimes this is the way they feel about themselves. In other words, the same image that provides working mothers with the reasons they should go out to work accounts for the ambivalence that stay-at-home mothers feel about staying at home.

A few stay-at-home mothers seem to feel absolutely secure in their position, but most do not. Many believe that they will seek paid work at some point, and almost all are made uncomfortable by the sense that the outside world does not value what they do. In all cases, their expressions of ambivalence about staying at home mimic the concerns of employed mothers. For instance, some women who stay at home also worry about becoming frumpy: "I'm not this heavy. I'm, like, twenty-seven pounds overweight. It sounds very vain of me, in my situation. It's like, I'm not used to being home all the time, I'm home twenty-four hours. I don't have that balance in my life anymore." And some stay-at-home mothers feel as if they are physically confined inside the home. This mother, for example, seems tired of meeting the children's demands and feels that she is losing her sense of self:

> There's a hard thing of being at home all the time. You have a lot of stress, because you're constantly in the house. I think having a job can relieve some of that stress and to make it a lot more enjoyable, to want to come home all the time. . . . My outings are [limited]. I'm excited when I have to go grocery shopping. Everything I pick is what they eat, everything they like, or what they should eat. Me, I'm just *there*. I'm there for them. I feel that I'm here for them.

Both of these stay-at-home mothers, like over one-third of the stay-at-home mothers in my sample, plan to go out to work as soon as they can find paid employment that offers sufficient rewards to compensate (both financially and ideologically) for sending the kids to day care. Most of the remaining mothers are committed to staying at home with the children through what they understand as formative years. The following mother shares that commitment, while also echoing many paid working mothers in her hopes that one day she will have a chance to be around adults and further her own growth:

Well, we could do more, we'd have more money, but that's really not the biggest reason I'd go back to work. I want to do things for myself, too. I want to go back and get my master's [degree] or something. I need to grow, and be around adults, too. I don't know when, but I think in the next two years I'll go back to work. The formative years—their personality is going to develop until they're about five. It's pretty much set by then. So I think it's pretty critical that you're around them during those times.

One mother stated explicitly that she can hardly wait until the kids are through their formative years:

At least talking to grown-ups is a little more fulfilling than ordering the kids around all day. My life right now is just all theirs. Sometimes it's a depressing thought because I think, "Where am I? I want my life back." . . . I mean, they are totally selfish. It's like an ice cream. They just gobble that down and say, "Let me have the cinnamon roll now."
   . . . [But] I had them, and I want them to be good people. So I've dedicated myself to them right now. Later on I get my life back. They won't always be these little sponges. I don't want any deficiency—well, nobody can cover all the loopholes—but I want to be comfortable in myself to know that I did everything that I could. It's the least I can do to do the best I can by them.

Mothers, she seems to be saying, are like confections that the kids just gobble down—and then they ask for more.

Thus, many stay-at-home moms experience the exhaustion of meeting the demands of children all day long, just as employed mothers fear they might. And many stay-at-home mothers also experience a loss of self. Part of the reason they feel like they are losing their identity is that they know the outside world does not recognize a mother's work as valuable. This woman, committed to staying at home until her youngest is at least three years old, explains:

You go through a period where you feel like you've lost all your marbles. Boy, you're not as smart as you used to be, and as sharp as you used to be, and not as respected as you used to be. And those things are really hard to swallow. But that's something I've discussed with other mothers who are willing to stay home with their kids, and we've formed a support group where we've said, "Boy, those people just don't know what they're talking about." We're like a support group for each other, which you have to have if you've decided to stay at home, because you have so many people almost pushing you to work, or asking "Why don't you work?" You're not somehow as good as anybody else 'cause you're staying at home; what you're doing isn't important. We have a lot of that in this society.

Another mother, this one determined to stay at home with her kids over the long haul, provides a concrete example of the subtle and not-so-subtle ways in which society pushes mothers to participate in the paid labor force, and of the discomfort such mothers experience as a result:

As a matter of fact, somebody said to me (I guess it was a principal from one of the schools) . . . "Well, what do you *do?* Do you have a *job?*" And it was just very funny to me that he was so uncomfortable trying to ask me what it was in our society that I did. I guess that they just assume that if you're a mom at home that it means nothing. I don't know, I just don't consider it that way. But it's kind of funny, worrying about what you're gonna say at a dinner party about what you do.

And it's not just that these mothers worry about being able to impress school principals and people at cocktail parties, of course. The following mother worries about being "interesting" to other women who do not have children:

> I find myself, now that I'm not working, not to have as much in common [with other women who don't have children]. We don't talk that much because I don't have that much to talk about. Like I feel I'm not an interesting person anymore.

In short, the world presents, and mothers experience, the image of the lazy mindless, dull housewife—and no mother wants to be included in that image.

THE TIME-CRUNCHED CAREER WOMAN AND THE PULL TOWARD HOME

Stay-at-home mothers use a number of strategies to support their position and combat the image of the frumpy housewife. Many moms who are committed to staying at home with their kids often become part of formal or informal support groups, providing them an opportunity to interact with other mothers who have made the same commitment. Others, if they can afford the cost of transportation and child care, engage in a variety of outside activities—as volunteers for churches, temples, and community groups, for instance, or in regular leisure activities and exercise programs. They then have a chance to communicate with other adults and to experience themselves as part of a larger social world (though one in which children generally occupy a central role).

But the primary way that stay-at-home mothers cope with their ambivalence is through ideological work. Like paid working mothers, they make a list of all the good reasons they do what they do. In this case, that list includes confirming their commitment to good mothering, emphasizing the importance of putting their children's needs ahead of their own, and telling stories about the problems that families, and especially children, experience when mothers go out to work for pay.

Many stay-at-home mothers argue that kids require guidance and should have those cookies cooling on the kitchen counter when they come home from school:

> The kids are the ones that suffer. The kids need guidance and stuff. And with two parents working, sometimes there isn't even a parent home when they come home from school. And that's one thing that got me too. I want to be home and I want to have cookies on the stove when they come home from school. Now we eat meals together all the time. It's more of a homey atmosphere. It's more of a *home* atmosphere.

Providing this homey atmosphere is difficult to do if one works elsewhere all day. And providing some period of so-called quality time in the evening, these mothers tell me, is not an adequate substitute. One mother elaborates on this point in response to a question about how she would feel if she was working outside the home:

Oh, guilty as anything. I know what I'm like after dinner, and I'm not at my best. And neither are my kids. And if that's all the time I had with them, it wouldn't be, quote, "quality time." I think it's a bunch of b.s. about quality time.

And quality time, even if it *is* of high quality, cannot make up for children's lack of a quantity of time with their mothers. This argument is often voiced in connection with the problem of paid caregiver arrangements. Most mothers, whether they work for pay or not, are concerned about the quality of day care, but stay-at-home mothers often use this concern to explain their commitment to staying at home. This mother, for example, argues that children who are shuffled off to a series of day-care providers simply will not get the love they need:

> I mean, if I'm going to have children I want to *raise* them. I feel really strongly about that. Really strongly. I wish more people did that. Myself, I think it's very underestimated the role the mother plays with the child. I really do. From zero to three [years], it's like their whole self-image. [Yet, working mothers will say,] "Well, okay, I've got a caretaker now," "Well, that nanny didn't work out." So by the time the children are three years old they've had four or five people who have supposedly said "I'll love you forever," and they're gone. I think that's really tough on the kids.

Since paid caregivers lack that deep and long-lasting love, I'm told, they won't ever be as committed to ministering to the child's needs as a mom will:

> I don't think anybody can give to children what a mother can give to her own children. I think there's a level of willingness to put up with hard days, crying days, cranky days, whining days, that most mothers are going to be able to tolerate just a little bit more than a caretaker would. I think there's more of a commitment of what a mother wants to give her children in terms of love, support, values, etcetera. A caretaker isn't going to feel quite the same way.

Stay-at-home mothers imply that all these problems of kids who lack guidance, love, and support are connected to the problem of mothers who put their own interests ahead of the interests of their children. A few stay-at-home mothers will explicitly argue, as this one does, that employed mothers are allowing material and power interests to take priority over the well-being of their kids:

> People are too interested in power, they just aren't interested in what happens to their kids. You know, "Fine, put them in day care." And I just feel sad. If you're so interested in money or a career or whatever, then why have kids? Why bring them into it?

Putting such interests ahead of one's children is not only somehow immoral; it also produces children with real problems. The following mother, echoing many stories about "bad mothers" that we have heard before, had this to say about her sister:

> My sister works full-time—she's a lawyer. And her kids are the most obnoxious, whiny kids. I can't stand it. They just hang on her. She thinks she's doing okay by them because they're in an expensive private school and they have expensive music lessons and they have

expensive clothes and expensive toys and expensive cars and an expensive house. I don't know. Time will tell, I guess. But I can't believe they're not going to have some insecurities. The thing that gets me is, they don't need it. I mean, he's a lawyer too. Basically, it's like, "Well, I like you guys, but I don't really want to be there all day with you, and I don't want to have to do the dirty work."

These are serious indictments indeed.

It is just these sorts of concerns that leave paid working mothers feeling inadequate and ambivalent about *their* position. Many of them wonder at times if their lives or the lives of their children might actually be better if they stayed at home with the kids. Above all, many of them feel guilty and wonder, "Am I doing it right?" or "Have I done all I can do?" These are the mothers who, we're told, have it all. It is impossible to have it all, however, when "all" includes two contradictory sets of requirements. To begin to get a deeper sense of how these supermoms do not always feel so super, two examples might be helpful.

Angela is a working-class mother who had expected to stay home with her son through his formative years. But after nine months she found herself bored, lonely, and eager to interact with other adults. She therefore went out and got a full-time job as a cashier. She begins by expressing her concern that she is not living up to the homemaking suggestions she reads in *Parenting* magazine, worrying that she may not be doing it right:

> I get *Parenting* magazine and I read it. I do what is comfortable for me and what I can do. I'm not very creative. Where they have all these cooking ideas, and who has time to do that, except for a mother who stays home all day? Most of this is for a mother who has five, six hours to spend with her child doing this kind of thing. I don't have time for that.
>
> So then that's when I go back to day care. And I know that she's doing this kind of stuff with him, teaching him things. You know, a lot of the stuff that they have is on schooling kinds of things, flash cards, that kind of thing. Just things that I don't do. That makes me feel bad. Then I think, "I should be doing this" and "Am I doing the right thing?" I know I have a lot of love for him.

Although she loves her son and believes that this is probably "the most important thing," she also feels guilty that she may not be spending a sufficient amount of time with him, simply because she gets so tired:

> I think sometimes that I feel like I don't spend enough time with him and that's my biggest [concern]. And when I am with him, sometimes I'm not really up to being with him. Even though I am with him, sometimes I want him to go away because I've been working all day and I'm exhausted. And I feel sometimes I'll stick him in bed early because I just don't want to deal with him that day. And I feel really guilty because I don't spend enough time with him as it is. When I do have the chance to spend time with him, I don't want to spend time with him, because I'm so tired and I just want to be with myself and by myself.

Even though Angela likes her paid work and does not want to give it up, the problems of providing both a quantity of time and the idealized image of quality time with her child, just like the challenge of applying the creative cooking and child-rearing ideas she finds in *Parenting* magazine, haunt her and leave her feeling both inadequate and guilty.

Linda is a professional-class mother with a well-paying and challenging job that gives her a lot of satisfaction. She spent months searching for the right preschool for her son and is relieved that he is now in a place where the caregivers share her values. Still, she worries and wonders if life might be better if she had made different choices:

> I have a friend. She's a very good mom. She seems very patient, and I never heard her raise her voice. And she's also not working. She gets to stay home with her children, which is another thing I admire. I guess I sort of envy that too. There never seems to be a time where we can just spend, like, playing a lot. I think that's what really bothers me, that I don't feel like I have the time to just sit down and, in a relaxing way, play with him. I can do it, but then I'm thinking "Okay, well I can do this for five minutes." So that's always in the back of my mind. Time, time, time. So I guess that's the biggest thing.
>
> And just like your question, "How many hours a day is he at preschool and how many hours do you spend per day as the primary caregiver?" just made me think, "Oh my gosh!" I mean they're watching him grow up more than I am. They're with him more than I am. And that makes me feel guilty in a way, and it makes me feel sad in a way. I mean I can just see him, slipping, just growing up before me. Maybe it's that quality-time stuff. I don't spend a lot of time, and I don't know if the time I do spend with him is quality.
>
> [But] if I just stay at home, I'll kind of lose, I don't know if I want to say my sense of identity, but I guess I'll lose my career identity. I'm afraid of that I guess. . . . My friend who stays at home, she had a career before she had her children, but I forget what it was. So that whole part of her, I can't even identify it now.

On the one hand, Linda envies and admires stay-at-home moms and worries about not spending enough quality time with her son, or enough play time. She is also upset that her day-care provider spends more hours with her son each day than she can. On the other hand, Linda worries that if she did stay at home she'd lose her identity as a professional and a member of the larger society. "Time, time, time," she says, there's never enough time to do it all—or at least to do it all "right."

The issue of time is a primary source of paid working mothers' ambivalence about their double shift. Attempting to juggle two commitments at once is, of course, very difficult and stressful. This mother's sense of how time pressures make her feel that she is always moving too fast would be recognizable to the majority of paid working mothers:

> I can see when I get together with my sister [who doesn't have a paid job] . . . that she's so easygoing with the kids, and she takes her time, and when I'm with her, I realize how stressed out I am sometimes trying to get things done.
>
> And I notice how much faster I move when I shop. . . . She's so relaxed, and I think I kind of envy that.

The problem of moving too fast when shopping is connected to the problem of moving too fast when raising children. Many paid working mothers envy those who can do such things at a more relaxed pace.

For a few employed mothers (two out of twenty in my sample) the problems of quality and quantity time outweigh the rewards of paid work, and they intend to leave their jobs as soon as they can afford to do so. This woman is one example:

> I believe there's a more cohesive family unit with maybe the mother staying at home. Because a woman tends to be a buffer, mediator, you name it. She pulls the family together.

But if she's working outside the home, sometimes there's not that opportunity anymore for her to pull everyone together. She's just as tired as the husband would be and, I don't know, maybe the children are feeling like they've been not necessarily abandoned but, well, I'm sure they accept it, especially if that's the only life they've seen. But my daughter has seen a change, even when I was only on maternity leave. I've seen a change in her and she seemed to just enjoy it and appreciate us as a family more than when I was working. So now she keeps telling me, "Mom, I miss you."

When this mother hears her daughter say "I miss you," she feels a tremendous pull toward staying at home. And when she talks about the way a family needs a mother to bring its members together, she is pointing to an idealized image of the family that, like quality and quantity time, weighs heavily in the minds of many mothers.

The following paid working mother also wishes she could stay at home with the kids and wishes she could be just like the television mom of the 1950s who bakes cookies every afternoon. But she knows she has to continue working for financial seasons:

Yes. I want to be Donna Reed, definitely. Or maybe Beaver Cleaver's mother, Jane Wyatt. Anybody in an apron and a pretty hairdo and a beautiful house. Yes. Getting out of the television set and making the most of reality is really what I have to do. Because I'll always have to work.

But the majority of paid working mothers, as I have stated, not only feel they need to work for financial reasons but also *want* to work, as Angela and Linda do. Nonetheless, their concerns about the effects of the double shift on their children match the concerns of those employed moms who wish they could stay at home as well as mimicking those of mothers who actually do stay at home. This mother, for instance, loves her paid work and does not want to give it up, but she does feel guilty, wondering if she's depriving her kids of the love and stimulation they need, particularly since she does not earn enough to justify the time she spends away:

Honestly, I don't make that much money. So that in itself brings a little bit of guilt, 'cause I know I work even though we don't have to. So there's some guilt associated. If kids are coming home to an empty house every day, they're not getting the intellectual stimulation [and] they're not getting the love and nurturing that other mothers are able to give their kids. So I think in the long run they're missing out on a lot of the love and the nurturing and the caring.

And this mother does not want it to seem that she is putting her child second, but she feels pressure to live up to the image of a supermom:

I felt really torn between what I wanted to do. Like a gut-wrenching decision. Like, what's more important? Of course your kids are important, but you know, there's so many outside pressures for women to work. Every ad you see in magazines or on television shows this working woman who's coming home with a briefcase and the kids are all dressed and clean. It's such a lie. I don't know of anybody who lives like that.

There's just a lot of pressure that you're not a fulfilled woman if you're not working outside of the home. But yet, it's just a real hard choice.

This feeling of being torn by a gut-wrenching decision comes up frequently:

> I'm constantly torn between what I feel I should be doing in my work and spending more time with them. . . . I think I would spend more time with them if I could. Sometimes I think it would be great not to work and be a mom and do that, and then I think, "well?"
>
> I think it's hard. Because I think you do need to have contact with your kid. You can't just see him in the morning and put him to bed at night because you work all day long. I think that's a real problem. You need to give your child guidance. You can't leave it to the schools. You can't leave it to churches. You need to be there. So, in some ways I'm really torn.

The overriding issue for this mother is guidance; seeing the children in the morning and putting them to bed at night is just not enough.

This problem, of course, is related to the problem of leaving kids with a paid caregiver all day. Paid working mothers do not like the idea of hearing their children cry when they leave them at day care any more than any other mother does. They are, as we have seen, just as concerned that their children will not get enough love, enough nurturing, enough of the right values, enough of the proper education, and enough of the right kind of discipline if they spend most of their time with a paid caregiver. To this list of concerns, paid working mothers add their feeling that when the kids are with a paid caregiver all day, it feels as if someone else is being the mother. One woman (who stayed at home until her son was two years old) elaborates:

> Well, I think it's really sad that kids have to be at day care forty hours a week. Because basically the person who's taking care of them is your day-care person. They're pretty much being the mother. It's really sad that this other person is raising your child, and it's basically like having this other person *adopting* your child. It's *awful* that we have to do that. I just think it's a crime basically. I wish we didn't have to do it. I wish everybody could stay home with their kids and have some kind of outlet. . . .
>
> And I think having a career is really important, but I think when it comes time to have children, you can take that time off and spend it with your kid. Because you can't go backwards, and time does fly with them. It's so sad . . . I hear people say, "Oh, my day-care lady said that so-and-so walked today or used a spoon or something." I mean it's just so devastating to hear that you didn't get to see that.

Leaving one's child with a paid caregiver for hours on end is therefore a potential problem not only because that "other mother" may not be a good mother but also because the real mother misses out on the joys that come from just being with the child and having a chance to watch him or her grow. This is a heart rending issue for many mothers who work outside the home.

Once again, the arguments used by stay-at-home mothers to affirm their commitment to staying home are mimicked by the arguments paid working mothers use to express their ambivalence about the time they spend away from their children. And again, though the reasoning of these women is grounded in their experiences, it is also drawn from a widely available cultural rhetoric regarding the proper behavior of mothers.

THE CURIOUS COINCIDENCE OF PAID WORK AND THE IDEOLOGY OF INTENSIVE MOTHERING

Both paid working moms and stay-at-home moms, then, do the ideological work of making their respective lists of the reasons they should work for pay and the reasons they should stay at home. Yet both groups also continue to experience and express some ambivalence about their current positions, feeling pushed and pulled in two directions. One would assume that they would cope with their ambivalence by simply returning to their list of good reasons for doing what they do. And stay-at-home mothers do just that: they respond to the push toward work in the paid labor force by arguing that their kids need them to be at home. But, as I will demonstrate, working mothers do not use the mirror strategy. The vast majority of these women do not respond to the pull toward staying at home by arguing that kids are a pain in the neck and that paid work is more enjoyable. Instead, they respond by creating a new list of all the reasons that they are good mothers even though they work outside the home. In other words, the ideological work meant to resolve mothers' ambivalence generally points in the direction of intensive mothering.

Most paid working mothers cope with the ambivalence by arguing that their participation in the labor force is ultimately good for their kids. They make this point in a number of ways. For instance, one mother thinks that the example she provides may help to teach her kids the work ethic. Another says that with the "outside constraints" imposed by her work schedule, she's "more organized and effective" as a mom. Yet another mother suggests that her second child takes just as much time and energy away from her first child as her career does:

> I think the only negative effect [of my employment] is just [that] generally when I'm over-stressed I don't do as well as a mother. But work is only one of the things that gets me overstressed. In fact it probably stresses me less than some other things. I think I do feel guilty about working 'cause it takes time away from [my oldest daughter]. But it struck me that it's acceptable to have a second child that takes just as much time away from the other child. *That* I'm not supposed to feel guilty about. But in some ways this [pointing to the infant she is holding] takes my time away from her more than my work does. Because this is constant.

More often, however, paid working mothers share a set of more standard explanations for why their labor-force participation is actually what's best for their kids. First, just as Rachel feels that her income provides for her daughter's toys, clothing, outings, and education, and just as Jacqueline argues, "I have weeks when I don't spend enough time with them and they suffer, but those are also the weeks I bring home the biggest paychecks," many mothers point out that their paid work provides the financial resources necessary for the well-being of their children:

> How am I supposed to send her to college without saving up? And also the money that I make from working helps pay for her toys, things that she needs, clothes. I never have to say, "Oh, I'm on a budget, I can't go buy this pair of shoes." I want the best for her.

Some mothers express a related concern—namely, what would happen to the family if they did not have paying jobs and their husbands should die or divorce them? One women expressed it this way:

> Well, my dad was a fireman, so I guess there was a little bit of fear, well, if anything happened to him, how are we gonna go on? And I always kind of wished that [my mother] had something to fall back on. I think that has a lot to do with why I continue to work after the kids. I've always just felt the need to have something to hold on to.

The second standard argument given by employed mothers is that paid caregiver arrangements can help to further children's development. With respect to other people's kids, I'm told, these arrangements can keep them from being smothered by their mothers or can temporarily remove them from bad family situations. With reference to their own children, mothers emphasize that good day care provides kids with the opportunity to interact with adults, gives them access to "new experiences" and "different activities," "encourages their independence," and allows them to play with other kids—which is very important, especially now that neighborhoods no longer provide the sort of community life they once did:

> They do say that kids in preschool these days are growing up a little more neurotic, but I don't think that my daughter would have had a better life. In fact I think her life would have been a thousand times worse if I was a low-income mother who stayed home and she only got to play with the kids at the park. Because I think that preschool is really good for them. Maybe not a holding tank, but a nice preschool where they play nice games with them and they have the opportunity to play with the same kids over and over again. I think that's really good for them. Back in the 1950s, everybody stayed home and there were kids all over the block to play with. It's not that way now. The neighborhoods are deserted during the week.

Third, several mothers tell me that the quality of the time they spend with their kids actually seems to increase when they have a chance to be away from them for a part of the day. Listen to these mothers:

> When I'm with them too long I tend to lose my patience and start yelling at them. This way we both get out. And we're glad to see each other when we come home.

> If women were only allowed to work maybe ten to fifteen hours a week, they would appreciate their kids more and they'd have more quality time with them, rather than having to always just scold them.

> I think I have even less patience [when I stay home with the children], because it's like, "Oh, is this all there is?" . . . Whereas when I go to work and come home, I'm glad to see him. You know, you hear people say that they're better parents when they work because they spend more quality time, all those clichés, or whatever. For me that happens to be true.

> And now when I come home from work (although I wish I could get off earlier from work), I think I'm a better mom. There you go! Because when I come home from work, I don't

have *all* day, just being with the kids. It's just that when I'm working I feel like I'm competent, I'm a person!

Getting this break from the kids, a break that reinforces your feeling of competence and therefore results in more rewarding time with your children is closely connected to the final way paid working mothers commonly attempt to resolve their ambivalence. Their children's happiness, they explain, is dependent upon their *own* happiness as mothers. One hears this again and again: "Happy moms make happy children"; "If I'm happy in my work then I think I can be a better mom"; and "I have to be happy with myself in order to make the children happy." One mother explains it this way:

> In some ways working is good. It's definitely got its positive side, because I get a break. I mean, now what I'm doing [working part-time] is perfect. I go to work. I have time to myself. I get to go to the bathroom when I need to go to the bathroom. I come home and I'm very happy to see my kids again. What's good for the mother and makes the mother happy is definitely good for the kids.

In all these explanations for why their participation in the paid labor force is actually good for their kids, these mothers want to make it clear that they still consider children their primary interest. They are definitely not placing a higher value on material success or power, they say. Nor are they putting their own interests above the interests of their children. They want the children to get all they need. But part of what children need, they argue, is financial security, the material goods required for proper development, some time away from their mothers, more quality time when they are with their mothers, and mothers who are happy in what they do. In all of these statements, paid working mothers clearly recognize the ideology of intensive mothering and testify that they are committed to fulfilling its requirements.

To underline the significance of this point, let me remind the reader that these paid working mothers use methods of child rearing that are just as child-centered, expert-guided, emotionally absorbing, labor-intensive, and financially expensive as their stay-at-home counterparts; they hold the child just as sacred, and they are just as likely to consider themselves as primarily responsible for the present and future well-being of their children. These are also the very same mothers who put a tremendous amount of time and energy into finding appropriate paid caregiver arrangements. Yet for all that they do to meet the needs of their children, they still express some ambivalence about working outside the home. And they still resolve this ambivalence by returning to the logic of intensive mothering and reminding the observer that ultimately they are most interested in what is best for their kids. This is striking.

CONTINUING CONTRADICTIONS

All this ideological work is a measure of the power of the pushes and pulls experienced by American mothers today. A woman can be a stay-at-home mother and claim to follow tradition, but not without paying the price of being treated as an outsider in the larger public world of the market. Or a woman can be a paid worker who participates in that larger world, but she must then pay the price of an impossible double shift. In both cases, women are enjoined to maintain the logic of intensive mothering. These contradictory pressures mimic the contradictory logics operating in this society, and almost all mothers experience them. The complex strategies mothers use to cope with these contradictory logics highlight the emotional, cognitive, and physical toll they take on contemporary mothers.

As I have argued, these strategies also highlight something more. The ways mothers explain their decisions to stay at home or work in the paid labor force, like the pushes and pulls they feel, run in opposite directions. Yet the ways they attempt to resolve the ambivalence they experience as a result of those decisions run in the *same* direction. Stay-at-home mothers, as I have shown, reaffirm their commitment to good mothering, and employed mothers maintain that they are good mothers even though they work. Paid working mothers do not, for instance, claim that child rearing is a relatively meaningless task, that personal profit is their primary goal, and that children are more efficiently raised in child-care centers. If you are a mother, in other words, although both the logic of the workplace and the logic of mothering operate in your life, the logic of intensive mothering has a *stronger* claim.

This phenomenon is particularly curious. The fact that there is no way for either type of mother to get it right would seem all the more reason to give up the logic of intensive mothering, especially since both groups of mothers recognize that paid employment confers more status than motherhood in the larger world. Yet images of freshly baked cookies and *Leave It to Beaver* seem to haunt mothers more often than the housewives' "problem that has no name" (Friedan 1963), and far more often than the image of a corporate manager with a big office, a large staff, and lots of perks. Although these mothers do not want to be defined as "mere" housewives and do want to achieve recognition in the outside world, most would also like to be there when the kids come home from school. Mothers surely try to balance their own desires against the requirements of appropriate child rearing, but in the world of mothering, it is socially unacceptable for them (in word if not in deed) to place their own needs above the needs of their children. A good mother certainly would never simply put her child aside for her own convenience. And placing material wealth or power on a higher plane than the well-being of children is strictly forbidden. It is clear that the two groups come together in holding these values as primary, despite the social devaluation of mothering and despite the glorification of wealth and power.

The portrait of the mommy wars, then, is overdrawn. Although the ideological strategies these groups use to explain their choice of home or paid work include an implicit critique of those "on the other side," this is almost always qualified, and both groups, at least at times, discuss their envy or admiration for the others. More important, as should now be abundantly clear, both groups ultimately share the same set of beliefs and the same set of concerns. Over half the women in my sample explicitly state that the choice between home and paid work depends on the individual woman, her interests, desires, and circumstances. Nearly all the rest argue that home is more important than paid work because children are simply more important than careers or the pursuit of financial gain. The paid working women in my sample were actually twice as likely as their stay-at-home counterparts to respond that home and children are more important and rewarding than paid work. Ideologically speaking, at least, home and children actually seem to become more important to a mother the more time she spends away from them.

There *are* significant differences among mothers—ranging from individual differences to more systematic differences of class, race, and employment. But in the present context, what is most significant is the commitment to the ideology of intensive mothering that women share in spite of their differences. In this, the cultural contradictions of motherhood persist.

The case of paid working mothers is particularly important in this regard, since these are the very mothers who, arguably, have the most to gain from redefining motherhood in such a way as to lighten their load on the second shift. As we have seen, however, this is not exactly what they do. It is true, as Gerson (1985) argues, that there are ways in which paid working mothers do redefine motherhood and lighten their load—for instance, by sending their kids to day care, spending less time with them than their stay-at-home counterparts, legitimating their paid labor-force participation, and engaging in any number of practical strategies to make child-rearing tasks less energy- and time-consuming. But, as I have argued, this does not mean that these mothers have given up the ideology of intensive mothering. Rather, it means that, whether or not they actually do, they feel they should spend a good deal of time looking for appropriate paid caregivers, trying to make up for the lack of quantity time by focusing their energy on providing quality time, and remaining attentive to the central tenets of the ideology of intensive child rearing. It also means that many are left feeling pressed for time, a little guilty, a bit inadequate, and somewhat ambivalent about their position. These stresses and the strain toward compensatory strategies should actually be taken as a measure of the persistent strength of the ideology of intensive mothering.

To deepen the sense of paradox further, one final point should be repeated. There are reasons to expect middle-class mothers to be in the vanguard of transforming ideas about child rearing away from an intensive model. First, middle-class women were historically in the vanguard of transforming child-rearing ideologies. Second, while many poor and working-class women have had to carry a double shift of wage labor and domestic chores for generations, middle-class mothers have had little practice, historically speaking, in juggling paid work and home and therefore might be eager to avoid it. Finally, one could argue that employed mothers in the middle class have more to gain from reconstructing ideas about appropriate child rearing than any other group—not only because their higher salaries mean that more money is at stake, but also because intensive mothering potentially interferes with their career trajectories in a more damaging way than is true of less high-status occupations. But, as I have suggested, middle-class women are, in some respects, those who go about the task of child rearing with the greatest intensity.

When women's increasing participation in the labor force, the cultural ambivalence regarding paid working and stay-at-home mothers, the particular intensity of middle-class mothering, and the demanding character of the cultural model of appropriate child rearing are taken together, it becomes clear that the cultural contradictions of motherhood have been deepened rather than resolved. The history of child-rearing ideas demonstrates that the more powerful the logic of the rationalized market became, so too did its ideological opposition in the logic of intensive mothering. The words of contemporary mothers demonstrate that this trend persists in the day-to-day lives of women.

Editors' Note: *References for this reading can be found in the original source.*

■READING 5

Decline of the Family: Conservative, Liberal, and Feminist Views

Janet Z. Giele

In the 1990s the state of American families and children became a new and urgent topic. Everyone recognized that families had changed. Divorce rates had risen dramatically. More women were in the labor force. Evidence on rising teenage suicides, high rates of teen births, and disturbing levels of addiction and violence had put children at risk.

Conservatives have held that these problems can be traced to a culture of toleration and an expanding welfare state that undercut self-reliance and community standards. They focus on the family as a caregiving institution and try to restore its strengths by changing the culture of marriage and parenthood. Liberals center on the disappearance of manual jobs that throws less educated men out of work and undercuts their status in the family as well as rising hours of work among the middle class that makes stable two-parent families more difficult to maintain. Liberals argue that structural changes are needed outside the family in the public world of employment and schools.

The feminist vision combines both the reality of human interdependence in the family and individualism of the workplace. Feminists want to protect diverse family forms that allow realization of freedom and equality while at the same time nurturing the children of the next generation.

THE CONSERVATIVE EXPLANATION: SELFISHNESS AND MORAL DECLINE

The new family advocates turn their spotlight on the breakdown in the two-parent family, saying that rising divorce, illegitimacy, and father absence have put children at greater risk of school failure, unemployment, and antisocial behavior. The remedy is to restore religious faith and family commitment as well as to cut welfare payments to unwed mothers and mother-headed families.

Conservative Model

| Cultural and moral weakening | → | Family breakdown, divorce, family decline | → | Father absence, school failure, poverty, crime, drug use |

Cultural and Moral Weakening

To many conservatives, the modern secularization of religious practice and the decline of religious affiliation have undermined the norms of sexual abstinence before marriage and the prohibitions of adultery or divorce thereafter. Sanctions against illegitimacy or divorce have been made to seem narrow-minded and prejudiced. In addition, daytime television and the infamous example of Murphy Brown, a single mother having a child out of wedlock, helped to obscure simple notions of right and wrong. Barbara Dafoe Whitehead's controversial article in the *Atlantic* entitled "Dan Quayle Was Right" is an example of this argument.[1]

Gradual changes in marriage law have also diminished the hold of tradition. Restrictions against waiting periods, race dissimilarity, and varying degrees of consanguinity were gradually disappearing all over the United States and Europe.[2] While Mary Ann Glendon viewed the change cautiously but relativistically—as a process that waxed and waned across the centuries—others have interpreted these changes as a movement from status to contract (i.e., from attention to the particular individual's characteristics to reliance on the impersonal considerations of the market place).[3] The resulting transformation lessened the family's distinctive capacity to serve as a bastion of private freedom against the leveling effect and impersonality of public bureaucracy.

Erosion of the Two-Parent Family

To conservatives, one of the most visible causes of family erosion was government welfare payments, which made fatherless families a viable option. In *Losing Ground*, Charles Murray used the rise in teenage illegitimate births as proof that government-sponsored welfare programs had actually contributed to the breakdown of marriage.[4] Statistics on rising divorce and mother-headed families appeared to provide ample proof that the two-parent family was under siege. The proportion of all households headed by married couples fell from 77 percent in 1950 to 61 percent in 1980 and 55 percent in 1993.[5] Rising cohabitation, divorce rates, and births out of wedlock all contributed to the trend. The rise in single-person households was also significant, from only 12 percent of all households in 1950 to 27 percent in 1980, a trend fed by rising affluence and the undoubling of living arrangements that occurred with the expansion of the housing supply after World War II.[6]

The growth of single-parent households, however, was the most worrisome to policymakers because of their strong links to child poverty. In 1988, 50 percent of all children were found in mother-only families compared with 20 percent in 1950. The parental situation of children in poverty changed accordingly. Of all poor children in 1959, 73 percent had two parents present and 20 percent had a mother only. By 1988, only 35 percent of children in poverty lived with two parents and 57 percent lived with a mother only. These developments were fed by rising rates of divorce and out-of-wedlock births. Between 1940 and 1990, the divorce rate rose from 8.8 to 21 per thousand married women. Out-of-wedlock births exploded from 5 percent in 1960 to 26 percent in 1990.[7]

To explain these changes, conservatives emphasize the breakdown of individual and cultural commitment to marriage and the loss of stigma for divorce and illegitimacy. They understand both trends to be the result of greater emphasis on short-term gratification and on adults' personal desires rather than on what is good for children. A young woman brings a child into the world without thinking about who will support it. A husband divorces his wife and forms another household, possibly with other children, and leaves children of the earlier family behind without necessarily feeling obliged to be present in their upbringing or to provide them with financial support.

Negative Consequences for Children

To cultural conservatives there appears to be a strong connection between erosion of the two-parent family and the rise of health and social problems in children. Parental investment in children has declined—especially in the time available for supervision and companionship. Parents had roughly 10 fewer hours per week for their children in 1986 than in 1960, largely because more married women were employed (up from 24 percent in 1940 to 52 percent in 1983) and more mothers of young children (under age six) were working (up from 12 percent in 1940 to 50 percent in 1983). By the late 1980s just over half of mothers of children under a year old were in the labor force for at least part of the year.[8] At the same time fathers were increasingly absent from the family because of desertion, divorce, or failure to marry. In 1980, 15 percent of white children, 50 percent of black children, and 27 percent of children of Hispanic origin had no father present. Today 36 percent of children are living apart from their biological fathers compared with only 17 percent in 1960.[9]

Without a parent to supervise children after school, keep them from watching television all day, or prevent them from playing in dangerous neighborhoods, many more children appear to be falling by the wayside, victims of drugs, obesity, violence, suicide, or failure in school. During the 1960s and 1970s the suicide rate for persons aged fifteen to nineteen more than doubled. The proportion of obese children between the ages of six and eleven rose from 18 to 27 percent. Average SAT scores fell, and 25 percent of all high school students failed to graduate.[10] In 1995 the Council on Families in America reported, "Recent surveys have found that children from broken homes, when they become teenagers, have 2 to 3 times more behavioral and psychological problems than do children from intact homes."[11] Father absence is blamed by the fatherhood movement for the rise in violence among young males. David Blankenhorn and others reason that the lack of a positive and productive male role model has contributed to an uncertain masculine identity which then uses violence and aggression to prove itself. Every child deserves a father and "in a good society, men prove their masculinity not by killing other people, impregnating lots of women, or amassing large fortunes, but rather by being committed fathers and loving husbands."[12]

Psychologist David Elkind, in *The Hurried Child*, suggests that parents' work and time constraints have pushed down the developmental timetable to younger ages so that small children are being expected to take care of themselves and perform at levels which are robbing them of their childhood. The consequences are depression, discouragement, and a loss of joy at learning and growing into maturity.[13]

Reinvention of Marriage

According to the conservative analysis, the solution to a breakdown in family values is to revitalize and reinstitutionalize marriage. The culture should change to give higher priority to marriage and parenting. The legal code should favor marriage and encourage parental responsibility on the part of fathers as well as mothers. Government should cut back welfare programs which have supported alternate family forms.

The cultural approach to revitalizing marriage is to raise the overall priority given to family activities relative to work, material consumption, or leisure. Marriage is seen as the basic building block of civil society, which helps to hold together the fabric of volunteer activity and mutual support that underpins any democratic society.[14] Some advocates are unapologetically judgmental toward families who fall outside the two-parent mold. According to a 1995 *Newsweek* article on "The Return of Shame," David Blankenhorn believes "a stronger sense of shame about illegitimacy and divorce would do more than any tax cut or any new governmental program to maximize the life circumstances of children." But he also adds that the ultimate goal is "to move beyond stigmatizing only teenage mothers toward an understanding of the terrible message sent by all of us when we minimize the importance of fathers or contribute to the breakup of families."[15]

Another means to marriage and family revitalization is some form of taking a "pledge." Prevention programs for teenage pregnancy affirm the ideal of chastity before marriage. Athletes for Abstinence, an organization founded by a professional basketball player, preaches that young people should "save sex for marriage." A Baptist-led national program called True Love Waits has gathered an abstinence pledge from hundreds of thousands of teenagers since it was begun in the spring of 1993. More than 2,000 school districts now offer an abstinence-based sex education curriculum entitled "Sex Respect." Parents who are desperate about their children's sexual behavior are at last seeing ways that society can resist the continued sexualization of childhood.[16]

The new fatherhood movement encourages fathers to promise that they will spend more time with their children. The National Fatherhood Initiative argues that men's roles as fathers should not simply duplicate women's roles as mothers but should teach those essential qualities which are perhaps uniquely conveyed by fathers—the ability to take risks, contain emotions, and be decisive. In addition, fathers fulfill a time-honored role of providing for children as well as teaching them.[17]

Full-time mothers have likewise formed support groups to reassure themselves that not having a job and being at home full-time for their children is an honorable choice, although it is typically undervalued and perhaps even scorned by dual-earner couples and women with careers. A 1994 *Barron's* article claimed that young people in their twenties ("generation X,") were turning away from the two-paycheck family and scaling down their consumption so that young mothers could stay at home. Although Labor Department statistics show no such trend but only a flattening of the upward rise of women's employment, a variety of poll data does suggest that Americans would rather spend less time at work and more time with their families.[18] Such groups as Mothers at Home (with 15,000 members) and Mothers' Home Business Network (with 6,000 members) are trying to create a sea change that reverses the priority given to paid work outside the home relative to unpaid caregiving work inside the family.[19]

Conservatives see government cutbacks as one of the major strategies for strengthening marriage and restoring family values. In the words of Lawrence Mead, we have "taxed Peter to pay Paula."[20] According to a *Wall Street Journal* editorial, the "relinquishment of personal responsibility" among people who bring children into the world without any visible means of support is at the root of educational, health, and emotional problems of children from one-parent families, their higher accident and mortality rates, and rising crime.[21]

The new congressional solution is to cut back on the benefits to young men and women who "violate social convention by having children they cannot support."[22] Sociologist Brigitte Berger notes that the increase in children and women on welfare coincided with the explosion of federal child welfare programs—family planning, prenatal and postnatal care, child nutrition, child abuse prevention and treatment, child health and guidance, day care, Head Start, and Aid to Families with Dependent Children (AFDC), Medicaid, and Food Stamps. The solution is to turn back the debilitating culture of welfare dependency by decentralizing the power of the federal government and restoring the role of intermediary community institutions such as the neighborhood and the church. The mechanism for change would be block grants to the states which would change the welfare culture from the ground up.[23] Robert Rector of the American Heritage Foundation explains that the states would use these funds for a wide variety of alternative programs to discourage illegitimate births and to care for children born out of wedlock, such as promoting adoption, closely supervised group homes for unmarried mothers and their children, and pregnancy prevention programs (except abortion).[24]

Government programs, however, are only one way to bring about cultural change. The Council on Families in America puts its hope in grassroots social movements to change the hearts and minds of religious and civil leaders, employers, human service professionals, courts, and the media and entertainment industry. The Council enunciates four ideals: marital permanence, childbearing confined to marriage, every child's right to have a father, and limitation of parents' total work time (60 hours per week) to permit adequate time with their families.[25] To restore the cultural ideal of the two-parent family, they would make all other types of family life less attractive and more difficult.

ECONOMIC RESTRUCTURING: LIBERAL ANALYSIS OF FAMILY CHANGE

Liberals agree that there are serious problems in America's social health and the condition of its children. But they pinpoint economic and structural changes that have placed new demands on the family without providing countervailing social supports. The economy has become ever more specialized with rapid technological change undercutting established occupations. More women have entered the labor force as their child-free years have increased due to a shorter childbearing period and longer lifespan. The family has lost economic functions to the urban workplace and socialization functions to the school. What is left is the intimate relationship between the marital couple, which, unbuffered by the traditional economic division of labor between men and women, is subject to even higher demands for emotional fulfillment and is thus more vulnerable to breakdown when it falls short of those demands.

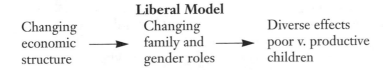

Liberal Model

Changing economic structure → Changing family and gender roles → Diverse effects poor v. productive children

The current family crisis thus stems from structural more than cultural change—changes in the economy, a paired-down nuclear family, and less parental time at home. Market forces have led to a new ethic of individual flexibility and autonomy. More dual-earner couples and single-parent families have broadened the variety of family forms. More single-parent families and more working mothers have decreased the time available for parenting. Loss of the father's income through separation and divorce has forced many women and children into poverty with inadequate health care, poor education, and inability to save for future economic needs. The solution that most liberals espouse is a government-sponsored safety net which will facilitate women's employment, mute the effects of poverty, and help women and children to become economically secure.

Recent Changes in the Labor Market

Liberals attribute the dramatic changes in the family to the intrusion of the money economy rather than cultural and moral decline. In a capitalist society individual behavior follows the market. Adam Smith's "invisible hand" brings together buyers and sellers who maximize their satisfaction through an exchange of resources in the marketplace. Jobs are now with an employer, not with the family business or family farm as in preindustrial times. The cash economy has, in the words of Robert Bellah, "invaded" the diffuse personal relationships of trust between family and community members and transformed them into specific impersonal transactions. In an agricultural economy husbands and wives and parents and children were bound together in relationships of exchange that served each others' mutual interests. But modern society erodes this social capital of organization, trust among individuals, and mutual obligation that enhances both productivity and parenting.[26]

The market has also eroded community by encouraging maximum mobility of goods and services. Cheaper labor in the South, lower fuel prices, and deeper tax breaks attracted first textile factories, then the shoe industry, and later automobile assembly plants which had begun in the North. Eventually, many of these jobs left the country. Loss of manufacturing jobs has had dramatic consequences for employment of young men without a college education and their capacity to support a family. In the 1970s, 68 percent of male high school graduates had a full-time, year-round job compared with only 51 percent in the 1980s. Many new jobs are located in clerical work, sales, or other service occupations traditionally associated with women. The upshot is a deteriorating employment picture for less well educated male workers at the same time that there are rising opportunities for women. Not surprisingly, even more middle income men and women combine forces to construct a two-paycheck family wage.[27]

Changing Family Forms

Whereas the farm economy dictated a two-parent family and several children as the most efficient work group, the market economy gives rise to a much wider variety of family forms. A woman on the frontier in the 1800s had few other options even if she were married to a drunken, violent, or improvident husband. In today's economy this woman may have enough education to get a clerical job that will support her and her children in a small apartment where the family will be able to use public schools and other public amenities.[28]

Despite its corrosive effect on family relations, the modern economy has also been a liberating force. Women could escape patriarchal domination; the young could seek their fortune without waiting for an inheritance from their elders—all a process that a century ago was aligned with a cultural shift that Fred Weinstein and Gerald Platt termed "the wish to be free."[29] Dramatic improvements took place in the status of women as they gained the right to higher education, entry into the professions, and the elective franchise.[30] Similarly, children were released from sometimes cruel and exploitive labor and became the object of deliberate parental investment and consumption.[31] Elders gained pensions for maintenance and care that made them economically independent of their adult children. All these developments could be understood as part of what William J. Goode has referred to as the "world revolution in family patterns" which resulted in liberation and equality of formerly oppressed groups.[32]

The current assessment of change in family forms is, however, mostly negative because of the consequences for children. More parental investment in work outside the family has meant less time for children. According to liberals, parents separate or divorce or have children outside of marriage because of the economic structure, not because they have become less moral or more selfish. Young women have children out of wedlock when the young men whom they might marry have few economic prospects and when the women themselves have little hope for their own education or employment.[33] Change in the family thus begins with jobs. Advocates of current government programs therefore challenge the conservatives' assertion that welfare caused the breakup of two-parent families by supporting mothers with dependent children. According to William Julius Wilson, it is partly the lack of manual labor jobs for the would-be male breadwinner in inner-city Chicago—the scarcity of "marriageable males"—which drives up the illegitimacy rate.[34]

Among educated women, it is well known that the opportunity costs of foregone income from staying home became so high during the 1950s and 1960s that ever increasing numbers of women deserted full-time homemaking to take paid employment.[35] In the 1990s several social scientists have further noted that Richard Easterlin's prediction that women will return to the home during the 1980s never happened. Instead, women continued in the labor force because of irreversible normative changes surrounding women's equality and the need for women's income to finance children's expensive college education.[36] Moreover, in light of globalization of the economy and increasing job insecurity in the face of corporate downsizing, economists and sociologists are questioning Gary Becker's thesis that the lower waged worker in a household (typically the woman) will tend to become a full-time homemaker while the higher waged partner becomes the primary breadwinner. Data from Germany and the United States on the trend toward women's multiple roles suggests that uncertainty about the future has made women invest more strongly than ever in their own careers. They know that if they drop out for very long they will have difficulty reentering if they have to tide over the family when the main breadwinner loses his job.[37]

Consequences for Children

The ideal family in the liberal economic model, according to political philosopher Iris Young, is one which has sufficient income to support the parents and the children and "to foster in those children the emotional and intellectual capacities to acquire such well-paid, secure jobs themselves, and also sufficient to finance a retirement."[38] Dependent families do not have self-sufficient income but must rely on friends, relatives, charity, or the state to carry out their contribution to bringing up children and being good citizens.

Among liberals there is an emerging consensus that the current economic structure leads to two kinds of underinvestment in children that are implicated in their later dependency—material poverty, characteristic of the poor, and "time" poverty, characteristic of the middle class.

Thirty years ago Daniel Patrick Moynihan perceived that material poverty and job loss for a man put strain on the marriage, sometimes to the point that he would leave. His children also did less well in school.[39] Rand Conger, in his studies of Iowa families who lost their farms during the 1980s, found that economic hardship not only puts strain on the marriage but leads to harsh parenting practices and poorer outcomes for children.[40] Thus it appears possible that poverty may not just be the result of family separation, divorce, and ineffective childrearing practices; it may also be the *cause* of the irritability, quarrels, and violence which lead to marital breakdown. Material underinvestment in children is visible not just with the poor but in the changing ratio of per capita income of children and adults in U.S. society as a whole. As the proportion of households without children has doubled over the last century (from 30 to 65 percent), per capita income of children has fallen from 71 percent of adult income in 1870 to 63 percent in 1930 and 51 percent in 1983.[41]

The problem of "time" poverty used to be almost exclusively associated with mothers' employment. Numerous studies explored whether younger children did better if their mother was a full-time homemaker rather than employed outside the home but found no clear results.[42] Lately the lack of parental time for children has become much more acute because parents are working a total of twenty-one hours more per week than in 1970 and because there are more single-parent families. In 1965 the average child spent about thirty hours a week interacting with a parent, compared with seventeen hours in the 1980s.[43] Moreover, parents are less dependent on their children to provide support for them during old age, and children feel less obligated to do so. As skilled craftsmanship, the trades, and the family farms have disappeared, children's upbringing can no longer be easily or cheaply combined with what parents are already doing. So adults are no longer so invested in children's futures. The result is that where the social capital of group affiliations and mutual obligations is the lowest (in the form of continuity of neighborhoods, a two-parent family, or a parent's interest in higher education for her children), children are 20 percent more likely to drop out of high school.[44]

It is not that parents prefer their current feelings of being rushed, working too many hours, and having too little time with their families. Economist Juliet Schor reports that at least two-thirds of persons she surveyed about their desires for more family time versus more salary would take a cut in salary if it could mean more time with their families. Since this option is not realistically open to many, what parents appear to do is spend more money on their children as a substitute for spending more time with them.[45]

Fixing the Safety Net

Since liberals believe in a market economy with sufficient government regulation to assure justice and equality of opportunity, they support those measures which will eradicate the worst poverty and assure the healthy reproduction of the next generation.[46] What particularly worries them, however, is Charles Murray's observation that since

1970 the growth of government welfare programs has been associated with a *rise* in poverty among children. Payments to poor families with children, while not generous, have nevertheless enabled adults to be supported by attachment to their children.[47] Society is faced with a dilemma between addressing material poverty through further government subsidy and time poverty through policies on parental leave and working hours. It turns out that the United States is trying to do both.

Measures for addressing material poverty would stimulate various kinds of training and job opportunities. The Family Support Act of 1988 would move AFDC mothers off the welfare rolls by giving them job training and requiring them to join the labor force. Such action would bring their economic responsibility for supporting their children into line with their parental authority. A whole program of integrated supports for health insurance, job training, earned income tax credits for the working poor, child support by the noncustodial parent, and supported work is put forward by economist David Ellwood in *Poor Support*.[48] An opposite strategy is to consolidate authority over children with the state's economic responsibility for their care by encouraging group homes and adoption for children whose parents cannot support them economically.[49]

Means for addressing time poverty are evident in such legislative initiatives as the Family and Medical Leave Act of 1993. By encouraging employers to grant parental leave or other forms of flexible work time, government policy is recognizing the value of parents having more time with their children, but the beneficiaries of such change are largely middle-class families who can afford an unpaid parental leave.[50] Another tactic is to reform the tax law to discourage marital splitting. In a couple with two children in which the father earns $16,000 annually and the mother $9,000, joint tax filing gives them no special consideration. But if they file separately, each taking one child as a dependent, the woman will receive about $5,000 in Earned Income Tax Credit and an extra $2,000 in food stamps.[51] Changing the tax law to remove the incentives for splitting, establishing paternity of children born out of wedlock, and intensifying child support enforcement to recover economic support from fathers are all examples of state efforts to strengthen the kinship unit.

INTERDEPENDENCE: THE FEMINIST VISION OF WORK AND CAREGIVING

A feminist perspective has elements in common with both conservatives and liberals: a respect for the family as an institution (shared with the conservatives) and an appreciation of modernity (valued by the liberals). In addition, a feminist perspective grapples with the problem of women's traditionally subordinate status and how to improve it through both a "relational" and an "individualist" strategy while also sustaining family life and the healthy rearing of children.[52] At the same time feminists are skeptical of both conservative and liberal solutions. Traditionalists have so often relied on women as the exploited and underpaid caregivers in the family to enable men's activities in the public realm. Liberals are sometimes guilty of a "male" bias in focusing on the independent individual actor in the marketplace who does not realize that his so-called "independence," is possible only because he is actually *dependent* on all kinds of relationships that made possible his education and life in a stable social order.[53]

By articulating the value of caregiving along with the ideal of women's autonomy, feminists are in a position to examine modern capitalism critically for its effects on families and to offer alternative policies that place greater value on the quality of life and human relationships. They judge family strength not by their *form* (whether they have two-parents) but by their functioning (whether they promote human satisfaction and development) and whether both women and men are able to be family caregivers as well as productive workers. They attribute difficulties of children less to the absence of the two-parent family than to low-wage work of single mothers, inadequate child care, and inhospitable housing and neighborhoods.

Feminist Model

Lack of cooperation among community, family, and work	→	Families where adults are stressed and overburdened	→	Children lack sufficient care and attention from parents

Accordingly, feminists would work for reforms that build and maintain the social capital of volunteer groups, neighborhoods, and communities because a healthy civil society promotes the well-being of families and individuals as well as economic prosperity and a democratic state. They would also recognize greater role flexibility across the life cycle so that both men and women could engage in caregiving, and they would encourage education and employment among women as well as among men.

Disappearance of Community

From a feminist perspective, family values have become an issue because individualism has driven out the sense of collective responsibility in our national culture. American institutions and social policies have not properly implemented a concern for all citizens. Comparative research on family structure, teenage pregnancy, poverty, and child outcomes in other countries demonstrates that where support is generous to help *all* families and children, there are higher levels of health and general education and lower levels of violence and child deviance than in the United States.[54]

Liberal thinking and the focus on the free market have made it seem that citizens make their greatest contribution when they are self-sufficient, thereby keeping themselves off the public dole. But feminist theorist Iris Young argues that many of the activities that are basic to a healthy democratic society (such as cultural production, caretaking, political organizing, and charitable activities) will never be profitable in a private market. Yet many of the recipients of welfare and Social Security such as homemakers, single mothers, and retirees are doing important volunteer work caring for children and helping others in their communities. Thus the social worth of a person's contribution is not just in earning a paycheck that allows economic independence but also in making a social contribution. Such caretaking of other dependent citizens and of the body politic should be regarded as honorable, not inferior, and worthy of society's support and subsidy.[55]

In fact it appears that married women's rising labor force participation from 41 percent in 1970 to 58 percent in 1990 may have been associated with their withdrawal from unpaid work in the home and community.[56] Volunteer membership in everything from the PTA to bowling leagues declined by over 25 percent between 1969 and 1993. There is now considerable concern that the very basis that Alexis de Tocqueville thought necessary to democracy is under siege.[57] To reverse this trend, social observers suggest that it will be necessary to guard time for families and leisure that is currently being sucked into the maw of paid employment. What is needed is a reorientation of priorities to give greater value to unpaid family and community work by both men and women.

National policies should also be reoriented to give universal support to children at every economic level of society, but especially to poor children. In a comparison of countries in the Organization for Economic Cooperation and Development, the United States ranks at the top in average male wages but near the bottom in its provision for disposable income for children. In comparison with the $700 per month available to children in Norway, France, or the Netherlands in 1992, U.S. children of a single nonemployed mother received only slightly under $200.[58] The discrepancy is explained by very unequal distribution of U.S. income, with the top quintile, the "fortunate fifth," gaining 47 percent of the national income while the bottom fifth receives only 3.6 percent.[59] This sharp inequality is, in turn, explained by an ideology of individualism that justifies the disproportionate gains of the few for their innovation and productivity and the meager income of the poor for their low initiative or competence. Lack of access to jobs and the low pay accruing to many contingent service occupations simply worsen the picture.

Feminists are skeptical of explanations that ascribe higher productivity to the higher paid and more successful leading actors while ignoring the efforts and contribution of the supporting cast. They know that being an invisible helper is the situation of many women. This insight is congruent with new ideas about the importance "social capital" to the health of a society that have been put forward recently by a number of social scientists.[60] Corporations cannot be solely responsible for maintaining the web of community, although they are already being asked to serve as extended family, neighborhood support group, and national health service.

Diversity of Family Forms

Those who are concerned for strengthening the civil society immediately turn to the changing nature of the family as being a key building block. Feminists worry that seemingly sensible efforts to reverse the trend of rising divorce and single parenthood will privilege the two-parent family to the detriment of women; they propose instead that family values be understood in a broader sense as valuing the family's unique capacity for giving emotional and material support rather than implying simply a two–parent form.

The debate between conservatives, liberals, and feminists on the issue of the two-parent family has been most starkly stated by sociologist Judith Stacey and political philosopher Iris Young.[61] They regard the requirement that all women stay in a marriage as an invitation to coercion and subordination and an assault on the principles of freedom and self-determination that are at the foundation of democracy. Moreover, as Christopher Jencks and Kathryn Edin conclude from their study of several hundred welfare families, the current welfare reform rhetoric that no couple should have a child unless they can support it, does not take into account the uncertainty of life in which people who start out married or with adequate income not always remain so. In the face of the worldwide dethronement of the two-parent family (approximately one-quarter to one-third of all families around the globe are headed by women), marriage should not be seen as the cure for child poverty. Mothers should not be seen as less than full citizens if they are not married or not employed (in 1989 there were only 16 million males between the ages of 25 and 34 who made over $12,000 compared with 20 million females of the same age who either had a child or wanted one).[62] National family policy should instead begin with a value on women's autonomy and self-determination that includes the right to bear children. Mother-citizens are helping to reproduce the next generation for the whole society, and in that responsibility they deserve at least partial support.

From a feminist perspective the goal of the family is not only to bring up a healthy and productive new generation; families also provide the intimate and supportive group of kin or fictive kin that foster the health and well-being of every person—young or old, male or female, heterosexual, homosexual, or celibate. Recognition as "family" should therefore not be confined to the traditional two-parent unit connected by blood, marriage, or adoption, but should be extended to include kin of a divorced spouse (as Stacey documented in her study of Silicon Valley families), same-sex partnerships, congregate households of retired persons, group living arrangements, and so on.[63] Twenty years ago economist Nancy Barrett noted that such diversity in family and household form was already present. Among all U.S. households in 1976, no one of the six major types constituted more than 15–20 percent: couples with and without children under eighteen with the wife in the labor force (15.4 and 13.3 percent respectively); couples with or without children under 18 with the wife not in the labor force (19.1 and 17.1 percent); female- or male-headed households (14.4 percent); and single persons living alone (20.6 percent).[64]

Such diversity both describes and informs contemporary "family values" in the United States. Each family type is numerous enough to have a legitimacy of its own, yet no single form is the dominant one. As a result the larger value system has evolved to encompass beliefs and rules that legitimate each type on the spectrum. The regressive alternative is "fundamentalism" that treats the two-parent family with children as the only legitimate form, single-parent families as unworthy of support, and the nontraditional forms as illegitimate. In 1995 the general population appears to have accepted diversity of family forms as normal. A Harris poll of 1,502 women and 460 men found that only 2 percent of women and 1 percent of men defined family as "being about the traditional nuclear family," One out of ten women defined family values as loving, taking care of, and supporting each other, knowing right from wrong or having good values, and nine out of ten said society should value all types of families.[65] It appears most Americans believe that an Aunt Polly single-parent type of family for a Huck Finn that provides economic support, shelter, meals, a place to sleep and to withdraw, is better than no family at all.

Amidst gradual acceptance of greater diversity in family form, the gender-role revolution is also loosening the sex-role expectations traditionally associated with breadwinning and homemaking. Feminists believe that men and women can each do both.[66] In addition, women in advanced industrial nations have by and large converged upon a new life pattern of multiple roles by which they combine work and family life. The negative outcome is an almost universal "double burden" for working women in which they spend eighty-four hours per week on paid and family work, married men spend seventy-two hours, and single persons without children spend fifty hours.[67] The positive consequence, however, appears to be improved physical and mental health for those women who, though stressed, combine work and family roles.[68] In addition, where a woman's husband helps her more with the housework, she is less likely to think of getting a divorce.[69]

The Precarious Situation of Children

The principal remedy that conservatives and liberals would apply to the problems of children is to restore the two-parent family by reducing out-of-wedlock births, increasing the presence of fathers, and encouraging couples who are having marital difficulties to avoid divorce for the sake of their children. Feminists, on the other hand, are skeptical that illegitimacy, father absence, or divorce are the principal culprits they are made out to be. Leon Eisenberg reports that over half of all births in Sweden and one-quarter of births in France are to unmarried women, but without the disastrous correlated effects observed in the United States. Arlene Skolnick and Stacey Rosencrantz cite longitudinal studies showing that most children recover from the immediate negative effects of divorce.[70]

How then, while supporting the principle that some fraction of women should be able to head families as single parents, do feminists analyze the problem of ill health, antisocial behavior, and poverty among children? Their answer focuses on the *lack of institutional supports* for the new type of dual-earner and single-parent families that are more prevalent today. Rather than attempt to force families back into the traditional mold, feminists note that divorce, lone-mother families, and women's employment are on the rise in every industrialized nation. But other countries have not seen the same devastating decline in child well-being, teen pregnancy, suicides and violent death, school failure, and a rising population of children in poverty. These other countries have four key elements of social and family policy which protect all children and their mothers: (1) work guarantees and other economic supports; (2) child care; (3) health care; and (4) housing subsidies. In the United States these benefits are scattered and uneven; those who can pay their way do so; only those who are poor or disabled receive AFDC for economic support, some help with child care, Medicaid for health care, and government-subsidized housing.

A first line of defense is to raise women's wages through raising the minimum wage, then provide them greater access to male-dominated occupations with higher wages. One-half of working women do not earn a wage adequate to support a family of four above the poverty line. Moreover, women in low-wage occupations are subject to frequent lay-offs and lack of benefits. Training to improve their human capital, provision of child care, and broadening of benefits would help raise women's capacity to support a family. Eisenberg reports that the Human Development Index of the United Nations (HDI), which ranks countries by such indicators as life expectancy, educational levels, and per capita income, places the United States fifth and Sweden sixth in the world. But when the HDI is recalculated to take into account equity of treatment of women, Sweden rises to first place and the United States falls to ninth. Therefore, one of the obvious places to begin raising children's status is to "raise the economic status and earning power of their mothers."[71]

A second major benefit which is not assured to working mothers is child care. Among school-age children up to thirteen years of age, one-eighth lack any kind of after-school child care. Children come to the factories where their mothers work and wait on the lawn or in the lobby until their mothers are finished working. If a child is sick, some mothers risk losing a job if they stay home. Others are latchkey kids or in unknown circumstances such as sleeping in their parents' cars or loitering on the streets. Although 60 percent of mothers of the 22 million preschool children are working, there are only 10 million child care places available, a shortfall of one to three million slots.[72] Lack of good quality care for her children not only distracts a mother, adds to her absences from work, and make her less productive, it also exposes the child to a lack of attention and care that leads to violent and antisocial behavior and poor performance in school.

Lack of medical benefits is a third gaping hole for poor children and lone-parent families. Jencks and Edin analyze what happens to a Chicago-area working woman's income if she goes off welfare. Her total income in 1993 dollars on AFDC (with food stamps, unreported earnings, help from family and friends) adds up to $12,355, in addition to which she receives Medicaid and child care. At a $6 per hour full-time job, however, without AFDC, with less than half as much from food stamps, with an Earned Income Tax Credit, and help from relatives, her total income would add to $20,853. But she would have to pay for her own medical care, bringing her effective income down to $14,745 if she found free child care, and $9,801 if she had to pay for child care herself.[73]

Some housing subsidies or low-income housing are available to low-income families. But the neighborhoods and schools are frequently of poor quality and plagued by violence. To bring up children in a setting where they cannot safely play with others introduces important risk factors that cannot simply be attributed to divorce and single parenthood. Rather than being protected and being allowed to be innocent, children must learn to be competent at a very early age. The family, rather than being child-centered, must be adult-centered, not because parents are selfish or self-centered but because the institutions of the society have changed the context of family life.[74] These demands may be too much for children, and depression, violence, teen suicide, teen pregnancy, and school failure may result. But it would be myopic to think that simply restoring the two-parent family would be enough to solve all these problems.

Constructing Institutions for the Good Society

What is to be done? Rather than try to restore the two-parent family as the conservatives suggest or change the economy to provide more jobs as recommended by the liberals, the feminists focus on the need to revise and construct institutions to accommodate the new realities of work and family life. Such an undertaking requires, however, a broader interpretation of family values, a recognition that families benefit not only their members but the public interest, and fresh thinking about how to schedule work and family demands of everyday life as well as the entire life cycle of men and women.

The understanding of family values has to be extended in two ways. First, American values should be stretched to embrace all citizens, their children and families, whether they are poor, white, or people of color, or living in a one-parent family. In 1977, Kenneth Keniston titled the report of the Carnegie Commission on Children *All Our Children.* Today many Americans still speak and act politically in ways suggesting that they *disown* other people's children as the next generation who will inherit the land and support the economy. Yet in the view of most feminists and other progressive reformers, all these children should be embraced for the long-term good of the nation.[75] By a commitment to "family values" feminists secondly intend to valorize the family as a distinctive intimate group of many forms that is needed by persons of all ages but especially children. To serve the needs of children and other dependent persons, the family must be given support and encouragement by the state to carry out its unique functions. Iris Young contends that marriage should not be used to reduce the ultimate need for the state to serve as a means to distribute needed supports to the families of those less fortunate.[76] Compare the example of the GI Bill of Rights after World War II, which provided educational benefits to those who had served their country in the military. Why should there not be a similar approach to the contribution that a parent makes in raising a healthy and productive youngster?[77]

At the community level families should be embraced by all the institutions of the civil society—schools, hospitals, churches, and employers—as the hidden but necessary complement to the bureaucratic and impersonal workings of these formal organizations. Schools rely on parents for the child's "school readiness." Hospitals send home patients who need considerable home care before becoming completely well. The work of the church is carried out and reinforced in the family; and when families fail, it is the unconditional love and intimacy of family that the church tries to replicate. Employers depend on families to give the rest, shelter, emotional support, and other maintenance of human capital that will motivate workers and make them productive. Increasingly, the professionals and managers in these formal organizations are realizing that they need to work more closely with parents and family members if they are to succeed.

Feminists would especially like to see the reintegration of work and family life that was torn apart at the time of the industrial revolution when productive work moved out of the home and into the factory. Several proposals appear repeatedly: parental leave (which now is possible through the Family and Medical Leave Act of 1993); flexible hours and part-time work shared by working parents but without loss of benefits and promotion opportunities; home-based work; child care for sick children and after-school supervision. Although some progress has been made, acceptance of these reforms has been very slow. Parental leave is still *unpaid.* The culture of the workplace discourages many persons from taking advantage of the more flexible options which do exist because they fear they will be seen as less serious and dedicated workers. In addition, most programs are aimed at mothers and at managers, although there is growing feeling that fathers and hourly workers should be included as well.[78]

Ultimately these trends may alter the shape of women's and men's life cycles. Increasingly, a new ideal for the life course is being held up as the model that society should work toward. Lotte Bailyn proposes reorganization of careers in which young couples trade off periods of intense work commitment with each other while they establish their families so that either or both can spend more time at home.[79] Right now both women and men feel they must work so intensely to establish their careers that they have too little time for their children.[80] For the poor and untrained, the problem is the opposite: childbearing and childrearing are far more satisfying and validating than a low-paying, dead-end job. The question is how to reorient educators or employers to factor in time with family as an important obligation to society (much as one would factor in military service, for example). Such institutional reorganization is necessary to give families and childrearing their proper place in the modern postindustrial society.

CONCLUSION

A review of the conservative, liberal, and feminist perspectives on the changing nature of the American family suggests that future policy should combine the distinctive contributions of all three. From the conservatives comes a critique of modernity that recognizes the important role of the family in maintaining child health and preventing child failure. Although their understanding of "family values" is too narrow, they deserve credit for raising the issue of family function and form to public debate. Liberals see clearly the overwhelming power of the economy to deny employment, make demands on parents as workers, and drive a wedge between employers' needs for competitiveness and families' needs for connection and community.

Surprising although it may seem, since feminists are often imagined to be "way out," the most comprehensive plan for restoring family to its rightful place is put forward by the feminists who appreciate both the inherently premodern nature of the family and at the same time its inevitable interdependence with a fast-changing world economy. Feminists will not turn back to the past because they know that the traditional family was often a straightjacket for women. But they also know that family cannot be turned into a formal organization or have its functions performed by government or other public institutions that are incapable of giving needed succor to children, adults, and old people which only the family can give.

The feminist synthesis accepts both the inherent particularism and emotional nature of the family and the inevitable specialization and impersonality of the modern economy. Feminists are different from conservatives in accepting diversity of the family to respond to the needs of the modern economy. They are different from the liberals in recognizing that intimate nurturing relationships such as parenting cannot all be turned into a safety net of formal care. The most promising social policies for families and children take their direction from inclusive values that confirm the good life and the well-being of every individual as the ultimate goal of the nation. The policy challenge is to adjust the partnership between the family and its surrounding institutions so that together they combine the best of private initiative with public concern.

Notes

1. Barbara Dafoe Whitehead, "Dan Qayle Was Right," *Atlantic Monthly* (April 1993): 47. Her chapter in [*Promises to Keep: Decline and Renewal of Marriage in America*, edited by D. Popenoe, J. B. Elshtain, and D. Blankenhorn] on the "Story of Marriage" continues the theme of an erosion of values for cultural diversity.

2. Mary Ann Glenn, "Marriage and the State: The Withering Away of Marriage," *Virginia Law Review* 62 (May 1976): 663–729.

3. See chapters by Milton Regan and Carl Schneider in [*Promises to Keep: Decline and Renewal of Marriage in America*, edited by D. Popenoe, J. B. Elshtain, and D. Blankenhorn].

4. Charles A. Murray, *Losing Ground: American Social Policy: 1950–1980* (New York: Basic Books, 1984). Critics point out that the rise in out-of-wedlock births continues, even though welfare payments have declined in size over the last several decades, thereby casting doubt on the perverse incentive theory of rising illegitimacy.

5. U.S. Bureau of the Census. *Statistical Abstract of the United States: 1994*, 114th ed. (Washington, DC: 1994), 59.

6. Suzanne M. Bianchi and Daphne Spain, *American Women in Transition* (New York: Russell Sage Foundation, 1986), 88.

7. Donald J. Hernandez, *America's Children: Resources from Family, Government, and the Economy* (New York: Russell Sage Foundation, 1993), 284, 70. Janet Zollinger Giele, "Woman's Role Change and Adaptation: 1920–1990," in *Women's Lives through Time: Educated American Women of the Twentieth Century*, ed. K Hulbert and D. Schuster (San Francisco Jossey-Bass. 1993), 40.

8. Victor Fuchs, "Are Americas Underinvesting in Children?" in *Rebuilding the Nest*, ed. David Blankenhorn, Stephen Bayme, and Jean Bethke Elshtain (Milwaukee: Family Service America, 1990), 66. Bianchi and Spain, *American Women in Transition*, 141, 201, 226. Janet Zollinger Giele, "Gender and Sex Roles," in *Handbook of Sociology*, ed. N. J. Smelser (Beverly Hills, CA: Sage Publications, 1988), 300.

9. Hernandez, *America's Children*, 130. Council on Families in America, *Marriage in America* (New York: Institute for American Values. 1995), 7.

10. Fuchs, "Are Americans Underinvesting in Children?" 61. Some would say, however, that the decline was due in part to a larger and more heterogeneous group taking the tests.

11. Council on Families in America, *Marriage in America*, 6. The report cites research by Nicholas Zill and Charlotte A. Schoenborn, "Developmental, Learning and Emotional Problems: Health of Our Nation's Children, United States, 1988." *Advance Data*, National Center for Health Statistics, Publication #120, November 1990. See also, Sara McLanahan and Gary Sandefur, *Growing Up with a Single Parent* (Cambridge, MA: Harvard University Press, 1994).

12. Edward Gilbreath, "Manhood's Great Awakening," *Christianity Today* (February 6, 1995): 27.

13. David Elkind, *The Hurried Child: Growing Up Too Fast Too Soon* (Reading, MA: Addison-Wesley, 1981).

14. Jean Bethke Elshtain, *Democracy on Trial* (New York: Basic Books, 1995).

15. Jonathan Alter and Pat Wingert, "The Return of Shame," *Newsweek* (February 6. 1995): 25.

16. Tom McNichol, "The New Sex Vow: 'I won't' until 'I do'," USA Weekend, March 25–27, 1994, 4 ff. Lee Smith. "The New Wave of Illegitimacy," *Fortune* (April 18, 1994): 81 ff.

17. Susan Chira, "War over Role of American Fathers," *New York Times*, June 19, 1994, 22.

18. Juliet Schor, "Consumerism and the Decline of Family and Community: Preliminary Statistics from a Survey on Time, Money, and Values." Harvard Divinity School, Seminar on Families and Family Policy, April 4, 1995.

19. Karen S. Peterson, "In Balancing Act, Scale Tips toward Family," *USA Today*, January 25, 1995.

20. Lawrence Mead, "Taxing Peter to Pay Paula," *Wall Street Journal*, November 2, 1994.

21. Tom G. Palmer, "English Lessons: Britain Rethinks the Welfare State," *Wall Street Journal*, November 2, 1994.

22. Robert Pear, "G.O.P. Affirms Plan to Stop Money for Unwed Mothers," *New York Times*, January 21, 1995, 9.

23. Brigitte Berger. "Block Grants: Changing the Welfare Culture from the Ground Up," *Dialogue* (Boston: Pioneer Institute for Public Policy Research), no. 3, March 1995.

24. Robert Rector, "Welfare," *Issues '94: The Candidate's Briefing Book* (Washington, DC: American Heritage Foundation, 1994), chap. 13.

25. Council on Families in America, *Marriage in America*, 13–16.

26. Robert Bellah, "Invasion of the Money World," in *Rebuilding the Nest*, ed. David Blankenhorn, Steven Bayme, and Jean Bethke Elshtain (Milwaukee: Family Service America, 1990), 227–36. James Coleman, *Foundations of Social Theory* (Cambridge, MA: Harvard University Press, 1990).

27. Sylvia Nasar, "More Men in Prime of Life Spend Less Time Working," *New York Times*, December 1, 1994, Al.

28. John Scanzoni, *Power Politics in the American Marriage* (Englewood Cliffs. NJ: Prentice-Hall, 1972). Ruth A. Wallace and Alison Wolf, *Contemporary Sociological Theory* (Englewood Cliffs, NJ: Prentice-Hall, 1991), 176.

29. Fred Weinstein and Gerald M. Platt, *The Wish to Be Free: Society, Psyche, and Value Change* (Berkeley, CA: University of California Press, 1969).

30. Kingsley Davis, "Wives and Work: A Theory of the Sex-Role Revolution and Its Consequenecs," in *Feminism, Children, and the New Families*, ed. S. M. Dornbusch and M. H. Strober (New York: Guilford Press. 1988), 67–86. Janet Zollinger Giele, *Two Paths to Women's Equality: Temperance, Suffrage, and the Origins of American Feminism* (New York: Twayne Publishers, Macmillan, 1995).

31. Vivianna A. Zelizer, *Pricing the Priceless Child: The Changing Social Value of Children* (New York: Basic Books, 1985).

32. William J. Goode, *World Revolution in Family Patterns* (New York: The Free Press, 1963).

33. Constance Willard Williams, *Black Teenage Mothers: Pregnancy and Child Rearing from Their Perspective* (Lexington, MA: Lexington Books, 1990).

34. William Julius Wilson, *The Truly Disadvantaged: The Inner City, the Underclass, and Public Policy* (Chicago: University of Chicago Press, 1987).

35. Jacob Mincer, "Labor-Force Participation of Married Women: A Study of Labor Supply," in *Aspects of Labor Economics*, Report of the National Bureau of Economic Research (Princeton, NJ: Universities-National Bureau Committee of Economic Research, 1962). Glen G. Cain. *Married Women in the Labor Force: An Economic Analysis* (Chicago: University of Chicago Press, 1966).

36. Richard A. Easterlin, *Birth and Fortune: The Impact of Numbers on Personal Welfare* (New York: Basic Books, 1980). Valerie K. Oppenheimer, "Structural Sources of Economic Pressure for Wives to Work— Analytic Framework," *Journal of Family History* 4, no. 2 (1979): 177–99. Valerie K. Oppenheimer, *Work and the Family: A Study in Social Demography* (New York: Academic Press, 1982).

37. Janet Z. Giele and Rainer Pischner, "The Emergence of Multiple Role Patterns Among Women: A Comparison of Germany and the United States," *Vierteljahrshefte zur Wirtschaftsforschung* (Applied Economics Quarterly) (Heft 1–2, 1994). Alice S. Rossi, "The Future in the Making," *American Journal of Orthopsychiatry* 63, no. 2 (1993): 166–76. Notburga Ott, *Intrafamily Bargaining and Household Decisions* (Berlin: Springer-Verlag, 1992).

38. Iris Young, "Mothers, Citizenship and Independence: A Critique of Pure Family Values," *Ethics* 105, no. 3 (1995): 535–56. Young critiques the liberal stance of William Galston, *Liberal Purposes* (New York: Cambridge University Press, 1991).

39. Lee Rainwater and William L. Yancey, *The Moynihan Report and the Politics of Controversy* (Cambridge, MA: MIT Press, 1967).

40. Glen H. Elder, Jr., *Children of the Great Depression* (Chicago: University of Chicago Press, 1974). Rand D. Conger, Xiao-Jia Ge, and Frederick O. Lorenz, "Economic Stress and Marital Relations," in *Families in Troubled Times: Adapting to Change in Rural America*, ed. R. D. Conger and G. H. Elder, Jr. (New York: Aldine de Gruyter, 1994), 187–203.

41. Coleman, *Foundations of Social Theory*, 590.

42. Elizabeth G. Menaghan and Toby L. Parcel, "Employed Mothers and Children's Home Environments," *Journal of Marriage and the Family* 53, no. 2 (1991): 417–31. Lois Hoffman, "The Effects on Children of Maternal and Paternal Employment," in *Families and Work*, ed. Naomi Gerstel and Harriet Engel Gross (Philadelphia: Temple University Press, 1987), 362–95.

43. Juliet Schor, *The Overworked American: The Unexpected Decline of Leisure* (New York: Basic Books, 1991). Robert Haveman and Barbara Wolfe, *Succeeding Generations: On the Effects of Investments in Children* (New York: Russell Sage Foundation, 1994), 239.

44. Coleman, *Foundations of Social Theory*, 596–97.

45. Schor, "Consumerism and Decline of Family."

46. Iris Young, "Mothers, Citizenship and Independence," puts Elshtain, Etzioni, Galston, and Whitehead in this category.

47. Coleman, *Foundations of Social Theory*, 597–609.

48. Sherry Wexler, "To Work and To Mother: A Comparison of the Family Support Act and the Family and Medical Leave Act" (Ph.D. diss. draft, Brandeis University, 1995). David T. Ellwood, *Poor Support: Poverty in the American Family* (New York: Basic Books, 1988).

49. Coleman, *Foundations of Social Theory*, 300–21. Coleman, known for rational choice theory in sociology, put forward these theoretical possibilities in 1990, fully four years ahead of what in 1994 was voiced in the Republican Contract with America.

50. Wexler, "To Work and To Mother."

51. Robert Lerman, "Marketplace," National Public Radio, April 18, 1995.

52. Karen Offen, "Defining Feminism: A Comparative Historical Approach," *Signs* 14, no. 1 (1988): 119–51.

53. Young, "Mothers, Citizenship and Independence."

54. Robert N. Bellah et al., *Habits of the Heart* (Berkeley, CA: University of California Press, 1985), 250–71. Gosta Esping-Andersen, *The Three Worlds of Welfare Capitalism* (Princeton, NJ: Princeton University Press, 1990). Susan Pedersen, *Family, Dependence, and the Origins of the Welfare State: Britain and France, 1914–1945* (New York: Cambridge University Press, 1993).

55. Young, "Mothers, Citizenship and Independence."

56. Giele, "Woman's Role Change and Adaptation" presents these historical statistics.

57. Elshtain, *Democracy on Trial*. Robert N. Bellah et al., *The Good Society* (New York: Knopf, 1991), 210. Robert D. Putnam, "Bowling Alone: America's Declining Social Capital," *Journal of Democracy* 4, no. 1 (1995): 65–78.

58. Heather McCallum, "Mind the Gap" (paper presented to the Family and Children's Policy Center colloquium, Waltham, MA, Brandeis University, March 23, 1995). The sum was markedly better for children of employed single mothers, around $700 per mother in the United States. But this figure corresponded with over $1,000 in eleven other countries, with only Greece and Portugal lower than the U.S. Concerning the high U.S. rates of teen pregnancy, see Planned Parenthood advertisement, "Let's Get Serious About Ending Teen Childbearing," *New York Times*, April 4, 1995, A25.

59. Ruth Walker, "Secretary Reich and the Disintegrating Middle Class," *Christian Science Monitor*, November 2, 1994, 19.

60. For reference to "social capital," see Coleman, *Foundations of Social Theory*; Elshtain, *Democracy on Trial*; and Putnam, "Bowling Alone." For "emotional capital," see Arlie Russell Hochschild, *The Managed Heart: The Commercialization of Human Feeling* (Berkeley, CA: University of California Press, 1983). For "cultural capital," see work by Pierre Bourdieu and Jurgen Habermas.

61. Judith Stacey, "Dan Quayle's Revenge: The New Family Values Crusaders," *The Nation*, July 25/August 1, 1994, 119–22. Iris Marion Young, "Making Single Motherhood Normal," *Dissent* (Winter 1994): 88–93.

62. Christopher Jencks and Kathryn Edin, "Do Poor Women Have a Right to Bear Children," *The American Prospect* (Winter 1995): 43–52.

63. Stacey, "Dan Quayle's Revenge." Arlene Skolnick and Stacey Rosencrantz, "The New Crusade for the Old Family," *The American Prospect* (Summer 1994): 59–65.

64. Nancy Smith Barrett, "Data Needs for Evaluating the Labor Market Status of Women," in *Census Bureau Conference on Federal Statistical Needs Relating to Women*, ed. Barbara B. Reagan (U.S. Bureau of the Census, 1979), Current Population Reports, Special Studies, Series P-23, no. 83, pp. 10–19. These figures belie the familiar but misleading statement that "only 7 percent" of all American families are of the traditional nuclear type because "traditional" is defined so narrowly—as husband and wife with two children under 18 where the wife is not employed outside the home. For more recent figures and a similar argument for more universal family ethic, see Christine Winquist Nord and Nicholas Zill, "American Households in Demographic Perspective," working paper no. 5, Institute for American Values, New York, 1991.

65. Tamar Levin, "Women Are Becoming Equal Providers," *New York Times*, May 11, 1995, A27.

66. Marianne A. Ferber and Julie A. Nelson, *Beyond Economic Man: Feminist Theory and Economics* (Chicago: University of Chicago Press, 1993).

67. Fran Sussner Rodgers and Charles Rodgers, "Business and the Facts of Family Life," *Harvard Business Review*, no. 6 (1989): 199–213, especially 206.

68. Ravenna Helson and S. Picano, "Is the Traditional Role Bad for Women?" *Journal of Personality and Social Psychology* 59 (1990): 311–20. Rosalind C. Barnett, "Home-to-Work Spillover Revisited: A Study of Full-Time Employed Women in Dual-Earner Couples," *Journal of Marriage and the Family* 56 (August 1994): 647–56.

69. Arlie Hochschild, "The Fractured Family," *The American Prospect* (Summer 1991): 106–15.

70. Leon Eisenberg, "Is the Family Obsolete?" *The Key Reporter* 60, no. 3 (1995): 1–5. Arlene Skolnick and Stacey Rosencrantz, "The New Crusade for the Old Family," *The American Prospect* (Summer 1994): 59–65.

71. Roberta M. Spalter-Roth, Heidi I. Hartmann, and Linda M. Andrews, "Mothers, Children, and Low-Wage Work: The Ability to Earn a Family Wage," in *Sociology and the Public Agenda*, ed. W. J. Wilson (Newbury Park, CA: Sage Publications, 1993), 316–38.

72. Louis Uchitelle, "Lacking Child Care, Parents Take Their Children to Work," *New York Times*, December 23, 1994, 1.

73. Jencks and Edin, "Do Poor Women Have a Right," 50.

74. David Elkind, *Ties That Stress: The New Family in Balance* (Boston: Harvard University Press, 1994).

75. It is frequently noted that the U.S. is a much more racially diverse nation than, say, Sweden, which has a concerted family and children's policy. Symptomatic of the potential for race and class division that

impedes recognition of all children as the nation's children is the book by Richard J. Herrnstein and Charles A. Murray, *The Bell Curve: Intelligence and Class Structure in American Life* (New York: The Free Press, 1994).

76. Young, "Making Single Motherhood Normal," 93.

77. If the objection is that the wrong people will have children, as Herrnstein and Murray suggest in *The Bell Curve*, then the challenge is to find ways for poor women to make money or have some other more exciting career that will offset the rewards of having children, "such as becoming the bride of Christ or the head of a Fortune 500 corporation," to quote Jencks and Edin, "Do Poor Women Have a Right," 48.

78. Beth M. Miller, "Private Welfare: The Distubutive Equity of Family Benefits in America" (Ph.D. thesis, Brandeis University, 1992). Sue Shellenbarger, "Family-Friendly Firms Often Leave Fathers Out of the Picture," *Wall Street Journal*, November 2, 1994. Richard T. Gill and T. Grandon Gill, *Of Familes, Children, and a Parental Bill of Rights* (New York: Institute for American Values, 1993). For gathering information on these new work-family policies, I wish to acknowledge help of students in my 1994–95 Family Policy Seminar at Brandeis University, particularly Cathleen O'Brien, Deborah Gurewich, Alissa Starr, and Pamela Swain, as well as the insights of two Ph.D students, Mindy Fried and Sherry Wexler.

79. Lotte Bailyn, *Breaking the Mold: Women, Men and Time in the New Corporate World* (New York: The Free Press, 1994).

80. Penelope Leach, *Children First: What Our Society Must Do and Is Doing* (New York: Random House, 1994).

II *The Sexes*

American society has experienced both a sexual revolution and a gender revolution. The first has liberalized attitudes toward erotic behavior and expression; the second has changed the roles and status of women and men in the direction of greater equality. Both revolutions have been brought about by the rapid social changes in recent years, and both revolutions have challenged traditional conceptions of marriage.

The traditional idea of sexuality defines sex as a powerful biological drive continually struggling for gratification against restraints imposed by civilization. The notion of sexual instincts also implies a kind of innate knowledge: A person intuitively knows his or her own identity as male or female, he or she knows how to act accordingly, and he or she is attracted to the "proper" sex object—a person of the opposite gender. In other words, the view of sex as biological drive pure and simple implies "that sexuality has a magical ability, possessed by no other capacity, that allows biological drives to be expressed directly in psychological and social behaviors" (Gagnon and Simon, 1970, p. 24).

The whole issue of the relative importance of biological versus psychological and social factors in sexuality and sex differences has been obscured by polemics. On the one hand, there are the strict biological determinists who declare that anatomy is destiny. On the other hand, there are those who argue that all aspects of sexuality and sex-role differences are matters of learning and social construction.

There are two essential points to be made about the nature-versus-nurture argument. First, modern genetic theory views biology and environment as interacting, not opposing forces. Second, both biological determinists and their opponents assume that if a biological force exists, it must be overwhelmingly strong. But the most sophisticated evidence concerning both gender development *and* erotic arousal suggests that physiological forces are gentle rather than powerful. Despite all the media stories about a "gay gene" or "a gene for lung cancer," the scientific reality is more complicated. As one researcher wrote recently, "the scientists have identified a number of genes that may, under certain circumstances, make an individual more or less susceptible to the action of a variety of environmental agents" (cited in Berwick, 1998, p. 4).

In terms of scholarship, the main effect of the sex-role and sexual revolutions has been on awareness and consciousness. For example, much early social science writing was revealed to have been based on sexist assumptions. Many sociologists and psychologists took it for granted that women's roles and functions in society reflect universal physiological and temperamental traits. Since in practically every society women were subordinate to men, inequality was interpreted as an inescapable necessity of organized social life. Such analysis suffered from the same intellectual flaw as the idea that discrimination against nonwhites implies their innate inferiority. All such explanations failed to analyze the social institutions and forces producing and supporting the observed differences.

But as Robert M. Jackson points out, modern economic and political institutions have been moving toward gender equality. For example, both the modern workplace and the state have increasingly come to treat people as workers or voters without regard for their gender or their family status. Educational institutions from nursery school to graduate school are open to both sexes. Whether or not men who have traditionally run these institutions were in favor of gender inequality, their actions eventually improved women's status in society. Women have not yet attained full quality, but in Jackson's view, the trend in that direction is irreversible.

One reason the trend toward greater gender equality will persist is that young people born since the 1970s have grown up in a more equal society than their parents' generation. Kathleen Gerson reports on a number of findings from her study of 18- to 30-year-old "children of the gender revolution." First, she finds that whether a mother works or the number of parents in the home is not the major determinant of children's experience in the home. What seems to matter is, first, family process—how family members interact with one another. Second, life changes such as a major illness, alcoholism, job loss, or family move can have a major impact on a child, but can occur in any family structure. She finds that young adults of both sexes have similar high aspirations for themselves in work and family, valuing both commitment and autonomy. They understand that these are difficult goals, and that there is a lack of social and community resources, such as child care, in support of working families. But Gerson finds a loss of political vision in this generation; they see only private solutions to work and family issues.

In their article, Scott Coltrane and Michele Adams examine some reasons why the home lags behind other institutions in the shift toward greater symmetry in male–female roles. Although men are doing more housework than they did twenty years ago, they are still doing much less than women. Partly, the answer is that men retain a good deal of power in marriage because of their greater earning capacity. But there is also a culture lag; most people in the United States are ambivalent about women's equality in marriage and family life. And many feel uncomfortable about a man who works fewer hours to devote more time to his home and children.

Many Americans, yearning for some lost golden age of traditional families, imagine that Japan still embodies that ideal. Sumiko Iwao shows how wrong that image is. A "battle of the sexes" rages even more strongly there than it does here, and the Japanese government has become concerned about declining birth rates. Instead of trying to force women back into the home however, the government is trying to build a gender-neutral but family-friendly society, one with a balance of work and family for both men and women.

The transformation of gender is intertwined with changes in sex and marriage. In her article, Beth Bailey presents a historian's overview of the most recent sexual revolution. She finds that it was composed of at least three separate strands. First, there has been a gradual increase, over the course of the twentieth century, in sexual imagery and openness about sexual matters in the media and in public life generally. Second, in the 1960s and 1970s, premarital sex, which had always been part of dating, came to include intercourse, and even living together before or without marriage. The flamboyant sex radicals of the sixties' counterculture were the loudest but the least numerous part of the sexual revolution.

The sexual revolution raises questions about the nature of human sexuality and the meaning of "normality." One way to look for answers is to examine the anthropological evidence. Burton Pasternak and Carol and Melvin Ember reveal the great variation that exists in sexual attitudes and practices of different cultures around the world. Some are more permissive than the United States today; some are far more restrictive. Some regard sex as a duty, some as a pleasure, and some regard it as dangerous and fearful. Some societies deny homosexuality exists, others tolerate it, still others actually prescribe homosexual relationships between boys and older men. These authors also discuss some of the explanations anthropologists have offered to explain such widely divergent customs.

For many people, the recent changes in sexual norms, especially the spread of premarital sex to teenagers, is the most worrisome aspect of recent social change. And those adults who grew up in the era of "traditional" dating—which began in the 1920s—wonder how young people these days connect with one another for romantic relationships. In his article, Don Merten presents an anthropological study of young adolescents "going with" one another.

Public anxiety about the future of marriage, as Frank F. Furstenberg Jr. points out in his article, sometimes approaches hysterical levels. He argues that recent changes are not signs that marriage is disappearing or in a severe state of crisis, but that there *is* cause for concern. The traditional marriage bargain, he explains, in which women exchanged their domestic services for financial support, is no longer valid. Now that women work outside the home, they are no longer as dependent on men as they used to be. Further, most men no longer have jobs that pay enough to support a family. Both men and women say they believe in greater equality in marriage, but in practice, most women still do the lion's share of housework and child care.

While people in all walks of life are grappling with new expectations of gender equality, for many young adults with low incomes, marriage has become a luxury item. Furstenberg finds that people still value marriage, but that living together or single parenthood has become "the budget way to start a family." Restoring marriage to its former status will require moving toward a society that provides secure jobs and better child-care options.

Elaborating on this theme, Kathryn Edin examines various theories about why poor women find it hard to find men who might make good husbands, no matter how much they would like to be married.

What would a truly equal marriage look like? Are there any couples with genuinely egalitarian relationships? In her article, Pepper Schwartz reports on her study of "peer marriages"—couples who believe strongly in equality and who share the childrearing, housework, and control over money. She found that there is no single blueprint for a successful peer marriage, but keeping such a marriage going takes a lot of effort in a society that does not offer much support for these nontraditional arrangements.

Along with the sexual revolution, the sharp increase in divorce rates since the 1960s has given rise to public alarm about the future of the family, and even proposals to make divorces harder to get. But as the article by Mavis Hetherington and colleagues shows, divorce is not a single event, but a long process. It is a complex chain of events and life experiences that begins long before the divorce itself and continues long after. Although divorce is an emotionally wrenching process for all concerned, it's difficult to make blanket statements about its long-term effects. Divorce tends to be a different experience for men, women, and children; and individual reactions to it vary enormously.

What does it mean for married couples to be living in a time when divorce has become a commonplace, no longer shameful, event? Do high divorce rates signify a decline in such family values as commitment and responsibility? Karla B. Hackstaff explores these questions through in-depth interviews contrasting couples who married in the 1950s and those who married in the 1970s. She finds that the issue of divorce is inseparably intertwined with the issue of gender equality. Historically, marriage has been a male-dominated institution. The 50s wives accepted this, yet they tended to think about divorce far more than their husbands did. The 70s couples try to work out more egalitarian arrangements, and have developed a "marital work ethic" to counter the threat of divorce. Hackstaff concludes that today's "divorce culture" may be a temporary phenomenon, part of the transition toward greater equality in all aspects of marriage.

Gender issues also haunt stepfamily relationships, as Ann C. Bernstein reports in her article. Remarriages generate a complex array of family structures and kinship arrangements, and they also vary by class, race, ethnicity, and sexual orientation. White middle-class stepfamilies have been the most studied. Many of the problems stepfamilies face stem from the persistence of older cultural notions and narratives. For example, members of stepfamilies often use the *Ozzie and Harriet* or *Father Knows Best* family model as a yardstick, and see themselves as deficient. Also, the older cultural tradition of seeing stepmothers as wicked witches, stepchildren as Cinderellas, and "real" mothers as fairy godmothers adds to people's ambivalence. Stepfathers do not have such a negative image. Moreover, their roles as father and stepfather do not differ as much as the roles of mother and stepmother do. Nevertheless, Bernstein reminds us, the majority of parents and stepparents are both satisfied and involved with their families.

Despite all its difficulties, marriage is not likely to go out of style in the near future. Ultimately we agree with Jessie Bernard (1982), who, after a devastating critique of traditional marriage from the point of view of a sociologist who is also a feminist, said this:

> The future of marriage is as assured as any social form can be. . . . For men and women will continue to want intimacy, they will continue to want to celebrate their mutuality, to experience the mystic unity which once led the church to consider marriage a sacrament. . . . There is hardly any probability such commitments will disappear or that all relationships between them will become merely casual or transient. (p. 301)

References

Bernard, Jessie. 1982. *The Future of Marriage.* New York: World.
Berwick, Robert C. 1998. The doors of perception. *The Los Angeles Times Book Review.* March 15.
Gagnon, J. H., and W. Simon. 1970. *The Sexual Scene.* Chicago: Aldine/Transaction.

3 Changing Gender Roles

■ READING 6

Destined for Equality

Robert M. Jackson

Over the past two centuries, women's long, conspicuous struggle for better treatment has masked a surprising condition. Men's social dominance was doomed from the beginning. Gender inequality could not adapt successfully to modern economic and political institutions. No one planned this. Indeed, for a long time, the impending extinction of gender inequality was hidden from all.

In the middle of the nineteenth century, few said that equality between women and men was possible or desirable. The new forms of business, government, schools, and the family seemed to fit nicely with the existing division between women's roles and men's roles. Men controlled them all, and they showed no signs of losing belief in their natural superiority. If anything, women's subordination seemed likely to grow worse as they remained attached to the household while business and politics became a separate, distinctively masculine, realm.

Nonetheless, 150 years later, seemingly against all odds, women are well on the way to becoming men's equals. Now, few say that gender equality is impossible or undesirable. Somehow our expectations have been turned upside down.

Women's rising status is an enigmatic paradox. For millennia women were subordinate to men under the most diverse economic, political, and cultural conditions. Although the specific content of gender-based roles and the degree of inequality between the sexes varied considerably across time and place, men everywhere held power and status over women. Moreover, people believed that men's dominance was a natural and unchangeable part of life. Yet over the past two centuries, gender inequality has declined across the world.

The driving force behind this transformation has been the migration of economic and political power outside households and its reorganization around business and political interests detached from gender. Women (and their male supporters) have fought against prejudice and discrimination throughout American history, but social conditions governed the intensity and effectiveness of their efforts. Behind the very visible conflicts between women and male-dominated institutions, fundamental processes concerning economic and political organization have been paving the way for women's success. Throughout these years, while many women struggled to improve their status and many men resisted those efforts, institutional changes haltingly, often imperceptibly, but persistently undermined gender inequality. Responding to the emergent imperatives of large-scale, bureaucratic organizations, men with economic or political power intermittently adopted policies that favored greater equality, often without anticipating the implications of their actions. Gradually responding to the changing demands and possibilities of households without economic activity, men acting as individuals reduced their resistance to wives and daughters extending their roles, although men rarely recognized they were doing something different from their fathers' generation.

Social theorists have long taught us that institutions have unanticipated consequences, particularly when the combined effect of many people's actions diverges from their individual aims. Adam Smith, the renowned theorist of early capitalism, proposed that capitalist markets shared a remarkable characteristic. Many people pursuing only selfish, private interests could further the good of all. Subsequently, Karl Marx, considering the capitalist economy, proposed an equally remarkable but contradictory assessment. Systems of inequality fueled by rational self-interest, he argued, inevitably produce irrational crises that threaten to destroy the social order. Both ideas have suffered many critical blows, but they still capture our imaginations by their extraordinary insight. They teach us how unanticipated effects often ensue when disparate people and organizations each follow their own short-sighted interests.

Through a similar unanticipated and uncontrolled process, the changing actions of men, women, and powerful institutions have gradually but irresistibly reduced gender inequality. Women had always resisted their constraints and inferior status. Over the past 150 years, however, their individual strivings and organized resistance became increasingly effective. Men long continued to oppose the loss of their privileged status. Nonetheless, although men and male-controlled institutions did not adopt egalitarian values, their actions changed because their interests changed. Men's resistance to women's aspirations diminished, and they found new advantages in strategies that also benefited women.

Modern economic and political organization propelled this transformation by slowly dissociating social power from its allegiance to gender inequality. The power over economic resources, legal rights, the allocation of positions, legitimating values, and setting priorities once present in families shifted into businesses and government organizations. In these organizations, profit, efficiency, political legitimacy, organizational stability, competitiveness, and similar considerations mattered more than male privileges vis-à-vis females. Men who had power because of their positions in these organizations gradually adopted policies ruled more by institutional interests than by personal prejudices. Over the long run, institutional needs and opportunities produced policies that worked against gender inequality. Simultaneously, ordinary men (those without economic or political power) resisted women's advancements less. They had fewer resources to use against the women in their lives, and less to gain from keeping women subordinate. Male politicians seeking more power, businessmen pursuing wealth and success, and ordinary men pursuing their self-interest all contributed to the gradual decline of gender inequality.

Structural developments produced ever more inconsistencies with the requirements for continued gender inequality. Both the economy and the state increasingly treated people as potential workers or voters without reference to their family status. To the disinterested, and often rationalized, authority within these institutions, sex inequality was just one more consideration with calculating strategies for profit and political advantage. For these institutions, men and women embodied similar problems of control, exploitation, and legitimation.

Seeking to further their own interests, powerful men launched institutional changes that eventually reduced the discrimination against women. Politicians passed laws giving married women property rights. Employers hired women in ever-increasing numbers. Educators opened their doors to women. These examples and many others show powerful men pursuing their interests in preserving and expanding their economic and political power, yet also improving women's social standing.

The economy and state did not systematically oppose inequality. On the contrary, each institution needed and aggressively supported some forms of inequality, such as income differentials and the legal authority of state officials, that gave them strength. Other forms of inequality received neither automatic support nor automatic opposition. Over time, the responses to other kinds of inequality depended on how well they met institutional interests and how contested they became.

When men adopted organizational policies that eventually improved women's status, they consciously sought to increase profits, end labor shortages, get more votes, and increase social order. They imposed concrete solutions to short-term economic and political problems and to conflicts associated with them. These men usually did not envision, and probably did not care, that the cumulative effect of these policies would be to curtail male dominance.

Only when they were responding to explicitly egalitarian demands from women such as suffrage did men with power consistently examine the implications of their actions for gender inequality. Even then, as when responding to women's explicit demands for legal changes, most legislators were concerned more about their political interests than the fate of gender inequality. When legislatures did pass laws responding to public pressure about women's rights, few male legislators expected the laws could dramatically alter gender inequality.

Powerful men adopted various policies that ultimately would undermine gender inequality because such policies seemed to further their private interests and to address inescapable economic, political, and organizational problems. The structure and integral logic of development within modern political and economic institutions shaped the problems, interests, and apparent solutions. Without regard to what either women or men wanted, industrial capitalism and rational legal government eroded gender inequality.

MAPPING GENDER INEQUALITY'S DECLINE

When a band of men committed to revolutionary change self-consciously designed the American institutional framework, they did not imagine or desire that it would lead toward gender equality. In 1776 a small group of men claimed equality for themselves and similar men by signing the Declaration of Independence. In throwing off British sovereignty, they inaugurated the American ideal of equality. Yet after the success of their revolution, its leaders and like-minded property-owning white men created a nation that subjugated women, enslaved blacks, and withheld suffrage from men without property.

These men understood the egalitarian ideals they espoused through the culture and experiences dictated by their own historical circumstances. Everyone then accepted that women and men were absolutely and inalterably different. Although Abigail Adams admonished her husband that they should "remember the ladies," when these "fathers" of the American nation established its most basic rights and laws, the prospect of fuller citizenship for women was not even credible enough to warrant the effort of rejection. These nation builders could not foresee that their political and economic institutions would eventually erode some forms of inequality much more emphatically than had their revolutionary vision. They could not know that the social structure would eventually extend egalitarian social relations much further than they might ever have thought desirable or possible.

By the 1830s, a half-century after the American Revolution, little had changed. In the era of Jacksonian democracy, women still could not vote or hold political office. They had to cede legal control of their inherited property and their income to their husbands. With few exceptions, they could not make legal contracts or escape a marriage through divorce. They could not enter college. Dependence on men was perpetual and inescapable. Household toil and family welfare monopolized women's time and energies. Civil society recognized women not as individuals but as adjuncts to men. Like the democracy of ancient Athens, the American democracy limited political equality to men.

Today women enjoy independent citizenship; they have the same liberty as men to control their person and property. If they choose or need to do so, women can live without a husband. They can discard an unwanted husband to seek a better alternative. Women vote and occupy political offices. They hold jobs almost as often as men do. Ever more women have managerial and professional positions. Our culture has adopted more affirmative images for women, particularly as models of such values as independence, public advocacy, economic success, and thoughtfulness. Although these changes have not removed all inequities, women now have greater resources, more choices in life, and a higher social status than in the past.

In terms of the varied events and processes that have so dramatically changed women's place in society, the past 150 years of American history can be divided into three half-century periods. The *era of separate spheres* covers roughly 1840–1890, from the era of Jacksonian democracy to the Gilded Age. The *era of egalitarian illusions*, roughly 1890–1940, extends from the Progressive Era to the beginning of World War II. The third period, the *era of assimilation*, covers the time from World War II to the present (see Table 1).

Over the three periods, notable changes altered women's legal, political, and economic status, women's access to higher education and to divorce, women's sexuality, and the cultural images of women and men. Most analysts agree that people's legal, political, and economic status largely define their social status, and we will focus on the changes in these. Of course, like gender, other personal characteristics such as race and age also define an individual's status, because they similarly influence legal, political, and economic rights and resources. Under most circumstances, however, women and men are

TABLE 1 *The Decline of Gender Inequality in American Society*

	1840–1890 The Era of Separate Spheres	1890–1940 The Era of Egalitarian Illusions	1940–1990 The Era of Assimilation	1990–? Residual Inequities
Legal and political status	Formal legal equality instituted	Formal political equality instituted	Formal economic equality instituted	Women rare in high political offices
Economic opportunity	Working-class jobs for single women only	Some jobs for married women and educated women	All kinds of jobs available to all kinds of women	"Glass ceiling" and domestic duties hold women back
Higher education	A few women admitted to public universities and new women's colleges	Increasing college; little graduate or professional education	Full access at all levels	Some prestigious fields remain largely male domains
Divorce	Almost none, but available for dire circumstances	Increasingly available, but difficult	Freely available and accepted	Women typically suffer greater costs
Sexuality and reproductive control	Repressive sexuality; little reproductive control	Positive sexuality but double standard; increasing reproductive control	High sexual freedom; full reproductive control	Sexual harassment and fear of rape still widespread
Cultural image	Virtuous domesticity and subordination	Educated motherhood, capable for employment & public service	Careers, marital equality	Sexes still perceived as inherently different

not systematically differentiated by other kinds of inequality based on personal characteristics, because these other differences, such as race and age, cut across gender lines. Educational institutions have played an ever-larger role in regulating people's access to opportunities over the last century. Changes in access to divorce, women's sexuality, and cultural images of gender will not play a central role in this study. They are important indicators of women's status, but they are derivative rather than formative. They reveal inequality's burden.

The creation of separate spheres for women and men dominated the history of gender inequality during the first period, 1840–1890. The cultural doctrine of separate spheres emerged in the mid-nineteenth century. It declared emphatically that women and men belonged to different worlds. Women were identified with the household and maintenance of family life. Men were associated with income-generating employment and public life. Popular ideas attributed greater religious virtue to women but greater civic virtue to men. Women were hailed as guardians of private morality while men were regarded as the protectors of the public good. These cultural and ideological inventions were responses to a fundamental institutional transition, the movement of economic activity out of households into independent enterprises. The concept of separate spheres legitimated women's exclusion from the public realm, although it gave them some autonomy and authority within their homes.

Women's status was not stagnant in this period. The cultural wedge driven between women's and men's worlds obscured diverse and significant changes that did erode inequality. The state gave married women the right to control their property and income. Jobs became available for some, mainly single, women, giving them some economic independence and an identity apart from the household. Secondary education similar to that offered to men became available to women, and colleges began to admit some women for higher learning. Divorce became a possible, though still difficult, strategy for the first time and led social commentators to bemoan the increasing rate of marital dissolution. In short, women's opportunities moved slowly forward in diverse ways.

From 1890 to 1940 women's opportunities continued to improve, and many claimed that women had won equality. Still, the opportunities were never enough to enable women to transcend their subordinate position. The passage of the Woman Suffrage Amendment stands out as the high point of changes during this period, yet women could make little headway in government while husbands and male politicians belittled and rejected their political aspirations. Women entered the labor market in ever-increasing numbers, educated women could get white-collar positions for the first time, and employers extended hiring to married women. Still, employers rarely considered women for high-status jobs, and explicit discrimination was an accepted practice. Although women's college opportunities became more like men's, professional and advanced degree programs still excluded women. Married women gained widespread access to effective contraception. Although popular opinion expected women to pursue and enjoy sex within marriage, social mores still denied them sex outside it. While divorce became more socially acceptable and practically available, laws still restricted divorce by demanding that one spouse prove that the other was morally repugnant. Movies portrayed glamorous women as smart, sexually provocative, professionally talented, and ambitious, but even they, if they were good women, were driven by an overwhelming desire to marry, bear children, and dedicate themselves to their homes.

Writing at the end of this period, the sociologist Mirra Komarovsky captured its implications splendidly. After studying affluent college students during World War II, Komarovsky concluded that young women were beset by "serious contradictions between two roles." The first was the feminine role, with its expectations of deference to men and a future focused on familial activities. The second was the "modern" role that "partly obliterates the differentiation in sex," presumably because the emphasis on education made the universal qualities of ability and accomplishment seem the only reasonable limitations on future activities. Women who absorbed the egalitarian implications of modern education felt confused, burdened, and irritated by the contrary expectations that they display a subordinate femininity. The intrinsic contradictions between these two role expectations could only end, Komarovsky declared, when women's real adult role was redefined to make it "consistent with the socioeconomic and ideological modern society."[1]

Since 1940, many of these contradictions have been resolved. At an accelerating pace, women have continually gained greater access to the activities, positions, and statuses formerly reserved to men.

Despite the tremendous gains women have experienced, they have not achieved complete equality, nor is it imminent. The improvement of women's status has been uneven, seesawing between setbacks and advances. Women still bear the major responsibility for raising children. They suffer from lingering harassment, intimidation, and disguised discrimination. Women in the United States still get poorer jobs and lower income. They have less access to economic or political power. The higher echelons of previously male social hierarchies have assimilated women slowest and least completely. For example, in blue-collar hierarchies they find it hard to get skilled jobs or join craft unions; in white-collar hierarchies they rarely reach top management; and in politics the barriers to women's entry seem to rise with the power of the office they seek. Yet when we compare the status of American women today with their status in the past, the movement toward greater equality is striking.

While women have not gained full equality, the formal structural barriers holding them back have largely collapsed and those left are crumbling. New government policies have discouraged sex discrimination by most organizations and in most areas of life outside the family. The political and economic systems have accepted ever more women and have promoted them to positions with more influence and higher status. Education at all levels has become equally available to women. Women have gained great control over their reproductive processes, and their sexual freedom has come to resemble that of men. It has become easy and socially acceptable to end unsatisfactory marriages with divorce. Popular culture has come close to portraying women as men's legitimate equal. Television, our most dynamic communication media, regularly portrays discrimination as wrong and male abuse or male dominance as nasty. The prevailing theme of this recent period has been women's assimilation into all the activities and positions once denied them.

This book [this reading was taken from] focuses on the dominant patterns and the groups that had the most decisive and most public roles in the processes that changed women's status: middle-class whites and, secondarily, the white working class. The histories of gender inequality among racial and ethnic minorities are too diverse to address adequately here.[2] Similarly, this analysis neglects other distinctive groups, especially lesbians and heterosexual women who avoided marriage, whose changing circumstances also deserve extended study.

While these minorities all have distinctive histories, the major trends considered here have influenced all groups. Every group had to respond to the same changing political and economic structures that defined the opportunities and constraints for all people in the society. Also, whatever their particular history, the members of each group understood their gender relations against the backdrop of the white, middle-class family's cultural preeminence. Even when people in higher or lower-class positions or people in ethnic communities expressed contempt for these values, they were familiar with the middle-class ideals and thought of them as leading ideas in the society. The focus on the white middle classes is simply an analytical and practical strategy. The history of dominant groups has no greater inherent or moral worth. Still, except in cases of open, successful rebellion, the ideas and actions of dominant groups usually affect history much more than the ideas and actions of subordinate groups. This fact is an inevitable effect of inequality.

THE MEANING OF INEQUALITY AND ITS DECLINE

We will think differently about women's status under two theoretical agendas. Either we can try to evaluate how short from equality women now fall, or we can try to understand how far they have come from past deprivations.

Looking at women's place in society today from these two vantage points yields remarkably different perspectives. They accentuate different aspects of women's status by altering the background against which we compare it. Temporal and analytical differences separate these two vantage points, not distinctive moral positions, although people sometimes confuse these differences with competing moral positions.

If we want to assess and criticize women's disadvantages today, we usually compare their existing status with an imagined future when complete equality reigns. Using this ideal standard of complete equality, we would find varied shortcomings in women's status today. These shortcomings include women's absence from positions of political or economic power, men's preponderance in the better-paid and higher-status occupations, women's lower average income, women's greater family responsibilities, the higher status commonly attached to male activities, and the dearth of institutions or policies supporting dual-earner couples.

Alternatively, if we want to evaluate how women's social status has improved, we must turn in the other direction and face the past. We look back to a time when women were legal and political outcasts, working only in a few low-status jobs, and always deferring to male authority. From this perspective, women's status today seems much brighter. Compared with the nineteenth century, women now have a nearly equal legal and political status, far more women hold jobs, women can succeed at almost any occupation, women usually get paid as much as men in the same position (in the same firm), women have as much educational opportunity as men, and both sexes normally expect women to pursue jobs and careers.

As we seek to understand the decline of gender inequality, we will necessarily stress the improvements in women's status. We will always want to remember, however, that gender inequality today stands somewhere between extreme inequality and complete equality. To analyze the modern history of gender inequality fully, we must be able to look at this middle ground from both sides. It is seriously deficient when measured against full equality. It is a remarkable improvement when measured against past inequality.

Editors' Note: *Notes for this reading can be found in the original source.*

■READING 7

Children of the Gender Revolution: Some Theoretical Questions and Findings from the Field

Kathleen Gerson

As a new century commences, it is clear that fundamental changes in family, work, and gender arrangements have transformed the experience of growing up in American society. Only several decades ago, an American child was likely to grow to adulthood in a two-parent home with a mother who worked outside the home either intermittently or not at all. No such common situation unites children today. With less than fourteen percent of American households containing a married couple with a breadwinning husband and homemaking wife, children living in a "traditional family" now form a distinct minority (Ahlburg and De Vita, 1992; Gerson, 1993). Regardless of race, ethnicity, or class, most younger Americans have lived, or will live, in a family situation that departs significantly from a pattern once thought to be enduring. Many have grown up in a two-parent home in which both parents have pursued strong and sustained ties to work outside the home. Others have lived through marital disruptions and perhaps the remarriage of one or both parents. Still others have been raised by a single mother who never married the father of her children. Most of these children have experienced shifting circumstances, in which some substantial change occurred in their family situation before they left their parents' home.

This revolution in the experience of childhood has provided an unprecedented opportunity to unravel the processes of human development and better understand the consequences of growing up in diverse family situations. We are living through a natural social experiment that makes it possible to assess the effects of family arrangements as well as other social and cultural institutions on the lives of children. As the recipients of widespread gender and family change, this generation is ideally positioned to shed light on a number of important theoretical questions.

First, what is the relationship between family composition and children's welfare? Is family structure, as measured by the household's composition and gender division of labor, the most consequential aspect of a child's developmental environment, as has been generally assumed, or is family form mediated by other factors, such as interactional processes within the home and contextual factors outside it? Second, what are the links between parental choices and children's reactions? How do children make sense of their family situations and their parents' circumstances, and what strategies do they develop to cope with their situations? Are children inclined to adopt their parents' choices and beliefs, and when and under what circumstances are they more likely to reject or modify them?

Third, what part do institutions outside the family, and especially community, educational, and labor market structures, play in shaping a child's outlook and developmental trajectory? And, finally, as new generations of women and men respond to widespread cultural changes outside the home and shifting dynamics within it, what personal, social, and political strategies are they developing to cope with the new contingencies wrought by the family and gender revolutions? What do the experiences of this pivotal generation portend for the future of gender—as a cultural belief and a lived experience?

The "children of the gender revolution" have grown to adulthood in a wide range of circumstances, and their experiences offer a window through which to glimpse both general processes of human development and historically embedded social shifts. By taking a careful look at the developmental paths and personal conflicts of this generation, we can untangle the role that family structure plays in children's lives and discover the other processes and factors that either mitigate or explain its effects. And since members of this generation are now negotiating the transition to adulthood and thus poised to craft their own work and family strategies, they offer important clues to the future course of the transformation in family, work, and gender patterns begun by their parents.

CHANGES IN CHILDREN'S LIVES: CONTENDING WITH THEORETICAL APPROACHES AND THE "FAMILY VALUES" DEBATE

The diversification of family forms has produced disputes among American social scientists (as well as among politicians and ordinary citizens) about the effects of family and gender transformations on the welfare of children. These debates have been framed in "either/or" terms, in which those who decry the decline of the homemaker–breadwinner family have clashed with those who defend and, to some extent, celebrate the rise of alternative family forms.

Analysts concerned that family and gender transformations threaten children's welfare and undermine the larger social fabric have developed a perspective that emphasizes "family decline." (See, for example, Blankenhorn, 1994; Popenoe, 1989 and 1996; Whitehead, 1997.) This approach tends to view the "traditional family," characterized by permanent heterosexual commitment and a clear sexual division of labor between stay-at-home mothers and breadwinning fathers, as the ideal family form. The rise in divorce, out-of-wedlock parenthood, and employment among mothers thus represent a serious family breakdown that is putting new generations of younger Americans at risk. From this perspective, "nontraditional families," such as dual-earner and single-parent households, are part of a wider moral breakdown, in which the spread of an individualistic ethos has encouraged adults to pursue their own self-interest at the expense of children.

While compelling, the "family decline" contains both logical and empirical deficiencies. First, it treats family change as if it were a cause rather than an effect. Yet new family forms are inescapable reactions to basic economic and social shifts that have propelled women into the workplace and expanded the options for personal development in adulthood. By idealizing the mid-twentieth century homemaker–breadwinner household, this perspective also tends to downplay the positive aspects of change and especially the expansion of options for women. We now know, however, that family life in the past rarely conformed to our nostalgic images and that many homemaker–breadwinner families were rife with unhappiness and abuse (Coontz, 1992).

In response to the critique of family change, less pessimistic analysts have responded that family life is not declining but rather adapting, as it has always done in response to new social and economic exigencies. These analysts point out that a return to family forms marked by significant gender inequality is neither possible nor desirable and would not solve the predicaments parents and children now face. (See, for example, Skolnick, 1991; Stacey, 1990 and 1996; Coontz, 1997.) The roots of the family and gender revolution extend deep into the foundations of the economy, the society, and the culture. Single parents and employed mothers have thus become scapegoats for social ills with deeper economic and political roots.

Despite the polarized nature of the American "family values" debate, both perspectives have tended to focus on family structure as the crucial arena of contention. Yet research suggests that family structure, taken alone, cannot explain or predict outcomes for children. While children living with both biological parents appear on average to fare better than children in one-parent homes, most of the difference can be traced to the lower economic and social resources available to single parents as well as to factors such as high family conflict that promote parental break-up in the first place (Cherlin et al., 1991; McLanahan and Gary Sandefur, 1994).

In the case of employed mothers, circumstantial factors also appear to trump family structure. Despite the persisting concern that children are harmed when their mothers work outside the home, decades of research have yielded virtually no support for this claim. Instead, the critical ingredients in providing for children's welfare are such factors as a mother's satisfaction with her situation, the quality of care a child receives, and the involvement of fathers and other supportive caretakers (Barnett and Rivers, 1996; Hoffman, 1987). Even comparisons between oft-labeled "traditional" and "nontraditional" families show that diversity within family types is generally as large as differences between them (Acock and Demo, 1994).

The focus on family structure has thus obscured a number of more basic questions about the short- and long-run consequences of these complicated and deeply rooted social changes. While it is clear that a return to a world marked by a clear sexual division of labor, an unquestioned acceptance of gender inequality, and the predominance of patriarchal families, is neither desirable nor possible, it is less clear what new social forms will or should emerge. To understand this process, we need to delve beneath the polarized controversy over family values to clarify the consequences of diversifying family forms, increasing female autonomy, and shifting adult commitments to those who are the most direct recipients of change. How has the generation born during this period of rapid and tumultuous change experienced, interpreted, and responded to the gender revolution forged by their parents?

UNDERSTANDING THE CHILDREN OF THE GENDER REVOLUTION

To answer these questions, I have interviewed a group that can be considered the "children of the gender revolution." These late adolescents and young adults, between the ages of 18 and 30, are members of the generation that is young enough to have experienced the dynamics of family change at close hand, yet old enough to have a perspective on their childhood circumstances and to be formulating their own plans for the future. Since family change may have been experienced differently in different economic and social contexts, the group has been drawn from a range of racial and ethnic backgrounds and a variety of poor, working-class, and middle-class communities. Of the 120 people interviewed, approximately 56% are non-Hispanic white, 20% are African-American, 18% are Hispanic, and 6% are Asian. They were randomly selected from a range of urban and suburban neighborhoods in the New York metropolitan area. (Most respondents were selected by a random sampling procedure as part of a larger study of the children of immigrants and native-born Americans. To ensure that the parents of my respondents had been born and grown up amid the changing family circumstances of American society, my sample was drawn entirely from the native-born group. (See Mollenkopf et al. for a description of the study and sampling techniques.)

To illuminate how these "children of the gender revolution" have made sense of their childhoods and are formulating strategies for adulthood, in-depth, life-history interviews elicited information on their experiences growing up, their strategies for coping with past and present difficulties, and their outlooks on the future. Most lived in some form of "nontraditional" family arrangement before reaching eighteen. About a third lived in a single-parent home at some point in their childhood, and an additional 40% grew up in homes in which both parents held full-time jobs for a sustained period of time. Even the remaining group, who described their families as generally "traditional," were likely to grow up in homes that underwent some form of notable change as mothers went to work or marriages faced crises. As a whole, this diverse group experienced the full range of changes now emerging in U.S. family and gender arrangements.

The experiences of these strategically placed young women and men call into question a number of long-held assumptions about the primacy of family structure in human development. Their life paths and outlooks point, instead, to the importance of processes of family change, the shape of opportunities outside the family, and children's active strategies to cope with their circumstances amid inescapable but uncertain social shifts.

FAMILY STRUCTURE OR FAMILY TRAJECTORIES?

Despite the theoretical focus on "family structure," which generally refers to the composition and division of labor in the household, these young women and men offer a different view of how they formed their sense of self and their outlook on the future. From their perspective, what matters instead are more subtle family processes and pathways. Indeed, simple family typologies, based on differences among homemaker–breadwinner, dual-earner, and single-parent homes, mask important variations within such family forms. Indeed, regardless of the apparent "structure" of the household, most children experience some form of change in their family life over time. While a minority can point to stable, supportive family environments marked by few noticeable changes, the more common experience involves transitions, sometimes abrupt and always consequential, from one "family environment" to another. Surprisingly, this experience of change applies to many whose parents remained married and not just to those whose households underwent a break-up. More important than household structure at one point in time are the "trajectories" that families follow as they develop throughout the life of a child.

From the time a child is born to the time she or he leaves home, the family environment can develop in different ways. From the point of view of the child, these family experiences assume the form of family trajectories, or pathways, that can either remain stable or move in different directions over time. A "stable" trajectory may remain relatively harmonious, supportive, and secure, or it may remain chronically conflictual and unsupportive. A "changing" trajectory may become more stable and supportive as family conditions improve over the span of childhood and adolescence, or it may become more conflictual and insecure as family conditions deteriorate.

These trajectories are important, but they are not closely linked to prevailing notions of "traditional" and "nontraditional" family structures. While classical theories might predict that traditional households would be more stable and harmonious than nontraditional ones, the experiences of these young women and men reveal no such clear relationship. For example, a number of apparently stable "traditional" households are actually marked by chronic conflict or some kind of less readily noticeable change. In one case, a family's outward stability masked chronic parental addictions and abuse that never improved, despite their status as a two-parent home. In another case, a drug-addicted, distant father moved out of the family home in response to his wife's demand that he break his addiction or leave. Several years later, after a successful recovery, he returned to become a supportive, involved parent. This outwardly stable but internally riven "traditional" family thus became more harmonious and secure over time.

A comparable diversity of processes and practices can be found in nontraditional households. While all children undergo some kind of change if their parents separate or divorce, the transition can bring improvement or deterioration. One young woman, for example, felt relieved when her father divorced her neglectful, emotionally abusive mother, and she found stability and support when he remarried a nurturing, economically successful woman.

Static categories of "family type" thus offer limited clues about the dynamics between parents and children or the unfolding nature of family life. Children rarely perceive their families as fixed arrangements, but rather as a range of situations in flux, which either offer or deny them support over time. These processes are important in providing for a child's welfare, but they are not simple reflections of family structure. A breadwinner–homemaker arrangement does not guarantee a stable or supportive home, and those with dual-earning, single, or stepparents are clearly able to provide support and care.

EMPLOYED MOTHERS AND OTHER PARENTS

If family process is more important than family structure, then a mother's well-being is also more important than whether or not she works outside the home. While most of these young women and men grew up in homes in which their mothers were strongly involved in earning a living, the fact of working or not working mattered less than whether or not mothers (and fathers) appeared satisfied with their lives as workers and parents.

Young women and men reared by work-committed mothers generally agreed that the ensuing benefits outweighed any hypothetical losses. In many cases, a mother's job kept the family from falling into poverty, and in some, it helped propel the household up the class ladder. A mother's employment also gave both parents increased autonomy and appeared to enhance parental equality. While some worried that their mothers and fathers had to toil at difficult, demanding, and low-paying jobs, no one felt neglected. To the contrary, they were appreciative of their mothers' efforts to provide for their own and their family's welfare. Working outside the home thus provided a way for mothers as well as fathers to become "good" parents.

Those whose mothers did not pursue independent avenues outside the domestic sphere expressed more ambivalence. While some were pleased to have their mothers' attention focused exclusively on home and family, others were concerned that the choice had been an unnecessary sacrifice. In these cases, when a homemaking mother seemed frustrated or unhappy, the child's reaction was more likely to center on guilt and minor resentment than on gratitude.

More important than the choice to work or stay home, however, is the child's perception about why the choice was made. When a parent, whether mother or father, appeared to work for the family's welfare as well as his or her own needs, the child accepted these choices as unproblematic. If, in contrast, a mother's choice appeared to contradict her family's needs or her own desires, the child responded with concern and doubt. Children felt supported when parents made choices that provided for everyone's needs and did not pit the wishes of mothers against the needs of children. They fared better, however, when contextual supports helped working parents resolve the conflicts between family and work. Most important were reliable, neighborhood-based child care resources, involvement from committed fathers, and satisfying and flexible jobs for both parents.

BEYOND FAMILY STRUCTURE: FAMILY PROCESSES AND OPPORTUNITY CONTEXTS

How did children from these diverse family situations fare as they negotiated the challenges and dangers of childhood and adolescence? Their diverse fates ranged from successful young adults who were able to launch promising college and work careers to those who became entangled in less felicitous patterns, such as school failure, involvement in crime, and early parenthood. Why were some able to negotiate the risks of adolescence while others were propelled down perilous paths? While it may be tempting to attribute these disparate outcomes to family structure, that does not appear to be the explanation. Not only were people from all types of families, including traditional ones, socially and emotionally sidetracked, but many from "nontraditional" households were able to avoid or overcome the dangers they faced.

Several important, interacting factors influence individual trajectories. First, processes within the family either provided or denied emotional and social support to the child. Second, social and economic resources outside the family, including neighborhood-based resources such as peer groups and schools and class-based resources such as economic support, provided or denied financial and "social capital" to either avoid or escape dangerous situations. Structural and cultural contexts outside the family thus influenced children's outlooks and trajectories, regardless of the kinds of families in which they lived.

School experiences, for example, ranged from academic involvement and success to minor alienation to school failure. Those who fared poorly were likely to have parents who lacked either the will, the skills, or the money to make a special effort to hold the child to reasonable standards, to fight for a child in the face of an indifferent bureaucracy, or to make financial sacrifices (such as choosing a parochial or private school). Those who succeeded, on the other hand, were fortunate in a variety of ways. Most possessed either class-related resources that provided access to good schools and the social pressures and expectations of school success. In the absence of class resources, the support of only one person who believed in and would fight for the child could made a crucial difference.

Yet single mothers, many of whom were poor, and dual-income parents with time-consuming jobs were just as likely as traditional families to provide these pressures and supports. For example, one young man attributed his college and graduate degrees to his struggling but feisty single mother, who fought against a school bureaucracy determined to consign him to the category of "learning disabled."

Experiences outside of school also ranged from engagement in constructive activities, such as organized sports and social service, to involvement in dangerous pursuits, such as crime, drugs, and sexual risk-taking. While opportunities to experiment in risky ways were more prevalent in poor and minority communities, there were inducements in all types of neighborhoods. Those who fell prey to more dangerous lifestyles were not more likely to live in nontraditional homes, but they were more likely to become integrated into peer groups that countered a family's influence. Indeed, avoiding risky behavior often required resisting local temptations, such as a street culture centered around illicit activities. Neighborhoods matter and can thwart the efforts of parents to protect their children from the influences of a burgeoning youth culture outside the home.

Class resources, however, offer a consequential buffer. Middle-class children were more likely to be shielded by their parents and their communities while they passed through a stage of adolescent experimentation, whether it involved drugs, sex, or petty crimes. Poor and minority children were more likely to "get caught," to become ensnared in a punitive system, and to pay a higher long-term price for youthful indiscretions. In all of these ways, class resources and family processes (especially in the form of parental support) provide the context for family life and tend to supercede family structure as crucial shapers of children's life chances and developmental trajectories.

CHILDREN'S INTERPRETIVE FRAMEWORKS AND COPING STRATEGIES

Family processes and class resources form the context for children's experiences, but these contexts are always sifted through a child's interpretive framework and personal coping strategies. These strategies and frameworks represent active efforts on the part of children to give meaning to the actions of others and to craft their own choices amid the uncertainties of changing circumstances.

As this strategic generation has confronted the ideas, opportunities, and models of work and family institutions in flux, most people have had to cope with a world in which high hopes and aspirations are colliding with subtle fears and constricted realities. Regardless of race or class position, most women and men strongly support those aspects of change that have opened up opportunities for women and created new possibilities for redefining gender. Yet these hopes co-exist with concerns about the difficulty of combining work and family, the dangers of economic insecurity, and the lack of institutionalized supports for nontraditional choices. Whether the issue is work, family, or how to combine the two, the men and women emerging from the gender revolution perceive both new opportunities and a new set of dilemmas with few clear resolutions. While most hold egalitarian and pluralist ideals, at least in the abstract, they are less sanguine about whether or how these ideals can be achieved. (In a study of children living in gender-equal families, Risman, 1998, also finds a gap between children's egalitarian ideals and their identities.)

Work

Among women and men of all classes, almost everyone aspires to better jobs than their parents secured or they have yet been able to find. However, if the desire for a good, well-paying, white-collar job or career is nearly universal, the expectation of achieving it is not. Rather, these young women and men are divided in their optimism about the future. These divisions reveal blurring gender boundaries even as class boundaries persist. Women and men alike thus hold high aspirations for work careers, although those with constricted opportunities are less confident about reaching them. Optimism seems well-founded for some (e.g., college-educated whites) and ill-founded for others (e.g., young, single mothers and high school drop-outs). Most are hoping to find "satisfying jobs," willing to settle for "economic security," and not confident that they will be able to achieve either.

The skepticism about long-term economic prospects is reflected in men's and women's expectations of each other. Both groups view their economic prospects in "individualist" terms. Since men generally do not expect to earn enough to support wives and families alone, and women do not expect to be able to rely on male breadwinners, both groups believe their economic fate depends on their own job market achievements rather than on forging a lasting commitment with one partner. Women are thus as likely as men to express high job aspirations, and men are as likely as women to long for respite from the demands of earning a living. Despite these shared aspirations, women remain aware that their opportunities are more constricted than men's. A common refrain is thus that, "Women have it better today than in the past, but men still have it better and probably always will."

Marriage

If economic security and job options remain a concern, most nevertheless believe it is easier to shape their own labor market fate than to control the fate of their personal relationships. The vast majority of women *and* men view egalitarian marriage as the ideal, not only because dual-earner marriages appear to provide the best economic alternative but also because they offer the best hope for balancing personal autonomy with mutual commitment. These are high standards for defining a "good marriage," and many are skeptical that they will be able to achieve it.

Gender provides a lens through which similar expectations are experienced differently. While women and men are equally skeptical of creating lasting commitments, women are more aware of the consequences for work and family. They are more likely to see the possibility of raising children alone and more likely to link this possibility to the need for economic autonomy. Yet women agree with men that it is better to go it alone than to become enmeshed in an unhappy or narrowly confining commitment. Even those few—mostly men—who view traditional marriage as the ideal are more wishful than certain. In the face of these ideals, however, women remain skeptical that men can be counted on to shoulder their fair share, and men doubt they will have the job flexibility to do so.

Parenthood

Changing views of marriage provide the context for shifting orientations toward parenthood. For most women and men, the best parenting appears to be equal parenting. The rise of employed mothers and dual-earning couples thus appears to be good for children—bringing in more family income, fostering happier marriages, and providing better examples of women's autonomy and gender justice. Most (though not all) have concluded that "ideal mothers" and "ideal fathers" are fundamentally indistinguishable, and, across races and classes, the majority are skeptical of family arrangements based on rigid or insurmountable gender differences.

Regardless of their own family experience, moreover, everyone agrees that a committed partnership and happy marriage provide the best context for raising a child. The problem, however, is that a happy marriage is difficult to achieve. Most also agree, therefore, in the context of a deteriorating or chronically conflictual marriage, a child cannot thrive. The key for this generation is that both parents remain involved and supportive even if they find they cannot sustain a commitment to each other.

Views of Gender

Larger cultural shifts, and especially the rising acceptance of and need for women's economic independence, have permeated everywhere, leaving children from all classes and family situations exposed to changing definitions of gender and new work and family options. Most support these changes, arguing that while women have gained considerable opportunities, they have not done so at men's expense.

Women as well as men place a high value on autonomy, and men are equally likely to espouse egalitarian ideals at home and at work. These ideals clash, however, with institutional options that put many of them out of reach. If egalitarian ideologies, support for diversity, and a desire for personal choice predominate, behavioral strategies may stray far from these ideals.

Despite the desire to span the perceived gap between goals and opportunities, few can envision effective social, institutional, or political resolutions to these intractable dilemmas. When asked whether employers or the government can or should help families, most reply that individuals in American society are on their own. The protracted political battle over "family values" has left this generation with little faith that political action can make a difference or that "personal" problems can have social causes and institutional solutions.

Self and Society Amid the Gender Revolution

A diverse and shifting set of experiences are sending these children of the gender revolution in a variety of new and unclear directions. Most hold high aspirations for the future but are also skeptical about the possibilities for achieving their fondest dreams. And because they do not generally see the link between their own seemingly intractable dilemmas and the larger social–structural forces that are shaping the contours of change, they lack a vision of the possibilities for social solutions to what are experienced as very personal problems.

Prepared to face a gap between ideals and options, they are determined to exercise some choice over which trade-offs to make—between work and family, parenthood and career, marriage and going it alone. If their work and family ideals prove to be false promises, they reserve the right to change their circumstances. Despite the uncertainty ahead, however, most agree that the future will not and should not bring a return to the idealized past of separate spheres for men and women. From their perspective, the era when most marriages were permanent, women stayed home with children, and men wielded unquestioned power is irretrievable and undesirable.

BEYOND THE "FAMILY VALUES" DEBATE

The emergence of diverse family arrangements in the United States offers a unique opportunity to develop a better theoretical grasp of the link between the institutions of child rearing, the experiences of growing up, and the long-term trajectories of children. While debate has focused on the importance of family structure, the developmental trajectories of those who have grown up amid these changes reveals a more complicated picture. The lessons gleaned from these lives suggest expansions to and reformulations of prevailing theoretical frameworks.

First, family processes and trajectories matter more than family structure. Not only can conflict and neglect be found in all types of families, including those that may appear outwardly stable and secure, but processes of nurturance and support also emerge in a range of family contexts. More important than a family's structure at one point in time are processes of family change over time. Does a child's family context involve increasing support and declining conflict or, in contrast, declining support and continuing or rising conflict? From the child's perspective, what matters in the long run are emotional and economic sustenance, mutually respectful dynamics within the home, and caring bonds with their parents and other caretakers. Traditional families cannot guarantee these conditions, and nontraditional ones are often able to provide them.

Similarly, the employment status of mothers matters less than the overall context in which mothers—and fathers—create their lives. Across classes and gender groups, children are less concerned about whether their mothers work outside the home than about why their mothers work (or do not work), how their mothers feel about working (or not working), and what kind of caretaking arrangements their mothers and fathers can rely on. On balance, children see their mothers' employment as a benefit on many levels. Mothers' jobs offer families greater economic security and increased resources, enhance mothers' satisfaction and autonomy, and provide an example worthy of emulation. Children do worry, however, about their mothers' and fathers' abilities to obtain jobs with good economic prospects, supportive working conditions, and enough flexibility for combining work with family life.

Given the varied and ambiguous influence of family structure, it is time to focus theoretical attention on the institutional arrangements and social processes that matter for children, regardless of the family form in which they happen to live. Community and economic resources are crucial, providing the context for family life and either opening opportunities or posing risks and dangers. Resources such as educational and work opportunities, child care services, and personal networks of adults and peers help shape parents' strategies for rearing their children and children's abilities to cope with difficult circumstances.

Finally, children are not passive recipients of parental and social influences. They actively interpret and respond to their social worlds, often in unexpected ways. As social actors facing unforeseen contingencies, they must make new sense out of received messages and develop a variety of innovative coping strategies. They are crafting these strategies in a changing cultural context, where new views of gender and shifting work and family opportunities are as likely to influence their outlooks as are immediate family experiences.

The trajectories and experiences of these "children of the gender revolution" suggest that a search for one "best" family form provides neither a fruitful theoretical avenue nor a useful practical agenda. Instead, the challenge is to understand how children experience and respond to family conditions that are usually in flux and always embedded in wider institutions. Regardless of a child's family circumstance, contextual supports are essential for enabling parents and children to cope with change in a satisfying way.

For those who have grown to adulthood during this era of fluid personal paths and family arrangements, the fundamental aspects of change appear irreversible and, on balance, desirable. The dismantling of the homemaker–breadwinner ideal has widened options that few are prepared to surrender. These changes in family life and women's options have not, however, been met with comparable changes in the workplace and community life. And although most have adopted nontraditional, egalitarian ideals, few can envision support from employers or the government for achieving their goals. Lacking faith in work or political institutions, they are resolved to seek individual solutions to unprecedented social dilemmas and to develop new ways of negotiating adulthood. The experiences and responses of this new generation are especially important in this era of irrevocable but incomplete transformation. They may be the inheritors of change, but their strategies for responding to their parents' choices and their own dilemmas will shape their future course.

References

Acock, Alan C., and David H. Demo. 1994. *Family Diversity and Well-Being.* Thousand Oaks, CA: Sage Publications.

Ahlburg, Dennis A., and Carol J. De Vita. 1992. "New Realities of the American Family." *Population Bulletin* 47 (2) (August): 1–44.

Barnett, Rosalind, and Caryl Rivers. 1996. *She Works/He Works: How Two-Income Families Are Happier, Healthier, and Better Off.* San Francisco, CA: HarperSanFrancisco.

Blankenhorn, David. 1994. *Fatherless America: Confronting Our Most Urgent Social Problem.* New York: Basic Books.

Cherlin, Andrew, et al. 1991. "Longitudinal Studies of Effects of Divorce on Children in Great Britain and the United States." *Science* 252 (June): 1386–1389.

Coontz, Stephanie. 1992. *The Way We Never Were: American Families and the Nostalgia Trap.* New York: Basic Books.

———. 1997. *The Way We Really Are: Coming to Terms with America's Changing Families.* New York: Basic Books.

Crosby, Faye J., ed. 1987. *Spouse, Parent, Worker: On Gender and Multiple Roles.* New Haven: Yale University Press.

Gerson, Kathleen. 1993. *No Man's Land: Men's Changing Commitments to Family and Work.* New York: Basic Books.

Hoffman, Lois. 1987. "The Effects on Children of Maternal and Paternal Employment." Pp. 362–395 in *Families and Work,* edited by Naomi Gerstel and Harriet Engel Gross. Philadelphia: Temple University Press.

McLanahan, Sara, and Gary Sandefur. 1994. *Growing Up with a Single Parent: What Hurts, What Helps.* Cambridge, MA: Harvard University Press.

Mollenkopf, John, Philip Kasinitz, and Mary Waters. 1997. "The School to Work Transition of Second Generation Immigrants in Metropolitan New York: Some Preliminary Findings." Paper presented at Levy Institute Conference on the Second Generation (October). New York: Bard College.

Popenoe, David. 1989. *Disturbing the Nest: Family Change and Decline in Modern Societies.* New York: Aldine de Gruyter.

———. 1996. *Life without Father: Compelling New Evidence that Fatherhood and Marriage Are Indispensable for the Good of Children and Society.* New York: Free Press.

Risman, Barbara J. 1998. *Gender Vertigo: American Families in Transition.* New Haven and London: Yale University Press.

Skolnick, Arlene. 1991. *Embattled Paradise: The American Family in an Age of Uncertainty.* New York: Basic Books.

Stacey, Judith. 1990. *Brave New Families: Stories of Domestic Upheaval in Late 20th Century America.* New York: Basic Books.

———. 1996. *In the Name of the Family: Rethinking Family Values in a Postmodern Age.* Boston: Beacon Press.

Whitehead, Barbara D. 1997. *The Divorce Culture.* New York: Alfred A. Knopf.

■READING 8

Men's Family Work: Child-Centered Fathering and the Sharing of Domestic Labor

Scott Coltrane and Michele Adams

According to popular wisdom, housework is so trivial that it is not worthy of serious discussion. According to recent scholarship from sociology and women's studies, however, examining the allocation of housework may tell us more about marital power and gender relations than almost any other subject. Families cannot function unless someone does the routine shopping, cooking, and cleaning that it takes to run a household. Identifying who avoids doing these household tasks is often an excellent indicator of who has the highest status in the couple or family. Who feels entitled to household services, who is obligated to perform them, and how couples evaluate the fairness of divisions of labor can tell us something important about the subtle exercise of power in intimate relationships. And such seemingly trivial household matters can also help us understand how and why gender inequity is perpetuated in the society-at-large.

Modern history shows that it has been women who have done most of the routine family housework, including shopping, cooking, meal cleanup, house cleaning, and laundry. In this chapter, we will see that the cultural ideal of separate spheres, which suggests that women belong in the private/home sphere and men belong in the public/work sphere, has encouraged this unbalanced distribution of household labor. More recently, however, as wives have moved into the paid labor force and started to share the breadwinning role with their husbands, social scientists have generally expected men to begin to share in housework responsibilities. Unfortunately for working women, this has not been the case, as most women have instead been expected to shoulder the burden of a "second shift" of housework on top of their employment responsibilities (Hochschild with Machung 1989).

In recent years, there have been some shifts in who is doing the housework in American families. Generally speaking, the amount of time per week that men spend doing housework has increased slightly. At the same time, women are now doing less housework than they used to, and, therefore, the percent of total housework which is being performed by men has increased. Nevertheless, the overall changes in men's contributions have been small. Thus, today, housework continues to be unequally distributed, with women spending roughly twice as much time on routine household tasks as men. In this chapter, we will look at the unbalanced distribution of housework, how it got to be that way, how it is changing, and how we think these changes will affect the balance of power between men and women in the future.

A BRIEF HISTORY OF SEPARATE SPHERES

In preindustrial America, which was largely rural and agricultural, husbands and wives (and children) generally worked on the family farm, producing most of the food, goods, and services needed for the family's survival. Through bartering and trading with other nearby farmers or in the village at small artisans' shops, families were able to obtain the goods and services that couldn't be produced at home. With the spread of the industrial revolution in the 1800s, however, items which had been produced at home and in village artisans' shops began to be replaced by goods and services produced in urban factories. Family farms and businesses found they could no longer compete with factory production. Farmers and artisans, finding themselves without a means of livelihood, began to monopolize factory jobs. When men later found their control over jobs threatened by women's entry into waged labor, the cult of domesticity (also known as the cult of true womanhood) developed to bolster the notion of separate spheres for men and women. According to these emergent cultural ideals, frail but morally pure women were expected to find true happiness and fulfillment in their domestic roles as wives and mothers, while rugged "manly" men left home each day to earn a family wage. The ideal middle-class woman was supposed to take care of the home (with help from servants), tend to her children, and humanize her husband, giving him respite from the cruel and competitive world beyond the family.

The boundary between home and work was never as distinct as these ideals implied, especially for poor and working-class families, but the romantic image of separate spheres gained widespread popularity. Moreover, belief in separate spheres for men and women functioned to structure access to the labor market; while women were expected to stay at home in the "private" sphere, men (especially middle-class white men) could have relatively unconstrained access to high-paying jobs in the public realm. Throughout modern history, separate spheres ideology has been revived periodically to encourage women to focus on domestic responsibilities, particularly in times of high unemployment when men are especially fearful of competing with women for jobs (Jackson 1992; Kimmel 1996).

Separate spheres ideology and the cult of domesticity were firmly embedded in the public consciousness by the beginning of the twentieth century. At the same time, a steadily increasing number of women were entering the paid labor force, with this increase becoming particularly steep after the onset of World War II. The rapid influx of women into paid labor served as a countervailing force to separate spheres thinking, although "modernized" versions of the cult of domesticity have continued to be invoked at certain periods throughout the century. Even today, remnants of separate spheres ideology affect how men and women view women's roles both in the home and in the workplace, with the result that women often question their own dedication to housework and hesitate to ask men to do more.

Nevertheless, married women continue to enter the paid labor force in record numbers, with the biggest increases seen for mothers of young children. Between 1960 and 1997, the percent of married women over 16 participating in the United States labor force nearly doubled, from 31.9 to 61.6 percent (*Statistical Abstract of the United States: 1998*, tables 652, 653). By 1997, nearly 78 percent of married women with school-aged children and 65 percent of those with preschool children were employed (*Statistical Abstract of the United States: 1998*, tables 654, 655).

CONTEMPORARY DIVISIONS
OF HOUSEWORK

Most women enter the paid labor force because they need the money, but employment also provides personal satisfaction and fulfillment (Coontz 1997:58). Additionally, national and global economic restructuring has resulted in a substantial growth in service sector jobs and a decreased need for workers in agriculture and manufacturing (Coltrane 1998:72). Moreover, according to the U.S. Bureau of the Census, women's real wages increased between 1995 and 1996, while men's decreased slightly (U.S. Bureau of the Census 1997, Current Population Reports: Consumer Income P60-197). For these reasons, it is generally agreed that two incomes are necessary to maintain a middle-class standard of living, and dual-earner families are now the norm in the United States. In fact, in 1996, nearly 64 percent of families with children under 18 years old included both an employed father and an employed mother (*Statistical Abstract of the United States: 1998*, table 656). Working women, wives, and mothers, therefore, have less time available to perform household tasks which they routinely performed in the past.

Neither are working wives inclined to leave their paid employment. A recent national survey found that less than a third of working women would prefer to stay home even if money were no object (Coontz 1997:58). Other polls have found that over two-thirds of both men and women disagree that women should return to the role of stay-at-home housewife (Skolnick 1991:189; see also Coltrane 1998:74). Research on housework over the last several decades, therefore, has focused on how much of the housework slack men have taken up as women have moved into waged employment. In response to the rapid increase in women's labor force participation, and with opinion polls showing more people endorsing equality for women, many observers predicted that the division of household labor would rapidly become more gender-neutral. Contrary to this expectation, housework studies performed in the 1970s, 1980s, and 1990s offered little evidence that major changes were occurring (Coltrane 1999; Miller and Garrison 1982; Thompson and Walker 1989). Most studies find that women continue to do roughly two-thirds of the family's routine housework, generally taking responsibility for monitoring and supervising the work as well, even when they pay for domestic services or assign tasks to other family members. Moreover, married women, and those who have children, tend to perform an even greater proportion of housework than single women and those without children.

To get a sense of how housework is divided by gender across the country, researchers have examined the amount of time spent doing specific household tasks (see Blair and Lichter 1991). Studies have found that wives perform over 96 percent of the cooking, 92 percent of the dishwashing, 90 percent of the vacuuming, and 94 percent of bed making (Blair and Lichter 1991; see also Berk and Berk 1979; and Berk 1985). Men, in contrast, do over 86 percent of household repairs, 75 percent of lawn mowing, and 77 percent of snow shoveling (Blair and Lichter 1991; see also Schooler, Miller, Miller, and Richtand 1984).

The exasperation experienced by working women whose husbands contribute little to the more routine housework is captured in books such as Francine M. Deutsch's *Halving It All* (1999). One woman she interviewed, employed fifty-two hours a week, still did virtually all of the housework:

> Although tired and stressed, working a double day, Carol doesn't expect [her husband] to do much: "I just want him to pick up after himself. I don't particularly expect that he is going to vacuum . . . My husband doesn't even know how dishes go in the dishwasher . . . All I would really like him to do is pick up behind himself." (Deutsch 1999:67)

Another woman employed full-time singled out laundry as a particularly troublesome task: "I get so sick of doing laundry. I do laundry constantly . . . he won't . . . lay a finger on laundry" (Deutsch 1999:67). Vacuuming, washing dishes, and doing laundry, which these women's husbands refused to do, are household chores that women are typically expected to perform. Auto repairs and lawn maintenance, on the other hand, are chores which men are expected to do (Blair and Lichter 1991). How are these gendered expectations related? One husband explained to Deutsch that he "rides" on taking care of the cars when his wife is insistent that he clean up the house: "If the cars have needed a lot of work lately, I can ride on that for a bit because then I can have something quantifiable I point to that I have been doing" (Deutsch 1999:71). At the microlevel, this segregation of household tasks reinforces power differences between men and women by associating women's tasks with the most routine, least enjoyable family chores. At the macrolevel, a similar segregation of tasks is reflected in the gendered nature of particular occupations, with service and support jobs labeled "women's work." Similar to women's household tasks, "women's work" in the paid labor force is generally less prestigious and paid less than men's work (Coltrane 1998).

In fact, some household chores are more likely to be considered "housework" than others. Household labor includes a number of different tasks, some occurring inside the home and others taking place outside of it. There are five "indoor" chores that have repeatedly been shown to be the most time-consuming, and which we refer to as "housework" or "routine housework." These tasks involve meal preparation or cooking, house cleaning, shopping for groceries and household goods, washing dishes or cleaning up after meals, and laundry (including washing, ironing, and mending clothes) (Blair and Lichter 1991; Robinson and Godbey 1997). These chores are more time-consuming, less optional, and less able to be put off than other household tasks such as lawn care or house repairs. Although some people do see this routine work (particularly the cooking) as pleasant, most men and women report that they do not like doing housework (Devault 1991; Robinson and Milkie 1997, 1998). On the other hand, most people find other tasks such as household repairs and yard care to be more flexible, more discretionary, and more enjoyable than everyday routine housework tasks (Coltrane 1998; Larson, Richards, and Perry-Jenkins 1994).

These patterns of household labor allocation tend to generate feelings of entitlement among men. When Deutsch asked Carol's husband how he responds to his more-than-full-time-employed wife's pleas for help around the house, he said, "I just chuckle" (Deutsch 1999:67). And the husband in Deutsch's study who refused to do laundry said he felt entitled to relax after work and on the weekends:

> She probably won't sit still on a Sunday . . . Sundays I usually relax . . . She's not happy unless she's doing something. That's the difference between her and I. She's not happy unless she's making a cake, making supper, doing laundry. She very rarely can sit down and

watch television, take a break . . . She's not happy unless she's doing something. I'm different. I can relax. (Deutsch 1999:68)

Not surprisingly, some people, mostly men, consider housework to be trivial. In a now classic article that was one of the first to consider the political significance of housework, Pat Mainardi (1970) noted that men resort to a number of verbal ploys to avoid it. Mainardi's husband insisted, for example, "I don't mind sharing the housework, but I don't do it very well. We should each do the things we're best at." And, "I don't mind sharing the housework, but you'll have to show me how to do it." Or, "I *hate* it more than you. You don't mind it so much." Then, finally, "Housework is too trivial to even talk about" (Mainardi 1970:449–450). Although men have used their superior bargaining position to trivialize and avoid housework, it remains essential to human well-being. The routine activities that provide food, clothing, shelter, and care for both children and adults are vital for survival. In fact, domestic work is just as important to maintaining society as is the productive work occurring in the formal market economy. Recent studies suggest that the total amount of time spent in family work (including child care, housework, and other household labor) is about equal to the time spent in paid labor (Robinson and Godbey 1997).

MEN'S PARTICIPATION IN HOUSEWORK

Relatively few cultural images exist which suggest that men could possibly be "as good" at housework as women are. With few exceptions, comic strips, television shows, and movies show us how inept men are when they attempt to perform "women's work." From Dagwood Bumstead in *Blondie* to Tim Allen on *Home Improvement*, men are shown as comic buffoons when it comes to doing the housework. Even films that celebrate fathers' efforts to care for their children, like Michael Keaton in *Mr. Mom*, Dustin Hoffman in *Kramer vs. Kramer*, and Robin Williams in *Mrs. Doubtfire* illustrate how ill-prepared men are for performing mundane domestic work. Thus, there are few cultural role models for boys or men to follow in assuming greater responsibility for household tasks. Scholars argue about whether media images mimic everyday life and promote or inhibit social change, but in the area of housework, it is clear that popular culture is not pushing most men to do more (Coltrane and Adams 1997; Coltrane and Allan 1994).

In real life, men's self-proclaimed ineptitude at doing housework often becomes an excuse for them to avoid it. One wife's exasperation at her husband's (feigned) incompetence is expressed by Deutsch:

He plays, you know, "How do you do this kind of thing?" and asks me fifteen questions so it would almost be easier for me to do it myself than to sit there and answer all his questions. That makes me angry because I feel like he's just playing stupid because he doesn't want to do it. (Deutsch 1999:77)

And, Deutsch notes, there are men who use praise of their wife as the "flip side" of their self-professed incompetence, as does the following father:

> She's wonderful (as a mother) . . . Some women, like I say, are geared to be business-women; Florence is geared to be a mother. She loves it. She's good at it. I feel real lucky to have her as a partner because it takes a lot of the burden off me. (Deutsch 1999:77)

By extolling Florence's virtues as a mother, her husband symbolically removes her from the public realm of business while at the same time praising her for allowing him unfettered access to it. Separate spheres ideology and the cult of domesticity never had it so good.

Why does men's participation in housework remain so far behind their wives' in spite of women's paid employment? A number of reasons have been suggested for men's "housework lag." Some researchers believe that women may act as "gatekeepers" to men's involvement in family work, using their traditional role as household managers to restrict men's opportunities to learn how to do housework. By setting rigid standards for housecleaning which men are unable (or unwilling) to maintain, it is argued, women may be able to sustain their (conceptual) dominance in the private sphere (see Allen and Hawkins 1999; Coltrane 1996, 1989; Feree 1991; Greenstein 1996). For example, Deutsch notes the benefits of "doing it all" for a school psychologist who works forty-five hours a week: "Embarrassed, Peg [said]: 'Another thing I can't ignore is I'm in control. That sounds terrible. That's not how I mean it, but I mean I'm able to structure things . . . I feel like I want to be in control' " (Deutsch 1999:55). While Peg's admission that she wants to be in control may represent an example of maternal gatekeeping, it is also likely a response to her husband's refusal to participate in family work in the first place (see Allen and Hawkins 1999). Ethan, Peg's husband, observes:

> It's hard for me to do anything during the week. If I come home at six-thirty, seven, I'm tired, basically fatigued . . . so when 6 A.M. rolls around and the kids are getting up, the last thing I think I really want to volunteer for is extra duties. I shouldn't say extra duties, but [I'm] certainly not going out of my way. (Deutsch 1999:53)

Most theories examining why men's housework continues to lag behind women's involve the issue of power in families and focus on the relative resources of husband and wife, time availability, economic dependency, and gender ideology (Coltrane 1999; Greenstein 1996; Vannoy-Hiller 1982). Theories using relative resource models suggest that the person with more income (generally the husband) will do less housework, while time availability theories imply that when people spend more time in paid work they will spend less time doing housework. The economic dependency model of housework suggests that women make a contract with their husbands to exchange household labor in return for economic support from a main breadwinner (Brines 1994). Finally, theories drawing on gender ideology suggest that people brought up to believe in the gender-segregation of work will conform to those beliefs when they later marry.

The difference in power between men and women in families has important implications for each of these theories, and suggests that the partner with the most power in the relationship will be the one who can tacitly set the terms of the division of labor in the family. Because most people (men and women alike) do not find housework to be particularly enjoyable and most men have relatively higher earnings and social power, it is usually men who "opt out" of doing routine domestic chores. Moreover, power in marriage is not just about conflict or other overt behavior, but also includes "invisible" or "hidden" power that relies on what Gramsci (1971) called "ideological hegemony." This notion suggests that both men and women tend to accept the idea that what is in the husband's best interest, is in the wife's best interest as well. The invisible power that promotes an acceptance of men's interests as primary also encourages both husbands and wives to "buy into" men's reduced participation in housework (Komter 1989) and their excuses for doing little (Pyke and Coltrane 1996). Wives are, therefore, often inadvertently complicit in permitting their husbands to avoid housework, protecting men from tasks that they find onerous. In this sense, it is not unusual for a woman to intentionally avoid asking her husband to do chores that she anticipates he will hate (Braverman 1991).

On the other hand, men are doing more housework now than they were twenty years ago, although they still do much less than their wives. Since the 1970s, men's contribution to cooking, cleaning, and washing has increased from about 2 to 3 hours per week to about 5 to 8 hours per week (different estimates result from different ways of collecting household labor data). While men's participation has increased, women have decreased the amount of time they spend in these tasks. In addition, employed women have shifted considerable housework to the weekends and now do about one-third less family work than other women (Robinson and Godbey 1997). Combining women's reductions with men's increases, we can say that men's percentage of contribution to housework in the average American household has more than doubled in two decades (Coltrane 1999).

What chores are men performing? Men have begun to take on at least a portion of the responsibility for some of the routine tasks normally identified with women, such as grocery shopping, cooking, and meal clean-up. On the other hand, there have been only modest increases in men's share of housecleaning, laundry, and other repetitive indoor housekeeping tasks. Studies show that men are still reluctant to take full responsibility for housework tasks, but are sometimes more willing to do them if they can act as "helpers" to their wives. With the increased attention paid to studying housework in the past two decades, we now know that men perform more housework and child care when they are employed fewer hours, when their wives work longer hours or earn more money, and when both spouses believe in gender equity (Coltrane 1999).

Studies also show us that sharing housework is usually a practical response to work and childcare demands. In general, substantial sharing between husbands and wives occurs only after wives actively bargain for it. If couples deliberately divide tasks early in the relationship, a pattern of sharing develops and becomes self-perpetuating. If, however, couples make the assumption that sharing will happen on its own, the tendency is for women to end up doing virtually everything (Coltrane 1996).

FAIRNESS AND ENTITLEMENT IN HOUSEWORK

A recent public opinion poll showed that fully 88 percent of women and 78 percent of men believe that women do more of the household chores in their family (To the Contrary Poll 1997). Interestingly, however, 60 percent of the women and 71 percent of the men answered "yes" to the question, "Is the way that you and your spouse share household chores fair to both of you?" This poll confirms what previous studies have suggested: In spite of the fact that the burden of housework falls disproportionately on women, a majority of both men and women consider it to be fair.

Fairness in household labor does not automatically mean sharing tasks equally or putting in the same amount of time. To evaluate just how much housework is considered to be fair, sociologists Mary Clare Lennon and Sarah Rosenfield (1994) examined the amount of household labor that men and women are willing to do before they see the task division as unfair to themselves. According to Lennon and Rosenfield, women are willing to do roughly two-thirds of the household labor (about 66 percent) before they start to see it as unfair to themselves. Men, on the other hand, will do approximately 36 percent of the household labor before they begin to see it as unfair to themselves. Thus, there appears to be general acceptance of highly unbalanced divisions of household labor, with both sexes expecting women to put in many more hours than men on domestic tasks. The relevant question then becomes: Why are women willing to accept such an unequal division of housework?

Social theories suggest that wives label unbalanced divisions of household labor as fair because they have less power (including invisible power) in the marriage. One reason wives continue to perceive lopsided housework distribution as fair is because of differences in their sense of entitlement relative to that of their spouse (see Ferree 1990; Hochschild 1989; Major 1987, 1993; and Thompson 1991). As noted above, men often see themselves as entitled to household services, a fact which sometimes makes women hesitant to ask for the help they need.

Sociologist Arlie Hochschild has described a "marital economy of gratitude" whereby husbands' and wives' images of themselves as masculine or feminine encourage them to see some actions in their marriage as gifts and others as burdens; for example, a man may see his wife's employment as either a gift or a burden, depending on how he views himself as a man (Hochschild with Machung 1989:18). This "emotional economy of marriage" includes feelings about entitlements, as well (Pyke and Coltrane 1996). While marital economies of gratitude are constantly negotiated in all couples, the more powerful spouse usually sets the terms for such negotiations. Thus, when one spouse is grateful for the actions of the other, he or she feels indebted and obligated to reciprocate. When, however, that spouse is displeased with the others' actions, he or she expects a spouse to compensate for the displeasing acts by doing more.

As suggested previously, it is generally the husband who is the more powerful spouse, due in large part to his greater financial and social leverage in the relationship. Therefore, the husband's pleasure or displeasure usually drives feelings of entitlement. These feelings of entitlement then reflect "invisible power" that leads both women and men to see fairness where fairness does not objectively exist. Men's culturally and economically driven feelings of entitlement to women's domestic services, therefore, may be important sources of women's acceptance of unbalanced distributions of housework.

Other factors may contribute to a perception of fairness in the distribution of housework, as well, such as the outcomes that are desired (more time, certain standards of cleanliness, care, or "keeping the peace," for example) (Major 1993; Thompson 1991). Also, whether an individual compares their household contributions to their partner's (cross-gender comparison), or to other women's or men's (within-gender comparison), may significantly impact their fairness evaluations (Thompson 1991; Coltrane 1990). Commenting on a father's boast that "Very few men on the face of this earth ever diapered as many bottoms as I have," Deutsch observes that it is easy to see these fathers as "extraordinary if you compare them to other men, but once the standard shifts to a comparison with their wives, their pride and the applause seem misplaced" (1999:103). Fathers who help out with child care are often praised and described in glowing terms for performing tasks that go unnoticed if performed by mothers. In an interview study of role-sharing parents, one woman said that she "appreciated her husband's willingness to help, [but] friends who called him perfect were a little out of touch" (Coltrane 1996:138). Men's contributions to housework, likewise, tend to be noticed and applauded, whereas women's are generally taken for granted (Robinson and Spitze 1992). Finally, whether the procedures that created the existing unbalanced distribution of housework are considered appropriate also contributes to perceptions of fairness, including, for example, forgiving a partner's lack of housework because of supposed ineptitude or because a prior joint decision was made about who should do the work.

The more hours women work in the paid labor force, the less fair they see the division of labor in the home (see Greenstein 1996; Sanchez 1994; Sanchez and Kane 1996). A number of studies also show that both men and women with more egalitarian gender attitudes tend to see the existing division of household labor as more unfair to the wife (Blair and Johnson 1992; DeMaris and Longmore 1996; Sanchez and Kane 1996). Interestingly, when measuring gender ideology by asking if employed spouses should share housework, egalitarian men rate the existing division of household labor as more fair to their wives, but egalitarian wives rate the existing division of labor as less fair to themselves (DeMaris and Longmore 1996). Apparently, egalitarian husbands are hesitant to admit to an unbalanced distribution of housework which contradicts their belief in equality. For egalitarian wives, on the other hand, an unequal division of tasks is likely to be particularly salient because of their belief in sharing, and their attitudes, therefore, are more likely to generate criticism of the present situation.

Women (and sometimes men) often see both their own and their spouse's housework as carrying emotional messages, such as love, caring, or appreciation. Symbolically equating housework with care can lead to demands for more task performance on the one hand, but it can also encourage women to consider men's expressions of affection or intent to do housework as sufficient (without actually *doing* the work), thereby encouraging these women to assess current unbalanced labor arrangements as fair. One woman who gave up a promising career to stay home with her children, asked only that her husband show some appreciation for her sacrifice and recognition of her domestic contributions: "You are at work with all these bigwigs and I'm home with children playing blocks. I've had a hard day too" (Deutsch 1999:69).

Perceptions of fairness may also intervene between the division of household labor and personal or marital well-being. When housework is believed to be fair, wives display fewer symptoms of depression, but when it is perceived as unfair, women are more depressed (Glass and Fujimoto 1994; Lennon and Rosenfield 1994). Being satisfied with one's husband's contribution to housework is also related to better marital interaction and more marital closeness, less marital conflict, and fewer thoughts of divorce (Piña and Bengtson 1993). Moreover, while perceived unfairness predicts both unhappiness and distress for women, it predicts neither for men (Robinson and Spitze 1992).

Men are almost universally satisfied with the division of housework, whereas women, particularly egalitarian women who are content with their paid work, are typically less satisfied (Baxter and Western 1998). In the end, the single most important predictor of how fair a wife sees the distribution of housework to be is what portion of the routine housework (cooking, cleaning, and laundry) her husband contributes. And, while husbands are making some limited progress in these areas, these also seem to be the areas where they are most resistant to change.

LINKING PAID WORK AND HOUSEWORK

Economist Heidi Hartmann once said that the family is "a primary arena where men exercise their patriarchal power over women's labor" (1981:377). That power is played out in the family at least partly through the unbalanced distribution of housework. In spite of recent endorsement of women's equality as shown in opinion polls, the division of labor in the home continues to disadvantage women.

The Victorian ideal of separate spheres for men and women relegated women to the "private sphere," where they were expected to care for their husband, their children, and their house. Men, on the other hand, were sent to the "public sphere" to earn wages outside of the home. In recent decades, women have moved into the paid labor force in record numbers, but their jobs have not relieved them of obligation to maintain the home. Many experience a "double day" because they work in paid employment during the day and, during the evening, perform the housework and "caring" work that is expected of them as wives, mothers, and daughters. Although women have reduced the number of hours they spend performing housework, men have not been as willing to take up the slack in domestic responsibilities.

On the other hand, men are doing more housework these days than they did in the past and, when coupled with women's reduction in household labor, they are actually doing a larger percentage of the housework as well. However, the changes in men's housework contributions have been small. Women continue to perform roughly two-thirds of the housework that is being done in America's families. Moreover, men and women both tend to see this imbalance as fair; the "tipping point" for women's sense of fairness is at about 66 percent of the household labor. Men, on the other hand, feel the housework division to be unfair to them when they do more than 36 percent of the total household labor. This general acceptance of the unequal nature of housework attests to a hidden power imbalance in families. Men feel entitled to benefit from women's labor in the home and women feel a corresponding sense of obligation to perform this labor in gratitude for the economic support which men (at least conceptually) provide. The power of housework lies in its ability to create a "Catch 22" for women: The more housework they do, the less able they are to participate in the waged workforce and provide their own economic support; relatedly, the less they participate in the waged workforce, the more housework they must perform in gratitude for economic support from their husbands. Not surprisingly, economists find that lower wages for women are directly related to women's greater responsibility for housework (Hersch and Stratton 1994, 1997).

Although most men feel that housework is a trivial concern, most women do not. As Hartmann (1981) and others suggest, housework links men's control of women in the private sphere to their control of women in the public sphere. Sharing housework equally would begin to break this link and reduce men's control over women. Men, however, are rarely motivated to break this link because they gain leisure time and other benefits from assuming that housework is women's work (Goode 1992).

Americans now accept the idea that women should work to (help) support the family, but most still assume that only certain jobs or public activities are appropriate for women. Few Americans admit that job discrimination against women is acceptable, yet most feel uncomfortable with a woman as a combat soldier, an auto mechanic, or an airline pilot. More women have been elected to public office than ever before, but most of them still sit on local school boards and city councils, rather than in state legislatures or in Congress. Most Americans say they would vote for a woman for president, but no woman has ever been nominated for that office by a major party. And Americans tend to be even more ambivalent about women's equality when it comes to marriage and family life. Although young women are now encouraged to be independent and professional, they are still expected to be generous and self-sacrificing within their marriages. Most Americans want to have it both ways.

Even though more women are going to college, taking jobs, and pursuing careers, they are still held accountable for what was once called "women's work." If their houses are a mess, their children are left alone, or worse, if they forego marriage altogether, they are subject to blame (Schur 1984). Similar equivocal feelings emerge about fathers and paid work. Although eight out of ten Americans now believe it is OK for women to hold jobs, half still think that men should be the *real* breadwinners (Wilkie 1993). By definition, men's jobs are supposed to be more important than women's jobs, and most people get uncomfortable if a wife makes more money than her husband (Gerson 1993). Americans want men to be more involved in family life, but most still feel uncomfortable if a father takes time off work "just" to be with his kids, or if a husband does most of the cooking and housekeeping (Coltrane 1996). Employers, too, are ambivalent about men's desires to be home instead of on the job. When men take advantage of parental leaves or part-time work, they are often considered unreliable or not serious and most "work-family" programs in the United States are tacitly designed to be used only by working mothers (Pleck 1993). It seems that the ideal of separate work spheres for men and women is still with us, even though the economic and social factors underlying it are in the midst of change.

Job segregation and unequal pay, along with women's lower employment levels, are associated with marriage bargains that include wives' obligation to perform domestic labor and husbands' sense of entitlement to receive unpaid domestic services. Nevertheless, we are beginning to see changes in both the private and public arenas. Not only are men doing a little more housework and women somewhat less, but the underlying factors associated with more equal power in marriages are becoming more common. For example, the gender wage gap is narrowing. Women's wages in the United States have shown steady increases since the 1970s, at the same time that men's wages have remained stagnant or declined. As of 1997, women who worked full-time, year-round were making 74 percent of what full-time, year-round men workers were making (U.S. Bureau of the Census, Women's Bureau 1998). This is far from equal, but women's relative earnings are significantly higher than in the 1970s, when they were earning just 59 percent of what men made.

With a further narrowing of the gender gap in employment levels and pay scales, we should see a movement toward more sharing of housework between husbands and wives. Cross-cultural studies show that societies with significant public participation by women also have significant domestic participation by men (Coltrane 1996). We suggest that the link between the two goes in both directions: when women have more money and public power, they can encourage more domestic participation from men; and when men cooperate with women in doing housework and child care, it encourages their acceptance of women as powerful public figures. If American men began doing substantially more of the housework and child care, we would see a further weakening of the separate spheres assumption that women should be paid less on the job, or be tracked into "women's" occupations. Such a movement would challenge the idea that it is "natural" for women to care for homes and "unnatural" for men to do this work. In this sense, housework is far from trivial.

References

Allen, Sarah M. and Alan J. Hawkins. 1999. "Maternal Gatekeeping: Mothers' Beliefs and Behaviors That Inhibit Greater Father Involvement in Family Work." *Journal of Marriage and the Family* 61:199–212.

Baxter, Janeen and Mark Western. 1998. "Satisfaction with Housework: Examining the Paradox." *Sociology* 32:101–120.

Berk, Richard A. and Sarah Fenstermaker Berk. 1979. *Labor and Leisure at Home: Content and Organization of the Household Day.* Beverly Hills, CA: Sage.

Berk, Sarah Fenstermaker. 1985. *The Gender Factory: The Apportionment of Work in American Households.* New York: Plenum.

Blair, Sampson Lee and Michael P. Johnson. 1992. "Wives' Perceptions of the Fairness of the Division of Household Labor: The Intersection of Housework and Ideology." *Journal of Marriage and the Family* 54:570–581.

Blair, Sampson Lee and Daniel T. Lichter. 1991. "Measuring the Division of Household labor: Gender Segregation of Housework Among American Couples." *Journal of Family Issues* 2(1):91–113.

Braverman, Lois. 1991. "The Dilemma of Housework: A Feminist Response to Gottman, Napier, and Pittman." *Journal of Marital and Family Therapy* 17(1):25–28.

Brines, Julie. 1994. "Economic Dependency, Gender, and the Division of Labor at Home." *American Journal of Sociology* 100:652–688.

Coltrane, Scott. 1999. "Research on Household Labor: Modeling and Measuring the Social Embeddedness of Routine Family Work." *Journal of Marriage and the Family.* In press.

Coltrane, Scott. 1998. *Gender and Families.* Thousand Oaks: Pine Forge Press.

Coltrane, Scott. 1996. *Family Man: Fatherhood, Housework, and Gender Equity.* New York: Oxford University Press.

Coltrane, Scott. 1990. "Birth Timing and the Division of Labor in Dual-Earner Families: Exploratory Findings and Suggestions for Future Research." *Journal of Family Issues* 11:157–181.

Coltrane, Scott. 1989. "Household Labor and the Routine Production of Gender." *Social Problems* 36:473–490.

Coltrane, Scott and Michele Adams. 1997. "Work-Family Imagery and Gender Stereotypes: Television and the Reproduction of Difference." *Journal of Vocational Behavior* 50(2):323–347.

Coltrane, Scott and Kenneth Allan. 1994. " 'New' Fathers and Old Stereotypes: Representations of Masculinity in 1980s Television Advertising." *masculinities* 2(4):43–66.

Coontz, Stephanie. 1997. *The Way We Really Are: Coming to Terms with America's Changing Families.* New York: BasicBooks.

DeMaris, Alfred and Monica A. Longmore. 1996. "Ideology, Power, and Equity: Testing Competing Explanations for the Perception of Fairness in Household Labor." *Social Forces* 74:1043–1071.

Deutsch, Francine M. 1999. *Halving It All.* Cambridge, MA: Harvard University Press.

DeVault, Marjorie. 1991. *Feeding the Family: The Social Organization of Caring and Gendered Work.* Chicago, IL: University of Chicago Press.

Ferree, Myra Marx. 1991. "The Gender Division of Labor in Two-Earner Marriages: Dimensions of Variability and Change." *Journal of Family Issues* 12:158–180.

Ferree, Myra Marx. 1990. "Beyond Separate Spheres: Feminism and Family Research." *Journal of Marriage and Family* 52:866–884.

Gerson, Kathleen. 1993. *No Man's Land: Men's Changing Committments to Family and Work.* New York: BasicBooks.

Glass, Jennifer and Fujimoto, Tetsushi. (1994). "Housework, Paid Work, and Depression among Husbands and Wives." *Journal of Health and Social Behavior* 35:179–191.

Goode, William J. 1992. "Why Men Resist." In B. Thorne with M. Yalom (Eds.), *Rethinking the Family: Some Feminist Questions* (pp. 287–310). Boston, MA: Northeastern University Press.

Gramsci, Antonio. 1971. *Selections from the Prison Notebooks*, edited and translated by Q. Hoare and G. Nowell-Smith. London: Lawrence and Wishart.

Greenstein, Theodore N. 1996. "Gender Ideology and Perceptions of the Fairness of the Division of Household Labor: Effects on Marital Quality." *Social Forces* 74:1029–1042.

Hartmann, Heidi I. 1981. "The Family as the Locus of Gender, Class, and Political Struggle: The Example of Housework." *Signs: Journal of Women in Culture and Society* 6(3):366–394.

Hersch, Joni and Leslie S. Stratton. 1997. "Housework, Fixed Effects, and Wages of Married Workers." *Journal of Human Resources* 32:285–307.

Hersch, Joni and Leslie S. Stratton. 1994. "Housework, Wages, and the Division of Housework Time for Employed Spouses." *American Economic Review* 84:120–125.

Hochschild, Arlie with Anne Machung. 1989. *The Second Shift.* New York: Avon Books.

Jackson, Stevi. 1992. "Towards a Historical Sociology of Housework: A Materialist Feminist Analysis." *Women's Studies International Forum* 15(2):153–172.

Kimmel, Michael S. 1996. *Manhood in America: A Cultural History.* New York: Free Press.

Komter, Aafke. 1989. "Hidden Power in Marriage." *Gender and Society* 3(2):187–216.

Larson, Reed W., Maryse H. Richards, and Maureen Perry-Jenkins. 1994. "Divergent Worlds: The Daily Emotional Experience of Mothers and Fathers in the Domestic and Public Spheres." *Journal of Personality and Social Psychology* 67:1034–1046.

Lennon, Mary Clare and Sarah Rosenfield. 1994. "Relative Fairness and the Division of Housework: The Importance of Opinions." *American Journal of Sociology* 100:506–531.

Mainardi, Pat. 1970. "The Politics of Housework." In R. Morgan (Ed.), *Sisterhood Is Powerful: An Anthology of Writings from the Women's Liberation Movement* (pp. 447–453). New York: Random House.

Major, Brenda. 1993. "Gender, Entitlement, and the Distribution of Family Labor." *Journal of Social Issues* 49:141–159.

Major, Brenda. 1987. "Gender, Justice, and the Psychology of Entitlement." In P. Shaver and C. Hendricks (Eds.), *Review of Personality and Social Psychology* (pp. 124–140). Newbury Park, CA: Sage.

Miller, Joanne and Howard H. Garrison. 1982. "Sex Roles: The Division of Labor at Home and in the Workplace." *Annual Review of Sociology* 8:237–262.

Piña, Darlene L. and Vern L. Bengtson. 1993. "The Division of Household Labor and Wive's Happiness—Ideology, Employment, and Perceptions of Support." *Journal of Marriage and the Family* 55:901–912.

Pleck, Joseph. 1993. "Are 'Family-Supportive' Employer Policies Relevant to Men?" In J. C. Hood (Ed.), *Men, Work, and Family* (pp. 251–333). Newbury Park, CA: Sage.

Pyke, Karen and Scott Coltrane. 1996. "Entitlement, Obligation, and Gratitude in Family Work." *Journal of Family Issues* 17(1):60–82.

Robinson, John and Geoffrey Godbey. 1997. *Time for Life.* University Park, PA: Pennsylvania State University Press.

Robinson, John and Glenna Spitze. 1992. "Whistle While You Work? The Effect of Household Task Performance on Women's and Men's Well-Being." *Social Science Quarterly* 73:844–861.

Robinson, John P. and Melissa Milkie. 1997. "Dances with Dust Bunnies: Housecleaning in America." *American Demographics* 37–40, 59.

Robinson, John P. and Melissa A. Milkie. 1998. "Back to the Basics: Trends in and Role Determinants of Women's Attitudes Toward Housework." *Journal of Marriage and the Family* 60:205–218.

Sanchez, Laura. 1994. "Gender, Labor Allocations, and the Psychology of Entitlement Within the Home." *Social Forces* 73:533–553.

Sanchez, Laura and Emily W. Kane. 1996. "Women's and Men's Constructions of Perceptions of Housework Fairness." *Journal of Family Issues* 17:358–387.

Schooler, Carmi, Joanne Miller, Karen A. Miller, and Carol N. Richtand. 1984. "Work for the Household: Its Nature and Consequences for Husbands and Wives." *American Journal of Sociology* 90:97–124.

Schur, Edwin M. 1984. *Labeling Women Deviant: Gender, Stigma, and Social Control.* Philadelphia, PA: Temple University Press.

Skolnick, Arlene. 1991. *Embattled Paradise: The American Family in an Age of Uncertainty.* New York: Basic Books.

Thompson, Linda. 1991. "Family Work: Women's Sense of Fairness." *Journal of Family Issues* 12:181–196.

Thompson, Linda and Alexis J. Walker. 1989. "Gender in Families: Women and Men in Marriage, Work, and Parenthood." *Journal of Marriage and the Family* 51:845–871.

To the Contrary Poll. 1997. <http://www.pbs.org/ttc/speakup/pollresults.html> 5 March, 1999.

U.S. Bureau of the Census. 1997. *Money Income in the United States: 1996* (Current Population Reports: Household Economic Studies, Series P-60). Washington DC: Government Printing Office.

U.S. Bureau of the Census. 1998. *Statistical Abstract of the United States, 1998.* Washington, DC: Government Printing Office.

U.S. Bureau of the Census, Women's Bureau. 1998. "Women's Earnings as Percent of Men's, 1979–1996." (Current Population Reports, Series P-60, selected issues). Washington, DC: Government Printing Office. <www.dol.gov/dol/wb/> 5 May, 1999.

Vannoy-Hiller, Dana. 1982. "Power Dependence and Division of Family Work." *Sex Roles* 10(11/12): 1003–1019.

Wilkie, Jane Riblett. 1993. "Changes in U.S. Men's Attitudes Toward the Family Provider Role, 1972–1989." *Gender and Society* 7(2):261–279.

■ READING 9

Japan's Battle of the Sexes: The Search for Common Ground

Sumiko Iwao

Today, many younger Japanese women feel that the distribution of time and energy spent by men and women on paid and unpaid work is off-balance and unfair. In the past, the main burden of unpaid work related to the home—housework and parenting—has fallen on women, regardless of whether or not they are also involved in paid work. Young Japanese women today are in revolt—unless there is a more equitable redistribution, more and more young women look set to postpone the joys associated with marriage and having children. Personal choices are becoming public problems. Already, the birth rate is low enough in Japan for the government to belatedly propose various ways of creating a social and economic climate that induces single people to want to marry and have children.

THE GOOD OLD DAYS

When men were the sole breadwinners for the family, they were excused from unpaid work at home, including looking after themselves. They depended on their wives for their daily needs. Women, on the other hand, thought their place was in the home and were economically dependent upon their husbands; they focused their responsibilities on unpaid work and looked after family and home. Both men and women depended on each other for survival and an asymmetrical equilibrium was maintained.

When women did not participate in paid work, a husband's earnings were handed over to his wife more or less intact; these she spent as she thought fit for the family and he, in turn, was given a monthly allowance by his wife.

This traditional pattern is somewhat different to the pattern in Europe where typically it was the stay-at-home wife who received a housekeeping allowance. In Japan, the traditional wife was responsible for managing daily family expenses with the husband's income, and if it was not sufficient, she was expected to use her talents to make ends meet, for example, by earning extra money herself or by bringing her belongings to a pawn shop. (Thus, Japanese women traditionally became very keen on "saving for rainy days," manifested in Japan's high savings rate.) As long as men brought their salary home, they had the freedom to spend long hours outside of the home and consequently not participate in unpaid work at home. Many Japanese women, on the other hand, enjoyed the autonomy given to them by the "absent husband" and welcomed the situation by saying "good husbands are healthy and absent."

Such a division of life's spheres by gender typically works until men retire and invade the sphere run by women. As a result, women's autonomy and freedom is curbed, which can sometimes become intolerable to emotionally independent women. These women are then likely to seek divorce rather than face life with man who has not developed the skills to participate in unpaid work and leisure pursuits. Therefore, it is necessary to consider the balance between paid and unpaid work and leisure/cultural activities over the entire life course rather than only during the employed period.

STRESSFUL TRANSITION
TO A NEW STYLE FAMILY

But there is another problem—the new patterns of family life are generating more stress and strain. With more women participating in both paid and unpaid work, life styles and financial arrangements in the family are changing. However, even to this day, families where the husband is the major breadwinner more or less follow the traditional pattern of the wife holding the purse strings. With double income families, however, where the incomes are of more or less equal size, both husband and wife equally share both earning and spending responsibilities

Not only has the financial relationship between husband and wife changed today, so has the attitude toward marriage. Marriage, once considered a necessity, has more and more become one of life's options, especially with young single women. Rather than husband and wife playing different roles as in the past, young women today hope to share both economic and family responsibilities with their spouses—an equal partnership is what they want.

But there are a range of problems—men's attitudes have been slower to catch up in the domestic sphere and workplace cultures have been slow to shift leaving women with a double burden. Just as in many other countries today, an increasing number of Japanese women are employed. About 40 per cent of the employed paid workers now are women; of them, 57 per cent are married and 33 per cent are single. Many of the paid working women who are married with families are carrying a double burden of paid and unpaid work, while men and working women who can relegate unpaid work to others (such as their wives, mothers or paid help) are carrying only the single burden of paid work. If women with a double burden have to compete with men and women who are carrying one burden, it is clearly unfair. They also have difficulties at work. Many workplaces still expect their employees to place work before family, which makes it impossible to keep work-family balance. If one wants to keep a balance among work/family/ leisure activities, time is never sufficient and stress is great. Some women have sought to balance paid and unpaid work by being part-time workers, which now makes up 36.5 per cent of employed women, but these women still are carrying a double burden because they do the vast majority of unpaid work at home.

Japanese men for their part are also hampered from playing a greater role at home. The long working hours culture in Japan is well known—many men feel they must stay at their workplace for long hours, thus putting the workplace before the family, where most unpaid work is performed. The workplace culture interferes with their ability to achieve a better balance between paid and unpaid work. In addition, the long commuting hours that many men (and increasingly full time working women) must put in to reach their workplace further prevents them from participating in unpaid work at home; this adds to the existing imbalance in paid/unpaid work and cultural pursuits.

The amount of time both men and women spend on paid work and on unpaid work has been researched and illustrates the problem. According to a survey conducted by the NHK (Japan's public broadcasting station), Japanese men, on average, spend seven hours daily on paid work and only thirty-one minutes on unpaid work. Japanese women, by contrast, spend three hours and forty-one minutes on paid work and four hours and forty-one minutes on unpaid work—or housework—daily.[1]

PRIVATE CHOICES BECOME PUBLIC PROBLEMS

Today's young single women live in an information age. They can easily imagine what sort of life is waiting for them after marriage and after childbirth. They know that even with good intentions to share unpaid work more evenly, their future husbands are unlikely to be able to carry out what they intended. Demands from the workplace will always have priority. At the same time, today's young women believe companionship with their spouse is most important for a good marriage; otherwise, they don't feel that marriage offers enough rewards to justify the plunge. They are children of affluence and know the taste of overseas vacations and expensive restaurants, but they also know that their regular paid employment is necessary for such luxuries. Thus, there is some reluctance or hesitation to marry and have children.

The trends show this clearly. In 1975, the average age for a first marriage in Japan was 25.9 for men and 23 for women, but it went up to 28.5 for men and 26.3 for women in 1995. Also in that year, the percentage of single women 25 to 29 years old reached 48 per cent, and for those 30 to 34 year old it reached 20 per cent. Women know that if they quit paid work on the birth of a child, the opportunity costs for them are very high. Thus, their hesitation to marry or have children is quite understandable, yet the declining birthrate, which affects the country as a whole, cannot be ignored by policymakers.

Though the choice is entirely a private matter, the resultant postponement of marriage (as these figures imply) has a wide social and economic impact. For example, unless more women marry earlier, a decline in birthrate is expected (children born out of wedlock are still quite rare in Japan). Japan's population will reach its peak in the year 2007, then start declining. A birthrate of about 2.08 is needed to maintain the population at its current size. However, at the current birthrate of 1.38, Japan's population will be less than half its present size within 100 years. The lower birthrate has serious economic as well as socio-cultural implications. Labour shortages, shrinking markets, and the difficulty of maintaining public pension schemes and children's culture (some children's books are no longer available due to shrinking markets) are some such implications. These trends are all the more worrying because Japan has been becoming an aged society at a faster rate than any other nation in the world.

JAPAN'S WORK–LIFE AGENDA

In responding to this challenge, the Japanese government has put great efforts into providing life-long learning opportunities in addition to various courses offered by business organizations. Right now, middle-aged or older women, who tend to have more free time than men, are the major recipient of such opportunities. But the government needs to do much more. Indeed, to really tackle this problem, the Japanese government must find a way of satisfying women's desires to maintain paid work, while getting men to share unpaid work more equitably as a good companion.

The Japanese government has made two fundamental efforts to create a work–family balance for men and women, as well as providing an environment that is attractive enough for people to want to marry and have children.

Promoting Gender Equality

The first initiative was the passage in June 1999 of the Basic Law for Building a Gender-Neutral Society, which states that both men and women be given equal opportunity to find both paid and unpaid work. Now they are working on specific measures to implement this law based on recommendations from the Council for Gender Equality.

There have already been some important initiatives. The economic value of unpaid work has been quantified. In 1996, the Japanese Economic Planning Agency calculated the monetary value of unpaid work for Japan to be 116 billion yen ($1,392,000) of which 85 per cent (98 billion yen) were contributed by women. The Agency estimated that, on average, the unpaid work carried out by one woman has an annual average monetary value of $23,000. By putting a price on the economic value of unpaid work, the Japanese government has made women's traditional work visible, and has valued it.

They have also tried to tackle the other issue—namely how to bring about a shift in male responsibility. Earlier this year, the Japanese Ministry of Health and Welfare produced a poster that captured an unusual amount of public attention compared with other government-run campaigns. The poster features a popular male dancer holding his baby boy; the mother is a nationally admired young pop singer. The caption reads: "We don't call a man who does not take care of his children a father. Just 17 minutes a day is the average time Japanese fathers spend for childcare." The poster was produced to urge men to share household responsibilities so that women alone do not shoulder the full load of childcare and house work. Its explicit objective was to achieve a better balance for both men and women between paid work and unpaid work related to the family. Some male politicians in the National Diet were obviously irritated by this poster. They summoned the ministry's staffs for an explanation. They seemed to think that they were qualified to be fathers simply by being the breadwinners in the family. Thankfully the government no longer seems to subscribe to this view.

Tackling the Low Birthrate

The other key policy initiative focuses on measures to reverse the declining birthrate. In addition to parental leave and the expansion of services at day care centres, the prime minister has also formed a task force for solving the problems of the declining birthrate. The task force submitted a report to the prime minister in December 1998 with over one hundred concrete suggestions for reforming work styles and making family life more attractive. For example, more efficient work styles are encouraged so that workers can leave the office early enough to participate in unpaid work at home. Another example is the setting up of "consultation service stations" to help parents with problems they might face in raising children. Parents who came from small families with only one or no siblings may not have experienced even holding a small child until they themselves became parents and are scared of failing to produce "perfect" children. They have more than enough information about the serious difficulties that face parents and children, which makes them hesitate to have children.

Clearly, many interrelated problems are reflected in the declining birthrate. Government, as well as politicians and the business community—which are primarily composed of and run by men—are finally and slowly realising the importance of those problems that they have neglected, and they cannot solve them without women's cooperation. Lower birthrates clearly imply a dwindling market for the business community, and a dwindling economy overall. It is this business case for pursuing gender equity which is bringing about government and business action. Looking to the future, I believe that the great challenge for Japanese society in the twenty-first century will be about achieving genuine synergy between paid and unpaid work, between the sexes and across the generations. Long term economic prosperity clearly depends on much greater gender equality and a far better work–life balance, and both are the keys to solving the problems of an ageing population, low birth rate and the negative effects of workplace culture on women, men and family life.

Editors' Note: *Notes for this reading can be found in the original source.*

4 Sexuality and Society

Sexual Revolution(s)

Beth Bailey

In 1957 America's favorite TV couple, the safely married Ricky and Lucy Ricardo, slept in twin beds. Having beds at all was probably progressive—as late as 1962 June and Ward Cleaver did not even have a bedroom. Elvis's pelvis was censored in each of his three appearances on the *Ed Sullivan Show* in 1956, leaving his oddly disembodied upper torso and head thrashing about on the TV screen. But the sensuality in his eyes, his lips, his lyrics was unmistakable, and his genitals were all the more important in their absence. There was, likewise, no mistaking Mick Jagger's meaning when he grimaced ostentatiously and sang "Let's spend some *time* together" on *Ed Sullivan* in 1967. Much of the audience knew that the line was really "Let's spend the night together," and the rest quickly got the idea. The viewing public could see absence and hear silence—and therein lay the seeds of the sexual revolution.

What we call the sexual revolution grew from these tensions between public and private—not only from tensions manifest in public culture, but also from tensions between private behaviors and the public rules and ideologies that were meant to govern behavior. By the 1950s the gulf between private acts and public norms was often quite wide—and the distance was crucial. People had sex outside marriage, but very, very few acknowledged that publicly. A woman who married the only man with whom she had had premarital sex still worried years later: "I was afraid someone might have learned that we had intercourse before marriage and I'd be disgraced." The consequences, however, were not just psychological. Young women (and sometimes men) discovered to be having premarital sex were routinely expelled from school or college; gay men risked jail for engaging in consensual sex. There were real penalties for sexual misconduct, and while many deviated from the sexual orthodoxy of the day, all but a few did so furtively, careful not to get "caught."

Few episodes demonstrate the tensions between the public and private dimensions of sexuality in midcentury America better than the furor that surrounded the publication of the studies of sexual behavior collectively referred to as the "Kinsey Reports." Though a dry, social scientific report, *Sexual Behavior in the Human Male* (1948) had sold over a quarter of a million copies by 1953, when the companion volume on the human female came out. The male volume was controversial, but the female volume was, in *Look* magazine's characterization, "stronger stuff." Kinsey made it clear that he understood the social implications of his study, introducing a section on "the pre-marital coital behavior of the female sample which has been available for this study" with the following qualification: "Because of this public condemnation of pre-marital coitus, one might believe that such contacts would be rare among American females and males. But this is only the overt culture, the things that people openly profess to believe and do. Our previous report (1948) on the male has indicated how far publicly expressed attitudes may depart from the realities of behavior—the covert culture, what males actually do."

Kinsey, a biologist who had begun his career with much less controversial studies of the gall wasp, drew fire from many quarters, but throughout the criticism is evident concern about his uncomfortable juxtaposition of public and private. "What price biological science . . . to reveal intimacies of one's private sex life and to draw conclusions from inscriptions on the walls of public toilets?" asked one American in a letter to the editor of *Look* magazine.

Much of the reaction to Kinsey did hinge on the distance between the "overt" and the "covert." People were shocked to learn how many men and women were doing what they were not supposed to be doing. Kinsey found that 50 percent of the women in his sample had had premarital sex (even though between 80 percent and 89 percent of his sample disapproved of premarital sex on "moral grounds"), that 61 percent of college-educated men and 84 percent of men who had completed only high school had had premarital sex, that over one-third of the married women in the sample had "engaged in petting" with more than ten different men, that approximately half of the married couples had engaged in "oral stimulation" of both male and female genitalia, and that at least 37 percent of American men had had "some homosexual experience" during their lifetimes.

By pulling the sheets back, so to speak, Kinsey had publicized the private. Many people must have been reassured by the knowledge that they were not alone, that their sexual behaviors were not individual deviant acts but part of widespread social trends. But others saw danger in what Kinsey had done. By demonstrating the distance between the overt and the covert cultures, Kinsey had further undermined what was manifestly a beleaguered set of rules. *Time* magazine warned its readers against the attitude that "there is morality in numbers," the *Chicago Tribune* called Kinsey a "menace to society," and the *Ladies' Home Journal* ran an article with the disclaimer: "The facts of behavior reported . . . are not to be interpreted as moral or social justification for individual acts."

Looking back to the century's midpoint, it is clear that the coherence of (to use Kinsey's terms) covert and overt sexual cultures was strained beyond repair. The sexual revolution of the 1960s emerged from these tensions, and to that extent it was not revolutionary, but evolutionary. As much as anything else, we see the overt coming to terms with the covert. But the revision of revolution to evolution would miss a crucial point. It is not historians who have labeled these changes "sexual revolution"—it was people at the time, those who participated and those who watched. And they called it that before much of what we would see as revolutionary really emerged—before gay liberation and the women's movement and Alex Comfort's *The Joy of Sex* (1972) and "promiscuity" and singles' bars. The term was in general use by 1963—earlier than one might expect.

To make any sense of the sexual revolution, we have to pay attention to the label people gave it. Revolutions, for good or ill, are moments of danger. It matters that a metaphor of revolution gave structure to the myriad changes taking place in American society. The changes in sexual mores and behaviors could as easily have been cast as evolutionary—but they were not.

Looking back, the question of whether or not the sexual revolution was revolutionary is not easy to answer; it depends partly on one's political (defined broadly) position. Part of the trouble, though, is that the sexual revolution was not one movement. It was instead a set of movements, movements that were closely linked, even intertwined, but which often made uneasy bedfellows. Here I hope to do some untangling, laying out three of the most important strands of the sexual revolution and showing their historical origins, continuities, and disruptions.

The first strand, which transcended youth, might be cast as both evolutionary and revolutionary. Throughout the twentieth century, picking up speed in the 1920s, the 1940s and the 1960s, we have seen a sexualization of America's culture. Sexual images have become more and more a part of public life, and sex—or more accurately, the representation of sex—is used to great effect in a marketplace that offers Americans fulfillment through consumption. Although the blatancy of today's sexual images would be shocking to someone transported from an earlier era, such representations developed gradually and generally did not challenge more "traditional" understandings of sex and of men's and women's respective roles in sex or in society.

The second strand was the most modest in aspect but perhaps the most revolutionary in implication. In the 1960s and early 1970s an increasing number of young people began to live together "without benefit of matrimony," as the phrase went at the time. While sex was usually a part of the relationship (and probably a more important part than most people acknowledged), few called on concepts of "free love" or "pleasure" but instead used words like "honesty," "commitment," and "family." Many of the young people who lived together could have passed for young marrieds and in that sense were pursuing fairly traditional arrangements. At the same time, self-consciously or not, they challenged the tattered remnants of a Victorian epistemological and ideological system that still, in the early 1960s, fundamentally structured the public sexual mores of the American middle class.

The third strand was more self-consciously revolutionary, as sex was *actively claimed* by young people and used not only for pleasure, but also for power in a new form of cultural politics that shook the nation. As those who threw themselves into the "youth revolution" (a label that did not stick) knew so well, the struggle for America's future would take place not in the structure of electoral politics, but on the battlefield of cultural meaning. Sex was an incendiary tool of a revolution that was more than political. But not even the cultural revolutionaries agreed on goals, or on the role and meaning of sex in the revolution.

These last two strands had to do primarily with young people, and that is significant. The changes that took place in America's sexual mores and behaviors in the sixties were *experienced* and *defined* as revolutionary in large part because they were so closely tied to youth. The nation's young, according to common wisdom and the mass media, were in revolt. Of course, the sexual revolution was not limited to youth, and sex was only one part of the revolutionary claims of youth. Still, it was the intersection of sex and youth that signaled danger. And the fact that these were often middle-class youths, the ones reared in a culture of respectability (told that a single sexual misstep could jeopardize their bright futures), made their frontal challenges to sexual mores all the more inexplicable and alarming.

Each of these strands is complex, and I make no pretense to be exhaustive. Thus, rather than attempting to provide a complete picture of changes in behaviors or ideologies, I will examine several manifestations of seemingly larger trends. The sexualization of culture (the first strand) is illustrated by the emergence of *Playboy* and *Cosmo* magazines. For the "modest revolutionaries" (the second strand), I look to the national scandal over a Barnard College junior's "arrangement" in 1968 and the efforts of University of Kansas students to establish a coed dormitory. Finally, the cultural radicals (the third strand) are represented by the writings of a few counterculture figures.

By focusing on the 1960s, we lose much of the "sexual revolution." In many ways, the most important decade of that revolution was the 1970s, when the "strands" of the 1960s joined with gay liberation, the women's movement, and powerful assertions of the importance of cultural differences in America. Yet, by concentrating on the early years of the sexual revolution, we see its tangled roots—the sexual ideologies and behaviors that gave it birth. We can also understand how little had been resolved—even begun—by the end of the 1960s.

BEFORE THE REVOLUTION: YOUTH AND SEX

Like many of the protest movements that challenged American tranquility in the sixties, the sexual revolution developed within the protected space and intensified atmosphere of the college campus. An American historian recalls returning to Harvard University in 1966 after a year of postgraduate study in England. Off balance from culture shock and travel fatigue, he entered Harvard Yard and knew with absolute certainty that he had "missed the sexual revolution." One can imagine a single symbolic act of copulation signaling the beginning of the revolution (it has a nicely ironic echo of "the shot heard round the world"). The single act and the revolution complete in 1966 are fanciful constructions; not everything began or ended at Harvard even in those glory years. But events there and at other elite colleges and universities, if only because of the national attention they received, provide a way into the public intersections of sex, youth and cultural politics.

Harvard had set a precedent in student freedom in 1952, when girls (the contemporary term) were allowed to visit in Harvard men's rooms. The freedom offered was not supposed to be sexual—or at least not flagrantly so. But by 1963 Dean Jon Monro complained that he was "badly shaken up by some severe violations," for a once "pleasant privilege" had come to be "considered a license to use the college rooms for wild parties or sexual intercourse." The controversy went public with the aid of *Time* magazine, which fanned the flames by quoting a senior's statement that "morality is a relative concept projecting certain mythologies associated with magico-religious beliefs." The Parietals Committee of the Harvard Council for Undergraduate Affairs, according to the

Boston Herald, concluded that "if these deep emotional commitments and ties occasionally lead to sexual intercourse, surely even that is more healthy than the situation a generation ago when 'nice girls' were dated under largely artificial circumstances and sexual needs were gratified at a brothel." Both justifications seemed fundamentally troubling in different ways, but at least the controversy focused on men. The sexual double standard was strong. When the spotlight turned on women, the stakes seemed even higher.

The media had a field day when the president of Vassar College, Sarah Blanding, said unequivocally that if a student wished to engage in premarital sex, she must withdraw from the college. The oft-quoted student reply to her dictum chilled the hearts of middle-class parents throughout the country: "If Vassar is to become the Poughkeepsie Victorian Seminary for young Virgins, then the change of policy had better be made explicit in admissions catalogs."

Such challenges to authority and to conventional morality were reported to eager audiences around the nation. None of this, of course, was new. National audiences had been scandalized by the panty raid epidemic of the early 1950s; the antics and petting parties of college youth had provided sensational fodder for hungry journalists in the 1920s. The parents—and grandparents—of these young people had chipped away at the system of sexual controls themselves. But they had not directly and publicly denied the very foundations of sexual morality. With few exceptions, they had evaded the controls and circumvented the rules, climbing into dorm rooms through open windows, signing out to the library and going to motels, carefully maintaining virginity in the technical sense while engaging in every caress known to married couples. The evasions often succeeded, but that does not mean that the controls had no effect. On the contrary, they had a great impact on the ways people experienced sex.

There were, in fact, two major systems of sexual control, one structural and one ideological. These systems worked to reinforce one another, but they affected the lives of those they touched differently.

The structural system was the more practical of the two but probably the less successful. It worked by limiting opportunities for the unmarried to have intercourse. Parents of teenagers set curfews and promoted double dating, hoping that by preventing privacy they would limit sexual exploration. Colleges, acting in loco parentis, used several tactics: visitation hours, parietals, security patrols, and restrictions on students' use of cars. When Oberlin students mounted a protest against the college's policy on cars in 1963, one male student observed that the issue was not transportation but privacy: "We wouldn't care if the cars had no wheels, just so long as they had doors."

The rules governing hours applied only to women and, to some extent, were meant to guarantee women's safety by keeping track of their comings and goings. But the larger rationale clearly had to do with sexual conduct. Men were not allowed in women's rooms but were received in lounges or "date rooms," where privacy was never assured. By setting curfew hours and requiring women to sign out from their dormitories, indicating who they were with and where they were going, college authorities meant to limit possibilities for privacy. Rules for men were not deemed necessary—because of a sexual double standard, because men's safety and well-being seemed less threatened in general, and because the colleges and universities were primarily concerned with controlling their own populations. If women were supervised or chaperoned and in by 11:00 P.M., the men would not have partners—at least, not partners drawn from the population that mattered.

Throughout the 1950s, the structural controls became increasingly complex; by the early 1960s they were so elaborate as to be ludicrous. At the University of Michigan in 1962, the student handbook devoted nine of its fifteen pages to rules for women. Curfews varied by the night of the week, by the student's year in college, and even, in some places, by her grade point average. Students could claim Automatic Late Permissions (ALPs) but only under certain conditions. Penalties at Michigan (an institutional version of "grounding") began when a student had eleven "late minutes"—but the late minutes could be acquired one at a time throughout the semester. At the University of Kansas in the late 1950s, one sorority asked the new dean of women to discipline two women who had flagrantly disregarded curfew. The dean, investigating, discovered that the women in question had been between one and three minutes late signing in on three occasions.

The myriad of rules, as anyone who lived through this period well knows, did not prevent sexual relations between students so much as they structured the times and places and ways that students could have sexual contact. Students said extended good-nights on the porches of houses, they petted in dormitory lounges while struggling to keep three feet on the floor and clothing in some semblance of order, and they had intercourse in cars, keeping an eye out for police patrols. What could be done after eleven could be done before eleven, and sex need not occur behind a closed door and in a bed—but this set of rules had a profound impact on the *ways* college students and many young people living in their parents homes *experienced sex*.

The overelaboration of rules, in itself, offers evidence that the controls were beleaguered. Nonetheless, the rules were rarely challenged frontally and thus they offered some illusion of control. This system of rules, in all its inconsistency, arbitrariness, and blindness, helped to preserve the distinction between public and private, the coexistence of overt and covert, that defines midcentury American sexuality.

The ideological system of controls was more pervasive than the structured system and probably more effective. This system centered on ideas of difference: men and women were fundamentally different creatures, with different roles and interests in sex. Whether one adopted a psychoanalytic or an essentialist approach, whether one looked to scholarly or popular analysis, the final conclusion pointed to *difference*. In sex (as in life), women were the limit setters and men the aggressors.

The proper limits naturally depended on one's marital status, but even within marriage sex was to be structured along lines of difference rather than of commonality. Marital advice books since the 1920s had [emphasized] the importance of female orgasm, insisting that men must satisfy their wives, but even these calls for orgasm equality posited male and female pleasure as competing interests. The language of difference in postwar America, which was often quite extreme, can be seen as a defensive reaction to changing gender roles in American society.

One influential psychoanalytic study, provocatively titled *Modern Woman: The Lost Sex*, condemned women who tried to be men and argued the natural difference between men and women by comparing their roles in sexual intercourse. The woman's role is "passive," the authors asserted. "[Sex] is not as easy as rolling off a log for her. It is easier. It is as easy as being the log itself. She cannot fail to deliver a masterly performance, by doing nothing whatever except being duly appreciative and allowing nature to take its course." For the man, in contrast, sexuality is "overt, apparent and urgent, outward and ever-present," fostered by psychological and physiological pressures toward orgasm.

Men might experiment sexually with few or no consequences and no diminution of plea-sure. Women, on the other hand, could not: "The strong desire for children or lack of it in a woman has a crucial bearing on how much enjoyment she derives from the sex-ual act. . . . Woman cannot make . . . pleasure an end in itself without inducing a decline in the pleasure."

These experts argued from a psychoanalytic framework, but much less theoretical work also insisted on the fundamental difference between men and women, and on their fundamentally different interests in sex. Texts used in marriage courses in American high schools and college typically included chapters on the difference between men and women—and these difference were not limited to their reproductive systems.

Woman did in fact have a different and more imperative interest in controlling sex than men, for women could become pregnant. Few doctors would fit an unmarried woman with a diaphragm, though one might get by in the anonymity of a city with a cheap "gold" ring from a drugstore or by pretending to be preparing for an impending honeymoon. Relying on the ubiquitous condom in the wallet was risky and douching (Coca-Cola had a short-lived popularity) even more so. Abortion was illegal, and though many abortions took place, they were dangerous, expensive, and usually frightening and degrading experiences. Dependable and *available* birth control might have made a dif-ference (many would later attribute "the sexual revolution" to the "pill"), but sexual be-haviors and sexual mores were not based simply on the threat of illegitimate pregnancy. Kinsey found that only 44 percent of the women in his sample said that they "restricted their pre-marital coitus" because of fear of pregnancy, whereas 80 percent cited "moral reasons." Interestingly, 44 percent of the sample also noted their "fear of public opinion."

Women who were too "free" with sexual favors could lose value and even threaten their marriageability. In this society, a woman's future socioeconomic status depended primarily on her husband's occupation and earning power. While a girl was expected to "pet to be popular," girls and women who went "too far" risked their futures. Advice books and columns from the 1940s and 1950s linked girls' and womens' "value" to their "virtue," arguing in explicitly economic terms that "free" kisses destroyed a woman's value in the dating system: "The boys find her easy to afford. She doesn't put a high value on herself." The exchange was even clearer in the marriage market. In chilling language, a teen adviser asked: "Who wants second hand goods?"

It was not only the advisers and experts who equated virtue and value. Fifty percent of the male respondents in Kinsey's study wanted to marry a virgin. Even though a rela-tively high percentage of women had intercourse before marriage, and a greater number engaged in "petting," most of these women at least *expected* to marry the man, and many did. Still, there might be consequences. Elaine Tyler May, who analyzed responses to a large, ongoing psychological study of married couples in the postwar era, found that many couples struggled with the psychological burdens of premarital intimacy for much of their married lives. In the context of a social/cultural system that insisted that "nice girls don't," many reported a legacy of guilt or mistrust. One woman wrote of her hus-band: "I think he felt that because we had been intimate before marriage that I could be as easily interested in any man that came along."

Of course, sexual mores and behaviors were highly conditioned by the sexual dou-ble standard. Lip service was paid to the ideal of male premarital chastity, but that ideal was usually obviated by the notion, strong in peer culture and implicitly acknowledged in the larger culture, that sexual intercourse was a male rite of passage. Middle-class boys pushed at the limits set by middle-class girls, but they generally looked elsewhere for "experience." A man who went to high school in the early 1960s (and did not lose his virginity until his first year of college) recalls the system with a kind of horror: "You slept with one kind of woman, and dated another kind, and the women you slept with, you didn't have much respect for, generally."

The distinction was often based on class—middle-class boys and men had sex with girls and women of the lower classes, or even with prostitutes. They did not really expect to have intercourse with a woman of their own class unless they were to be married. Samuel Hynes, in his memoir of coming of age as a navy flier during World War II, describes that certain knowledge: "There were nice girls in our lives, too. Being middle-class is more than a social station, it's kind of destiny. A middle-class boy from Minneapolis will seek out nice middle-class girls, in Memphis or anywhere else, will take them out on middle-class dates and try to put their hand inside their middle-class underpants. And he will fail. It was all a story that had already been written."

Dating, for middle-class youth, was a process of sexual negotiation. "Good girls" had to keep their virginity yet still contend with their own sexual desires or with boys who expected at least some petting as a "return" on the cost of the date. Petting was virtually universal in the world of heterosexual dating. A 1959 *Atlantic* article, "Sex and the College Girl," described the ideal as having "done every possible kind of petting without actually having intercourse."

For most middle-class youth in the postwar era, sex involved a series of skirmishes that centered around lines and boundaries: kissing, necking, petting above the waist, petting below the waist, petting through clothes, petting under clothes, mild petting, heavy petting. The progression of sexual intimacy had emerged as a highly ordered system. Each act constituted a stage, ordered in a strict hierarchy (first base, second base, and so forth), with vaginal penetration as the ultimate step. But in their attempts to preserve technical virginity, many young people engaged in sexual behaviors that, in the sexual hierarchy of the larger culture, should have been more forbidden than vaginal intercourse. One woman remembers: "We went pretty far, very far; everything but intercourse. But it was very frustrating. . . . Sex was out of the question. I had it in mind that I was going to be a virgin. So I came up with oral sex. . . . I thought I invented it."

Many young men and women acted in defiance of the rules, but that does not make the rules irrelevant. The same physical act can have very different meanings depending on its emotional and social/cultural contexts. For America's large middle class and for all those who aspired to "respectability" in the prerevolutionary twentieth century, sex was overwhelmingly secret or furtive. Sex was a set of acts with high stakes and possibly serious consequences, acts that emphasized and reinforced the different roles of men and women in American society. We do not know how each person felt about his or her private acts, but we do know that few were willing or able to publicly reject the system of sexual controls.

The members of the generation that would be labeled "the sixties" were revolutionary in that they called fundamental principles of sexual morality and control into question. The system of controls they had inherited and lived within was based on a set of presumptions rooted in the previous century. In an evolving set of arguments and actions (which never became thoroughly coherent or unified), they rejected a system of sexual controls organized around concepts of difference and hierarchy.

Both systems of control—the structural and the ideological—were firmly rooted in a Victorian epistemology that had, in most areas of life, broken down by the early twentieth century. This system was based on a belief in absolute truth and a passion for order and control. Victorian thought, as Joseph Singal has argued persuasively, insisted on "preserving absolute standards based on a radical dichotomy between that which was deemed 'human' and that regarded as 'animal.' " On the "human" side were all forces of civilization; on the "animal," all instincts, passions, and desires that threatened order and self-control. Sex clearly fell into the latter category. But the Victorian romance was not restricted to human versus animal, civilized versus savage. The moral dichotomy "fostered a tendency to see the world in polar terms." Thus we find rigid dichotomous pairs not only of good and evil, but of men and women, body and soul, home and world, public and private.

Victorian epistemology, with its remarkably comfortable and comforting certainties and its stifling absolutes, was shaken by the rise of a new science that looked to "dynamic process" and "relativism" instead of the rigid dichotomies of Victorian thought. It was challenged from within by those children of Victorianism who "yearned to smash the glass and breathe freely," as Jackson Lears argued in his study of antimodernism. And most fundamentally, it was undermined by the realities of an urban industrial society. American Victorian culture was, as much as anything, a strategy of the emerging middle classes. Overwhelmed by the chaos of the social order that had produced them and that they sought to manage, the middling classes had attempted to separate themselves from disorder and corruption. This separation, finally, was untenable.

The Victorian order was overthrown and replaced by a self-consciously "modern culture." One place we point to demonstrate the decline of Victorianism is the change in sexual "manners and mores" in the early twentieth century. Nonetheless, sex may be the place that Victorian thought least relinquished its hold. This is not to say that prudishness reigned—the continuity is more subtle and more fundamental. Skirts rose above the knee, couples dated and petted, sexologists and psychologists acknowledged that women were not naturally "passionless," and the good judge Ben Lindsey called for the "companionate marriage." But the systems of control that regulated and structured sex were Victorian at their core, with science replacing religion to authorize absolute truth, and with inflexible bipolar constructions somewhat reformulated but intact. The system of public controls over premarital sex was based on rigid dichotomous pairings: men and women, public and private. This distinction would be rejected—or at least recast—in the cultural and sexual struggles of the sixties.

REVOLUTIONARIES

All those who rejected the sexual mores of the postwar era did not reject the fundamental premises that gave them shape. *Playboy* magazine played an enormously important (if symbolic) role in the sexual revolution, or at least in preparing the ground for the sexual revolution. *Playboy* was a men's magazine in the tradition of *Esquire* (for which its founder had worked briefly) but laid claim to a revolutionary stance partly by replacing *Esquire's* airbrushed drawings with airbrushed flesh.

Begun by Hugh Hefner in 1953 with an initial print run of 70,000, *Playboy* passed the one million circulation mark in three years. By the mid-1960s Hefner had amassed a fortune of $100 million, including a lasciviously appointed forty-eight-room mansion staffed by thirty Playboy "bunnies" ("fuck like bunnies" is a phrase we have largely left behind, but most people at the time caught the allusion). Playboy clubs, also staffed by large-breasted and long-legged women in bunny ears and cottontails, flourished throughout the country. Though *Playboy* offered quality writing and advice for those aspiring to sophistication, the greatest selling point of the magazine was undoubtedly its illustrations.

Playboy, however, offered more than masturbatory opportunities. Between the pages of coyly arranged female bodies—more, inscribed in the coyly arranged female bodies—flourished a strong and relatively coherent ideology. Hefner called it a philosophy and wrote quite a few articles expounding it (a philosophy professor in North Carolina took it seriously enough to describe his course as "philosophy from Socrates to Hefner").

Hefner saw his naked women as "a symbol of disobedience, a triumph of sexuality, an end of Puritanism." He saw his magazines as an attack on "our ferocious anti-sexuality, our dark antieroticism." But his thrust toward pleasure and light was not to be undertaken in partnership. The Playboy philosophy, according to Hefner, had less to do with sex and more to do with sex roles. American society increasingly "blurred distinctions between the sexes . . . not only in business, but in such diverse realms as household chores, leisure activities, smoking and drinking habits, clothing styles, upswinging homosexuality and the sex-obliterating aspects of togetherness," concluded the "Playboy Panel" in June 1962. In Part 19 of his extended essay on the Playboy philosophy, Hefner wrote: "*Playboy* stresses a strongly heterosexual concept of society—in which the separate roles of men and women are clearly defined and compatible."

Read without context, Hefner's call does not necessarily preclude sex as a common interest between men and women. He is certainly advocating heterosexual sex. But the models of sex offered are not partnerships. Ever innovative in marketing and design, *Playboy* offered in one issue a special "coloring book" section. A page featuring three excessively voluptuous women was captioned: "Make one of the girls a blonde. Make one of the girls a brunette. Make one of the girls a redhead. It does not matter which is which. The girls' haircolors are interchangeable. So are the girls."

Sex, in the Playboy mode, was a contest—not of wills, in the model of the male seducer and the virtuous female, but of exploitative intent, as in the playboy and the would-be wife. In *Playboy's* world, women were out to ensnare men, to entangle them in a web of responsibility and obligation (not the least of which was financial). Barbara Ehrenreich has convincingly argued that *Playboy* was an integral part of a male-initiated revolution in sex roles, for it advocated that men reject burdensome responsibility (mainly in the shape of wives) for lives of pleasure through consumption. Sex, of course, was part of this pleasurable universe. In *Playboy*, sex was located in the realm of consumption, and women were interchangeable objects, mute, making no demands, each airbrushed beauty supplanted by the next month's model.

It was not only to men that sexual freedom was sold through exploitative visions. When Helen Gurley Brown revitalized the traditional women's magazine that was *Cosmopolitan* in 1965, she compared her magazine to *Playboy*—and *Cosmo* did celebrate the pleasures of single womanhood and "sexual and material consumerism." But before Brown ran *Cosmo*, she had made her contribution to the sexual revolution with *Sex and the Single Girl*, published in May 1962. By April 1963, 150,000 hard-cover copies had been sold, garnering Brown much media attention and a syndicated newspaper column, "Woman Alone."

The claim of *Sex and the Single Girl* was, quite simply, "nice, single girls *do*." Brown's radical message to a society in which twenty-three-year-olds were called old maids was that singleness is good. Marriage, she insisted, should not be an immediate goal. The Single Girl sounds like the Playboy's dream, but she was more likely a nightmare revisited. Marriage, Brown advised, is "insurance for the worst years of your life. During the best years you don't need a husband." But she quickly amended that statement: "You do need a man every step of the way, and they are often cheaper emotionally and more fun by the dozen." That fun explicitly included sex, and on the woman's terms. But Brown's celebration of the joys of single life still posed men and women as adversaries. "She need never be bored with one man per lifetime," she enthused. "Her choice of partners is endless and they seek *her* . . . Her married friends refer to her pursuers as wolves, but actually many of them turn out to be lambs—to be shorn and worn by her."

Brown's celebration of the single "girl" actually began with a success story—her own. "I married for the first time at thirty-seven. I got the man I wanted," begins *Sex and the Single Girl*. Brown's description of that union is instructive: "David is a motion picture producer, forty-four, brainy, charming and sexy. He was sought after by many a Hollywood starlet as well as some less flamboyant but more deadly types. And I got him! We have two Mercedes-Benzes, one hundred acres of virgin forest near San Francisco, a Mediterranean house overlooking the Pacific, a full-time maid and a good life."

While Brown believes "her body wants to" is a sufficient reason for a woman to have an "affair," she is not positing identical interests of men and women in sex. Instead, she asserts the validity of women's interests—interests that include Mercedes-Benzes, full-time maids, lunch ("Anyone can take you to lunch. How bored can you be for an hour?"), vacations, and vicuna coats. But by offering a female version of the Playboy ethic, she greatly strengthened its message.

Unlike the youths who called for honesty, who sought to blur the boundaries between male and female, *Playboy* and *Cosmo* offered a vision of sexual freedom based on difference and deceit, but within a shared universe of an intensely competitive market economy. They were revolutionary in their claiming of sex as a legitimate pleasure and in the directness they brought to portraying sex as an arena for struggle and exploitation that could be enjoined by men and women alike (though in different ways and to different ends). Without this strand, the sexual revolution would have looked very different. In many ways *Playboy* was a necessary condition for "revolution," for it linked sex to the emerging culture of consumption and the rites of the marketplace. As it fed into the sexual reconfigurations of the sixties, *Playboy* helped make sex more—or less—than a rite of youth.

In the revolutionary spring of 1968, *Life* magazine looked from the student protests at Columbia across the street to Barnard College: "A sexual anthropologist of some future century, analyzing the pill, the drive-in, the works of Harold Robbins, the Tween-Bra and all the other artifacts of the American Sexual Revolution, may consider the case of Linda LeClair and her boyfriend, Peter Behr, as a moment in which the morality of an era changed."

The LeClair affair, as it was heralded in newspaper headlines and syndicated columns around the country, was indeed such a moment. Linda LeClair and Peter Behr were accidental revolutionaries, but as *Life* not so kindly noted, "history will often have its little joke. And so it was this spring when it found as its symbol of the revolution a champion as staunch, as bold and as unalluring as Linda LeClair." The significance of the moment is not to be found in the actions of LeClair and Behr, who certainly lacked revolutionary glamour despite all the headlines about "Free Love," but in the contest over the meaning of those actions.

The facts of the case were simple. On 4 March 1968 the *New York Times* ran an article called "An Arrangement: Living Together for Convenience, Security, Sex." (The piece ran full-page width; below it appeared articles on "How to Duck the Hemline Issue" and "A Cook's Guide to the Shallot.") An "arrangement," the author informs us, was one of the current euphemisms for what was otherwise known as "shacking up" or, more innocuously, "living together." The article, which offers a fairly sympathetic portrait of several unmarried student couples who lived together in New York City, features an interview with a Barnard sophomore, "Susan," who lived with her boyfriend "Peter" in an off-campus apartment. Though Barnard had strict housing regulations and parietals (the curfew was midnight on weekends and ten o'clock on weeknights, and students were meant to live either at home or in Barnard housing), Susan had received permission to live off campus by accepting a job listed through Barnard's employment office as a "live-in maid." The job had, in fact, been listed by a young married woman who was a good friend of "Susan's."

Not surprisingly, the feature article caught the attention of Barnard administrators, who had little trouble identifying "Susan" as Linda LeClair. LeClair was brought before the Judiciary Council—not for her sexual conduct, but for lying to Barnard about her housing arrangements. Her choice of roommate was certainly an issue; if she had been found to be living alone or, as one Barnard student confessed to the *Times*, with a female cat, she would not have been headline-worthy.

Linda, however, was versed in campus politics, and she and Peter owned a mimeograph machine. She played it both ways, appearing for her hearings in a demure, knee-length pastel dress and churning out pamphlets on what she and Peter called "A Victorian Drama." She and Peter distributed a survey on campus, garnering three hundred replies, most of which admitted to some violation of Barnard's parietals or housing regulations. Sixty women were willing to go public and signed forms that read: "I am a student of Barnard College and I have violated the Barnard Housing Regulations. . . . In the interest of fairness I request that an investigation be made of my disobedience."

Linda LeClair had not done anything especially unusual, as several letters from alumnae to Barnard's president, Martha Peterson, testified. But her case was a symbol of change, and it tells us much about how people understood the incident. The president's office received over two hundred telephone calls (most demanding LeClair's expulsion) and over one hundred letters; editorials ran in newspapers, large and small, throughout the country. Some of the letters were vehement in their condemnation of LeClair and of the college. Francis Beamen of Needham, Massachusetts, suggested that Barnard should be renamed "BARNYARD"; Charles Orsinger wrote (on good quality letterhead), "If you let Linda stay in college, I can finally prove to my wife with a front page news story about that bunch of glorified whores going to eastern colleges." An unsigned letter began: "SUBJECT: Barnard College—and the kow-tow to female 'students' who practice prostitution, PUBLICLY!"

Though the term "alley cat" cropped up more than once, a majority of the letters were thoughtful attempts to come to terms with the changing morality of America's youth. Many were from parents who understood the symbolic import of the case. Overwhelmingly, those who did not simply rant about "whoredom" structured their comments around concepts of public and private. The word *flaunt* appeared over and over in the letters to President Peterson. Linda was "flaunting her sneering attitude"; Linda and Peter were "openly flaunting their disregard of moral codes"; they were "openly flaunting rules of civilized society." Mrs. Bruce Bromley, Jr., wrote her first such letter on a public issue to recommend, "Do not let Miss LeClair attend Barnard as long as she flaunts immorality in your face." David Abrahamson, M.D., identifying himself as a former Columbia faculty member, offered "any help in this difficult case." He advised President Peterson, "Undoubtedly the girl's behavior must be regarded as exhibitionism, as her tendency is to be in the limelight which clearly indicates some emotional disturbance or upset."

The public–private question *was* the issue in this case—the letter writers were correct. Most were willing to acknowledge that "mistakes" can happen; many were willing to allow for some "discreet" sex among the unmarried young. But Linda LeClair *claimed* the right to determine her own "private" life; she rejected the private–public dichotomy *as it was framed around sex*, casting her case as an issue of individual right versus institutional authority.

But public response to the case is interesting in another way. When a woman wrote President Peterson that "it is time for these young people to put sex back in its proper place, instead of something to be flaunted" and William F. Buckley condemned the "delinquency of this pathetic little girl, so gluttonous for sex and publicity," they were not listening. Sex was not what Linda and Peter talked about. Sex was not mentioned. Security was, and "family." "Peter is my family," said Linda. "It's a very united married type of relationship—it's the most important one in each of our lives. And our lives are very much intertwined."

Of course they had sex. They were young and in love, and their peer culture accepted sex within such relationships. But what they claimed was partnership—a partnership that obviated the larger culture's insistence on the difference between men and women. The letters suggesting that young women would "welcome a strong rule against living with men to protect them against doing that" made no sense in LeClair's universe. When she claimed that Barnard's rules were discriminatory because Columbia men had no such rules, that "Barnard College was founded on the principle of equality between women and men," and asked, "If women are able, intelligent people, why must we be supervised and curfewed?" she was denying that men and women had different interests and needs. Just as the private–public dichotomy was a cornerstone of sexual control in the postwar era, the much-touted differences between men and women were a crucial part of the system.

Many people in the 1960s and 1970s struggled with questions of equality and difference in sophisticated and hard-thought ways. Neither Peter Behr nor Linda LeClair was especially gifted in that respect. What they argued was commonplace to them—a natural language and set of assumptions that nonetheless had revolutionary implications.

It is when a set of assumptions becomes natural and unself-conscious, when a language appears in the private comments of a wide variety or people that it is worth taking seriously. The unity of interests that Behr and LeClair called upon as they obviated the male-female dichotomy was not restricted to students in the progressive institutions on either coast.

In 1969 the administration at the University of Kansas (KU), a state institution dependent on a conservative, though populist, legislature for its funding, attempted to establish a coed dormitory for some of its scholarship students. KU had tried coed living as an experiment in the 1964 summer session and found students well satisfied, though some complained that it was awkward to go downstairs to the candy machines with one's hair in curlers. Curlers were out of fashion by 1969, and the administration moved forward with caution.

A survey on attitudes toward coed housing was given to those who lived in the scholarship halls, and the answers of the men survive. The results of the survey go against conventional wisdom about the provinces. Only one man (of the 124 responses recorded) said his parents objected to the arrangement ("Pending further discussion," he noted). But what is most striking is the language in which the men supported and opposed the plan. "As a stereotypical answer," one man wrote, "I already am able to do all the role-playing socially I need, and see communication now as an ultimate goal." A sophomore who listed his classification as both "soph." and "4-F I hope" responded: "I believe that the segregation of the sexes is unnatural. I would like to associate with women on a basis other than dating roles. This tradition of segregation is discriminatory and promotes inequality of mankind." One man thought coed living would make the hall "more homey." Another said it would be "more humane." Many used the word "natural." The most eloquent of the sophomores wrote: "[It would] allow them to meet and interact with one another in a situation relatively free of sexual overtones; that is, the participating individuals would be free to encounter one another as human beings, rather than having to play the traditional stereotyped male and female roles. I feel that coed living is the only feasible way to allow people to escape this stereotypical role behavior."

The student-generated proposal that went forward in December 1970 stressed these (as they defined them) "philosophical" justifications. The system "would *not* be an arrangement for increased boy-meets-girl contact or for convenience in finding dates," the committee insisted. Instead, coed living would "contribute to the development of each resident as a full human being." Through "interpersonal relationships based on friendship and cooperative efforts rather than on the male/female roles we usually play in dating situations" students would try to develop "a human concern that transcends membership in one or the other sex.

While the students disavowed " 'boy-meets-girl' contact" as motivation, no one seriously believed that sex was going to disappear. The most cogently stated argument against the plan came from a young man who insisted: "[You] can't ignore the sexual overtones involved in coed living; after all, sex is the basic motivation for your plan. (I didn't say lust, I said sex)." Yet the language in which they framed their proposal was significant: They called for relationships (including sexual) based on a common humanity.

Like Peter Behr and Linda LeClair, these students at the University of Kansas were attempting to redefine both sex and sex roles. Sex should not be negotiated through the dichotomous pairings of male and female, public and private. Instead, they attempted to formulate and articulate a new standard that looked to a model of "togetherness" un-dreamed of and likely undesired by their parents. The *Life* magazine issue with which this essay began characterized the "sexual revolution" as "dull." "Love still makes the world go square," the author concluded, for the revolutionaries he interviewed subscribed to a philosophy "less indebted to *Playboy* than Peanuts, in which sex is not so much a pleasure as a warm puppy." To his amusement, one "California girl" told him: "Besides being my lover, Bob is my best friend in all the world," and a young man insisted, "We are not sleeping together, we are living together."

For those to whom *Playboy* promised revolution, this attitude was undoubtedly tame. And in the context of the cultural revolution taking place among America's youth, and documented in titillating detail by magazines such as *Life*, these were modest revo-lutionaries indeed, seeming almost already out of step with their generation. But the issue, to these "dull" revolutionaries, as to their more flamboyant brothers and sister, was larger than sex. They understood that the line between public and private had utility; that the personal was political.

In 1967, The Summer of Love

It was a "holy pilgrimage," according to the Council for a Summer of Love. In the streets of Haight-Ashbury, thousands and thousands of "pilgrims" acted out a street theater of costumed fantasy, drugs and music and sex that was unimaginable in the neat suburban streets of their earlier youth. Visionaries and revolutionaries had preceded the deluge; few of them drowned. Others did. But the tide flowed in the vague countercultural yearn-ings, drawn by the pop hit "San Francisco (Be Sure to Wear Flowers in Your Hair)" and its promise of a "love-in," by the pictures in *Life* magazine or in *Look* magazine or in *Time* magazine, by the proclamations of the underground press that San Francisco would be "the love-guerilla training school for drop-outs from mainstream America . . . where the new world, a human world of the 21st century is being constructed." Here sexual free-dom would be explored; not cohabitation, not "arrangements," not "living together" in ways that looked a lot like marriage except for the lack of a piece of paper that symbol-ized the sanction of the state. Sex in the Haight was revolutionary.

In neat suburban houses on neat suburban streets, people came to imagine this new world, helped by television and by the color pictures in glossy-paper magazines (a joke in the Haight told of "bead-wearing *Look* reporters interviewing bead-wearing *Life* re-porters"). Everyone knew that these pilgrims represented a tiny fraction of America's young, but the images reverberated. America felt itself in revolution.

Todd Gitlin, in his soul-searching memoir of the sixties, argues the cultural signif-icance of the few:

> Youth culture seemed a counterculture. There were many more weekend dope-smokers than hard-core "heads"; many more readers of the *Oracle* than writers for it; many more co-habitors than orgiasts; many more turners-on than droppers-out. Thanks to the sheer number and concentration of youth, the torrent of drugs, the sexual revolution, the trau-matic war, the general stampede away from authority, and the trend-spotting media, it was easy to assume that all the styles of revolt and disaffection were spilling together tribu-taries into a common torrent of youth and euphoria, life against death, joy over sacrifice, now over later, remaking the whole bleeding world.

Youth culture and counterculture, as Gitlin argues so well, were not synonymous, and for many the culture itself was more a matter of lifestyle than revolutionary intent. But the strands flowed together in the chaos of the age, and the few and the marginal provided archetypes that were read into the youth culture by an American public that did not see the lines of division. "Hippies, yippies, flippies," said Mayor Richard Daley of Chicago. "Free Love," screamed the headlines about Barnard's Linda LeClair.

But even the truly revolutionary youths were not unified, no more on the subject of sex than on anything else. Members of the New Left, revolutionary but rarely counter-cultural, had sex but did not talk about it all the time. They consigned sex to a relatively "private" sphere. Denizens of Haight-Ashbury lived a Dionysian sexuality, most looking nowhere but to immediate pleasure. Some political-cultural revolutionaries, however, claimed sex and used it for the revolution. They capitalized on the sexual chaos and fears of the nation, attempting to use sex to politicize youth and to challenge "Amerika."

In March 1968 the *Sun*, a Detroit people's paper put out by a "community of artists and lovers" (most notably John Sinclair of the rock group MC5), declared a "Total Assault on the Culture." Sinclair, in his "editorial statement," disavowed any prescriptive intent but informed his readers: "We *have* found that there are three essential human activities of the greatest importance to all persons, and that people are well and healthy in proportion to their involvement in these activities: rock and roll, dope, and fucking in the streets. . . . We suggest the three in combination, all the time."

He meant it. He meant it partly because it was outrageous, but there was more to it. "Fucking" helps you "escape the hangups that are drilled into us in this weirdo country"—it negates "private lives," "feels good," and so destroys an economy of pain and scarcity. Lapsing into inappropriately programmatic language, Sinclair argued:

> Our position is that all people must be free to fuck freely, whenever and wherever they want to, or not to fuck if they don't wanna—in bed, on the floor, in the chair, on the streets, in the parks and fields, "back seat boogie for the high school kids" sing the Fugs who brought it all out in the open on stage and on records, fuck whoever wants to fuck you and everybody else do the same. America's silly sexual "mores" are the end-product of thousands of years of deprivation and sickness, of marriage and companionship based on the ridiculous misconception that one person can "belong" to another person, that "love" is something that has to do with being "hurt," sacrificing, holding out, "teardrops on your pillow," and all that shit.

Sinclair was not alone in his paean to copulation. Other countercultural seekers believed that they had to remake love and reclaim sex to create community. These few struggled, with varying degrees of honesty and sincerity, over the significance of sex in the beloved community.

For others, sex was less a philosophy than a weapon. In the spring of 1968, the revolutionary potential of sex also suffused the claims of the Yippies as they struggled to stage a "Festival of Life" to counter the "Death Convention" in Chicago. "How can you separate politics and sex?" Jerry Rubin asked with indignation after the fact. Yippies lived by that creed. Sex was a double-edged sword, to be played two ways. Sex was a lure to youth; it was part of their attempt to tap the youth market, to "sell a revolutionary consciousness." It was also a challenge, "flaunted in the face" (as it were) of America.

The first Yippie manifesto, released in January 1968, summoned the tribes of Chicago. It played well in the underground press, with its promise of "50,000 of us dancing in the streets, throbbing with amplifiers and harmony . . . making love in the parks." Sex was a politics of pleasure, a politics of abundance that made sense to young middle-class whites who had been raised in the world without limits that was postwar America.

Sex was also incendiary, and the Yippies knew that well. It guaranteed attention. Thus the "top secret" plans for the convention that Abbie Hoffman mimeographed and distributed to the press promised a barbecue and lovemaking by the lake, followed by "Pin the Tail on the Donkey," "Pin the Rubber on the Pope," and "other normal and healthy games." Grandstanding before a crowd of Chicago reporters, the Yippies presented a city official with an official document wrapped in a *Playboy* centerfold inscribed, "To Dick with love, the Yippies." The *Playboy* centerfold in the Yippies' hands was an awkward nexus between the old and the new sexuality. As a symbolic act, it did not proffer freedom so much as challenge authority. It was a sign of disrespect—to Mayor Richard Daley and to straight America.

While America was full of young people sporting long hair and beads, the committed revolutionaries (of cultural stripe) were few in number and marginal at best. It is telling that the LeClair affair could still be a scandal in a nation that had weathered the Summer of Love. But the lines were blurred in sixties America. One might ask with Todd Gitlin, "What was marginal anymore, where was the mainstream anyway?" when the Beatles were singing, "Why Don't We Do It in the Road?"

CONCLUSION

The battles of the sexual revolution were hard fought, its victories ambiguous, its outcome still unclear. What we call the sexual revolution was an amalgam of movements that flowed together in an unsettled era. They were often at odds with one another, rarely well thought out, and usually without a clear agenda.

The sexual revolution was built on equal measures of hypocrisy and honesty, equality and exploitation. Indeed, the individual strands contain mixed motivations and ideological charges. Even the most heartfelt or best intentions did not always work out for the good when put into practice by mere humans with physical and psychological frailties. As we struggle over the meaning of the "revolution" and ask ourselves who, in fact, *won*, it helps to untangle the threads and reject the conflation of radically different impulses into a singular revolution.

■READING 11

Culture Channels Sexuality

Burton Pasternak, Carol R. Ember, and Melvin Ember

Although sexuality is part of human nature, no society leaves it to nature alone; all have rules and attitudes channeling proper conduct. When it comes to how much and what sorts of sexual activity societies allow or encourage before marriage, outside marriage, and even within marriage, there is considerable variation. Societies also differ in their tolerance of homosexual sexuality. We also find that restrictions of one sort or another may not apply throughout life, or to all aspects of sex. Moreover, the various cultural rules governing sexual behavior are not haphazard; within societies there seems to be some consistency among them. For example, societies that frown on sexual expression in young children are also likely to punish premarital and postmarital sex.

Customs may also change over time. In our own society, attitudes were becoming more permissive until the AIDS epidemic. During the 1970s, American behavior and attitudes suggested that acceptance and frequency of premarital sex had increased markedly since Kinsey's surveys in the 1940s. Surprisingly, attitudes toward extramarital sex had not changed much from the 1940s to the 1970s; the vast majority surveyed in the 1970s still objected to it. More recent surveys in the 1990s indicate a large drop in the frequency of both extramarital and premarital sex.

What do we know about how sexuality and sexual relations are regulated cross-culturally? How uniform or varied are customs governing childhood sexuality, premarital sex, and sex after marriage? Do people everywhere disapprove of sexual relations among persons of the same sex? It is to these questions that we now turn. As many of our examples illustrate, acceptance of sexuality is not an all-or-nothing matter; societies differ in the sorts of heterosexual relationships they tolerate (or encourage), and with whom such relationships are proper. So in our discussion of attitudes toward sexuality, it will be useful to consider various kinds of sexuality separately.

It is important to keep in mind that the customs of a society may be reported by an ethnographer as of the time she or he was there, but often (if the culture had been severely disrupted) the ethnography pertains to an earlier time, such as before the people were confined to a reservation. So the customs of a society may have changed substantially after the ethnographic report which we refer to in our discussion.

CHILDHOOD SEXUALITY

One thing we know is that the sexual curiosity of children is not worrisome to all people; in many societies people greet it with tolerance and openness. An ethnographer working among the Aymara of Peru described a people for whom sexual relations in general were considered "normal, natural, and pleasurable." From early childhood the sexes were unsegregated and related easily and freely. Children slept near their parents and were, from early childhood, aware of adult sexuality. The Aymara viewed the sex play of young children with tolerant amusement. Masturbation was not actively disapproved and evoked neither guilt nor shame. Heterosexual activity on the part of children, too, was generally ignored, and if noted, evoked only amusement or mild ridicule. Girls and boys alike usually had considerable sexual experience by the time they reached puberty—in this society virginity had no special value.

Similarly, the Cubeo Indians of the northwest Amazon considered masturbation and sex play between same sex children neither shameful nor worthy of discouragement. We are told that Cubeo boys sometimes indulged in mutual masturbation, while girls might stroke one another's nipples to produce erection. While younger people participated in this "mild form of homosexual eroticism," however, "true homosexuality" was rare.

Not all societies are so permissive when it comes to sex in general or to masturbation in particular. Consider the people of East Bay, a South Pacific island, who exhibited "great concern for sexual propriety." They discouraged children from touching their genitalia in public—the boys through good-natured ridicule, the girls by scolding. By age five, children had learned to avoid all physical contact with the opposite sex and had become highly sensitive to lapses in modesty. Girls and boys were careful to maintain proper distance at all times. Among the Ashanti of Ghana, a father warned his son against the evils of masturbation, of "making a pestle of his penis." And among the Chinese of Taiwan, masturbation was also greeted with strong disapproval:

> If a child is discovered masturbating he is severely scolded and beaten. He is threatened with what will happen if he continues; he will be unable to urinate, or he will go crazy. Children are also expected to conceal their genitalia from the eyes of others. If a boy urinates outside, he must use his hand to conceal his genitals, while girls past the age of four are expected to use the privacy of the benjo [toilet] where no one can see them. They are reprimanded with slaps and scoldings if they expose themselves.

Childhood sexuality is not just about allowing or encouraging children to be autoerotic or sexual with others of their own age. We should also consider attitudes about sexuality involving adults and children. In our society most people consider any sexual behavior involving an adult and child to be child abuse and strongly condemn it. But some societies are more tolerant of sexual behavior between adults and children. We are told that Thai mothers often tickled their sons' genitalia while feeding or playing with them, for example. Among the Kogi of Colombia, mothers taught their sons how to masturbate, using this method from about age five to calm them and make them sleep. What is especially interesting about the Kogi is that fathers' attitudes toward masturbation were very different from mothers'. Fathers considered masturbation a serious transgression and punished it harshly. They were especially concerned about it because of the belief that a child's masturbation endangered the father's health:

> A father condemns in general the manifestations of infantile sexuality in both sexes, but a mother does not. She, in addition to masturbating her son, shows a lively interest in the erotic pleasures which her daughter derives from her body and takes a certain pride in the fact that this instinct is developing in her children. Both parents nevertheless try to avoid having the children observe the sexual activities of the adults, since these are carried out almost solely at night and outside the house, the children evidently do not have any occasion to learn about them.

Some societies also allowed older people special license with respect to sex with young children. Here, for example, is a description of a practice among the Truk of the South Pacific:

> Among older people no longer able for physical or social reasons to have heterosexual liaisons, two practices are reported by a number of informants. Older men not infrequently perform cunnilingus on preadolescent girls; both are said to enjoy this, the men because it is their only sexual outlet and the girls because it is so gentle . . . [the Trukese refer to such behavior] with tolerant amusement over the dilemma of these old people who have to resort to such devices in order to obtain sexual satisfaction.

While this description might suggest that any sexuality was permitted, the Trukese were much less permissive about certain kinds of sex. When children three or four years in age were observed masturbating they were crossly told to stop, although reproofs did not go beyond "mild pats and somewhat angry sounding remarks." They believed that heterosexual activity made children sick, and that notion extended to masturbation. Yet, as the ethnographers pointed out,

> we may be fairly sure that the prohibition does not reflect disapproval of masturbation as such for this activity is permitted adults with only the restrictions of modesty which apply, for example, to urination, provided the people nearby are of the same sex.

As we have seen, people are not always consistent regarding the kinds of sexual activities allowed infants and children. However, there is a general tendency for societies that allow children to express their sexuality with each other before puberty to be fairly tolerant of premarital and extramarital intercourse as well. Such societies also tend not to insist on modesty in dress and do not constrain their talk about sex around children. Still, no society is entirely free and open about sex. Even the most permissive societies do not allow sexual intercourse between parents and children or between brothers and sisters.

HETEROSEXUALITY IN ADOLESCENCE

Do relatively permissive societies alter their attitudes toward sexuality when pregnancy becomes possible? Mostly they do not; as we have seen, tolerance of childhood sexuality generally predicts tolerance for premarital sex. Many societies permissive of childhood sexuality get girls to marry before or shortly after puberty, so premarital pregnancy is not usually a problem. Some make a clear distinction between sexual play and intercourse before marriage. For example, among the Kikuyu of Kenya, premarital sex was traditionally encouraged as long as intercourse was avoided. Adolescents practiced *ngweko* which involved "platonic love and fondling." Girls wore an *apron* over their genitals and adults taught them, and the boys, how to intertwine legs so as to enjoy sex without intercourse. Traditionally, they learned to do this after initiation into an age-set, but now that the initiation and age-set system has broken down, the practice of ngweko has diminished. Sexual activity has not decreased, however, and premarital pregnancy is not now unusual.

More permissive than the Kikuyu were the Trobriand Islanders who permitted sexual intercourse before marriage. Girls were expected to have sex with boys visiting from other villages, and could have as many lovers as they wished. This was still the case during the 1970s and 1980s when Annette B. Weiner did fieldwork among the Trobriand Islanders. As she describes it,

> in the Trobriands, adultery is a crime, but premarital love affairs are not. For unmarried young people, each decorative element is carefully chosen to catch the eye of a possible lover, as each use of magic is calculated to "make someone want to sleep with you." Attraction and seduction are adolescent pursuits, and the presence of young people walking through Losuia, laughing, singing, and teasing, made Saturdays almost as celebratory as traditional yam harvest feasts.
>
> Even while involved in the daily village routine, young people are preoccupied with their own plans and negotiations. Throughout the day, lovers send messages back and forth to arrange evening meeting places. Conversations between young people are filled with sexual metaphors that express a person's intention. Questions such as "Can I have a coconut to drink?" or "Can I ride your bicycle?" are Trobriand ways to say, "Will you sleep with me?" Dabweyowa once told me, "Women's eyes are different than men's. When I talk to a girl I watch her eyes. If she looks straight at me, I know she wants me." Young women are just as assertive and dominant as men in their pursuit or refusal of a lover.

Given the frequency of premarital sex among the Trobrianders, Malinowski was puzzled about why there was so little premarital pregnancy. Whiting et al. suggest its rarity was perhaps due to adolescent subfecundity—Trobriand girls remained unmarried for only about three years after puberty. Trobriand Islanders believed that pregnancy was unrelated to copulation, perhaps because the frequent sex did not often result in pregnancy.

Among the Tikopia of the Pacific, masturbation was an acceptable alternative to intercourse for the young of both sexes. Their only reservation was that masturbation makes the hands unclean for food preparation. In the case of men, masturbation could involve self or mutual stimulation, and a girl might masturbate herself if she

> cannot get a man to have intercourse with her, or is too shy to ask the one she wants. It is said that only women who have already tasted sex pleasure will act thus. Such a woman "remembers the male organ," and with her finger, or a manioc root, or a peeled banana, rubs herself. She does so with increasing energy as her desire climbs up. It is because of the force used that it is customary to peel the banana; otherwise her genitals would become sore.

Allowing premarital sex does not always mean that anxiety about sex is absent. For example, even though premarital sex on the Micronesian island of Truk was allowed during the late 1940s and early 1950s, courting usually involved trysts in the bush and secret visits at night to the girl's home. Discovery evoked teasing, even if there was no punishment. The Trukese believed men should initiate sex. But for young men, getting a sexual relationship started, and keeping it going, could be quite stressful. For one thing, it was not easy to find unmarried women with whom to "practice" because girls married early, usually around the time of puberty. It was easier to establish illicit relationships with married women. That was always a bit risky; if discovered, such relationships could be embarrassing, especially for the young man. Courting an unmarried (or married) woman usually required skill at writing love letters. Gladwin and Sarason noted: "It is ironic that, in terms of quantity at least, the most important use to which the art of writing has been put by the Trukese since it was taught them so painfully by missionaries and administration alike is the writing of love letters." A woman could pick and choose among potential lovers, who struggled and competed to satisfy her sexual needs:

> Sexual intercourse, without which a lover's relationship has no meaning for the Trukese, by its very nature requires the expression of strong emotion not only by the man, but also by the woman. In some societies the occurrence or nonoccurrence of female orgasm is not considered of major importance; on Truk, however, it is important, particularly for more accomplished or serious lovers, and its occurrence is a function of the contribution of both partners to the relationship. For the man it determines the success or failure of his performance: If he reaches his climax before the woman he not only leaves her in some degree unsatisfied, but more importantly from his standpoint has "lost" in the contest.

The woman could also exert some control over her lover by virtue of the fact that she possessed his letters, by their nature clear evidence of his intent to consummate a sexual liaison. Their purpose was unambiguous, and by answering a letter a woman essentially agreed to sex. Were she later to become displeased with her lover, she could publicize the letters to his discomfort. All-around, sexual liaisons were far more difficult and sensitive for the man (although not less exciting for that reason):

> It is the woman whose position is at every turn secure and the man who exposes himself to hazards. A man has committed himself by writing the first letter; the woman holds and can expose the incriminating document. With the entry into the house and his approach to the woman it is again the man who runs the risk: of being discovered or of being rejected. And finally during the intercourse itself it is the man who stands to "lose" if he ejaculates too soon; it must furthermore be noted that it is under these circumstances that the type of intercourse least likely to produce rapid orgasm in the woman is used.

Not all peoples are as tolerant of premarital sex as those we have been describing. The Chinese certainly valued premarital chastity and wifely fidelity after marriage. They traditionally took pains to control the perambulation of women, and to limit their contact with the opposite sex. These efforts were not always successful. Constant watchfulness notwithstanding, girls did (and do) have affairs and even get pregnant before marriage, courting discovery, punishment, shame, and possibly reducing bride-wealth value. It was a heavy burden for any family to discover, after a son's marriage, that his bride was not a virgin. But, as one of Pasternak's Taiwan informants put it, "rice already cooked cannot be returned to the storage bin." Such a family usually tries to contain and hide their discovery, but the daughter-in-law can expect to pay for her indiscretion.

Watchfulness was essential among the Tepoztlan of Mexico as well, where a girl's life became "crabbed, cribbed, confined" from her first menstruation. From then on she was not to speak to or encourage boys in the least way. It was a mother's burden to guard her daughters' chastity and reputation. One mother confided to the ethnographer that she wished her fifteen-year-old daughter would marry soon because it was inconvenient to "spy" on her all the time. Indeed, virginity at marriage was (and often still is) important in many cultures. In many Muslim societies, it used to be customary to display bloodstained sheets after the wedding night as proof of a bride's virginity.

With increased education, attitudes toward female/male relationships are often relaxed. In the small Moroccan town of Zawiya, adolescent girls and boys can now walk to school and study together, although dating is still taboo and marriages are still largely arranged (as of the mid–1980s). In the previous generation, just talking together was considered shameful. Even now a girl risks her reputation if people see her too often in a boy's company; they invariably suspect the worst. And a boy might well eliminate as potential mate any girl who has kissed him before. Zawiya town clearly has a double standard, constraining girls more than boys. But surprisingly it is not common for societies to have a double standard regarding premarital sex.

What sorts of societies are more accepting of premarital sex than others, and why? Comparative research work by Suzanne G. Frayser provides some indications. To begin with, her research revealed that more societies allow premarital sex for one or both sexes than do not, and that where there are restraints, they are considerably more likely to apply to sex before marriage than to extramarital sex. Further, societies that restrict sex before marriage are likely to restrict extramarital sex as well. When the rules differ for women and men, it is always in the direction of allowing greater freedom to males. As Frayser put it, "the double standard operates only in one direction."

But why should there be more interest in restricting women's sexual relationships, or in confining them to the reproductive context (to marriage) in some societies but not in others? In this connection, Frayser draws our attention to the fact that women are more obviously linked to their offspring than men, through childbirth, nursing, and the like. For men, the linkage must be assured in other ways:

> If a man has a continuing relationship with a woman who confines her sexual relations exclusively to him, he can more easily identify any children she bears as his own. Therefore, a man indirectly affirms his physical link to his child by creating a close, social bond with the woman whose children he wishes to claim as his own. Cultural beliefs about his role in conception and the restriction of the woman's sexual relations to him further strengthen the basis for his connection with the child.

Still, why are some people more concerned about paternity than others? It is clear that societies vary in the degree to which social groups have an interest in the reproductive potential of women. Consider two examples Frayser provides, one a society in which there is little interest, the other in which interest is considerable.

Among the Kimam, inhabitants of an island off New Guinea, women may have premarital sex and even take the initiative in that regard. There is considerable extramarital liberty as well, for women as well as men. It is not that having children is of no concern; everyone wants sons to work the gardens and to provide support in old age. They need daughters, too, to exchange for daughters-in-law. Interest in childbirth is so strong that a man can divorce or kill his wife for aborting her child.

Although the Kimam appreciate the biological contribution women and men make to childbearing, they base rights to children on other considerations. As Frayser puts it, "conceiving or giving birth to a child is not sufficient reason to claim the right of parenthood; people acquire this right by taking care of the child." For that reason, a barren woman need not fear shame or retribution. Adoption provides an easy solution; few refuse to give a child. Establishment of paternity may not be so much an issue because adoption is acceptable. A man helps support his sister's children and has the right to adopt the sister's child.

Consider now the Kenuzi Nubians, on Egypt's Nile River, among whom strict control over women's sexuality begins early. When a girl is three or four, the custom is to remove her clitoris and practically seal her vaginal opening to guarantee virginity at marriage. And once married she can have sex only with her husband, who often spends long periods working far from home. Husbands sometimes insist that their wives' vaginas be sewn up during long absences. A husband may kill his wife at the slightest suspicion of infidelity, so conception during his absence is to be avoided at all cost.

Like the Kimam, the Kenuzi want children; women to ensure continuation of marriage (and husband's economic support), men to provide for continuity of their descent groups. In fact, reproduction is so much a group concern among the Kenuzi that a man is under pressure to remarry if his wife bears no sons. (This is a source of considerable anxiety for wives, especially given that one-third to one-half of Kenuzi children die young.) Sons, as in all patrilineal societies, belong to the kin groups of their father. For these reasons, men may feel it important to establish paternity and they attempt to do so by strictly controlling the sexuality of women. However, societies that emphasize the mother in kinship (matrilineal societies) have no comparable problem. Identification of the mother is critical for access to kin group resources but maternity is hardly problematic. Knowing the identity of the father is not vital, so controlling his sexuality is probably not as necessary in societies that have kin groups oriented around women.

Where descent is traced through women, then, establishing paternity may be less vital. There, a man's responsibility is to his sister's children; children belong to their mother's group, which is also that of the mother's brother. A man's own offspring belong to a different group—to that of his wife. Thus, a husband's contribution to reproduction can be relatively brief and limited. The link between mother and child is crucial, but motherhood requires no special confirmation.

Is the patterning of kinship crucial to the control of sexuality, then? Frayser's data do confirm that patrilineal systems are more likely to restrict women's sexual relations, and confine their reproductive potential to one man, than matrilineal systems. We find the opposite where descent is traced through women: low confinement of women's sexual and reproductive relationships to one man.

But what of societies in which descent is not traced exclusively through women or men, or in which there are no descent groups at all? Such societies, like patrilineal ones, also tend to emphasize father-child bonds. Frayser suggests this may be because most of these societies require a woman to live with or near her husband's family (patrilocally) when she marries:

> Paternity would be most important in patrilocal groups, because it is the only residence pattern whereby an individual's postmarital residence depends upon where the person's father lives. In addition, patrilocal residence means that the raw materials for community organization consist of clusters of related males.

The comparative evidence confirms that patrilocality is significantly related to restrictions on women's sexual and reproductive relationships. It is even more strongly related to such restrictions than patrilineal descent is related to such restrictions. In fact, patrilineal societies may have these constraints because they are usually also patrilocal.

The nature of kinship organization clearly has an impact, but environmental factors too may play a role. The Circum-Mediterranean area is especially restrictive when it comes to female sexuality, with strong prohibitions against both premarital and extramarital sex. Divorces are difficult to obtain, and where granted the basis is usually barrenness. Remarriage after divorce or death of a husband is difficult. And, as Jane Schneider has pointed out, considerable attention is given in this region to matters of honor, shame, and virginity. There is also considerable competition for pastoral and agricultural resources, resulting in conflict within and between groups, and weak political integration. In the face of competition and social fragmentation, family and descent groups are unstable. Lacking effective political controls, codes of honor and shame provide some degree of social control. In Frayser's view, there may be good reason for women to abide by these codes as well:

> In Circum-Mediterranean societies, a woman's contribution to subsistence relative to a man's is lowest in comparison with all other world areas. Therefore, if a woman's husband divorces her, her consequent economic deprivation would be of major proportions. This economic loss could over-shadow a woman's temptation to violate the regulations placed upon her sexual or reproductive relationships.

Are similar sorts of societies likely, then, to be more or less permissive when it comes to premarital sex? Indeed, in societies where property and other rights are passed to children through males (patrilineal descent) and where married couples live with or near the husband's parents (patrilocal residence), premarital pregnancies tend to evoke considerable disapproval.

In such societies, an unmarried woman who becomes pregnant puts her child at a severe economic as well as social disadvantage. However, if rights to property pass through the mother (matrilineal descent) and women live with or near their own kin when they marry (matrilocal residence), then illegitimate children usually enjoy access to resources.

Societies with dowry, goods and money given by the bride's family to the bride or the couple, are also likely to be restrictive of premarital sex. And, as we will see in the chapter on getting married, dowry is common in socially stratified societies, where families often use large dowries to attract high-status sons-in-law. That strategy may well fail, however, if a daughter has had sex with and become pregnant by a low-status male. So, one reason families guard daughters may be to defend against social climbers attempting to use seduction and pregnancy to force a marriage.

Cross-cultural studies do indicate that complex societies—those with political hierarchies, part- or full-time craft specialists, cities and towns, and class stratification—are especially likely to restrict premarital sex. Perhaps with increasing social inequality, parents become increasingly concerned about their children avoiding marriage with people "beneath them." Permissive premarital sex could complicate matters if it leads to inappropriate emotional attachments. Even worse, unsuitable liaisons resulting in pregnancy could make it difficult or impossible for a girl to marry well. Consistent with this notion, we find that societies with little premarital sex also tend to have arranged marriages.

The degree to which premarital and extramarital sexuality are regulated in society are clearly not matters of chance or accident. These customs and practices are related to each other, to characteristics of kinship and political organization, and perhaps to ecological adaptations as well. Our understanding of the connections is still rudimentary, however, and much more research still needs to be done.

HOMOSEXUALITY

We discuss homosexuality separately because societal attitudes toward it are apparently unrelated to those governing heterosexuality. Because many societies deny homosexuality exists and many ethnographers have ignored it, the incidence or prevalence of homosexuality cross-culturally is difficult to estimate. It is easier simply to determine whether a society permits or prohibits homosexuality. We know less about female homosexuality (less often discussed in ethnographies), but we do know that if it is permitted for adolescent girls, it is almost always also permitted for adolescent boys. We are also aware that permissiveness of homosexuality in adolescence almost always predicts tolerance of it in adulthood.

The consensus now is that homosexuality is not a unitary phenomenon. Some researchers suggest that different types of male homosexuality should be distinguished. In some societies, for example, homosexuality is *mandatory* during a phase of the life cycle. This is the case in parts of Melanesia, where homosexuality is commonly associated with the initiation rites which all adolescent boys undergo. Here, younger participants receive semen from older men in homosexual episodes. They subsequently become the inseminators of younger boys. Later still, they marry heterosexually and have children. Some examples follow.

Among the Big Nambas of Malekula, an island in eastern Melanesia, boys become lovers of older men. The custom is that, after a decision to hold circumcision rites, fathers find guardians for their sons, guardians who will possess exclusive sexual rights over the boys. The guardian becomes the boy's "husband," in a relationship that is very close and usually monogamous. (Chiefs are different; they may take many boy lovers just as they may have many wives.) The boy accompanies his guardian everywhere, and should one die, the survivor would mourn him deeply.

Homosexual liaisons elsewhere in Melanesia are not as intimate or monogamous as among the Big Nambas. Those of the Keraki, in the Trans-Fly area of Papua New Guinea, are more transitory. With respect to the Keraki, Creed tells us that

> sodomy was fully sanctioned by male society, universally practiced, and . . . homosexuality was actually regarded as essential to a boy's bodily growth. Boys are initiated at the bull-roarer ceremony at about the age of thirteen. On the night of the ceremony the initiate is turned over to a youth of the previous group of initiates who introduces the boy to homosexual intercourse. In all cases . . . the older youth was the mother's brother's son or the father's sister's son of the new initiate. After this, the boy is available to fellow villagers or visitors of the opposite moiety who wish to have homosexual relations with him.

During this time the initiates live together in a seclusion hut for several months, during which they are supposed to grow rapidly with the aid of homosexual activities. At the end of the seclusion the youth becomes a "bachelor." He associates more freely with the elders and shows an increased interest in hunting, but he continues to play the passive role in homosexual relations for a year or so.

Initiates then go through a ceremony during which lime is poured down their throats. People believe the burns which result ensure that the boys have not become pregnant as a result of their homosexual relationships. From that time sexual passivity is over; newly initiated youths now become the inseminators of other boys until, in time, they marry heterosexually.

The expectation that all boys will engage in homosexual relationships with older men is not limited to Melanesia. Other societies have this custom as well. For example, the Siwans of Egypt expected all unmarried males to have homosexual relations, which their fathers arranged. The custom was not entirely permissive, however, since it limited a man to one boy. Although the government eventually prohibited Siwan homosexuality, it was practiced quite openly until 1909. Almost all older men reported having had homosexual relationships as boys. Later, between sixteen and twenty years of age, they invariably married girls. As in Melanesia, then, homosexuality was a phase in every man's life.

The mandatory homosexuality we have been describing usually involves relationships between older men and boys. But homosexuality finds acceptance even in societies where it is not mandatory; some researchers suggest that it commonly occurs as a form of adolescent experimentation. As we noted in our earlier discussion of childhood sexuality, some societies allow casual homosexual play. Still others have special times when homosexuality can be expressed. For example, the Papago of the southwestern United States had "nights of saturnalia," during which males could have brief homosexual relationships. Quite a few North American Indian societies also accommodated male transvestites, commonly referred to as *berdaches*. These men assumed the dress, occupations, and many of the behaviors of women. But whether they were homosexual as well is not clear. The evidence in the ethnographic literature suggests quite a bit of variability. In some societies, like the Papago, Crow, Mohave, and Santee, berdaches reportedly did engage in homosexual behavior. However, informants denied they were homosexual among the Flathead, Pima, Plains Cree, Chiracahua Apache, and Bella Coola. Also variable was the extent to which berdaches married. Where they did, in some societies they customarily married nonberdache men and assumed a woman's role; in other cases they married women and established heterosexual relationships.

In some native North American societies, females too could adopt transvestite roles, but this was much less often accepted. One survey found reports of female transvestites in 30 native North American societies, compared to 113 with male transvestites. And in societies with both female and male berdaches, the females were usually far less common than their male counterparts. Female berdaches often cross-dressed and took up some male pursuits, like hunting. Homosexuality is mentioned in connection with them in some North American societies, but in others their sexual proclivities are not clearly described.

Sexuality is not necessarily either heterosexual or homosexual. The notion of gender does not invariably involve just two categories—female and male—and berdache-like roles are not limited to North America. In a survey of 186 societies, Richley H. Crapo found such statuses in 41 or 22 percent of them, and about half were outside North America. Only eight societies (3 percent) provided evidence of female berdaches. Just as accounts more often describe male berdaches, so do they more often report male homosexuality than lesbianism. Without more research on lesbianism in societies around the world, there is no way to know whether it is reported less often than male homosexuality because it really is so, or because ethnographers have neglected to investigate the phenomenon and the members of many societies are more reluctant to discuss it.

The fact that societies accepting homosexuality in childhood are generally also tolerant of it in adulthood does not imply that expectations about sexual behavior do not change in adulthood. Reproduction requires heterosexual relationships, so it is hardly surprising that, once individuals are able to reproduce, societies expect and prefer them to do so. Indeed, even in societies where most or all individuals have homosexual experiences during an early stage of their lives, most adults marry and have heterosexual intercourse. And even where people may adopt roles atypical for their sex, such individuals are rare. There are actually very few societies in which people prefer homosexuality over heterosexuality in adulthood. The Etoro of New Guinea were one such society. Although most men married and had heterosexual sex, the Etoro actually prohibited heterosexual sex for as many as 260 days a year, and never allowed it in or near the house or gardens. There were no restrictions on male homosexuality, however; the Etoro believed it made crops flourish and boys strong.

While people tolerate homosexuality in most societies, in some they condemn or ridicule it, or consider it incomprehensible. A few societies even eliminate persons discovered engaging in homosexual acts. For example, the Eastern Apache executed homosexuals, considering them dangerous witches. However, they did not consider cross-dressing synonymous with homosexuality; they ridiculed berdaches, but did not execute them unless they were homosexual as well. Among the Azande of the Sudan, too, the reaction was severe. Lesbianism among women in princely households was punishable by death, flogging the likely response in poorer families.

Several cross-cultural studies have attempted to discover why some societies are more accepting of homosexuality than others. The findings, unfortunately, have been contradictory. Part of the problem may be that most researchers have not distinguished different kinds of male homosexuality. If degree of acceptance varies according to type, then failing to make such distinctions could well obscure the results. Nonetheless, an intriguing study by Dennis Werner found that societies with evidence of population pressure on resources, and therefore with reason to limit reproduction, are more likely to tolerate male homosexuality.

The presumption is, of course, that more homosexuality translates into less heterosexuality and, therefore, a lower reproductive rate. By way of contrast, societies that forbid abortion and infanticide for married women (most permit these practices for illegitimate births) are likely to disapprove of male homosexuality, suggesting that it may be less acceptable in societies struggling to increase their populations. These societies may discourage any behavior that inhibits population growth. Widespread homosexuality would have that effect to the extent that it decreased heterosexual relations. Another bit of evidence in support of the population pressure interpretation is that societies with famines and severe food shortages, indirect indicators of excess population, are also more likely to allow homosexuality.

Policy changes in the former Soviet Union were consistent with this interpretation. In 1917, during the turmoil of revolution, the government encouraged people to have fewer children, and also revoked laws prohibiting abortion and homosexuality. Later, when a pronatalist policy emerged (1934–1936), the Soviet government rewarded mothers with many children, and once again declared abortion and homosexuality illegal.

Population pressure may not be the only inducement to more relaxed attitudes toward homosexuality. We know, for example, that societies with customary rites of passage from boyhood to manhood (usually including genital operations) are also more likely to condone or encourage homosexuality, although the reasons are unclear. It is important to keep in mind, as well, that while problems of population growth (too little or too much) may have something to do with *societal* attitudes toward homosexuality, such problems cannot explain why certain *individuals* become homosexual.

Let us return, now, to the matter of types. Have comparative studies thrown any light on the conditions under which different forms of homosexuality are more or less likely to occur? In one study, Richley H. Crapo compared mandatory intergenerational homosexuality (which he calls mentorship homosexuality) with voluntary same generation homosexuality, and found that they occur in different types of societies. The mentorship variety appears in societies with male-centered kin groups, a good deal of segregation of the sexes in childhood, and clear role distinctions between males and females.

This is consistent with earlier suggestions that mentorship homosexuality is part of a larger syndrome reflecting strong male power and authority. Where older men exercise strong control over women and younger males, institutionalizing homosexuality for younger males may increase their prospects of acquiring multiple wives. If this is so, mentorship homosexuality may have more to do with control than with some fundamental homosexual orientation or desire. Societies with voluntary same generation homosexuality (or at least a tolerance of male transvestites) may be different. Although early theorists thought that male transvestism was a way for some males to escape oppressive sex-role requirements (such as aggressive warrior roles), subsequent research by Munroe, Whiting, and Hally found that male transvestism was actually more likely where sex-role distinctions are *minimal.* In societies that emphasize female-male role differences, people seem to consider transvestism less acceptable.

We have been talking about the degree to which societies allow or tolerate different kinds of sex, but we have not yet considered how people *think* of sex—as desirable and pleasurable, or as a duty and perhaps even frightening? Just because a society allows a certain type of sex with a certain type of person does not mean people generally desire it. On the other hand, even forbidden sex may be illicitly enjoyed by some. When it comes to attitudes toward sexuality, too, we find considerable variation, as the following examples will show.

Sex, according to the Chukchee of Siberia, was the "best thing" in the world, while for the Cayapa of Ecuador it was "a little like work." And earlier in this chapter, we discussed the Aymara and Trukese, who clearly also considered sex pleasurable and desirable. Where people think of sex as pleasurable, it is not necessarily so for one sex alone. This was clearly the case on Truk, where men went to great lengths to ensure orgasm in their partners. And among the Bemba of Africa,

> puberty is eagerly looked forward to by the girls. They and their parents watch the growth of their breasts with interest and excitement and openly discuss the approach of

womanhood. Girls are enthusiastic about the prospect of marriage and are taught that sex relations are pleasant and that it is their duty to give pleasure to their husbands. They do not seem to fear the first act of intercourse or to apprehend that it will be painful.

Malinowski tells us that for Trobriand Islanders the most important idea about sex was that it is "purely a source of pleasure." Here is an informant's account, a description of lovemaking which clearly conveys the pleasure derived by women and men alike:

> When I sleep with Dabugera I embrace her, I hug her with my whole body, I rub noses with her. We suck each other's lower lip, so that we are stirred to passion. We suck each other's tongues, we bite each other's noses, we bite each other's chins, we bite cheeks and caress the armpit and the groin. Then she will say: "O my lover, it itches very much . . . push on again, my whole body melts with pleasure . . . do it vigorously, be quick, so that the fluids may discharge . . . tread on again, my body feels so pleasant."

In some societies men take special pains to assure the pleasure of their sex partners. This was clearly also the case among the Toradja, a people of Central Celebes, according to the account provided by Adriani and Kruyte:

> for the purpose of increasing sensual pleasure, the penis is sometimes mutilated. . . . One man from there even claimed that someone whose penis is not mutilated is not desired by the women. This mutilation is done by inserting under the skin of the glans of the penis little marbles of about five millimeters in diameter, which are ground from shells. The men of Kawanga had this operation done in a woods located between this place and Mo-engkoe-lande. The skin of the glans of the penis is pinched in a split piece of wood, so that it protrudes above. Then the skin is pierced and the little balls are pushed into the cut, after which this is rubbed with horse manure. These little marbles are called *kandoekoe* (*makamloekoe*, "uneven, bumpy"). At each operation two or three little balls are inserted, up to seven in all. (It is said that there are girls who inquire about the number of kandoekoe that a young man who asks to marry them has, with the words: "How many guests do you have" (*bara sangkoedja linggonamoe*). They are said to be inserted in such a way that, when the penis is limp, the little marbles are on the under side of it, and with an erection they come to lie on the upper side. The operation takes place without any ceremony. When the wound has healed, the person must not eat any peas (*tibesi*), fern greens (*bate'a*), or slimy vegetables; otherwise the little marbles will fall out.

While many people consider sex pleasurable, there are also those who find it dangerous and fearful. The Mae Enga, in Highland New Guinea, are an example of a society in which men are afraid to have sex with women, even in marriage. Before and after heterosexual sex, men engage in various rituals to protect themselves against harm. Mervyn Meggitt described the situation as follows:

> Each act of coitus increases a man's chances of being contaminated . . . copulation is in itself detrimental to male well-being. Men believe that the vital fluid residing in a man's skin makes it sound and handsome, a condition that determines and reflects his mental vigor and self-confidence. This fluid also manifests itself as his semen. Hence, every ejaculation depletes his vitality, and over-indulgence must dull his mind and leave his body permanently exhausted and withered.

We do not have research yet on why some societies think of sex as a pleasure versus a duty, but we do know quite a bit about the conditions under which men will fear sex with women. Relatively few societies express fears as strong as the Mae Enga, but we find evidence of a milder fear of sex in many societies around the world. During planting, sex may spoil the harvest; dreams about sex can bring bad luck; sex before sports may result in losing the game. Carol R. Ember has conducted cross-cultural research to evaluate four explanations of men's fear of sex with women. She limited herself to men's attitudes only because women's views are not often described in ethnographies.

One explanation, suggested by Meggitt on the basis of data from various places in New Guinea, is that men may fear sex with women if they usually obtain wives from their enemies, as the Mae Enga did (along with many other societies in Papua New Guinea's Western Highlands.) On the other hand, fear of sex with women is likely to be absent if marriage is not with traditional enemies (as in the Central Highlands of Papua New Guinea).

A second hypothesis Ember tested was that of Shirley Lindenbaum, who proposed that fear of sex with women may be a cultural device that serves to restrain population growth where resources are endangered. If Lindenbaum is right, fear of sex with women should be found in the presence of population pressure.

Beatrice B. Whiting suggested a third possibility: If men are conflicted about their sexual identity, they are likely to exhibit exaggerated masculine behavior as well as antagonism toward, and fear of, women. We might expect problems of sexual identity where there is an initial unconscious feminine identification and a subsequent (more conscious) identification with men. That sequence is likely where, early in life, boys have almost exclusive contact with mothers who exert almost complete control over them. That situation could lead to an initial feminine identification. When they later become aware that men actually control the society's important resources, boys might shift their identification to men. Accordingly, men's fear of sex with women should be particularly likely where they initially have a cross-sex identification.

The fourth proposal Ember tested was that of William N. Stephens, who suggested that some societies may produce an exaggerated *Oedipus complex*, which in turn is conducive to a fear of sex with women. The idea here is that anxiety about heterosexual sex should emerge where we find an unconscious equation of *mother* with *sex partner*. If a boy's sexual interest in his mother were heightened for some reason, he would be especially frightened because of the incest taboo (fearing retaliation by the father). Under what circumstances might the Oedipus complex be exaggerated? Stephens suggests this might occur where custom frustrates a mother's sexual expression, causing her to redirect some of her sexual interest toward her son. This could happen, for example, where there is a long postpartum sex taboo (a mother avoiding sex for a year or more after she gives birth). But whatever the reason, the closer the relationship between mother and son, and the more contact between them, the more likely his Oedipal impulses will be enhanced, and the more likely he will fear sex with women (generalizing from his fear of sex with his mother).

When Ember tested the predictive value of these four hypotheses cross-culturally, she found support for all four. The more a society marries its enemies, the more likely men will fear sex with women. The more evidence of population pressure (food shortages or famine), the more likely men will be afraid of sex with women. Where mothers sleep closer to their infants than to their husbands *and* live with or near their husbands' families when they marry (a combination that presumably produces conflict over male

sex identity), men tend to fear sex with women. As for the Oedipal interpretation, duration of the postpartum sex taboo does not by itself predict that men will fear sex with
women, but Ember did find that men are likely to fear sex with women in societies where
mothers customarily sleep closer physically (in the same bed or room) to their babies than
to their husbands. Because all of the hypotheses tested were supported, Ember suggests
the following theory to integrate them:

> "Marrying enemies" (with food shortage as a partial cause) creates emotional distance (in-
> cluding sleeping distance) between husbands and wives. This in turn may exaggerate a
> boy's unconscious sexual interest in his mother, which becomes frightening in view of the
> incest taboo. Given the incest taboo, this exaggerated interest may result in a general fear
> of sex with women.

Reanalyzing Ember's data, Michio Kitahara has offered a different interpretation.
He suggests that food shortages may have a more direct effect on men's fear of sex than
Ember supposed; anxiety about food itself may inhibit sexual desire. (The Embers now
speculate that, lacking an adequate diet, people might experience dizziness and weakness
during and after sex, reactions that could lead to the conclusion that sex is dangerous.)
Societies in which men fear sex with women may have considerable stress of one kind or
another. Food shortage is only one kind of stress; there are others. For example, if people find mates in nearby villages with which they are periodically at war, marriage with
women from enemy villages might well promote sexual anxiety. We should keep in mind,
however, that the risk of famine and marriage with enemies are likely to be stressful for
both parties, for the women as well as the men. If Kitahara's theory is right, then, we
would expect both genders to fear heterosexual sex. Unfortunately, we do not yet have
comparative research that might enable us to confirm or refute this theory. One reason
may be that ethnographic accounts are generally deficient about women's thoughts on
sexual attitudes, probably because most of them have been written by men.

Fear of women is not only manifested in reluctance to have sex. The Mae Enga also
believe that menstrual blood is dangerous, that contact with it can "sicken a man and cause
persistent vomiting, turn his blood black, corrupt his vital juices so that his skin darkens
and wrinkles as his flesh wastes, permanently dull his wits, and eventually lead to a slow decline and death." The Onge of Little Andaman are also among those who refrain during
menses, believing that swelling of the arms and legs would follow. Among the Chinese, too,
sex is prohibited during menstruation; women in this state are considered polluting, as they
are for one month after childbirth, when sex would "endanger the health of all concerned."

The notion that menstrual blood is dangerous is actually fairly common around the
world, and most often the danger is to men or to the community at large. Rarely are risks
to women mentioned in ethnographic accounts. This raises the possibility that men's fear
of sex with women, and fear of menstrual blood, may both be part of a more general pattern of husband-wife avoidance and aloofness. It should also be noted that societies in which
sex is enjoyable rather than frightening, and in which marital relationships are likely to be
intimate, are generally also those in which social organization does not center on men. We
will return to the issue of marital intimacy and aloofness later, in our chapter on marital relationships. But first let us shift gears to pursue at greater length a matter only vaguely suggested thus far. At a number of points in this chapter, we noted that societies vary in terms
of how sharply they define different roles for women and men. Just what is the relationship
between sex and social roles, or between them and characteristics of personality? . . .

5 Courtship and Marriage

Going-With: The Role of a Social Form in Early Romance

Don E. Merten

In American culture, the ideal of romantic love (Peele 1988) is nearly as pervasive as it is difficult to realize. For example, Moss and Schwebel (1993) find that "[F]ailure to obtain satisfactory levels of intimacy in a romantic relationship has been identified as the largest category of problem which motivates people to obtain psychotherapy . . . and as the most frequent reason given by couples for their divorce" (p. 31). From accounts of college and high school students, it appears that problems with romance emerge early. Yet in order to examine the initial enculturation into romantic social forms, it is necessary to move further down the educational structure. This article describes the experiences of early adolescents as they "go with" each other during junior high school.

The few ethnographic studies that consider romance usually involve adolescents, since dating is a defining feature of American adolescence and is the most common social form in which romance is pursued. Ethnographic studies tend to focus on late adolescence/college (Holland and Eisenhart 1990; Moffatt 1989) and more commonly on middle adolescence/high school (Canaan 1986; Henry 1965; Schwartz and Merten 1980). Early adolescent romance has seldom been the focus of ethnographic research even though there is evidence that romantic interaction is moving further down the age structure (Roscoe, Diana, and Brooks 1987). A notable exception is the work of Simon, Eder, and Evans (1992) who describe how middle-school girls develop and transmit *feeling norms* regarding romance (see also Eisenhart and Holland 1983; Thorne 1993). Simon and her coauthors (1992), however, do not specifically focus on the *social form* associated with romance, that is, the arrangement that gives meaning to the interaction of individuals who

Author's Note: Funding for this research was provided by National Institute of Mental Health grants MH 33599 and RO-MH 39686. I wish to acknowledge the contributions of my colleagues—especially Drs. Gary Schwartz and Robert Bursik—to the larger study upon which this article draws. My wife, Nina, deserves special thanks for proofreading this and earlier versions of the article.

151

are attracted to each other. Nevertheless, their middle-school girls are involved in a social form the girls refer to as "going together."

This article examines a similar social form, going-with, that is used by students in a junior high school. Going-with is hyphenated to emphasize its integrity as a social form and to highlight its usage. Other terms such as going together, going out, and so forth are less often used variants of going-with. Usually these datinglike social forms are treated as activities. Considered as an activity, going-with is thought to bring two people together whereupon they work out a relationship. Concomitantly, the failure to forge a good relationship is thought to be caused by individual characteristics of the participants (e.g., she was too possessive, he was not attentive). Treating going-with as an activity, however, neglects the role the form itself plays in shaping the interaction and experience of participants. As Hebdige (1979) points out, "Social relations and processes are . . . appropriated by individuals only through the forms in which they are represented to those individuals" (p. 13). By participating in this form, individuals learn about romance—a strongly experienced attraction combined with emotional intimacy—as particular meanings are given to the actions they undertake in the name of going-with somebody. From the descriptions offered by junior high school students, one is struck by the disparity between the emotional energy they put into going-with someone compared to how little emotional return they derive. The cultural construction of this social form, it is argued here, is an important element for understanding the difficulties individuals encounter when going-with each other.

SETTING AND METHOD

The larger context in which going-with is examined is a junior high school in a middle- to upper-middle-class suburb. Located about an hour from Chicago, this suburb has a population of approximately 30,000. Like many such suburbs in this large metropolitan area, it is populated by successful adults who want to see their children match their success. In keeping with this expectation, the community provides an environment that is rich in opportunities for its children to develop their academic, social, and athletic skills. While the school offers a broad array of extracurricular activities, these are also supplemented by community-based activities (Adler and Adler 1994).

This suburb has a half-dozen elementary schools feeding into one junior high school. In turn, the junior high school sends its students to a large well-equipped high school that prepares many of them to attend prestigious colleges. The junior high school houses seventh and eighth grades with an enrollment of over 700 students. Going to junior high school is considered a major transition by parents, students, and teachers. For instance, much of sixth grade is spent communicating to students how different junior high school will be, a warning that seems to be borne out by research (Berndt 1983; Merten 1994; Simmons and Blyth 1987). The transition is viewed as a movement from a neighborhood school to a community school, and from childhood to adolescence. Teachers in junior high school (Schwartz, Merten, and Bursik 1987) expect students to be independent, self-motivated, and responsible for themselves. At the same time, students have many more opportunities to participate in clubs, sports teams, cheerleading, and school dances. School dances are the venue in which the school officially sanctions students' growing romantic interests.

Before presenting students' accounts of going-with, it is necessary to describe briefly how these data were gathered. A two-year longitudinal study followed a cohort of early adolescents as they entered junior high school (seventh grade) through their graduation from the eighth grade. Two ethnographers spent three years interviewing and observing students (the first year was prior to the study cohort's arrival). The ethnographers were young female teachers who received intensive ethnographic training plus extensive weekly supervision from senior researchers. Supervision consisted of reviewing field notes and interviews, identifying future questions to pursue, and discussing current concerns of the ethnographers. Both individuals were from outside the school district and unknown to participants prior to the study. Because they had access to all areas of the school, they were able to observe and talk to students casually in many settings. Being able to observe a wide range of student interaction and activities grounded questions about junior high school life in commonplace events.

Interviews were conducted in a room set aside for that purpose and were open-ended inquiries that sought to elicit the students' views and experiences of their world. Of special importance were the meanings students bestowed on various emic categories, which they used to identify and evaluate their peers. Interviews built upon themselves to provide extended accounts of what was happening in a student's life at home, in school, and especially with peers. The cohort data consisted of over 600 interviews, which were conducted with slightly more than 160 students. Most students were interviewed several times and some more than a dozen times.[1] The interviews were tape-recorded and later transcribed, as were field notes of observations and casual conversations. In order to have ongoing contact with two homeroom groups, the ethnographers each taught one class each semester. Students, as well as teachers and parents, were aware of their dual role in this setting. Despite prior concerns that there might be role conflict, the interviews with students they taught showed no discernible differences in openness or candor from interviews with students who were not in their class.

GOING-WITH AS A SOCIAL FORM

Whyte (1966) states about form that it is "very important and yet tantalizingly subtle" (p. 1). While Whyte is referring to physical form, Simmel's extensive work with social forms also captures their subtlety (see Lawrence 1976). Simmel's (1971) analysis of sociability stands as a classic treatment of how social form shapes behavior and consciousness. For example, he writes that the essence of sociability occurs when external motives and interests fall away and interpersonal interaction pursued for its own sake and its own pleasure. Likewise, in order for a social form like going-with to set the stage for an intimate experience, it is necessary that unrelated interests (e.g., prestige concerns) be held at bay.

Social form is conceptualized here as a culturally created and recognized pattern of interaction. Going-with, as a social form, is the expression of ideas and images about how individuals who are attracted romantically to each other should pursue that attraction. Social forms such as casual dating, steady dating, and engagement are thought to lead to, and to express, varying levels of romantic involvement. These are forms within which symbols having romantic meanings are expected to produce romantic feelings. To these better known forms one can add going-with. Because these forms facilitate the interaction of two individuals who are romantically attracted to each other, to participate in them is to publicly express one's romantic interest.

The transition to junior high school brings with it a set of new expectations about social life. For example, Eckert (1989) reports that at the end of elementary school, "The shift from mixed friendship group to dating was apparently part of the conscious preparation for junior high school" (p. 83). Thorne (1993) too observes the increased importance of girl-boy attraction prior to junior high school by noting that "in the upper grades of elementary school . . . some kids start to publicly affirm themselves as sexual or at least romantic actors. By fifth and especially sixth grades the ritual of 'goin' with' becomes a central activity" (p. 151). Thus romantic interests precede the transition to junior high school for some students. Nevertheless, upon entering junior high school, students feel more compelled to explore datinglike relationships. Simmons and Blyth (1987) find that "[T]he junior high school seventh graders are significantly more likely than K-8 counterparts . . . to report that their peers expect them to be more interested in the opposite sex" p. 233). The anticipation of junior high school and entry into it contributes to the pressure students feel to become involved with an opposite sex peer. In this junior high school, going-with provides the form that allows boys and girls to be romantically involved. In the following sections, various aspects of going-with are described: the establishment of contact with opposite sex peers to whom one is attracted; the relationship of going-with to other peer involvements; the presentation of self that going-with encourages; the role of physical intimacy; and the termination of going-with relationships.

Making Contact

Bringing themselves to take the perceived risks (Hatfield 1984) of making public their feelings of attraction prevents some adolescents from going-with someone. The risks, for example embarrassment, stem from not knowing how one should talk to the person one wants to go-with. When even socially sophisticated students are afraid to initiate contact with a person they want to go-with, unsophisticated students like William find the process especially daunting. When asked if he would call a girl he likes, William replies,

> I don't know. That seems pretty weird calling up somebody, "Hi, this is William"—I would have to have a reason to call her.

Asked how he would feel if she called him, he responds,

> I would be so happy. I would start talking, but I want to know what to talk about. I wouldn't have the slightest idea what to talk about.

William believes that he simply cannot communicate in a ordinary way with someone he wants to go-with. From his perspective, there must be a *special* way of talking and acting that goes beyond routine dialogue and interaction. While he would like to participate in this social form, he expects that going-with demands the use of specific, but as yet largely unknown, discourse in order to participate competently. He cannot just talk to someone because he likes them without risking embarrassment. As William becomes more familiar with the social form of going-with, he will use his friends to initiate contact with a girl he likes.

Some individuals are already aware that friends can help prevent the embarrassment that comes from disclosing attraction that is not mutual. Dancy takes Diana's offer to undertake this task as a sign of friendship.

> Diana just was really nice to me. I liked this one kid and she goes, "Well, don't worry, I'll try to get him to like you." If you like someone and they don't know, you usually have one of your friends call him and say, "Hey, so and so likes you and you should like her. She's really nice." Sometimes it's not good though. They sorta get forced and they don't really like you.

The basis for going-with someone is that one is attracted that person and that person to you—or as students phrase it you "like" each other. Yet the expectation that going-with will produce emotional closeness as two people get to know each other better is seldom realized. Most students find going-with someone to be less than the term implies; there is neither much shared activity (go) nor much sense of relationship (with). A rather typical relationship is described by Grace, who went with Dale during the summer between seventh and eighth grade:

> I went with Dale Walters, that's John's brother. He was really nice and he's really cute. But I didn't go with him for that long. It wasn't like I had a boyfriend because he never called. The only time I saw him was at the pool. He was really shy and I never talked to him.

Unlike Grace, who treats her lack of communication with Dale in a matter-of-fact manner, Christi's ironic tone in describing her relationship with George reflects her awareness of how divergent the image of going-with is from the reality of their relationship.

> Well, I was going out with George. He was really sweet in school. He never called me and he would hardly talk to me. I would go, "Hi, George," and he goes, "Oh, hi, Christi, right?" I'm going, "Yeah, right!" He was just quiet about the whole thing. We went out for two weeks and he never called me.

Christi talks of how shallow her relationship with George is—both with regard to the lack of emotional closeness and also with regard to the many other expectations that accompany going-with, for example, that notes will be exchanged, phone calls made, public acknowledgments extended, and exclusivity observed. However, even when individuals engage in actions that are congruent with the image of going-with, the actions still may lack substance. Brenda indicates as much when she notes, "I tell boys, 'I love you so much. You are such a babe.' It's not true. I say that to everybody I go-with." Thus the importance students bestow on going-with someone frequently belies the rather shallow relationship they share.

Relational Priorities

Despite the widespread desire of students to go-with someone, there are many complications and drawbacks. One that is frequently mentioned is knowing how to fit such a relationship into one's life. Choosing between going-with and other commitments is enough to immobilize some students. Simon and her colleagues (1992) found that making the relationship "important but not everything in life" (p. 33) was a feeling norm that most girls learn. According to Jennifer, boys too need to learn to place going-with alongside their other relationships. She describes her experience:

> I think that he [Jerry] is nice and everything. It's hard to explain. He is really nice at school and everything. But when he is with his friends, he just won't talk to me. I guess that he is just embarrassed or something. Like he doesn't know who to pick from. Like if I'm walking with him in the halls, and if it is just us two, he will talk to me. But if we are in the hall with his friends, he will talk to them.

According to Jennifer, she and Jerry broke up

> Because he said we never talked or anything. We never talked about that we were having problems or anything. We talked and everything after we broke up.

Couples like Jennifer and Jerry have to establish what priority to give going-with relative to their friendship relationships. Furthermore, they have to figure out how to negotiate this issue with both their friends and their partner.

Even if a satisfactory allocation of time has been devised, a relationship may be difficult to sustain. Beth and Scott have been going together for several months and according to Beth have spent a great deal of time "hanging around' with each other at school and outside of school. They expect this because time together symbolizes, to their peers and to themselves, a good relationship, and decreased time together signals problems. Yet as Beth points out, it is necessary to have both friends and a partner:

> Scott wasn't as good as Dan about balancing his outside relationships with his buddies. I think sometimes like with what I'm going through now, that I need my friends more than I need a boyfriend. But if I'm going with someone, I need both 'cause I need somebody to tell, "Oh guess what he did today" and then I need somebody to say, "I love you."

Despite the emphasis going-with places on time spent together, Beth observes that going-with someone is still embedded in the larger social world of friends and peers (Fine 1987). Thus finding a balance when both romantic and friendship relations are constantly changing is a formidable challenge.

Ideal Relationships and Ideal Selves

Having to consciously modify and monitor their behavior when around their partner is a problem frequently mentioned by students. Students indicate that they must be more controlled, polite, sensitive, and mature when with their partners. This constraint on going-with is noted by Rick when asked if it would be difficult to go-with someone in his homeroom.

> Yeah. It would be hard to have one [a girlfriend] in your section because you would have to be on your best behavior all the time. In school, you clown around most of the time.

A classmate of Rick's, Cindy, describes how she would feel going-with someone in her section.

> I could never live with having my boyfriend in the same section with me. Because I'm afraid that he would see me as a jerk or something. You would always have to talk and al-

ways work together. I don't think I could do that with my boyfriend. I would feel so queer. I don't want to give a bad impression or anything, like I'm queer or something. But around my friends, I can act any way that I want to and it doesn't really matter.

Going-with modifies the meaning of activities undertaken with one's partner. For example, one is not just going swimming but is going swimming with someone to whom one is attracted and for whom one's attraction is publicly acknowledged. This makes going-with a *special* peer relationship. As Rick and Cindy suggest, going-with is special insofar as it requires one's best behavior around one's partner; one must present an ideal self. I use the term *ideal* self to refer to what students consider being on their "best behavior" and avoiding behavior that would "embarrass" them. This is a situated self that is connected to this social form and a self that students contrast to their more ordinary selves, which they can display with their close friends. But how does this idealized presentation affect interaction with the person one is going-with?

Even though early adolescents assume that going-with results in getting to know one's partner, it is clear that this form also can impede open communication. Brad, who has gone with a dozen or so girls, compares his relationship with his friend Jane with another friend who is a boy:

> Like Jane Parsons, she's probably my best friend now. Everybody thinks that [she is my girl-friend]. I can talk to her about anything. We just get along real good. We can go places together and just be friends—that's what I like about her. With a boy I could joke around more I guess, but with a girl I guess it's a little bit more serious and you gotta tell her more of your problems, 'cause you can't really tell guys your problems. It just doesn't work that way.

When asked to compare a girlfriend to Jane, a girl who is a friend, Brad went on to say,

> I don't think it's as meaningful really, as it is with just having a regular friend. You can't joke around with a girlfriend. I mean, you never want to embarrass yourself. With Jane, we never get embarrassed in front of each other or anything.

Brad's comments suggest that he is more self-disclosing and open with Jane than with his male friends—even though he jokes more with the latter. He symbolizes his closeness to Jane by saying he can tell her anything and even feels he should tell her his problems.[2] This closeness leads their friends to conclude that they are going-with each other, because the relationship that Brad has with Jane is what going-with someone is *supposed* to be like. Their relationship also makes clear that early adolescents are capable of establishing emotional intimacy and can do so with members of the opposite sex. He is least open and least himself around his girlfriend, the person he is going-with. Brad links his guarded behavior around his girlfriend to his concern with embarrassing himself in her presence.

Even though Brad and Jane achieved significant closeness as friends, the shift from friendship to going-with often alters the interpersonal dynamic and makes the relationship less close. Dancy tells of her experience in this regard:

> Sometimes it is not that good if you know each other too well. Sometimes I'm too good of friends with some guys to probably ever go with them. I would feel weird. If you do go with them, it is like you ignore each other and it is like, "We were such good friends

before, what changed?" That was how it was with me and Marc last year. 'Cause we were really good friends and we were in the same section. He asked me out and I was embarrassed and I wasn't like that before.

Despite going-with's various problems, it occasionally produces a relationship that far exceeds the experience of most students. Sarah and Ron have such a relationship. Sarah is a popular cheerleader who takes going-with a boy seriously. Her relationships have much greater longevity than those of her peers—something of which she is proud. Her enthusiasm for the boys she goes-with is obvious in her interviews:

> Ron is a massive babe! He is such a babe! I love him sooo much. We have been going out for four months and three weeks. That's pretty good, at least I think so.

She goes on to say,

> Last night when I was talking to Ron, I asked him if he thought we would go out for longer than a year and he said, "God yes! A lot longer!" I was so happy, then he goes, "I really like you a lot and I'm not going to break up with you." He is so sweet! I really honestly, truly, totally love him a lot, lot, lot; that is the truth. Then I asked him if he thought that since he got mad at me, that we had gotten closer and he said "yes." He is so nice. When we usually talk, we don't really say anything too exciting. But this week we've really been talking about feelings and stuff. He's been exceptionally nice to me.

Sarah's account of her relationship with Ron emphasizes her high evaluation of him as a "babe" and repeatedly characterizes him as "sweet" and "nice." She is especially pleased and happy when he talks about how he feels regarding their relationship. However, Ron is seldom so forthcoming. Sarah observes,

> Sometimes I get really mad because he just sits there. I always say stuff and I feel like he doesn't even care what I say. It is like, "Will you shut up Sarah." I ask him everyday, How was school? "It's ok." How is football? "Why?" I don't know, I'm just asking. "It was ok." That is exactly how he talks. . . . Sometimes we talk about things that are important but not a lot.

Even though Sarah works assiduously at going-with Ron, and even though she emphasizes the importance of communication, it is not always easy to get Ron to participate. While she values talking about "important" things, it is difficult, at times, to talk about even everyday occurrences. Going-with does not seem to promote communication between individuals even when the relationship is outstanding by junior high school standards. Given the expectations of going-with, however, long-term relationships present their own problems.

Physical Intimacy

Besides the emotional intimacy that individuals seek from going-with someone, there is also the matter of physical intimacy. In this junior high school, most physical intimacy is referred to in terms of the "bases." Students refer to degrees of physical intimacy by using a baseball metaphor—first base involves kissing; second base refers to petting above the waist ("going up the shirt"); third base involves petting below the waist ("going down the pants"); home refers to sexual intercourse. It is worth noting that even though both males and females routinely use these references, they do so only when describing what males do to females.

The degree of physical intimacy is expected to correspond roughly to the length of time two individuals have been going together. For example, Sandy says, "If you go out real long like me and Kyle, it is better. 'Cause you don't feel like a slut. You get closer and everything." Generally it is acceptable for a girl to go to "second" if she has been going-with a boy for a couple of months. The acceptability of going to "third" is less clear: no one seems to think going to "home" is acceptable, even though some students have. For the most part, girls say that they are the recipients of physical intimacy. The following account is an exception—Beth describes her actions with the boy she is going-with:

> I gave him a handjob, it was like I really didn't mind or anything. It was after one of the basketball games, behind the garbage thing [dumpster). We had our arms around each other and were walking around and talking and then we were alone. We just started looking at each other and then we started making out and then . . .

The tone of Beth's comments is similar to that used by other girls when describing physical intimacy: trepidation blended with matter-of-factness. She continues:

> I didn't mind. We were both kind of afraid someone would walk in, it's kind of embarrassing. But I didn't necessarily want to get it over with.

In interviews, students seldom volunteer the details of their sexual experiences or those of their close friends. This discretion is not accorded individuals who engage in sexual activities with someone they are not going-with or who do so in short-term relationships. Such behaviors provide the basis for gossip and censure. Sarah describes a situation in which her classmates, Jenny and Karen, tell about their exploits:

> They tell Laura and I something different everyday that has happened to them. They must think that we do all that stuff too. But god, we don't! Jenny likes Dan and somebody told her that he likes her, but he really doesn't. . . . I heard that she let him do what he did because she likes him—he fingered her. I mean they weren't going out. If you've been going with someone for a long while, then I guess it's ok, but I don't know. It's pretty bad if you aren't even going out. But it's not just Jenny, it's Karen too. She's just like Jenny, but she's usually going out with the guy. But they usually don't go out for a really long time—maybe two weeks, that's not long at all.

Sarah makes the above evaluation even though she has gone to "third" with her boyfriend Ron; she is not against physical intimacy in principle. Jenny and Karen, however, are far from the most notorious of the junior high girls. That dubious honor goes to girls who engage in types of intimacy that most of their female peers think of as perverse with boys they barely know. They, using Canaan's (1986) term, engage in "kinky sex." The latter removes physical intimacy from romance by placing it *both* outside going-with and also outside the conventional expressions of physical intimacy.

Finally, the expectation that sexual intimacy is part of going-with is enough to discourage some individuals from participating in this form. Louise is vocal about her disapproval of what some of her peers do. She offers the following comments when asked what it takes to be like the girls who go-with someone:

> Let boys touch private parts, which is very gross. You should see them in class, they are so bad. They go up to girls and they go like that [touching buttocks or breasts]. Lisa and I look at each other and go, "Oh, how sick." We just don't want any part of that. It's so babyish; I just don't see any purpose in it.

Louise and early adolescents who openly disapprove of the sexual behavior involved in going-with consider such actions as "baby-ish" (i.e., these individuals lack the self-control associated with maturity). The peers Louise characterizes as babies, in turn, return the insult by pointing out that her compliance to adult expectations makes her the baby. In contesting the meaning of going-with, Louise finds very little peer support for her interpretation.

Conflict and Breaking Up

In junior high school, breaking up experiences are as frequent as going-with someone. Reasons given for breaking up usually entail violating the form's expectations, such as failing to observe exclusivity by being romantically involved with more than one person. When a relationship begins to dissolve, the process is frequently ambiguous. Participants, therefore, look for signs that a breakup is in the offing so they can act first. Sandy identifies signs of a weakening relationship:

> When they don't call you or when they don't wait for you in the hall, that's what usually happens. This is what Beth tells me—that when they get off the phone, she'll go, "I like you so much" and she'll talk real sensitive to him and he'll just go, "yeah" and he used to say it back. They used to be real close.

Reciprocal sensitivity in communication is a potent symbol of a couple's openness to each other and a sign that the relationship is going well. A decline in reciprocity or effort to be together generally signals problems and the weakening of the relationship. Because the difficulties are thought to reside in the other individual, breaking up seldom provides usable insight as to how to make one's next relationship better.

The difficulty couples encounter in going-with extends beyond specific conflicts. Beth echoes a common refrain as to how various dissatisfactions of one partner affect the other and ultimately threaten the relationship. She describes what it is like for her when Scott is in a bad mood:

> Whenever he's upset, I always wonder what I did. Whenever he's mad at something, he kind of takes it out on me, by just not talking to me. I'll talk to him and he'll just shrug his shoulders. I mean if I'm going with somebody, I'd want them to care whether or not I was upset.

Beth tends to assume that Scott is mad at *her* when he is upset. Moreover, she believes that rebuffing her attempts to console him violates what individuals *should* do when they are going-with each other. Beth also thinks that her contributions to the relationship far exceed those of Scott. She compares the two:

> I give more than enough. [He gives] nothing practically. Nothing now at least. I use to write him a note and he'd write back. Now I write him a note, [and] a note, [and] a note, and I don't get anything back.

Scott at this point has reduced his participation and, as Beth describes it, is contributing nothing. Despite Scott's frustration with the relationship, he seems unable to break up with Beth. She says,

> Monday night Scott called me up and said that he just wanted to be friends. He said that he was sick of trying to make our relationship work and that he was sick of everything. I go, "I know, so am I." He goes, "You know, you make me feel real good" and he said it sarcastically, 'cause I was a little upset. What does he want of me? So then Tuesday morning he calls me at 7:00 and says he was sorry and asked me out again. So I said, "Yeah." So then Tuesday night he called me and broke up with me.

Whereas it is not altogether clear what it means to make going-with "work," it is very clear that Scott feels he has been committed to their relationship and tells Beth one reason for his dissatisfaction.

> He said, "There's so many things going on in my life right now that I can't give you my full attention" and then I go, "I don't want your full attention but just some of it." He goes, "Well I feel bad when I don't give it to you."

For individuals like Beth and Scott who take going-with seriously, the form's expectations make it difficult to sustain a relationship. As Scott understands going-with, he needs to devote his full-time attention to the person he is going-with. Honoring this expectation leads to experiencing the relationship as all or nothing. Thus he feels bad when he does not live up to the form's demands.

DISCUSSION

The most striking characteristic of going-with is the superficial, even empty, quality of the interaction. For every emotionally open relationship like Sarah and Ron's, there are perhaps fifty like Christi and George that are largely without emotional substance. Nevertheless, these junior high school students are beginning their "education in romance" (Holland and Eisenhart 1990) by going-with someone. The question is, What are they learning from participating in this social form? In other words, regardless of whether they are "ready" for romance, they are learning something about a cultural domain in which they are likely to participate for many years. Therefore the role this social form plays in their early enculturation requires further examination.

Going-with as a social form serves as both a "model of" and "model for" romantic intimacy (Geertz 1973). That is, participation both results from and symbolizes the attraction two individuals have for each other and in that respect going-with serves as a model *of* that attraction. On the other hand, going-with serves as a model *for* romance insofar as it provides expectations as to what people who are attracted to each other should do to express and develop that attraction. Romantic involvement between junior high school students is therefore mediated by going-with as a model *of* and *for* romantic intimacy. Students who are attracted to each other and seek intimacy are obliged to act in terms of this culturally identified form or risk encountering unfavorable evaluations of their actions.

Going-with is also a symbol that takes its meaning from the larger context in which it is found. Its primary contextual meaning arises from junior high school as a transitional institution and especially as a move from childhood to adolescence. Because a quintessential social feature of adolescence is dating, those who go-with someone see themselves, and are seen by their peers, as no longer children. Moreover, their claim to adolescent status is indirectly strengthened by their few peers, like Louise, who object to going-with. Because most of these latter students are *not* attuned to junior high school culture and are considered childish, their objection to going-with enhances its salience as a symbol of adolescence.

When going-with is used largely as a symbol of adolescence, it subverts the romantic meaning of this form. At the very least, a form that finds its primary meaning in romance is being used for another purpose.[3] That is, the pressure to express one's "adolescent-ness" takes precedence over attraction as the reason to go-with someone. Thus the contextual meaning (transition) of going-with and its use to enhance one's identity as an adolescent diminish its effectiveness as a romantic social form by reversing the process that Simmel (1971) considered necessary to realize a form's essence: instead of stripping away concerns and interests extraneous to intimacy, extraneous concerns such as one's identity as an adolescent are being added. This results in mixed meanings that are difficult to disentangle.

If individuals, as Hebdige (1979) suggests, appropriate social relations and social processes through the form in which they are embedded, then the form as it is used to foster intimate relationships should be the focus of inquiry. Go-with as a form is constituted by the *expectations* that constitute it and the meanings that these expectations carry. A key expectation is going-with's insistence on exclusivity (i.e., one is permitted to go-with only one person at a time). As an integral part of going-with, exclusivity shapes the interaction between early adolescents in a number of ways. For example, exclusivity plays an important role in legitimating behavior that occurs within the going-with form, that when undertaken outside of it is strongly disparaged. Reiss (1973) notes that "Western society has for centuries been developing an association of sexual behavior with mutual affection" (p. 293). Since in junior high school, mutual affection is expected to result in going-with someone, to engage in physical intimacy outside this form is to break this important cultural association. The reverse, however, is also true in the sense that going-with entails an expectation of intimacy—both emotional and physical. To not engage in physical intimacy is to risk being labeled "cold" or "queer."

In addition, because going-with becomes one's primary peer relationship—at least from the standpoint of visibility and peer interest—considerable pressure is exerted on the relationship. The pressure results from the critical peer scrutiny that focuses on the single individual whom one is going-with. More importantly, by going-with only one person, expectations of this social form are activated any time the two people encounter each other. It is not that two people are going-with each other *only* when they are doing "datelike" things together (e.g., going to a school dance with each other), but also when they are in class together, see each other in the lunchroom, or pass each other in the hall. In this respect, the exclusivity of going-with has the effect of making it an encompassing relationship—one that is largely unbounded by time, place, or activity. Thus the exclusivity that the social form demands produces performance pressures insofar as individuals experience themselves and their relationships as continually under scrutiny.

Another expectation of going-with is that the two people engage each other as ideal selves. Time and again students mentioned the difficulty of being around the person they were going-with because they had to be on their best behavior. This is why many students found it unthinkable to go-with someone in their homeroom (i.e., peers they are with most of the day). The idealization of self in going-with has significant implications for how students interact. First, according to students, it discourages them from being "themselves" and acting spontaneously. Whereas spontaneity is an important symbolic feature of adolescence, having to control carefully one's behavior diminishes this aspect of adolescence. In addition, feeling compelled to present an ideal version of oneself does not allow the two people to come to know each other as the complex individuals they are.

Camarena, Sarigiani, and Petersen (1990) point out that intimacy can develop along two paths: shared experience and self-disclosure. Given the limits on what early adolescents can do together or the places they can go together, the development of intimacy by sharing experiences is not promising. However, self-disclosure is possible because students have ample opportunity to communicate with each other. Yet feeling compelled to present an ideal self largely precludes the sort of self-disclosure and openness that leads to intimacy. Thus going-with includes expectations that impede the development of emotional intimacy between its early adolescent participants. As long as one has to enact an ideal self rather than less ideal self-representations, there seems to be little basis for self-disclosure and therefore intimacy. For going-with to contribute to intimacy, it must protect the disclosure of less than ideal selves, not demand that individuals present ideal selves to their partners.

To consider an alternative source (i.e., other than the form itself) for the difficulties participants experience in going-with, one might look to the earlier antagonisms and estrangements between boys and girls in elementary school (Thorne 1993). Even though agonistic responses can be observed around going-with, it seems that they do not so much cause problems but rather represent a response that is taken when going-with does not succeed. When relationships dissolve, both boys and girls rally around their same-sexed friends and castigate the ex-partners for the breakup. It would be, however, a mistake to locate the main source of going-with's difficulties in prior male/female antagonisms. While the earlier gender antagonisms are far from optimal preparation for establishing closeness and intimacy between boys and girls who now seek to go-with each other, the fact that intimacy occurs between boys and girls as friends (recall Brad and Jane) suggests that the earlier antagonisms do not preclude intimacy. Nor is intimacy between friends a guarantee that going-with each other will sustain that intimacy much less enhance it (recall Dancy and Marc). Thus the form itself qua its expectations, it is argued here, is the primary source of the difficulties students experience in going-with relationships.

Another more speculative interpretation for the problems of going-with suggests that the emptiness of going-with is *not a failure* of the form even though the interaction does not live up to the ideals of romantic imagery. Instead of a failure, the emptiness might be an adaptation to the circumstances in which mainstream Americans find themselves. For example, Bellah and his coauthors (1985) point to the prominence of "empty selves" in America as being somewhat adaptive in a highly mobile and rapidly changing society. It is not much of a stretch to suggest that empty selves may find empty forms of romance acceptable, even if not entirely satisfying. Edward Sapir (1963), in formulating his concept of "spurious culture," and Jules Henry (1965), in describing how culture can be used against its carriers, have both provided insights into how actions that are contrary to espoused values exist in society. One can wonder if pushing romantic forms further and further down the age structure contributes to the generation of spurious culture and the creation of empty selves participating in empty forms.

The above speculation is consistent with the nature of social forms as conceptualized by Hebdige (1979), who argues that social forms are "by no means transparent. They are shrouded in 'common sense' which simultaneously validates and mystifies them" (p. 13). This formulation fits going-with as it is pursued by junior high school students. Their commonsense interpretation assumes that going-with should lead to developing an intimate relationship and in those cases where such a relationship is achieved, the efficacy of the form is validated. Concomitantly, when the emptiness of a relationship can no longer be denied or overlooked, the blame is placed on the incompatibility of the individuals—thus mystifying and obscuring the role of the form. Thus to neglect the role that social forms have in constituting romantic relationships may also obscure a source of their difficulties. While it is not possible to say what the long-term effect of early enculturation into going-with is, it is likely that achieving intimacy in future relationships will occur despite this form, not because of it.

Notes

1. Personal names in the text are pseudonyms and are used to protect the confidentiality of the data.
2. Fischer (1981) reports that late adolescent females socialize their boyfriends into intimate relationships based on intimate relationships with their same-sex friends. See also Schwartz and Merten (1980).
3. Such distortion is not uncommon since one routinely sees romantic images used to sell a broad array of commercial products.

References

Adler, P. A., and P. Adler. 1994. Social reproduction and the corporate other: The institutionalization of afterschool activities. *Sociological Quarterly* 35:309–28.
Bellah, R., R. Madsen, W. Sullivan, A. Swidler, and S. Tipton. 1985. *Habits of the heart: Individualism and commitment in American life*. New York: Harper & Row.
Berndt, T. J. 1983. Correlates and causes of sociometric status in childhood: A commentary on six current studies of popular, rejected, and neglected children. *Merrill-Palmer Quarterly* 29:439–48.
Camarena, P. M., P. A. Sarigiani, and A. C. Petersen. 1990. Gender-specific pathways to intimacy in early adolescence. *Journal of Youth and Adolescence* 19:19–32.
Canaan, J. 1986. Why a "slut" is a "slut": Cautionary tales of midde-class teenage girls' morality. In *Symbolizing America*, edited by H. Varenne, 184–208. Lincoln: University of Nebraska Press.
Eckert, P. 1989. *Jocks and burnouts: Social categories and identity in high school*. New York: Teachers College Press.

Eisenhart, M. A., and D. C. Holland. 1983. Learning from peers: The role of peer groups in the cultural transmission of gander. *Human Organization* 42:321–2.

Fine, G. A. 1987. *With the boys: Little league baseball and pro-adolescent culture.* Chicago: University of Chicago Press.

Fischer, J. L. 1981. Transitions in relationship style from adolescence to young adulthood. *Journal of Youth and Adolescence* 10:11–23.

Geertz, C., ed. 1973. Religion as a cultural system. In *The interpretation of cultures*, 87–125. New York: Basic Books.

Hatfield, E. 1984. The dangers of intimacy. In *Communication, intimacy, and close relationships*, edited by V. Derlega, 207–20. New York: Academic Press.

Hebdige, D. 1979. *Subculture: The meaning of style.* New York: Methuen.

Henry, J. 1965. *Culture against man.* New York: Random House.

Holland, D., and M. Eisenhart. 1990. *Educated in romance: Women, achievement, and college culture.* Chicago: University of Chicago Press.

Lawrence, P. A. 1976. *Georg Simmel: Sociologist and European.* New York: Barnes and Noble.

Merten, D. E. 1994. The cultural context of aggression: The transition to junior high school. *Anthropology and Education Quarterly* 25:29–43.

Moffatt, M. 1989. *Coming of age in New Jersey: College and American culture.* New Brunswick, NJ: Rutgers University Press.

Moss, B. F., and A. I. Schwebel. 1993. Defining intimacy in romantic relationships. *Family Relations* 42:31–7.

Peele, S. 1988. Fools for love: The romantic ideal, psychological theory, and addictive love. In *The psychology of love*, edited by R. J. Stemberg and M. L. Barnes, 159–88. New Haven, CT: Yale University Press.

Reiss, I. 1973. Sexual codes in teen-age culture. In *The sociology of youth: Evolution and revolution*, edited by H. Silverstein, 292–302. New York: Macmillian.

Roscoe, B., M. S. Diana, and R. H. Brooks II. 1987. Early, middle, and late adolescents' views on dating and factors influencing partner selection. *Adolescence* 22:59–68.

Sapir, E. 1963. Culture, genuine and spurious. In *Selected writings of Edward Sapir in language, culture, and personality*, edited by D. G. Mandelbaum, 308–31. Berkeley: University of California Press.

Schwartz, G. H., and D. E. Merten. 1980. *Love and commitment.* Beverly Hills, CA: Sage.

Schwartz, G. H., D. E. Marten, and R. J. Bursik. 1987. Teaching styles and performance values in junior high school: The impersonal, nonpersonal, and personal. *American Journal of Education* 95:346–70.

Simmel, G. 1971. Sociability. In *Georg Simmel: On individuality and social forms*, edited by D. N. Levine, 127–40. Chicago: University of Chicago Press.

Simmons, R. G., and D. A. Blyth. 1987. *Moving into adolescence: The impact of pubertal change and school context.* New York: Aldine de Gruyter.

Simon, R. W., D. Eder, and C. Evans. 1992. The development of feeling norms underlying romantic love among adolescent females. *Social Psychological Quarterly* 55:29–46.

Thorne, B. 1993. *Gender play: Girls and boys in school.* New Brunswick, NJ: Rutgers University Press.

Whyte, L. L. 1966. *Aspects of form: A symposium on form in nature and art*, edited by L. L. Whyte. Bloomington: Indiana University Press.

■ READING 13

The Future of Marriage

Frank F. Furstenberg, Jr.

It's clear that the institution of family is undergoing a major overhaul. Perhaps you've recently been to a wedding where the bride and groom have invited their former spouses to join the festivities. Or maybe a family member told you that your 37-year-old unmarried cousin is pregnant by artificial insemination. Or you heard that your 75-year-old widowed grandfather just moved in with his 68-year-old woman friend. To those of us who grew up in the 1950s, the married-couple family is beginning to look like the Model T Ford.

Public concern over changes in the practice of marriage is approaching hysteria. An avalanche of books and articles declares that the American family is in a severe state of crisis. Yet little agreement exists among experts on what the crisis is about, why it has occurred, or what could be done to restore confidence in matrimony. I believe that the current situation falls somewhere between those who embrace the changes with complete sanguinity and an increasingly vocal group who see the meltdown of the so-called traditional family as an unmitigated disaster.

Social scientists agree that we have seen a startling amount of change in nuptial practices in the past half century. The shift is producing an especially striking contrast from the 1940s, because the period just after World War II was a time of remarkable domestication. The post-war period followed several decades of turbulence in marriage patterns initiated by rapid urbanization during World War I, and the Great Depression.

Many of the complaints about family life in the 1990s sound an awful lot like those voiced in the 1950s, an era we look upon with nostalgia. We often forget that the current gold standard of family life—the family built upon an intimate marital relationship—was regarded with great suspicion when it made its debut. The middle-class nuclear family that became the norm at mid-century was a stripped-down version of the extended families of previous decades. Kingsley Davis observed that a host of social ills could be traced to this new form of family: " . . . The family union has been reduced to its lowest common denominator—married couple and children. The family aspect of our culture has become couple-centered with only one or two children eventually entering the charmed circle," he wrote.

Ernest Burgess, one of the most respected sociologists of his generation, wrote in 1953 that urbanization, greater mobilization, individualization, increased secularization, and the emancipation of women had transformed the family from an institution based on law and custom to one based on companionship and love. Despite believing that the changes taking place in the family were largely beneficial to society, Burgess acknowledged that enormous pressure would be placed on the marital relationship to meet new expectations for intimacy. Burgess and Davis correctly predicted that divorce would rise because of the tremendous strain placed on couples to manage the growing demands for congeniality and cooperation.

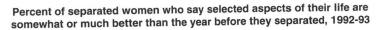

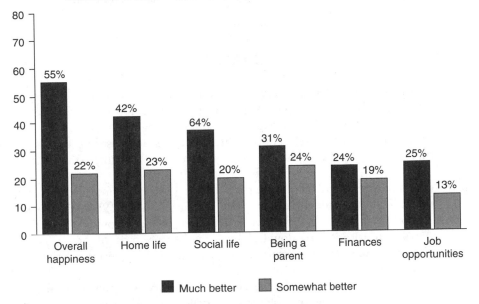

FIGURE 1 *The Trade-Offs of Ending a Marriage.*
Recently separated women are more likely to perceive improvement in their parenting and social lives than in their financial well-being. *Note:* Separated women are those who split from their husbands since the last survey was taken in 1987–88.

Source: National Survey of Families and Households, 1992–93.

Marriage is not in immediate danger of extinction, though. In 1960, 94 percent of women had been married at least once by age 45. The share in 1994 was 91 percent. In other words, the vast majority of Americans are still willing to try marriage at some point. What has changed from the 1960s is when, how, and for how long.

The median age at marriage has risen from a low of 20.3 for women and 22.5 for men in 1960, to 24.5 for women and 26.7 for men in 1994. The proportion of women never married by their late 20s tripled from a historical low of 11 percent in 1960 to a high of 33 percent in 1993. The divorce rate among ever-married women more than doubled between the early 1960s and late 1980s, although it has since leveled off.

The number of children living in married-couple families dropped from 88 percent in 1960 to 69 percent in 1994. Divorce plays a role in this decline, but much of the rise in single-parent families results from the sharp increase in nonmarital childbearing. The proportion of births occurring out of wedlock jumped from 5 percent in 1960 to 31 percent in 1993. While some of these births occur among couples who are living together, the vast majority are to single parents.

The increase in single-parenthood due to divorce and out-of-wedlock births may be the most telling sign that Americans are losing confidence in marriage. Ironically, some of today's most vitriolic political rhetoric is directed toward gay couples who want the right to marry, just as the cultural legitimacy of marriage has been declining.

WHAT WE GET OUT OF MARRIAGE

What has transformed societal attitudes toward marriage so that young people delay it, older people get out of it, and some skip it altogether? Before attempting to answer these questions, a few cautions are in order. Demographers and sociologists, like climatologists, are pretty good at short-term forecasts, but have little ability to forecast into the distant future. In truth, no one can predict what marriage patterns will look like 50 years from now.

Virtually no one foresaw the "marriage rush" of the 1940s that preceded the baby boom. And few predicted the sudden decline of the institution in the 1960s. If our society alternates periods of embracing and rejecting marriage, then we could be poised on the cusp of a marriage restoration. It's doubtful, however, because most of the forces that have worked to reduce the strength of marital bonds are unlikely to reverse in the near future.

The biggest stress on marriage in the late 20th century is a transition from a clearcut gender-based division of labor to a much less focused one. For a century or more, men were assigned to the work force and women to domestic duties. This social arrangement is becoming defunct. Women are only moderately less likely than men to be gainfully employed. Even women with young children are more likely than not to be working. In 1994, 55 percent of women with children under age 6 were currently employed, compared with 19 percent in 1960.

Women's participation in the labor force has reduced their economic dependency on men. The traditional bargain struck between men and women—financial support in exchange for domestic services—is no longer valid. Men now expect women to help bring home the bacon. And women expect men to help cook the bacon, feed the kids, and clean up afterward. In addition, the old status order that granted men a privileged position in the family is crumbling.

These dramatic alterations in the marriage contract are widely endorsed in theory by men and women alike. The share of both who say their ideal marriage is one in which spouses share household and work responsibilities has increased since the 1970s, according to the 1995 Virginia Slims Opinion Poll. Yet in practice, moves toward gender equality have come with a price. Both men and women enter marriage with higher expectations for interpersonal communication, intimacy, and sexual gratification. If these expectations are not met, they feel freer than they once did to dissolve the relationship and seek a new partner.

Being out of marriage has its downside, too, of course. About four in ten recently separated women say they are worse off financially than they were while married, according to the 1992–93 National Survey of Families and Households. This longitudinal study asked women who separated from their husbands since the previous survey in 1987–88 to evaluate several aspects of their lives. At the same time, 43 percent of separated women say their finances are better than during marriage.

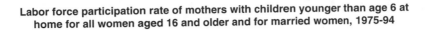

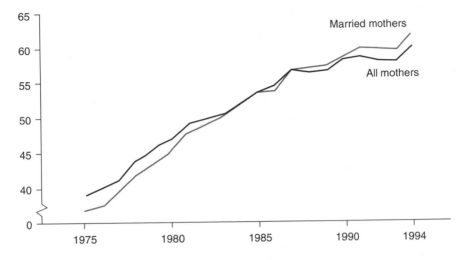

FIGURE 2   *Mom Learns to Juggle.*
Married mothers of preschoolers are more likely than all mothers to be in the labor force.
Source: Bureau of Labor Statistics.

Ending an unhappy marriage obviously brings about other positive changes. If it didn't, people wouldn't divorce. Being a single parent isn't easy. Yet more than half of separated women say that being a parent is better than before their split-up; 52 percent say care of children is better. Sixty-five percent say their overall home life is better, and 49 percent say their leisure time has improved. This may not mean they have more leisure time than while married, but perhaps the quality of that time is more fulfilling.

The increase in the share of women who work is not the only reason why Americans readily leave marriages that don't suit them. Legal reform and social trends have made divorce and nonmarital childbearing easier and more acceptable. Safe, affordable contraception enables couples to engage in sex outside of marriage with minimal risk of pregnancy. Women's college-enrollment rates have risen sharply in the past two decades, while public policies and societal attitudes have helped increase their involvement in politics and government. These changes have spurred women to greater autonomy. Each has affected marriage in a different way, but they have all worked in concert toward the same result: to make marriage less imperative and more discretionary.

Some Americans vigorously object to this "take-it-or-leave-it" approach to marriage on moral grounds, hoping to reverse the course of recent history by restoring "traditional" family values. Yet changes in the practice of marriage are not peculiar to the U.S. The decline of marriage as it was practiced in the 1940s in the United States has occurred in virtually all Western societies.

MARRIAGE AS A LUXURY ITEM

The rise of delayed marriage, divorce, and out-of-wedlock childbearing disturbs the moral sensibilities of many observers. Others may not object on moral grounds, but they fear that the byproducts of intimate relationships—children—are no longer safeguarded by the family. Their fears are well-founded. A great deal of research shows that children are disadvantaged by our society's high level of marital flux.

A wealth of data shows that married men and women have lower incidences of alcohol related problems and other health risks than do divorced and widowed people. Men especially seem to enjoy health benefits from marriage. Experts believe this is because wives often monitor health behavior, and because marriage provides incentives for men to avoid high-risk behaviors.

Marriage gives all parties involved an economic boost. In fact, stable marriages could be perpetuating the growing division in American society between the haves and have-nots. Marriage, quite simply, is a form of having. Children growing up with both of their biological parents are likely to be more educated, and to have better job skills and a more secure sense of themselves. Thus, they enter adulthood with greater chances of success and a greater likelihood of finding a mate with a similar profile.

This does not mean, however, that children are better off with married parents. Some think that men and women today lack the capacity to sacrifice for children as they did a generation ago. Maybe they do. But if sacrifice means remaining in stressful, hostile, and abusive environment, it's not necessarily worth it. Even so, I doubt if failure to compromise one's own needs for the good of others is the main reason why fewer couples are getting married and staying married.

In my research on low-income families, I hear men and women talking about the virtues of marriage. Nearly all endorse the idea that children are better off when they grow up with both biological parents, although this is probably said in the context of assuming that the marriage is a "good" one.

Plenty of young people have seen "bad" marriages as they've grown up, which has given them an understandable fear of committing themselves and children to such a situation. "Most of my girlfriends, they got married when they was 20," says one woman. "Now they divorced. They got children. Fathers don't do nothing for them, so then, it was a toss-up. Either to go ahead and start out on the wrong foot or get on the right foot and then fall down." In other words, if you plan to have children, it may not matter too much whether you get married first, because you may not get anything out of the marriage, either financially or emotionally.

Although women may not depend on men's economic support as much as they used to, they still expect something out of the bargain. Young adults in low-income populations feel that they don't have the wherewithal to enter marriage. It's as if marriage has become a luxury consumer item, available only to those with the means to bring it off. Living together or single-parenthood has become the budget way to start a family. Most low-income people I talk to would prefer the luxury model. They just can't afford it.

Marriage is both a cause and a consequence of economic, cultural, and psychological stratification in American society. The recent apparent increase in income inequality in the U.S. means that the population may continue to sort itself between those who are eligible for marriage and a growing number who are deemed ineligible to marry.

There is little to suggest that marriage will become more accessible and enduring in the next century. The unpredictability and insecurity of the job market is likely to have an unsettling effect on marriage in the short term by making marriage a risky proposition, and in the long term by generating larger numbers of people who are the products of unstable family situations. Men are making some progress in taking on household tasks, including child care, but women still shoulder most of the burden in families, causing continued marital stress.

While this may sound unduly pessimistic, marriage may change for the better if people are committed to making the institution work, albeit in a new format. The end of the 20th century may eventually be recognized as the period when this new form of family—the symmetrical marriage—first appeared.

It's no longer noteworthy to see a man pushing a stroller or for preschoolers to be just as curious about mommy's job as daddy's. As with many social trends, well-educated couples appear to be leading the way in developing marriages based on equal sharing of economic and family responsibilities. It may be a little easier for them, too, because they are more likely to have the resources to hire people to do the things they choose not to do themselves.

FIGURE 3   *The Perfect Family, 1974–95.*
Both men and women are more likely now than 20 years ago to say an egalitarian marriage is ideal, but they are also more likely to favor alternatives to marriage.
Source: Virginia Slims Opinion Poll.

The move toward symmetry may be more challenging for average Americans of more modest means. Couples who work split shifts because they can't afford child care may be sharing the economic and household load, but they don't spend much time with their spouses.

Single parents who have no one with whom to share the load might have little sympathy for couples who argue about whose turn it is to do the dishes, but at least they are spared the arguing. Single people supporting themselves may feel that their finances are strapped, but when a married person loses his or her job, more than one person is adversely affected.

I am often struck by the fact that we have generous ways—both public and private—of aiding communities beset by natural disasters. Yet we do practically nothing for the same communities when a private industry abandons them, or when their young people can't find work, no matter how hard they look. Restoring marriage to an institution of enduring, compassionate relationships will require more than sanctimonious calls for traditional, communitarian, and family values. We should back up our words with resources. This includes moving toward a society that offers secure, remunerative jobs, as well as better child-care options and more flexible schedules so people can accept those jobs. Otherwise, the institution of marriage as we knew it in this century will in the 21st century become a practice of the privileged. Marriage could become a luxury item that most Americans cannot afford.

■ READING 14

Few Good Men: Why Poor Mothers Stay Single

Kathryn Edin

It is no secret that the institution of marriage is in trouble. The median age at first marriage is at its highest since the United States began keeping reliable statistics: 24 for women and 26 for men. Nearly six of every 10 new marriages will end in divorce, and the propensity to remarry has also declined. Though these trends cut across race, ethnic, and class lines, poor adults from disadvantaged minority groups marry and remarry far less than others.

Whether these trends are a cause for concern or celebration is in the eye of the beholder. Some happily take them as an indication that women can now survive without men who beat them, abuse their children, or are otherwise difficult to live with. Others lament the moral effect on the fabric of American society. Still others worry because of the strong association between growing up with a single parent and a host of negative outcomes for children. Sara McLanahan and Gary Sandefur's work reveals that half the disadvantage these children face reflects the poverty so often associated with single parenthood (almost 50 percent of all unmarried mothers have family incomes below the poverty line); the other half reflects such factors as lower parental involvement and supervision, and greater residential mobility in mother-only families. Why, then, do low-income women continue to have and raise children outside marriage, in the face of these daunting circumstances?

In 1990 I began publishing the results of a study of low-income single mothers that showed it was nearly impossible for these women to make ends meet on either a welfare check or a low-wage job [see Kathryn Edin and Christopher Jencks, "The Real Welfare Problem," *TAP*, Spring 1990]. Drawing data from in-depth multiple interviews with nearly 400 low-income single mothers in four U.S. cities, my research collaborator Laura Lein and I documented large monthly budget deficits for single mothers, whether on welfare or in low-wage employment. Even though they were clever at devising strategies to make up their budget shortfalls, these strategies took a great deal of time and energy; they were highly unstable and sometimes illegal. The women's situations resembled a continually unraveling patchwork quilt. Because of the budget gaps and the instability of the strategies used to bridge them, these single mothers and their children often went without items most Americans would consider necessities: adequate food or shelter, clothing, heat, electricity, telephone service, and adequate health care or health insurance.

In the mid-1990s, Lein and I began to appear as guests on radio talk shows around the country. When we told the story of the hardship these single mothers and their children faced, callers invariably asked two questions. First, if things were so bad for these single mothers, callers wondered, why did they have children in the first place? Second, wouldn't these women be better off if they simply got married? For these listeners, both *motherhood* and *singleness* were choices low-income women had made, and these choices had led to the hardships. I had inadvertently touched upon a raw nerve in a large segment of Americans; their anger and incomprehension went very deep. I decided it was worth asking these questions of low-income single mothers themselves.

People's ideas about children and marriage presumably emerge out of interactions they have with one another in a given ecological context (a family, kinship group, or neighborhood)—a context that may have distinctive cultural and structural features. The Philadelphia metropolitan area, where my colleagues and I conducted our most recent interviews, contains many poor neighborhoods that tend to be segregated by race and ethnicity. We tried to ensure a balanced representation of whites, African Americans, and Puerto Ricans, the three main racial and ethnic groups in the area. In Philadelphia single parents headed nearly 23 percent of white family households with children under eighteen in 1990. The rate was 44 percent for Hispanics and 63 percent for African Americans. These rates are not unlike those in the rest of the country (18 percent, 29 percent, and 53 percent respectively).

THEORIES ABOUT MARRIAGE

Four theories of nonmarriage hold currency among scholars. First, Gary Becker and others point to the increasing economic independence of women. According to Becker's economic theory of the family, women who can earn a living on their own will find marriage less attractive than those financially dependent on men. Though this explanation for declining marriage rates makes intuitive sense, the evidence is mixed. While more women have indeed been entering the paid labor force during the years when marriage has been declining, the effect on low-income women may be paradoxical. Some analyses show that for low-income women, marriage and earnings are positively related—as a woman's income rises, so does the probability that she will be married.

Starting from the other side of the relationship, William Julius Wilson has looked at changes in men's economic position, assuming that a man must be stably employed for a woman to consider him marriage material. He points to the declines in unskilled men's employment over the past 30 years and to large decreases in unskilled wages. Wilson argues that shrinking labor force participation and declining wages create an imbalance in marriage markets, particularly among African Americans, whose male employment rates and wages remain lower than those of other groups. While this theory is broadly persuasive, the declines in marriage are even greater than the theory would predict.

Third, Charles Murray and others blame welfare. As welfare became more generous, women increasingly traded dependence on a man for dependence on the government. In the early 1970s, the Supreme Court struck down the man-in-the-house rule (which had prohibited female welfare recipients from cohabiting with a man). In Murray's estimation, cohabiting while remaining unmarried became the rational option for a poor couple because they could combine his earnings with her welfare allotment. Nonmarital childbearing did rise in the 1960s and 1970s. However, welfare benefits shrank in real terms from the mid-1970s to the 1990s, while nonmarital childbearing still continued to increase. And there is not much empirical association between the relative generosity of welfare benefits state by state and changes in marriage rates.

Fourth, some observers cite cultural factors. Arguably, the women's movement and women's entry into the paid labor force have revolutionized women's notions of gender roles. There is certainly evidence that among lower-income adults, women's views have changed far more dramatically than men's, and the result is a mismatch in sex role expectations of poor men and women. Yet I know of no analyses that have looked directly at how changes in sex role expectations have influenced marriage rates per se.

There is even more confusion and disagreement on the question of why poor single women have babies. Some scholars and advocates view this as a dysfunctional act, to be remedied by more intensive education on the wisdom of using birth control and deferring pregnancy. Other research has found that given the available alternatives, having a baby may not be all that irrational for some single poor women. Arlene Geronimous and Sanders Korenman found that comparable women who waited to have babies were no better off economically than those who had babies as teens. The *Prospect* has addressed this issue [see Kristin Luker, "Dubious Conceptions: The Controversy over Teen Pregnancy," *TAP*, Spring 1991.]

LISTENING TO THE POOR

So we are still left with more questions than answers. How do low-income single mothers feel about marriage? What factors do they believe prevent them from marrying? To what extent does the marriage norm still operate in poor communities?

One way to get at the often subtle and complex meanings of marriage in poor communities is to listen to residents at length, observe and take part in their daily routines, and immerse oneself in their world. Thus far, my colleagues and I have talked with over 130 black, white, and Puerto Rican mothers in nine neighborhoods across the Philadelphia metropolitan area. These interviews reveal four major motives for nonmarriage among the poor: affordability, respectability, trust, and control. Some of these motives fit with current theories of nonmarriage, but some do not. Overall, the interviews show that although mothers still aspire to marriage, they feel that it entails far more risks than rewards—at least marriage to the kind of men who fathered their children and live in their neighborhoods. Mothers say these risks may be diminished if they can find the "right" man—and they define "rightness" in both economic and noneconomic terms. In sum, they say they are willing and even eager to wed if the marriage represents substantial economic upward mobility and their husband doesn't beat them, abuse their children, insist on making all the decisions, or "fool around" with other women. If they cannot find such a man, most would rather remain single.

AFFORDABILITY

Mothers see economic stability on the part of a prospective partner as a necessary precondition for marriage. Welfare-reliant and low-wage working mothers worry a great deal about money simply because they have to. The price for not balancing their budgets is high: the stability of the household and the well-being of their children. Though men frequently contribute to mothers' households, their employment situations are often unstable and their contributions vary. Mothers' consistent needs for supplemental income, combined with men's erratic employment and earnings, mean that couples often break up over money or fail to marry because of it.

Mothers aren't completely cold and calculating when they weigh the costs and benefits of keeping a man around. Many say they try to take into account the effort their men put into finding and keeping a job. But if the man quits or loses his job for reasons the woman views as his own fault, he often loses the right to co-reside in the household, share in family meals, or even to maintain any romantic relationship with her. Mothers whose boyfriends live with them almost always told us they impose a "pay and stay" rule—if the men are out of work and not contributing to household expenses, they eventually lose the right to co-reside. One Puerto Rican mother said,

> I didn't want to be mean or anything, [but when he didn't work], I didn't let him eat my food. I would tell him, "If you can't put any food here, you can't eat here. These are your kids, and you should want to help your kids, so if you come here, you can't eat their food." Finally, I told him he couldn't stay here either.

Since these men can seldom afford their own apartment and are not eligible for housing subsidies because they have no custodial children, they are often powerfully motivated to try and maintain a place in their girlfriend's household. Often, their only alternatives are to move back in with their own mother or to live on the streets. No low-income single mother we have spoken to has allowed a nonpaying male partner to sponge off her welfare or paycheck for any substantial length of time simply because neither welfare nor low-wage employment pay enough to make this an affordable option.

One might expect that, given their economic needs, mothers would pressure their men into engaging in any form of employment available, including the drug trade. But virtually all tell us that "drug money" cannot buy marriage or even long-term co-residence. In fact, it is often a father's entry into the drug trade that breaks young couples up (except when the woman herself is addicted, in which case she usually loses custody of the children). Mothers fear that if their man gets involved in drug dealing, he might stash weapons, drugs, or drug proceeds in the household, that the violence of street life might follow him into the household, that he will end up in prison, or that he will start "using his product." Mothers consider these outcomes inevitable for anyone who participates in the drug trade for long. Even more worrisome for mothers is the negative role model a drug-dealing husband would provide their children. One African-American mother recounted, "The baby came home and [my child's father] was still selling drugs. I kept on telling him, 'Well, it's time for you to get a job now. . . . The kid's home now, and its time for you to get a job . . . and a job where you're not gonna get hurt or you're not gonna get locked up.' "

The somewhat mercenary nature of mothers' marriage views does not mean they do not care deeply about the men in their lives. Indeed, holding men to economic standards even the mothers recognize are hard to attain is often emotionally wrenching. One Puerto Rican mother admitted,

> There was a struggle going on inside of me. I mean, he lost his job at the auto body shop when they went [bankrupt] and closed down. Then he couldn't find another one. But it was months and months, and I was trying to live on my welfare check and it just wasn't enough. Finally, I couldn't do it anymore [because] it was just too much pressure on me [even though] he is the love of my life. I told him he had to leave even though I knew it wasn't really his fault that [he wasn't working]. But I had nothing in the house to feed the kids, no money to pay the bills, nothing. And he was just sitting there not working. I couldn't take it, so I made him leave.

This dilemma is particularly stark in the neighborhoods we are studying, where unemployment rates are three or four times higher than the national average. Deferring or avoiding marriage allows mothers to substitute an economically productive male for an unproductive one, should the need arise. Divorce takes both time and money, both of which these mothers find in short supply.

RESPECTABILITY

Many middle-class Americans, like the talk-show callers, believe that the marriage norm no longer operates within poor communities because these men and women think too *little* of marriage. Our interviews revealed the opposite. Women often said they avoid marriage because they think too *much* of it. Indeed, marriage often had a kind of sacred significance in the communities we studied, a marker of respectability. However, marriage signals respectability for low-skilled mothers only if accompanied by financial stability and some measure of upward mobility. As one young African-American mother declared, "I'm not marrying nobody until they can move me into my own apartment or my own house."

Marriage to an economically unproductive or erratically employed man, on the other hand, makes the mother a "fool" in the eyes of her friends and neighbors. Mothers find it somewhat more respectable to remain single and hold out hope that they will eventually make a respectable match. Even for mothers who could technically afford to marry a "low-class" man, such a union would entail a diminished level of class respectability. Like the young white mother in the following quote, our respondents tended to group marriage together with other status markers such as diplomas, careers, savings accounts, and houses:

> I want a big wedding. I want to be set—out of school, have a career, and then go from there. . . . Yeah, my friends that have children, my one girlfriend, she's engaged, but they're not getting married . . . until they have some money put aside. My other girlfriend, she wants to get a house first and be ready with that and then decide.

In these communities (as in much of America), a wife appropriates the class standing of her husband. Marriage to an economically unproductive male means, in these mothers' view, permanently taking on his very low status. A woman who marries a poor or economically unstable man makes a profound statement to the larger community (and to herself): "This is the best I can do." Such a choice will garner the ridicule rather than the respect of neighbors and kin. By avoiding marriage to men with attributes similar to their own, mothers hope they will someday find a man through whom they can gain enhanced class standing and respectability. As one white mother succinctly put it, "I just want [a marriage] that will take me up to where I want to go."

TRUST

Though many of our respondents have given up on marriage altogether, this is more because of their low view of the men they know than because they reject the institution of marriage itself. Among the low-income couples we observed, the battle between the sexes often looks more like outright war, and many women say that they regard men simply as "children," "no good," or "low-down dirty dogs." Women tend to believe men are untrustworthy in several respects. First, they fear that the men will not (or cannot, in some women's view) be sexually faithful. One young African-American mother stated, "I feel like this: A married man, a single man, a man that's in a relationship for a certain amount of time—they're still gonna run around. A man is gonna be a man." Another said, "There's a shortage of men, so they think, 'I can have more than one woman. I'm gonna go around to this one or that one, and I'm gonna have two or three of them.' " Like these mothers, many women view infidelity as almost inevitable (part of men's "nature"), but they are not willing to accept it as a natural part of marriage.

Women believe the best way to avoid being deceived by an unfaithful spouse is to either avoid marriage altogether (being cheated on by a boyfriend generally entails less loss of face because the woman has not publicly tied herself to the man "for life") or delay marriage while observing and evaluating a potential spouse's behavior over time. If he fails to confirm her fears after several years or shows improvement, she might consider him "marriage material." A white respondent admitted, "Living with [a man] would be fine. If after I lived with him for a couple of years and I see that nothing's gonna change in the relationship, then maybe I'll marry him. But he's gotta be somebody that's got [enough] money to take care of me."

Mothers also mistrust men's ability to handle money. While mothers are hard-pressed to pay their bills each month and therefore budget their money carefully, many view men as prone toward wasteful or selfish spending. An African-American mother re-counted, "I gave [my child's father] the money to go buy my son's Pampers. He went on some street with his cousin [and] they were down there partying, drinking, everything. He spent my son's Pamper money [on partying]."

Most mothers understand that a married couple has joint responsibility for either party's debt, while unmarried partners need not assume such responsibility. When a mother considers marriage, she usually begins to demand financial accountability of her partner (which not only ensures that the bills get paid but also makes it harder for him to maintain a relationship with a woman "on the side"). Perhaps not surprisingly, a prospective husband may resent these financial demands and might not always comply, thus confirming her view of his financial irresponsibility.

Additionally, mothers often do not trust men with their children. Respondents tell us stories about men (both their children's fathers and other boyfriends) who leave chil-dren home alone, engage in unsuitable activities (heavy drinking or smoking crack, for example) in front of them, neglect to feed or otherwise care for a child in their charge, or even physically or sexually abuse a child. A white respondent recounted a time when she let her children's father take them on a short trip: "I let him take them down the shore. He got into a fight with his girlfriend, beat her up, got locked up. I didn't know where my kids were [and] I didn't find out until 9:00 [the next morning]."

While mothers feel that the experience of parenthood has matured them, fathers without primary custody have never been forced to stop "rippin' and runnin' the streets" and to "settle down." Indeed, most mothers we talk with say their children's fathers have not perceptibly "changed their ways" since they became parents. When asked about her baby's father, one white mother said, "He's 25, but he still likes to run the streets and go out with his friends all the time. I just can't be bothered with that." An African-American mother stated, "Sometimes men don't grow up as fast as women. He's still a kid in part— a kid, period, to be honest with you." Another white mother was even more caustic: "They're stupid. They're still little boys. You think you can get one and mold him into a man, [but] they turn out to be assholes. All men are. They're good for one thing and one thing only, and it ain't supporting me."

While mothers express profound distrust toward men in many ways, they have not always held these attitudes. Many described loving and even committed relationships to their children's fathers or other male partners in the past, and often used the terms "love of my life" or "first love" to describe how they felt (and sometimes still feel) about these relationships. The story differs somewhat for the divorced mothers and those who never married.

Many never-married mothers often related that, prior to their pregnancy, relation-ships with their children's fathers were warm, romantic, and loving; a good number said they had even planned to marry. But as the pregnancy progressed, many mothers say that their boyfriend's behavior changed dramatically: Boyfriends who had been warm and lov-ing often became panicked, hostile, and uncommunicative. One African-American mother said, "That first stage of me being pregnant was so stressful. . . . He would call up [and say that] I was cheating on him and it wasn't his baby. I went through that the whole [pregnancy, with him calling me a] cheater." A startling number of women tell us that their boyfriends beat them while they're pregnant (often by punching them in the stomach or pushing them down the stairs). One young white mother recalled,

> He started really beating me up. I was pregnant and he beat the shit out of me. . . . I must have been like four, five months pregnant. . . . By then I had a belly. . . . He's on top of me—a grown six-foot-two man, 205 pounds, [and] I'm five feet and maybe 120 pounds because of the fact that I was pregnant—him on top of me, beating me up, punching me, hitting me. And I got a belly [with] his child.

These relationships deteriorate partly because, as the woman's pregnancy advances, her sense of what she and the baby will need materially grows more concrete. Though an intermittently employed boyfriend might have adequate funds to play the role of boyfriend, a pregnant girlfriend quickly realizes that these meager earnings cannot support a family. A young man who may have been completely acceptable six months prior is suddenly viewed as "no good" by his girlfriend, even when his behavior may not have changed in any way.

Mothers often describe a golden period in their relationship with the child's father once their child is born. Often, the father comes to the hospital during or after the birth, and the couple renews their desire to stay together and perhaps marry. However, the new mother, who necessarily begins to deal with the practical demands of raising the child, again places increased financial demands on the father. One African-American mother recalled that after the baby was born,

> That's when everything started blowing up. I didn't wanna be with him no more 'cause he wasn't working and he was getting on my nerves. . . . He just never gave me no money. I would tell him, you know, "Well, the baby needs diapers." "Well, I don't have no money." "The baby needs milk." "Well, I don't have no money." I just started getting mad. I had to buy milk and diapers so I just told him to leave me alone.

Fathers in tight economic straits grow increasingly resentful, and the relationship quickly deteriorates—sometimes within days of the birth. Many of the same fathers that talked of romance and marriage at the hospital often deny that they are the father of the child soon after. They accuse their baby's mother of "stepping out," "sleeping around," or "whoring" behind their back. Some demand a blood test before buying anything for the baby. Not surprisingly, these scenarios increase women's mistrust. One African-American mother said, "[When] a woman gets pregnant, right away the man [says], 'It's not mine.' I mean, if you're together eight years, how come it's not yours all of a sudden?"

For married women, the devastation is perhaps deeper because their expectations are often higher. Most say they had expected their marriages to last "forever" and had often given up educational or occupational goals to wed and to raise children. These women seldom suffer through the harsh pregnancy experiences and subsequent denial of paternity the unmarried women report, but the public humiliation that relational failure can bring is perhaps greater. Separated or divorced mothers described painful breakups due to infidelity, financial irresponsibility, domestic violence, alcoholism or drug abuse, or child abuse—precisely echoing the fears of the unmarried women. These mothers' experiences also leave them unwilling or unable to trust men.

CONTROL

When we ask mothers what they like best about being a single mother, many tell us that they enjoy being in control. Some of the previously married women have at one time been almost completely dependent on a man, having moved directly from their natal household to their husband's with little or no work experience in between. Having not worked full time for years, these women have forgone investments in human capital that might have resulted in higher wages. The period of economic shock and near-destitution that oftentimes follows the marital breakup is a painful one, and mothers say that every inch of economic independence they currently enjoy has been hard won. These lessons convince most mothers that it simply isn't safe to completely depend on a man again. One divorced African-American woman said, "One guy was like, 'Marry me, I want a baby.' I don't want to have to depend on anybody. No way. I [would rather] work. [If I married him and had his baby], I'd [have to quit work and] be dependent again. It's too scary."

For never-married mothers, the story is somewhat different. Some of these women are taught life's hard lessons by their own mothers, older sisters, aunts, and other older female kin, whose boyfriends or husbands beat them, cheat on them, abuse their children, or "drink or smoke up their paychecks." For others, enrollment in the school of hard knocks began during pregnancy or after childbirth, for reasons described above. Having and caring for a child often reveals in unmarried mothers competencies they did not know that they possessed. Yet they feel that men often do not respect these competencies and want to be in control. Unmarried male partners cannot fully exert this control because they know their female partners can get rid of them at any time. As one white woman asserted, "I can kick him out whenever I want to kick him out. This is my life. No one can tell me what to do." Once marriage vows are taken, mothers are afraid all that might change. A divorced white mother stated,

> They think that piece of paper says they own you. You are their personal slave. Cook their meals, clean their house, do their laundry. Who did it before I came along, you know? That's why they get married. A man gets married to have somebody to take care of them cause their mommy can't do it anymore.

Most low-income single mothers don't want to be owned or to "slave" for their husbands. They want marriages that are partnerships of equals. Most believe that the best way to maintain power in a romantic relationship is to make sure they are contributing financially to the household economy. A white woman described an ideal marriage this way: "It will be me and my husband [both] working. We both work, [while] the children are in school." A good marriage from the woman's point of view is one where she contributes financially so that she has a say in the decision making. The greater her financial contribution, the more say she believes she is entitled to.

Since mothers also believe that childbearing and the early child-rearing years mandate at least a partial withdrawal from the labor market, mothers equate the early child-rearing years with relational vulnerability. A marriage that occurs prior to or during the prime family-building years, when the mother is least able to contribute financially to the household, is likely to leave a mother quite powerless in her relationship with her husband. Waiting until all of the children are in school (or even out on their own) means that mothers can focus more of their energies on paid labor and increase their chances of entering into a marital relationship with more control. Such marriages, they feel, are more likely to be both satisfying and sustainable over time. As a young African-American mother said,

> I want to have a nice job, [so] that I know if he walked out I have something to fall back on. The mortgage [and] everything [else] is going to be in my name. That's how I want it to be. . . . I do want to get married, but I'm going to get myself stabilized and get everything together with me and [my daughter] before I even take that route.

Since the 1970s, a sharply declining proportion of unskilled men has been able to earn enough to support a family. As the accounts of Philadelphia-area, low-income, single mothers illustrate, these trends have had a profound influence on marriage: Women simply cannot afford to keep an economically unproductive or intermittently employed man around the house. Unless a prospective marriage partner has the resources to ensure a mother some level of social mobility, she will not generally consider marriage even if she could "afford" to do so. I know of no data that demonstrate that gender mistrust has grown over time, but certainly the risk of divorce—and the economic destitution for women that so often accompanies it—has grown.

Beyond affordability, respectability, and trust, these interviews suggest a wide gap between low-income men and women's expectations in regard to gender roles. Women who have proven their competencies though the hard lessons of single parenthood aren't generally willing to enter subservient roles—they want to maintain power in subsequent relationships. Those who plan on marrying generally assume they will put off marriage until their children are in school, and until they are working steadily. By waiting to marry until after early child-rearing and the temporary labor market withdrawal that accompanies it, mothers feel they can minimize these risks and enhance their bargaining power within marriage.

In relation to theories of the retreat from marriage, I find little support for the argument that these women are eschewing marriage because of their enhanced prospects for economic independence outside of marriage (though the theory could well be true for higher-skilled women). Indeed, poor women seem to view economic independence almost as a *prerequisite* for marriage. I also find virtually no support for the welfare disincentives argument, since very few mothers say that they have avoided marriage or remarriage to maintain eligibility for welfare, even when asked directly.

In short, these low-income single mothers believe that marriage will probably make their lives more difficult. They do not, by and large, perceive any special stigma to remaining single. If they cannot enjoy economic stability and respectability from marriage, they see little reason to expose themselves or their children to men's lack of trustworthiness and sometimes violent behavior, or to risk the loss of control they fear marriage might exact from them. Unless low-skilled men's economic situations improve and they begin to change their behaviors toward women, it is quite likely that large numbers of low-income women will continue to resist marriage.

■ READING 15

Peer Marriage: What Does It Take to Create a Truly Egalitarian Relationship?

Pepper Schwartz

When I told people that I was beginning a research study of couples who evenly divided parenting and housework responsibilities, the usual reaction was mock curiosity—how was I going to find the three existing egalitarian couples in the universe? Despite several decades of dissecting the sexism and inequities inherent in traditional marriage, as a society, we have yet to develop a clear picture of how more balanced marital partnerships actually work. Some critics even argue that the practice of true equality in marriage is not much more common today than it was 30 years ago. In fact, authors like Arlie Hochschild have suggested that women's liberation has made prospects for equity worse. The basic theme of her provocative book, *The Second Shift*, is that women now have two jobs—their old, traditional marital roles and their new responsibilities in the work force. A look at the spectacular divorce rates and lower marriage rate for successful women provides further fuel for the argument that equality has just brought wives more, not less, burdens.

All of this figured heavily in my own commitment to exploring the alternative possibilities for marital partnership. Ten years ago this began with *American Couples: Money, Work and Sex*, a study I did with Phillip Blumstein that compared more than 6,000 couples—married, cohabiting, gay males and lesbians—looking for, among other things, what aspects of gendered behavior contributed to relationship satisfaction and durability. This study contained within it a small number of egalitarian couples, who fascinated and inspired me. We discussed them rather briefly in the book, but our editor encouraged us to make them the subject of a second study that would examine how couples manage to sustain an egalitarian partnership over time. Unfortunately, my co-author was not able to continue the project and it was not until three years ago that I began the research on what I came to call Peer Marriage. I began looking for couples who had worked out no worse than a 60–40 split on childrearing, housework and control of discretionary funds and who considered themselves to have "equal status or standing in the relationship."

I started out interviewing some of the couples originally studied for *American Couples* and then, using what sociologists call a "snowball sample," I asked those couples if they knew anyone else like themselves that I could interview. After talking to a few couples in a given network, I then would look for a different kind of couple (different class, race, educational background, etc.) in order to extend the range of my sample. I interviewed 57 egalitarian couples, but even after the formal study was over, I kept running into couples that fit my specifications and did 10 more partial interviews.

While initially my design included only Peer Marriages, I also began to interview a lot of couples who others thought to be egalitarian, but who did not meet my criteria.

Instead of throwing them out of the sample, I used them as a base of comparison, dividing them into two additional categories: "Traditionals" and "Near Peers." Traditionals were couples in which the man usually had veto power over decision-making (except with the children) and in which the wife felt that she did not have—nor did she want—equal status. The Near Peers were couples who, while they believed in equality, felt derailed from their initial goal of an egalitarian marriage because of the realities of raising children and/or the need or desire to maximize male income. As a result, the husband could not be anywhere near as participatory a father as the couple had initially envisioned. These two groups proved to be a fortuitous addition to the design. It is sometimes hard to understand what peer couples are doing that allows them to fulfill an egalitarian agenda without understanding what keeps other couples from doing the same.

Even though I consider myself to be in a Peer Marriage, I found many surprises among the Peer Couples I studied. Of course, as a researcher, one is never supposed to extrapolate from one's own experience, but it is almost impossible not to unconsciously put one's presuppositions into the hypothesis phase of the research. Clearly, people make their marital bargains for many different reasons, and face different challenges in sustaining them. Here are some of the discoveries I made that I thought might be of use to therapists.

I assumed most couples would, like myself, come to egalitarianism out of the women's movement or feminist ideology. Nevertheless, while approximately 40 percent of the women and about 20 percent of the men cited feminism and a desire to be in a nonhierarchical relationship, the majority of couples mentioned other reasons. These included a desire to avoid parental models that they found oppressive in their own upbringing, the *other* partner's strong preference for an egalitarian marriage, some emotional turmoil that had led to their rethinking their relationship, or an intense desire for co-parenting. Women in particular often mentioned their own parents as a negative model. One woman said, "I want a husband who knows how to pack his own suitcase, who puts away his own clothes, who can't tell me to shut up at will . . . My mother may have been happy with this kind of marriage, but I'm still angry at my father for treating my mother like that—and angry at her for letting him." A 25-year-old husband told me, on a different theme, "My main objective in having an equal relationship was not to be the kind of father I had. I want my kids to know me before they are adults. I want them to be able to talk to me. I want them to run to me if they hurt themselves. I want our conversations to be more than me telling them they could do better on a test or that I was disappointed they didn't make the team. I want to be all the things to my kids that my dad was not. I want us to have hugged many, many times and not just on birthdays or their wedding day."

Quite a few men in Peer Marriages said they really had no strong feelings about being in either traditional or egalitarian marriages, but had merely followed their wives' lead. Typical of this group was a high school basketball coach who said he had had a very traditional first marriage because that was the only arrangement that he and his wife could envision even when it wasn't working. But when he met his current wife, a policewoman who had been single quite a while, her demands for equality seemed perfectly reasonable to him. He just, more or less, fell into line with his future wife's ideas about the relationship. Many of these men told me they had always expected a woman to be the emotional architect of a relationship and were predisposed to let her set the rules.

Most of the couples, however, did have strong ideas about marriage and placed particular emphasis on equity and equality. Even if they didn't start out with a common agenda, most ended up sharing a high degree of conscious purpose. People's particular personal philosophies about marriage mattered less than the fact that their philosophies differentiated their family from a culture that reinforced the general belief that equality is neither possible nor even in the long-term interests of couples. Many people talked about how easy it is to slide into old and familiar roles or follow economic opportunities that started to whittle away at male participation in childrearing. It takes an intense desire to keep a couple on the nontraditional track and a clear sense of purpose to justify the economic sacrifices and daily complications it takes to co-parent. As one wife of 10 years said, "We always try to make sure that we don't start getting traditional. It's so easy to do. But we really want this extraordinary empathy and respect we have. I just know it wouldn't be there if we did this marriage any other way."

Important as relationship idealogy is, Peer Marriages depend at least as much on coordinating work with home and childraising responsibilities and not letting a higher earner be exempt from daily participation. Previous research had shown me the connection between a husband's and wife's relative income and their likelihood of being egalitarian. So I assumed that most of the couples I interviewed would be working couples, and have relatively similar incomes. This was mostly true, although I was struck by the couples who were exceptions. Four husbands in the study had non-working wives. The men didn't want to dominate those relationships because they felt very strongly that money did not legitimately confer power. For example, one husband had inherited a great deal of money but didn't feel it was any more his than his wife's. She stayed at home with the children, but he took over in the late afternoon and on weekends. He also was the primary cook and cleaner. In another case, a husband who earned a good deal more than his wife put all the money in a joint account and put investments in her name as well as his. Over time, she had assets equal to his. While these triumphs over income differentials were exceptions, it did make me respect the fact that truly determined couples could overcome being seduced by the power of economic advantage.

However, many Peer Marriages had a significant income differential and husbands and wives had to negotiate a lot just to make sure they didn't fall into the trap of letting the higher earner be the senior decision-maker. Even more tricky, according to many, was not letting work set the emotional and task agenda of the household. The couples needed to keep their eyes on what was the tail and what was the dog so that their relationship was not sidetracked by career opportunities or job pressures. Many Peer Couples had gone through periods in which they realized that they were beginning to have no time for each other, or that one of them was more consistently taking care of the children while the other was consumed with job demands. But what distinguished those couples from more traditional marriages was that they had a competing ideology of economic or career success that guided them when their egalitarianism began to get out of kilter.

One husband, who had an architectural practice designing and building airports, had begun to travel for longer and longer periods of time until it was clear that he was no longer a true co-parent or a full partner in the marriage. After long and painful discussions, he quit his job and opened up a home office so he could spend more time with his wife and children. Both partners realized this would cause some economic privations and, in fact, it took the husband five years to get a modestly successful practice going while the wife struggled to support the family. Without minimizing how tough this period had been, the couple felt they had done the right thing. "After all," the husband said, "we saved our marriage."

This attitude helped explain another surprise in this study. I had presumed that most of the Peer Marriages I would find would be yuppie or post-yuppie couples, mostly young or baby boom professionals who were "having it all." In fact, most of them were solidly middle class: small-business owners, social workers, school teachers, health professionals (but not doctors). Apparently, people on career fast tracks were less willing to endanger their potential income and opportunities for promotion. There may be child-rearing Peer Marriages out there comprised of litigators, investment bankers and brain surgeons—but I didn't find them. The closest I came to finding fast trackers in a Peer Marriage and family were high-earning women who had husbands who were extremely pleased with their partner's success and were willing to be the more primary parent in order to support her career.

When these women negotiated issues with their husbands in front of me, they seemed more sensitive about their husbands' feelings than men of comparable accomplishment with lower earning wives. For example, they did not interrupt as much as high-earning men in traditional marriages, and they seemed to quite consciously not pull rank when I asked them jointly to solve a financial problem. They told me, however, that they consciously had to work at being less controlling than they sometimes thought they deserved to be. A very successful woman attorney, married to another, significantly-less-prominent attorney, told me that they had some problems because he wasn't used to picking up the slack when she was called away suddenly to represent a Fortune 500 company. She found herself battling her own ambitions in order to be sensitive to his desire for her to let up a bit. As she noted, "We [women] are not prepared to be the major providers and it's easy to want all the privileges and leeway that men have always gotten for the role. But our bargain to raise the kids together and be respectful of one another holds me back from being like every other lawyer who would have this powerful a job. Still, it's hard."

The other fast track exception was very successful men in their second marriages who had sacrificed their first in their climb to the top. Mostly these were men who talked about dependent ex-wives, their unhappiness at paying substantial support and their determination not to repeat the mistakes of their first marriages. One 50-year-old man, who had traveled constantly in his first marriage raising money for pension funds, told me he was through being the high earner for the company and wanted more family time in the second part of his life. As he put it, "I consciously went looking for someone who I could spend time with, who I had a lot in common with, who would want me to stop having to be the big earner all the time. I don't want to die before I've been a real partner to somebody who can stand on her own two feet . . . and I've been a real father."

When I first realized how often the desire to co-parent led couples into an egalitarian ideology, I thought this might also lead couples to prioritize their parenting responsibilities over their husband-and-wife relationship. But these were not marriages in which husbands and wives called each other "Mom" and "Dad." For the most part, these couples avoided the rigidly territorial approach I saw in Traditional and Near Peer marriages. In both of these types of couples, I observed mothers who were much more absorbed in their children, which both partners regarded as a primarily female responsibility. As a result, women had sole control over decisions about their children's daily life and used the children as a main source of intimacy, affection and unshared secrets. They related stories about things the children told them that "they would never dare tell their father." While quite a few of the mothers talked about how "close" their husbands were with their children, they would also, usually in the same story, tell me how much closer their children were with them. What surprised me was that while these traditional moms complained about father absence, very few really wanted to change the situation. Most often, it was explained that, while it would be great to have their husband home, they "couldn't afford it." But of course "afford" is a relative term and I sensed that the women really did not want the men interfering with their control over parenting. Or they would have liked more fatherly engagement but definitely not at the cost of loss of income. One young, working Near Peer Couple with four kids was discussing the husband's lesser parenting responsibilities with me when he said, "You know, I could come home early and get the kids by 3:30. I'd like to do that." The wife's response was to straightforwardly insist that with four kids going to private school, his energies were best used paying for their tuitions. She preferred a double shift to a shared one because her financial priorities and her vision of what most profited her children were clear.

But there was an unexpected downside for the couples who did manage to co-parent. I was unprepared for how often Peer Couples mentioned serious conflict over childrearing. Because each partner felt very strongly about the children's upbringing, differences of opinion were not easily resolved. As one peer wife said, "We are both capable of stepping up to the line and staying there screaming at each other." Another husband said, "If you only talked to us about how we deal with disagreements about the kids, you might think we were a deeply conflicted marriage. We're not. But unfortunately, we have very different ideas about discipline and we can get pretty intense with one another and it might look bad. We went to counseling about the kids and this therapist wanted to look at our whole relationship and we had to say, 'You don't get it. This really is the only thing we argue about like this.' "

Peers may, in fact, have more conflict about children than more Traditional partners because unlike Traditional Marriage, there is no territory that is automatically ceded to the other person and conflict cannot be resolved by one person claiming the greater right to have the final word. I wondered if these arguments threatened the relationship. In the majority of the Peer marriages where such conflicts occurred, the couples talked about how they ultimately, if not in the heat of battle, followed their usual pattern of talking until an agreement was reached. What usually forced them to continue to communicate and reach a joint answer was their pledge to give the other partner equal standing in the relationship. Occasionally, a few people told me, they just couldn't reach a mutually satisfying answer and let their partner "win one" out of trust in his or her good judgment, not because they agreed on a given issue.

The couples that I felt might be in more trouble had recurring disagreements that they were never able to resolve over punishments, educational or religious choices or how much freedom to give kids. Furthermore, in each instance at least one partner said that the other partner's approach was beginning to erode the respect that made their relationship possible. Moreover, this particular kind of conflict was deeply troubling since many of them had organized their marriage around the expectation of being great co-parents. It may be that co-parenting requires that parenting philosophies be similar or grow together. Co-parents may have a particular need for good negotiating and communication skills so that they can resolve their differences without threatening the basis of their relationship.

In contrast with traditional or Near Peer Couples, the partners in Peer Marriages never complained about lack of affection or intimacy in their relationships. What they did mention, that other couples did not, was the problem of becoming so familiar with each other that they felt more like siblings than lovers. Some researchers have theorized that sexual arousal is often caused or intensified by anxiety, fear and tension. Many others have written about how sexual desire depends on "Yin" and "Yang"—mystery and difference. And quite a few women and men I talked to rather guiltily confessed that while they wanted equal partners, all their sexual socialization had been to having sex in a hierarchical relationship: Women had fantasies of being "taken" or mildly dominated; men had learned very early on that they were expected to be the orchestrators of any given sexual encounter and that masculinity required sexual directiveness. For men, sexual arousal was often connected with a strong desire to protect or control.

Peer couples complained that they often forgot to include sex in their daily lives. Unlike Traditional or Near Peers, their sexual frequency did not slow down because of unresolved issues or continuing anger, at least not in any systematic ways. These couples may start to lose interest in sex even more than the other kinds of marriages because sex is not their main way of getting close. Many Traditional and some Near Peer Couples mentioned that the only time they felt that they got through to each other was in bed. Perhaps the more emotional distance couples feel with one another, the larger the role sexuality plays in helping them feel they still have the capacity for intimacy. Being less dependent on this pathway to intimacy, partners in Peer Marriage may be more willing to tolerate a less satisfactory sexual relationship.

One husband, who worked with his wife in their own advertising firm, even talked about having developed "an incest taboo," which had led to the couple entering therapy. They were such buddies during the daytime, he had trouble treating her as anything else in the evening. The therapist this couple consulted encouraged them to assume new personas in the bedroom. For example, he told them to take turns being the dominant partner, to create scenarios where they created new characters and then behaved as they thought the person they were impersonating would behave. He gave them "homework," such as putting themselves in romantic or sexy environments and allowing themselves to imagine meeting there the first time. The wife was encouraged to dress outrageously for bed every now and then; the husband occasionally to be stereotypically directive. The therapist reminded both partners that their emotional bargain was safe: they loved and respected each other. That meant they could use sex as recreation, release and exploration. They were good pupils and felt they had really learned something for a lifetime.

In another couple, it was the wife who mentioned the problem. Her husband had been the dominant partner in his previous marriage and had enjoyed that role in bed. However, she liked more reciprocity and role-sharing in sex, so he tried to be accommodating. However, early on in the relationship he began treating her, as she put it, "too darn respectfully . . . it was almost as if we were having politically correct sex . . . I had to remember that he wasn't my brother and it was okay to be sexually far out with him."

On the other hand, Peer Couples with satisfying sexual relationships often mentioned their equality as a source of sexual strength. These couples felt their emotional security with one another allowed them to be more uninhibited and made sex more likely since both people were responsible for making it happen. Women with unhappy sexual experiences with sexist men mentioned that for the first time in their lives they could use any sexual position without worrying about any larger meaning in the act. Being on the bottom just meant being on the bottom; it was not about surrendering in a more cosmic way. Being a sex kitten was a role for the evening—and not part of a larger submissive persona.

Many of the Peer Couples I interviewed had terrific sexual lives. The women, especially, felt they had finally met men with whom they could be vulnerable and uninhibited. As one woman said, "I used to be a real market for women's books. I wanted men who fit the stereotype of Clark Gable or Kevin Costner—few words, and when they are delivered, they are real ringers, and there is a lot of eye contact and passion, and that's about as much talking as you get. Maybe it was dating all these guys who were really like that, but even as fantasy objects, I got tired of men who didn't want to explore a feeling or who were only loving when they had a hard-on. I fell in love the first time sharing *Prince of Tides* with the guy I was dating, and fell in love with Eric [her husband] over a discussion of *Eyes on the Prize*. The sexy thing was the conversation and the quality of our minds . . . I can't imagine anything more boring or ultimately unsexy than a man—and I don't care if he looked like Robert Redford and earned like Donald Trump—who had nothing to say or if he did, didn't get turned on by what I was saying."

Equality brings with it the tools to have a great erotic relationship and also, at the same time, the pitfalls that can lead to sexual boredom. If couples learn that their sexual lives need not be constrained by any preconceived idea of what is "egalitarian sex" or appropriate sexual roles, there is no reason that their equality can't work for them. But couples who cannot separate their nights and days, who cannot transcend their identities in everyday life, may need guidance from a knowledgeable counselor.

What enables couples to sustain a style of egalitarian relationship in a world that encourages families to link their economic destiny with the male's career and casts women in an auxiliary worker role so that they can take responsibility for everyday childcare and household chores? In Peer Couples, a sense of shared purpose helps guide the couple back to why they are putting up with all the problems that come from putting together a new model of relationship without societal or familiar supports.

Otherwise it is all too easy for mothers to fall in love with their children and assume primary responsibility for their upbringing or for men to allow their careers to sweep them out of the home, away from their children and back into the more familiar territory they have been trained to inhabit. When this begins to happen, a couple's ideology, almost like an organization's mission statement, helps remind them what their central goal is: the marital intimacy that comes from being part of a well-matched, equally empowered, equally participatory team.

But avoiding traditional hierarchy involves a constant struggle to resist the power of money to define each partner's family roles. Peer Couples continually have to evaluate the role of work in their lives and how much it can infringe on parenting and household responsibilities. If one partner earns or starts to earn a lot more money, and the job starts to take up more time, the couple has to face what this means for their relationship—how much it might distort what they have set out to create.

Peer Couples check in with each other an extraordinary amount to keep their relationship on track. They each have to take responsibility for making sure that they are not drifting too far away from reciprocity. Peer Couples manage to maintain equity in small ways that make sure the balance in their marriage is more than an ideology. If one person has been picking up the kids, the other is planning their summer activities and getting their clothes. Or if one partner has been responsible lately for making sure extended family members are contacted, the other person takes it over for a while. If one partner really decides he or she likes to cook, then the other partner takes on some other equally functional and time-consuming job. There's no reason that each partner can't specialize, but both are careful that one of them doesn't take over all the high-prestige, undemanding jobs while the other ends up with the classically stigmatized assignments (like cleaning bathrooms, or whatever is personally loathed by that person).

Besides monitoring jobs and sharing, couples have to monitor their attitude. Is the wife being treated as a subordinate? Does one person carry around the anger so often seen in someone who feels discounted and unappreciated? Is one person's voice considered more important than the other person's? Is the relationship getting distant and is the couple starting to lead parallel lives? Do they put in the time required to be best friends and family collaborators? Are they treating each other in the ways that would support a non-romantic relationship of freely associating friends?

There is nothing "natural" or automatic about keeping Peer Marriages going. There will be role discomfort when newly inhabiting the other gender's world. That is why some research shows that men who start being involved with a child from prenatal classes show more easy attachment and participation in childrearing activities later. While men become comfortable with mothering over time, some need a lot of help. Children will sense who is the primary parent and that will be the person to whom they run, make demands, and from whom they seek daily counsel. One direct way of helping fathers evaluate how they are doing is to help the partners measure how much the children treat them as equally viable sources of comfort and help.

Likewise, being a serious provider is a responsibility some women find absolutely crushing. Most middle-class women were raised to feel that working would be voluntary. After they have made a bargain to do their share of keeping the family economically afloat, they may regret the pressures it puts on them. The old deal of staying at home and being supported can look pretty good after a bad day at the office. But only the exceptional relationship seems to be able to make that traditional provider/mother deal for very long and still sustain a marriage where partners have equal standing in each other's eyes. Couples have to keep reminding themselves how much intimacy, respect and mutual interest they earn in exchange for learning new roles and sustaining the less enjoyable elements of new responsibilities.

Couples who live as peers often attract others like themselves and the building of a supportive community can modify the impact of the lack of support in the larger world. Like-minded others who have made similar decisions help a lot, especially when critical turning points are reached: such as re-evaluating a career track when it becomes painfully clear that it will not accommodate Peer Family life.

This study yielded no single blueprint for successful Peer Marriage. As in all couples, partners in Peer Marriages require a good measure of honesty, a dedication to fair play, flexibility, generosity and maturity. But most of all, they need to remember what they set out to do and why it is important, at least for them. If they can keep their eyes and hearts on the purpose of it all—if we help them do that—more Peer Marriages will endure and provide a model for others exploring the still-unchartered territory of egalitarian relationships.

6 Divorce and Remarriage

Divorce Culture: A Quest for Relational Equality in Marriage

Karla B. Hackstaff

When people marry they do not simply tie a knot, but weave a complex of relationships according to pre-existing patterns. In U.S. history, the institution of marriage has been like a loom through which several threads of social relations have been woven. Marriage has been a monogamous, lifelong commitment that has regulated gender, sexuality, and the physical and social reproduction of the generations. This Western marital pattern is being redesigned. We are still responding to the tapestry of old, but the various threads are being disaggregated and rewoven. Our society is deeply divided regarding the value and meaning of these new and partially woven designs.

Over the past decade, family scholars have debated whether we should be optimistic or pessimistic about marital and family life (Glenn 1987, 349).[1] Optimistic theorists have argued that families are not falling apart, but simply changing and adapting to new socioeconomic conditions (Riley 1991; Scanzoni 1987; Skolnick 1991). They stress the value of embracing family diversity and removing structural obstacles for the well-being of all families. Optimists emphasize the oppression that has attended women's sacrifices in marriage and point to the potential for greater self-determination and happier relationships today (Cancian 1987; Coontz 1992, 1997; Riessman 1990; Skolnick 1991; Stacey 1990, 1996). These theorists are concerned about threads that have regulated gender and sexuality and have subordinated women in marriage.

Pessimistic theorists have argued that the institution of marriage is a cause for concern—that divorce rates signify an unraveling of social bonds (Bellah et al. 1985; Glenn 1987; Lasch 1979; Popenoe 1988; Popenoe, Elshtain, and Blankenhorn 1996; Spanier 1989; Whitehead 1997a). Above all, pessimists argue that divorce suggests an increasingly tenuous thread of commitment and a growing "individualism" among today's adults, particularly since marital dissolution by divorce, rather than death, entails individual choice. In this view, marriage represents the singular commitment that sustains intergenerational family relationships, especially parenthood. Indeed, several recent books urge a return to lifelong marriage for the sake of children (Blankenhorn 1995a, 1995b; Popenoe, Elshtain, and Blankenhorn 1996; Whitehead 1997a).

Pessimists fear that with the advent of divorce culture we have forsaken nurturance, commitment, and responsibility. Because these are the very virtues that have traditionally been valorized in women, these divorce debates are always implicitly, if not explicitly, about gender. As one optimistic scholar has argued, "when commentators lament the collapse of traditional family commitments and values, they almost invariably mean the uniquely female duties associated with the doctrine of separate spheres for men and women" (Coontz 1992, 40). Critics of divorce do not always or necessarily reject gender equality in marriage, but they do tend to set it apart. Many scholars assume that the thread of gender ideology can be easily disentangled from the thread of commitment.

The middle-class '50s and '70s couples in this study, in combination with those in other studies, enhance our knowledge of the newly constructed meanings of marriage. Among the '70s spouses, I found a reproduction of divorce culture among the married, a growth in a marital work ethic, and fluid, even contradictory, beliefs regarding marital and gender ideologies. These findings validate the concerns of both optimists and pessimists.

Pessimists may be dismayed by the sense of contingency in the talk of married couples and may be confirmed in their belief that commitments are unraveling. On the other hand, optimists may feel validated in their views that spouses do not take divorce lightly; rather, "working" on marriages is the prevailing belief among spouses—though wives are still trying to equalize this work. A full-blown marital work ethic has arisen because of divorce anxiety and marital instability, yet it has also arisen because of instabilities in beliefs about gender. Spouses must be reflexive about the nature of marriage since the authority of marriage culture and male dominance have lost their hegemonic hold. The fluid beliefs among '70s spouses suggest that spouses do not wholly embrace either marriage or divorce culture. This may disturb pessimists more—at least those who would like to see marriage culture regain the hegemony of generations past.

At this point in time, marriage does not seem to be forever for almost half of all marriages. Is this a result of culture and the decline of values such as commitment, or are there other factors contributing to marital contingency today? Could divorce culture be transitional—a means to the goals of equality and new tapestries of commitment, rather than an end in itself? While the individualism of divorce culture has brought new problems, we should neither overlook the structural sources of these troubles nor forget the costs of marriage culture, particularly to women.

THE COSTS OF MARRIAGE CULTURE

Women's greater participation in the labor force, increased activity in the political sphere, and greater initiation of divorces suggest that women like Mia Turner and Roxanne Kason-Morris are claiming their rights and appropriating a model of individualism. However, my research suggests that women's increasing "individualism" needs to be understood in context. Because we proceed from a history of male-dominated marriages, individualism does not *mean* the same thing for women as for men.

Historically, we know that as heads of the household, even when not primary bread-winners, most husbands have had greater authority, and therefore greater freedom to be independent, than wives. Economic and legal structures have not only firmly anchored a white man's family authority in the public sphere, but have recognized and applauded his individualism. His autonomy, integrity, rights, and self-expression were never constrained to the same degree as those of wives, though he carried heavy financial responsibilities. Not all men have been able to accomplish or benefit from the provider role—working-class men and men of color have often been thwarted by economic and racial injustice. However, for those able to realize the ideal of the male provider role, these responsibilities have optimized men's freedoms and prerogatives.

Wives who are more individualistic are often trying to counter the legacy of male dominance in marriage. At face value, "contingent marriage" dilutes commitment by making it conditional. Marital commitment and contingency stand in an uneasy relation to one another. The unconditional commitment requires flexibility and a long-range view of reciprocity and rewards over time; it permits conflict, serendipity, and unforeseen developments without threatening the commitment; it builds trust that only a sustained history can provide. Yet, "marriage as forever" can also obscure the latent terms of commitment that have prevailed under conditions of male dominance. Paradoxically, a sense of contingency can enable wives to elicit values such as commitment, responsibility, caretaking, and equality. In short, it provides a powerful lever to set the terms of marriage.[2]

Of course, both men and women can use the lever of contingency in heterosexual marriage. Indeed, a male-dominated divorce culture may be a greater threat to the values of responsibility, caretaking, and equality than a male-dominated marriage culture. Yet, as I have suggested, securing power through individualism is not a new means for men within divorce culture. Thus, this lever is more important for women, who have had less economic and political power in the marital relationship. In fact, contingent marriage may be crucial for redefining marriage in an egalitarian direction. Most women are hungry not for power but for "the absence of domination" (M. Johnson 1988, 261). Yet, how can wives challenge domination without engaging the power of individualism?

A belief in equality is more widespread today—the '70s spouses did not generally embrace male dominance as their '50s counterparts did, but rather voiced support for gender equality.[3] Yet, ongoing conflicts over gender equality are apparent in husbands' and wives' "hidden agendas." When there is evidence of rights equality—such as a wives' participation in the labor force—husbands tend to assume that equality has been achieved; they are unaware of ongoing inequalities, such as marital work, and their enduring privileges to set the terms of marriage. Rights equality has more often been a masculinist discourse in U.S. law and culture (Arendell 1995; Coltrane and Hickman 1992; Weitzman 1985).

Many wives also embrace rights equality, yet women's conventional responsibilities for caretaking, child rearing, kin work, and marital work continue to incline women toward a vision of equality that focuses upon relational responsibilities, expressiveness, equity, and interdependence. Relational equality has been more often feminized in U.S. society (Cancian 1987; Riessman 1990). It is not that women are "essentially" relational, but rather that they have been expected and positioned to accomplish relationality. While some women are undoubtedly more individualistic today, as critics of divorce culture argue (Hewlett and West 1998, 200; Whitehead 1997a, 172, 181), more women increasingly want to share the marital and family labors that optimists have documented. Women are frustrated by men's lack of participation in marital work—and the emotion work, kin work, and housework that such reflexive assessment encompasses (Blaisure and Allen 1995; Cancian 1987; DeVault 1987; di Leonardo 1987; Goldscheider and Waite 1991; Hochschild 1983; Hochschild with Maching 1989; Oliker 1989; Thompson and Walker 1989; Thompson 1991).

These gendered marital visions are also apparent in the retrospective accounts of the divorced. Among divorced women and men, Riessman (1990, 164–65, 184) found that "freedom" encapsulated the positive meaning of divorce, but this gateway to freedom did not necessarily hold the same meaning. Women reported a freedom from subordination and the freedom for self-development—reflecting limits to equality in marriage; men reported freedom from obligations demanded by wives and a freedom from wives' scrutiny—reflecting some dissatisfaction with marital labors. Also, while former wives described their "transformations in identity" as learning to balance relatedness with self-reliance, former husbands discovered the value of "talk" and becoming more relational (199). This latter change by some husbands is ironic for former wives if, as I have argued, relational inequality contributes to marital instability and contingency.

In their suburban divorced sample, Kitson and Holmes (1992) found that ex-husbands and ex-wives similarly ranked a "lack of communication or understanding" as the top marital complaint (though wives ranked this higher) and similarly ranked "joint conflict over roles" as a key complaint.[4] Most interesting, however, was a notable gender difference on the marital complaint "not sure what happened"; for ex-husbands it ranked third, for ex-wives it ranked 28th (123). This suggests that men were less attuned to what the marriage lacked—a prerequisite for doing marital work.

Some '70s husbands—such as Robert Leonetti, Gordon Walker, and Paul Nakato—do marital work. Yet, more often than not, wives initiate and try to redistribute the actual "marital work" of communicating, caring, fulfilling needs, adjusting, and planning for marital well-being. To advocate shared marital work is to de-gender the rights and responsibilities conventionally attached to marital practices, to challenge male authority, and to disrupt power relations. Recent research that aims to predict marital happiness and divorce, as well as to improve the efficacy of marital therapy, reveals that a husband's refusal to accept influence from his wife is a key factor for predicting divorce (Gottman et al. 1998, 14, 19).

The above research suggests that marital work and the relational equality that it entails may be as important as rights equality for wives in a culture of divorce. The cultural irony is that even though wives may want a relational marriage, they may need to draw upon individualism to secure it. If secured, that is, if husbands keep up with wives' changes, wives may change the power dynamics of their marriage. Yet, ultimately what many wives want is not freedom from commitment, but freedom within an egalitarian and relational marriage. However, if relationality is unsecured, these wives may choose the gateway of divorce.

It is worth recalling that it was primarily the wives and not the husbands who thought about divorce among '50s couples ensconced in marriage culture. What does this reveal about the gendered costs of marriage culture? Writing about marriage and the nuclear family, Stacey (1996, 69) noted: "It seems a poignant commentary on the benefits to women of that family system that, even in a period when women retain primary responsibility for maintaining children and other kin, when most women continue to earn significantly less than men with equivalent cultural capital, and when women and their children suffer substantial economic decline after divorce, that in spite of all this, so many regard divorce as the lesser of evils." In light of women's postdivorce commitments to children, to charge such mothers with an egoistic or self-centered individualism reveals a refusal to recognize the costs of marriage culture to women.

Are there no costs for men in marriage culture? While research continues to find that marriage is better for men than women in terms of overall health and mortality rates (Hu and Goldman 1990), men are adjusting to new gender ideologies and practices too. Historically, the ability to provide and the ability to head a household have rooted men's identities. Working women and growing beliefs in equality are increasingly uprooting these means to manhood, as distinct from womanhood. As Furstenberg (1988, 239) has observed: "Men looking at marriage today may sense that it offers them a less good deal than it once did. This is the inevitable result of reducing male privileges, female deference to men, and a range of services that were customarily provided as part of the conjugal bargain. The loss of these privileges has persuaded some men to opt out of family life altogether." Paul Nakato's observation that some '70s men would rather be "right" than "married"—echoes Goode (1992, 124) on the sociology of superordinates: "Men view even small losses of deference, advantages, or opportunities as large threats and losses." Craig Kason-Morris felt increasingly underappreciated for all his work; yet his solution was to devote more energy to breadwinning, risking the relational needs of his marriage.

If we ignore the emotional costs of marriage culture and its connection to gender inequality, we will fail to see that divorce culture is a transitional phenomenon. We will also advance the costs of divorce culture—the impoverished single mothers, estranged fathers, and affected children—of concern to pessimists and optimists alike.

THE COSTS OF DIVORCE CULTURE

The gendered patterns of divorce follow from those of marriage. Just as women usually do the primary parenting during a marriage, they generally obtain custody of children after divorce. Fathers are overwhelmingly noncustodial parents—only 14 percent of custodial parents are fathers (Sugarman 1998, 15). Just as fathers help support children during marriage, they are expected to contribute to child support upon divorce. Yet, many noncustodial fathers have become estranged from their children and delinquent on child support. Single, custodial mothers must often raise children on one slim paycheck. More widespread divorce seems to have increased women's and children's impoverishment, undermined fathers' economic and emotional commitment to children, and deprived children of the emotional and economic goods that two parents can provide.

Pessimists acknowledge structural impediments to marital commitments—the decline of the male wage and the need for two wage earners in a postindustrial economy. Yet, they see the decline in cultural and family values, such as commitment, as the more pivotal factor fostering these new social problems. On the other hand, optimists regularly argue that our failure to respond to the new global and postindustrial economy—the low priority given to families by corporate and government entities—is more basic to these problems, and that these new conditions demand solutions that do not discriminate on the basis of marital status. Although structural solutions are central, optimists are also concerned with cultural and family values—though the values of equality or justice are of greater concern than commitment.

Optimists and pessimists alike are concerned about the economic costs of divorce for mothers and their children. About a third of female-headed households are in poverty—six times the rate of married-couple households (U.S. Bureau of the Census 1995, P60-187). A re-evaluation of one study's claims about the economic consequences of divorce a year after divorce, finds that women's standard of living declines by 27 percent and men's increases by 10 percent (Peterson 1996, 534).[5]

A key solution to poverty for many pessimistic family scholars is reinforcing marriage and the nuclear family structure (Blankenhorn 1995b; Hewlett and West 1998; Popenoe et al. 1996; Whitehead 1997a). Marriage has functioned to redistribute economic resources in the past.[6] Also, today more than ever, two earners are necessary to secure a middle-class standard of living. However, to imply that unmarried motherhood or divorce are the *cause* of poverty among women and children, and marriage the only solution, is to use family structure to solve problems generated by the social structure. Such an approach overlooks the enduring gender inequality in economic structures. Also, marriage does not necessarily reverse poverty, particularly for working-class women and women of color. For instance, Brewer (1988, 344) noted that "an emphasis on female-headed households misses an essential truth about black women's poverty: black women are also poor in households with male heads." Higher wages in female-dominated jobs may be a more effective solution than marriage. This would not only help married, nuclear family households, but all families and households.

Similarly, marriage culture will not solve the larger economic problem of declining wages for working- and middle-class men brought by a postindustrial, service, and global economy.[7] Indeed, we could transform divorce culture by repairing wage declines for those most disadvantaged by this postindustrial economy—including many working-class men, especially men of color. This could remove sources of conflict and resentment within and across family groups. Yet, to address structural sources of inequality would only mitigate, and not reverse, divorce culture unless we attend to cultural beliefs about gender as well.

Pessimists advocate marriage culture in part because it would seem to solve so many problems of divorce culture at once, most especially divorced men's failure to provide and care for their children. Of all policies, child support has received the most attention by legislators and media over the last two decades. Only about half of custodial mothers with child support orders receive the full amount (Arendell 1995, 39). In 1991 the "average monthly child support paid by divorced fathers contributing economic support" was only $302 (for an estimated 1.5 children), and "child support payments amounted to only about 16% of the incomes of divorced mothers and their children" (Arendell 1997, 162). As a result of the Family Support Act of 1988, the mechanisms for securing child support from fathers have become more rigorous (Furstenberg and Cherlin 1991, 109); there are established formulas for calculating child support payments and, since 1994, all new child support payments are withheld from the paychecks of absent parents (mostly fathers). Yet, as Hewlett and West (1998, 180) observe, in spite of all the policies and prison terms, "the number of deadbeat dads has declined only slightly since 1978."[8]

We need new ways to address fathers' "failure to provide"—clearly, some fathers partly withdraw from marriage and children because they cannot be "good providers."[9] Yet, to focus on the provider role is to limit fatherhood to a model that evolved during the industrial era and is at odds with a postindustrial economy. One could say that this approach merely exchanges a "fragmented" fatherhood for its predecessor: a "shrinking" fatherhood (Blankenhorn 1995a).[10] Indeed, to focus on providing alone will only sustain men's detachment from parenting. "Studies do show that fathers who visit more regularly pay more in child support" (Furstenberg and Cherlin 1991, 274). Whether these payments are due to visiting or greater commitment, attention to the relational aspects of fathering would seem crucial.

Both optimistic and pessimistic scholars are concerned about the lack of paternal participation in children's lives. Most research shows a substantial and unacceptable decline over time in father-child contact after a divorce (Furstenberg and Cherlin 1991). Data from the recent National Survey of Families and Households reveals that about 30 percent of children of divorce have not seen their fathers at all in the preceding year and many more see their fathers irregularly and infrequently (Arendell 1995, 38). Speaking of unmarried as well as divorced fathers, Hewlett and West (1988, 168) report that "close to half of all fathers lose contact with their children."

Thus, all family scholars see a need to revitalize and redefine fatherhood. For example, a supporter of divorce culture, Arendell (1995, 251) protests: "Why should it be so difficult to be a nurturing, engaged father? Where are the institutional and ideological supports for parenting?" Arendell adds: "That caring fathers are subject to criticism and stigmatization points to a seriously flawed ideological system" (251). Also, advocates of marriage culture Hewlett and West (1998, 173) assert that "a withering of the father-child bond devastates children, stunts men, and seriously erodes our social capital." In spite of shared concerns, the means to a revitalized fatherhood are contested.

Just as critics of divorce culture suggest that marriage will alleviate the impoverishment of single mothers, they argue that fathers cannot be effective parents outside of the marriage structure (Blankenhorn 1995a; Hewlett and West 1998; Popenoe 1996; Wallerstein and Blakeslee 1989; Whitehead 1997a). For example, Hewlett and West (1998, 171–72) note that single males are more likely to die prematurely due to self-neglect, more likely to abuse drugs and alcohol, and are responsible for a disproportionate share of violence—including murder, robbery, and rape. They reason, like Durkheim, that marriage and children have a "civilizing" effect upon men.[11] In Blankenhorn's (1995a) view, both co-residence and a parental alliance with the mother are preconditions for effective fatherhood.

Undoubtedly, co-residence assists in the building of relationships—including, and especially, parent-child relationships. Yet, there is evidence to suggest it is not a precondition for effective fatherhood. In her study of divorced fathers, Arendell (1995) describes "innovative" divorced fathers (not all of whom had single custody) who were able to detach being a father from being a partner, separate anger at an ex-wife from their love for their children, focus on the children's needs rather than adult rights, and combine breadwinning with caretaking in ways that developed their nurturing and relational skills. While such fathers are too rare, fathers who parent effectively after divorce suggest that marriage or co-residence are not prerequisites—though alliances between parents do seem to be important whether outside or inside the marriage structure. Further, studies on nonresidential mothers show they are more active participants in their children's lives (Maccoby and Mnookin 1992, 212; Arendell 1997, 170). Finally, even if custody determinations were divided equally between women and men, co-residence would not always be an option for father and child. Suggesting marriage as the solution for divorce—and effective fathering—is empty advice for those compelled to divorce.[12]

Divorced fathers' flagging commitment seems to have exposed a tenuous responsibility for children in the first place. This may represent a "male flight from commitment" that started in the 1950s (Ehrenreich 1984); even so, this too should be understood as a legacy of separate spheres that identified masculinity with the provider role and devalued men's caretaking capacities (Bernard 1981; Coontz 1992). Since women still do the bulk of child rearing during a marriage, many divorced fathers have to learn how to be a primary parent after divorce (Arendell 1997, 163). As optimists and pessimists alike have observed, men appear to depend upon wives to mediate their relationship to their children (Arendell 1995, 33; Furstenberg and Cherlin 1991, 275; Wallerstein and Blakeslee 1989; Whitehead 1997b).[13] This may explain why marriage seems like the only solution for effective fathering for the pessimists.

Another route for expanding paternal participation—and overcoming the historical equivalence between breadwinning and masculinity[14]—would be to construct men as nurturers, caretakers, and responsible fathers. Arendell (1995, 251) calls for "a more vocal and widespread critique of the conventions of masculinity." A construction of masculinity that goes beyond putting all of men's eggs into one "breadwinner" basket (Bernard 1981) is long overdue. Perhaps marriage has an important "civilizing function" for men because of a flawed construction of masculinity in the first place; men have been deprived of the expectation or opportunity to advance their relationality—from boyhood to manhood.

Reinforcing marriage by compelling "divorce as a last resort" would obscure, not solve, this paternal disability. Rather than advocating marriage or reinforcing the provider role as pessimists do, many optimists argue that men need to combine providing with caretaking just as women have combined caretaking with providing. In the aggregate, women are changing faster than men. To keep up with wives' changes means that husbands must be willing to recognize the legitimacy of a wife's relational concerns, embrace what has been largely a devalued sphere, and to share power with their wives.

If a redistribution of relational responsibilities were to take place in marriage, this might extend fathers' involvement with their children in the event of divorce. More important, this could prevent divorces based on relational inequalities in the first place.[15] Indeed, in my research, paternal participation is part of the "marital labor" that egalitarian wives wanted to share. Reconstructing masculinity (and therefore gender in marriage) might provide the stronger deterrent to divorce for which pessimists have been searching.

IS DIVORCE EVER A GATEWAY FOR CHILDREN?

Given children's attenuated relations with their fathers and the downward mobility most children share with their mothers, is divorce ever a gateway for children? Not only do two-thirds of divorces involve children (U.S. Bureau of the Census 1995, P60-187), but few people object to divorce by childless couples today. Because it is children that electrify the divorce debates, I only sampled married parents. Are children paying the price for adults' individualism and lapsed family values, as the critics of divorce culture would argue? Or, could they be paying the costs of marriage culture and the quest for equality—interpersonal and institutional—that I have described?

Divorce is rarely experienced as a "gateway" for children—even perhaps, when it should be. It is, however, a turning point that is distinct from the adult experience. There is a tendency in the debates about the effects of divorce upon children to project adult experiences and capacities onto children. One recent study found that parents' and children's experiences were generally "out of synch" (Stewart et al. 1997, cited in Arendell 1998, 227). Parents may overestimate their child's well-being. Kitson with Holmes (1992, 227) found that most parents attribute very low levels of distress to their children, even though we know that the early period is hard for children. Whether divorce is due to a spouse's adultery, violence, or self-centeredness, the decision is not the child's to make. Of course, children survive and thrive after the temporary crisis of parental divorce, just as they survive other crises. Yet, the assumption that children are resilient should be tempered with the view that the endurance of parental relationships (even if they divorce) matters to children. Neither "divorce as a last resort" nor "divorce as a gateway" capture the divorce turning point for children, because they both presume some choice in the matter.[16]

Many studies agree upon some costs borne by children after a parental divorce, yet the source, extent, and meaning of these costs are fiercely debated (Wallerstein and Kelly 1980; Wallerstein and Blakeslee 1989; Amato and Booth 1997; Maccoby and Mnookin 1992; Hetherington, Law, and O'Connor 1993; Furstenberg and Cherlin 1991; Whitehead 1997a). The conditions preceding, surrounding, and following divorce matter a great deal, including the quality of parent-child relationships, custodial arrangements, the quality of the ex-spousal and coparenting relationships, the economic and social supports available, and the child's own psychological strengths (Furstenberg and Cherlin 1991; Kelly 1988, 134). The age and gender of the child may matter—though gender effects have been questioned (Arendell 1997, 175; Wallerstein and Kelly 1980; Kelly 1988; Wallerstein and Blakeslee 1989). Remarriage and new stepfamily relations affect a child's adjustment over time; indeed, some research suggests remarriage may be more of an adjustment than divorce (Ahrons and Rodgers 1987, 257).

Drawing upon an analysis of 92 studies involving 13,000 children, Amato (1994, 145) reports consistent findings that children of divorce experience "lower academic achievement, more behavioral problems, poorer psychological adjustment, more negative self-concepts, more social difficulties, and more problematic relationships with both mothers and fathers. Also, children of divorce are reported to become pregnant outside of marriage, marry young, and divorce upon becoming adults (McLanahan and Bumpass 1988; Glenn and Kramer 1987).

Taken together, these findings would seem to be alarming. The pessimists are alarmed. Yet, we should not assume that divorce is the "cause" when divorce is correlated with undesirable effects among children. Research on the adverse effects of divorce for children consistently finds that other factors that accompany divorce may be more important than the divorce itself. For example, "income differences account for almost 50 percent of the disadvantage faced by children in single-parent households" (McLanahan and Sandefur 1994; Coontz 1997, 101). Changes of residence and schools help to explain the other 50 percent of disadvantage. Above all, prospective and longitudinal studies of families suggest that marital conflict is more crucial than divorce in explaining behavioral and emotional problems for those children who are troubled (Amato and Booth 1996, 1997; Block, Block, and Gjerde, 1986; Coontz 1997, 102). Longitudinal studies have discovered that children's problems are apparent over a decade before the parents' divorce. Thus, in some cases, divorce and a single-parent household is better for children than continued marital conflict (Amato, Loomis, and Booth 1995).

Furthermore, Amato's (1994) analysis of multiple studies also reveals that the effects of divorce are very weak and that differences between children of divorce and children in continuously intact families are quite small (Amato and Keith 1991; Amato 1994; Amato and Booth 1996, 1997). As the optimist Coontz (1997, 99) clarifies, this research does not suggest that children of divorced parents have *more problems*, rather that *more children* of divorced parents have problems than do children of married parents. Yet, children of divorce show greater variability in their adjustment (Amato 1994). This means that some children of divorce do better thin children of married parents. Children from all kinds of families fare well and poorly. When we focus on the difference between family structures, we overlook the extensive overlap in children's well-being across family structures. Further, research increasingly suggests that the quality and consistency of family life, and not family structure, influences children's well-being (Arendell 1997, 187).

Most of the '70s couples I interviewed did not believe in staying together "for the sake of the children" if there was marital conflict. Parents sense that if their marriage is continuously in conflict, then this harms children too. Divorce is not a singular solution to conflict or violence since both can be exacerbated upon separation and divorce (Arendell and Kurz, 1999). Yet the gateway is crucial for such troubled marriages. Recall that the '50s Dominicks stayed together miserably for thirty years in spite of extramarital affairs, separation, and indications of violence—all for the sake of the children. These were justifiable conditions under the terms of marriage culture. One wonders to what degree the "sake of the children," among other deterrents, inhibited divorces that should have been when marriage culture reigned uncontested.[17]

Kurz's (1995, 52) random sample of divorced mothers revealed that 19 percent pursued divorce specifically because of violence; however, an astonishing 70 percent reported at least one incident of violence during the marriage or separation. Most research shows that violence remains a graver problem for wives than husbands—particularly in terms of injuries (Gelles and Straus 1988; Kurz 1989; Straton 1994). Also, research increasingly finds that witnessing spouse abuse *is* child abuse—even when a child is not physically violated (Holden, Geffner, and Jouriles 1998). Thus, removing children from the perpetrator, however much he (or she) is loved, is arguably for the sake of the children.

Believers in "divorce as a gateway" may want to make parental happiness equivalent to children's happiness when it is not. Pessimists correctly stress that the child's experience of divorce is distinct from the parents' experience. Thus, scholars are increasingly advocating parenting education classes for divorcing parents (Arendell 1995; Wallerstein 1998). Yet, believers in "divorce as a last resort" also mistakenly presume that the maintenance of marriage and a nuclear family is equivalent to children's happiness. We should not ignore the injuries that have attended marriage culture—particularly a male-dominated marriage culture. When egalitarian spouses become parents there is often a shift toward "increased traditionality of family and work roles in families of the 1980s and 1990s," and this "tends to be associated with *more* individual and marital distress for parents" (Cowan and Cowan 1998, 184). This represents the pinch between egalitarian beliefs and the structural impediments to equality in practice. Further, to the degree that we idealize a male-dominated, nuclear family model we cannot fail to reproduce such constructions of inequality among children. While some children are paying a price for the quest for equality, children also pay a price when the thread of commitment is tangled with the thread of male dominance. Moreover, children do find happiness and another vision of equality in alternative family forms.

THE FUTURE OF DIVORCE CULTURE

From Durkheim (1961) to Giddens (1979, 1991), sociologists have regularly addressed transitional periods such as our own. Norms, ideals, and authorities that guided our marital practices in the past are inadequate to families' needs in today's socioeconomic context. Could divorce culture represent a new tapestry of ideals and norms for guiding today's family lives? Even as the practices of '70s spouses are shaped by novel conditions, spouses attempt to shape them in turn—drawing alternatively, selectively, and even haphazardly on available ideologies and practices. Although divorce culture seems to be replacing marriage culture, it should be seen as a transitional means for "people to make sense of the circumstances in which they find themselves" (Mullings 1986), providing alternative strategies for action when marriage culture falls short. Still, like the '70s spouses, many people are ambivalent about divorce culture. Moreover, marriage culture endures.

Because divorce culture is new and unsettling there is a tendency to inflate its power and prevalence. Marriage culture is widely embraced. "Marriage as forever" is a belief that is not only sustained by married couples, but also the divorced (Riessman 1990). The reintroduction of grounds in "covenant marriages" represents a political effort to value the old tapestry that sustained "divorce as a last resort." Finally, "marrying as a given" lives on. While rates of marriage and remarriage have decreased since the mid-1960s (U.S. Bureau of the Census, 1992, P23-180, 8)—suggesting that fewer people experience marriage as an imperative—the majority of people eventually marry. Also, the two-parent family continues to be the predominant family form—so concern with its decline can be overstated (Cowan and Cowan 1998, 189).

Marriage culture also lives on in the next generation's aspirations. The majority of young people say they value marriage and plan to marry (Landis-Kleine et al. 1995). A 1992 survey showed that of all extremely important goals in life, the most valued by 78 percent of the high school respondents was "having a good marriage and family life" (Glenn 1996, 21). "Being able to find steady work" was ranked a close second by 77 percent of these students, and "being successful in my line of work" and "being able to give my children better opportunities than I've had" tied for third, at 66 percent.

Will the '90s spouses continue, reverse, or transcend the advance of divorce culture? How will they cope with the rise of divorce culture and its problems? Because a culture of divorce creates "divorce anxiety," premarital counseling would seem to be increasingly important. One valuable component of "covenant marriage" advanced by pessimists (in spite of critiques of therapeutic culture) has been to encourage religious or secular premarital counseling. Instituting therapy before marriage might prepare '90s spouses for the reflexive process and the marital work that characterizes marriage in an era of change, choice, and uncertainty.[18] Such counseling should not only attune spouses to one another's hopes, dreams, and desires, but should also provide information on the social conditions faced by married couples today. For example, the arrival of children is a vulnerable period of transition in marriage even when children are deeply desired (Cowan and Cowan 1998). Also, '90s spouses should know that aspirations for lifetime marriage, for thriving children, and a good job are not new; most people getting married share these hopes for themselves even as they harbor doubts about others. What thwarts their resolve and aspirations? Do they simply become individualistic?

This analysis of divorce culture has tried to situate the charges that a high divorce rate represents increased individualism in recent generations. On the one hand, like the pessimists, I agree that divorce culture is marked by individualism. Individualism clearly links and underlies the tenets of divorce culture: the choice to marry, to set conditions, and the chance to unmarry all speak to the primacy of the individual to redesign his or her life. However, my research complicates these claims. Individualism is not in a zero-sum relationship with commitment. It can be morally responsible rather than egoistic, it has not been absent for men in marriage culture, and it is not necessarily an end in itself. Divorce culture exposes how the terms of marital commitment reflect a legacy of male dominance. For married women, individualism can be a tool to resist old and enforce new terms of marital commitment—including nurturance, commitment, and relational responsibility shared by both spouses. When mothers use the power of individualism for relational ends—by working to provide, by removing children from violent households, or by refusing to be subordinated—individualism is neither an end in itself nor easily severed from committed responsibility. The meaning of pulling the individualistic lever of divorce culture cannot be stripped from interactional or institutional contexts. Thus '90s spouses would also do well to take the insights of optimists into account. Our quest for equality is ongoing.

Finally, an overemphasis on the individualism of women or men diverts our attention from the ways our social structures obstruct this quest for equality. The variety of families today may not represent a failure of commitment as much as individuals' valiant struggles to sustain commitments in a society that withholds structural supports from workers and families. Indeed, until the 1993 Family and Medical Leave Act, the United States had no family policy at all.[19] Other scholars have suggested an array of family policies—from easing work and family conflicts to providing economic and social supports—for today's burdened families, which I will not repeat here (see Arendell 1995; Burggraf 1997; Hewlett and West 1998; Hochschild 1997; Mason, Skolnick, and Sugarman 1998). Yet, two things are clear—when we allow corporate and government policies to neglect the needs of working parents, we are undermining marriage culture, and when we ignore enduring gender inequalities we advance divorce culture.

While divorce culture is flawed, I see it as a means to propel marital and family relationships in an egalitarian direction. Both "optional marriage" and "divorce as a gateway" recognize commitments apart from marriage, expose the costs of marriage culture, and legitimate diverse family arrangements. Critics of divorce culture advocate a return to the singular design of the nuclear family structure; however, in many ways this sustains a white, middle-class ethnocentrism,[20] and a heterosexism[21] that has marked our family ideals. By challenging "marriage as a given" and "divorce as a last resort," divorce culture helps to destigmatize unmarried families.

As we reconstruct the terms of marriage culture with the tool of divorce culture, we risk sacrificing relationality for rights equality. Rights language is essential for justice, dignity, and self-determination. Yet, it is not an unmitigated good, and only the young, childless, wealthy, or powerful can indulge in a sense of independence and obscure interdependence by relying upon others to sustain the illusion. Only when the relational responsibilities, still constructed as "feminine," are practiced and valued by men, and by the society at large, will we be able to move beyond the individualism of divorce culture and beyond a notion of equality limited to individual rights and obscuring relational responsibilities. Whether divorce culture eventually supplants rather than contests marriage culture, or generates "family cultures" that transcend this contestation, will depend upon social structural change and the quest for relational equality in the next generation.

Editors' Note: *References and Notes for this reading can be found in the original source.*

Women in Stepfamilies: The Fairy Godmother, the Wicked Witch, and Cinderella Reconstructed

Anne C. Bernstein

The two Barbaras were sitting at either end of the couch in my office. Both are bright, engaging, caring women. Although they would not be mistaken for sisters, they are of the same physical "type": tall, brunette, and robust. They are mother and stepmother to the same child.

It was early in my work with stepfamilies, and I had foolishly decided—after meeting with mother and child, with father and child, with the child alone, with mother and father, and with father and stepmother—that a meeting between these two smart, personable women would be an opportunity to dispel mutual suspicion. The mother was convinced that the stepmother was childishly competitive with her daughter for her father's attention; the stepmother believed that the mother was instigating her daughter to cold-shoulder her, leaving her feeling like an unwelcome guest in her own home. How could they fail to see their mutual interest in the welfare of a 10-year-old girl they both loved? "I want to make Susan's time with us happier for her," the stepmother ventured in one way after another throughout the session. And each time the mother's response was, in variation, "Susan's interest is in her father, not you." The stepmother called me that evening in tears, distraught that once again her role in the girl's life was dismissed as inconsequential. Although my intention was to dispel myths of ill will and incompetence—a goal accomplished in prior cases by meeting with ex-spouses and their new partners—I wondered whether I had failed to account adequately for how gender is a key player in the stepfamily scenario.

In proposing to recontextualize the stepfamily, I must first contextualize myself: I became active in the feminist movement in the late 1960s, a family psychologist in the early 1970s, and a stepmother and a mother in the early 1980s. In this chapter, I explore how and why women's experience of stepfamily differs from men's, thus introducing gender into the clinical discourse. I first consider the stepfamily in its evolving societal context, highlighting how stepfamily stories—those we are told and those we tell ourselves—inform our experience and shape our relationships.

THE STEPFAMILY IN CONTEXT

Much of the dissatisfaction for all participants in stepfamilies comes from their employing a user-friendly yardstick—the "Ozzie and Harriet," "Father Knows Best" version of American family life. A "nuclear" family, comprised of a breadwinner father, homemaker mother, and their dependent children, has been both the implicit and explicit frame of reference in assessing stepfamily experience. This results in a "deficit comparison" model, whereby the stepfamily is seen as a less effective constellation. It is important to remember here, as with the reports of stepfamily outcome research that follow, that significant differences between groups can overshadow the most important finding of all: that majorities of parents and stepparents of both sexes are both involved in and satisfied with stepfamily life.

Clinical thinking about working with stepfamilies often begins with addressing the ways in which stepfamilies differ from first-marriage families. We are repeatedly reminded how important it is to underline the differences between nuclear families and stepfamilies in thinking about what is functional and dysfunctional, normal or abnormal; family members themselves are urged to accept that their relationships with stepkin cannot and should not be forced into the nuclear mold. As welcome antidotes to the handicapping expectation that stepfamilies can be "just the same" as those formed from first marriages, these psychoeducational efforts have helped stepfamily members avoid the misery that comes with falling short of impossible goals. But while we have been busily encouraging stepkin to hold themselves to a different measure, the basis for comparison has itself been transformed: The deviant behavior has become the norm, and what we have long held to be normal is itself aberrant.

Demographic Shifts

By the early 1990s, residential married-couple stepfamilies outnumbered "traditional nuclear families" with provider husbands and homemaker wives, and projections for the year 2000 are that stepfamilies will outnumber any other single family type (Furstenberg & Cherlin, 1991). Americans born in the 1980s have a probability of one in two that they will be members of stepfamilies, either in their childhood or as adults (Furstenberg,

1980). Moreover, official statistics do not include part-time stepfamilies; remarried families with younger children, in which the older stepchildren have already left home; or *de facto* stepfamilies not involving remarriage (e.g., the first marriage of a formerly unmarried parent, or the long-term cohabitation of parents with heterosexual or lesbian/gay partners). Taken together, we are talking about more families having stepkin than not.

Traditional, Modern, or Old-Fashioned?

Contemporary socioeconomic issues, combined with these demographic trends, show that the "traditional nuclear family" that forms the basis for the deficit comparison model has outlived its historical moment. In fact, it is not traditional at all. It is a "modern" form that developed in conjunction with the industrialization of society, not achieving predominance until the post-World War II period.

In *Brave New Families*, Judith Stacey (1990) describes the decline of the modern family as a response to postindustrial economic conditions, including the shift away from productive employment and the failure of most jobs to pay a family-supporting wage, without which the gendered roles that are the linchpins of the modern family cannot be sustained. Feminist criticism of the family views women's economic dependency as disempowering, and the narrowing definition of women's realm as housework, consumption, and raising fewer and fewer children as exploitative and constricting. This critique has provided ideological support for women's entering the labor market, accelerating postindustrial economic trends. Entry into the work world has given women both the ability to envision other possibilities and the economic wherewithal to make leaving unsatisfying marriages feasible, contributing to the divorce rate, leading to the proliferation of female-headed households, and rendering the "modern" family "old-fashioned."

The "postmodern" family, viewed by Stacey (1990) as "a normless gender order, one in which parenting arrangements, sexuality, and the distribution of work, responsibility, and resources are all negotiable and constantly renegotiable, can also invite considerable conflict and insecurity" (p. 258). The postmodern perspective embraces uncertainty and doubt; old patterns or ideas are implicitly discarded or radically transformed, while the shape and significance of what is to follow remain unfathomable. In employing this concept to characterize changing family and gender arrangements, Stacey's ethnography illustrates that "no longer is there a single culturally dominant family pattern to which the majority of Americans conform and most of the rest aspire" (p. 17).

Thinking about stepfamilies can follow a similar course. The "traditional" stepfamily, epitomized by a remarriage following bereavement, was a variant of the "modern" family, with the stepparent as a replacement for the dead parent in an attempt to recreate the original family. The division of parental labor was gender-specific, following the Parsonian model of a partnership between an "instrumental" male and an "expressive" female (Stacey, 1990, p. 10). The "modern" family map was superimposed on the stepfamily terrain, with roles and rules that conspired to make stepfamily members feel deprived and dysfunctional. But in their variety and complexity, in the ambiguity of both membership and family roles, and in the prevalence of experiential uncertainty, insecurity, and doubt, stepfamilies constitute a prototype of the "postmodern" family.

Considerations of Class, Race, and Sexual Preference

Most of the stepfamily literature describes white middle-class stepfamilies that seek psychotherapy or participate in research. About the "white" part of it, there is little ambiguity, but "middle-class" is increasingly a catch-all term claimed by all but the indigent and the superrich. One household may contain blue-, white-, and pink-collar workers; family income may depend more on how many members are bringing home paychecks than on the occupational or educational standing of any individual. Although definitive statements about the impact of social class on stepfamily process may be impossible given this ambiguity, this blurring of boundaries seems to point to a greater generalizability of findings than might otherwise be expected.

Racial differences are another story. There is a dramatic dearth of information about African-American and other minority stepfamilies. As psychologist Nancy Boyd-Franklin (personal communication, February 29, 1992) has said, pointing to how social science has pathologized black experience, "whites are described as having stepfamilies, African-Americans as coming from 'broken homes.'" Demographers tell us that African-Americans are more likely than whites to experience marital disruption in both first and second marriages, and, women especially, are less likely to remarry following divorce (Fine, McKenry, Donnelly, & Voydanoff, 1992). The percentage of all families that are stepfamilies is higher for whites than for blacks, indicating that African-Americans who remarry constitute a smaller segment of the black community. When nonmarital or "boyfriend" families are taken into account, the proportion of African-American stepfamilies increases, but their numbers are still limited by the greater numbers of eligible women relative to men.

In one of the few empirical studies, Fine et al. (1992) concluded that African-American stepfather families were generally similar in parent and child adjustment to both white stepfather families and African-American first-marriage families, although they differed from each comparison group in some ways. A fuller discussion of the interaction of race and stepfamily dynamics awaits more data, but there is evidence that demographic family patterns among blacks are being replicated among whites at a slower rate (Walker, 1988).

Other unexplored groups, usually not included in the ranks of stepfamilies by demographers, are gay and lesbian stepfamilies.[1] Although reliable demographic data are difficult to locate, estimates are that 10% of gays and 20% of lesbians have children, typically from prior heterosexual partnerships. Patterson (1992) estimates that in the United States there are between 1 and 5 million lesbian mothers, between 1 and 3 million gay fathers, and between 6 and 14 million children of either. Any subsequent residential partnership creates a stepfamily.

Although a comprehensive discussion of this subject is beyond the scope of this chapter, lesbian and gay stepfamilies are both like and unlike their heterosexual counterparts. In the therapist's office, many of their experiences will be similar to the referring stories of male–female stepfamilies. There are, however, important differences. These stepfamilies are even less "institutionalized" than those formed by remarriage, and often are closeted to avoid discrimination. Ambiguous to begin with, the "stepparent" role is still more improvisational in lesbian and gay families, where parenthood is less likely to be part of a partner's expectations for relationships. Studies comparing gay and lesbian couples with heterosexual couples report that what differences do exist are mostly reflective of differences in gender socialization (Blumstein & Schwartz, 1983). In looking at stepcouples who are lesbian or gay, we might expect that most of the differences from their heterosexual counterparts stem from being households headed by two women or by two men, and/or from the added stress of confronting societal homophobia.

WOMEN'S EXPERIENCE OF STEPFAMILY LIFE[2]

In the past decade, researchers (Pasley & Ibinger-Tallman, 1987; Hetherington, 1987; Zaslow, 1988, 1989) have confirmed what clinicians (Visher & Visher, 1979; Keshet, 1987) who work with remarried families have noted for years: that females in stepfamilies—be they mothers, stepmothers, or stepdaughters—experience more stress, less satisfaction, and more symptoms than their male counterparts.

What is so hard for females living in stepfamilies? Is it really more difficult to be a stepmother than a stepfather? A stepdaughter than a stepson? A remarried mother than a remarried father? And if these findings accurately reflect the experience of those who occupy those roles, why?

Differences among Stepfamilies

In talking about stepfamilies, we are considering not a single family type but an array of possible kinship systems. A parent, who has been widowed, divorced, or previously unmarried, creates a household with another adult who has been widowed, divorced, or never before married. The new mate may or may not already be a parent, and they may or may not go on to have a child together. Children from prior unions may reside with the new couple, may visit on alternate weekends or during vacations, or may divide their time nearly equally between two households. A stepparent and stepchild may become acquainted any time between the child's infancy and adulthood, or even beyond. All these factors create important differences in the experience of all family members in the process of stepfamily formation and integration.

Both because mothers retain custody of their children in 90% of contemporary divorces and because many stepfather families include a previously single mother, residential stepmother families are far less prevalent than those families in which children live with their mothers and stepfathers (Furstenberg & Cherlin, 1991). As a result, residential stepmother families face a great number of risk factors. The stepchildren are more likely to have experienced profound disruptions in their relationships with their parents: loss of their mothers through death; being the objects of custody battles; separations from their siblings in what is called "split custody"; and changes in custody. In many cases, they have moved in with their fathers because their single mothers could not manage their behavior problems (Greif, 1985; Glick, 1980; Spanier & Glick, 1980; Risman, 1986). As a result of greater disruption, conflict, and loss, these children are more likely to have problems that precede stepfamily formation. In addition, because they do not live with their mothers, they are more apt to see themselves as deviant at a time of life when being "like everyone else" is highly valued.

Another way that stepmother families differ structurally from stepfather families is in greater boundary ambiguity within the "binuclear family" (Ahrons & Rodgers, 1987). Because a stepmother family is usually not the primary residence for the father's children, their membership in the household and status as family "insiders" can be ambiguous. Nor is the separation between households as clearly bounded as that between a stepfather family and a father's home. Mothers are more of a presence in stepmother households, calling to keep contact with their children and to make arrangements for the myriad activities for which they typically take responsibility. Even when the children live with their fathers and stepmothers, mothers remain more involved with their children than do noncustodial fathers (Furstenberg, Nord, Peterson, & Zill, 1983). Because the relationship between parents more often deteriorates with remarriage, especially if only the fathers have remarried, this greater contact will result in more prolonged conflict and stress between parents and stepparents in stepmother families, complicating children's relationship with their stepmothers (Ahrons & Rodgers, 1987; Furstenberg & Nord, 1985; Ibinger-Tallman & Pasley, 1987).

Women's and Men's Experience of Stepparenthood

In summarizing the greater stress and negative outcome for children in stepmother families, Pasley and Ibinger-Tallman (1987) concluded:

> . . . stepmothers are less satisfied with their relationship to their stepchildren, feel that their marital relationship is negatively affected by their husband's children, are more dissatisfied with their role, and feel that the relationship between them and the biological mother is more difficult. Stepmothers also report themselves to be less involved with their stepchildren and have more conflictual relationships with them. (p. 310)

Stepfathers, who have been far more extensively studied, have traditionally been described as "detached" in their relationships with their stepchildren (Duberman, 1975, Hetherington, 1987). Yet those few studies that compare stepmothers with stepfathers show that stepmothers feel still less involved than stepfathers (Ahrons & Wallisch, 1987; Ahrons & Rodgers, 1987). But are they?

Why these grey-tinted glasses on the the part of the women? I suggest that one answer may be that stepmothers hold themselves to a higher standard and care more about the quality of relationships than do stepfathers. In trying to meet their own and others' relational needs, all stepfamily members struggle with role ambiguity and the almost inevitable mismatch in what members expect of one another, making reciprocity a significant challenge. Females may be more sensitive to the quality of relationship within each family dyad; their emotional seismographs identify problems earlier, when the difficulties are more subtle, and their dissatisfaction with family relationships matters more in reckoning their general life satisfaction.

The character Joanie Caucus in the comic strip *Doonesbury*, a congressional aide and remarried mother of a mutual child, sits up one night in bed and asks her husband: "Rick, I know you love Jeff as much as I do. So why don't you seem as torn up about not being able to spend time with him?" Not even opening his eyes, he replies: "Well, it may be because I'm spending a whole lot more time on family than my father did, and you're spending far less time than your mother did. Consequently," he goes on in the next frame, "you feel incredibly guilty, while I naturally feel pretty proud of myself. I think that's all it really amounts to, don't you?" Still not fully roused, he tells her to try and get some sleep, oblivious to the lamp she is hurling in his direction (Trudeau, 1985).

This example suggests how women expect more of themselves as parents, and, I propose, as stepparents. When stepfathers measure their involvement with their stepchildren, their basis of comparison is how involved they think fathers are with their children, whereas stepmothers compare their own involvement with what they think mothers would do or feel. When stepfathers report that they are "very" involved with their stepchildren in greater numbers than do stepmothers, what we may be witnessing is their employing very different standards.

Stepfathers are more like fathers because their roles are essentially similar. Despite a great deal of media attention to fathers' more active participation in child care, the trend toward shared parenting is still a limited phenomenon (Ehrensaft, 1987); women are still primarily responsible for the care of children. The mother–child relationship may be the most monogamous of all. The expression "a face only a mother could love" says it all. Stepmothers do not offer that level of acceptance—nor, we must remember, do all mothers—but neither fathers nor stepfathers are expected to provide unconditional acceptance. Less than unconditional love is thus felt as more of a deficit in a stepmother than in a stepfather.

Children in stepmother families appear to underestimate their stepmothers' involvement even as they overestimate their mothers' involvement in their lives; this may testify to children's need to preserve the image of a mother who is always there. In a study of full-time stepmothers who were sharing many child-rearing activities with their husbands and struggling to establish good relationships with their stepchildren, Santrock and Sitterle (1987) found that

> despite the stepmothers' persistent efforts to become involved, their stepchildren tenaciously held onto the view of them as somewhat detached, unsupportive and uninvolved in their lives. Not surprisingly, stepmothers seemed to have reached a similar conclusion about their role in the family system. (p. 291)

Although few, if any, little girls go to bed at night hugging their pillows and dreaming that "someday I'll be a stepmother," part of what it means to grow up female is to try on—even if only to be later discarded—the role of mother as a core component of feminine identity. In thinking of herself as a mother, every woman confronts powerful cultural imperatives: to be always available, to be all-giving, to do it all. It is the very impossibility of measuring up to this societal ideal, reflected in the splitting of "good mother/fairy godmother" and "bad mother/wicked stepmother" in the fairy tales that introduced us all to what stepfamily life might be expected to be. Faulting themselves for not feeling or doing all that they assume *real* mothers feel or do, stepmothers often do not realize that being a mother forces every woman to accept her limitations. Women who are stepmothers without first being mothers base their maternal self-esteem on experience with stepchildren and have a harder time gaining a sense of themselves as "good enough" mothers.

Although custodial remarried fathers are more actively involved in their children's daily lives than are fathers in general, they leave more "mothering" tasks undone than do their female counterparts (Santrock & Sitterle, 1987; Guisinger, Cowan, & Schuldberg, 1989). In her study of shared parenting, Ehrensaft (1987) found that women care more about how the children's appearance reflects on them, worry more, and do more of the psychological management, keeping track of what needs to be done for the children and when. Similarly, stepmothers compare the parenting that fathers provide with their own internalized templates of what needs to be done, and find that there is "mothering" work left undone. Because "mothering" means more contact between stepparent and stepchild, and because more contact (especially when it entails the traditional tasks of socialization) makes for more opportunities for conflict, the results are greater stress, anxiety, depression, and anger in stepmother families.

When stepmothers withdraw, it is more reactive than disengaged, more of a cutoff than a modest backing away. Stepmothers who describe having been actively involved with their stepchildren at the beginning of a remarriage and later retreating in frustration, hurt, anger, and disappointment, date an improvement in the stepparent–stepchild relationship to the time of their retreat from "trying too hard." Children, however, do not always agree, registering the loss of a prior level of involvement they did not seem to appreciate at the time (Bernstein, 1989b). The question remains, however, as to whether those stepmothers who see themselves as less involved with their stepchildren, using as their referent an earlier unrealistic or unworkable model, are actually any less involved than the stepfathers who did not demand as much of themselves to begin with.

The more disengaged masculine style of relating may be an asset for a stepparent in the early stages of a remarriage, during which time clinicians generally advise that stepparents not directly offer guidance or discipline (Visher & Visher, 1988; Bray, 1990). Traditionally more involved in the external world of work and achievement, men invest less of their identities in family role status than women do. Men are thus better able to remain "relatively pleasant in spite of the adverse behavior they encounter" with stepchildren (Hetherington, 1987, p. 196). Stepmothers, however, consistently report to clinicians their pain in feeling peripheral to family emotional life; they complain of feeling exploited by stepchildren who eat their meals and leave towels on their bathroom floors while remaining personally disengaged, if not hostile.

Mothers in the Middle

Even remarried mothers who are not stepmothers are less satisfied with both their marriages and life in general than are remarried fathers (Hetherington, 1987). As is true of stepmothers and women in general, their experience of one relationship within the household is contingent on their satisfaction with each of the others.

Unlike stepmothers, however, mothers in stepfather families have more influence with the children; they have both more power and more responsibility. Socialized to see the maintenance of relational quality as their job, mothers feel the need to satisfy everyone's needs, even when competing demands make that impossible. A mother may shuttle between faulting her partner for not fulfilling her dream of giving her children a full-time Daddy, and not wanting to put too many demands on her new husband for fear of making the "package deal" so onerous that he takes flight. Seeking relief from the responsibilities of single parenting, a mother can be torn between wanting her new partner to take over and shutting him (or her) out, protecting her children from the discipline of someone she cannot trust to love them as she does. Wanting the children to be well cared for, she nonetheless can be impatient as their needs seem to preclude couple time and resentful that they are an issue of contention with a new partner.

Marie, the lesbian mother of 19-year-old Debbie, described the stress she feels in being the person to whom all family members turn:

> "There is this push-pull thing between your partner and your child. It feels like you're trying to mother two people—sibling rivalry, in a way. I feel I have to make decisions where Sally will perceive that I'm taking Debbie's side, and Debbie will perceive that I'm taking Sally's side, based on Debbie's feeling not included and Sally's feeling that it's probably not the appropriate way for a parent to act. I feel constantly in the middle and always have. It doesn't seem like it ever goes away."

Because it is less obvious to the community that they are in stepfamilies, mothers may attempt to pass their families off as first-marriage families. In a consultation about problems with her 11-year-old son, for example, Marge began to see the ill effects of her insistence on always being in the middle between the boy and his stepfather, as well as her elation when a fight at his father's house led to Sam's being with her full-time, making her feel as if she had won the "best parent" award. In a follow-up interview, she told me:

> "I feel that I denied for a long time that we were a stepfamily, and that Sam's place in it was any different than that of our two younger children. Even though Sam can be a real pain in the neck—on an outing, for instance, he'll complain, whine, and fall down more often than you would expect—I still wanted him there because this was my family. And if someone said, 'Oh, you have two kids,' I'd correct them, 'No, I have three kids.'' I pretended that we were a nuclear family, and if we made believe that that other out there didn't exist, it would go away and we could put up our white picket fence and be fine. But it didn't work that way."

Stepdaughters at Risk

Stepdaughters, too, fare less well in remarried families than do stepsons. A review of the literature by Zaslow (1988, 1989) concluded that girls with remarried mothers showed more externalized symptoms (behavior problems, hostility, acting out) and internalized symptoms (anxiety, depression, withdrawal, dependence) than did boys in the same family configuration—a reversal of the pre-remarriage picture of the boys' more negative responses to parental divorce. Although there is less information available about remarried fathers, this differential outcome by stepchild and gender seems to apply to these families as well: Stepmothers and stepdaughters reported abiding conflict (Furstenberg, 1987), and stepmother–stepdaughter relationships were more detached and negative than stepmother–stepson relationships (Clingempeel, Brand, and Ievoli, 1984).

A daughter typically experiences more of a sense of loss when a parent enters a new partnership than does a son. Daughters have more often been close confidants of their single mothers. The greater the intimacy in a mother's new partnership, the less access a daughter feels to her mother, and the more she misses the exclusivity she enjoyed earlier. Talking with Debbie, the teenage daughter in the lesbian family above, conveys this sense of loss:

> "You really feel like your mother's gone, that the person takes your mother. Sally spends more time with my mother; my mother sleeps with her. We used to spend time watching

TV together, and now she spends time with Sally, alone in the room, and she goes out more."

When it is a father who remarries, a stepdaughter's loss may be still more bitter. Not only are single fathers more indulgent and more permissive with their daughters than with their sons, but daughters of single fathers are more apt than their brothers to cast themselves in a partnership role in their fathers' households, making the entry of stepmothers more of a usurpation (Santrock & Sitterle, 1987).

Just as stepmother–mother relations are more intense and conflictual than stepfather–father relations, stepmother–stepdaughter relationships may be more difficult than stepmother–stepson relationships because they include at least two people in ambiguous roles with a heightened sensitivity to the relational context. Their relationships may be rated as more problematic because they are subjecting the quality of the relationship to greater scrutiny and have higher expectations to begin with. It is possible that there may be a continuum of stepparent–stepchild relationships, with both the positive and negative extremes of the continuum occupied by stepmother–stepdaughter pairs. In other words, stepmother–stepdaughter relationships may be both worse and better than stepmother–stepson relationships, which may be more affable and more disengaged.

Stepmothers, Stepdaughters, and Mothers

Having been a girl herself, the childless stepmother is more confident of her ability to parent stepdaughters than stepsons—a confidence that has its underside, however, in trying too hard too soon to make a difference in the girls' lives. As females, both stepmothers and stepdaughters may have a harder time defining boundaries. Stepmothers are more likely to see their stepdaughters as extensions of themselves than their stepsons, whom they expect, by reason of gender, to be different. And a stepdaughter, more than a stepson, in developing a sense of her own identity, will be more judgmental of her stepmother's personal traits, seeing in the older woman's characteristics a model that must be adopted or discarded. Looking for and not finding in the other a reflection of the self can lead to estrangement or conflict.

Identity issues as part of stepmother–stepdaughter conflicts may not, however, be obvious to the participants. A stepmother who complains about her stepdaughter's appropriating her belongings is usually not thinking that in wearing the woman's clothes, the girl is trying to feel closer to her. Helen Coale (1993) describes how she defused a stepmother's anger at her stepdaughter's going through her drawers and and helping herself to lingerie and cosmetics: By hiding little gifts and notes in her drawers, the stepmother could playfully take control of what had felt out of control, making explicit the stepdaughter's indirect attempts at contact, changing her own response, and thereby changing the girl's behavior.

Intimately connected with the stepmother–stepdaughter relationship is a third female: the girl's mother, whose role though not so ambiguous as the stepmother's, becomes less clear when her children are (at least in part) in the care of another woman. Typically, it is no small adjustment for a mother to feel, for example, that her child is sick and she has no access to the child's bedside, when everything she knows and feels about being a mother dictates that she should be there for her child. Access to children can be an explosive issue in separating and separated families, and the entry of another woman into the parental field can intensify feelings of being displaced in mothers who do not see fathers as real competition or as standards for comparison.

Children, especially girls, need their mothers' permission to accept their stepmothers; otherwise, to welcome the stepmother is disloyally to abandon the mother. When a stepmother has been "the other woman" in a triangle that preceded the dissolution of the marriage, a mother faces a formidable obstacle to releasing her children to form an independent relationship with their father's new partner. When a mother has initiated the marital separation, or is happily settled in her own life, the blessing comes more easily.

Each woman, mother and stepmother, brings different challenges and vulnerabilities to the task of working out how they will acknowledge and respect each other's role in the lives of the children who travel between them. For the most part, mothers need to be less intrusive and stepmothers less territorial. Centrality in their children's lives is one of the few areas in which women generally feel empowered; for a mother who is already disempowered by the loss of a spouse, to relinquish any more power can be unbearable. To learn to be a divorced mother means to unlearn the idea that "wherever my children are is my space." Only when a stepmother can be consistently clear that she is not out to replace the mother's centrality in the children's affection can their mother find the resources to honor the boundaries of the stepfamily household. Conversely, a stepmother can only be inclusive when she feels that her needs count too.

In thinking about her evolving relationship with her stepchildren's mother, one stepmother recalled:

> "In the early days I was with my husband, we would be in bed, and we'd hear her walk down the hall and into the bathroom on the other side of the wall, because she'd forgotten to brush the boys' hair and let herself into the house they used to share to use a hairbrush. Even after we'd moved, she'd stop by in the morning to pick up a child, and before we knew it she'd be in the bathroom, talking to my husband while he took a shower. In those first few years, I felt like I had to be a sentry and meet her at the door before she could get up the stairs, or ask her to leave when I'd come home to what I thought would be an empty house and find her sitting there helping Carl with his homework. As those intrusions lessened and essentially disappeared, I find myself much readier to consult with her about decisions on 'my watch' and to insist that she participate when we're making plans for the boys."

This anecdote demonstrates how the children's needs are more likely to be met when the mother's need for access to her children is balanced with the stepmother's need for privacy and predictability.

THERAPY WITH STEPFAMILIES

Stepfamily therapy is not so much a question of technique as a way of engaging with the discourse about family life that "disrupt[s] " or "relax[es] . . . [the] complex of network of presuppositions" (James & McIntyre, 1989, p. 18) that create distress and foreclose possibilities. I am using the language of social construction (Gergen, 1985) and narrative approaches to therapy (Laird, 1989; White & Epston, 1990) to propose that therapy be grounded in the cocreation of new stepfamily stories—stories that enable family members to discover ways of thinking, feeling, and behaving that are both more personally satisfying and more congruent with the changed context of family life. By recontextualizing stepfamily life, the therapist invites the family to create inclusive and democratic solutions to family membership, to build empowering alliances, and to redistribute the emotional division of labor, both within a stepfamily household and between households linked in the remarriage chain.

Deconstructing Stepfamily Myths

A postmodern approach to therapy with stepfamilies calls for a radical deconstruction of the disabling family stories of failure, insufficiency, and neglect that have made 'stepchild' the popular image for any "person, organization, project, etc. that is not properly treated, supported or appreciated" (*Webster's College Dictionary*, 1991, p. 1311). By actively constructing stories that liberate our relationships from the legacy of the Brothers Grimm, and by redefining the meanings of "family" and "kinship" to create nurturing and empowering contexts for contemporary social life, we ease the pain for those whose life stories take place in the transition between the modern family and its successors.

Recent research has validated clinicians' long-held belief that teaching stepfamilies about normal and expectable differences from first-marriage families produces immediate relief and can generate changes that resound throughout the family system (Elion, 1990). Psychoeducation is the point of departure for effective therapy with stepfamily members. This involves dispelling myths, normalizing client's experiences, and locating them in a developmental framework that looks beyond the impasses of the present and provides strategies that have proven effective to others similarly situated.

I have discussed earlier how women's narratives of stepfamily life are more disappointed than men's. In storying their lives as stepfamily members, women can be encouraged to examine what they expect of themselves, what the men and children in their lives expect of them, and what cultural expectations they have absorbed. Are they facing demands and asking of themselves feelings and behaviors that are more appropriate to first-marriage families? How do these expectations fit current opportunities and inclinations? Which beliefs are remnants from ill-fitting hand-me-down fashions, and what might they design to fit their lives as they are living them?

Beyond Categories, Toward Connection

Workable stepfamily narratives need to entertain the possibility that the relationship between two people is not totally circumscribed by social categories. Using stepkin labels as an explanatory frame may be reducing reality to its barest outlines, obscuring the influence of developmental factors, and serving as a shield against a more personal connection.

Hare-Mustin (1987) has proposed two ways to err in creating therapeutic models: "Alpha prejudice" exaggerates differences between groups of people, while "beta prejudice" ignores differences when they do exist. In thinking about stepfamilies, most writers have attacked the beta prejudice of a stepfamily's pretending to be a family formed from a first marriage, and it is in countering this set of distortions that the psychoeducation is most helpful. But there is another side to the situation—the alpha prejudice of making too much of the differences that do exist. Although differentiations from the nuclear model must be made in both descriptive and prescriptive conceptualizations about stepfamilies, overuse of the "step-" qualifier in relationships in remarried families can also be problematic.

Delia, for example, attributed feeling estranged as a teenager to Irene's being her stepmother. Had she entertained the possibility that they could be close, albeit stepkin, she could have approached Irene and said, "I know you're busy, but I'd really like to go shopping and have lunch with you, like my friends do with their mothers." Irene, too, held back, feeling that she did not have the legitimacy to push too hard for her stepchildren to adopt her values. Delia recounts,

> "Irene would say to Dad, 'Go tell your daughter.' Later, I asked her, 'Why?' She said, 'I felt that I couldn't do that with you kids, because I wasn't your mother.' But I think it would have been better if she had. I really wanted a mother."

In the same vein, conflicts within stepfamilies can be too easily diverted to stepfamily status (e.g., "You wouldn't treat me like this if you were my real parent/child"). If what is undesirable (e.g., a particular behavior) is a necessary function of what is immutable (i.e., being a stepparent/stepchild), change, by definition, cannot occur. Commenting on his wife's calling his then 16-year-old daughter "the Ice Princess" and attributing her teenage uncooperativeness to their not being mother and daughter, one father I interviewed philosophized,

> "Part of having a good blended family is having a good myth: that it's possible; that the kids will be okay, you'll be okay, and that it will all work out reasonably well. Everyone has problems, and theirs may not be substantially worse than anybody else's."

In hearing the family story, the therapist listens for superimpositions of paragraphs or even chapters that have been cut and pasted, out of context, from other families' stories; normalizes the emotional discrepancy created by the mismatch; explores possibilities for moving beyond the current impasse; and then helps family members to work through the transition, both interpersonally by renegotiating relationships and intrapersonally by understanding how echoes of old scripts intrude on the current scene.

For example, a stepmother struggling with feeling excluded by her husband's relationship with his children is validated in her pain at being the outsider to an intimacy that precedes her entry into the family. She is helped to understand that stepfamily integration is a process that takes time. She and the children's father then are assisted in negotiating ways to make her feel that she matters, creating "both–and" solutions to what appeared to be an "either–or" choice of attending to wife or children. She may also need to explore how family-of-origin issues have made belonging and exclusion particularly salient issues for her in a more personal way. (See the case example of Nell, Ken, and Darla, below.)

Differentiating between which aspects of the presenting problem pertain to stepfamily status and which are particular to the individuals involved is the initial challenge of the therapy. The effects of stepfamily dynamics are not always obvious to participants, who may either overplay or underplay such issues in the initial contact. Emotionally and logistically central to their families, mothers who are not themselves in steprelationships may not think of theirs as stepfamilies. In contrast to stepmothers and stepdaughters, who tend to overuse stepkin status as an explanatory frame for family problems, mothers may neglect to mention being part of stepfamilies, simply reporting children's symptoms. For example, a mother calling for help in managing her pubescent son may not consider that the family dynamics of his being the only mutual child of her remarriage play a part in the problem and have some bearing on the solution.

Recreating Roles: Toward Inclusivity and Empowerment

Role ambiguity is another source of distress that brings stepfamily members to therapy, either because stepparents are unsure and uneasy about how to relate to their stepchildren or because their preferences are rejected by partners and/or children. The consulting room is an arena in which all parties can compare and contrast their expectations of what appropriate and comfortable roles might be, working toward agreement.

Although lack of role clarity is normal in stepfamilies, and clarification among family members can decrease conflict and improve relationships, there is virtual consensus that new stepparents should go slowly in being "parental" to their partners' children. With stepfamily integration, the evolution of parental authority is usually toward shared responsibility: Parents and stepparents will never be equals in this regard, but they usually become more balanced.

Some styles of stepparenting yield better results than others, especially in the first few years of remarriage. Bray (1990) and his colleagues found that "parental monitoring" by stepfathers—being aware of where and what the children were doing and upholding the rules set by the parents, much like babysitters or child care providers—was associated with fewer behavior problems in stepchildren. Such monitoring requires parents to let children know clearly what their expectations are and that they have deputized stepparents to see to it that these are met in the parents' absence.

One approach in working with stepfamilies is to advocate drastic revisions of traditional family gender roles, so that stepmothers do not end up "wicked" and depressed from failed attempts to make up to the children for their family losses, and so that stepfathers do not become depressed "ogres" from taking on all the responsibility for providing discipline and financial stability. Instead, parents are asked to "own a full range of parenting tasks for the children: so that 'moms' are not needed to nurture and 'dads' are not needed to discipline" (Webb, 1990, p. 21).

There is much to be said for this approach, and for efforts to redistribute the division of labor (both physical and emotional) within stepfamilies, as within other households. Caution must be taken, however, to ensure that it not be used to disempower women further. Mothers left with the sole responsibility for nurturing and discipline may be overburdened, functioning as virtual single parents despite the presence of their partners. And stepmothers, relieved of the "traditional" female child-rearing tasks, may be left relationally underemployed and tangential, helplessly sidelined as their stepchildren are underparented. This does not mean that stepmothers want to take over primary responsibility for the children. When the division of labor is along traditional gender lines, they become increasingly dissatisfied with their marriages and are most content when both child care and household tasks are shared (Guisinger et al., 1989).

Accomplishing a shift in gender roles can also be a therapeutic challenge. Telling people to do things differently is generally insufficient, as gender roles are deeply structured and cannot be casually rearranged. Partners frequently take issue with each other's attempts at assuming nontraditional parental functions. Stepmothers, like women in general, see men as not covering the bases when the "mothering" is left to them (Ehrensaft, 1987), and stepfathers chide mothers for "letting the kids walk all over them." Anticipating that there will be difficulties in making the transition, as men assume primary responsibility for nurturing and women for limit setting, helps prevent precipitous interventions by stepparents who see partners avoiding or struggling with tasks that they feel they could do better. Both for men and women, the temptation in such a position is to jump in to fill the void—or, conversely, to withdraw from the field, cutting off either physically or emotionally.

Preparing a couple to work out a system of consultation, so that the "expertise" of one gender is seen as a resource that can be shared with the other without fear of being put down, can accomplish this shift while keeping the couple connected and attending to the children's needs. "Consultation" implies imparting information and experience to a less experienced but respected colleague. The challenge, to paraphrase Keshet (1989), is to work out a role division within a stepfamily that respects and challenges both the biological ties of the parent and children and the gender roles for which men and women have been socialized. It is not enough to tell stepparents what not to do; in order for them to feel connected to their stepchildren, they must be helped to discover how they can make a significant contribution to family relatedness.

Extending Inclusivity and Democracy between Households

In working with stepfamilies, clinicians who can extend the strategy of inclusivity to relations between households help create the basis for a parental coalition among all the adults that reduces conflict and improves child outcome (Visher & Visher, 1989). Addressing issues of power and control, therapy can help in working out flexible yet protective boundaries, with mother respecting the integrity of the new marriage and stepmother honoring the irreplaceable precedence of the mother. Each sees the other as more powerful than either experiences herself. A mother feels diminished by not being able to live out her culturally created expectations of centrality and control. And a stepmother is hungry for acknowledgment as a contributor to the children's welfare. Both women need to learn that they occupy different spaces in the children's lives and that taking care of children is not a zero-sum game: What one is able to give does not diminish what the other can contribute.

To appreciate what their stepmother does for her children, a mother needs to feel that she does not have to compete for primacy in the children's affection; to be able to reassure the mother that a stepmother is not taking over her role, the stepmother needs to feel that the mother values her participation. Women in stepfamilies learn earlier than most that even a mother's control or possession of her children is limited, that it is shared with the larger social context.

One difficulty in reassuring mothers that stepmothers are not out to replace them is fathers' dramatic devaluation of their former wives (Schuldberg & Guisinger, 1991), so that a mother often correctly perceives that a father fantasizes that his remarriage can recreate a family in which the mother plays no part. He complains to his new wife, who gets angry both at his ex-wife on his behalf and at him for the passive resignation that frequently accompanies his extreme negativity. By focusing on the "outrageousness" of an ex-wife, a stepmother misdirects her energy and attention from the unresolved issues within the new marriage. Similarly, a mother who targets her ex-husband's new wife as responsible for his uncooperativeness or for her disappointment in how her children are cared for in his home is diverting accountability from where it belongs: with the children's father. Frequently, both women find it less dangerous to scapegoat each other than to risk an open confrontation with the man who occasions their participation in each other's lives.

Building empathy between a mother and stepmother can be a challenge, but the payoff more than rewards the cost. The higher the regard in which a stepmother and her husband hold his ex-wife, the happier both are with the current marriage (Guisinger et al., 1989). And the more respect a mother has for her children's stepmother, the easier it is for the stepmother to be open-hearted and open-handed to her stepchildren. Most mothers would be astonished by how much their children's stepmothers long for the mothers' acceptance and approval, and how moved they are when these are forthcoming.

Detriangulating

Another important component of the therapeutic work with stepfamilies is sorting out and working through conflicts by proxy, whereby family members take on others' emotional work. Women are typically more expressive of men's unvoiced issues, and children typically carry their parents' pain, resentment, and guilt.

> Ten-year-old Susan was referred to me by her pediatrician for headaches that were making her miss school. Her parents had been divorced for more than 7 years, but her kinetic family drawing depicted herself, her mother, Barbara, and her father, Eric, who is remarried: They are the family in the case example with which I opened this chapter. Susan frequently called Eric to intercede on her behalf in arguments between mother and daughter, but she was loath to tell Eric directly when she was angry at or hurt by him, complaining to her mother instead. When she was at Eric's house, she wanted his exclusive attention; on alternate weekends, her stepmother felt the maid. Eric wanted to please everyone and ended up with everyone angry at him.
>
> The initial therapy, conducted in ones, twos, and threes, resolved Susan's somatic symptoms and began the process of disengagement in the incomplete divorce. The mother's life had been centered around Susan; as her roles narrowed from wife and mother to simply mother, she became determined to be the best one possible. When Barbara shifted her approach to respond only minimally to Susan's symptoms, they diminished in frequency and severity and no longer interfered with her school attendance. We then worked on redefining boundaries between the two households. Instead of giving herself permission to consult Eric as Susan's coparent about whether their daughter was old enough to walk to school, Barbara felt compelled to raise with him their daughter's complaints about events at his house. When Mom told Susan that she could not do anything about things that happened at Dad's house, suggesting that Susan speak directly to Eric, Susan mustered the courage to talk with her father about her own needs, both in my office and at home. In an individual therapy that resumed 2 years later to deal with her own

depression, Barbara told me that the earlier sessions had been the first time that she had crossed the line to not wanting Eric back. From that time forward, they were able to collaborate as parents to make decisions together in their daughter's best interests. And as Barbara began to feel better about herself, she was able to have pleasant, casual contact with the other Barbara, Susan's stepmother, as well.

Presented with any stepfamily dyad experiencing conflict, it is important to look at whether another twosome is avoiding conflict. The stepparent can be a free-fire zone in families, diverting children's anger from the parent. For example, one 13-year-old boy made it clear that he enjoyed getting his stepmother worked up; it was obviously safer to provoke her than his father, who was stricter with him and whom he both loved and feared. Even as adults, stepchildren may focus on the stepparent as the cause of either childhood or continued unhappiness, diverting their gaze from their parent's complicity in the process. For example, a young adult stepdaughter saw her stepmother's hand in everything her father did, picturing him as a pushover to a manipulative and demanding woman, and underestimating his ability to make his own choices.

Redistributing the Division of Emotional Labor

Another therapeutic task is redistributing the emotional division of labor. This involves getting men to do their own emotional work, instead of drafting their often all-too-willing partners into acting as their proxies. In such situations, husbands and fathers emerge unscathed as feelings fly fast and furious, only to complain how irrational women are. Whether the two women in question are past and present wives or wife and daughter, a man who is slow to know his own feelings and unaccustomed to emotional expression may unwittingly orchestrate a real-life psychodrama in which his female kin play out his own angers or fears.

Nell and Ken were referred for marital issues after she pummeled him awake, so furious was she at feeling an outsider in her own home. They had been married for several years; it was a second marriage for both. Ken got along fine with Nell's adult sons, while she had more trouble with his daughter, Darla, then a college student. Ken reported great anguish in feeling he could not make his daughter welcome in his home.

For years Darla had made a point of letting Nell know she was not her friend—grunting in response to questions and refusing invitations to join them at the table, only to re-enter noisily to prepare her own meal 10 minutes later. Nell felt exploited when her resources were used and she was excluded. But what compounded her hurt was how much she was also left out by Ken's style of responding to conflict with paralysis; feeling mortified and helpless, he did nothing when Darla was rude or Nell distraught, leaving Nell feeling abandoned and enraged.

We worked out ways for the couple to respond to Darla's provocations, so that whether or not these were designed to divide them (as Nell suspected), Darla could not get between them. Ken had dismissed efforts to request change of Darla as doomed to failure, feeling that his directives would foment her rebellion. Asked whether he could instead frame a request for change as a consideration he would appreciate as a loving father, Ken shared a long history of difficulty in talking about his feelings. The son of a father who did not appear to have any feelings and a mother who appeared to use hers only to manipulate him, he was suspicious of feelings in general and scared of his own "shadow feelings," discounting them whenever possible: "It's nothing really, only my reaction."

A few weeks into the therapy, Nell told her story of the difficult night that led them to seek help, recounting her experience of loneliness and abandonment. Recalling how scared he had been of her anger, needing to walk away in order not to respond in kind, Ken pictured Nell as a raging maniac, running down the street trying to kill him. I invited him to think of her as running after him to get him to see and hear and understand her. We talked about how when one member of a couple overreacts it can mean that the other is underreacting, and Ken recognized himself in that formulation. His strategy—of keeping his fear a secret and trying to distract her—had not worked.

It was not easy for him, but Ken made an effort to talk to Nell and was pleased by her response. More confident that Ken loved her and was dedicated to working things out with her, Nell offered to wipe the slate clean and start over with Darla. She surprised Ken by not being upset that Darla had taken pillows from the house without asking, or that they had to drive home separately from a meeting so that he could do a favor for his daughter. She did not know why, she reported; it just was not an issue for her.

Instead of brooding about the possibility, Ken mustered the courage to discuss his worry that Darla would interrupt a dinner party by enlisting him to move her belongings during the only inconvenient evening that week. Nell appreciated hearing of his concern, and they negotiated a plan for him both to help his daughter and to protect their social time. Six weeks into the therapy, Darla departed for school, after giving a gift she made a point of saying was for both of them and hugging her stepmother as the older woman left for work. At the next session, Ken announced that he had his own issues with Darla. Brokering between the two women had been an unpleasant but "safer" option. The distraction of stepmother–stepdaughter conflict had abated, and he was faced with having to look into himself in ways that left him "shivering."

This pattern of diverting a family's emotional tasks to its female members can occur across households in the remarriage chain, so that stepmother and mother can redirect their dissatisfactions with their present/past partner toward each other, and he can avoid responsibility for his own actions and desires by enlisting one (or, less frequently, both) as his agent(s). The mother may blame the stepmother for the father's unavailability to his children; the stepmother may blame the mother for turning her life upside down with capricious changes in plans. Each sees the other as controlling her ex- or present spouse, who "neglects my needs and gives in to hers," rescuing him from having to come to terms with himself and assert on his own behalf.

CONCLUSION

In reading about the stepfamilies discussed in this chapter, some of us see our own family stories played in variation; others see "the decline of western civilization." It is important to recognize that family change is not the result of its members' devaluing the family. The dramatic and far-reaching changes in how people organize their family lives is neither a matter of personal depravity nor of ideological agenda; families exist in a cultural context. Some families continue to approximate "traditional" models. Other families work hard to bring about deliberate changes in a structure experienced as oppressive. Perhaps the majority, to paraphrase Shakespeare, have change thrust upon them.

Working through the pain and discovering the promise of change in our family possibilities constitute the special province of therapy—our contribution to the discourse on families in transition. Finding acceptable narratives for stepfamilies in therapy may depend on developing a new appreciation for both ambiguity and ambivalence; neither can be found in the psychological and cultural stepfamily legacy that stepchildren are mistreated Cinderellas, stepmothers are wicked witches, and mothers should be fairy godmothers who can make things all better with the touch of a wand. There is much to be ambivalent about in postmodern family life. People in stepfamilies are tyrannized by a demand to embrace an unambivalent narrative—a demand that they make of themselves and of each other. Allowing for an ambivalent story enables family members to move beyond begrudging how current realities are discrepant with past expectations and to discover new ways to nurture caring and connection.

ACKNOWLEDGMENTS

I would like to thank Jane Ariel, Hendon Chubb, Diane Ehrensaft, Conn Hallinan, Casi Kushel, Marsha Pravder Mirkin, Phyllis Nauts, Roz Spafford, and Mary Whiteside for their thoughtful suggestions on earlier drafts of this chapter.

Notes

1. In talking about homosexual stepfamilies, I am not referring to the families of the "lesbian baby boom." When homosexual partners choose to have a baby together, although only one can be the biological parent, this is not considered a stepfamily because the couple relationship precedes the birth.
2. An expanded form of this section can be found in Bernstein (1989a).

References

Ahrons, C. R., & Rodgers, R. H. (1987). *Divorced families: A multidisciplinary developmental view.* New York: Norton.

Ahrons, C. R., & Wallisch, L. (1987). Parenting in the binuclear family: Relationships between biological and stepparents. In K. Pasley & M. Ihinger-Tallman (Eds.), *Remarriage and stepparenting: Current research and theory* (pp. 225–256). New York: Guilford Press.

Bernstein, A. C. (1989a). Gender and stepfamily life: A review. *Journal of Feminist Family Therapy, 1*(4), 1–27.

Bernstein, A. C. (1989b) *Yours, mine and ours: How families change when remarried parents have a child together.* New York: Scribner's.

Blumstein, P., & Schwartz, P. (1983). *American couples: Money, work, sex.* New York: William Morrow.

Bray, J. H. (1990). Overview of the developmental issues in stepfamilies research project. *INSTEP: Newsletter from the StepFamily Research Project* (Baylor College of Medicine, Houston, TX), *1*(1), 1–7.

Clingempeel, W. G., Brand, E., & Ievoli, R. (1984). Stepparent–stepchild relationships in stepmother and stepfather families: A multimethod study. *Family Relations, 33*, 465–474.

Coale, H. (1993, January) Use of humor in stepfamily therapy. *Stepfamilies: The Bulletin of the Stepfamily Association of America*, pp. 10–11.

Duberman, L. (1975). *The reconstituted family: A study of remarried couples and their children.* Chicago: Nelson-Hall.

Ehrensaft, D. (1987). *Parenting together: Men and women sharing the care of their children.* New York: Free Press.

Elion, D. (1990). *Therapy with remarriage families with children: Positive interventions from the client perspective.* Unpublished master's thesis, University of Wisconsin–Stout.

Fine, M. A., McKenry, P. C. Donnelly, B. W., & Voydanoff, P. (1992). Perceived adjustment of parents and children: Variations by family structure, race, and gender. *Journal of Marriage and the Family, 54*, 118–127.

Furstenberg, F. F. (1980). Reflections of remarriage. *Journal of Family Issues, 1*, 443–453.

Furstenberg, F. F. (1987). The new extended family: The experience of parents and children after remarriage. In K. Pasley & M. Ihinger-Tallman (Eds.), *Remarriage and stepparenting: Current research and theory* (pp. 19–41). New York: Guilford Press.

Furstenberg, F. F., & Cherlin, A. J. (1991). *Divided families: What happens to children when parents part.* Cambridge, MA: Harvard University Press.

Furstenberg, F. F., & Nord, C. W. (1985). Parenting apart: Patterns of childrearing after divorce. *Journal of Marriage and the Family, 47*, 893–904.

Furstenberg, F. F., Nord, C. W., Peterson, J. L., & Zill, N. (1983). The life course of children of divorce: Marital disruption and parental contact. *American Sociological Review, 48*, 656–668.

Gergen, K. J. (1985). The social constructionist movement in psychology. *American Psychologist, 40*, 266–275.

Glick, P. C. (1980) Remarriage: Some recent changes and variations. *Journal of Family Issues, 1*, 455–478.

Greif, G. L. (1985). Single fathers rearing children. *Journal of Marriage and the Family, 47*, 185–191.

Guisinger, S., Cowan, P. A., & Schuldberg, D. (1989). Changing parent and spouse relations in the first years of remarriage of divorced fathers. *Journal of Marriage and the Family, 51*(2), 445–456.

Hare-Mustin, R. T. (1987). The problem of gender in family therapy theory. *Family Process, 26*, 15–27.

Hetherington, E. M. (1987). Family relations six years after divorce. In K. Pasley & M. Ihinger-Tallman (Eds.), *Remarriage and stepparenting: Current research and theory* (pp. 185–205). New York: Guilford Press.

Ihinger-Tallman, M., & Pasley, K. (1987). *Remarriage.* Newbury Park, CA: Sage.

James, K., & McIntyre, D. (1989). A momentary gleam of enlightenment: Towards a model of feminist family therapy. *Journal of Feminist Family Therapy, 1*(3), 3–24.

Keshet, J. K. (1987). *Love and power in the stepfamily: A practical guide.* New York: McGraw-Hill.

Keshet, J. K. (1989). Gender and biological models of role division in stepmother families. *Journal of Feminist Family Therapy, 1*(4), 29–50.

Laird, J. (1989). Women and stories: Restoring women's self-constructions. In M. McGoldrick, C. Anderson, & F. Walsh (Eds.), *Women in families* (pp. 427–450). New York: Norton.

Pasley, K., & Ihinger-Tallman, M. (1987). The evolution of a field of investigation: Issues and concepts. In K. Pasley & M. Ihinger-Tallman (Eds.), *Remarriage and stepparenting: Current research and theory* (pp. 303–313). New York: Guilford Press.

Patterson, C. J. (1992). Children of lesbian and gay parents. *Child Development, 63*, 1025–1042.

Risman, B. L. (1986). Can men "mother"? Life as a single father. *Family Relations, 35*, 95–102.

Santrock, J. W., & Sitterle, K. A. (1987). Parent–child relationships in stepmother families. In K. Pasley & M. Ihinger-Tallman (Eds.), *Remarriage and stepparenting: Current research and theory* (pp. 273-299). New York: Guilford Press.

Schuldberg, D., & Guisinger, S. (1991). Divorced fathers describe their former wives: Devaluation and contrast. *Journal of Divorce and Remarriage, 14*(3–4), 61–87.

Spanier, G., & Glick, P. (1980). Paths to remarriage. *Journal of Divorce, 3*, 283–298.

Stacey, J. (1990). *Brave new families: Stories of domestic upheaval in late twentieth century America.* New York: Basic Books.

Trudeau, G. (1985, June 13). *Doonesbury* [Comic strip.] *San Francisco Chronicle.*

Visher, E. B., & Visher, J. S. (1979). *Stepfamilies: A guide to working with stepparents and stepchildren.* New York: Brunner/Mazel.

Visher, E. B., & Visher, J. S. (1988). *Old loyalties, new ties: Therapeutic strategies with stepfamilies.* New York: Brunner/Mazel.

Visher, E. B., & Visher, J. S. (1989). Parenting coalitions after remarriage: Dynamics and therapeutic guidelines. *Family Relations, 38*(1), 65–70.

Walker, H. A. (1988) Black–white differences in marriage and family patterns. In S. M. Dornbusch & M. H. Strober (Eds.), *Feminism, children, and the new families* (pp. 297–326). New York: Guilford Press.

Webb, C. (1990, May–June). Stepfamilies require special FT handling. *Family Therapy News*, pp. 21–22.

Webster's College Dictionary. (1991). New York: Random House.

White, M., & Epston, D. (1990). *Narrative means to therapeutic ends.* New York: Norton.

Zaslow, M. J. (1988). Sex differences in children's response to parental divorce: 1. Research methodology and postdivorce family forms. *American Journal of Orthopsychiatry, 58*(3), 355-378.

Zalsow, M. J. (1989). Sex differences in children's response to parental divorce: 2. Samples, variables, ages, and sources. *American Journal of Orthopsychiatry, 59*(1), 118–141.

Suggested Readings

Ariel, J., & Stearns, S. M. (1992). Challenges facing gay and lesbian families. In S. Dworkin and F. Gutierrez (Eds.), *Counseling gay men and lesbians* (pp. 95–114). Alexandria, VA: American Association for Counseling and Development.

Baptiste, J. A. (1987). Psychotherapy with gay/lesbian couples and their children in "stepfamilies": A challenge for marriage and family therapists. *Journal of Homosexuality, 14*(1–2), 223–238.

Bernstein, A. C. (1988). Unravelling the tangles: Children's understanding of stepfamily kinship. In W. Beer (Ed.), *Relative strangers: Studies of stepfamily processes* (pp. 83–111). Totowa, NJ: Rowman & Littlefield.

Crosbie-Burnett, M., Skyles, A., & Becker-Haven, J. (1988). Exploring stepfamilies from a feminist perspective. In S. M. Dornbusch & M. H. Strober (Eds.), *Feminism, children, and the new families* (pp. 297–326). New York: Guilford Press.

Keshet, J., & Mirkin, M. P. (1985). Troubled adolescents in divorced and remarried families. In M. P. Mirkin and S. L. Koman (Eds.), *Handbook of adolescent and family therapy* (pp. 273–293). Boston: Allyn & Bacon.

Maglin, N. B., & Schniedewind, N. (Eds.). (1989). *Women and stepfamilies: Voices of love and anger.* Philadelphia: Temple University Press.

Whiteside, M., & Campbell, P. (1993, Summer). Stepparenting in gay and lesbian families: Integrity, safety, and the real world out there. *Stepfamilies: The Bulletin of the Stepfamily Association of America*, pp. 13–14.

Whiteside, M. (1988). Creation of family identity through ritual performance in early remarriage. In E. Imber-Black, J. Roberts, & R. Whiting (Eds.), *Rituals in families and family therapy* (pp. 276–304). New York: Norton.

■READING 18

Divorce: Challenges, Changes, and New Chances

E. Mavis Hetherington, Tracy C. Law, and Thomas G. O'Connor

Studies of the effects of divorce on family members traditionally have centered around the development of problem behaviors subsequent to marital dissolution. Recent findings, however, have emphasized the wide variation in responses to stressful experiences and life transitions, including divorce and remarriage (e.g., Rutter, 1987; Werner, 1987; Hether-

ington, 1991a). Although debate still exists over the question of the magnitude and duration of the effects of parental divorce on children, work in the past 10 years has converged
in suggesting that the interaction among individual differences in personal and familial
characteristics and extrafamilial factors that support or undermine coping efforts by family members must be examined in order to understand the spectrum of responses to divorce. This spectrum can range from enhanced competence to clinical levels of problem
behavior (Hetherington, 1989, 1991a; Stolberg, Camplair, Currier, & Wells, 1987).

In addition, it is becoming increasingly apparent that divorce should be viewed not
as a discrete event but as part of a series of family transitions and changes in family relationships. The response to any family transition will depend both on what precedes and
follows it. The response to divorce and life in a single-parent household will be influenced by individual adjustment and the quality of family relationships before the divorce
as well as circumstances surrounding and following the divorce. In many families, divorce
may trigger a series of adverse transactional factors such as economic decline, parenting
stress, and physical and psychological dysfunction in family members. For others, it may
present an escape from conflict and an unsatisfying marital relationship, a chance to form
more gratifying and harmonious relationships, and an opportunity for personal growth
and individuation (Gore & Eckenroade, 1992; Hetherington, 1989).

The recognition that divorce is part of a chain of marital transitions and shifting
life experiences, and that individual responses to these experiences demonstrate marked
variability, has been a powerful influence on recent theoretical models developed to explain children's adjustment to parental divorce. In understanding these findings, many researchers have adopted a developmental contextual framework (Gore & Eckenroade,
1992; Nock, 1982; Hetherington & Clingempeel, 1992; Hetherington & Martin, 1986).
This approach examines adjustment across time, and on multiple levels, including interactions among the overarching social and historical context, changing dynamics within
the family system, individual ontogenic characteristics of child and parent, and influences
external to the family such as the extended family, peer relationships, and the educational,
occupational, mental health, legal, religious, and welfare systems.

The purpose of this chapter is not to present a comprehensive review of research
and clinical findings concerning the adjustment to divorce. Selected recent research examples and a developmental, contextual, interactive model will be used as an organizational framework in which to examine factors that contribute to individual differences in
the way family members negotiate the changes and challenges associated with divorce.
Many of the research findings will be drawn from the longitudinal studies of Hetherington and her colleagues. Before discussing the factors implicated in a developmental, contextual, interactive approach, it is important to place the findings in the larger context of
demographic and social changes that have occurred in the last 20 years.

THE CHANGING WORLD OF THE FAMILY: DEMOGRAPHIC AND SOCIAL FORCES

Although the divorce rate doubled between 1960 and 1980, it has leveled off and even
declined slightly in the past decade (Glick, 1988). Currently, it is estimated that half of
all marriages will end in divorce and that approximately 60% of these dissolutions will

involve children. Although the percentage of marriages ending in divorce has not changed appreciably since the early 1980s, the number of children affected by parental divorce, as well as the number of children from divorced families now of marriageable age themselves, has continued to increase (Bumpass, 1984). It has been estimated that 38% of white children and 75% of African-American children born to married parents in the United States will experience their parents' divorce before their 16th birthday (Bumpass, 1984). In addition, African-Americans not only have a higher rate of divorce than whites, they are also more likely to separate but not go through a legal divorce procedure, to experience a longer time-lag between time of separation and divorce, and are less likely to remarry (Glick, 1988; Teachman, Polonko, & Scanzoni, 1987). Although families who are poor, African-American, and suffering multiple life stresses are more likely to divorce, the rise in economic independence for well-educated women also has led to a greater likelihood that these women will divorce compared to their less-educated peers. Furthermore, since most divorced men and women remarry, and since the rate of divorce in second marriages is even higher than in first marriages (61% of men and 54% of women go through a second divorce), many children and parents encounter a series of marital transitions and reorganizations in family roles and relationships (Glick, 1988; Chase-Lansdale & Hetherington, 1990). These statistics indicate that divorce, once considered an atypical family event, is now a "normative," even if not a "normal," experience in the life cycle of many contemporary American families (Emery & Forehand, 1992).

Shifting social and historical factors affect patterns of both marriage and divorce (Cherlin, 1981; Teachman et al., 1987; Glick, 1988). Wars, whether the Civil War, World War II, the Korean War, or the Vietnam War, have been associated with hasty marriages followed by increased rates of divorce (Glick, 1988). Current high rates of divorce have also been attributed to greater labor force participation and economic independence of women, improved contraception, the emergence of the welfare system, an increase in the proportion of marriages involving premarital births, changing ideologies associated with the women's movement, and the liberalization of divorce laws. The family is being reshaped in response to transformations in social values and roles. Greater diversity in attitudes and accepted behaviors are found not only in family and gender roles but also in other social systems—in law, politics, religion, education, and the workplace. Divorce and the concomitant experiences of family members are only one reflection of the need for social institutions, such as the family, to adapt to historical and social change.

WHY MARRIAGES FAIL: THE PRECURSORS OF DIVORCE

Neither marital satisfaction nor sheer frequency of disagreements is a good predictor of divorce. Instead, styles of conflict resolution involving disengagement, stonewalling, contempt, denial, and blaming are likely to be associated with divorce (Gottman, 1994; Hetherington, 1989). One of the most common patterns of marital relations leading to divorce is a conflict-confronting, conflict-avoiding pattern where one spouse, usually the wife, confronts areas of concern and disagreements in the marriage and expresses her feelings about these problems, while the other spouse responds with defensiveness, avoidance, withdrawal, whining, and, if prodded, with resentment and anger. A second common marital pattern associated with later divorce is one in which couples have little overt conflict, but have different expectations and perceptions about family life, marriage and their children, and have few shared interests, activities, or friends (Hetherington & Tryon, 1989; Notarius & Vanzetti, 1983).

These patterns of relating in dysfunctional couples means that many children before the divorce are likely to have been exposed to unresolved disagreements, resentment, anger, and ineffective marital problem solving. Prospective studies indicate that troubled marital relations and interparental tension accompanied by unsupportive parenting and high rates of behavior problems in children occur years before the dissolution of the marriage (Block, Block, & Gjerde, 1986, 1988; Cherlin et al., 1991). The inept parenting and behavior disorders usually attributed to divorce and life in a one-parent household may, to some extent, be a continuation of predivorce functioning and be associated with disrupted processes in the nuclear family. Although the popular interpretation of these findings is that marital tension, alienation and conflict cause inept parenting and behavior problems in children, it may be that the stress of dealing with a difficult, noncompliant, antisocial child helps to undermine an already fragile marriage and precipitates divorce.

Recently, another explanation, based on the findings of twin studies, has been proposed. It suggests that divorce and problem behaviors in children are genetically linked, and that this may help to explain the slightly higher rates of divorce found in offspring of divorced parents (McGue & Lykken, in press). Irritable, antisocial behavior in parents may provoke marital problems and be genetically associated with behavior problems in children, with the subsequent marital difficulties of adult offspring of divorced parents, and with the intergenerational transmission of divorce. Whatever the reasons may be for the dysfunctional precursors of divorce, it is against a background of disrupted family relationships and disordered behavior in parents and children that family members move into the changes and challenges associated with separation, divorce, and life in a one-parent household.

CHANGES IN THE LIVING SITUATION

An established family system can be viewed as a mechanism for identifying and framing the roles, activities, and daily life of each family member. When a divorce occurs, it means not only the loss of patterns of everyday family interaction and a family member, but loss of a way of life. Pervasive alterations in expectations, life experiences, and the sense of self in parents and children are associated with the uncertainty, found not only in divorce, but also in other transitions, such as loss of a family member through death (Silverman, 1988) or even with the addition of a family member through remarriage (Hetherington, in press).

Immediately following divorce, household routines and roles break down and parents experience task overload as a single parent attempts to perform the tasks usually assumed by two parents. In such situations, children, especially daughters, in divorced families are often asked to assume responsibility for household chores and care of younger siblings. Many of the interactions between custodial mothers and their children, are instrumental in nature and occur in the context of shared tasks. The problems of overwhelming responsibility for parent and child are often exacerbated when divorced mothers must begin working or increase their workload because of economic necessity (Duncan & Hoffman, 1985).

In the first year following divorce, the average family income of women decreases by almost 40%. Although income relative to needs gradually increases, even 5 years after divorce, the income of divorced mothers remains at 94% of their predivorced income, in contrast to 130% for divorced fathers and 125% for remarried women (Duncan & Hoffman, 1985). This is the result, in part, of partial or intermittent payment, or nonpayment, of child support by 70% of divorced noncustodial fathers. This loss of income following martial dissolution often determines where families live, where children go to school, the quality of neighborhoods and peer groups, and the accessibility of jobs, health care, and support networks. Although income level or loss explains only a small amount of the variance related to children's adjustment following divorce, poverty does increase the probability of encountering these other transactional factors associated with the ability of parents and children to manage stress successfully and with developmental outcomes for children. Negative life stresses are most marked for members of divorced families in the first 2 years following divorce and gradually decline with time; however, they always remain higher than those in nondivorced families (Forgatch, Patterson, & Ray, in press; Hetherington, Cox, & Cox, 1985). An unexpected bill, illness, or a school closing may present a greater emergency for a divorced mother than for parents in a two-parent household with mutual support and greater resources.

In spite of the difficulties encountered by divorced women, by 2 years after divorce, whether or not they initiated the divorce, the vast majority of women report being more satisfied with their family situation than they had been in the last year of their marriage. Furthermore, although divorced mothers report more child-rearing stress than do non-divorced mothers, they also say that parenting is easier without a nonsupportive spouse who undermines or disagrees with their parenting practices. The balance between increased risk and stressors and positive life changes must be considered in examining the response to divorce (Hetherington, in press).

CUSTODY, CONTACT, AND CO-PARENTAL RELATIONS

In the vast majority of divorces, the mother is awarded custody of children; only 13% of fathers are awarded sole custody of their children at the time of divorce (Emery, 1988). In these cases, it is often because mothers are deemed incompetent, do not want custody of their children, or because male or adolescent children are involved. In spite of the overt or covert legal preference for mothers as custodians under the guise of best interests of the child or primary caregivers guidelines, there is no consistent evidence that fathers who seek custody are less competent parents than mothers (Warshak, 1992). In fact, by 2 years after divorce, custodial fathers report better family relations and fewer problems with their children than do custodial mothers (Furstenberg, 1988). This may be because custodial fathers, in contrast to custodial mothers, have higher incomes, more available supports, and are more likely to be caring for older children. In addition, fathers may be less sensitive and responsive than mothers to family dysfunction and behavior problems in children. However, reluctant fathers who assent to assume custody because of their wives' inability or disinclination to care for their children are less involved and able parents. A finding relevant to decisions involving custody is that, although there is some continuity in the pre- and postdivorce quality of parenting for mothers, there is little for fathers (Hetherington, Cox, & Cox, 1982). Some custodial fathers seem to exhibit a *Kramer vs. Kramer* response and develop an involvement and parenting skills they had not had before the divorce, but some intensely attached noncustodial fathers find intermittent parenting painful and withdraw from their children. On the other hand, a substantial number of noncustodial fathers report that their relationship with their children improves after divorce.

On the average, noncustodial fathers become increasingly less available to their children. In the most recent national study using a probability sample, mothers reported that, following divorce, only one-quarter of children see their fathers once a week or more, and over a third do not see their father at all or see them only a few times a year (Seltzer, 1991). Physical distance in residence, low socioeconomic status, remarriage, and having only female rather than male children are associated with less visitation by noncustodial fathers. Noncustodial mothers are more likely to maintain contact with their children than are noncustodial fathers (Furstenberg, 1988; Zill, 1988). This leads to the rather intriguing issue as to whether differences found in children in a mother's custody, and a father's custody are attributable to the relationship with the custodial parent or to differences in the child's contact with the noncustodial parent and additional support in childrearing for custodial fathers provided by noncustodial mothers.

The move toward facilitating visitation and joint custody has been based on the premises that continued contact with both parents is desirable and that noncustodial parents with joint custody will be more likely to maintain contact and financial support. The response to the first premise must be that it depends on who is doing the visiting and on the relationship between the parents. If the noncustodial parent is reasonably well-adjusted, competent in parenting, and has a close relationship with the child, and if the child is not exposed to conflict between the two parents, continued contact can have a salutary effect on the child's adjustment. However, it takes an exceptionally close relationship with a noncustodial parent to buffer a child from the deleterious effects of a conflictual, nonsupportive relationship with a custodial parent (Hetherington et al., 1982). If there is high conflict between the parents, joint custody and continued contact can have adverse effects on the child (Maccoby, Depner, & Mnookin, 1988; Wallerstein & Blakeslee, 1989). Furthermore, there is some evidence that, after remarriage, although continued involvement of the noncustodial father with the child does not interfere with family functioning in the stepfamily, frequent visits by the noncustodial mother may be associated with negative relations between children, especially daughters, and their stepmothers (Brand, Clingempeel, & Bowen-Woodward, 1988).

Although cooperative, consensual coparenting following divorce is the ideal relationship (Camara & Resnick, 1988), in most cases the best that can be attained is one of independent but noninterfering parental relations. In a substantial group of families, conflict is sustained or accelerates following divorce (Hetherington et al., 1982; Kline, Johnston, & Tschan, 1991; Maccoby, Depner, & Mnookin, 1990). Interparental conflict in the long run is related to diminished contact and fewer child support payments by noncustodial fathers (Seltzer, 1991). In addition, in such conflicted relationships, children may feel caught in the middle as they are sometimes asked to carry messages between parents, to inform each parent of the other's activities, to defend one parent against the other's disparaging remarks, or to justify wanting to spend time with the other parent (Buchanon, Maccoby, & Dombusch, 1991; Hetherington, in press). Being "caught in the middle," rather than divorce per se, or loss of contact with a noncustodial parent, has the most adverse effect on children's behavior and psychological well-being. Parental conflict provides children with an opportunity to exploit parents and play one off against the other, and when they are older, to escape careful monitoring of their activities. However children, especially older children, are able to function well over time in independent, noninterfering households. As long as they are not involved in parental conflict, children are able to cope well even if these households have different rules and expectations. Children are able to learn the differing role demands and constraints required in relating to diverse people in a variety of social situations such as in the peer group, church, the classroom, on the playing field, or at grandmother's house. In view of children's adaptability and differentiated responses to a broad range of social situations, the resistance to recognizing that children can cope with two different home situations is remarkable. Problems in joint custody come when parents interfere in each other's childrearing, and when children don't want to leave their friends, neighborhoods, or regular routines. In the rare cases where joint custody requires shifts between schools, this too may become a burden. Difficulty in visitation under any custody arrangement may emerge as children grow older and want to spend more time with their peers and less with parents.

Joint custody does tend to promote greater contact and financial support by non-custodial parents (Maccoby et al., 1988). Noncustodial fathers or fathers with joint custody are more likely to support children when they feel they have power in decisions relating to their children's life circumstances and activities. However, under conditions of high conflict, the increased contact associated with joint custody can be detrimental to the well-being of the child. Under conditions of low or encapsulated conflict, or emotional distancing between the parents, the effects of contact will be positive or at least neutral. Most children want to maintain contact with both parents and are more satisfied with continued contact. However, if the custodial parent has formed a hostile alliance with the child against the noncustodial parent, if the child feels caught in the middle of the parental conflict, or if the noncustodial parent has been extremely dysfunctional (e.g., abusive), children may seek to limit their contact with the nonresidential parent.

ADJUSTMENT OF DIVORCED PARENTS

Separation and divorce place both men and women at risk for psychological and physical dysfunction (Chase-Lansdale & Hetherington, 1990). In the immediate aftermath of marital dissolution, both men and women often exhibit extreme emotional lability, anger, depression, anxiety, and impulsive, and antisocial behavior, but for most this is gone by 2 years following divorce. However, even in the long run, alcoholism, drug abuse, psychosomatic problems, accidents, depression, and antisocial behavior are more common in divorced than nondivorced adults (Bloom, Asher, & White, 1978). Furthermore, recent research suggests that marital disruption alters the immune system, making divorced persons more vulnerable to disease, infection, chronic and acute medical problems, and even death (Kiecolt-Glaser et al., 1987). Some of these postdivorce symptoms in adults, such as depression and antisocial behavior, seem likely to have been present before divorce and even to have contributed to a distressed marriage and to marital dissolution. Depression and antisocial behavior are related to irritable, conflictual marital interactions. Adults exhibiting antisocial behavior are more likely to have disordered social relationships, to encounter negative life events, and to undergo multiple marital transitions (Forgatch et al., in press). Our own work, examining couples who later divorced, suggests that, especially for women in distant or hostile, conflicted marriages, depression is likely to decline following divorce, whereas antisocial behavior is likely to remain constant or to increase. Continued attachment to the ex-spouse is associated both with health problems and depression (Kiecolt-Glaser et al., 1987). This connection, however, declines with repartnering and the formation of a close meaningful relationship (Hetherington et al., 1982; Forgatch et al., in press).

We spoke earlier of divorce, like death of a spouse, involving loss of a way of life. It also involves loss of aspects of the self sustained by that way of life (Silverman, 1988). Because of this, the early years of separation and divorce offer great opportunity for positive and negative change. In this early phase, separated and divorced men and women often complain of being disoriented, of not knowing who they are or who they want to be, and of behaving in ego alien ways. They speak of having "not me experiences" where previously rational, self-controlled individuals report such things as smearing dog feces on their ex-spouse's face, following them and peering into their bedroom windows, defacing their property, fantasizing and sometimes acting out violent impulses, or whining and begging for reconciliation. "I can't believe I did that" or "That wasn't really me" is repeatedly heard in interviews with divorcing adults. Many noncustodial fathers feel rootless, disoriented, shut out of regular contact with their children and nurture unrealistic fantasies of reconciliation. Others throw themselves into a frenzy of social activity and try to develop a more open, free-living persona.

Conventional women have more problems in adapting to their new life situation than do less conventional, more internally controlled, androgynous, or working women. Nonemployed women in traditional marriages have often organized their identities around the achievements of their husbands and children. One said, "I used to be Mrs. John Jones, the bank manager's wife. Now I'm Mary Jones! Who is Mary Jones?" In spite of the problems with income, housing, inadequate childcare, loneliness, and limited resources and support encountered by many divorced women, our work shows that about 70%, in the long run, prefer their new life to an unsatisfying marriage. Most think that divorce and raising children alone have provided an experience of personal growth, albeit sometimes painful growth. Some of these women were competent, autonomous women before the divorce. Others, in coping with the demands of their new situation, discovered strengths, developed skills, and attained levels of individuation that might never have emerged if they had remained in the constraints of a dysfunctional marriage. It should be noted, however, that in comparison to married women, divorced women are overrepresented at both extremes of competence and adjustment. Some are found in a group with high self-esteem and few psychological problems who function ably in social situations, in the workplace, and in the family. Others seem permanently overwhelmed by the losses and changes in their lives, show little adequate coping behavior, and exhibit low self-esteem and multiple problems such as depression, antisocial behavior, substance abuse, and repeated, unsuccessful intimate relationships. Job training, continued education, and professional enhancement play important roles not only in the economic, but also the psychological, well-being of women. Adequate childcare is critical in facilitating these activities (Burns, 1992). Although work satisfaction plays an important role in the self-esteem of divorced adults, most custodial mothers and fathers restrict their social, and to some extent, work activities, and organize their lives around providing and caring for their children. Adequacy in these roles is central to their self-esteem.

Repartnering is the single factor that contributes most to the life satisfaction of divorced men and women; however, it seems more critical to men. Divorced fathers are less likely than divorced mothers to show marked personal growth and individuation while they are single. Men show more positive development in the security of a marriage.

The significance for children of these psychological, emotional, and physical changes in parents is that, in the early years following divorce, children are encountering an altered parent at a time when they need stability in a rapidly changing life situation. A physically ill, emotionally disturbed, or preoccupied parent and a distressed, demanding, angry child may have difficulty giving each other support or solace. Over time, the well-being of the child is associated with the adjustment of the custodial parent, and this is largely an indirect path mediated by parenting behaviors. If parent distress, low self-esteem, depression, or antisocial behavior results in disrupted parenting, behavior problems in children increase (Hetherington & Clingempeel, 1992; Patterson & Bank, 1989; Forgatch et al., in press). If a disturbed parent is able to maintain authoritative qualities, such as responsiveness, warmth, firm control, monitoring, and communication, adverse effects on children are less likely to occur.

Editor's Note: *References for this reading can be found in the original source.*

III *Parents and Children*

No aspect of childhood seems more natural, universal, and changeless than the relationship between parents and child. Yet historical and cross-cultural evidence reveals major changes in conceptions of childhood and adulthood and in the psychological relationships between children and parents. For example, the shift from an agrarian to an industrial society over the past 200 years has revolutionized parent–child relations and the conditions of child development.

Among the changes associated with this transformation of childhood are: the decline of agriculture as a way of life; the elimination of child labor; the fall in infant mortality; the spread of literacy and mass schooling; and a focus on childhood as a distinct and valuable stage of life. As a result of these changes, industrial-era parents bear fewer children, make greater emotional and economic investments in them, and expect less in return than their agrarian counterparts. Agrarian parents were not expected to emphasize emotional bonds or the value of children as unique individuals. Parents and children were bound together by economic necessity: children were an essential source of labor in the family economy and a source of support in an old age. Today, almost all children are economic liabilities. But they now have profound emotional significance. Parents hope offspring will provide intimacy, even genetic immortality. Although today's children have become economically worthless, they have become emotionally "priceless" (Zelizer, 1985).

No matter how eagerly an emotionally priceless child is awaited, becoming a parent is usually experienced as one of life's major "normal" crises. In a classic article, Alice Rossi (1968) was one of the first to point out that the transition to parenthood is often one of life's difficult passages. Since Rossi's article first appeared more than three decades ago, a large body of research literature has developed, most of which supports her view that the early years of parenting can be a period of stress and change as well as joy.

Parenthood itself has changed since Rossi wrote. As Carolyn and Phillip Cowan observe, becoming a parent may be more difficult now than it used to be. The Cowans studied couples before and after the births of their first children. Because of the rapid and dramatic social changes of the past decades, young parents today are like pioneers in a new, uncharted territory. For example, the vast majority of today's couples come to parenthood with both husband and wife in the workforce, and most have expectations of a more egalitarian relationship than their own parents had. But the balance in their lives and their relationship has to shift dramatically after the baby is born. Most couples cannot afford the traditional pattern of the wife staying home full time; nor is this arrangement free of strain for those who try it. Young families thus face more burdens than in the past, yet supportive family policies such as visiting nurses, paid parental leave, and the like that exist in other countries are lacking in the United States.

Mothers are still the principal nurturers and caretakers of their children, but the norms of parenthood have shifted—as the growing use of the term "parenting" suggests. Views of fatherhood in the research literature are changing along with the actual behavior of fathers and children in real life. Until recently, a father could feel he was fulfilling his parental obligations merely by supporting his family. He was expected to spend time with his children when his work schedule permitted, to generally oversee their upbringing, and to discipline them when necessary. Even scholars of the family and of child development tended to ignore the role of the father except as breadwinner and role model. His family participation did not call for direct involvement in the daily round of child rearing, especially when the children were babies. By contrast, scholars expressed the extreme importance of the mother and the dangers of maternal deprivation. Today, however, the role of father is beginning to demand much more active involvement in the life of the family, especially with regard to child rearing. Rosanna Hertz reports on the different ways dual-earner couples arrange for the care of their young children. In her study, she found three different patterns. In the "mothering approach," the couple agree that it is best for the mother to care for the children in the home; even if the mother must work outside the home, she arranges her schedule so as to maximize her time with the children. In the "parenting approach," both parents share the care of the children, and organize their work lives so as to maximize the time they have with their children. In the "market approach," the couple uses professional caregivers to look after their children. Hertz observes that only the shared parenting approaches challenge traditional gender roles and the traditional demands of the workplace.

Helen Ragoné examines the meaning of parenting through surrogate motherhood— a practice that seems a radical departure from traditional understandings of motherhood, fatherhood, and biological relatedness. She finds, however, that all participants in the process try to define their actions in terms of traditional values. For example, surrogate mothers explain that by having a child for a childless couple they are "giving the gift of life," and not simply getting pregnant in exchange for money. The surrogate mother and a woman who will adopt her child often form an emotional bond with one another, and the adoptive mother sees herself as conceiving the child "in her heart" before it was formed in the surrogate's body. In short, all the participants in surrogacy emphasize the importance of traditional values such as love of children and family.

While most of us tend to overestimate the amount of change in families since the 1960s, we tend to think that the lives of parents and children were fairly stable in earlier times. But Donald Hernandez shows that there have been revolutionary transformations in children's lives since the country was founded. The first major change was the shift away from the working farm family to the father-as-breadwinner, mother-as-homemaker arrangement. The second major change, linked to the first, was a dramatic decline in the number of large families. In 1865, the median adolescent had more than seven siblings, whereas by 1930, most children had only one or two. The third revolution in children's lives was an enormous increase in years of education. Most recently, childhood in the United States has been transformed by the entrance of mothers into the workplace, along with the increase in single-parent families and the increasing ethnic and cultural diversity of the child population.

In her article, Ellen Galinsky addresses the issue of work-and-parenting through a research method that is remarkably rare in studies of family life—going to the children and asking them. Among her many findings, perhaps the most surprising is a discrepancy between the opinions of working parents and their children as to whether they are spending too little time together. Most people assume that the issue of time spent with children is about mothers. But although a majority of working mothers feel they are spending too little time with their offspring, the children themselves have a different view. A majority feel they have enough time with their mothers, but not enough with their fathers. These findings, Galinsky argues, show why it is so important to ask children directly about how family issues affect them, rather than rely on our own assumptions.

References

Rossi, A. 1968. Transition to parenthood. *Journal of Marriage and the Family* 30, 26–39.
Zelizer, V. A. 1985. *Pricing the Priceless Child*. New York: Basic Books.

7 *Parenthood*

Becoming a Parent

Carolyn P. Cowan and Phillip A. Cowan

Sharon: I did a home pregnancy test. I felt really crummy that day, and stayed home from work. I set the container with the urine sample on a bookcase and managed to stay out of the room until the last few minutes. Finally, I walked in and it looked positive. And I went to check the information on the box and, sure enough, it *was* positive. I was so excited. Then I went back to look and see if maybe it has disappeared; you know, maybe the test was false. Then I just sat down on the sofa and kept thinking, "I'm pregnant. I'm really pregnant. I'm going to have a baby!"

Daniel: I knew she was pregnant. She didn't need the test as far as I was concerned. I was excited too, at first, but then I started to worry. I don't know how I'm going to handle being there at the birth, especially if anything goes wrong. And Sharon's going to quit work soon. I don't know when she's going to go back, and we're barely making it as it is.

Sharon: My mom never worked a day in her life for pay. She was home all the time, looking after *her* mother, and us, and cleaning the house. My dad left all of that to her. We're not going to do it that way. But I don't know how we're supposed to manage it all. Daniel promised that he's going to pitch in right along with me in taking care of the baby, but I don't know whether that's realistic. If he doesn't come through, I'm going to be a real bear about it. If I put all my energy into Daniel and the marriage and something happens, then I'll have to start all over again and that scares the hell out of me.

Sharon is beginning the third trimester of her first pregnancy. If her grandmother were to listen in on our conversation with Sharon and her husband, Daniel, and try to make sense of it, given the experience of her own pregnancy fifty years ago, she would surely have a lot of questions. Home pregnancy tests? Why would a woman with a new-born infant *want* to work if she didn't have to? What husband would share the house-work and care of the baby? Why would Sharon and Daniel worry about their marriage not surviving after they have a baby? Understandable questions for someone who made the transition to parenthood five decades ago, in a qualitatively different world. Unfor-tunately, the old trail maps are outmoded, and there are as yet no new ones to describe the final destination. They may not need covered wagons for their journey, but Sharon and Daniel are true pioneers.

Like many modern couples, they have two different fantasies about their journey. The first has them embarking on an exciting adventure to bring a new human being into the world, fill their lives with delight and wonder, and enrich their feeling of closeness as a couple. In the second, their path from couple to family is strewn with unexpected ob-stacles, hazardous conditions, and potential marital strife. Our work suggests that, like most fantasy scenarios, these represent extreme and somewhat exaggerated versions of what really happens when partners become parents. . . .

THE FIVE DOMAINS OF FAMILY LIFE

The responses of one couple to our interview questions offer a preview of how the five domains in our model capture the changes that most couples contend with as they make their transition to parenthood. Natalie and Victor have lived in the San Francisco Bay Area most of their lives. At the time of their initial interview, Natalie, age twenty-nine, is in her fifth month of pregnancy. Victor, her husband of six years, is thirty-four. When their daughter, Kim, is six months old, they visit us again for a follow-up interview. Arranged around each of the five domains, the following excerpts from our second in-terview reveal some universal themes of early parenthood.

Changes in Identity and Inner Life

After settling comfortably with cups of coffee and tea, we ask both Natalie and Victor whether they feel that their sense of self has shifted in any way since Kim was born. As would be typical in our interviews, Mother and Father focus on different aspects of per-sonal change:

> *Natalie:*   There's not much "me" left to think about right now. Most of the time, even when I'm not nursing, I see myself as attached to this little being with only the milk flowing between us.
>
> *Victor:*   I've earned money since I was sixteen, but being a father means that I've become the family breadwinner. I've got this new sense of myself as having to go out there in the world to make sure that my wife and daughter are going to be safe and looked after. I mean, I'm concerned about advancing in my job—and we've even bought insurance policies for the first time! This "protector" role feels exciting *and* frightening.

Another change that often occurs in partners' inner lives during a major life transition is a shift in what C. Murray Parkes (1971) describes as our "assumptive world." Men's and women's assumptions about how the world works or how families operate sometimes change radically during the transition from couple to family.

Natalie: I used to be completely apathetic about political things. I wasn't sure of my congressman's name. Now I'm writing him about once a month because I feel I need to help clean up some of the mess this country is in before Kim grows up.

Victor: What's changed for me is what I think families and fathers are all about. When we were pregnant, I had these pictures of coming home each night as the tired warrior, playing with the baby for a little while and putting my feet up for the rest of the evening. It's not just that there's more work to do than I ever imagined, but I'm so much more a part of the action every night.

Clearly, Natalie and Victor are experiencing qualitatively different shifts in their sense of self and in how vulnerable or safe each feels in the world. These shifts are tied not only to their new life as parents but also to a new sense of their identities as providers and protectors. Even though most of these changes are positive, they can lead to moments when the couple's relationship feels a bit shaky.

Shifts in the Roles and Relationships within the Marriage

Victor: After Kim was born, I noticed that something was bugging Natalie, and I kept saying, "What is bothering you?" Finally we went out to dinner without the baby and it came out. And it was because of small things that I never even think about. Like I always used to leave my running shorts in the bathroom . . .

Natalie: He'd just undress and drop everything!

Victor: . . . and Nat never made a fuss. In fact she *used* to just pick them up and put them in the hamper. And then that night at dinner she said, "When you leave your shorts there, or your wet towel, and don't pick them up—I get furious." At first I didn't believe what she was saying because it never used to bother her at all, but now I say, "OK, fine, no problem. I'll pick up the shorts and hang them up. I'll be very conscientious." And I have been trying.

Natalie: You have, but you still don't quite get it. I think my quick trigger has something to do with my feeling so dependent on you and having the baby so dependent on me—and my being stuck here day in and day out. You at least get to go out to do your work, and you bring home a paycheck to show for it. I work here all day long and by the end of the day I feel that all I have to show for it is my exhaustion.

In addition to their distinctive inner changes, men's and women's roles change in very different ways when partners become parents. The division of labor in taking care of the baby, the household, the meals, the laundry, the shopping, calling parents and friends, and earning the money to keep the family fed, clothed, and sheltered is a hot topic for couples (C. Cowan and P. Cowan 1988; Hochschild 1989). It seems to come as a great surprise to most of them that changes in some of their major roles affect their feelings about their overall relationship.

In a domino effect, both partners have to make major adjustments of time and energy as individuals during a period when they are getting less sleep and fewer opportunities to be together. As with Natalie and Victor, they are apt to find that they have less patience with things that didn't seem annoying before. Their frustration often focuses on each other. For couples who thought that having a baby was going to bring them closer together, this is especially confusing and disappointing.

> *Natalie:*   It's strange. I feel that we're much closer *and* more distant than we have ever been. I think we communicate more, because there's so much to work out, especially about Kim, but it doesn't always feel very good. And we're both so busy that we're not getting much snuggling or loving time.
>
> *Victor:*   We're fighting more too. But I'm still not sure why.

Victor and Natalie are so involved in what is happening to them that even though they can identify some of the sources of their disenchantment, they cannot really make sense of all of it. They are playing out a scenario that was very common for the couples in our study during the first year of parenthood. Both men and women are experiencing a changing sense of self *and* a shift in the atmosphere in the relationship between them. The nurturance that partners might ordinarily get from one another is in very short supply. As if this were not enough to adjust to, almost all of the new parents in our study say that their other key relationships are shifting too.

Shifts in the Three-Generational Roles and Relationships

> *Victor:*   It was really weird to see my father's reaction to Kim's birth. The week before Natalie's due date, my father all of a sudden decided that he was going to Seattle, and he took off with my mom and some other people. Well, the next day Natalie went into labor and we had the baby, and my mother kept calling, saying she wanted to get back here. But my dad seemed to be playing games and made it stretch out for two or three days. Finally, when they came back and the whole period was past, it turned out that my father was *jealous* of my mother's relationship with the baby. He didn't want my mother to take time away from him to be with Kim! He's gotten over it now. He holds Kim and plays with her, and doesn't want to go home after a visit. But my dad and me, we're still sort of recovering from what happened. And when things don't go well with me and Dad, Natalie sometimes gets it in the neck.
>
> *Natalie:*   I'll say.

For Victor's father, becoming a first-time grandfather is something that is happening *to* him. His son and daughter-in-law are having a baby and he is becoming grandfather, ready or not. Many men and women in Victor's parents' position have mixed feelings about becoming grandparents (Lowe 1991), but rarely know how to deal with them. As Victor searches for ways to become comfortable with his new identity as a father, like so many of the men we spoke to, he is desperately hoping that it will bring him closer to his father.

As father and son struggle with these separate inner changes, they feel a strain in the relationship between them, a strain they feel they cannot mention. Some of it spills over into the relationship between Victor and Natalie: After a visit with his parents, they realize, they are much more likely to get into a fight.

Changing Roles and Relationships Outside the Family

Natalie: While Victor has been dealing with his dad, I've been struggling with my boss. After a long set of negotiations on the phone, he reluctantly agreed to let me come back four days a week instead of full-time. I haven't gone back officially yet, but I dropped in to see him. He always used to have time for me, but this week, after just a few minutes of small talk, he told me that he had a meeting and practically bolted out of the room. He as much as said that he figured I wasn't serious about my job anymore.

Victor: Natalie's not getting much support from her friends, either. None of them have kids and they just don't seem to understand what she's going through. Who ever thought how lonely it can be to have a baby?

Although the burden of the shifts in roles and relationships outside the family affects both parents, it tends to fall more heavily on new mothers. It is women who tend to put their jobs and careers on hold, at least temporarily, after they have babies (Daniels and Weingarten 1982, 1988), and even though they may have more close friends than their husbands do, they find it difficult to make contact with them in the early months of new parenthood. It takes all of the energy new mothers have to cope with the ongoing care and feeding that a newborn requires and to replenish the energy spent undergoing labor or cesarean delivery. The unanticipated loss of support from friends and co-workers can leave new mothers feeling surprisingly isolated and vulnerable. New fathers' energies are on double duty too. Because they are the sole earners when their wives stop working or take maternity leave, men often work longer hours or take on extra jobs. Fatigue and limited availability means that fathers too get less support or comfort from co-workers or friends. This is one of many aspects of family life in which becoming a parent seems to involve more *loss* than either spouse anticipated—especially because they have been focused on the gain of the baby. Although it is not difficult for us to see how these shifts and losses might catch two tired parents off guard, most husbands and wives fail to recognize that these changes are affecting them as individuals and as a couple.

New Parenting Roles and Relationships

Natalie and Victor, unlike most of the other couples, had worked out a shared approach to household tasks from the time they moved in together. Whoever was available to do something would do it. And when Kim was born, they just continued that. During the week, Victor would get the baby up in the morning and then take over when he got home from work. Natalie put her to bed at night. During the weekends the responsibilities were reversed.

It was not surprising that Natalie and Victor expected their egalitarian system—a rare arrangement—to carry over to the care of their baby. What is surprising to us is that a majority of the couples predicted that they would share the care of their baby much more equally than they were sharing their housework and family tasks *before* they became parents. Even though they are unusually collaborative in their care of Kim, Natalie and Victor are not protected from the fact that, like most couples, their different ideas about what a baby needs create some conflict and disagreement:

Victor: I tend to be a little more . . . what would you say?

Natalie: Crazy.

Victor: A little more crazy with Kim. I like to put her on my bicycle and go for a ride real fast. I like the thought of the wind blowing on her and her eyes watering. I want her to feel the rain hitting her face. Natalie would cover her head, put a thick jacket on her, you know, make sure she's warm and dry.

Natalie: At the beginning, we argued a lot about things like that. More than we ever did. Some of them seemed trivial at the time. The argument wouldn't last more than a day. It would all build up, explode, and then be over. One night, though, Victor simply walked out. He took a long drive, and then came back. It was a bad day for both of us. We just had to get it out, regardless of the fact that it was three A.M.

Victor: I think it was at that point that I realized that couples who start off with a bad relationship would really be in trouble. As it was, it wasn't too pleasant for us, but we got through it.

Despite the fact that their emotional focus had been on the baby during pregnancy and the early months of parenthood, Victor and Natalie were not prepared for the way their relationship with the baby affected and was affected by the changes they had been experiencing all along as individuals, at work, in their marriage, and in their relationships with their parents, friends, and co-workers—the spillover effects. They sometimes have new and serious disagreements, but both of them convey a sense that they have the ability to prevent their occasional blowups from escalating into serious and long-lasting tensions.

As we follow them over time, Victor and Natalie describe periods in which their goodwill toward each other wears thin, but their down periods are typically followed by genuine ups. It seems that one of them always finds a way to come back to discuss the painful issues when they are not in so much distress. In subsequent visits, for example, the shorts-in-the-bathroom episode, retold with much laughter, becomes a shorthand symbol for the times when tensions erupt between them. They give themselves time to cool down, they come back to talk about what was so upsetting, and having heard each other out, they go on to find a solution to the problem that satisfies both of their needs. This, we know, is the key to a couple's stable and satisfying relationship (Gottman and Krokoff 1989).

Compared to the other couples, one of the unusual strengths in Natalie and Victor's life together is their ability to come back to problem issues after they have calmed down. Many couples are afraid to rock the boat once their heated feelings have cooled down. Even more unusual is their trust that they will both be listened to sympathetically when they try to sort out what happened. Because Natalie and Victor each dare to raise issues that concern them, they end up feeling that they are on the same side when it comes to the most important things in life (cf. Ball 1984). This is what makes it possible for them to engage in conflict and yet maintain their positive feelings about their relationship.

Most important, perhaps, for the long-term outcome of their journey to parenthood is that the good feeling between Victor and Natalie spills over to their daughter. Throughout Kim's preschool years and into her first year of kindergarten, we see the threesome as an active, involved family in which the members are fully engaged with one another in both serious and playful activities.

WHAT MAKES PARENTHOOD HARDER NOW

Natalie and Victor are charting new territory. They are trying to create a family based on the new, egalitarian ideology in which both of them work *and* share the tasks of managing the household and caring for their daughter. They have already embraced less traditional roles than most of the couples in our study. Although the world they live in has changed a great deal since they were children, it has not shifted sufficiently to support them in realizing their ideals easily. Their journey seems to require heroic effort.

Would a more traditional version of family life be less stressful? Couples who arrange things so that the woman tends the hearth and baby and the man provides the income to support them are also showing signs of strain. They struggle financially because it often takes more than one parent's income to maintain a family. They feel drained emotionally because they rely almost entirely on their relationship to satisfy most of their psychological needs. Contemporary parents find themselves in double jeopardy. Significant historical shifts in the family landscape of the last century, particularly of the last few decades, have created additional burdens for them. As couples set foot on the trails of this challenging journey, they become disoriented because society's map of the territory has been redrawn. Becoming a family today is more difficult than it used to be.

In recent decades there has been a steady ripple of revolutionary social change. Birth control technology has been transformed. Small nuclear families live more isolated lives in crowded cities, often feeling cut off from extended family and friends. Mothers of young children are entering the work force earlier and in ever larger numbers. Choices about how to create life as a family are much greater then they used to be. Men and women are having a difficult time regaining their balance as couples after they have babies, in part because the radical shifts in the circumstances surrounding family life in America demand new arrangements to accommodate the increasing demands on parents of young children. But new social arrangements and roles have simply not kept pace with these changes, leaving couples on their own to manage the demands of work and family.

More Choice

Compared with the experiences of their parents and grandparents, couples today have many more choices about whether and when to bring a child into their lives. New forms of birth control have given most couples the means to engage in an active sex life with some confidence, though no guarantee, that they can avoid unwanted pregnancy. In addition, despite recent challenges in American courts and legislatures, the 1973 Supreme Court decision legalizing abortion has given couples a second chance to decide whether to become parents if birth control fails or is not used.

But along with modern birth control techniques come reports of newly discovered hazards. We now know that using birth control pills, intrauterine devices, the cervical cap, the sponge, and even the diaphragm poses some risk to a woman's health. The decision to abort a fetus brings with it both public controversy and the private anguish of the physical, psychological, and moral consequences of ending a pregnancy (see Nathanson 1989). Men and women today may enjoy more choice about parenthood than any previous generation, but the couples in our studies are finding it quite difficult to navigate this new family-making terrain.

Sharon, who was eagerly awaiting the results of her home pregnancy test when we met her at the beginning of this reading, had not been nearly as eager to become a mother three years earlier.

> *Sharon:*   Actually, we fought about it a lot. Daniel already had a child, Hallie, from his first marriage. "Let's have one of our own. It'll be easy," he said. And I said, "Yeah, and what happened before Hallie was two? You were out the door."
>
> *Daniel:*   I told you, that had nothing to do with Hallie. She was great. It was my ex that was the problem. I just knew that for us a baby would be right.
>
> *Sharon:*   I wasn't sure. What was I going to do about a career? What was I going to do about me? I wasn't ready to put things on hold. I wasn't even convinced, then, that I wanted to become a mother. It wouldn't have been good for me, and it sure wouldn't have been good for the baby, to go ahead and give in to Daniel when I was feeling that way.

In past times, fewer choices meant less conflict between spouses, at least at the outset. Now, with each partner expecting to have a free choice in the matter, planning a family can become the occasion for sensitive and delicate treaty negotiations. First, couples who want to live together must decide whether they want to get married. One partner may be for it, the other not. Second, the timing of childbirth has changed. For couples married in 1950–54, the majority (60 percent) would have a baby within two years. Now, almost one-third of couples are marrying *after* having a child, and those who marry before becoming parents are marrying later in life. Only a minority of them have their first child within two years. Some delay parenthood for more than a decade (Teachman, Polonko, and Scanzoni 1987).

Couples are also having smaller families. The decline in fertility has for the first time reduced the birthrate below the replacement level of zero population growth—less than two children per family.* And because couples are having fewer children and having them later, more seems to be at stake in each decision about whether and when to have a child. What was once a natural progression has become a series of choice points, each with a potential for serious disagreement between the partners.

Alice is in the last trimester of her pregnancy. In our initial interview, she and Andy described a profound struggle between them that is not over yet.

> *Alice:*　This pregnancy was a life and death issue for me. I'd already had two abortions with a man I'd lived with before, because it was very clear that we could not deal with raising a child. Although I'd known Andy for years, we had been together only four months when I became pregnant unexpectedly. I loved him, I was thirty-four years old, and I wasn't going to risk the possibility of another abortion and maybe never being able to have children. So when I became pregnant this time, I said, "I'm having this baby with you or without you. But I'd much rather have it with you."

> *Andy:*　Well, I'm only twenty-seven and I haven't gotten on track with my own life. Alice was using a diaphragm and I thought it was safe. For months after she became pregnant, I was just pissed off that this was happening to me, to us, but I gradually calmed down. If it was just up to me, I'd wait for a number of years yet because I don't feel ready, but I want to be with her, and you can hear that she's determined to have this baby.

Clearly, more choice has not necessarily made life easier for couples who are becoming a family.

Isolation

The living environments of families with children have changed dramatically. In 1850, 75 percent of American families lived in rural settings. By 1970, 75 percent were living in urban or suburban environments, and the migration from farm to city is continuing.

We began our own family in Toronto, Canada, the city we had grown up in, with both sets of parents living nearby. Today we live some distance from our parents, relatives, and childhood friends, as do the majority of couples in North America. Increasingly, at least in the middle- and upper-income brackets, couples are living in unfamiliar surroundings, bringing newborns home to be reared in single-family apartments or houses, where their neighbors are strangers. Becoming a parent, then, can quickly result in social isolation, especially for the parent who stays at home with the baby.

John and Shannon are one of the younger couples in our study. He is twenty-four and she is twenty-three.

> *John:*　My sister in Dallas lives down the block from our mother. Whenever she and her husband want a night out, they just call up and either they take the baby over to Mom's house or Mom comes right over to my sister's. Our friends help

---

*There are indications, however, that the birthrate of the United States is now on the rise.

us out once in a while, but you have to reach out and ask them and a lot of times they aren't in a position to respond. Some of them don't have kids, so they don't really understand what it's like for us. They keep calling us and suggesting that we go for a picnic or out for pizza, and we have to remind them that we have this baby to take care of.

Shannon: All the uncles, aunts, and cousins in my family used to get together every Sunday. Most of the time I don't miss that because they were intrusive and gossipy and into everybody else's business. But sometimes it would be nice to have someone to talk to who cares about me, and who lived through all the baby throw-up and ear infections and lack of sleep, and could just say, "Don't worry, Shannon, it's going to get better soon."

Women's Roles

Since we began our family thirty years ago, mothers have been joining the labor force in ever-increasing numbers, even when they have young babies. Women have always worked, but economic necessity in the middle as well as the working classes, and increased training and education among women, propelled them into the work force in record numbers. In 1960, 18 percent of mothers with children under six were working at least part-time outside the home. By 1970, that figure had grown to 30 percent, and by 1980 it was 45 percent. Today, the majority of women with children under *three* work at least part-time, and recent research suggests that this figure will soon extend to a majority of mothers of one-year-olds (Teachman, Polonko, and Scanzoni 1987).

With the enormous increase in women's choices and opportunities in the work world, many women are caught between traditional and modern conceptions of how they should be living their lives. It is a common refrain in our couples groups.

Joan: It's ironic. My mother knew that she was supposed to be a mom and not a career woman. But she suffered from that. She was a capable woman with more business sense than my dad, but she felt it was her job to stay home with us kids. And she was *very* depressed some of the time. But I'm *supposed* to be a career woman. I feel that I just need to stay home right now. I'm really happy with that decision, but I struggled with it for months.

Tanya: I know what Joan means, but it's the opposite for me. I'm doing what I want, going back to work, but it's driving me crazy. All day as I'm working, I'm wondering what's happening to Kevin. Is he OK, is he doing some new thing that I'm missing, is he getting enough individual attention? And when I get home, I'm tired, Jackson's tired, Kevin's tired. I have to get dinner on the table and Kevin ready for bed. And then I'm exhausted and Jackson's exhausted and I just hit the pillow and I'm out. We haven't made love in three months. I know Jackson's frustrated. *I'm* frustrated. I didn't know it was going to be like this.

News media accounts of family-oriented men imply that as mothers have taken on more of a role in the world of paid work, fathers have taken on a comparable load of family work. But this simply hasn't happened. As Arlie Hochschild (1989) demonstrates, working mothers are coming home to face a "second shift"—running the household and caring for the children. Although there are studies suggesting that fathers are taking on a little more housework and care of the children than they used to (Pleck 1985), mothers who are employed full-time still have far greater responsibility for managing the family work and child rearing than their husbands do (C. Cowan 1988). It is not simply that men's and women's roles are unequal that seems to be causing distress for couples, but rather that they are so clearly discrepant from what both spouses expected them to be.

Women are getting the short end of what Hochschild calls the "stalled revolution": Their work roles have changed but their family roles have not. Well-intentioned and confused husbands feel guilty, while their overburdened wives feel angry. It does not take much imagination to see how these emotions can fuel the fire of marital conflict.

Social Policy

The stress that Joan and Tanya talk about comes not only from internal conflict and from difficulties in coping with life inside the family but from factors outside the family as well. Joan might consider working part-time if she felt that she and her husband could get high-quality, affordable child care for their son. Tanya might consider working different shifts or part-time if her company had more flexible working arrangements for parents of young children. But few of the business and government policies that affect parents and children are supportive of anything beyond the most traditional family arrangements.

We see a few couples, like Natalie and Victor, who strike out on their own to make their ideology of more balanced roles a reality. These couples believe that they and their children will reap the rewards of their innovation, but they are exhausted from bucking the strong winds of opposition—from parents, from bosses, from co-workers. Six months after the birth of her daughter, Natalie mentioned receiving a lukewarm reception from her boss after negotiating a four-day work week.

> *Natalie:*   He made me feel terrible. I'm going to have to work *very* hard to make things go, but I think I can do it. What worries me, though, is that the people I used to supervise aren't very supportive either. They keep raising these issues, "Well, what if so-and-so happens, and you're not there?" Well, sometimes I wasn't there before because I was traveling for the company, and nobody got in a snit. Now that I've got a baby, somehow my being away from the office at a particular moment is a problem.
>
> *Victor:*   My boss is flexible about when I come in and when I leave, but he keeps asking me questions. He can't understand why I want to be at home with Kim some of the time that Natalie's at work.

It would seem to be in the interest of business and government to develop policies that are supportive of the family. Satisfied workers are more productive. Healthy families drain scarce economic resources less than unhealthy ones, and make more of a contribution to the welfare of society at large. Yet, the United States is the only country in the Western world without a semblance of explicit family policy. This lack is felt most severely by parents of young children. There are no resources to help new parents deal with their anxieties about child rearing (such as the visiting public health nurses in England), unless the situation is serious enough to warrant medical or psychiatric attention. If both parents want or need to work, they would be less conflicted if they could expect to have adequate parental leave when their babies are born (as in Sweden and other countries), flexible work hours to accommodate the needs of young children, and access to reasonably priced, competent child care. These policies and provisions are simply not available in most American businesses and communities (Catalyst 1988).

The absence of family policy also takes its toll on traditional family arrangements, which are not supported by income supplements or family allowances (as they are in Canada and Britain) as a financial cushion for the single-earner family. The lack of supportive policy and family-oriented resources results in increased stress on new parents just when their energies are needed to care for their children. It is almost inevitable that this kind of stress spills over into the couple's negotiations and conflicts about how they will divide the housework and care of the children.

The Need for New Role Models

Based on recent statistics, the modern family norm is neither the Norman Rockwell *Saturday Evening Post* cover family nor the "Leave It to Beaver" scenario with Dad going out to work and Mom staying at home to look after the children. Only about 6 percent of all American households today have a husband as the sole breadwinner and a wife and two or more children at home—"the typical American family" of earlier times. Patterns from earlier generations are often irrelevant to the challenges faced by dual-worker couples in today's marketplace.

After setting out on the family journey, partners often discover that they have conflicting values, needs, expectations, and plans for their destination. This may not be an altogether new phenomenon, but it creates additional strain for a couple.

> *James:* My parents were old-school Swedes who settled in Minnesota on a farm. It was cold outside in the winters, but it was cold inside too. Nobody said anything unless they had to. My mom was home all the time. She worked hard to support my dad and keep the farm going, but she never really had anything of her own. I'm determined to support Cindy going back to school as soon as she's ready.

> *Cindy:* My parents were as different from James's as any two parents could be. When they were home with us, they were all touchy-feely, but they were hardly ever around. During the days my mom and dad both worked. At night, they went out with their friends. I really don't want that to happen to Eddie. So, James and I are having a thing about it now. He wants me to go back to school. I don't want to. I'm working about ten hours a week, partly because he nags at me so much. If it were just up to me, I'd stay home until Eddie gets into first grade.

Cindy and James each feel that they have the freedom to do things differently than their parents did. The problem is that the things each of them wants to be different are on a collision course. James is trying to be supportive of Cindy's educational ambitions so his new family will feel different than the one he grew up in. Given her history, Cindy does not experience this as support. Her picture of the family she wanted to create and James's picture do not match. Like so many of the couples in our study, both partners are finding it difficult to establish a new pattern because the models from the families they grew up in are so different from the families they want to create.

Increased Emotional Burden

The historical changes we have been describing have increased the burden on both men and women with respect to the emotional side of married life. Not quite the equal sharers of breadwinning and family management they hoped to be, husbands and wives now expect to be each other's major suppliers of emotional warmth and support. Especially in the early months as a family, they look to their marriage as a "haven in a heartless world." Deprived of regular daily contact with extended family members and lifelong friends, wives and husbands look to each other to "be there" for them—to pick up the slack when energies flag, to work collaboratively on solving problems, to provide comfort when it is needed, and to share the highs and lows of life inside and outside the family. While this mutual expectation may sound reasonable to modern couples, it is very difficult to live up to in an intimate relationship that is already vulnerable to disappointment from within and pressure from without.

The greatest emotional pressure on the couple, we believe, comes from the culture's increasing emphasis on self-fulfillment and self-development (Bellah et al. 1985). The vocabulary of individualism, endemic to American society from its beginnings, has become even more pervasive in recent decades. It is increasingly difficult for two people to make a commitment to each other if they believe that ultimately they are alone, and that personal development and success in life must be achieved through individual efforts. As this individualistic vocabulary plays out within the family, it makes it even more difficult for partners to subordinate some of their personal interests to the common good of the relationship. When "my needs" and "your needs" appear to be in conflict, partners can wind up feeling more like adversaries than family collaborators.

The vocabulary of individualism also makes it likely that today's parents will be blamed for any disarray in American families. In the spirit of Ben Franklin and Horatio Alger, new parents feel that they ought to be able to make it on their own, without help. Couples are quick to blame themselves if something goes wrong. When the expectable tensions increase as partners become parents, their tendency is to blame each other for not doing a better job. We believe that pioneers will inevitably find themselves in difficulty at some points on a strenuous journey. If societal policies do not become more responsive to parents and children, many of them will lose their way.

Editor's Note: *References for this reading can be found in the original source.*

■READING 20

A Typology of Approaches to Child Care: The Centerpiece of Organizing Family Life for Dual-Earner Couples

Rosanna Hertz

Child rearing tends to be regarded as an individualistic concern for parents in the United States. Society may purport to be so-called profamily but, judging by the small number of policies and programs that pertain to child care, society largely ignores how young children spend their days despite widespread recognition that women's labor force participation has increased dramatically over the past several decades.[1] Indeed, it has become quite popular for political contenders to voice support for family values but to sidestep the sticky questions about how children are being cared for when mothers (and fathers) must work for pay outside the home.

With the exception of Head Start programs, when compared with other industrialized nations, the United States has little government-sponsored or subsidized day care (Benin & Chong, 1993; Kamerman & Kahn, 1991; Zigler, 1990). We lack the extensive system of day care that exists in other industrialized countries (Ferber & O'Farrell, 1991; Moen, 1989) because of ideological conflicts over the government's involvement in family life (Hartmann & Spalter-Roth, 1994).[2] The invocation of family values to indicate a belief in the strength of families to organize independently their lives to maximize the care and nurturance of the young (and elderly) rings hollow when studies find that affordable good quality day care arrangements would reduce both economic hardships and distress couples face in trying to balance the simultaneous child care and workplace demands (Bird, 1995). The lack of affordable child care in the United States is a serious problem for all social classes (Bianchi & Spain, 1986); but its consequences for low-income families are perhaps the greatest of all (Ferber & O'Farrell, 1991, pp. 74–84).[3]

Child care should be a leading social issue addressed at workplaces, in communities and at the state and federal levels of government. But without an array of good solutions to preschool child care (e.g., quality, affordability, certification, etc.), couples attempt to resolve this work/family dilemma through individual solutions. This article explores in a systematic way the different approaches dual-earner couples implement to care for their children. It also seeks to understand in context the critical factors that explain couples' choice of day care arrangements. The data presented suggest that a combination of a priori beliefs and economic resources explains the choice of child care practice. Only in rare instances do beliefs or resources alone play the determining role

Author's Note: I thank Faith I. T. Ferguson, who helped interview some of the couples with me, and I thank Wellesley College for a faculty award for tape transcriptions. I also thank Robert J. Thomas for helpful comments on this manuscript. A version of this article was presented at the British Psychological Society, London, 1996.

in selecting child care practices. However, there is no clear-cut relationship between beliefs and economic resources. In the absence of strong evidence regarding the relationship between beliefs and economic resources, I propose a typology of approaches to child care that reflects the interaction of ideology and economic factors. From a sample of dual-earner couples, I suggest that there are three general approaches to child care: (a) the "mothering" approach, (b) the parenting approach, and (c) the market approach. In addition to exploring diverse views of child rearing that exist in the United States, I will analyze how sentiments about mothering influence the ways couples organize and integrate family and work lives.

THE STUDY AND THE INTERVIEW SAMPLE

This article is part of an in-depth study of 95 dual-earner couples, with the majority (88 couples) having at least one child still living in the home in eastern Massachusetts. Each husband and wife was individually interviewed; the majority of couples were also interviewed simultaneously (Hertz, 1995).[4] Husbands and wives were told that we were interested in studying how couples make decisions about child care, finances, and work. The interviews lasted a minimum of 2 hours, with a smaller number of interviews lasting up to 4 hours. There are two parts to the interview: a longer-in-depth open-ended guide with extensive probes and then a shorter division of labor survey adapted from Huber and Spitzer (1983).

Because the primary focus of the study was looking at how women's labor force participation has altered family life—particularly authority surrounding decision making in the home—I decided to use a stratified quota sample. Different strategies were used to find different segments of the study's population. In general, access to individual couples was obtained either through other professionals who identified couples fitting the study's parameters or through mailings to day care parents in several communities.

I used a combination of factors to decide who belongs in each social class stratum; these included the income of both spouses combined. Families in the upper middle class had a combined income of at least $100,000 annually and professional or managerial occupations; middle-class couples had a combined income of between $40,000 and $100,000, and most were in white-collar jobs in service professions or middle-management occupations; and working-class couples had incomes that overlapped those earned by the middle class, but these couples were distinguished by their occupations. I tried to locate couples for this segment employed in traditional working-class occupations or trades, such as painter, policeman, nurse, waitress, factory worker.

A total of 36% of the couples are working class; the other three fifths are middle and upper middle class. Within the working class, 30 couples are White and 4 couples are of other races. Within the middle and upper middle class, 35 couples are White and 21 couples are of other races. An additional 5 couples do not share the same race as their spouse; they are all middle- to upper middle-class couples. There are no "cross-class" couples (husbands and wives who differ in occupational prestige). For purposes of this article, social class is only mentioned. Racial differences in the three approaches to mothering appear not to be as important for this article as social class. For instance, upper middle-class African American families were as likely to have a professional approach to child rearing as their White counterparts. Racial differences are relevant when it comes to deciding between types of non-kin care and selecting between settings, which I have discussed in another article (Hertz & Ferguson, 1996). Therefore, I have not used race as a way of identifying respondents; I have instead used occupations as a signifier of the social class of each respondent.

At the time of the interview, each spouse within a couple had a minimum of one job. This does not mean, however, that at the time of having young children (preschool or elementary age) there were two full-time jobs. In most cases, women did not leave the labor force for more than 1 year; but in a small number of cases, women were not employed in the labor force when their children were preschool age or younger. More likely among this small group of couples, women worked outside the home for fewer hours than a full-time job. The decision to stay home longer than a year is not related to social class. That is, regardless of social class, it is possible to organize family life around a mothering approach (discussed below) provided that there are enough economic resources to live on one salary for a period of time. It is questionable whether younger couples can afford to do this today except perhaps among the upper middle and upper classes. At the time of the interviews, just over 60% of the couples were between their late 30s and middle 40s.[5] But there is great variation within this group as to the age when they had their first children. For those couples who had children in early decades, having children may have led to greater economic ability for the wife to stay at home. There were also fewer day care services available then; the growth of day care in the United States has mushroomed in the last 10 years. For those couples who have had children in the last 5 years, most remain in the paid labor force, with wives typically taking only brief maternity leaves.[6]

Independent of what age couples are now, I am interested in the relationship between child care beliefs and practices and social class at the time each couple had young children. At the time of the interview, 63 couples (66%) had at least one child age 5 or younger. An additional 25 couples (26%) had children living at home older than age 5. I indicate age of the respondents and their children's ages as part of the lead-ins to quotes so the reader can assess the historical factors (labor force and day care options) that inform each couple's story. I have deliberately selected quotes and respondents in each type who presently have young children as well as those whose children are older to give the reader information about couples presently undergoing child care decision making and couples who are reflecting back to this period in their family lives.

The focal points of this article are based on an analysis of responses to one open-ended question: "Tell me a history of your child care arrangements." Probes included likes and dislikes about child care arrangements but not anything about motherhood. Other topics emerge from the dialogue between interviewer and interviewee. Demographic facts and information are also used to analyze the responses to this question. Because I am particularly interested in the women's and men's views, I have relied heavily on their words and descriptions of family life to demonstrate the diverse beliefs about caring for young children in the United States today.

THE MOTHERING APPROACH

The mothering approach assumes that the person who is best suited to raise the couple's children is the wife, who should be with them at home. According to this approach, only the family can give its children the right values and moral upbringing. These couples uniformly believe that what will create successful adults is a childhood steeped in love, caring, and nurturing properly provided only by the insular world of the family. In this regard, the child's future is tied to a certain kind of early mothering practice.[7]

To maximize wives' abilities to devote themselves to the upbringing of the children, husbands work either overtime or they supplement a primary job with a second one, sacrificing their own leisure and time with children and spouses. But even the additional work hours were insufficient to pay the bills and keep wives out of the paid labor force. For the few lucky families who 15 years ago could get by financially on his earnings, as men reached their late 30s and early 40s, "burn-out" and being physically forced to slow down commonly occurred. Some worked less overtime; others found less strenuous work with less income. Even these men's wives eventually went back to paid work to take the pressure off him and to make their family's life less of an economic struggle to pay bills on time and to perhaps put a little money aside for a vacation. In 53% of working-class couples at the time of the interview, at least one spouse, typically the husband, worked overtime or held a second part-time job, totaling at minimum 60 hours a week.

This ideological belief about child rearing rarely exists for long in practice. Few couples could economically afford to have wives at home and out of the paid labor force. Yet, this central family belief in mother as the best person to raise children fuels how they arrange their work schedules and jobs to attempt not to compromise their children's upbringing. Child rearing—and keeping children within the family circle—is the priority, and work schedules of wives are critical to meeting this approach. Most of these women were employed even when their children were infants and toddlers, but talk about that only emerges once the conversation shifts to paid employment.

Beyond the early childhood years, even mothers who stayed out of the paid workforce, returned to paid employment at least part-time when the youngest entered kindergarten. In other families, however, wives remained in the paid workforce but changed to working shifts (Presser & Cain, 1983; Presser, 1988). To be available to young children, women worked nights giving the appearance of stay-at-home traditional moms to make highly visible their identities as mothers (Garey, 1995). Wives adjusted their work schedules, changing shifts as their children aged, placing their ability to care for children over spending time with husbands (Hertz & Charlton, 1989). Scheduling of work hours for both spouses to maximize mother care is more important than the wife's job mobility or workplace loyalty.

To permit a continued belief in a division of labor in which wives raise children, couples redefine their circumstances. That is, it is not the husband's fault that he does not earn enough. The economy is to blame. Placing blame on an external force does not damage their views of masculinity as tied to being a good provider. Economic explanations also become more congruent with couples' expectations that wives are picking up overtime because of cutbacks or due to erosion of wages so that families can avoid a decline in their standard of living (Ferber & O'Farrell, 1991). Put differently, locating blame external to the couple exempts husbands from feeling they are not good providers and wives from resenting their husbands for having jobs that do not pay enough, forcing them to seek paid employment.

It is interesting that these couples have yet to adjust their ideal view of family life to the reality they are living. But there is reason for this nested in a set of beliefs about family primacy. Even though these couples speak a language of traditional gender roles whereby spouses share the belief that child rearing is the wife's primary responsibility, their practices contradict these beliefs. For the most part, husbands strongly favor their wives' paid employment. It not only relieves the men of economic pressure but also means that the family is not living as tightly. They continue to live paycheck to paycheck but without worrying—especially for wives who typically pay the bills—about meeting monthly payments. But the ideological emphasis for them is not on gender equality as a larger value; instead, family is the critical variable. As a result of wives' paid employment, couples discuss parenting while emphasizing mothering. In this regard, there has been a shift by White working-class couples with traditional values of exclusive mothering to now resemble more the mother practices of earlier generations of minority working-class couples in this study;[8] now family values are about the family doing for itself in terms of raising its children, and whatever couples can do for themselves (without external supports, including everything from day care to welfare) is achieving family values.

Constructing Family Life to Maximize the Mother at Home

Despite hardship at times, keeping the mother/child dyad together is an organizing principal belief of these families. Sometimes, respondents phrased this belief as the mother's need to be with her child; other times, the belief appears as part of what is essential to so-called good mothering in addition to the glue that keeps the family unit strong. Put differently, the wife's status as mother becomes the pivotal point around which all other statuses (e.g., employee) revolve. Because the work of caring for family members is ignored (DeVault, 1991) or regarded as part of what might be called the invisible work (Daniels, 1988) of family life that women do, women's visible presence elevates mothering and other aspects of household work.

This wife, who once managed an office, thought when she was pregnant that she would return to work full-time. But becoming a mother is different than fantasizing about what it might feel like. Now 42 years old and the mother of two children, ages 1 and 10, she reflects back to how dramatically her beliefs changed about the kind of mother she wanted to be:

> I can remember, I always laugh with a girl friend who had a baby a year before me, and she'd say to me, "Are you still going back [to work]?" I go, "Oh ya, I'm gonna go back. No offense Ann, I really don't mean any offense, I really don't know what you do all day." And then once I had my baby, and was home for a couple of weeks with her, I never went back. (Interviewer: Really?) All of a sudden this thing took over me and it was there was no one in this world that could possibly raise this child like I was going to.

Other couples talked quite candidly about this division of labor as a taken-for-granted aspect of their marriage. Another husband, a policeman, age 44 with three children between the ages of 10 and 17, gave a typical response to why it was essential for mothers to be home:

> She's never worked full-time since we had our children. That's a decision we made. She took a maternity leave and decided not to go back to her job. Raising our children was too

important. . . . We had had a firm commitment to my children's being raised by my wife. Because we're firm believers in a strong foundation for children. I mean first through age 6. To me, it's like a building. If the foundation isn't strong, you're asking for trouble later, as you build.

His wife, age 42, who presently works part-time as a secretary and cares for a relative's child in her home 2 days a week, told us that it was an implicit part of their marriage that she stay home when the children were born.

> (Interviewer: Why did you make the decision to stay home?)
> Oh God. I guess because that was just the way it was. I guess I figured when I had children, I'd stay home with them. I had a great job. And I actually probably made more money than my husband did at the time, but it wasn't a question.
> (Was it something the two of you talked about at all?)
> Not really, it was just I would stay home. . . .
> (Were there any family members who could have watched the children?)
> My husband's mother never worked, so she probably could have, if I had decided to ever do that, but I really enjoy being here. I really didn't—I wanted to be with them.

In another family, with children ages 10 and 18, the husband, age 37, had been a factory worker since he was 19 years old. High school sweethearts, he and his 36-year-old wife (presently a medical transcriber who has had a series of different jobs) have both always had to work to make ends meet. He explains the couple's philosophy about raising children even though these beliefs were at times thwarted, as is often the case among working-class couples when the inability to pay bills forces the wife back to work—even part-time—and someone else watches the child, which is less of a concern when older siblings or relatives help out:

> It's very important to both of us that one, mainly that she should be—you know, because I was the primary breadwinner, I had the steady job—that she be home with our son [the second child], especially. With our daughter, it was hard because when she was born, I was making a lot less money. . . We always tried to put both our kids first. But when my daughter was a baby we had someone watching her—we've always both felt very strongly that if we're going to have children, that we should be with them, it's as simple as that. Not shuffling him off—it was never a "you have to go here [day care] every single day when you get home from school." . . . My daughter sometimes gets him [the son] in the afternoon, she helps a lot or his grandfather who lives down the street or we try to always have someone home for him in the afternoons.

In a fourth example, this mother, age 37, with three children between the ages of 10 and 16, returned to work waitressing after a 3-month maternity leave. Below, she explains why she shifted from working day hours to night hours:

> I really didn't want to leave my kids with someone else. You know . . . I did try to go to work during the day when Eric was about 3 months old. When I decided I want—needed to go back to work for the money. And an old job was available that I had had, and they really wanted me to come back. It was waitressing again. I worked 4 days and couldn't do it. I cried and it was just too much, I just couldn't be away from him during the day. Didn't

bother me to go in the evening when I knew he was with Mark [his father], sleeping most of the time and that was fine. Actually I've always liked working, but um . . . no, it wasn't for me. And it was tough when I just went to work a few years ago during the day. You know, because I wasn't here in the morning to get them off to school and it was difficult for my youngest. They've done great.

Night work did not compete with being a good mother in ways that being a day-working mom did (Garey, 1995). To meet the ideology of the stay-at-home mom, women are employed outside the home during hours that do not count: when children are in school and asleep. This allows these families to meet this kind of mothering expectation without challenging women's primary identities. Further, child care decisions (and the choice to limit paid child care services) define the boundaries of what is necessary for them to retain their sense of being good mothers as well as an important part of their families' lives (Hertz & Ferguson, 1996).

Her husband, age 36, a factory worker who leaves home at 6:00 a.m. and returns at 3:30 in the afternoon, during periods when there is no overtime also works as a custodian for a restaurant before his factory job on Thursdays and Fridays. He simplified all his wife's job arrangements to make his point about their shared beliefs regarding child raising as a family-centered activity. Note that his identity is not tied to fathering but his talk is about what is critical to children's upbringing:

> She got a job at night, I worked during the day. The key to good parenting is one parent being with the child at ALL times. That's what we always thought. . . . Cause kids like to see their parents when they get home. I mean, cause they run through the door and they got so many things to tell you. They just, they don't have anybody to blab it out to.

As their family grew, neighbors watched the children in the transition from mom's leaving to work and dad's returning home from work. Neighbors continue to be a source of help during transition points in the day. At the time of the interview, her oldest children were teenagers and she went back to working the dayshift. Below, she describes why she shifted back:

> Because I always hated . . . I hated when I worked nights and weekends. Um, because it was the weekends. I mean I went to work when everybody else was home, basically. And especially when all of the kids were in school, they would come home, even though it was only a couple nights a week, Thursday and Friday.

She felt like an invisible part of the family. Even though much of the evening and weekend time is devoted to team sports that her husband coaches and that she admits to not really enjoying, it was important to her to be a spectator and cheer the family on rather than work during this time. Being visible represents good mothering. Similarly, the woman above who does secretarial work part-time, in addition to caring for a niece 2 days a week, had just filled out an application to work during the day at a store part-time at the time of the interview. Worried about how they will pay the tuition so their oldest daughter can commute to college to study nursing, she explains why she is applying for this particular job:

So, I recently put in an application at a candy shop. See if I could sort of have two part-time jobs. I really still want to be home when my youngest gets out of school [elementary]. I FIRMLY believe that somebody needs to be home. As a matter of fact, even as they get older I really want to be around. I'm there for my older two [in high school].

The medical transcriber, who has a skill in high demand, requested hours to complement her children's school schedule. Flexibility in work scheduling allows women to assert the salience of their identity as mothers who place a priority on a particular kind of child rearing. Below, she explains the work arrangement she negotiated:

Now I work days. But once summer vacation comes, I may end up working second shift again. Once again, I don't want to put him in a day care home. . . . I stressed with my boss that I needed flexibility. [She told her boss,] "Yes, I will go full-time, but school vacations, summer vacations, I may have to completely change my schedule and you'll have to go along with that." And that was fine with him.

Even though couples articulate the importance of the wife's being the central care provider, all the women quoted above worked some hours each week from the birth of the first child. But what they did was leave well-paying jobs, often earning more than husbands, to find work with better hours, meaning hours that allowed their husbands (or if possible another relative) to watch the children for at least part of her shift while she went to her job. Neighbors or acquaintances, often members in the same church, cared for children during transition times as part of the patchwork of child care coverage. These "custodial" caregivers did not compete with the mother as the central nurturer (Uttal, 1996). The woman above, who was once an office manager, never really stayed home. This couple needed her income to qualify for a mortgage, so she took a night job as a tax auditor briefly and since then has worked steadily as a phone service operator during weekend evenings and some week nights. He said,

I'd get out of work at 3:30. Then she'd leave for work. I think she worked 4 to midnight. We might pass in the driveway or my mother-in-law would take care of the baby until I got home at night.

When their mortgage was approved, he was laid off. Finally, finding work as a truck driver, she needed weekend work hours because he was gone during the week. She took her present job as an answering service operator because she needed both a flexible schedule and some time out of the house. Below, she tells about this and her perfect job hours:

It's probably the lowest paying job I've ever had and the most abusive in that people who call want to get whomever they want to get, not you. But it's the only thing that fits into my schedule. But my ideal is that I'd like to work for 5 nights a week—Sunday to Thursday night—and I'd like to work 6–11. You know, if I could. That's what I'd like to do.

Work histories for more than one third of the women in this group included several years as child care providers. Economically, couples noted this was a way not to have to place several children in the care of others and, equally important, it continued to position women in the world of the home, not the external labor force (Fitz Gibbon, 1993; Nelson, 1994). Some were licensed as family providers; others, such as the secretary quoted earlier, were paid to care for relatives' or friends' children (and for a brief period, even the medical transcriber watched children). Between shifting from a night schedule to a day one, the waitress above also worked out of her home, a culturally desirable place for her to be, to approximate a full-time homemaker mom caring for her children:

> When my youngest was born, I did day care myself. I did day care for two years. . . . I said to my girlfriend, "I don't know what I'm gonna DO, I don't really want to go back to work with three kids and leaving them. It's just too much." And she said, "Well, you know, I was thinking about getting back into day care and doing it up here. Why don't you get licensed?" So I ended up in day care and ah. It was okay. It served the purpose, you know, with Ann a baby and Eric only 2, being able to be home. But, um, I got burnt out really fast. Really fast, cause I had so many babies. . . . And actually when I gave it up and decided that I wanted to work outside the home, I did keep one little girl and my niece. I kept them and still babysat during the day time and waitressed a couple nights a week. . . . Four years that I babysat. It was the hardest work I ever did.

But it is not simply mothers who do all the nurturing. Fathers are active participants in these households, particularly when it comes to scheduling their work so wives can earn as well. The police officer mentioned earlier followed up his comment about his wife's staying at home with the following comment:

> I work nights now. I've worked days. If she has something to go to, we work it out so one of us is around. I mean, we had babysitters, but there's never been a time when both of us worked that we needed day care.

The waitress described her husband's involvement with the children:

> Mark actually does more of the after-school activities than I do. He is the one who takes them to all their meets and practices and spends afternoons hearing about their day. Since I wasn't home during dinner, he gave them supper but now I do it.

According to the medical transcriber's detailed account, her husband is now doing the thinking work of running their household, instead of simply serving the meals she prepared when she worked nights and her first child was young. When she was asked to commit to full-time hours by her employer, they had a long conversation about how the division of labor between them would change:

> But we did talk about it a lot and he was very well aware of the added responsibility that he would have, not just with my son but with the household things. Because when I was working evenings, I would do everything in the house during the day. . . . I was always the one responsible for the housework, cooking, laundry. And now, especially now that I'm working full-time, my husband does just as much, maybe more sometimes, than I do. . . . In fact, my husband did all the laundry last night. He left it for me to fold and put away, but it was clean and dry. . . . Normally, I work 10:30 to 7:00 at night. He gets home at 3:30 or 4:00. So my husband does the majority of the cooking during the week. . . . But if I'm

going to be late, then he'll eat. And him and my daughter play cribbage or yahtzee to see who does the dishes. And on the weekends, if the house is a real pit, it's like "let's get up Saturday morning and clean the house." We just all chip in.

Finally, the good mother is juxtaposed to leaving children with strangers. Below, the trucker driver husband explains a common reason why the mother is preferred:

> We feel that we see the difference in the children that are being raised by their parents and children that are being raised by, you know, an outside entity. (Interviewer: In what ways?) Mostly, I think the way they do it is to let their kids do everything and anything. And ah, my wife is, I have to say, she's home with the children more and she does the disciplinary measures 90% of the time. Only because she's there when it's needed and I have very well-behaved children I am told. I feel they are. I'm not ashamed to take my children anywhere . . . my nephew is in day care and they can't go out to dinner unless there are special provisions because he can't sit in a restaurant. . . . (You think that's because he's in day care?) They, they're not spending, he's not getting the quality motherhood. I don't feel he is, ya. And I don't feel it's the day care people's job to, to instill these things in them. She's being paid to watch this child. She'd gonna do what she has to do to get through her day in a sane manner. She's not going to be a disciplinarian, or she shouldn't be there to, ah, to teach everything . . . my wife places our children in the playpen for several hours each day so she can get things done and the children learn to play by themselves. Other children who are in day care come here to play and they don't know how to entertain themselves.

Beliefs about motherhood remain entrenched in an essentialist argument that the only person qualified to care for young children is either the biological or adoptive mother (Hertz & Ferguson, 1996). Not only are strangers problematic as nurturers but they are less likely, these couples believe, to instill a strong foundation of values they share and believe to be necessary for adulthood. Even though fathers are essential to providing round-the-clock home care for children, it is the mother's visible presence that continues to be at the core of this construction of family life.

THE PARENTING APPROACH

The parenting approach is exemplified in the belief that the family ought to be organized around caring for the children with the critical distinction that both parents are full participants. Couples who adopt the parenting approach create new ways of combining family and work by seeking less demanding jobs or by negotiating more flexible arrangements with present employers (at least during the early years of their children's lives.) Some couples, particularly those who have middle-class occupations, are choosing to push employment in new directions. But for others, particularly those with working-class occupations, underemployment becomes a catalyst for rethinking traditional gender-based divisions of labor. These couples are crafting strategic responses to a shrinking labor market.

Regardless of how they came to share parenting, at the time of the interviews, these couples did not essentialize the mother as the only parent capable of nurturing children. For couples who chose to modify rigid work structures out of a belief that the responsibility for child rearing must be shared between mother and father, they talk about parenting with expectations that both parents are essential as nurturers and providers, though parents are not androgynous. Even among those couples wherein the men have lost full-time jobs and are presently doing less challenging work or working part-time, they also come to admit that men can care for children, throwing into question prior ideological beliefs about the dichotomy that conflates manhood and fatherhood with economic provision and womanhood and motherhood with nurturing activities. (Even though new practices of work/family divisions emerge, it does not necessarily follow that underemployed men view caring for their children as a substitute for their present employment situations.)

Emphasizing the sharing of child rearing between parents limits the need to use external child care providers. When it is used, they attempt to control the kind of child care that supplements their own involvement with children prior to their children's entry into the public schools. Some use only a few hours a week of day care or babysitters; others find cooperative exchanges between families with young children.

Restructuring Employment to Maximize Parenting

This group of parents shares a belief about parental superiority in raising children. They believe that men and women should work outside and inside the home and also share responsibility for child rearing. Individuals attempt to modify their jobs and employment commitments to regulate on their own terms the demands that paid work makes and thus restore some semblance of control, even if it means loss of income (Hertz & Ferguson, 1996).

Couples emphasize that men have historically been short-changed as nurturers, and they are seeking parity with wives in their desire to experience fatherhood (cf. Coltrane, 1989). Men explained their efforts to modify their work schedules to be actively involved in child care. One man, age 37, employed in a social service agency, explains why he decided to reorganize his work schedule to have 1 day a week at home when his first child was born. He was able to reorganize which 40 hours he worked to not cut back on his pay, to have 1 day a week at home and occasionally to hold staff meetings in his home with his infant daughter present:

> Why did I do it? I think I was a new father, I wanted to spend time with my child, first year of life. I also sort of figured I might not have this opportunity again. I thought this was unique. I knew I wasn't going to forever stay at this job and I just had immense flexibility. I still was working very hard, but I had immense flexibility and control because I was the director, so I could really set the policy, and I did. But it was just important to me to spend some time and not have either a professional caregiver or have it so my wife had some time.
>
> It also worked in terms of our hours. Partly there was some pragmatism here in terms of—we wanted to minimize the day care she was in, maximize our time with her, certainly in that first year.

Another unusual arrangement that highlights the prioritizing of family togetherness over full-time work is a middle-class couple who both work part-time day hours: she as a social worker and he as a patient advocate. The wife, age 33, explains that initially she thought she would remain at home, but they each negotiated part-time work hours in their respective jobs to share child rearing. Understanding her husband's desire to be with their child, she reported that they figured out the following solution:

> I had negotiated, at my job, to go back part-time after my maternity leave, but I thought in my heart that I might not go back at all. Then when Andy went back to work, he missed Sam so much that he felt like he really wanted to be home more. And what we were able to figure out was that if I went back part-time and he cut back his hours—so he decided he'd work 30 hours and I'd work 20 hours. And we could always be home with him. So that was what we did, and that's what we've done. . . . He worked 3 mornings and 2 afternoons and I worked 3 afternoons and 2 mornings. He worked 6 hours a day and I worked 4 hours a day.

Below, she explains why parental child rearing and part-time jobs better matched their desires:

> I don't have criticisms of people who use day care. I just couldn't bear the thought. But it just felt, for me, that I really wanted to be with Sam and I wanted Andy to be with Sam and I feel like I got the absolute best of all possible worlds. Because I think it would have been really hard for me to be home full-time and have Andy work full-time. And working part-time is just the perfect balance. So to be able to work, and to have Sam home with Andy, we just couldn't ask for more. . . . I thought it was better for him to be with one of his parents.

The husband, age 39, explains the price he has paid and the confusion this arrangement has caused at the agency where he is employed:

> I felt really stressed out initially. When I started working part-time, it was incredibly difficult because the expectations of myself were that I could do what I used to do just in less time. . . . I think more than anybody else at my office, I have had to scale back my expectations of myself. And I feel like people have been very supportive. . . . But it was frustrating. I'd post my schedule for everybody and give them a list. We'd try to set up a staff meeting and if we're going to do it on a Tuesday, do we do it in the morning or the afternoon? . . . And initially I'd have to scratch my own head and wonder when I was going to be in.

Some middle-class couples find a way to implement even more atypical arrangements, such as mutual exchanges, whereby families swap child care and keep track of hours. Administering part-time two different social services, the couple quoted below, ages 47 and 42, are making ends meet, placing themselves at the economic fringes of the middle class and conscious of their own downward mobility relative to their own parents. They know they could earn more money but as she put it,

> We want to maximize as much as possible these first 5 years of being with him. So I would say the first thing is values about the amount of day care. It is also more expensive and it makes you work more. . . . I would say the driving factor was about values. We didn't want him to be in a lot of day care. I figured the longer he had more intimate settings, the better.

Their present arrangements are described below:

> Now what we do is on Mondays I take care of a little girl in the morning and then her mom takes care of Mark in the afternoon. On Tuesdays and Thursdays, I bring Mark to a friend's house and that little girl's dad takes care of Mark and walks him to preschool with his little daughter and then picks them up and takes care of him. Then on Wednesdays, I take care of both little girls: the little girl whose mom takes care of Mark on Monday and the little girl whose dad takes care of Mark on Tuesdays and Thursdays. Then on Fridays, I take care of the little girl whose dad walked Mark to preschool. I take care of her on Friday mornings. So that evens out that because we get 2 afternoons and we give a day in the mornings. And then Friday afternoon, I pay the little girl's mother $20 to take care of him.

It is more common in this study sample for women to be the part-time worker or ask for special arrangements for them to combine motherhood and work, trading a solid middle-class standard of living for a more modest one. One woman, age 36, found a job working part-time as a lawyer. Below, she explains why:

> I've seen the way other people's lives had been crazy and I wanted to have a good time with my kids. I just kept hearing from people all the time: "These are the most precious years, don't give them up, hold onto them." . . . there's some truth to that and I really wanted to cherish the time I had with them. . . . I wanted to go back to work because I needed the intellectual stimulation and the respect.

But in many ways, the couples quoted above are labor force elites: They can shift the number of hours they work or change jobs without facing permanent career penalties. Eventually, the men and some of the women in these families shifted back to full-time work when their children entered preschool or grade school. But at least during the early years, they restructured the gender system to make fathering and mothering essential to childhood socialization.

Underemployment as a Route to Shared Parenting

For others, the downward economy and downsizing by corporations beginning in the 1980s (Hodson & Sullivan, 1990) led couples to piece together new work arrangements with active fathering a by-product. These latter couples did not make conscious choices to work less (and earn less) to do more for their children directly. They worry about spiraling downward even further. One father, age 39, with two children and presently working part-time as a home health aid, explains how his employment history has devolved:

> No. I think like MANY of the long-term unemployed, people like me who don't show up in the statistics, life goes on. So you do other things, you work part-time, either delivering pizza, which I did for 3 years, or bundling mail for the post office, whatever. But life goes on, so you have to adjust yourself because first of all, no one's gonna hire you. Once you're over 30, no one's gonna hire you for any real job. So what's the sense? . . . Your buddy who mows lawns for a living is offering you $10 an hour. So you do what you have to do. And you just fall into a whole other world that you forget exists when you worked for a large company, working 9–5 for 6 years.

The wife, age 35, a nurse who typically works the 7:00 P.M. to 7:00 A.M. night shift, worries that if she loses her overtime she will have to find a second nursing job. She added to her husband's comments her thoughts on how underemployment has affected her husband's sense of masculinity: "And of course his ego was all shot to hell. He's not the family provider he wants to be and he's not doing exactly what he wanted, what he set in his mind. All his goals are rearranged."

Couples in which the wife was working full-time and the husband part-time often wished that the wife could opt to work fewer hours. Whereas middle-class White women continue to think about their lives as having the option of staying at home or working full-time, ideological and structural barriers prevent men from having similar choices (Gerson, 1993). Another mother, age 40, an office manager with two children ages 5 and 9, assumed that there would be two full-time paychecks. She now carries the economic burden and wishes she could have a more flexible work schedule.

> When I decided I would have children, I knew I would always be working, but I thought there would be more flexibility in my work schedule that would allow me to take extended vacations with my children, sometimes come home, be available after school to go to a school function with my son, sometimes be able to go to a soccer practice in the afternoon on a Thursday, be able to go to my daughter's ballet classes with her, that kind of thing. I don't feel like I have that kind of flexibility in my life. . . . In the nicer part of the year, I'll arrive home at 6:30 and they've just come from a baseball practice and they're rosy cheeked and they're laughing about what happened, and I'm not a part of that. So I guess over a period of time you do build up a little resentment. It goes away. But that's what I'm missing.

Another man, age 37, who presently works part-time as a postal worker, was laid off from a factory job after a dozen years at his company. His inability to find a full-time job for the past several years made it necessary for his wife to remain employed full-time. Because she is the carrier of the medical benefits, they feel unable to reduce her work to part-time because they would lose these benefits. Despite his positive experiences caring for his 3-year-old son since he was an infant, this father describes the deep ambivalence he feels about contributing in atypical ways to family life:

> I was sort of thrust into the role. Thrust into it by job circumstances. . . . Sometimes it does bother me [not to be the main breadwinner]. . . . I just don't feel like I'm with the crowd. Not that I have to be with the crowd. . . . I realize that most men my age are probably established in careers now and I'm not. But, I just have that vague sense that, ah . . . like the world is going on out there and I'm here.
>
> I know it's more accepted now in society, but still I feel like I'm in the vast minority when it comes to my role. . . . I've more or less settled into the routine of taking care of my son. At first, it was quite an adjustment. . . . It's been kind of a metamorphosis for me. I've gone from being scared to death of it, to, ah, being actually quite comfortable now. Maybe that's why I stopped looking for full-time work, I don't know.

His wife, age 31, explains how her fantasies of the kind of family life she thought about have not materialized:

> It's funny because I guess we all have an idea of what's going to happen when you get married and all this. All my friends had it easy, you know, got married and then they did have

the kids and then they stayed home. So I figured that would just happen to me, too. But it was tough. The first year that I was at work it was hard. I think we had a lot of arguments. And I didn't think he could do anything right. When we were both with him it was like, "What are we DOING now?" There was no set of instructions or anything that come with a baby. I always felt I was better with him. As an infant, he felt very awkward with him. And actually, he's done very well with him. I can't, you know, knock him now. But you know, at that time I was very resentful. VERY resentful. And the thing is I had a job I didn't like and I had a manager I didn't like, he was terrible to me, very demanding, and he was very chauvinistic about women.

Even though mothering is a kind of craft or practice (Ruddick, 1980), the ideology that only mothers are really capable of maternal thinking is powerful and, as a result, many women do not necessarily want to share the work of mothering. The last woman quoted admits that mothering does not come naturally and it is only through practice that we learn how to do it. She concedes that her husband has mastered maternal practice; that is, he is engaged in sharing the work of parental love, a kind of work he never imagined himself doing. It is ironic that the couples who are on the cutting edge of transforming maternal thinking are doing so not because of an ideological belief as much as structural constraints of a shrinking labor force that catapult men into learning the work of child rearing. In the process, couples rethink family life, particularly caring for children, as they cobble together identities that are no longer unidimensional. Underemployed couples continue to wish their home and work time could be more evenly divided but not because they wish wives would become full-time mothers.

The Rise of Fathering

Fathering emerges but without a separate language from mothering, although the practice of it is markedly different from the White middle-class breadwinning fathers of a past generation (Bernard, 1981; Goode, 1982). Regardless of the route to sharing child care, the practice of fathering transformed these men into more nurturing and sensitive caregivers who are teaching their young children how to navigate the world (Coltrane, 1989). These men report wanting to be different than their own fathers. The husband of the couple who swap child care put it this way: "I didn't want to be the same kind of father my father had been. I wanted to be a more involved father. So, it seemed to me the way to do that was that I would work less and spend more time with [my child]."

The patient advocate quoted earlier talked about what he feels he has gained by taking care of his child:

When James was born, I was smitten, I was blown away by the strong feelings I had toward him. It was kind of like falling in love with a lover for me. I was really—I was shocked by that feeling, by how strong my feelings are and were. . . . But I also feel that I really—it's been a window for me, it's been watching him learn about the world and how much of an influence I have over that. I feel a tremendous amount of responsibility and I feel really eager to help him explore the world. I want him to do it on his own, but I know that I also have a lot of say in how things get set up, presentations that are made. But it's exciting to be part of that and I really love his discovery of things.

Even though the home health worker quoted above wishes he could return to full-time work to take some of the work pressure off his wife, he also was very eloquent about what it meant to be a father. The detailed response about infants he gives was once re-served for mothers only:

> Let's see. I don't think it's that different than being a mother. It's very stressful, very, at the same time it's very rewarding. And . . . but I think to have a lot of your father's influence is a good experience for a lot of children. Because I would take her places that my wife normally wouldn't take her. Like down to the auto parts store. . . . It got a lot harder when my second was born. It's twice as hard, ya. Especially right now, he is cutting teeth. He can't walk and he can't talk and so he can't TELL you anything. And he's at that time when he's trying to rearrange his clock to sleep at night so he's up, like last night he was up at midnight. So I brought him to bed with me. And I put him back to bed around 2 and he was up at 4, so like 3 or 4 times a night. And lack of sleep more than anything else gets you. Then the older one wakes up. Sometimes ARGGGGHHHH. I feel like a lioness with cubs crawling all around. . . . Fatherhood, it's a lot of hard work but it can also be a lot of fun too. . . . As they get older, you can play more and you can put them in a car and go for a ride and it's a lot easier once they're older.

The father, who presently works part-time as a postal worker, explains that what he feels is most important is making a difference in his child's life:

> Mr. Mom? Um . . . it's frus . . . it's rewarding, but it's also very frustrating. It's, it's ah . . . it seems like after a day of being with my son all day, it's fun and all that, but sometimes, some days it just wears thin, and I need some adult interaction if you know what I mean? . . . But I feel like I'm in the role of teacher and ah . . . which is I think the most fun part. And just watching him develop and learn new things . . . to see the difference that I can sort of shape and mold my son's life it gives me some personal satisfaction. Nobody told me that.

In sum, the members of this group are testing and contesting the limits of their work environments. Whereas there are certainly career costs and unwanted underemployment, these couples are altering the landscape of traditional ways that couples have attempted to integrate work and family and, in the process, altering the gender system that locates women according to a primary identity as mother and men as economic providers. Men's caring work undermines the belief that mothering comes naturally to women. Further, caring for children elevates the status of parenting as a source of primary identity for both mothers and fathers; it even takes priority over workplace goals and job advancement. In short, changing labor force patterns and creating flexible jobs forced new family practices and in the process altered beliefs about child care and nurturing.

THE MARKET APPROACH

The market approach to caring for children involves hiring other people to care for one's own children. Both wife and husband are career oriented and they emphasize profes-sional caregivers who replace mothers. Unlike the two approaches discussed in preced-ing sections, wherein the use of non-kin child care is minimized, among these couples children spend their days with adult caregivers who are not family members.[9] Often, cou-ples have a combination of care providers[10] and commonly they shift from one type of arrangement to another, ostensibly in response to the child's developmental needs. As I and my coauthor, Faith Ferguson, have argued (Hertz & Ferguson, 1996), regardless of whether children are placed in center-based care or in family day care or a woman is hired to provide individual care, in using day care the mother has hired someone to replace herself at least part of the time and her essential contribution to the family has become *deskilled* (Braverman, 1974). But the new middle-class model for women continues to emphasize the achievements of the individual (i.e., the mother); women achieve this by deskilling motherhood, breaking apart a once presumed holistic pattern of practices.[11] In this study, it is typical for couples in which both are professionals working full-time with more than one child to have multiple child care arrangements. Below is a striking example of deskilling the mother role into several components: the woman who is loving and good with infants and drives the children and the woman who provides developmental stimulation and reads to her children:

> But once the kids were 2 or something, when they like to be read to, that sort of thing, I have sent them to a play group, which is a family day care, really down the street from me. They've each gone there 2 days a week. . . . The reason for this is that my babysitter, as lovely and caring a person as she is, is functionally illiterate, which is the downside of what I have. . . . By the time I figured out that she could barely manage to write a phone message, it was clear that she was so good with my infant that it really didn't matter at that point.
>
> Now, she is driving my daughter to . . . Brownies, ballet, that sort of thing. . . . And we don't have family in the area, so she's sort of a surrogate mother to them in that sense. She has a large family of her own, and my kids know all of the members of her family. . . . I think I have been incredibly lucky. The kids love her and she loves them.

The woman above, pregnant with her third child at age 36 and a doctor with a doctor husband, is quite typical of this group whose caregiving role is tied to finding surrogates. Because the mother remains responsible for patching together child care arrangements, she uses different criteria to select different women to replace herself. The love of one's child becomes the major criteria for how couples select providers, particularly nannies, but also family-based day care settings. These kinds of providers are a substitute for mother love (Hertz, 1986; Hertz & Ferguson, 1996; Wrigley, 1995). Yet, often conflicts emerge around dissimilar values between the provider and the couple because couples tend to hire women of different social class and racial backgrounds to care for their children (Hertz, 1986; Wrigley, 1995). Center-based day care providers (or preschool or nursery school programs) are termed *teachers* and they are expected to expose the child to a first learning environment. This enrichment experience is supposed to supplement parental teaching, though often it is also a substitute for early education the mother once provided. Credentials and professionalism are ways couples assess whether a program shares their views on learning (Hertz & Ferguson, 1963).[12] After-school programs are now the new neighborhoods. These institutional settings provide adult supervision, replacing the mom with milk and cookies but also replacing no-longer-safe neighborhoods where children once freely rode bikes and played pick-up games.

Whereas initially women believe that continuity of care is the best replacement for not being at home themselves, they eventually abandon this idea. In this study and in my prior work (Hertz, 1986), not one family kept the same child care arrangements for the first years of a child's life. Dissatisfaction materializes on either side of the provider/couple relationship: Sometimes the child care provider quits, but other times the reason for a change is couched in a language of child development and the need for a new kind of arrangement, as predicted by the child care professional mother of the woman quoted below:

> At 2 years old, it was clear there was way too much TV. I didn't care about it as an infant, I didn't care about it at 1 year old because they watch some of it but they run around. They are too interested in their own motor stuff. And my mom had told me when she saw Janie [the provider]—a lot of my education about child care has come from my mom [a nursery school director]—I said, "Isn't it great because Janie promised me she'll take care of the kid until she is in kindergarten if I want." And there were kids there until 4 years old. So, I kept thinking that would be continuity I wasn't providing my child by working. And my mom said, "You're not going to want her at Janie's after 2 [years old]." And I didn't know at that time, but how right she was.

Couples speak a new language of quasi-psychology that emphasizes developmentally appropriate educational experiences for preschoolers who are introduced to the rudiments of a structured day, develop positive peer group experiences, and begin to develop a positive relationship to learning. Professionals are looked toward to provide these enrichment experiences. In sum, former child care providers are discarded and new child care workers rationalized on the changing developmental stages of the child.

Women do feel guilty for not being with their child and they worry about the cost to their children. The woman below, age 37, when she had her first child 9 years ago, describes the kind of work hours she was expected to keep.

> I had two people coming in, 6-hour shifts. And then when Kyle was 6 months old, I just sat down with my husband and I just felt like this was really hurting Kyle. So, I decided that my career was interfering with my family. And I actually quit my internship. I came home distraught and I just said, "That's it." At that point I was working 100 hours a week, I would leave at 6:00 one morning and come home at 10:00 the next night if I was on call. I was on call every third to fourth night. It was very hard with a newborn, although I had my husband who was here taking care of the baby at night and other family members. I said to myself, "What are you doing? Is it worth it?"

This woman was lucky because a sister volunteered to come and care for her infant son, which lessened her guilt about not caring for her own child. But when she became pregnant with a second child, the sister said two children was one too many to watch and this couple eventually found non-relative live-in help.

But guilt was not shared by husbands who had similar occupations or male colleagues, as a woman doctor, age 31, reported:

> But you know, I've been a mother for 9 years so I've worked on the guilt a lot. . . . And I used to ask all these men I worked with, I said, "You know, when you go out the door in the morning, do you feel guilty when you say goodbye to your children?" And they would look at me as if to say, "What a dumb question that is." But every time I would go out it would tear me apart. So I've tried to lessen the guilt as the years go by.

Men did not mention feeling guilty about working full-time, which underscores the cultural asymmetry in the emphasis placed on the unique role of the mother/child dyad. The husbands of these women did mention the guilt their wives felt by not being available to their children. A professor with more flexible work hours, married to the doctor quoted above, began his discussion on day care with the following:

> My wife was essentially gone [the first year of the child's life]. I used to take the baby into the hospital in the middle of the night to see her mother. It was a rough year. I had a very free year—on sabbatical—which helped enormously and we had my in-laws close by. But my wife still feels that was a desertion, that she essentially deserted her baby 2 weeks after it was born.

The mothers who exemplify this approach are not the only ones in this study who feel guilty. Women in all three approaches feel guilty when they are unable to match their conception of motherhood and family life: Some try to alter shift scheduling; others try cutting back hours or find another type of work. But the ideal work load is rarely attained. I note the guilt in this section because the most career-oriented women have the least options because their work environments remain entrenched in a male trajectory despite recent claims of organizations' becoming more so-called family friendly (Gilbert, 1985; Hertz, 1986; Hochschild, 1971; Slater & Glazer, 1987). These women report that short of quitting professions in which they have invested heavily through years of school and training, hiring surrogates to replace themselves or deskilling motherhood are the only rational solutions.[13] Most mentioned wishing they could become part-time employees at least for a few years (the added income from their full-time employment was not essential to these families) but few employers agreed to experiment with such work arrangements. Some feel trapped as successful professionals wishing for more leisure time for themselves and time with their children.

Couples who select a market approach to child care also have a division of labor between themselves in which the wife does the work of finding the care, making the arrangements, and thinking through the various possibilities (Hertz, 1986; Hochschild & Machung, 1989; Nock & Kington, 1988). Husbands become sounding boards and only marginal participants in arranging the schedules of children. In this regard, women replace themselves and, in the process, the deskilling of tasks leaves mothers with changed relationships to their children, popularly dubbed "quality time" motherhood. Men's lives remain unaltered in these cases. Of the three approaches to child care, the men in this group are the least involved in child care. Masculinity remains tied to economic achievements and career goals. The mother/child dyad is altered by the insertion of another woman or professional day care setting. However, unlike the mothering approach, women's identities remain split between family and career. Gender relations between spouses are altered only because women buy out family commitments, not because men assume more responsibility (Hertz, 1986). Further, both mothers and fathers become primarily economic providers within their children's lives. During the week, it is others who love, nurture, and care for the children, and on weekends they become a family in which the mother might resume the craft of mothering while the men continue to devote themselves to career advancement.

CONCLUSIONS

Mothering does not mean that wives stop working for pay completely (i.e., they do not necessarily devote 100% of their time to caring for their children). It does mean, however, that a wife's status as mother becomes the pivotal point around which all other statuses (e.g., employee) revolve. Indeed, for many couples the arrival of children creates a paradox: One paid worker leaves the labor force at a time when the family's expenses increase dramatically. To maintain a (pre-child) standard of living, adjustments have to be made: Either (a) the husband increases the number of hours he works (which reduces his ability to share parenting) or (b) the wife continues to work but adjusts her job or hours to accommodate the children. In both instances, the basic parameters of work and family go unchallenged: (a) couples adjust their activities to sustain a pre-child standard of living; (b) they make little claim against employers or ask them to adjust in response to family needs; (c) they invoke mothering as either cause or a correlate of their actions.

The detailed exploration of couples who embrace the mothering approach suggests that the organization of gender conflates motherhood and womanhood. Not only does motherhood supersede all other dimensions of identity, it also allows women to claim a special place in the gender system. Just as couples ignore the wife's permanent labor force employment, they minimize the husband's involvement as co-participant in caring for children. Whereas child care work may be conceptualized as the wife's turf, and therefore the language of mothering dominates these interviews, fathers are not absent from the home nor solely economic providers. The emphasis is on an ideological presentation of family life that masks the present practices and a new division of labor between spouses.

Couples who adopt the parenting approach come to reorganize their work in response to placing family first. They are challenging and restructuring the workplace even if it is only temporary: (a) These couples attempt to restructure work to accommodate their family needs by making demands on employers; (b) both women and men are restructuring their work to be active parents at the expense of job mobility, career success, and economic sacrifice; (c) in the process, they are altering the organization of gender in ways that challenge mothering as the exclusive territory of women. In short, they are crafting new ways of parental thinking about child rearing. These couples personify family values as they attempt to push workplaces to care about families as much as they care about organizational goals.

A smaller group of couples back into the parental approach—forced into this reorganization of family and two jobs due to economic constraints. Decreasing jobs will lead more men to rethink their contributions to family life and to adapt to a shrinking economy by staying home or sharing child care, or both. Although the circumstances of their fathering may not be based on their own choice, these men are potential models for a future in which job uncertainty is likely to increase. On one hand, structural workforce constraints for men may alter motherhood ideals, giving rise to equally compelling arguments for men's greater involvement in sharing the work of child care. On the other hand, these data suggest that gender ideology is a powerful countervailing force to a shrinking labor market. Husbands and wives are not willing to agree that parenting is a substitute for men's paychecks. These couples craft shared parenting models but hope that this is a temporary family/work arrangement.

The market approach in many ways resembles the mothering approach in that couples resolve work/family dilemmas by parceling out the job of mothering. They rationalize this (with ambivalence) by placing a premium on professional child care knowledge over old-fashioned folk wisdom; these couples do not make claims against employers who continue to adhere to a masculine prototype of career trajectories, creating, at best, "mommy tracks"—as the major response to family needs. In this respect, husbands and wives may have more equal marriages but do little to alter the organization of gender between men and women. In fact, they only further inequalities between women whom they hire and themselves (Hertz, 1986; Rollins, 1985).

In addition to giving substance to a typology of alternative approaches to child care, the interviews conducted in this study provide valuable insights into the process through which choices among those alternatives are made. That is, as has been noted repeatedly in recent research on changing gender ideologies and child care (e.g., Hochschild & Machung, 1989; Uttal, 1996), it is vital to better understand the meaning women give to child care practices and the division of labor between spouses. By focusing on meaning (both supportive and contradictory), we are in a better position to assess how durable an approach might be or, if it creates conflicts (e.g., between traditional and nontraditional family gender ideologies), who will have to bend to resolve the conflict. A focus on child care choices helps us see what conflicts arise, how they are given meaning, and how they are resolved.

However, recent research in this area (including Garey, 1995; McMahon, 1995; Uttal, 1996) has overlooked the fact that these choices are rarely made by women alone. Whereas this new research is conceptually interesting, by focusing on the changing meaning of motherhood without considering the possibility of similar changes for the partners of these women, we learn little about the position of the partner as a participant or facilitator for social change in the family or workplace. As I have shown in this article, husbands often play an important role in the decision process. Yet, because most prior studies have tended to neglect husbands (e.g., by not interviewing them), they cannot realistically tell us a great deal about men's involvement in child care choices at either the levels of ideology or practice or about how couples may jointly decide or be forced to alter ideology or practice.

Thus, when we look back at the three different approaches to child care described in this article, it is not surprising that in many respects the parenting approach appears the most novel. Unlike mothering and market approaches, husbands play a visible and different role in child care choice. Their involvement is visible and different because they consciously challenge a traditional familial division of labor and a traditional definition of job and career. Neither the mothering nor the market approaches challenge tradition: The former reinforces tradition and the latter merely integrates another service into the family menu of consumption.

Notes

1. In 1993, fully 60% of all women with children under 6 were in the paid labor force. For those with children aged 6 to 17 years, 75% of all women were employed, representing a marked increase from 1966 when 44% of women with children this age were employed (Hayghe & Bianchi, 1994). For women between 15 and 44 who have had a child for the year 1994, 53% were in the labor force (Bachu, 1995).

2. Day care is regulated by individual states, which vary in licensing regulations and in enforcement (Benin & Chong, 1993). In Massachusetts, lists exist by town, giving the names of all licensed providers. We have no good information on how many family day care providers are illegal. But this assumes that a family would know enough to request a list from the town or know enough to realize that not all providers are licensed.

The vast majority of U.S. workplaces do not have child care provisions. Those that do have huge wait lists and most employees must go elsewhere for day care. Families in eastern Massachusetts who use center-based care put their children into either for-profit commercial day care and nonprofit centers housed within religious sites or universities and private nonprofit centers. In this area, after kin, family day care is the most often used type of care (Marshall et al., 1988).

3. Day care is also the second largest cost all couples have in this study after mortgages or rents. In 1995, for a preschooler in full-day center-based care in the greater Boston area, couples could expect to pay $12,000 per year for one child. Infant and toddler center-based care is even more costly.

4. See Hertz (1995) for a lengthy discussion of making sense of separate interviews and the rationale for this method.

5. The majority of couples in this study have been married to their present spouses at least 10 years. For the vast majority of individuals, these are first marriages. I note that I did not select couples on length of present marriage. I did, however, deliberately seek couples who still had children at home, when possible, so that child care and labor force decisions would not be distant memories.

6. With the exception of the upper middle-class professional women in this study, few women could afford to take a 12-week unpaid leave, which Massachusetts has had for quite some years. Most women did take a leave, but they were able to afford this by using their paid vacation time and sick days. In this study, few couples had enough money to cover the paychecks of a maternity leave. No man in this study took a formal paternity leave, though some men (the parental approach) did work out various arrangements with employers.

7. Because this is a study of dual-earner couples, there are no full time stay-at-home moms at the time of the interview who clearly favor this approach to early childhood care. There are a few women in the middle class who were home for a number of years until their youngest child entered elementary school. It is also possible for professional women to decide to leave the labor force permanently and stay home. I feature, in this section, women in working-class or lower middle-class jobs because they are more likely in this study to advance that approach.

8. White working-class mothers of both husbands and wives were typically in and out of the labor force. Mothers of minority spouses were overwhelmingly always in the labor force. Historically, women of color are more likely to work outside the home (Goldin, 1990, p. 18). In this study, working-class mothers of respondents are essential to the household. In addition to the importance of income contribution to the household for middle-class mothers of respondents, using talents and degrees to advance their race was also essential (Perkins, in press).

9. Children are collectively raised by professionally trained women in kibbutzim, which today resemble full-time center-based U.S. child care. Whereas economic necessity was the catalyst for the creation of the children's collective raising, the historical belief in professional knowledge as the best route to child rearing persists. My point here is two-fold: (a) The professional approach is not always tied to two-earner families, even though in the United States case, the emergence of (and rapidly growing) family and center-based day care is tied to the inability of most families to live on one wage as the family wage eroded; and (b) mothers are not essentialized in the kibbutz as the best caregivers of their own children. Professionally trained women are seen as more knowledgeable and suitable and, until recently, expertise superseded parents' wishes. Categorically, however, women rather than men do this work, gendering the job within the kibbutz and within the U.S. context.

10. Two national surveys indicate that approximately two fifths of preschool children with mothers in the paid labor force had multiple child care arrangements (Folk & Belier, 1993; Hofferth. Brayfield, Diech, & Holcomb, 1991).

11. Hertz and Ferguson (1996) argue that for Black couples in this study, deskilling of motherhood does not promote the same kind of crisis that it does for their White professional counterparts because historically Black women have always been employed outside the home and have had to work out arrangements for the care of children that did not permit nonexclusive mothering practices (Collins, 1990). However, even in this study Black women felt at times like they were the titular wives and mothers (Hertz

& Ferguson, 1996). The woman who solved her child care problems and returned to her internship when her sister volunteered to help was a Black woman whose mother had worked her entire life. The solutions to child care for the first child often included kin for women of color, which was less likely to occur among White women whose mothers (or other immediate relatives) were not willing to leave their own lives if they did not live locally. Even among White women whose mothers lived locally, it was less often in this study that they became the primary child care providers.

12. Regardless of race, the majority of families had multiple arrangements; however, there are differences between White women and women of color in how they found child care providers and how race factors into the selection of a particular arrangement (see Hertz & Ferguson, 1996, for a full discussion).

13. See especially Uttal (1996), who is interested in the meaning mothers assign to caregivers. The women who restructure the dominant cultural ideology of the mother as primary provider conceptualize the child care provider as either a surrogate or they define the child care provider as co-mothering in a coordinated effort that the mother orchestrates between herself and the provider.

References

Bachu, A. (1995). *Fertility of American women: June 1994* (P20-482, p. XVII). Washington, DC: U.S. Bureau of the Census.

Benin, M., & Chong, Y. (1993). Childcare concerns of employed mothers. In J. Frankel (Ed.), *The employed mother and the family context* (pp. 229–244). New York: Springer.

Bernard, J. (1981). The good-provider role: Its rise and fall. *The American Psychologist, 36,* 1–12.

Bianchi, S. M., & Spain, D. (1986). *American women in transition.* New York: Russell Sage Foundation.

Bird, C. E. (1995, March). *Gender parenthood and distress: Social and economic burdens of parenting.* Paper presented at the Eastern Sociological Society annual meetings, Philadelphia.

Braverman, H. (1974). *Labor and monopoly capital: The degradation of work in the twentieth century.* New York: Monthly Review Press.

Collins, P. H. (1990). *Black feminist thought: Knowledge, consciousness and the politics of empowerment.* New York: Routledge.

Coltrane, S. (1989). Household labor and the routine production of gender. *Social Problems, 36,* 473–490.

Daniels, A. K. (1988). *Invisible careers: Women civic leaders from the volunteer world.* Chicago: University of Chicago Press.

DeVault, M. L. (1991). *Feeding the family: The social organization of caring as gendered work.* Chicago: University of Chicago Press.

Ferber, M., & O'Farrell, B. (1991). Family-oriented programs in other countries. In M. Ferber, B. O'Farrell, & L. R. Allen (Eds.), *Work and family: Policies for a changing work force* (pp. 155–178). Washington, DC: National Academy Press.

Fitz Gibbon, H. (1993, August). Bridging spheres: The work of home daycare providers. Paper presented at the American Sociological Association Meetings, Miami.

Folk, K. F., & Beller, A. H. (1993). Part-time work and childcare choices for mothers of preschool children. *Journal of Marriage and the Family, 55,* 146–157.

Garey, A. I. (1995). Constructing motherhood on the night shift: "Working mothers" as "stay at home mom." *Qualitative Sociology, 18,* 415–437.

Gerson, K. (1993). *No man's land: Men's changing commitments to family and work.* New York: Basic Books.

Gilbert, L. (1985). *Men in dual career families.* Hillsdale, NJ: Lawrence Erlbaum.

Goldin, C. (1990). *Understanding the gender gap: An economic history of American women.* New York: Oxford University Press.

Goode, W. J. (1982). Why men resist. In B. Thorne & M. Yalom (Eds.), *Rethinking the family: Some feminist questions* (pp. 131–150). New York: Longman.

Hartmann, H., & Spalter-Roth, R. (1994, March). A feminist approach to policy making for women and families. Paper prepared for the Seminar on Future Directions for American Politics and Public Policy.

Hayghe, H. V., & Bianchi, S. M. (1994). Married mothers' work patterns: The job-family compromise. *U.S. Department of Labor Bureau of Labor Statistics, Monthly Labor Review, 117,* 24–30.

Hertz, R. (1986). *More equal than others: Women and men in dual-career marriages.* Berkeley: University of California Press.

Hertz, R. (1995). Separate but simultaneous interviewing of husbands and wives: Making sense of their stories. *Qualitative Inquiry, 1,* 429–451.

Hertz, R., & Charlton, J. (1989). Making family under a shiftwork schedule: Air Force security guards and their wives. *Social Problems, 36,* 491–507.

Hertz, R., & Ferguson, F.I.T. (1996). Childcare choices and constraints in the United States: Social class, race, and the influence of family views. *Journal of Comparative Family Studies, 27,* 249–280.

Hochschild, A., (1971). Inside the clockwork of male careers. In F. Howe (Ed.), *Women and the power to change* (pp. 47–80). New York: McGraw-Hill.

Hochschild, A., & Machung, A. (1989). *The second shift.* New York: Viking.

Hodson, R., & Sullivan, T. (1990). *The social organization of work.* Belmont, CA: Wadsworth.

Hofferth, S. L., Brayfield, A., Diech, S., & Holcomb, P. (1991). *National Childcare Survey 1990* (Urban Institute Report 91–5). Washington, DC: Urban Institute Press.

Huber, J., & Spitzer, G. (1983). *Sex stratification: Children, housework, and jobs.* New York: Academic Press.

Kamerman, S. B., & Kahn, A. J. (1991). Trends, issues and possible lessons. In S. B. Kamerman & A. J. Kahn (Eds.). *Childcare, parental leave, and the under three's: Policy innovation in Europe* (pp. 201–224). Westport. CT: Auburn House.

Marshall, N., Witte, A., Nichols, L., Marx, F., Mauser, E., Laws, B., & Silverstein, B. (1988). *Caring for our commonwealth: The economics of childcare in Massachusetts.* Boston: Office for Children.

McMahon, M. (1995). *Engendering motherhood: Identity and self-transformation in women's lives.* New York: Guilford.

Moen, P. (1989). *Working parents: Transformations in gender roles and public policies in Sweden.* Madison: University of Wisconsin Press.

Nelson, M. K. (1994). Family day care providers: Dilemmas of daily practice. In N. Glenn, G. Chang, & L. R. Forcey (Eds.), *Mothering ideology, experience and agency* (pp. 181–209). New York: Routledge.

Nock, S. L., & Kington, P. W. (1988). Time with children: The impact of couples' work-time commitments. *Social Forces, 67,* 59–85.

Perkins, L. M. (in press). For the good of the race: Married African American academics, a historical perspective. In M. A. Ferber & J. W. Loeb (Eds.), *Academic couples: Problems and promises.* Urbana-Champaign and Chicago: University of Illinois Press.

Presser, H. B. (1988). Shiftwork and childcare among young dual-earner American parents. *Journal of Marriage and the Family, 50,* 133–148.

Presser, H. B., & Cain, V. (1983). Shiftwork among dual-earner couples with children. *Science, 219,* 876–879.

Rollins, J. (1985). *Between women: Domestics and their employers.* Philadelphia: Temple University Press.

Ruddick, S. (1980). Maternal thinking. *Feminist Studies, 6,* 343–367.

Slater, M., & Galzer, P. M. (1987). Prescriptions for professional survival. *Daedalus, 116,* 119–135.

Uttal, L. (1996). Custodial care, surrogate care, and coordinated care: Employed mothers and the meaning of child care. *Gender & Society, 10,* 291–311.

Wrigley, J. (1995). *Other people's children.* New York: Basic Books.

Zigler, E. (1990). Shaping child care policies and programs in America. *American Journal of Community Psychology, 18,* 183–215.

■READING 21

Chasing the Blood Tie: Surrogate Mothers, Adoptive Mothers, and Fathers

Helena Ragoné

> An election that's about ideas and values is also about philosophy, and I have one. At the bright center is the individual, and radiating out from him or her is the family, the essential unit of closeness and love. For it's the family that communicates to our children, to the 21st century, our culture, our religious faith, our traditions, and our history.
> —George Bush, Presidential Nomination Acceptance Speech, 1989

In the wake of publicity created by the Baby M Case,[1] it seems unlikely that any in the United States can have remained unfamiliar with surrogate motherhood or have yet to form an opinion. The Baby M Case raised, and ultimately left unanswered, many questions about what constitutes motherhood, fatherhood, family reproduction, and kinship. Much of what has been written about surrogate motherhood has, however, been largely speculative or polemical in nature; it ranges from the view that surrogate motherhood is symptomatic of the dissolution of the American family[2] and the sanctity of motherhood, to charges that it reduces or assigns women to a breeder class structurally akin to prostitution (Dworkin 1978), or that it constitutes a form of commercial baby selling (Annas 1988; Neuhaus 1988).

In recent years a plethora of studies on reproduction has emerged in the field of anthropology (Browner 1986; Delaney 1986; 1991; Dolgin 1993; Ginsburg 1987, 1989; Martin 1987; Modell 1989; Newman 1985; Ragoné 1991, 1994; Rapp 1987, 1988, 1990; Scrimshaw 1978; Strathern 1991, 1992a, 1992b).[3] Not since the "virgin birth" controversy have so many theorists turned their attention to the subject (Leach 1967; Spiro 1968). Many of these studies represent a response to the interest generated by the emergence of what are collectively called assisted reproductive technologies, such as in vitro fertilization, surrogate motherhood, amniocentesis, and ultrasound. Much of the relevant research examines how these technologies are affecting the relationship between "Procreative beliefs and the wider context (worldview, cosmology, and culture)" (Delaney 1986:495), as exemplified by concepts and definitions of personhood and knowledge (Strathern 1991, 1992a). There nevertheless remains a paucity of ethnographic material about these technologies—in particular about surrogate motherhood, the subject of this article, which is based on fieldwork conducted at three different surrogate mother programs from 1988 to the present.

Historically there have been three profound shifts in the Western conceptualization of the categories of conception, reproduction, and parenthood. The first occurred in response to the separation of intercourse from reproduction through birth control methods (Snowden and Snowden 1983), a precedent that may have paved the way for surrogate motherhood in the 1980s (Andrews 1984:xiii). A second shift occurred in response to the emergence of assisted reproductive technologies and to the subsequent fragmentation of the unity of reproduction, when it became possible for pregnancy to occur without necessarily having been "preceded by sexual intercourse" (Snowden and Snowden 1983:5). The third shift occurred in response to further advances in reproductive medicine that called into question the "organic unity of fetus and mother" (Martin 1987:20). It was not, however, until the emergence of reproductive medicine that the fragmentation of motherhood became a reality; with that historical change, what was once the "single figure of the mother is dispersed among several potential figures, as the functions of maternal procreation—aspects of her physical parenthood—become dispersed" (Strathern 1991:32). As will be shown in the following section, the a priori acceptance of surrogates' stated motivations has often produced an incomplete profile of surrogate mothers.

SURROGATE MOTIVATIONS

When I began my field research in 1988, surrogate mother programs and directors had already become the subject of considerable media attention, a great deal of it sensationalized and negative in character. At that time there were ten established surrogate mother programs in the United States; in addition, there were also a number of small, part-time businesses (none of which were included in the study) in which lawyers, doctors, adoption agents, and others arranged occasional surrogate mother contracts.[4] In order to obtain as stable a sample as possible, I chose to include only firmly established programs in my study. The oldest of the programs was established in approximately 1980, and none of the programs included in my study had been in business for fewer than ten years as of 1994.

There are two types of surrogate mother programs: what I call "open" programs, in which surrogate and couple select one another and interact throughout the insemination and the pregnancy, and "closed" programs, in which couples select their surrogates from information—biological and medical information and a photograph of the surrogate—provided to them by the programs. After the child is born in a "closed" program, the couple and surrogate meet only to finalize the stepparent adoption.[5] I formally interviewed a total of 28 surrogates, from six different programs. Aside from these formal interviews I also engaged in countless conversations with surrogates, observing them as they interacted with their families, testified before legislative committees, worked in surrogate programs, and socialized at program gatherings with directors and others. Quite often I was an invited guest at the homes of program directors, a situation that provided me with a unique opportunity to observe directors interacting with their own spouses and children, with couples and surrogates, and with members of their staffs. The opportunity to observe the daily working of the surrogate mother programs provided me with invaluable data on the day-to-day operations of the programs. At one program, I attended staff meetings on a regular basis and observed consultations in which prospective couples and surrogates were interviewed singly by members of the staff such as the director, a psychologist, a medical coordinator, or the administrative coordinator.

A review of the literature on surrogate motherhood reveals that, until now, the primary research focus has been on the surrogate mother herself, and that there have been no ethnographic studies on surrogate mother programs and commissioning couples.

Studies of the surrogate population tend to focus, at times exclusively, on surrogates' stated motivations for becoming surrogate mothers (Parker 1983). Their stated reasons include the desire to help an infertile couple start a family, financial remuneration, and a love of pregnancy (Parker 1983:140). As I began my own research I soon observed a remarkable degree of consistency or uniformity in surrogates' responses to questions about their initial motivations for becoming surrogates; it was as if they had all been given a script in which they espoused many of the motivations earlier catalogued by Parker, motivations that also, as I will show, reflect culturally accepted ideas about reproduction, motherhood, and family and are fully reinforced by the programs.[6] I also began to uncover several areas of conflict between professed motivations and actual experiences, discovering, for example, that although surrogates claim to experience "easy pregnancies" and "problem-free labor," it was not unusual for surrogates to have experienced miscarriages, ectopic pregnancies, and related difficulties, as the following examples reveal. Jeannie, age 36, divorced with one child and employed in the entertainment industry, described the ectopic pregnancy she experienced while she was a surrogate in this manner: "I almost bled to death: I literally almost died for my couple." Nevertheless, she was again inseminating a second time for the same couple. As this and other examples demonstrate, even when their experiences are at odds with their stated motivations, surrogates tend not to acknowledge inconsistencies between their initially stated motivations and their subsequent experiences. This reformulation of motivation is seen in the following instance as well. Fran, age 27, divorced with one child and working as a dog trainer, described the difficulty of her delivery in this way: "I had a rough delivery, a C-section, and my lung collapsed because I had the flu, but it was worth every minute of it. If I were to die from childbirth, that's the best way to die. You died for a cause, a good one." As both these examples illustrate, some surrogates readily embrace the idea of meaningful suffering, heroism, or sacrifice, and although their stated motivations are of some interest they do not adequately account for the range of shifting motivations uncovered in my research.

One of the motivations most frequently assumed to be primary by the casual observer is remuneration, and I took considerable pains to try to evaluate its influence on surrogates. In the programs, surrogates receive between $10,000 and $15,000 (for three to four months of insemination and nine months of pregnancy, on average), a fee that has changed only nominally since the early 1980s.[7] As one program psychologist explained, the amount paid to surrogates is intentionally held at an artificially low rate by the programs so as to screen out women who might be motivated solely by monetary gain. One of the questions I sought to explore was whether surrogates were denying the importance of remuneration in order to cast their actions in a more culturally acceptable light, or whether they were motivated in part by remuneration and in part by other factors (with the importance of remuneration decreasing as the pregnancy progresses, the version of events put forth by both program staff and surrogates).

The opinion popular among both scholars and the general population, that surrogates are motivated primarily by financial gain, has tended to result in oversimplified analyses of surrogate motivations. The following are typical of surrogate explanations for the connection between the initial decision to become a surrogate and the remuneration they receive. Dismissals of the idea that remuneration serves as a primary source of motivation for surrogates of the kind expressed by Fran were frequent: "It [surrogacy] sounded so interesting and fun. The money wasn't enough to be pregnant for nine months."

Andrea, age 29, was married with three children. A high school graduate who worked as a motel night auditor, she expressly denied the idea that remuneration motivates most surrogates. As she said here, "I'm not doing it for the money. Take the money: that wouldn't stop me. It wouldn't stop the majority."

Sara, age 27, who attended two years of college, was married with two children and worked part-time as a tax examiner. Here she explains her feelings about remuneration:

> What's 10,000 bucks? You can't even buy a car. If it was just for the money you will want the baby. Money wasn't important. I possibly would have done it just for expenses, especially for the people I did it for. My father would have given me the money not to do it.

The issue of remuneration proved to be of particular interest in that, although surrogates do accept monetary compensation for their reproductive work, its role is a multifaceted one. The surrogate pregnancy, unlike a traditional pregnancy, is viewed by the surrogate and her family as work; as such, it is informed by the belief that work is something that occurs only within the context of paid occupations (Ferree 1984:72). It is interesting to note that surrogates rarely spend the money they earn on themselves. Not one of the surrogates I interviewed spent the money she earned on herself alone; the majority spend it on their children—as a contribution to their college education funds, for example—while others spend it on home improvement, gifts for their husbands, a family vacation, or simply to pay off "family debts."

One of the primary reasons that most surrogates do not spend the money they earn on themselves alone appears to stem from the fact that the money serves as a buffer against and/or reward to their families—in particular to their husbands, who make a number of compromises as a result of the surrogate arrangement. One of these compromises is obligatory abstention from sexual intercourse with their wives from the time insemination begins until a pregnancy has been confirmed (a period of time that lasts on average from three to four months in length, but that may be extended for as long as one year).

Surrogacy is viewed by surrogates as a part-time job in the sense that it allows a woman, especially a mother, to stay at home—to have, as one surrogate noted, "the luxury of staying home with my children," an idea that is also attractive to their husbands. The fact that a surrogate need not leave home on a routine basis or in any formalized way to earn money is perceived by the surrogate and her husband as a benefit; the surrogate, however, consequently spends less time with her family as a result of a new schedule that includes medical appointments, therapy sessions, social engagements with the commissioning couple. Thus surrogates are able to use the monetary compensation they receive as a means of procuring their husbands' support when and if they become less available to the family because of their employment.

The devaluation of the amount of the surrogate payment by surrogates as insufficient to compensate for "nine months of pregnancy" serves several important purposes. First, this view is representative of the cultural belief that children are "priceless" (Zelizer 1985); in this sense surrogates are merely reiterating a widely held cultural belief when they devalue the amount of remuneration they receive. When, for example, the largest and one of the most well-established surrogate mother programs changed the wording of its advertising copy from "Help an Infertile Couple" to "Give the Gift of Life," the vastly increased volume of response revealed that the program had discovered a successful formula with which to reach the surrogate population. With surrogacy, the gift is conceptualized as a child, a formulation that is widely used in Euro-American culture—for example, in blood (Titmuss 1971) and organ donation (Fox and Swazey 1992).

The gift formulation holds particular appeal for surrogates because it reinforces the idea that having a child for someone is an act that cannot be compensated for monetarily. As I have already mentioned, the "gift of life" theme is further enhanced by some surrogates to embrace the near-sacrifice of their own lives in childbirth.

Fran, whose dismissal of the importance of payment I have already quoted, also offered another, more revealing account of her decision to become a surrogate mother: "I wanted to do the ultimate thing for somebody, to give them the ultimate gift. Nobody can beat that, nobody can do anything nicer for them." Stella, age 38, married with two children, noted that the commissioning couples "consider it [the baby] a gift and I consider it a gift." Carolyn, age 33, married with two children and the owner of a house-cleaning company, discussed her feelings about remuneration and having a surrogate child in these terms: "It's a gift of love. I have always been a really giving person, and it's the ultimate way to give. I've always had babies so easily. It's the ultimate gift of love."

As we can see, when surrogates characterize the child they reproduce for couples as a "gift," they are also suggesting tacitly that mere monetary compensation would never be sufficient to repay the debt incurred. Although this formulation may at first appear to be a reiteration of the belief that children are culturally priceless, it also suggests that surrogates recognize that they are creating a state of enduring solidarity between themselves and their couples—precisely as in the practice of exogamy, where the end result is "more profound than the result of other gift transactions, because the relationship established is not just one of reciprocity, but one of kinship" (Rubin 1975:172). As Rubin summarizes Mauss's pioneering work on this subject, "The significance of gift giving is that [it] expresses, affirms, or creates a social link between the partners of exchange . . . confers upon its participants a special relationship of trust, solidarity and mutual aid" (1975:172).

Thus when surrogates frame the equation as one in which a gift is being proffered, the theme serves as a counterpoint to the business aspect of the arrangement, a reminder to them and to the commissioning couple that one of the symbolically central functions of money—the "removal of the personal element from human relationships through it(s) indifferent and objective nature" (Simmel 1978:297)—may be insufficient to erase certain kinds of relationships, and that the relational element may continue to surface despite the monetary exchange.

This formation of surrogacy as a matter of altruism versus remuneration has also proved to be a pivotal issue in legislative debates and discussions. Jan Sutton, the founder and spokeswoman of the National Association of Surrogate Mothers (a group of more than 100 surrogates who support legislation in favor of surrogacy), stated in her testimony before an information-gathering session of the California state legislature in 1989: "My organization and its members would all still be surrogates if no payment was involved" (Ragoné 1989). Her sentiment is not unrepresentative of those expressed by the surrogates interviewed for this study. Interestingly enough, once Sutton had informed the committee of that fact, several of the members of the panel who had previously voiced their opposition to surrogacy in its commercial form began to express praise for Sutton, indicating that her testimony had altered their opinion of surrogacy.

In direct response to her testimony, the committee began instead to discuss a proposal to ban commercial surrogacy but to allow for the practice of noncommercial surrogacy. In the latter practice the surrogate is barred from receiving financial compensation for her work, although physicians and lawyers involved are allowed their usual compensation for services rendered. In Britain, where commercial surrogacy has been declared illegal, the issue was framed often in moral terms: "The symbol of the pure surrogate who creates a child for love was pitted against the symbol of the wicked surrogate who prostitutes her maternity" (Cannell 1990:683). This dichotomous rendering in which "pure" surrogates are set in opposition to "wicked" surrogates is predicated on the idea that altruism precludes remuneration. In the Baby M Case, for example, the most decisive issue was the one concerning payment to the surrogate (Hull 1990:155).

Although surrogates overwhelmingly cast their actions in a traditional light, couching the desire to become a surrogate in conservative and traditionally feminine terms, it is clear that in many respects surrogate motherhood represents a departure from traditional motherhood. It transforms private motherhood into public motherhood, and it provides women with remuneration for their reproductive work—work that has in American culture been done, as Schneider has noted, for "love" rather than for "money" (Schneider 1968). It is this aspect that has unintendedly become one of the primary foci of consideration in state legislatures throughout the United States. Of the 15 states that now have surrogacy laws in place, the "most common regulations, applicable in 11 states . . . are statutes voiding paid surrogacy contracts" (Andrews 1992:50). The overwhelming acceptance of the idea of unpaid or noncommercial surrogacy (both in the United States and in Britain) can be attributed to the belief that it "duplicates maternity in culturally the most self-less manner" (Strathern 1991:31).

But what is perhaps even more important, the corresponding rejection of paid or commercial surrogacy may also be said to result from a cultural resistance to conflating the symbolic value of the family with the world of work to which it has long been held in opposition. From a legal perspective, commercial surrogacy has been viewed largely by the courts as a matter of "merg[ing] the family with the world of business and commerce" (Dolgin 1993:692), a prospect that presents a challenge to American cultural definitions in which the family has traditionally represented "the antithesis of the market relations of capitalism; it is also sacralized in our minds as the last stronghold against the state, as the symbolic refuge from the intrusion of a public domain that consistently threatens our sense of privacy and self determination" (Collier et al. 1982:37).

Resistance in U.S. society to merging these two realms, the domestic and the public, may be traced to the entrenched belief that the

> private realm [is] where women are most in evidence, where natural functions like sex and bodily functions related to procreation take place, where the affective content of relations is primary and [that] a public realm [is] where men are most in evidence, where culture is produced, where one's efficiency at producing goods or services takes precedence. [Martin 1987:15–16]

With the introduction of the phenomenon of public motherhood in the form of surrogacy, however, the separation of family and work has been irrevocably challenged. Over time it became clear to me that many of the women who chose to become surrogate mothers did so as a way to transcend the limitations of their domestic roles as wives, mothers, and homemakers while concomitantly attesting to the importance of those roles and to the satisfaction they derived from them. That idea indeed accounted for some of their contradictory statements. Surrogates, who are for the most part from predominantly working-class backgrounds, have, for example, often been denied access to prestigious roles and other avenues for attaining status and power. Surrogacy thus provides them with confirmation that motherhood is important and socially valued.[8] Surrogacy also introduces them to a world filled with social interaction with people who are deeply appreciative of the work that they do, and in this way surrogates receive validation and are rewarded for their reproductive work through their participation in this new form of public motherhood.

Of all the surrogates' stated motivations, remuneration proved to be the most problematic.[9] On a symbolic level, remuneration detracts from the idealized cultural image of women/mothers as selfless, nurturant, and altruistic, an image that surrogates have no wish to alter. Then, too, if surrogates were to acknowledge money as adequate compensation for their reproductive work, they would lose the sense that theirs is a gift that transcends all monetary compensation.[10] The fact that some surrogates had experienced difficult pregnancies and deliveries and were not thereby dissuaded from becoming surrogate mothers, coupled with their devaluation of remuneration and their tendency to characterize the child as a gift, suggested that current theories about surrogate motivations provided only a partial explanation for what was clearly a more complex phenomenon.

From the moment she places a telephone call to a surrogate mother program to the moment she delivers the child, the balance of power in a surrogate's personal life is altered radically. Her time can no longer be devoted exclusively to the care and nurture of her own family because she has entered into a legal and social contract to perform an important and economically rewarded task: helping an infertile couple to begin a family of their own. Unlike other types of employment, this activity cannot be regarded as unfeminine, selfish, or nonnurturant. As I have previously mentioned, the surrogate's husband must sign a consent form in which he agrees to abstain from sexual intercourse with his wife until a pregnancy has been confirmed. In so doing he agrees to relinquish both his sexual and procreative ties to his wife and thus is understood to be supporting his wife's decision to conceive and gestate another man's child (or another couple's child, in the case of gestational surrogacy). Once a surrogate enters a program, she also begins to recognize just how important having a child is to the commissioning couple. She sees with renewed clarity that no matter how much material success the couple has, their lives are emotionally impoverished because of their inability to have a child. In this way the surrogate's fertility serves as a leveling device for perceived, if unacknowledged, economic differences—and many surrogates begin to see themselves as altruistic or heroic figures who can rectify the imbalance in a couple's life.

FATHERS, ADOPTIVE MOTHERS, AND SURROGATE MOTHERS

Studies on surrogate motherhood have tended to characterize the couple's motivations as lacking in complexity; in other words, it is assumed that the primary motivation is to have a child that is biologically related to at least one member of the couple (in this case the father and, in the case of donor insemination, the mother) (Glover 1990). A tendency on the part of earlier researchers to accept this theory at face value may be said to stem from the influence of Euro-American kinship ideology, particularly from its emphasis on the centrality of biogenetic relatedness, and perhaps secondarily from the fact that researchers have not had ready access to this population. Biological relatedness thus continues to be accepted as a given, "one way of grounding the distinctiveness of kin relations . . . the natural facts of life that seem to lie prior to everything else" (Strathern 1992a:19).[11]

While genetic relatedness is clearly one of the primary motivations for couples' choice of surrogate motherhood, this view is something of a simplification unless one also acknowledges that surrogacy contradicts several cultural norms, not the least of which is that it involves procreation outside marriage. The case of surrogate motherhood requires that we go beyond the parameters that until now have delineated domains such as reproduction and kinship, to "pursue meaning[s] where they lead" (Delaney 1986:496). Although couples may be motivated initially by a desire to have a child that is biologically related to at least one of the partners, the fact that this can be achieved only by employing the services of a woman other than the wife introduces a host of dilemmas.

Fathers and adoptive mothers resolve the problems posed by surrogate motherhood through various and separate strategies. Their disparate concerns stem not only from the biogenetic relationship the father bears to the child and from the adoptive mother's lack of such a relationship, but also from the pressures of having to negotiate the landscape of this novel terrain. For the father the primary obstacle or issue posed by surrogate motherhood is that a woman other than his wife will be the "mother" of his child. The following quotations from fathers illustrate the considerable degree of ambiguity created by surrogate motherhood. They also reveal the couples' shared assumptions about American kinship ideology and how it is that "biological elements have primarily symbolic significance . . . [whose] meaning is not biology at all" (Schneider 1972:45).

Tom and his wife, for example, had experienced 17 years of infertility. Initially opposed to surrogate motherhood out of concern that his wife would feel "left out," Tom described his early reactions: "Yes, the whole thing was at first strange. I thought to myself; here she [the surrogate] is carrying my baby. Isn't she supposed to be my wife?"

Ed, a 45-year-old college professor, described a similar sense of confusion: "I felt weird about another woman carrying my child, but as we all got to know one another it didn't seem weird. It seemed strangely comfortable after a while."

Richard, age 43, a computer engineer, described similar feelings of awkwardness about the child's biological tie to the surrogate:

> Seeing Jane [the surrogate] in him [his son], it's literally a part of herself she gave. That's fairly profound. I developed an appreciation of the magnitude of what she did and the inappropriateness of approaching this as a business relationship. It didn't seem like such a big thing initially for another woman to carry my baby, a little awkward in not knowing how to relate to her and not wanting to interfere with her relationship with her husband. But after Tommy was born I can see Jane in his appearance and I had a feeling it was a strange thing we did not to have a relationship with Jane. But it's wearing off, and I'm not struck so much with: I've got a piece of Jane here.

Questions such as Tom's "Isn't she supposed to be my wife?" reflect the concern and confusion experienced by husbands, their ambivalence underscoring the continued symbolic centrality of sexual intercourse and procreation in American kinship, both of which continue to symbolize unity and love (Schneider 1968). The father's relationship to the surrogate, although strictly noncoital, is altered by the fact that it produces what was always, until the recent past, the product of a sexual union—namely, a child. Feelings of discomfort or "awkwardness," and concerns as to how to behave toward the surrogate and the surrogate's husband, stem from the idea that the father-surrogate relationship may be considered adultery by those unfamiliar with the particulars of the surrogate arrangement. For example, one program reported that a client from the Middle East arrived at the program office with the expectation that he would engage in sexual intercourse with the surrogate. One surrogate remarked on this ambivalence: "The general public thinks I went to bed with the father. They think I committed adultery!"

In addition to concerns about his relationship to the surrogate vis-a-vis the child, a father is aware that the child bears no genetic tie to his wife. The husband thus gains his inclusivity in the surrogate relationship through his biological contribution vis-a-vis the surrogate: he is both the genitor and pater; but it is the surrogate, not his wife, who is the genetrix. One of the primary strategies employed by both couples and surrogates is to deemphasize the husband's role precisely because it is the surrogate-father relationship that raises the specter of adultery or, more accurately, temporary polygandry and temporary polygyny. They also downplay the significance of his biological link to the child, focusing instead on the bond that develops between the adoptive and the surrogate mother.

THE SURROGATE AND ADOPTIVE MOTHER BOND

The adoptive mother attempts to resolve her lack of genetic relatedness to the child through what I have labeled her "mythic conception" of the child—that is, the notion that her desire to have a child is what first makes the surrogate arrangement a possibility. Cybil, an adoptive mother, explained the mythic conception in this way: "Ann is my baby; she was conceived in my heart before Lisa's [the surrogate's] body." Lucy, an adoptive mother, described the symbiotic relationship that developed between herself and her surrogate in a slightly different way: "She [the surrogate] represented that part of me that couldn't have a child."

The adoptive mother also experiences what can be described as a "pseudopregnancy" through which she experiences the state of pregnancy by proxy as close to the experience as an infertile woman can be. As one surrogate said of this relationship, "I had a closeness with Sue [the adoptive mother] that you would have with your husband. She took Lamaze class and went to the delivery room with me." In fact, when geographical proximity permits, it is expected in the open programs that adoptive mothers will accompany surrogates to all medical appointments and birthing classes, in addition to attending the delivery of the child in the hospital (where the biological father and the surrogate's husband are also present whenever possible).

Together, the surrogate and the adoptive mother thus define reproduction as "women's business," often reiterating the idea that their relationship is a natural and exclusive one. As Celeste, a surrogate mother, pointed out: "The whole miracle of birth would be lost if she [the adoptive mother] wasn't there. If women don't experience the birth of their children being born they would be alienated and they would be breeders." Mary, a surrogate whose adoptive mother gave her a heart-shaped necklace to commemorate the birth of the child, said, "I feel a sisterhood to all women of the world. I am doing this for her, looking to see her holding the baby."[12] Both of the adoptive mother's strategies, her mythic conception of the child and her pseudopregnancy, are—as these quotations demonstrate—greatly facilitated by the surrogate, who not only deemphasizes the importance of her physical pregnancy but also disavows the importance of her own biological link to the child. Celeste summed up the sentiment expressed by many surrogates when she stated, "She [the adoptive mother] was emotionally pregnant, and I was just *physically pregnant*" (emphasis added).

Without exception, when surrogates are asked whether they think of the child as their own, they say that they do not.[13] Kay, a surrogate, age 35 and divorced with two children, explained her feelings in this way: "I never think of the child as mine. After I had the baby, the mother came into the room and held the baby. I couldn't relate that it had any part of me."

Mary, age 37, married with three children, similarly stated, "I don't think of the baby as my child. I donated an egg I wasn't going to be using." Jeannie, yet another surrogate, described herself as having no connection to the child: "I feel like a vehicle, just like a cow; it's their baby, it's his sperm."

The surrogate's ability to deemphasize her own biological link to the child is made possible in part by her focus upon the folk theory of procreation in which paternity is viewed as the "primary, essential and creative role" (Delaney 1986:495). Even though in the realm of scientific knowledge women have long been identified as cocreators, "in Europe and America, the knowledge has not been encompassed symbolically. Symbols change slowly and the two levels of discourse are hardly ever brought into conjunction" (Delaney 1986:509).

With the "dominant folk theory of procreation in the West," paternity has been conceptualized as the "power to create and engender life" (Delaney 1986:510), whereas maternity has come to mean "giving nurturance and giving birth" (Delaney 1986:495). Surrogates, therefore, emphasize the importance of nurturance and consistently define that aspect of motherhood as a choice that one can elect to make or not make. This emphasis on nurturance is embraced readily by the surrogate and adoptive mother alike since "one of the central notions in the modern American construct of the family is that of nurturance" (Collier et al. 1982:34). In the United States nurturance until now has been considered "natural to women and [the] basis of their cultural authority" (Ginsburg 1987:629). Like other kinds of assisted reproduction, surrogate motherhood is understood to "fall into older cultural terrains, where women interpret their options in light of prior and contradictory meanings of pregnancy and childbearing" (Rapp 1990:41).

For this reason surrogates underplay their own biological contribution in order to bring to the fore the importance of the social, nurturant role played by the adoptive mother. The efforts of surrogates and adoptive mothers to separate social motherhood from biological motherhood can be seen to represent a reworking of the nature/culture dichotomy. A primary strategy an adoptive mother may employ in order to resolve her lack of genetic relatedness to the child is her use of the idea of intentionality, specifically of "conception in the heart"—that is, the idea that in the final analysis it is the adoptive mother's desire to have a child that brings the surrogate arrangement into being and ultimately results in the birth of a child. The surrogate thus devalues her own genetic/ physical contribution while highlighting the pseudopregnancy of the adoptive mother and the importance of the latter's role as nurturer. In this way motherhood is reinterpreted as primarily an important social role in order to sidestep problematic aspects of the surrogate's biogenetic relationship to the child and the adoptive mother's lack of a biogenetic link. This focus upon intentionality and nurturance by both surrogates and adoptive mothers is reflected in the following statement by Andy, a 39-year-old surrogate, who is the mother of two children and a full-time nurse:

> Parents are the ones who raise the child. I got that from my parents, who adopted children. My siblings were curious and my parents gave them the information they had and they never wanted to track down their biological parents. I don't think of the baby as mine; *it is the parents, the ones who raise the child*, that are important (emphasis added).

The adoptive mother and father of the child attempt to resolve the tensions inherent in the surrogate arrangement, in particular its rearrangement of boundaries through the blurring of the distinctions between pregnancy and motherhood, genetic relatedness and affective bonds, wife and mother, wife and husband, and wife and surrogate mother. The surrogate's role in achieving these goals is nevertheless essential. Through the process in which pregnancy and birth are defined as being exclusively women's business, the father's role is relegated to secondary status in the relational triangle. The surrogate plays a primary role in facilitating the adoptive mother's role as mother of the child, something that is made possible by her refusal to nurture the child to which she gives birth. In the interest of assisting this process the surrogate consistently devalues her biological contribution or genetic relationship to the child.

In this process of emphasizing the value of nurturance, surrogates describe motherhood as a role that one can adopt or refuse, and this concept of nurturance as choice is for them the single most important defining aspect of motherhood. Surrogates believe that, in the case of surrogacy, motherhood is comprised of two separable aspects: first, the biological process (insemination, pregnancy, and delivery); and second, the social process (nurturance). They reason that a woman can either choose to nurture—that is, to accept the role of social mother—or choose not to nurture, thereby rejecting the role of social mother.[14]

As we have seen, surrogates, couples, and surrogate mother programs work in concert to create a new idea of order and appropriate relations and boundaries by directing their attention to the sanctity of motherhood as it is illustrated in the surrogate and adoptive mother bond. The surrogate and adoptive mother work in unison, reinforcing one another's view that it is social rather than biological motherhood that ultimately creates a mother. Nurture, they reason together, is a far more important and central construct of motherhood than nature. The decision on the part of the surrogate not to nurture the child nullifies the value of biological motherhood, while the adoptive mother's choice to nurture activates or fully brings forth motherhood.

Because of the emphasis couples place on having a child that is biologically related to at least one partner, I was initially perplexed to learn that less than five percent of couples chose to have a paternity test performed once the child had been born (although this option is offered to every couple); surrogate contracts specifically state that the couple is under no obligation to accept the child until such a test has been performed. In view of the fact that couples spend between $40,000 and $45,000 in fees to have a child who is biologically related to them, such a lack of interest in the paternity test is initially perplexing. When asked about paternity testing, wives and husbands typically give responses such as these: "We knew she was ours from the minute we saw her," or "We decided that it really didn't matter; he was ours no matter what."

While these statements may initially appear to contradict the stated purpose of pursuing a partially biogenetic solution to childlessness, they can also be understood to fulfill two important purposes. From the wife's perspective, an element of doubt as to the child's paternity introduces a new variable that serves to equalize the issue of relatedness. The husband is of course aware that he has a decisive advantage over his wife in terms of his genetic relatedness to the child. Although paternal doubt is always present for males, in the case of surrogate motherhood paternal doubt is thereby culturally enhanced. Allowing paternal certainty to remain a mystery represents an attempt to redress symbolically the imbalance created between wife and husband through the surrogate arrangement. Before the advent of these reproductive technologies, the "figure of the mother provided a natural model for the social construction of the 'natural' facts" (Strathern 1991:5); motherhood was seen as a single, unified experience, combining both the social and biological aspects—unlike fatherhood, in which the father acquired a "double identity." With the separation of the social and biological elements, however, motherhood has, in the context of surrogacy, also acquired this double identity (Strathern 1991:4-5). In this way, surrogate motherhood thus produces the "maternal counterpart to the double identity of the father, certain in one mode and uncertain in another" (Strathern 1991:4).

All the participants in the surrogate motherhood triad work to downplay the importance of biological relatedness as it pertains to women. They tend to reinforce the idea of motherhood as nurturance so that the adoptive mother's inability to give birth or become a genetrix (both wife and mother) is of diminished importance. At the same time, the husband's relationship to the surrogate vis-a-vis the child, and his biological relationship to the child, is also deemphasized. The idea that the adoptive mother is a mother by virtue of her role as nurturer is frequently echoed by all parties concerned. In this sense motherhood, as it pertains to surrogacy, is redefined as a social role. This occludes the somewhat problematic issues of the surrogate's biogenetic relationship to the child and the adoptive mother's lack of such a relationship.

Thus the decision not to have a paternity test performed provides additional reinforcement for the idea of parenthood as a social construct rather than a biological phenomenon. The importance of the bond that develops between the surrogate and the adoptive mother is twofold: it merges the adoptive mother (or mater) and the surrogate (or genetrix) into one by reinforcing and maintaining the unity of experience, erasing the boundaries that surrogacy creates; and, at the same time, it establishes and maintains new boundaries as they are needed between surrogate and father.

I have attempted here to show that surrogates' stated motivations for choosing surrogate motherhood represent only one aspect of a whole complex of motivations. While surrogates do, as they say, enjoy being pregnant, desire to help an infertile couple to start a family of their own, and value the compensation they receive, there are other equally good—if not more—compelling reasons that motivate this unique group of women to become surrogate mothers. Biological relatedness is both the initial motivation for and the ultimate goal of surrogacy, and it is also that facet of surrogacy that makes it most consistent with the biogenetic basis of American kinship ideology. Nevertheless, it must be deemphasized—even devalued—by all the participants in order to make surrogacy consistent with American cultural values about appropriate relations between wives and husbands. In addition to broadening the scope of our understanding about the motivations of the couples who choose to pursue a surrogate solution, I hope that this article has illuminated the complexity of the couples' decision-making process as well as their motivation.

As we have seen, surrogates as a group tend to highlight only those aspects of surrogacy that are congruent with traditional values such as the importance of family. Like the couples, they also tend to deemphasize those aspects of the surrogate relationship that represent a departure from conventional beliefs about motherhood, reproduction, and the family. Interspersed with surrogates' assertions that surrogate motherhood is merely an extension of their conventional female roles as mother, however, are frequent interjections about the unique nature of what they are doing. The following quotation, for example, reflects surrogates' awareness of the radical, unusual, and adventurous nature of their actions: "Not everyone can do it. It's like the steelworkers who walk on beams ten floors up. Not everyone can do it; not everyone can be a surrogate."

It is thus not surprising, in view of their socialization, their life experiences, and their somewhat limited choices, that surrogates claim that it is their love of children, pregnancy and family, and their desire to help others that motivates them to become surrogates. To do otherwise would be to acknowledge that there may be inconsistencies within, and areas of conflict between, their traditional female roles as wives, mothers, and homemakers and their newfound public personae as surrogate mothers.

In conclusion, it can be said that all the participants involved in the surrogacy process wish to attain traditional ends, and are therefore willing to set aside their reservations about the means by which parenthood is attained. Placing surrogacy inside tradition, they attempt to circumvent some of the more difficult issues raised by the surrogacy process. In this way, programs and participants pick and choose among American cultural values about family, parenthood, and reproduction, now choosing biological relatedness, now nurture, according to their needs.

Notes

This article has benefited greatly from the comments, suggestions, and encouragement of many individuals. I would like to express my gratitude to the late David Schneider for his support of my work, and for his pioneering work on American kinship without which my own research would have been considerably less complete. I would also like to thank Marilyn Strathern for her encouragement. Many thanks to my anonymous reviewers for their incisive comments. Special thanks are due also to the following individuals: Robbie Apfel, William Beeman, Carole Browner, Sarah Franklin, Lina Fruzzetti, Louise Lamphere, Lucile Newman, Rayna Rapp, Susan Scrimshaw, Bennet Simon, and June Starr.

1. A couple, Willliam and Elizabeth Stern, contracted with a surrogate, Mary Beth Whitehead, to bear a child for them because Elizabeth Stern suffered from multiple sclerosis, a condition that can be exacerbated by pregnancy. Once the child was born, however, Whitehead refused to relinquish the child to the Sterns, and in 1987, William Stern, the biological father, filed suit against Whitehead in an effort to enforce the terms of the surrogate contract. The decision of the lower court to award custody to the biological father and to permit his wife to adopt the child was overturned by the New Jersey Supreme Court, which then awarded custody to William Stern, prohibiting Elizabeth Stern from adopting the child while granting visitation rights to Mary Beth Whitehead. These decisions mirrored public opinion about surrogacy (Hull 1990:154).

2. See Rapp (1978:279) and Gordon (1988:3) for a historical analysis of the idea of the demise of the American family.

3. For a more extensive review of the literature, see, for example, Ginsburg and Rapp 1991.

4. As of 1994, only seven of the original ten are now in existence. I have changed the names of programs, surrogates, couples, and directors in order to protect their identities.

5. Over the years I have interviewed surrogates who had been employed by closed programs, interviewed the administrative assistant at the largest closed program, and spoken with program directors who arrange either a closed or open arrangement (depending upon the couple's choice). Many of the data presented in this article were collected in the open programs.

6. See, for example, Ragoné 1994 for a detailed account of the role of the surrogate mother program.

7. One of the programs has, however, recently increased its rate to $15,000. Surrogates also receive an allowance for maternity clothing, remuneration for time lost from work (if they have employment outside of the home), and reimbursement for all babysitting fees incurred as a result of surrogate-related activities.

8. The quantifiable data reveal that surrogates are predominantly white, an average of 27 years of age, high school graduates, of Protestant or Catholic background, and married with an average of three children. Approximately 30 percent are full-time homemakers, and those surrogates who are employed outside the home tend to be employed in the service sector. A comparison of surrogate and couple statistics reveals pronounced differences in educational background, occupation, and income level. The average combined family income of commissioning couples is in excess of $100,000, as compared to $38,000 for married surrogates.

9. For example, Gullestad (1992) observed that girls who worked as babysitters in Norway tended to emphasize the extent to which their work was motivated by nurturance, deemphasizing the importance of the remuneration they received.

10. Surrogate motivations are diverse and overlapping, and surrogates express empathy for infertile couples as well as joy experienced during pregnancy.

11. Commissioning couples consistently articulate the belief that surrogacy is a superior alternative to adoption. Many couples have attempted to adopt, only to discover the shortage of healthy white infants and age limit criteria of adoption agencies: see Ragoné 1994. Surrogacy not only provides them with the highly desirable partial genetic link (through the father), but it also permits them to meet and interact with the biological mother—something that is usually not possible with adoption.

12. When Robert Winston, a pioneer in assisted reproductive technologies in Britain, revealed that he had facilitated a surrogate arrangement that involved two sisters, the case tended to elicit from the public "strong and sentimental approval" (Cannell 1990:675).

13. Prospective surrogates who find themselves unwilling to dismiss their biological link to a child frequently opt for gestational surrogacy rather than abandon the idea of surrogate motherhood altogether, even though the risk of medical complication is thereby greatly increased. Over a three-year period I observed that the rate of gestational surrogacy had increased from less than five percent to close to fifty percent at the largest of the surrogate mother programs and at another well-established program. I am currently in the process of researching gestational surrogacy.

14. Giddens' theory of structuration is understood as a corrective to both the exclusively rigid structuralist worldview (which tends to eliminate agency) and phenomenologists, symbolic interactionists, and ethnomethodologists who overemphasize the plasticity of society (Baber 1991:220). Giddens has articulated the view that "all structural properties of social systems are enabling as well as constraining" (1984:177), a phenomenon that can be seen in surrogate arrangements when surrogates and couples focus upon certain elements or aspects of parenthood while deemphasizing others. The way in which these different

idioms of nature and nurture are emphasized and deemphasized also parallels and substantiates Strathern's observations (1992c) about the selective weight of nature/nurture in the kinship context.

References

Annas, George. 1988. Fairy Tales Surrogate Mothers Tell. *In* Surrogate Motherhood: Politics and Privacy. Larry Gostin, ed. Pp. 43–55. Bloomington: Indiana University Press.

Andrews, Lori. 1984. New Conceptions: A Consumer's Guide to the Newest Infertility Treatments. New York: Ballantine. 1992. Surrogacy Wars. California Lawyer 12(10):42–49.

Baber, Zaheer. 1991. Beyond the Structure/Agency Dualism: An Evaluation of Giddens' Theory of Structuration. Sociological Inquiry 61(2):219–230

Browner, Carole. 1986. The Politics of Reproduction in a Mexican Village. Signs 11:710–724.

Cannell, Fenella. 1990. Concepts of Parenthood: The Warnock Report, the Gillick and Modern Myths. American Ethnologist 17:667–686.

Collier, Jane, Michelle Rosaldo, and Sylvia Yanagisako. 1982. Is There a Family? New Anthropological Views. *In* Rethinking the Family: Some Feminist Questions. Barrie Thorne and Marilyn Yalom, eds. Pp. 25–39. New York: Longman.

Delaney, Carol. 1986. The Meaning of Paternity and the Virgin Birth Debate. Man 24 (3):497–513. 1991. The Seed and the Soil: Gender and Cosmology in a Turkish Village Society. Berkeley: University of California Press.

Dolgin, Janet. 1993. Just a Gene: Judicial Assumptions about Parenthood. UCLA Law Review 40(3).

Dworkin, Andrea. 1978. Right-Wing Women. New York: Perigee Books.

Ferree, Myra. 1984. Sacrifice, Satisfaction and Social Change: Employment and the Family. *In* My Troubles Are Going to Have Trouble with Me. Karen Sacks and Dorothy Remy, eds. Pp. 61–79. New Brunswick, NJ: Rutgers University Press.

Fox, Reneé, and Judith Swazey. 1992. Spare Parts: Organ Replacement in American Society. Oxford: Oxford University Press.

Giddens, Anthony. 1984. The Constitution of Society. Berkeley: University of California Press.

Ginsburg, Faye. 1987. Procreation Stories: Reproduction, Nurturance and Procreation in Life Narratives of Abortion Activists. American Ethnologist 14(4):623–636. 1989. Contested Lives: The Abortion Debate in an American Community. Berkeley: University of California Press.

Ginsburg, Faye, and Rayna Rapp. 1991. The Politics of Reproduction. Annual Review of Anthropology 20:311–343.

Glover, Jonathan. 1990. Ethics of New Reproductive Technologies: The Glover Report to the European Commission. DeKalb: Northern Illinois Press.

Gordon, Linda. 1988. Heroes of Their Own Lives. New York: Viking.

Gullestad, Marianne. 1992. The Art of Social Relations. Oslo, Norway: Scandinavian Press.

Hull, Richard. 1990. Gestational Surrogacy and Surrogate Motherhood. *In* Ethical Issues in the New Reproductive Technologies. Richard Hull, ed. Pp. 150–155. Belmont, CA: Wadsworth Publishers.

Leach, Edmund R. 1967. Virgin Birth. *In* Proceedings of the Royal Anthropological Institute for 1966. Pp. 39–49. London: RAI.

Martin, Emily. 1987. The Woman in the Body: A Cultural Analysis of Reproduction. Boston: Beacon Press.

Modell, Judith. 1989. Last Chance Babies: Interpretations of Parenthood in an In Vitro Fertilization Program. Medical Anthropology Quarterly 3(2):124–138.

Neuhaus, Robert. 1988. Renting Women, Buying Babies and Class Struggles. Society 25(3):8–10.

Newman, Lucile, ed. 1985. Women's Medicine: A Cross-Cultural Study of Indigenous Fertility Regulations. New Brunswick, NJ: Rutgers University Press.

Parker, Philip. 1983. Motivation of Surrogate Mothers: Initial Findings. American Journal of Psychiatry 140:117–119.

Ragoné, Helena. 1989. Proceedings from an information-gathering committee to the California State Legislature. Unpublished notes. 1991. Surrogate Motherhood in America. Ph.D. dissertation,

Brown University. 1994. Surrogate Motherhood: Conception in the Heart. Boulder, CO, and Oxford: Westview Press/Basic Books.

Rapp, Rayna. 1978. Family and Class in Contemporary America: Notes toward an Understanding of Ideology. Science and Society 42(3):278–300. 1987. Moral Pioneers: Women, Men and Fetuses on a Frontier of Reproductive Technology. Women and Health 13(1/2):101–116. 1988. Chromosomes and Communication: The Disclosure of Genetic Counseling. Medical Anthropology Quarterly 2:143–157. 1990. Constructing Amniocentesis: Maternal and Medical Discourses. *In* Uncertain Terms: Negotiating Gender in American Culture. Faye Ginsburg and Anna Lowenhaupt Tsing, eds. Pp. 28–42. Boston: Beacon Press.

Rubin, Gayle. 1975. The Traffic in Woman: Notes on the Political Economy of Sex. *In* Toward an Anthropology of Women. Rayna Reiter, ed. Pp. 157–210. New York: Monthly Review Press.

Schneider, David. 1968. American Kinship: A Cultural Account. Englewood Cliffs, NJ: Prentice Hall. 1972. What Is Kinship All About? *In* Kinship Studies in the Morgan Centennial Year. Priscilla Reining, ed. Pp. 32–63. Washington, DC: Anthropological Society of Washington.

Scrimshaw, Susan. 1978. Infant Mortality and Behavior in the Regulation of Family Size. Population Development Review 4:383–403.

Simmel, Georg. 1978. The Philosophy of Money. London: Routledge and Kegan Paul.

Snowden, R. G. Mitchell, and E. Snowden. 1983. Artificial Reproduction: A Social Investigation. London: Allen and Unwin.

Spiro, Melford. 1968. Virgin Birth, Parthenogenesis, and Physiological Paternity: An Essay in Cultural Interpretation. Man (n.s.) 3:242–261.

Strathern, Marilyn. 1991. The Pursuit of Certainty: Investigating Kinship in the Late Twentieth Century. Paper presented at the 90th American Anthropological Association Annual Meeting, Chicago. 1992a. Reproducing the Future. New York: Routledge. 1992b. The Meaning of Assisted Kinship. *In* Changing Human Reproduction. Meg Stacey, ed. Pp. 148–169. London: Sage Publications. 1992c. After Nature: English Kinship in the Late Twentieth Century. Cambridge: Cambridge University Press.

Titmuss, Richard. 1971. The Gift Relationship: From Human Blood to Social Policy. New York: Pantheon Books.

Zelizer, Vivian. 1985. Pricing the Priceless Child. New York: Basic Books.

8 *Childhood*

■READING 22

Revolutions in Children's Lives

Donald Hernandez, with David E. Myers

INTRODUCTION

Revolutionary changes in the life course, the economy, and society have transformed childhood, and the resources available to children, during the past 150 years. A revolutionary decline in the number of siblings in the families of children occurred during the past 100 years. Historically, a substantial minority of children did not spend their entire childhood in a two-parent family, but this will expand to a majority for children born during the past decade. The role of grandparents in the home, as surrogate parents filling the gap left by absent parents, has been important but limited during at least the past half century.

The family economy was revolutionized twice during the past 150 years, first as fathers and then mothers left the home to spend much of the day away at jobs as family breadwinners. With these changes, with instability in fathers' work, and with increasing divorce and out-of-wedlock childbearing, never during the past half century were a majority of children born into "Ozzie and Harriet" families in which the father worked full-time year-round, the mother was a full-time homemaker, and all of the children were born after the parents' only marriage.

Corresponding revolutions in child care occurred first as children over age 5 and then as younger children began to spend increasing amounts of time in formal educational or other settings in the care of someone other than their parents. Since today's children are tomorrow's parents, the spread of universal compulsory education led to revolutionary increases in the educational attainments of parents during the past half century, to the benefit of successive cohorts of children. But as opportunities to complete at least a high school education became substantially more equal for children during the past century, opportunities to go beyond high school and complete at least one year of college became less equal.

The absolute income levels of families increased greatly after the Great Depression and World War II through the 1960s but have changed comparatively little since then. Meanwhile, childhood poverty and economic inequality declined after World War II through the 1960s, then increased mainly during the 1980s. Most poor children throughout the era lived in working-poor families, and only a minority of poor children were fully welfare-dependent.

FAMILY COMPOSITION

Because siblings are the family members who are usually closest in age, needs, and activities, they may be among a child's most important companions and most important competitors for family resources. The typical child born in 1890 lived, as an adolescent, in a family in which there were about 6.6 siblings, but the typical child born in 1994 is expected to live in a family that is only one-third as large—with 1.9 children.

About one-half of this decline in family size had occurred by 1945, and the typical child born during that year lived in a family that had 2.9 siblings. Subsequently, during the postwar baby boom that occurred between 1945 and 1957, the annual number of births jumped by 55 percent (from 2.7 to 4.3 million births per year) and the Total Fertility Rate jumped by 52 percent (from 2.4 to 3.7 births per woman), but the family size of the typical adolescent increased by only 17 percent (from 2.9 to 3.4 siblings).

Changes in the distribution of adolescents by family size tell a similar story. The proportion living in families in which there are 5 or more siblings is expected to decline from 77 percent for children born in 1890 to only 6 percent for children born in 1994. Again, about one-half of the decline had occurred for children born in 1945, 32 percent of whom as adolescents lived in families in which there were 5 or more children, and again the increase during the baby boom was comparatively small at about 6 percentage points. At the opposite extreme, the proportion of adolescents living in families in which there are only 1–2 children is expected to increase from only 7 percent for children born in 1890 to 57 percent for children born in 1994. Among children born in 1945, about 30 percent lived in such small families, and this fell by 10 percentage points to 20 percent during the baby boom.

Historically, black children have tended to live in families in which there were substantially larger numbers of siblings than did white children, but trends in the family sizes of both black and white children were generally similar between the Civil War and 1925. Then for about 20 years, however, the racial gap expanded, apparently because the comparatively large decline in tuberculosis and venereal disease led to increased family sizes among blacks. Since about 1945, the number of siblings in the families of both black and white children have been converging.

Among children born in 1994, family-size differences between blacks and whites, as well as between Hispanic children (of any race) and non-Hispanic children, are expected to essentially vanish. Of the racial convergence in family size that is expected to occur for children born between 1945 and 1994, more than two-thirds had occurred among children born in 1973 who are now about 18 years old and approaching college age.

What are the consequences of this decline for children? First, children with larger numbers of siblings have greater opportunities to experience caring, loving sibling companionship. Hence, the family-size revolution drastically reduced the number of siblings who were available as potential companions during childhood and through adulthood. On the other hand, childhood family size appears to have little effect on psychological well-being later during adulthood. But because children growing up in large families—especially families with 5 or more siblings—tend to complete fewer years of schooling than do children from smaller families, they are less likely to enter high-status occupations with high incomes when they reach adulthood. Hence, the family-size revolution led to greatly improved opportunities for educational, occupational, and economic advancement among successive cohorts of children. . . .

Most children depend mainly on the parents in their homes for financial support and day-to-day care. Hence, it would be surprising if important differences in current welfare and future life chances were not found when children who do spend their entire childhood in a two-parent family are compared with those who do not.

In the short run, for many children the separation or divorce of their parents brings a sharp drop in family income and substantial psychological trauma. When the lone parent in a one-parent family marries to form a stepfamily, however, the children often experience a sharp jump in family income. Still, children in stepfamilies are more likely to have a low family income than are children in intact two-parent families. In addition, since one parent is absent from the home in one-parent families, children in these families may receive substantially less day-to-day care and attention from parents than do children in two-parent families.

Children in one-parent families are more likely, on average, to be exposed to parental stress than are children in two-parent families, more likely to exhibit behavioral problems, more likely to receive or need professional psychological help, more likely to perform poorly in school, and more likely to have health problems. In addition, on average, stepchildren are virtually indistinguishable from children in one-parent families in their chances of having behavioral, psychological, academic, and health problems.

Over the long run, children who do not spend most of their childhood in an intact two-parent family tend, as they reach adulthood, to complete fewer years of schooling, enter lower-status occupations, and earn lower incomes than do adults who did spend most of their childhood in an intact two-parent family. Some children from one-parent families may finish fewer years of school because fathers who can afford to provide financial support in college do not in fact do so when the child reaches college age. Many of the disadvantages associated with living in a one-parent family may result from the low family incomes of many children who live in such families.

In view of the potential disadvantages of not living with two parents, how typical has it become for children not to spend their entire childhood in a two-parent family? Historically, about 90 percent of newborn children under age 1 have lived with both biological parents. Still, between the late 1800s and 1950, a large and nearly stable minority of about 33 percent spent part of their childhood before age 18 with fewer than two parents in the home. Little change occurred during the first half of the twentieth century, despite the rise in parental separation and divorce, because this rise was counterbalanced by declining parental mortality.

Since about 1950 the link between marriage and the bearing and rearing of children has loosened. Because of the rise in out-of-wedlock childbearing that occurred between 1950 and 1980, the proportion of newborn children under age 1 who did not live with two parents doubled, climbing from 9 to 19 percent. Combined with the rise in separation and divorce, the proportion of children who will ever live with fewer than two parents is expected to increase from about 33 percent for the era between the late 1800s and 1950 to about 55–60 percent of children born in 1980.

Since at least the Civil War, white and black children have been quite different in their chances of spending part of their childhood living with fewer than two parents. For example, in 1940 the proportion of newborn children under age 1 who did not live with two parents was about 25 percent for blacks, compared with 7 percent for whites. Historically, it appears that for children born between the late 1800s and 1940, a majority of blacks (55–60 percent) spent part of their childhood in families in which there were fewer than two parents. For whites born between the late 1800s and 1940, a minority (but a large minority of approximately 29–33 percent) spent part of their childhood in families in which there were fewer than two parents. . . .

FAMILY WORK AND EDUCATION

As children were experiencing a revolutionary decline in family size and a large increase in one-parent family living, they also were experiencing two distinct transformations in parents' work and living arrangements. On the family farm, economic production, parenting, and child care were combined, as parents and children worked together to support themselves. This changed with the Industrial Revolution, however. Fathers became breadwinners who took jobs located away from home in order to support the family, and mothers became homemakers who remained at home to personally care for the children as well as to clean, cook, and perform other domestic functions for the family. Following the Great Depression, parents' work and the family economy were again transformed. Today most children live either in dual-earner families in which both parents work at jobs away from home or in one-parent families.

More specifically, between about 1840 and 1920 the proportion of children who lived in two-parent farm families fell from at least two-thirds to about one-third, while the proportion who lived in breadwinner-homemaker families climbed from 15–20 percent to 50 percent. Although a majority of children lived in breadwinner-homemaker families between about 1920 and 1970, this figure never reached 60 percent.

In fact, even during the heyday of the breadwinner-homemaker family, a second transformation in parents' work was under way. Between 1920 and 1970, as the proportion of children living in two-parent farm families continued to fall, the proportion who had breadwinner mothers working at jobs that were located away from home increased, and after 1960 the proportion living in one-parent families with their mothers also increased. The rise in the proportion of children living in dual-earner or one-parent families was extremely rapid, since the increase from 15–20 percent to 50 percent required only 30 years—about one-third as long as the time required for the same rise in the breadwinner-homemaker family to take place.

By 1980, nearly 60 percent of children lived in dual-earner or one-parent families, by 1989 about 70 percent lived in such families, and by the year 2000, only 7 years from now, the proportion of children living in such families may exceed 80 percent. Equally striking is the fact that even between 1920 and 1970, only a minority of children aged 0–17 lived in families that conformed to the mid-twentieth century ideal portrayed, for example, on the "Ozzie and Harriet" television program (that is, a nonfarm breadwinner-homemaker family in which the father works full-time year-round, the mother is a full-time homemaker, and all of the children were born after the parents' only marriage).

In fact, only a minority of newborn children under age 1 lived in such families in any year between 1940 and 1980. During these years a large majority of newborns (75–86 percent) did live with employed fathers, but only 42–49 percent lived with two parents in families in which the father worked full-time year-round and all of the children were born after the parents' only marriage. Still smaller proportions of newborns lived with two parents in families in which the father worked full-time year-round, all of the children were born after the parents' only marriage, and the mother was a full-time homemaker. Between 1940 and 1960, 41–43 percent of newborns lived in such families, and with rising mothers' labor-force participation this fell to only 27 percent in 1980. By age 17, children were even less likely, historically, to live in such families, as the proportion declined from 31 to 15 percent between 1940 and 1980.

These estimates imply that for children born between 1940 and 1960, an average of 65–70 percent of their childhood years were spent in a family situation that did not conform to the mid-twentieth century ideal. Looking ahead, it appears that children born in 1980 may spend an average of 80 percent of their childhood in families that do not conform to this ideal. In addition, children who lived on farms were likely, historically, to experience a parental death or other parental loss, or the economic insecurity associated with drought, crop disease, collapse of commodity prices, and similar catastrophes. Consequently, it is clear that neither historically nor during the industrial era have a majority of children experienced the family stability, the economic stability, and the homemaking mother that was idealized in mid-twentieth century America.

For white children, the chances of living in an idealized "Ozzie and Harriet," breadwinner-homemaker family were only slightly larger than for children as a whole. Among newborn black children at least since 1940, however, no more than 25 percent lived in such idealized families, and this figure fell to only 8 percent for black newborns in 1980. By the end of childhood, among blacks born in 1922, only 15 percent still lived in such families by age 17, and among blacks born in 1962, only 3 percent still lived in such families by age 17. Looking across the entire childhood experience of black children, the average proportion of childhood years not spent in idealized "Ozzie and Harriet" families increased from about 70–80 percent for the 1920s cohort to at least 95 percent for the 1980s cohort.

In 1980 Hispanic children (of any race) were roughly midway between black and white children in their chances of living in an idealized "Ozzie and Harriet" family. Only 10 percent of Hispanic 17-year-olds (of any race) lived in such families in 1980, only 21 percent of Hispanic newborns (of any race) lived in such families in 1980, and among these newborns more than 85 percent of the childhood years will be spent in families that do not conform to the mid-twentieth century ideal.

With these two historic transformations in parents' work and living arrangements, children simultaneously experienced two revolutionary increases in nonparental care, first among those over age 5 and then among younger children.

As farming became overshadowed by an industrial economy in which fathers worked for pay at jobs located away from home, compulsory school attendance and child labor laws were enacted to ensure that children were protected from unsafe and unfair working conditions, that they were excluded from jobs that were needed for adults, and that they received at least a minimal level of education. Also, as time passed increasing affluence allowed families to support themselves without child labor, and higher educational attainments became increasingly necessary in order to obtain jobs that offered higher pay and higher social prestige.

Hence, in 1870 only 50 percent of children aged 5–19 were enrolled in school, and their attendance averaged only 21 percent of the total days in the year. But 70 years later, in 1940, 95 percent of children aged 7–13 were enrolled in school, 79 percent of children aged 14–17 were enrolled in school, and the average attendance amounted to 42 percent of the days in the year. Even as mothers were increasingly viewed as full-time child care providers and homemakers, the need for them to act as full-time child care providers was diminishing, both because of the revolutionary decline in family size and because of the quadrupling in the amount of nonparental child care provided by teachers in school.

Since a full adult workday amounted to about 8 hours per day, 5 days per week (plus commuting time) after 1940, a full adult work year amounted to about 65 percent of the days in a year. But by 1940, school days of 5–6 hours (plus commuting time) amounted to about two-thirds of a full workday for about two-thirds of a full work year. As of 1940, then, childhood school attendance had effectively released mothers from personal child care responsibilities for a time period equivalent to about two-thirds of a full-time adult work year, except for the few years before children entered elementary school.

By reducing the time required for a mother's most important homemaker responsibility—the personal care of her children—this first child care revolution contributed to the large increase in mothers' labor-force participation after 1940, not only for school-age children but for preschoolers as well. Increasing mothers' labor-force participation and the rise in one-parent families then ushered in the second child-care revolution for preschool children aged 0–5. Between 1940 and 1989, the proportion of children who had no specific parent at home full-time tripled for school-age children (from roughly 22 to 66 percent) and quadrupled for preschoolers (from about 13 percent to about 52 percent).

Today these proportions are probably fairly typical for children in industrial countries, since by 1980 labor-force participation rates for women who were in main parenting ages in the United States were average when compared with other industrial countries. For example, the labor-force participation rates for women aged 30–39 were 70–90 percent in Sweden, Denmark, and Norway, 60–70 percent in the United States, France, and Canada, and 45–60 percent in the United Kingdom, West Germany, Italy, Belgium, Switzerland, Australia, and Japan.[1]

[1]Data from the U.S. Bureau of the Census for the following years: 1985 (Norway), 1984 (France), 1983 (Sweden), 1982 (U.S.), 1981 (Canada, Denmark, United Kingdom, Italy, Australia), 1980 (Japan, West Germany, Switzerland), 1977 (Belgium).

The increase in the proportion of preschoolers who had no specific parent at home full-time effectively reduced the amount of parental time that was potentially available to care for preschoolers and effectively increased the need for nonparental care. Yet the proportion of preschoolers who had a relative other than a parent in the home who might act as a surrogate parent also declined. For preschoolers living in dual-earner families, the proportion with a potential surrogate parent in the home declined from 19–20 percent in 1940 to only 4–5 percent in 1980. Meanwhile, the proportion of preschoolers living in one-parent families in which there was a potential surrogate parent in the home declined from 51–57 to 20–25 percent.

Time-use studies of nonemployed mothers indicate that the actual time devoted to child care as a primary activity probably increased by about 50–100 percent between 1926–1935 and 1943 and may have increased a bit more during the 20 years that followed. But between the 1960s and the early 1980s, the average amount of time that all mothers of preschoolers devoted to child care as a primary activity declined because an increasing number of mothers were employed outside the home and because employed mothers of preschoolers devote about one-half as much time to child care as a primary activity as do nonemployed mothers (1.2 vs. 2.2 hours per day during the mid-1970s).

By 1989, then, about 48 percent of preschoolers had a specific nonemployed parent at home on a full-time basis (usually the mother), another 12 percent had dual-earner parents who personally provided for their preschoolers' care (often by working different hours or days), and the remaining 40 percent were cared for by someone other than their parents for a large portion of time. Since the proportion of preschoolers who have a specific parent at home full-time declined from about 80 to about 48 percent during the 29 years between 1960 and 1989, we appear to be halfway through the preschool child-care revolution, and we are probably within 30–40 years of its culmination and will then see a very large proportion of preschool children spending increasingly more time in the care of someone other than their parents.

Overall, black children in 1940 were 24 percentage points less likely to have a specific parent at home full-time than were white children, but this racial gap had narrowed to 12 percentage points by 1980. Essentially all of this convergence occurred among older children, since the racial gap among adolescents declined from 27 to 6 percentage points, while the racial gap among preschoolers remained nearly constant at 18–23 percentage points. In 1980, about one-half of the racial gap among preschoolers was accounted for by differences in parental employment, and about one-half was accounted for by differences in the proportion of preschoolers who have no parent in the home.

Also in 1980, Hispanic children (of any race) were generally quite similar to non-Hispanic white children in their parental working and living arrangements, except that Hispanics (of any race) were somewhat more likely to live in one-parent families in which the parent was not employed and somewhat less likely to live in dual-earner families in which at least one parent worked part-time.

The importance of mothers' employment in contributing to family income is discussed below, but what other consequences do mothers' employment and nonparental care have for preschoolers? Past research suggests, broadly, that mothers' employment and nonparental care are neither necessarily nor pervasively harmful to preschoolers. This research also suggests that nonparental care is not a form of maternal deprivation, since children can and do form attachments to multiple caregivers if the number of caregivers is limited, the child-caregiver relationships are long-lasting, and the caregivers are responsive to the individual child.

Available evidence also suggests that the quality of care that children receive is important, and that some children, especially those from low-income families, are in double jeopardy from psychological and economic stress at home as well as exposure to low-quality nonparental child care. Additional potentially beneficial and detrimental effects of mothers' employment and nonparental care for preschoolers have been identified, but most of the results must be viewed as preliminary and tentative. Overall, research on the consequences of nonparental care for preschoolers is itself in its infancy, and much remains to be done.

The first revolution in child care—that is, the advent of nearly universal elementary and high school enrollment between ages 6 and 17—as well as large increases in high school and college graduation, led in due course to a revolutionary increase in parents' education. For example, among children born during the 1920s, the proportions whose fathers completed only 0–8 years of schooling or 4 or more years of high school were 73 and 15 percent, respectively, but these proportions were nearly reversed (at 5 and 85 percent, respectively) among children born only 60 years later during the 1980s. For the same children, those with fathers who had completed 4 or more or 1 or more years of college climbed from 4 and 7 percent, respectively, to 28 and 47 percent. Increases were generally similar for mothers' education, except for a somewhat smaller rise in the proportion with mothers who were college-educated.

Black children, as well as white children, experienced revolutionary increases in parents' education, but blacks continued to lag behind whites, as the black disadvantage effectively shifted higher on the educational ladder but constricted substantially in size. For example, among the 1920s cohort, the maximum racial disadvantages of 38–43 percentage points were in the proportions whose fathers or mothers had completed at least 7–8 years of schooling. But among the 1980s cohort, the maximum racial gaps were only two-fifths as large at 15–16 percentage points, and were in the proportions whose fathers or mothers had completed 13–15 years of schooling.

Measured in terms of the number of decades by which blacks lagged behind whites, the 2–3 decades by which black children born during the 1940s and the 1950s lagged behind whites in having parents who received at least 8 years of education had essentially vanished for the 1970s cohort. But despite a temporary racial convergence among children born during the 1960s and the 1970s, black children born during the 1980s, like black children born during the 1940s and the 1950s, lagged about 2–3 decades behind whites in the proportion whose fathers and mothers had completed at least 4 years of college.

Old-family Hispanic children (of any race) born during the 1960s and the 1970s were fairly similar to non-Hispanic black children in their parents' educational attainments. But first-generation Hispanic children (of any race) were much less likely (by 32–42 percentage points) to have parents who had completed at least 8 years of schooling, presumably because many of their parents had immigrated from countries in which the general educational levels were much lower than those in the United States.

This revolution in parents' education, and continuing differentials by race and Hispanic origin, are important for children both in the short run and throughout their adult years. In the short run, parents with higher educational attainments are more likely to have higher incomes than those with lower educational attainments. In the long run, children whose parents have comparatively high educational attainments also tend, when they reach adulthood, to complete more years of education and thus obtain jobs that offer higher social prestige and income.

Consequently, successive cohorts of children benefited from increasing parents' education both because it contributed to the large increases in family income for children that occurred between World War II and approximately 1970, as described below, and because it contributed to increasing educational levels among children and therefore to higher prestige and income for successive cohorts of children when they reached adulthood. At the same time, the continuing disadvantage of black and Hispanic children (of any race) in their parents' educational attainments tends to limit their current family incomes and their future chances of achieving occupational and economic success during adulthood. . . .

FAMILY INCOME, POVERTY, AND WELFARE DEPENDENCE

Family income, another major feature of family origins, also has important consequences for children's current well-being and future life chances. On a day-to-day basis, whether children live in material deprivation, comfort, or luxury depends mainly on their family's income level. Of particular interest are children in low-income families because they may experience marked deprivation in such areas as nutrition, clothing, housing, or healthcare.

During the 1940s, 1950s, and 1960s, the absolute income levels of American families increased greatly, as real median family income jumped by 35–45 percent per decade, bringing corresponding decreases in absolute want. Associated with this rapid expansion in the ability to purchase consumer products was an unprecedented proliferation in the number and kinds of products that became available, as well as remarkable increases in the quality of these products. By the 1970s the typical American lived in a world of abundance that Americans 30 years earlier could hardly have imagined. Since the beginning of the 1970s, however, real family income has increased comparatively little, despite the ongoing revolution in labor force participation by wives and mothers, and during the 1970s and the 1980s median family income increased by only 5 and 1 percent, respectively.

Despite large improvements in absolute income levels between 1939 and 1969, however, these statistics tell us little about the extent to which children lived in relative deprivation or luxury compared with the standards of the time in which they grew up, because at a specific point in history, the measure of whether a family is judged to be living in deprivation or luxury is that family's income and whether it is especially low or especially high compared with typical families in the same historical period.

Measuring economic deprivation in comparison with median family income in various years, the "relative poverty rate" for children dropped sharply during the 1940s (from 38 to 27 percent) but then much more slowly (to 23 percent in 1969). Subsequently, the relative poverty rate for children increased—mostly during the 1980s—to 27 percent in 1988, reaching the same level experienced almost 40 years earlier in 1949. . . .

CONCLUSION

America's children experienced several interrelated revolutions in their life course, as the family, economy, and society were transformed during the past 150 years. Family size plummeted. One-parent family living jumped. Family farms nearly became extinct, as first fathers and then mothers left the home for much of the day in order to serve as family breadwinners. Formal schooling, nonparental care for children, and parents' educational attainments have increased greatly, although educational opportunities to go beyond high school have become less equal since the turn of the century.

Absolute family incomes multiplied, but the past two decades brought little change in average income and increasing economic inequality among children, despite increasing mothers' labor-force participation. Relative and official poverty rates for children climbed during the past decade. Welfare dependence increased during recent decades, but most poor children historically and today live in working-poor families.

Currently, it appears that many of these revolutionary changes will be most extreme among children born within a decade of this writing. By historical standards, family size can decline comparatively little below the level expected for children born in the mid-1990s. Divorce, the major contributor to one-parent family living, has changed little since the late 1970s. By the year 2000, a large majority of children will live in dual-earner or one-parent families, a majority of preschoolers will receive substantial nonparental care while parents work, and only a small minority, even among newborns, will live in idealized "Ozzie and Harriet" families. Future changes in parents' education, in real income, poverty, and income inequality, and in welfare recipiency appear less certain, partly because they may be more responsive to specific public policies than are family size, divorce, and whether fathers and mothers work outside the home.

Regardless of future public policies, however, it seems likely that the fundamental transformations that have occurred during the past 150 years in the family, the economy, and the society will not be undone. Today, as throughout America's history, most children live with their parents and rely on them to provide for their economic support and day-to-day care. Yet a majority of children—both historically and today—have experienced either the loss of a parent from the home or economic insecurity, or both. Nevertheless, as a result of 150 years of revolutionary change in parents' work, in the family economy, and in the broader economy and society, America's children have entered a new age.

■ READING 23

What Children Think about Their Working Parents

Ellen Galinsky

Despite all they hear and read proclaiming that working is okay or even good for children, if parents feel there is a problem about work and family life, they define the solution as *simply* having more time with their child.

We asked parents in our Ask the Children survey, "If *you* were granted one wish to change the way that your work affects your child's life, what would that wish be?" The largest proportion of parents—22 percent—wished to "have more time with their child." An additional 16 percent wished to "work less time."

We also asked parents another open-ended question: "If *your child* were granted one wish to change the way that your work affects his/her life, what would that wish be?" The largest proportion of parents—21 percent—thought their child would want "more time with me." An additional 19 percent thought their child would want them to work less time, and 16 percent thought their children would want them "not to have to go to work." Taken together, 56 percent of parents mentioned time.

In this chapter, we explore the issue of time. Why does the debate about quality time versus quantity time persist? Does the amount of time that children say that they have with their parents affect how they feel about their parents' parenting? Do other aspects of time matter, such as the kinds of activities parents and children do together and whether children's time with parents is rushed or calm? What does the research say about the impact of time together on children's development? Is this another either/or debate—quality time *or* quantity time—as many have portrayed it? And finally and very importantly, do children and parents feel the same way about having time together?

WHY WON'T THE DEBATE ABOUT QUALITY TIME VERSUS QUANTITY TIME GO AWAY?

This debate reminds me of a punching bag that is slugged, even beaten down, but rebounds right back up. For four decades, this debate has had real staying power. Clearly it strikes a resonant cord.

In the 1960s, researchers looked at children in orphanages who failed to thrive and extrapolated this result to children who experienced daily separations from their employed mothers. Others countered that it is not the *quantity* of time that matters, but what happens in that time—the *quality* of time—that is important. And besides, they noted, the prolonged separations children experience from parents in orphanages are not the same as daily separations. The embers of this debate were fanned into flame again in the 1980s when findings from a few studies found that infants whose mothers were away from them for more than 20 hours a week were at risk for being insecurely attached.

Many parents don't seem to like the notion of quality time. In our one-on-one interviews, some described it as a rationalization for parents to spend less time with their children. A cellular phone advertisement that ran in the late 1990s became a symbol—in fact, a lightning rod—for the issue of quality versus quantity time. In this ad, a child approaches her mother just before the mother is to leave for work. She and her siblings want to go to the beach. When the mother refuses, the child asks when she can be a "client." The mother pauses—then tells her children that they have 3 minutes to get ready to go the beach. The last shot shows the mother sitting on the beach making a conference call on her cellular phone while her children play nearby in the sand.

A mother of a 9-week-old child, who has just returned to work from maternity leave, comments:

> I would say that in general this generation of children may be getting signals that my generation didn't get—that they come in second. It is in this ad about this woman on the phone and the kid wants to go to the beach [and says to her mother,] "When am I going to be a client?" [The mother] gives such a mixed message. Instead of saying, "You're right. We are going to the beach," it's "We are going to the beach and I'm doing my conference call while you play around. And I'll [at least] make sure that you don't cut your foot on shells."

It is clear to many parents that one shouldn't make a distinction between the amount of time one spends with his or her children and what happens in that time. Both the quality and quantity of the time that parents and child share are important. Yet, when asked about their *one* wish to change the way their work affects their child, parents emphasize the *quantity* of time per se: They wish for "more time." What is going on?

WHAT IS GOING ON ABOUT TIME IN TODAY'S FAMILIES?

How Much Time Are Employed Parents Spending with Their Children?

To answer the question of time employed parents spend, let's compare two studies that were conducted 20 years apart: the Families and Work Institute's 1997 National Study of the Changing Workforce and the U.S. Department of Labor's 1977 Quality of Employment Survey (QES).[1]

My colleagues Terry Bond and Jennifer Swanberg and I find—no surprise—that in dual-earner families[2] with children under 18, mothers spend more time doing things and caring for children than fathers on workdays (3.2 hours for mothers versus 2.3 hours for fathers). We also find—again no surprise—that mothers today spend more time than fathers with their children on days off work (8.3 hours for mothers versus 6.4 hours for fathers).

But we find—to the surprise of many—that the gap between mothers and fathers in dual-earner families has narrowed considerably in the past 20 years. Although the amount of time that mothers spend with their children on workdays has not changed in a statistically significant way, fathers have increased the amount of time they spend with children by a half hour.

The 1997 National Study of the Changing Workforce also found that over the past 20 years fathers have increased the time they spend with their children by slightly more than 1 hour on nonwork days, whereas mothers' time has again remained the same.

When the Families and Work Institute released these findings in 1998, the media and public reactions were swift and strong. A few women wrote prominent editorials skeptical of the veracity of the findings, stating, for example, in *The New York Times* that "super dads need a reality check,"[3] whereas many men, like Matt Lauer, host of the *Today* show, gave the findings a high five sign. At last, good news for dads, he said to me.

The public reaction echoes the private fault line between men and women on the subject of time with children. Women ask, "Is he really caring for the children or is he just 'Dad, the helper,' 'Dad, the babysitter?' " "Why does he always wait until I ask him to be with the kids?" "Why doesn't he know what they like to eat for lunch and who their friends are?" Men ask, "Why does she always criticize what I do? When I try to do more, all I get are complaints, complaints, complaints." Or, "I am doing more, but nobody seems to notice."

Are men exaggerating? Are they really spending more time with their children? The 1997 National Study of the Changing Workforce didn't ask parents to keep time diaries, but it did have a reality check, as *The York Times* called it: We asked fathers and mothers how much time their *partners* spent with the children. Although of course our findings are estimates, we found—again a surprise to many—that mothers' estimates of their husbands parallel the amount of time fathers report spending with their children. So fathers do not seem to be exaggerating—at least according to wives.

Furthermore, because employed mothers have managed to keep constant the amount of time they spend with their children, because fathers have increased their time, and because families have fewer children today than they did 20 years ago, it appears that employed parents indeed are spending somewhat more time with their children than they were two decades ago.

Where do parents get more time? Certainly not from their workdays. For employed fathers with children under 18, the 40-hour workweek is a myth. On average, including paid and unpaid time and including part-time and full-time work, fathers work 50.9 hours per week and mothers work 41.4 hours. By our calculations, fathers' total work time has increased by 3.1 hours per week in the past 20 years, and mothers' time has increased by 5.2 hours.[4]

There has also been an increase in the amount of time that parents spend on their jobs while at home. Almost one in three parents spends time on a weekly basis doing work at home that is directly related to his or her job. The proportion of parents who take work home from the job once a week or more has increased 10 percent since 1977, while the proportion who never take work home from the job has decreased by 16 percent.

So if parents are spending more time at work and fathers are spending more time with their children, where has this increased time come from? Employed parents know the answer to that question. They are spending less time on themselves:

> I haven't set aside time for myself all these years. That's one thing I really need to start working on, just for my own sanity.

On average, fathers in dual-earner families report they have 1.2 hours for themselves on workdays. Mothers have about 18 minutes less—0.9 hour per workday. This figure has decreased quite significantly over the past 20 years. On average, fathers in dual-earner families in 1997 had 54 fewer minutes for themselves on workdays than fathers did in

1977, while mothers have 42 fewer minutes for themselves on workdays today than mothers did in 1977.[5]

Even on days off work, fathers' time for themselves has also decreased—from 5.1 hours to 3.3 hours, a change of 1.8 hours over the past 20 years. Mothers' time for themselves on days off work has also decreased from 3.3 hours to 2.5 hours, a change of 0.8 hour.[6] So while both parents are sacrificing "time for themselves" to spend more time with their children, fathers have done so more than mothers (who, granted, were spending more time with their children to begin with).

WHAT DID WE FIND ABOUT TIME, EMPLOYED PARENTS, AND CHILDREN?

How Much Time Are Employed Parents Spending with Individual Children?

In the Ask the Children study,[7] we looked at how much time employed parents spend with just one of their children, randomly selected. Overall, employed mothers report spending about an hour more with their child than employed fathers on workdays (3.8 hours for mothers compared with 2.7 hours for fathers). On nonworkdays, mothers also report spending about an hour more with their child than employed fathers: 7.7 hours for mothers and 6.6 hours for fathers.[8]

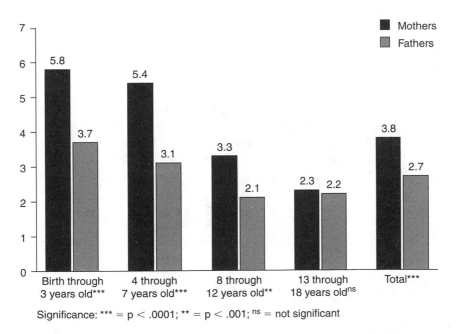

FIGURE 1   *Employed Parents: Hours Spent with Their Child on Workdays*

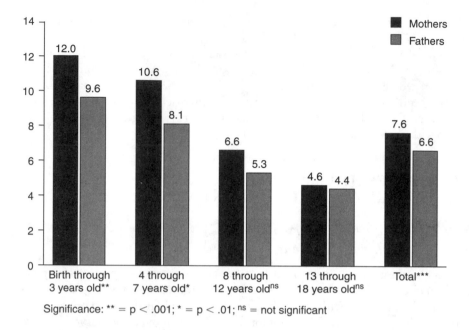

FIGURE 2   *Employed Parents: Hours Spent with Their Child on Nonworkdays*

When we look at the amount of time parents spend with children of different ages, there are shifts over time. Mothers spend more time with younger children than fathers do. By the teenage years, the amount of time that both parents spend declines—mothers' time more sharply than fathers'—to the point where there are no statistical differences in the amount of time mothers and fathers spend.

The same pattern applies to nonworkdays: Mothers reduce the amount of time they spend considerably as children age, dropping from 12 hours a day with a very young child to 4.6 hours with a teenager. Again, the difference in the amount of time mothers and fathers spend narrows and then disappears as the child grows up.[9] It is not simply that parents with an older child don't pay attention to that child; rather, children of these ages can be quite busy, doing their own thing. A mother with a teenage daughter says:

> I would like to be with my teenage daughter more, but she is so involved with schoolwork, activities, and her friends. Inevitably I will hang around the house weekend after weekend, and the one day that I make plans, she will come up to me and say, "Let's do something together today."

Since a few studies have found differences between how boys and girls are affected by their mothers' and fathers' work, I wondered whether there are gender differences here. I found that mothers spend more time with their daughters on workdays: 42.5 percent of mothers report spending 4.5 hours or more with their daughters on workdays compared with 24 percent who spend this much time with their sons. These differences occur during the teenage years, not when children are very young. In contrast, there is no difference in the amount of time mothers report spending with their daughters and their sons on nonworkdays. Moreover, there are no differences in the amount of time that fathers report spending with their sons and their daughters of all ages on workdays and nonworkdays.

How Much Time Do Children Say They Spend with Their Mothers and Fathers?

Now we turn full circle and look at children's estimates of the time they spend with their parents. Children in the third through twelfth grades were asked about how much time they spend with each of their parents—just the two of them or with other people—on a typical workday and on a typical nonworkday.[10]

Time Spent with Employed Parents on Workdays. The majority of children report spending considerable time with their mothers on workdays, although the amount of time fluctuates, depending on the age of the child. Twenty-nine percent of younger children (8 through 12 years old) say they spend 2 hours or less compared with 35 percent of older children (13 through 18 years old). At the other end of the spectrum, 47 percent of younger children and 35 percent of older children spend 5 hours or more with their mothers on workdays.

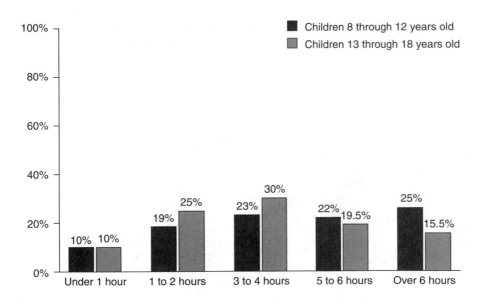

Significance: * = p < .01.

FIGURE 3 *Children Third through Twelfth Grades with Employed Mothers: Time Spent with Mother on Workdays*

There is no difference in the amount of time that sons and daughters report spending with their mothers on workdays (although recall that mothers report spending more time with their teenage daughters than their teenage sons). It is not clear to me why there is a discrepancy between children's and parents' viewpoints, though children have less reason to overestimate than parents.

Children spend less time with their fathers than their mothers on workdays. Overall, 44 percent of children ages 8 through 18 years old report spending 2 hours or less with their fathers on workdays while 27 percent spend 5 hours or more. Interestingly, there is no significant difference in the amount of time younger and older children report spending with their fathers. Neither are there differences between boys and girls

Time Spent with Parents on Nonworkdays.   An impressive 68.5 percent of both younger and older children say that they spend 5 hours or more with their mothers on nonworkdays. Although mothers do not report spending any more time with their daughters on nonworkdays than with their sons, children do report differences—girls say they spend more time with their mothers on nonworkdays than boys do. Here again, the discrepancy is hard to figure out.

Although children spend less time with their fathers than their mothers on nonworkdays, the amount of time they report spending with their fathers is still high: 66 percent of children—boys and girls alike—say that they spend 5 hours or more with their fathers on nonworkdays.

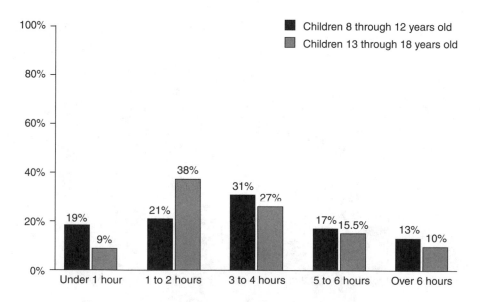

Significance: ns = not significant.

FIGURE 4   *Children Third through Twelfth Grades with Employed Fathers: Time Spent with Father on Workdays*

Do Parents and Children Feel They Have Enough Time Together?

Enough Time—According to Parents. It is one thing to know the *amount* of time that parents and children report spending together, but it is another to know the *psychological meaning* of that time. Do parents feel they have enough time with their child? Do children concur? I especially wondered about fathers. Since fathers spend less time with their children—both by their own and by their children's estimates—are they more likely than mothers to want more time?

Overall, 50 percent of parents with children, birth through 18 years old, say that they have too little time with their child; however, beneath this overall figure *fathers*—much more so than mothers—seem to be yearning to be with their child: 56 percent of fathers versus 44 percent of mothers feel deprived of time with their child!

Because fathers work longer hours, they have less time for their lives off the job. One father of a 9-year-old boy reflects on the fleeting nature of time:

> Time is something, once it's gone, it's gone forever. So, you can look back and think, "Well, gee, I wish I would have spent more time with my kids when they were younger, I wish I would've spent more time with them when they were in high school," whatever. But once time is gone, that's it.

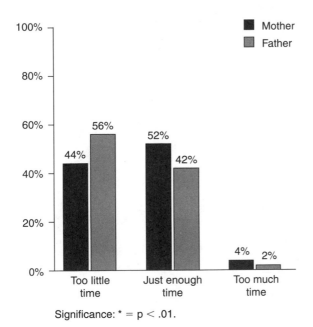

Significance: * = p < .01.

FIGURE 5 *Employed Parents with a Child Birth through 18: Enough Time with Their Child*

Mothers and fathers with a son or a daughter are equally likely to feel that they have too little time with this child. Moreover, parents of children of different ages—from infants to teenagers—are also equally likely to feel they have too little time.

Enough Time—According to Children.   The majority of children 8 through 18 years old feel that they have enough time with their employed mothers and fathers: 67 percent say that they have enough time with their mothers and 60 percent say they have enough time with their fathers. Paralleling the overall difference in the amount of time fathers and mothers spend with their children, children are more likely to feel that they have too little time with their *fathers* than with their mothers.

In our one-on-one interviews, a number of children talked about wanting more time with their fathers. One 12-year-old girl whose father takes frequent business trips says:

> I miss him. He's gone for short times. He calls from where he is. I'd rather have him at home during that time, but I know he has to do it because it's part of his job.

We heard a similar story from another girl whose father often works hard, including on weekends:

> I can't spend much time with him because he's working. Sometimes I go with him to work on the weekends. But I just wish that he wouldn't work so much.

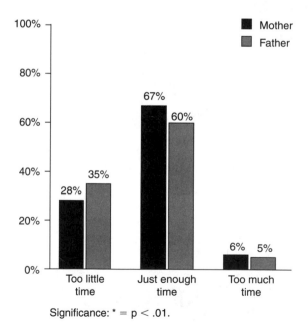

Significance: * = p < .01.

FIGURE 6   *Children Third through Twelfth Grades with Employed Parents: Enough Time with Mothers and Fathers*

Moreover, as has been the pattern thus far, children are far, far more likely to feel that they spend too little time with nonresident fathers (67 percent) than with resident fathers (35 percent).

These findings illustrate why it is so important to ask the children rather than to rely on our own assumptions. The issue of time with children has typically been framed in the public debate as mothers' issue. But when we ask the children, we see that fathers need to be front and center in this discussion as well.

Enough Time—Comparing Children's Views of Employed and Nonemployed Mothers. All of the analyses in this chapter focus on employed mothers, but we also asked the question about having enough time with parents of children who have non-employed mothers. Children with employed mothers are no more likely to feel they have too little time with their mothers than children with nonemployed mothers. Stated differently, children with mothers at home and children with mothers who work are equally likely to feel they have enough time with their mother.

Enough Time—Comparing Children and Mothers. What is also striking—and I must say unanticipated—is the discrepancy between the views of children and those of their mothers on whether they have enough time together. Almost half of mothers (49 percent) with a child 13 through 18 years old feel that they have too little time with their child, whereas less than one third of children (30 percent) this age concur. The results comparing mothers and younger children do not reach statistical significance but follow the same pattern. Perhaps mothers of teenagers anticipate the soon-to-occur loss of everyday contact with their child as the child grows up, goes to college, moves out. So they often long for more time, whereas children may be more eager (though ambivalently so) to separate from their mothers.

Enough Time—Comparing Children and Fathers. Teenagers are more likely than their younger counterparts to want more time with their fathers. Thirty-nine percent of children 13 through 18 years old feel they have too little time with their fathers compared with 29 percent of children 8 through 12 years old. On the other hand, children do not feel as strongly about this issue as fathers. For example, almost two thirds of fathers (64 percent) with a child 13 through 18 years feel that they have too little time with this child, but only 39 percent of children this age feel the same way about time with their fathers.

Unexpected Findings about Employed Parents and Time

In sum, while 53 percent of employed parents with a child 8 through 18 feel they have too little time with their child, only 31 percent of children with employed parents feel the same way.

Typically, when issues of employed parents and time are discussed, the focus is on comparing children with employed versus nonemployed mothers. When we "ask the children," however, we find that there is no statistically significant difference between these two groups of children in feeling that they have too little time with their mothers.

Second, the public discussion has been more concerned with mothers than with fathers. When we turn to children, we find that children 8 through 18 years old are more

TABLE 1 *Employed Mothers and Children with Employed Mothers: Enough Time Together*

	Children 8 through 12 years old	Children 13 through 18 years old
Too little time		
Mother	31%	49%
Child	24.5	30
Just enough time		
Mother	68%	50%
Child	69	65
Too much time		
Mother	1.5%	1%
Child	6.5	5
Significance:	*ns = not significant;*	*** = p < .0001.*

TABLE 2 *Employed Fathers and Children with Employed Fathers: Enough Time Together*

	Children 8 through 12 years old	Children 13 through 18 years old
Too little time		
Father	64%	64%
Child	29	39
Just enough time		
Father	35%	34%
Child	65	56
Too much time		
Father	1%	2%
Child	5.5	5
Significance:	*** = p < .0001;*	** = p < .001.*

likely to feel that they have too little time with their employed *fathers* than with their employed mothers. We also find that fathers—more so than mothers—feel they have too little time with their child.

Third, the public discussion about employed parents and time has centered on younger children, but we find that older children are more likely than younger children to feel that they have too little time with their fathers. Asking the children helps us see that the hidden story about working parents and time is about fathers and teenagers.

Editor's Note: *Notes for this reading can be found in the original source.*

IV Families in Society

During the 1950s and 1960s, family scholars and the mass media presented an image of the typical, normal, or model American family. It included a father, a mother, and two or three children living a middle-class existence in a single-family home in an area neither rural nor urban. Father was the breadwinner, and mother was a full-time homemaker. Both were, by implication, white.

No one denied that many families and individuals fell outside the standard nuclear model. Single persons, one-parent families, two-parent families in which both parents worked, three-generation families, and childless couples abounded. Three- or four-parent families were not uncommon, as one or both divorced spouses often remarried. Many families, moreover, neither white nor well-off, varied from the dominant image. White and seemingly middle-class families of particular ethnic, cultural, or sexual styles also differed from the model. The image scarcely reflected the increasing ratio of older people in the empty nest and retirement parts of the life cycle. But like poverty before its "rediscovery" in the mid-1960s, family complexity and variety existed on some dim fringe of semi-awareness.

When discussed, individuals or families departing from the standard model were analyzed in a context of pathology. Studies of one-parent families or working mothers, for example, focused on the harmful effects to children of such situations. Couples childless by choice were assumed to possess some basic personality inadequacy. Single persons were similarly interpreted, or else thought to be homosexual. Homosexuals symbolized evil, depravity, degradation, and mental illness.

Curiously, although social scientists have always emphasized the pluralism of American society in terms of ethnic groups, religion, and geographic region, the concept of pluralism had rarely been applied to the family.

In the wake of the social upheavals of the 1960s and 1970s, middle-class "mainstream" attitudes toward women's roles, sexuality, and the family were transformed. Despite the backlash that peaked in the 1980s, the "traditional" family did not return. American families became increasingly diverse, and Americans were increasingly willing to extend the notion of pluralism to family life.

The selections in this part of the book discuss not only diversity in families, but also the reality that families are both embedded in and sensitive to changes in the social structure and economics of American life. As Lillian B. Rubin writes in "Families on the Fault Line," words such as *downsizing*, *restructuring*, and *reengineering* have become all too familiar and even terrifying to blue-collar workers and their families. Rubin had carried

309

out a similar study of working-class families two decades earlier. In the 1970s, she found that while these families were never entirely secure, they felt they had a grasp of the American dream. Most owned their own homes, and expected that their children would do even better. In the more recent study, the people Rubin interviewed perceived a discontinuity between past and present, a sense that something had gone very wrong in the country.

Thirty-five percent of the men in the study were either unemployed at the time or had experienced bouts of unemployment. Parents and children had given up hope of upward mobility, or even that the children could own homes comparable to the one they had grown up in. The families, particularly the men, were angry, yet perplexed about who or what to blame—the government, high taxes, immigrants, minorities, women—for displacing men from the workplace.

The economic pressures on families since the mid-1970s have done as much as feminism to draw women into the paid workforce. The two-parent family in which both parents work is the form that now comes closest to being the "typical American family." In the 1950s, the working mother was considered deviant, even though many women were employed in the labor force. It was taken for granted that maternal employment must be harmful to children; much current research on working mothers still takes this "social problem" approach to the subject.

Cynthia Fuchs Epstein discusses how escalating time pressures in the professional workplace have created barriers to women's equality. A *true professional* is now defined by a willingness to commit oneself to overtime. As a result, today's lawyers, doctors, and managers, both men and women, are finding it difficult to build a career and a family at the same time. In addition, persisting stereotypes about gender roles influence both individual decision making and workplace policy. Epstein also argues that these continuing cultural stereotypes of gender roles are reinforced by the brand of feminism that emphasizes women's "difference."

What happens inside the family as women are expected to contribute to family income? Arlie Hochschild and Anne Machung take a close look at the emotional dynamics inside the family when both parents work full-time and the "second shift"—the work of caring for children and maintaining the home—is not shared equitably. The selection from their book portrays a painful dilemma shared by many couples in their study: The men saw themselves as having equal marriages; they were doing more work around the house than their fathers had done and more than they thought other men did. The women, whose lives were different from their own mothers', saw their husbands' contributions as falling far short of true equality. They resented having to carry more than their share of the "second shift," yet stifled their angry feelings in order to preserve their marriages. Still, this strategy took its toll on love and intimacy.

The next group of articles address family diversity along a number of dimensions—economic status, race, ethnicity, and sexual orientation. In recent years, family researchers have recognized that diversity is more complicated than previously thought. It's too simple to sort people into distinct categories—African Americans, Hispanics, Asians, European Americans, or gays. These aspects of diversity cross-cut one another, along with many other aspects of difference—such as social class, religion, region, family structure (e.g., stepfamilies), and many more. Further, as Roberto Suro points out, intermarriage between different groups has been increasing in recent years. For the first time, the forms for the 2000 census will allow people to identify themselves as belonging to many racial categories as they feel necessary.

There is also great diversity within groups. In his article Ronald L. Taylor explores diversity among African American families. He recalls being troubled that the stereotypes of black Americans that appeared in the media as well as in social science did not reflect the families he knew growing up in a small southern city. The dominant image of black families remains the low-income, single-parent family living in a crime-ridden inner-city neighborhood. Yet only a quarter of African American families fits that description. All African Americans share a common history of slavery and segregation, and they still face discrimination in housing and employment. Taylor discusses the impact of these past and present features on African American family life.

Latino families are now emerging as America's largest "minority." They are more diverse than other groups, as Maxine Baca Zinn and Barbara Wells show in their article. Mexican Americans are the largest group among Latinos and have been the most studied. But Puerto Ricans, Cubans, and Central and South Americans differ from those of Mexican background, and among themselves. These differences are not just cultural, but reflect the immigrants' social and economic status in their home country as well as the reasons for and the timing of their departure for the United States.

Sexual orientation—whether one is gay or straight—is an identity that cuts across all racial, ethnic, and class categories. Recently, homosexuality has become a major battleground in the culture wars, with the issue of gay marriage making headlines. In early 2000, the Vermont legislature debated whether same-sex partners should be granted the same right to marry as heterosexuals, or whether they should be granted "domestic partnerships" instead. These would include all the rights married couples enjoy except the name. In the end, lawmakers voted for domestic partnerships, making Vermont the first state to grant legal recognition of gay couples.

In her article, Laura Benkov analyzes the tension between traditional and emerging definitions of *family*. The first is based on heterosexual, procreative unions; the emerging one, based on the quality of relationships, can encompass gay and lesbian partners choosing to have children. Such children, she argues, should not have fewer legal rights than those born in more traditional families.

Another major change in family life is that people are living longer than ever before. In her article, Matilda White Riley discusses the new variations of family life resulting from the "revolution in longevity." During this century, life expectancy has risen from under 50 to over 70 years of age—and it continues to rise. This sharp increase in life expectancy has been accompanied by a greatly expanded kinship structure persisting through time. People used to have lots of relatives, but they didn't live long. Now people begin with smaller families, but these persist and grow through marriage, procreation, and remarriage. Kinship structures used to look like short, stubby, ephemeral bushes. Now they have sprouted into long, slender trees, with many branches. Riley argues optimistically that the new kinship structure offers more choice for selecting relationships that can provide emotional support.

In earlier years—the so-called good old days—when death took family members at relatively young ages, grandparents were a rare family species. Young people today, even adolescents and twenty- and thirty-somethings, grow up knowing grandparents, a phenomenon that has developed largely since World War II as a result of medical advances.

The grandfather of one of the editors of this volume had his life saved by the then–miracle drug, penicillin, and he went on to live to 98 years of age. Because grandparenthood is so common today, it should not, as Andrew J. Cherlin and Frank F. Furstenberg Jr. observe, be taken for granted. Widespread grandparenthood is a phenomenon of the last half-century, and, as they show, it is having a significant effect on contemporary family relations.

Scientific progress is usually positive, but, as with most things in life, there can be unanticipated and unwanted outcomes. As gender and family roles have changed, and as modern methods of contraception have become available, society has experienced a sexual revolution. Part of it, perhaps the most dramatic part, has been the increasing sexual activity of teenagers, especially of girls. Teenage girls who are having sex are also experiencing more pregnancies. In the first reading in Chapter 11 on family troubles, Kristin Luker argues that, while teenage pregnancy is indeed a problem, its causes are often misinterpreted. It is not, she argues, simply an issue of immorality or of young women out of control. Rather, she argues, it makes far more sense to understand that teenage pregnancy partly reflects limited opportunities for realizing personal achievement, fulfillment, and enhancement of self-esteem; and also results from changed cultural expectations about teenage sex and the tendencies of teens to take chances by not using birth control consistently.

Katherine S. Newman's article reports on her ethnographic studies of family life among the working poor in America's inner cities. She contrasts media images of "the underclass"—with its drug-addicted mothers and swaggering, criminal men who father children by as many different women as possible—with the realities she observed. She found that while there are families that unfortunately fit this description, they are a small minority. Moreover, such families are despised by the majority of inner-city residents and do not reflect the dominant family values of those communities. Nevertheless, despite their values, these families are not carbon copies of mainstream, middle-class ones. Newman shows how economic pressures at the bottom of the income scale affect the psychological and social functioning of people who are trying to "play by the rules."

The most dramatic and painful kind of family trouble is violence among family members. In their article, Neil Jacobson and John Gottman report on some findings from their program of research on men and women in abusive relationships. These authors observed more than 200 couples interacting, and discovered that many common beliefs about battering are mistaken—for example, that both men and women are batterers, or that women can control the violence of their partners by changing their own behavior.

In his article, Barry Glassner also debunks the "Husbands are Battered as Often as Wives" headlines that appear in the media from time to time. Glassner elaborates on the theme touched on earlier by Katherine Newman—the tendency of the media to feature frightening but misleading stories about recent family trends in the United States. He uses specific examples to show how problems such as teenage pregnancy—"babies having babies"—came to be seen as a major threat to the security and survival of the country. Glassner argues that such stories misdirect public attention from the actual causes of social problems. For example, it is teens who are already poor and attending bad schools who get pregnant in the first place (Luker makes the same point in her article). Nevertheless, stories about pregnant 10-year-olds or battered husbands never seem to die, even when they have been shown to be false.

9 *Work and Family*

Families on the Fault Line

Lillian B. Rubin

THE BARDOLINOS

It has been more than three years since I first met the Bardolino family, three years in which to grow accustomed to words like *downsizing, restructuring,* or the most recent one, *reengineering;* three years in which to learn to integrate them into the language so that they now fall easily from our lips. But these are no ordinary words, at least not for Marianne and Tony Bardolino.

The last time we talked, Tony had been unemployed for about three months and Marianne was working nights at the telephone company and dreaming about the day they could afford a new kitchen. They seemed like a stable couple then—a house, two children doing well in school, Marianne working without complaint, Tony taking on a reasonable share of the family work. Tony, who had been laid off from the chemical plant where he had worked for ten years, was still hoping he'd be called back and trying to convince himself their lives were on a short hold, not on a catastrophic downhill slide. But instead of calling workers back, the company kept cutting its work force. Shortly after our first meeting, it became clear: There would be no recall. Now, as I sit in the little cottage Marianne shares with her seventeen-year-old daughter, she tells the story of these last three years.

"When we got the word that they wouldn't be calling Tony back, that's when we really panicked; I mean *really* panicked. We didn't know what to do. Where was Tony going to find another job, with the recession and all that? It was like the bottom really dropped out. Before that, we really hoped he'd be called back any day. It wasn't just crazy; they told the guys when they laid them off, you know, that it would be three, four months at most. So we hoped. I mean, sure we worried; in these times, you'd be crazy not to worry. But he'd been laid off for a couple of months before and called back, so we thought maybe it's the same thing. Besides, Tony's boss was so sure the guys would be coming back in a couple of months; so you tried to believe it was true."

She stops speaking, takes a few sips of coffee from the mug she holds in her hand, then says with a sigh, "I don't really know where to start. So much happened, and sometimes you can't even keep track. Mostly what I remember is how scared we were. Tony started to look for a job, but there was nowhere to look. The union couldn't help; there were no jobs in the industry. So he looked in the papers, and he made the rounds of all the places around here. He even went all the way to San Francisco and some of the places down near the airport there. But there was nothing.

"At first, I kept thinking, *Don't panic; he'll find something.* But after his unemployment ran out, we couldn't pay the bills, so then you can't help getting panicked, can you?"

She stops again, this time staring directly at me, as if wanting something. But I'm not sure what, so I sit quietly and wait for her to continue. Finally, she demands, "Well, can you?"

I understand now; she wants reassurance that her anxiety wasn't out of line, that it's not she who's responsible for the rupture in the family. So I say, "It sounds as if you feel guilty because you were anxious about how the family would manage."

"Yeah, that's right," she replies as she fights her tears. "I keep thinking maybe if I hadn't been so awful, I wouldn't have driven Tony away." But as soon as the words are spoken, she wants to take them back. "I mean, I don't know, maybe I wasn't that bad. We were both so depressed and scared, maybe there's nothing I could have done. But I think about it a lot, and I didn't have to blame him so much and keep nagging at him about how worried I was. It wasn't his fault; he was trying.

"It was just that we looked at it so different. I kept thinking he should take anything, but he only wanted a job like the one he had. We fought about that a lot. I mean, what difference does it make what kind of job it is? No, I don't mean that; I know it makes a difference. But when you have to support a family, that should come first, shouldn't it?"

As I listen, I recall my meeting with Tony a few days earlier and how guiltily he, too, spoke about his behavior during that time. "I wasn't thinking about her at all," he explained. "I was just so mad about what happened; it was like the world came crashing down on me. I did a little too much drinking, and then I'd just crawl into a hole, wouldn't even know whether Marianne or the kids were there or not. She kept saying it was like I wasn't there. I guess she was right, because I sure didn't want to be there, not if I couldn't support them."

"Is that the only thing you were good for in the family?" I asked him.

"Good point," he replied laughing. "Maybe not, but it's hard to know what else you're good for when you can't do that."

I push these thoughts aside and turn my attention back to Marianne. "Tony told me that he did get a job after about a year," I remark.

"Yeah, did he tell you what kind of job it was?"

"Not exactly, only that it didn't work out."

"Sure, he didn't tell you because he's still so ashamed about it. He was out of work so long that even he finally got it that he didn't have a choice. So he took this job as a dishwasher in this restaurant. It's one of those new kind of places with an open kitchen, so there he was, standing there washing dishes in front of everybody. I mean, we used to go there to eat sometimes, and now he's washing the dishes and the whole town sees him doing it. He felt so ashamed, like it was such a comedown, that he'd come home even worse than when he wasn't working.

"That's when the drinking really started heavy. Before that he'd drink, but it wasn't so bad. After he went to work there, he'd come home and drink himself into a coma. I was working days by then, and I'd try to wait up until he came home. But it didn't matter; all he wanted to do was go for that bottle. He drank a lot during the day, too, so sometimes I'd come home and find him passed out on the couch and he never got to work that day. That's when I was maddest of all. I mean, I felt sorry for him having to do that work. But I was afraid he'd get fired."

"Did he?"

"No, he quit after a couple of months. He heard there was a chemical plant down near L.A. where he might get a job. So he left. I mean, we didn't exactly separate, but we didn't exactly not. He didn't ask me and the kids to go with him; he just went. It didn't make any difference. I didn't trust him by then, so why would I leave my job and pick up the kids and move when we didn't even know if he'd find work down there?

"I think he went because he had to get away. Anyway, he never found any decent work there either. I know he had some jobs, but I never knew exactly what he was doing. He'd call once in awhile, but we didn't have much to say to each other then. I always figured he wasn't making out so well because he didn't send much money the whole time he was gone."

As Tony tells it, he was in Los Angeles for nearly a year, every day an agony of guilt and shame. "I lived like a bum when I was down there. I had a room in a place that wasn't much better than a flop house, but it was like I couldn't get it together to go find something else. I wasn't making much money, but I had enough to live decent. I felt like what difference did it make how I lived?"

He sighs—a deep, sad sound—then continues, "I couldn't believe what I did, I mean that I really walked out on my family. My folks were mad as hell at me. When I told them what I was going to do, my father went nuts, said I shouldn't come back to his house until I got some sense again. But I couldn't stay around with Marianne blaming me all the time."

He stops abruptly, withdraws to someplace inside himself for a few moments, then turns back to me. "That's not fair. She wasn't the only one doing the blaming. I kept beating myself up, too, you know, blaming myself, like I did something wrong.

"Anyhow, I hated to see what it was doing to the kids; they were like caught in the middle with us fighting and hollering, or else I was passed out drunk. I didn't want them to have to see me like that, and I couldn't help it. So I got out."

For Marianne, Tony's departure was both a relief and a source of anguish. "At first I was glad he left; at least there was some peace in the house. But then I got so scared; I didn't know if I could make it alone with the kids. That's when I sold the house. We were behind in our payments, and I knew we'd never catch up. The bank was okay; they said they'd give us a little more time. But there was no point.

"That was really hard. It was our home; we worked so hard to get it. God, I hated to give it up. We were lucky, though. We found this place here. It's near where we used to live, so the kids didn't have to change schools, or anything like that. It's small, but at least it's a separate little house, not one of those grungy apartments." She interrupts herself with a laugh, "Well, 'house' makes it sound a lot more than it is, doesn't it?"

"How did your children manage all this?"

"It was real hard on them. My son had just turned thirteen when it all happened, and he was really attached to his father. He couldn't understand why Tony left us, and he was real angry for a long time. At first, I thought he'd be okay, you know, that he'd get over it. But then he got into some bad company. I think he was doing some drugs, although he still won't admit that. Anyway, one night he and some of his friends stole a car. I think they just wanted to go for a joyride; they didn't mean to really steal it forever. But they got caught, and he got sent to juvenile hall.

"I called Tony down in L.A. and told him what happened. It really shocked him; he started to cry on the phone. I never saw him cry before, not with all our trouble. But he just cried and cried. When he got off the phone, he took the first plane he could get, and he's been back up here ever since.

"Jimmy's trouble really changed everything around. When Tony came back, he didn't want to do anything to get Jimmy out of juvy right away. He thought he ought to stay there for a while; you know, like to teach him a lesson. I was mad at first because Jimmy wanted to come home so bad; he was so scared. But now I see Tony was right.

"Anyhow, we let Jimmy stay there for five whole days, then Tony's parents lent us the money to bail him out and get him a lawyer. He made a deal so that if Jimmy pleaded guilty, he'd get a suspended sentence. And that's what happened. But the judge laid down the law, told him if he got in one little bit of trouble again, he'd go to jail. It put the fear of God into the boy."

For Tony, his son's brush with the law was like a shot in the arm. "It was like I had something really important to do, to get that kid back on track. We talked it over and Marianne agreed it would be better if Jimmy came to live with me. She's too soft with the kids; I've got better control. And I wanted to make it up to him, too, to show him he could count on me again. I figured the whole trouble came because I left them, and I wanted to set it right.

"So when he got out of juvy, he went with me to my folks' house where I was staying. We lived there for awhile until I got this job. It's no great shakes, a kind of general handyman. But it's a job, and right from the start I made enough so we could move into this here apartment. So things are going pretty good right now."

"Pretty good" means that Jimmy, now sixteen, has settled down and is doing well enough in school to talk about going to college. For Tony, too, things have turned around. He set up his own business as an independent handyman several months ago and, although the work isn't yet regular enough to allow him to quit his job, his reputation as a man who can fix just about anything is growing. Last month the business actually made enough money to pay his bills. "I'll hang onto the job for a while, even if the business gets going real good, because we've got a lot of catching up to do. I don't mind working hard; I like it. And being my own boss, boy, that's really great," he concludes exultantly.

"Do you think you and Marianne will get together again?"

"I sure hope so; it's what I'm working for right now. She says she's not sure, but she's never made a move to get a divorce. That's a good sign, isn't it?"

When I ask Marianne the same question, she says, "Tony wants to, but I still feel a little scared. You know, I never thought I could manage without him, but then when I was forced to, I did. Now, I don't know what would happen if we got together again. It wouldn't be like it was before. I just got promoted to supervisor, so I have a lot of responsibility on my job. I'm a different person, and I don't know how Tony would like that. He says he likes it fine, but I figure we should wait a while and see what happens. I mean, what if things get tough again for him? I don't ever want to live through anything like these last few years."

"Yet you've never considered divorce."

She laughs, "You sound like Tony." Then more seriously, "I don't want a divorce if I can help it. Right now, I figure if we got through these last few years and still kind of like each other, maybe we've got a chance."

* * *

In the opening pages of this book, I wrote that when the economy falters, families tremble. The Bardolinos not only trembled, they cracked. Whether they can patch up the cracks and put the family back together again remains an open question. But the experience of families like those on the pages of this book provides undeniable evidence of the fundamental link between the public and private arenas of modern life.

No one has to tell the Bardolinos or their children about the many ways the structural changes in the economy affect family life. In the past, a worker like Tony Bardolino didn't need a high level of skill or literacy to hold down a well-paying semiskilled job in a steel mill or an automobile plant. A high school education, often even less, was enough. But an economy that relies most heavily on its service sector needs highly skilled and educated workers to fill its better-paying jobs, leaving people like Tony scrambling for jobs at the bottom of the economic order.

The shift from the manufacturing to the service sector, the restructuring of the corporate world, the competition from low-wage workers in underdeveloped countries that entices American corporations to produce their goods abroad, all have been going on for decades; all are expected to accelerate through the 1990s. The manufacturing sector, which employed just over 26 percent of American workers in 1970, already had fallen to nearly 18 percent by 1991. And experts predict a further drop to 12.5 percent by the year 2000. "This is the end of the post–World War boom era. We are never going back to what we knew," says employment analyst Dan Lacey, publisher of the newsletter *Workplace Trends*.

Yet the federal government has not only failed to offer the help working-class families need, but as a sponsor of a program to nurture capitalism elsewhere in the world it has become party to the exodus of American factories to foreign lands. Under the auspices of the U.S. Agency for International Development (AID), for example, Decaturville Sportswear, a company that used to be based in Tennessee, has moved to El Salvador. AID not only gave grants to trade organizations in El Salvador to recruit Decaturville but also subsidized the move by picking up the $5 million tab for the construction of a new plant, footing the bill for over $1 million worth of insurance, and providing low-interest loans for other expenses involved in the move.

It's a sweetheart deal for Decaturville Sportswear and the other companies that have been lured to move south of the border under this program. They build new factories at minimal cost to themselves, while their operating expenses drop dramatically. In El Salvador, Decaturville is exempted from corporate taxes and shipping duties. And best of all, the hourly wage for factory workers there is forty-five cents an hour; in the United States the minimum starting wage for workers doing the same job is $4.25.

True, like Tony Bardolino, many of the workers displaced by downsizing, restructuring, and corporate moves like these will eventually find other work. But like him also, they'll probably have to give up what little security they knew in the past. For the forty-hour-a-week steady job that pays a decent wage and provides good benefits is quickly becoming a thing of the past. Instead, as part of the new lean, clean, mean look of corporate America, we now have what the federal government and employment agencies call "contingent" workers—a more benign name for what some labor economists refer to as "disposable" or "throwaway" workers.

It's a labor strategy that comes in several forms. Generally, disposable workers are hired in part-time or temporary jobs to fill an organizational need and are released as soon as the work load lightens. But when union contracts call for employees to join the union after thirty days on the job, some unscrupulous employers fire contingent workers on the twenty-ninth day and bring in a new crew. However it's done, disposable workers earn less than those on the regular payroll and their jobs rarely come with benefits of any kind. Worse yet, they set off to work each morning fearful and uncertain, not knowing how the day will end, worrying that by nightfall they'll be out of a job.

The government's statistics on these workers are sketchy, but Labor Secretary Robert Reich estimates that they now make up nearly one-third of the existing work force. This means that about thirty-four million men and women, most of whom want steady, full-time work, start each day as contingent and/or part-time workers. Indeed, so widespread is this practice now that in some places temporary employment agencies are displacing the old ones that sought permanent placements for their clients.

Here again, class makes a difference. For while it's true that managers and professionals now also are finding themselves disposable, most of the workers who have become so easily expendable are in the lower reaches of the work order. And it's they who are likely to have the fewest options. These are the workers, the unskilled and the semiskilled—the welders, the forklift operators, the assemblers, the clerical workers, and the like—who are most likely to seem to management to be interchangeable. Their skills are limited; their job tasks are relatively simple and require little training. Therefore, they're able to move in and perform with reasonable efficiency soon after they come on the job. Whatever lost time or productivity a company may suffer by not having a steady crew of workers is compensated by the savings in wages and benefits the employment of throwaway workers permits. A resolution that brings short-term gains for the company at the long-term expense of both the workers and the nation. For when a person can't count on a permanent job, a critical element binding him or her to society is lost.

THE TOMALSONS

When I last met the Tomalsons, Gwen was working as a clerk in the office of a large Manhattan company and was also a student at a local college where she was studying nursing. George Tomalson, who had worked for three years in a furniture factory, where he laminated plastic to wooden frames, had been thrown out of a job when the company went bankrupt. He seemed a gentle man then, unhappy over the turn his life had taken but still wanting to believe that it would come out all right.

Now, as he sits before me in the still nearly bare apartment, George is angry. "If you're a black man in this country, you don't have a chance, that's all, not a chance. It's like no matter how hard you try, you're nothing but trash. I've been looking for work for over two years now, and there's nothing. White people are complaining all the time that black folks are getting a break. Yeah, well, I don't know who those people are, because it's not me or anybody else I know. People see a black man coming, they run the other way, that's what I know."

"You haven't found any work at all for two years?" I ask.

"Some temporary jobs, a few weeks sometimes, a couple of months once, mostly doing shit work for peanuts. Nothing I could count on."

"If you could do any kind of work you want, what would you do?"

He smiles, "That's easy; I'd be a carpenter. I'm good with my hands, and I know a lot about it," he says, holding his hands out, palms up, and looking at them proudly. But his mood shifts quickly; the smile disappears; his voice turns harsh. "But that's not going to happen. I tried to get into the union, but there's no room there for a black guy. And in this city, without being in the union, you don't have a chance at a construction job. They've got it all locked up, and they're making sure they keep it for themselves."

When I talk with Gwen later, she worries about the intensity of her husband's resentment. "It's not like George; he's always been a real even guy. But he's moody now, and he's so angry, I sometimes wonder what he might do. This place is a hell hole," she says, referring to the housing project they live in. "It's getting worse all the time; kids with guns, all the drugs, grown men out of work all around. I'll bet there's hardly a man in this whole place who's got a job, leave alone a good one."

"Just what is it you worry about?"

She hesitates, clearly wondering whether to speak, how much to tell me about her fears, then says with a shrug, "I don't know, everything, I guess. There's so much crime and drugs and stuff out there. You can't help wondering whether he'll get tempted." She stops herself, looks at me intently, and says, "Look, don't get me wrong; I know it's crazy to think like that. He's not that kind of person. But when you live in times like these, you can't help worrying about everything.

"We both worry a lot about the kids at school. Every time I hear about another kid shot while they're at school, I get like a raving lunatic. What's going on in this world that kids are killing kids? Doesn't anybody care that so many black kids are dying like that? It's like a black child's life doesn't count for anything. How do they expect our kids to grow up to be good citizens when nobody cares about them?

"It's one of the things that drives George crazy, worrying about the kids. There's no way you can keep them safe around here. Sometimes I wonder why we send them to school. They're not getting much of an education there. Michelle just started, but Julia's in the fifth grade, and believe me she's not learning much.

"We sit over her every night to make sure she does her homework and gets it right. But what good is it if the people at school aren't doing their job. Most of the teachers there don't give a damn. They just want the paycheck and the hell with the kids. Everybody knows it's not like that in the white schools; white people wouldn't stand for it.

"I keep thinking we've got to get out of here for the sake of the kids. I'd love to move someplace, anyplace out of the city where the schools aren't such a cesspool. But," she says dejectedly, "we'll never get out if George can't find a decent job. I'm just beginning my nursing career, and I know I've got a future now. But still, no matter what I do or how long I work at it, I can't make enough for that by myself."

George, too, has dreams of moving away, somewhere far from the city streets, away from the grime and the crime. "Look at this place," he says, his sweeping gesture taking in the whole landscape. "Is this any place to raise kids? Do you know what my little girls see every day they walk out the door? Filth, drugs, guys hanging on the corner waiting for trouble.

"If I could get any kind of a decent job, anything, we'd be out of here, far away, someplace outside the city where the kids could breathe clean and see a different life. It's so bad here, I take them over to my mother's a lot after school; it's a better neighborhood. Then we stay over there and eat sometimes. Mom likes it; she's lonely, and it helps us out. Not that she's got that much, but there's a little pension my father left."

"What about Gwen's family? Do they help out, too?"

"Her mother doesn't have anything to help with since her father died. He's long gone; he was killed by the cops when Gwen was a teenager," he says as calmly as if reporting the time of day.

"Killed by the cops." The words leap out at me and jangle my brain. But why do they startle me so? Surely with all the discussion of police violence in the black community in recent years, I can't be surprised to hear that a black man was "killed by the cops."

It's the calmness with which the news is relayed that gets to me. And it's the realization once again of the distance between the lives and experiences of blacks and others, even poor others. Not one white person in this study reported a violent death in the family. Nor did any of the Latino and Asian families, although the Latinos spoke of a difficult and often antagonistic relationship with Anglo authorities, especially the police. But four black families (13 percent) told of relatives who had been murdered, one of the families with two victims—a teenage son and a twenty-two-year-old daughter, both killed in violent street crimes.

But I'm also struck by the fact that Gwen never told me how her father died. True, I didn't ask. But I wonder now why she didn't offer the information. "Gwen didn't tell me," I say, as if trying to explain my surprise.

"She doesn't like to talk about it. Would you?" he replies somewhat curtly.

It's a moment or two before I can collect myself to speak again. Then I comment, "You talk about all this so calmly."

He leans forward, looks directly at me, and shakes his head. When he finally speaks, his voice is tight with the effort to control his rage. "What do you want? Should I rant and rave? You want me to say I want to go out and kill those mothers? Well, yeah, I do. They killed a good man just because he was black. He wasn't a criminal; he was a hard-working guy who just happened to be in the wrong place when the cops were looking for someone to shoot," he says, then sits back and stares stonily at the wall in front of him.

We both sit locked in silence until finally I break it. "How did it happen?"

He rouses himself at the sound of my voice. "They were after some dude who robbed a liquor store, and when they saw Gwen's dad, they didn't ask questions; they shot. The bastards. Then they said it was self-defense, that they saw a gun in his hand. That man never held a gun in his life, and nobody ever found one either. But nothing happens to them; it's no big deal, just another dead nigger," he concludes, his eyes blazing.

It's quiet again for a few moments, then, with a sardonic half smile, he says, "What would a nice, white middle-class lady like you know about any of that? You got all those degrees, writing books and all that. How are you going to write about people like us?"

"I was poor like you once, very poor," I say somewhat defensively.

He looks surprised, then retorts, "Poor and white; it's a big difference."

* * *

Thirty years before the beginning of the Civil War, Alexis de Tocqueville wrote: "If ever America undergoes great revolutions, they will be brought about by the presence of the black race on the soil of the United States; that is to say they will owe their origin, not to the equality, but to the inequality of condition." One hundred and sixty years later, relations between blacks and whites remain one of the great unresolved issues in American life, and "the inequality of condition" that de Tocqueville observed is still a primary part of the experience of black Americans.

I thought about de Tocqueville's words as I listened to George Tomalson and about how the years of unemployment had changed him from, as Gwen said, "a real even guy" to an angry and embittered one. And I was reminded, too, of de Tocqueville's observation that "the danger of conflict between the white and black inhabitants perpetually haunts the imagination of the [white] Americans, like a painful dream." Fifteen generations later we're still paying the cost of those years when Americans held slaves—whites still living in fear, blacks in rage. "People see a black man coming, they run the other way," says George Tomalson.

Yet however deep the cancer our racial history has left on the body of the nation, most Americans, including many blacks, believe that things are better today than they were a few decades ago–a belief that's both true and not true. There's no doubt that in ending the legal basis for discrimination and segregation, the nation took an important step toward fulfilling the promise of equality for all Americans. As more people meet as equals in the workplace, stereotypes begin to fall away and caricatures are transformed into real people. But it's also true that the economic problems of recent decades have raised the level of anxiety in American life to a new high. So although virtually all whites today give verbal assent to the need for racial justice and equality, they also find ways to resist the implementation of the belief when it seems to threaten their own status or economic well-being.

Our schizophrenia about race, our capacity to believe one thing and do another, is not new. Indeed, it is perhaps epitomized by Thomas Jefferson, the great liberator. For surely, as Gordon Wood writes in an essay in the *New York Review of Books*, "there is no greater irony in American history than the fact that America's supreme spokesman for liberty and equality was a lifelong aristocratic owner of slaves."

Jefferson spoke compellingly about the evils of slavery, but he bought, sold, bred, and flogged slaves. He wrote eloquently about equality but he was convinced that blacks were an inferior race and endorsed the racial stereotypes that have characterized African-Americans since their earliest days on this continent. He believed passionately in individual liberty, but he couldn't imagine free blacks living in America, maintaining instead that if the nation considered emancipating the slaves, it must also prepare for their expulsion.

No one talks seriously about expulsion anymore. Nor do many use the kind of language to describe African-Americans that was so common in Jefferson's day. But the duality he embodied—his belief in justice, liberty, and equality alongside his conviction of black inferiority—still lives.

THE RIVERAS

Once again Ana Rivera and I sit at the table in her bright and cheerful kitchen. She's sipping coffee; I'm drinking some bubbly water while we make small talk and get reacquainted. After a while, we begin to talk about the years since we last met. "I'm a grandmother now," she says, her face wreathed in a smile. "My daughter Karen got married and had a baby, and he's the sweetest little boy, smart, too. He's only two and a half, but you should hear him. He sounds like five."

"When I talked to her the last time I was here, Karen was planning to go to college. What happened?" I ask.

She flushes uncomfortably. "She got pregnant, so she had to get married. I was heartbroken at first. She was only nineteen, and I wanted her to get an education so bad. It was awful; she had been working for a whole year to save money for college, then she got pregnant and couldn't go."

"You say she had to get married. Did she ever consider an abortion?"

"I don't know; we never talked about it. We're Catholic," she says by way of explanation. "I mean, I don't believe in abortion." She hesitates, seeming uncertain about what more she wants to say, then adds, "I have to admit, at a time like that, you have to ask yourself what you really believe. I don't think anybody's got the right to take a child's life. But when I thought about what having that baby would do to Karen's life, I couldn't help thinking, *What if . . . ?*" She stops, unable to bring herself to finish the sentence.

"Did you ever say that to Karen?"

"No, I would *never* do that. I didn't even tell my husband I thought such things. But, you know," she adds, her voice dropping to nearly a whisper, "if she had done it, I don't think I would have said a word."

"What about the rest of the kids?"

"Paul's going to be nineteen soon; he's a problem," she sighs. "I mean, he's got a good head, but he won't use it. I don't know what's the matter with kids these days; it's like they want everything but they're not willing to work for anything. He hardly finished high school, so you can't talk to him about going to college. But what's he going to do? These days if you don't have a good education, you don't have a chance. No matter what we say, he doesn't listen, just goes on his smart-alecky way, hanging around the neighborhood with a bunch of no-good kids looking for trouble.

"Rick's so mad, he wants to throw him out of the house. But I say no, we can't do that because then what'll become of him? So we fight about that a lot, and I don't know what's going to happen."

"Does Paul work at all?"

"Sometimes, but mostly not. I'm afraid to think about where he gets money from. His father won't give him a dime. He borrows from me sometimes, but I don't have much to give him. And anyway, Rick would kill me if he knew."

I remember Paul as a gangly, shy sixteen-year-old, no macho posturing, none of the rage that shook his older brother, not a boy I would have thought would be heading for trouble. But then, Karen, too, had seemed so determined to grasp at a life that was different from the one her parents were living. What happens to these kids?

When I talk with Rick about these years, he, too, asks in bewilderment: What happened? "I don't know; we tried so hard to give the kids everything they needed. I mean, sure, we're not rich, and there's a lot of things we couldn't give them. But we were always here for them; we listened; we talked. What happened? First my daughter gets pregnant and has to get married; now my son is becoming a bum."

"Roberto—that's what we have to call him now," explains Rick, "he says it's what happens when people don't feel they've got respect. He says we'll keep losing our kids until they really believe they really have an equal chance. I don't know; I knew I had to *make* the Anglos respect me, and I had to make my chance. Why don't my kids see it like that?" he asks wearily, his shoulders seeming to sag lower with each sentence he speaks.

"I guess it's really different today, isn't it?" he sighs. "When I was coming up, you could still make your chance. I mean, I only went to high school, but I got a job and worked myself up. You can't do that anymore. Now you need to have some kind of special skills just to get a job that pays more than the minimum wage.

"And the schools, they don't teach kids anything anymore. I went to the same public schools my kids went to, but what a difference. It's like nobody cares anymore."

"How is Roberto doing?" I ask, remembering the hostile eighteen-year-old I interviewed several years earlier.

"He's still mad; he's always talking about injustice and things like that. But he's different than Paul. Roberto always had some goals. I used to worry about him because he's so angry all the time. But I see now that his anger helps him. He wants to fight for his people, to make things better for everybody. Paul, he's like the wind; nothing matters to him.

"Right now, Roberto has a job as an electrician's helper, learning the trade. He's been working there for a couple of years; he's pretty good at it. But I think—I hope—he's going to go to college. He heard that they're trying to get Chicano students to go to the university, so he applied. If he gets some aid, I think he'll go," Rick says, his face radiant at the thought that at least one of his children will fulfill his dream. "Ana and me, we tell him even if he doesn't get aid, he should go. We can't do a lot because we have to help Ana's parents and that takes a big hunk every month. But we'll help him, and he could work to make up the rest. I know it's hard to work and go to school, but people do it all the time, and he's smart; he could do it."

His gaze turns inward; then, as if talking to himself, he says, "I never thought I'd say this but I think Roberto's right. We've got something to learn from some of these kids. I told that to Roberto just the other day. He says Ana and me have been trying to pretend we're one of them all of our lives. I told him, 'I think you're right.' I kept thinking if I did everything right, I wouldn't be a 'greaser.' But after all these years, I'm still a 'greaser' in their eyes. It took my son to make me see it. Now I know. If I weren't I'd be head of the shipping department by now, not just one of the supervisors, and maybe Paul wouldn't be wasting his life on the corner."

* * *

We keep saying that family matters, that with a stable family and two caring parents children will grow to a satisfactory adulthood. But I've rarely met a family that's more constant or more concerned than the Riveras. Or one where both parents are so involved with their children. Ana was a full-time homemaker until Paul, their youngest, was twelve. Rick has been with the same company for more than twenty-five years, having worked his way up from clerk to shift supervisor in its shipping department. Whatever the conflicts in their marriage, theirs is clearly a warm, respectful, and caring relationship. Yet their daughter got pregnant and gave up her plans for college, and a son is idling his youth away on a street corner.

Obviously, then, something more than family matters. Growing up in a world where opportunities are available makes a difference. As does being able to afford to take advantage of an opportunity when it comes by. Getting an education that broadens horizons and prepares a child for a productive adulthood makes a difference. As does being able to find work that nourishes self-respect and pays a living wage. Living in a world that doesn't judge you by the color of your skin makes a difference. As does feeling the respect of the people around you.

This is not to suggest that there aren't also real problems inside American families that deserve our serious and sustained attention. But the constant focus on the failure of family life as the locus of both our personal and social difficulties has become a mindless litany, a dangerous diversion from the economic and social realities that make family life so difficult today and that so often destroy it.

THE KWANS

It's a rare sunny day in Seattle, so Andy Kwan and I are in his backyard, a lovely showcase for his talents as a landscape gardener. Although it has been only a few years since we first met, most of the people to whom I've returned in this round of interviews seem older, grayer, more careworn. Andy Kwan is no exception. The brilliant afternoon sunshine is cruel as it searches out every line of worry and age in his angular face. Since I interviewed his wife the day before, I already know that the recession has hurt his business. So I begin by saying, "Carol says that your business has been slow for the last couple of years."

"Yes," he sighs. "At first when the recession came, it didn't hurt me. I think Seattle didn't really get hit at the beginning. But the summer of 1991, that's when I began to feel it. It's as if everybody zipped up their wallets when it came to landscaping.

"A lot of my business has always been when people buy a new house. You know, they want to fix up the outside just like they like it. But nobody's been buying houses lately, and even if they do, they're not putting any money into landscaping. So it's been tight, real tight."

"How have you managed financially?"

"We get by, but it's hard. We have to cut back on a lot of stuff we used to take for granted, like going out to eat once in a while, or going to the movies, things like that. Clothes, nobody gets any new clothes anymore.

"I do a lot of regular gardening now—you know, the maintenance stuff. It helps; it takes up some of the slack, but it's not enough because it doesn't pay much. And the competition's pretty stiff, so you've got to keep your prices down. I mean, everybody knows that it's one of the things people can cut out when things get tough, so the gardeners around here try to hold on by cutting their prices. It gets pretty hairy, real cutthroat."

He gets up, walks over to a flower bed, and stands looking at it. Then, after a few quiet moments, he turns back to me and says, "It's a damned shame. I built my business like you build a house, brick by brick, and it was going real good. I finally got to the point where I wasn't doing much regular gardening anymore. I could concentrate on landscaping, and I was making a pretty good living. With Carol working, too, we were doing all right. I even hired two people and was keeping them busy most of the time. Then all of a sudden, it all came tumbling down.

"I felt real bad when I had to lay off my workers. They have families to feed, too. But what could I do? Now it's like I'm back where I started, an ordinary gardener again and even worrying about how long that'll last," he says disconsolately.

He walks back to his seat, sits down, and continues somewhat more philosophically, "Carol says I shouldn't complain because, with all the problems, we're lucky. She still has her job, and I'm making out. I mean, it's not great, but it could be a lot worse." He pauses, looks around blankly for a moment, sighs, and says, "I guess she's right. Her sister worked at Boeing for seven years and she got laid off a couple of months ago. No notice, nothing; just the pink slip. I mean, everybody knew there'd be layoffs there, but you know how it is. You don't think it's really going to happen to you.

"I try not to let it get me down. But it's hard to be thankful for not having bigger trouble than you've already got," he says ruefully. Then, a smile brightening his face for the first time, he adds, "But there's one thing I can be thankful for, and that's the kids; they're doing fine. I worry a little bit about what's going to happen, though. I guess you can't help it if you're a parent. Eric's the oldest; he's fifteen now, and you never know. Kids get into all kinds of trouble these days. But so far, he's okay. The girls, they're good kids. Carol worries about what'll happen when they get to those teenage years. But I think they'll be okay. We teach them decent values; they go to church every week. I have to believe that makes a difference."

"You say that you worry about Eric but that the girls will be fine because of the values of your family. Hasn't he been taught the same values?"

He thinks a moment, then says, "Did I say that? Yeah, I guess I did. I think maybe there's more ways for a boy to get in trouble than a girl." He laughs and says again, "Did I say *that?*" Then, more thoughtfully, "I don't know. I guess I worry about them all, but if you don't tell yourself that things'll work out okay, you go nuts. I mean, so much can go wrong with kids today.

"It used to be the Chinese family could really control the kids. When I was a kid, the family was law. My father was Chinese-born; he came here as a kid. My mother was born right here in this city. But the grandparents were all immigrants; everybody spoke Chinese at home; and we never lived more than a couple of blocks from both sides of the family. My parents were pretty Americanized everywhere but at home, at least while their parents were alive. My mother would go clean her mother's house for her because that's what a Chinese daughter did."

"Was that because your grandmother was old or sick?"

"No," he replies, shaking his head at the memory. "It's because that's what her mother expected her to do; that's the way Chinese families were then. We talk about that, Carol and me, and how things have changed. It's hard to imagine it, but that's the kind of control families had then.

"It's all changed now. Not that I'd want it that way. I want my kids to know respect for the family, but they shouldn't be servants. That's what my mother was, a servant for her mother.

"By the time my generation came along, things were already different. I couldn't wait to get away from all that family stuff. I mean, it was nice in some ways; there was always this big, noisy bunch of people around, and you knew you were part of something. That felt good. But Chinese families, boy, they don't let go. You felt like they were choking you.

"Now it's *really* different; it's like the kids aren't hardly Chinese any more. I mean, my kids are just like any other American kids. They never lived in a Chinese neighborhood like the one I grew up in, you know, the kind where the only Americans you see are the people who come to buy Chinese food or eat at the restaurants."

"You say they're ordinary American kids. What about the Chinese side? What kind of connection do they have to that?"

"It's funny," he muses. "We sent them to Chinese school because we wanted them to know about their history, and we thought they should know the language, at least a little bit. But they weren't really interested; they wanted to be like everybody else and eat peanut butter and jelly sandwiches. Lately it's a little different, but that's because they feel like they're picked on because they're Chinese. I mean, everybody's worrying about the Chinese kids being so smart and winning all the prizes at school, and the kids are angry about that, especially Eric. He says there's a lot of bad feelings about Chinese kids at school and that everybody's picking on them—the white kids and the black kids, all of them.

"So all of a sudden, he's becoming Chinese. It's like they're making him think about it because there's all this resentment about Asian kids all around. Until a couple of years ago, he had lots of white friends. Now he hangs out mostly with other Asian kids. I guess that's because they feel safer when they're together."

"How do you feel about this?"

The color rises in his face; his voice takes on an edge of agitation. "It's too bad. It's not the way I wanted it to be. I wanted my kids to know they're Chinese and be proud of it, but that's not what's going on now. It's more like . . . , " he stops, trying to find the words, then starts again. "It's like they have to defend themselves *because* they're Chinese. Know what I mean?" he asks. Then without waiting for an answer, he explains, "There's all this prejudice now, so then you can't forget you're Chinese.

"It makes me damn mad. You grow up here and they tell you everybody's equal and that any boy can grow up to be president. Not that I ever thought a Chinese kid could ever be president; any Chinese kid knows that's fairy tale. But I did believe the rest of it, you know, that if you're smart and work hard and do well, people will respect you and you'll be successful. Now, it looks like the smarter Chinese kids are, the more trouble they get."

"Do you think that prejudice against Chinese is different now than when you were growing up?"

"Yeah, I do. When I was a kid like Eric, nobody paid much attention to the Chinese. They left us alone, and we left them alone. But now all these Chinese kids are getting in the way of the white kids because there's so many of them, and they're getting better grades, and things like that. So then everybody gets mad because they think our kids are taking something from them."

He stops, weighs his last words, then says, "I guess they're right, too. When I was growing up, Chinese kids were lucky to graduate from high school, and we didn't get in anybody's way. Now so many Chinese kids are going to college that they're taking over places white kids used to have. I can understand that they don't like that. But that's not our problem; it's theirs. Why don't they work hard like Chinese kids do?

"It's not fair that they've got quotas for Asian kids because the people who run the colleges decided there's too many of them and not enough room for white kids. Nobody ever worried that there were too many white kids, did they?"

* * *

"It's not fair"—a cry from the heart, one I heard from nearly everyone in this study. For indeed, life has not been fair to the working-class people of America, no matter what their color or ethnic background. And it's precisely this sense that it's not fair, that there isn't enough to go around, that has stirred the racial and ethnic tensions that are so prevalent today.

In the face of such clear class disparities, how is it that our national discourse continues to focus on the middle class, denying the existence of a working class and rendering them invisible?

Whether a family or a nation, we all have myths that play tag with reality—myths that frame our thoughts, structure our beliefs, and organize our systems of denial. A myth encircles reality, encapsulates it, controls it. It allows us to know some things and to avoid knowing others, even when somewhere deep inside we really know what we don't want to know. Every parent has experienced this clash between myth and reality. We see signals that tell us a child is lying and explain them away. It isn't that we can't know; it's that we won't, that knowing is too difficult or painful, too discordant with the myth that defines the relationship, the one that says: *My child wouldn't lie to me.*

The same is true about a nation and its citizens. Myths are part of our national heritage, giving definition to the national character, offering guidance for both public and private behavior, comforting us in our moments of doubt. Not infrequently our myths trip over each other, providing a window into our often contradictory and ambivalently held beliefs. The myth that we are a nation of equals lives side-by-side in these United States with the belief in white supremacy. And, unlikely as it seems, it's quite possible to believe both at the same time. Sometimes we manage the conflict by shifting from one side to the other. More often, we simply redefine reality. The inequality of condition between whites and blacks isn't born in prejudice and discrimination, we insist; it's black inferiority that's the problem. Class distinctions have nothing to do with privilege, we say; it's merit that makes the difference.

It's not the outcome that counts, we maintain; it's the rules of the game. And since the rules say that everyone comes to the starting line equal, the different results are merely products of individual will and wit. The fact that working-class children usually grow up to be working-class parents doesn't make a dent in the belief system, nor does it lead to questions about why the written rule and the lived reality are at odds. Instead, with perfect circularity, the outcome reinforces the reasoning that says they're deficient, leaving those so labeled doubly wounded—first by the real problems in living they face, second by internalizing the blame for their estate.

Two decades ago, when I began the research for *Worlds of Pain*, we were living in the immediate aftermath of the civil rights revolution that had convulsed the nation since the mid-1950s. Significant gains had been won. And despite the tenacity with which this headway had been resisted by some, most white Americans were feeling good about themselves. No one expected the nation's racial problems and conflicts to dissolve easily or quickly. But there was also a sense that we were moving in the right direction, that there was a national commitment to redressing at least some of the worst aspects of black-white inequality.

In the intervening years, however, the national economy buckled under the weight of three recessions, while the nation's industrial base was undergoing a massive restructuring. At the same time, government policies requiring preferential treatment were enabling African-Americans and other minorities to make small but visible inroads into what had been, until then, largely white terrain. The sense of scarcity, always a part of American life but intensified sharply by the history of these economic upheavals, made minority gains seem particularly threatening to white working-class families.

It isn't, of course, just working-class whites who feel threatened by minority progress. Wherever racial minorities make inroads into formerly all-white territory, tensions increase. But it's working-class families who feel the fluctuations in the economy most quickly and most keenly. For them, these last decades have been like a bumpy roller coaster ride. "Every time we think we might be able to get ahead, it seems like we get knocked down again," declares Tom Ahmundsen, a forty-two-year-old white construction worker. "Things look a little better; there's a little more work; then all of a sudden, boom, the economy falls apart and it's gone. You can't count on anything; it really gets you down."

This is the story I heard repeatedly: Each small climb was followed by a fall, each glimmer of hope replaced by despair. As the economic vise tightened, despair turned to anger. But partly because we have so little concept of class resentment and conflict in America, this anger isn't directed so much at those above as at those below. And when whites at or near the bottom of the ladder look down in this nation, they generally see blacks and other minorities.

True, during all of the 1980s and into the 1990s, white ire was fostered by national administrations that fanned racial discord as a way of fending off white discontent—of diverting anger about the state of the economy and the declining quality of urban life to the foreigners and racial others in our midst. But our history of racial animosity coupled with our lack of class consciousness made this easier to accomplish than it might otherwise have been.

The difficult realities of white working-class life not withstanding, however, their whiteness has accorded them significant advantages—both materially and psychologically—over people of color. Racial discrimination and segregation in the workplace have kept competition for the best jobs at a minimum. They do, obviously, have to compete with each other for the resources available. But that's different. It's a competition among equals; they're all white. They don't think such things consciously, of course; they don't have to. It's understood, rooted in the culture and supported by the social contract that says they are the superior ones, the worthy ones. Indeed, this is precisely why, when the courts or the legislatures act in ways that seem to contravene that belief, whites experience themselves as victims.

From the earliest days of the republic, whiteness has been the ideal, and freedom and independence have been linked to being white. "Republicanism," writes labor historian David Roediger, "had long emphasized that the strength, virtue and resolve of a people guarded them from enslavement." And it was whites who had these qualities in abundance, as was evident, in the peculiarly circuitous reasoning of the time, in the fact that they were not slaves.

By this logic, the enslavement of blacks could be seen as stemming from their "slavishness" rather than from the institution of slavery. Slavery is gone now, but the reasoning lingers on in white America, which still insists that the lowly estate of people of color is due to their deficits, whether personal or cultural, rather than to the prejudice, discrimination, and institutionalized racism that has barred them from full participation in the society.

This is not to say that culture is irrelevant, whether among black Americans or any other group in our society. The lifeways of a people develop out of their experiences—out of the daily events, large and small, that define their lives; out of the resources that are available to them to meet both individual and group needs; out of the place in the social, cultural, and political systems within which group life is embedded. In the case of a significant proportion of blacks in America's inner cities, centuries of racism and economic discrimination have produced a subculture that is both personally and socially destructive. But to fault culture or the failure of individual responsibility without understanding the larger context within which such behaviors occur is to miss a vital piece of the picture. Nor does acknowledging the existence of certain destructive subcultural forms among some African-Americans disavow or diminish the causal connections between the structural inequalities at the social, political, and economic levels and the serious social problems at the community level.

In his study of "working-class lads" in Birmingham, England, for example, Paul Willis observes that their very acts of resistance to middle-class norms—the defiance with which these young men express their anger at class inequalities—help to reinforce the class structure by further entrenching them in their working-class status. The same can be said for some of the young men in the African-American community, whose active rejection of white norms and "in your face" behavior consigns them to the bottom of the American economic order.

To understand this doesn't make such behavior, whether in England or the United States, any more palatable. But it helps to explain the structural sources of cultural forms and to apprehend the social processes that undergird them. Like Willis's white "working-class lads," the hip-hoppers and rappers in the black community who are so determinedly "not white" are not just making a statement about black culture. They're also expressing their rage at white society for offering a promise of equality, then refusing to fulfill it. In the process, they're finding their own way to some accommodation and to a place in the world they can call their own, albeit one that ultimately reinforces their outsider status.

But, some might argue, white immigrants also suffered prejudice and discrimination in the years after they first arrived, but they found more socially acceptable ways to accommodate. It's true—and so do most of today's people of color, both immigrant and native born. Nevertheless, there's another truth as well. For wrenching as their early experiences were for white ethnics, they had an out. Writing about the Irish, for example, Roediger shows how they were able to insist upon their whiteness and to prove it by adopting the racist attitudes and behaviors of other whites, in the process often becoming leaders in the assault against blacks. With time and their growing political power, they won the prize they sought—recognition as whites. "The imperative to define themselves as white," writes Roediger, "came from the particular 'public and psychological wages' whiteness offered to a desperate rural and often preindustrial Irish population coming to labor in industrializing American cities."

Thus does whiteness bestow its psychological as well as material blessings on even the most demeaned. For no matter how far down the socioeconomic ladder whites may fall, the one thing they can't lose is their whiteness. No small matter because, as W. E. B. DuBois observed decades ago, the compensation of white workers includes a psychological wage, a bonus that enables them to believe in their inherent superiority over nonwhites.

It's also true, however, that this same psychological bonus that white workers prize so highly has cost them dearly. For along with the importation of an immigrant population, the separation of black and white workers has given American capital a reserve labor force to call upon whenever white workers seemed to them to get too "uppity." Thus, while racist ideology enables white workers to maintain the belief in their superiority, they have paid for that conviction by becoming far more vulnerable in the struggle for decent wages and working conditions than they might otherwise have been. . . .

■READING 25

The Family and Part-Time Work

Cynthia Fuchs Epstein, Carroll Seron,
Bonnie Oglensky, and Robert Sauté

THE ROLE OF PARENTS

Many of the issues that part-time professional work raises are linked to society's norms about the role of women and the care of children. Individual time and work priorities for parents, and especially working mothers, are shaped in part by questions of "family values," the sex division of labor, the rights of women, the needs of children, the "ideal family," and, of course, the psychologies of individual mothers and fathers. Although historically child care has been the responsibility of mothers, today fathers also are expected to share some of the obligations and to appreciate the attendant satisfactions of child care. But it continues to be defined as a woman's issue, and, as we have seen, it has generated pressures to institutionalize part-time work in the legal profession.

In the post-World War II era and for a time thereafter (Skolnick, 1991) the model of a stay-at-home, nonwage-earning mother caring for children represented an ideal in American society. Although women were actually moving into the workforce in ever-increasing numbers, the advent of the woman's movement in the late 1960s imbued women's presence in the labor force with a legitimacy that went beyond the economic pressures driving them there. At the same time, restrictions on their participation in high-prestige professions were seriously curbed through Title VII of the Civil Rights Act of 1964 and a series of landmark court cases. In the years that followed, women flocked to the legal profession (Epstein, [1981] 1993) as they did to medicine and other spheres from which they had been excluded in the past. Indeed, mothers all over America have gone back to work after the birth of their children in numbers that have increased sharply in recent years. Fifty-five percent of new mothers returned to the workforce in 1995 within 12 months of giving birth, compared with 31 percent in 1976 when the Bureau of Labor Statistics started to track these figures (Fiore, 1997). Seventy-seven percent of college-educated women ages 30 to 44 juggle work and child rearing.

Of course, this trend conflicts with today's norms of motherhood, which specify standards for "intensive mothering" that have become ever more demanding (Coser and Coser, 1974; Hays, 1996). Standards for "quality time" with children have also escalated the numbers of hours each week parents are supposed to devote to involvement in their children's education, psychological development, and leisure-time activities (Hays, 1996).

At the same time, child care —private and public day-care centers, all-day nurseries, agencies that supply nannies and baby-sitters for those who can afford private solutions— all cater to the child-care needs of working parents. However, there is not enough high-quality child care generally available to meet demand, and there are also cultural perspectives that make the use of surrogates (except for family members) problematic.

The backlash against working mothers has been reflected in a stream of books (Hewlett, 1986; Mack, 1997; Whitehead, 1997), newspaper and magazine articles, and television news stories. From the mainstream press to the publications of right-wing organizations and "foundations," features are published constantly decrying the use of surrogate care. Working women are directly or indirectly chastised for selfishness in articles such as "Day Careless" (Gallagher, 1998) in *National Review;* "Day Care: The Thalidomide of the 1980s" and "Working Moms, Failing Children," in publications of the Rockford Institute; and cover stories in national newsmagazines such as "The Myth of Quality Time: How We're Cheating Our Children" in *Newsweek* and "The Lies Parents Tell About Work, Kids, Money, Day Care and Ambition" in *US. News and World Report.* News coverage focuses on stories about inadequate, inappropriate, and even lethal caregivers (Barnett and Pivers, 1997). Sociologist Arlie Hochschild's (1997) claim that Americans prefer working to dealing with the stresses of parenting received much media attention, including a cover story in the *New York Times Magazine,* and evoked a lively public response faulting American women for their selfishness in preferring the workplace to the home. And the case of Louise Woodward, an English *au pair* worker acquitted in the death of an infant in her care in a Boston suburb, generated an avalanche of hate mail to the mother, a part-time physician, faulting her for not caring for her child herself.

The hostility and indifference expressed by the media to their child-care needs and the arrangements they make fuels guilt in working mothers and reinforces conventional negative attitudes about the advisability of full-time mothers' care for children (Faludi, 1991).

Women have written about the continuing conflict between their roles, seeing it as a war between their "selves." For example, in a book explaining her retreat from a high-powered publishing position to become a more attentive mother, Elizabeth Perle McKenna (1997:85) wrote:

> Every morning the bell would ring and out would come these two identities, sparring with one another, fighting for the minutes on the clock and for my attention.

Research that shows positive effects on the family well-being of dual-career couples (Barnett and Pivers, 1997; Parcel and Menanghan, 1994) does not evoke the same kind of media attention that bad experiences evoke, and virtually no media coverage focuses on the benefits to children of surrogate care or the successful management of roles by worker-mothers.

Thus, cultural contradictions of mothering have deepened rather than resolved concerns about the balancing of work and family obligations (Hays, 1996).

Though all the mothers among the lawyers interviewed for this study rely on at least part-time surrogate care, they are wary about delegating child care and seek to minimize it. Although even full-time working mothers express some ambivalence about assigning part of their mothering role to another person, part-timers have chosen reduced work schedules as a way to express their preferences and reduce their guilt, and, of course, to reduce role strain (Goode, 1960; Merton, 1957). A refrain common in many of the interviews with part-time lawyers was expressed by an associate at a large firm: "No one, no one, not a nanny, not a day-care center, will show my children as much love, and be able to care for my children the way that I can." Josh Levanthal, a supervising attorney in a government agency, worked part time to share in care for his children, as did his wife, Robin, another government attorney. Josh told us he agreed with his wife in thinking "a nonparent would not take the same sort of care that a parent would." Similarly, Sara Wright, an associate in a medium-size law firm whose office shelves were filled with photographs of her two toddlers, expressed concern that her children "have [my] moral values and not the babysitter's" and said this motivated her to take a part-time schedule.

Some of the lawyers interviewed expressed distrust of surrogates. Marina Goff, who cut back her work schedule after moving to a distant suburb so she could spend more time with her two-year-old son and five-year-old daughter, spoke of the "horror stories you hear, even from friends." Several other lawyers also spoke of the "absolute nightmare to find people who can watch your children." Fueled by newspaper accounts of horrible behavior by nannies, two of the attorneys interviewed admitted secretly videotaping their in-home child-care providers. Both were pleasantly relieved to discover that their children had exemplary care.

Of course, this cultural climate has had an effect on attitudes about how much commitment working mothers ought to have to their careers, and how much to the family. These cultural attitudes persuade many women to work less and a few to leave the workplace altogether for the sake of "motherhood," although discontent about the nature of their work may also contribute to retreat from career paths.

McKenna's (1997) study of women who decide to leave work found that when she scratched the surface, "women admitted that, yes, they wanted more flexibility and time for their children, but if they had been happier in their work, they would have figured it out somehow" (164). She pointed to the case of Alicia Daymans, who declared in an early part of an interview that she decided to leave the high-profile magazine she worked for because she wanted to spend more time with her daughter, but revealed later that the "real" reasons were the moral and philosophical differences she had with the publication's owners. Certainly, spending time with her preadolescent daughter was a big concern, but she admitted that this alone would not have prompted her to leave.

Certainly, many women feel it is appropriate to work full time and use child-care surrogates, and do. We interviewed scores of women attorneys in our study of lawyers in large corporate law firms (Epstein et al., 1995) who said they were comfortable with the balance of work and family in their lives and had worked with responsible and loving child-care surrogates who served their families well. This supported David Chambers's (1989) striking findings that women graduates of the Michigan Law School who were mothers showed the highest amount of contentment when compared with childless women (married and single) and with men. Although many of them worked part-time for some period after law school, many either consistently worked full-time or swiftly returned to full-time work after a brief leave. Consistent with our findings, women with children in Chambers's sample made more accommodations to career than men. Most for some period since law school ceased working outside the home or shifted to part-time work. A quarter of the mothers worked part-time or took leaves for periods totaling at least 18 months. But even women who do not feel guilty about sharing themselves with career and family must interact with others who question their behavior and punish them.

Several lawyer mothers complained that some "stay-at-home" mothers refused to make playdates with their children, if the nanny brought the child to their home. As a result many women are exposed to multiple and often contradictory messages. The women and the few men who choose part-time work, or the law jobs with "regular hours" considered less than the large-firm norm, are those who hope to reconcile the obligations and satisfactions of both spheres using an alternative equation. Part-timers particularly subscribe to the hands-on parenting norms popular today and are members of socioemotional communities that foster them. Pressures from spouses, children, coworkers, extended family members, and social acquaintances all affect what they say, believe, and do about balancing familial duties and professional calling.

It appears that the families of the lawyers who use part-time work in law firms to resolve the conflicts of work and child care are not so different structurally than the families of their full-time lawyer colleagues (Epstein *et al.*, 1995). They are about the same size and are headed by spouses who work in similar occupations, for example.

More than 80 percent (62 out of 75) of the lawyers in this study who work or have worked part time chose to do so for child-care reasons. They are mothers (with two exceptions) whose children ranged in age from infancy to 13 years old. Several mothers chose to work reduced hours from the time that they returned to work from maternity leave; others chose it as their children moved beyond infancy, and still others after the birth of a second child. About 40 percent either have returned or plan to return to full-time employment as their children mature (22 of 57), and 12 percent (7) are unsure of their plans. Almost half (28 lawyers) have no present intention of resuming full-time work. Additionally, most lawyers responding to a survey sent out by the Part-Time Network of the Association of the Bar of the City of New York (the LAWWS Network) (Schwab, 1994)—a group promoting part-time options in the legal profession—answered that they did not wish to return to full-time work in the future. A subset of our sample has migrated back and forth between full-time and part-time status as their families have increased in size, grown older, or been affected by other work or family pressures.

DECISIONS TO WORK PART-TIME FOR THE "JOYS OF MOTHERHOOD"

Just as these lawyers reported that their decisions to have children were worked out strategically in terms of their careers, more than half of the women part-timers in this study reported that when they were pregnant they were fairly certain that they would not return to work full-time after giving birth. Yet, of these, many told us that for strategic purposes, they behaved at work "as if" they were unsure about their postpartum plans. They did not want to reveal their intentions to work part-time prior to taking maternity leave because they did not want to lose quality work before they took leave, and they also believed they could negotiate a more favorable reduced-hours arrangement later. For most of the women in the study the decision to work part time was cushioned because they are wives of prosperous men. Thus, they were financially free to act on their feelings that it was necessary to spend more time at home.

Psychological reactions to motherhood compelled a number of lawyers interviewed to choose part-time work. Some reported their decisions to take extended periods of maternity leave or return on a part-time basis were spontaneous and emotionally unpredictable. As Patricia Clarke, a senior associate in a large Wall Street firm, described it:

> I fell madly in love with my son. . . . I just started to feel that I wouldn't be able to leave him every day and feel like someone else was raising my child. I didn't love my job enough to justify that. . . . It wasn't a trade-off worth making.

Cheryl Meany, a government attorney who left a position at a medium-size firm because she could not reduce her work schedule from four to three days a week, was agitated when she remarked, "I just felt desperate to be with my child." She admitted to being more traditional than other lawyers and wishing to stay home to take care of her two preschool-age daughters, but she was not alone in feeling "desperate."

Several mothers noted that the urge to work part time was fueled by jealous competition with their care providers. Gloria Mann, another government attorney, declared that she needed to spend "every waking hour" with her new son because:

> Being a mother to him . . . I felt like every minute, . . . every weekend I would be there for him to know that I was his mother, [not the] . . . baby-sitter.

Another mother admitted that she was heartbroken to find a local store clerk mistake her son's *au pair* for her.

Cultural lore stresses the value of witnessing a child's first steps or first words. The importance of these moments was internalized by many of the women (but was not reported by fathers in the same way). In her interview, Betty Forten, a full-time attorney, wept softly as she described her feelings at missing her son's first successful attempt at walking, a major regret of the women who worked full time. In her study of child-care providers, *Other People's Children* (1995), the sociologist Julia Wrigley found that nannies know the cultural importance of such infant milestones and that many refrain from telling parents when their children utter their first words or take their first steps, so that the mother or father will "discover" these achievements themselves.

The importance of witnessing and participating in the later development of a child was the rationale for their choice as Barbara Friedl, an eighth-year associate in a large, expanding firm, explained:

> I discovered that the more verbal they get, the more incredibly engaging they are. And the more my presence makes a difference to them. And right now, for a five-year-old . . . there is no one in the universe like me. . . . Her baby-sitter is wonderful and she adores her . . . but there is something absolutely extraordinary about having Mommy pick her up from school.

PROFILE OF FAMILIES AND CHILD-CARE ARRANGEMENTS

What do families in which the part-time lawyering choice is made look like? To draw this portrait we rely only on the 84 lawyers in the sample who returned questionnaires asking about their families and other socioeconomic data. The composition of their families and the child-care provisions they have made are as follows:

Marital status: Part-time lawyers typically are married. There is one single mother among the lawyers who answered the questionnaire and one childless single attorney whose part-time arrangement was negotiated to provide time to pursue other interests.

Employment of spouse: Most of the part-time lawyers' spouses were employed in law, finance, and other professional work. It seems evident that lawyers who choose to work part time rely on the income of a full-time working spouse. In general, women in households with higher levels of other income, either higher spousal earnings or larger amount of nonearned household income, are more likely to work part time than other women (Blank, 1990).

Size of family: The lawyers in this study have small families, with a norm of two children, like other professional families. About half (48 of 84) have two children. Eight of the lawyers in the sample had more than two children, and eight had none (although these were young and anticipated having children). Many of the women had not had children until they were past the age of 30.

Child-care arrangements: These lawyers use a wide variety of child-care arrangements. They rely on relatives, daily or live-in nannies, or day care. Almost one-half (32 of 69) of those for whom we have data use live-in or live-out full-time (i.e., full-week) care providers. Twenty-two families employ part-time providers as their primary child care, and the remaining 15 use baby-sitters, relatives, or day care.

A couple's resources of course affect the child-care arrangements they make. The high-income lawyers tend to use the most child care. Among families with high incomes, full-time or live-in nannies predominate. Of the 29 families for whom we have both income and employment sector data, 25 with family incomes of more than $150,000 have live-in nannies. Twenty-two of those lawyers are employed by large private law firms. A number of lawyers in large firms employ housekeepers as well as nannies, and some also have additional staff to take care of their country homes. Nannies were also employed by six lawyers who worked in the legal departments of corporations, by one self-employed lawyer, and by one government agency lawyer. About half (10 of the 22) of those who use part-time care providers work for government agencies, and four of the five using day care work in government agencies.

The nature of the attorneys' work is related closely to their incomes and thus is a determining factor in the type of child care they choose. The nature of the work may be a consideration in another way as well. Not only do attorneys in large firms and in corporate settings have the money to hire a nanny, but the demands on their time for schedule flexibility and the "on-call" nature of their work are believed to require it. Such flexibility typically cannot be put together at the last minute on an *ad hoc* basis. A few husbands have schedules that are predictable or flexible enough to permit them to pick up their children after school or day care or to relieve a sitter at the end of the day, and a small number of these part-time lawyers rely on them or on members of their extended families to do so. The more typical scenario, however, is that the husband's schedule is deemed to be more demanding than that of his wife, and she is expected to fill in the gaps in child care.

Seventeen sets of attorney couples were among the 32 families who employ full-time child-care providers. Five attorneys with full-time help have spouses who work in the financial sector. The lawyers whose spouses are academic professionals do not employ full-time or live-in nannies. But this lack of full-time coverage may be a reflection of the relatively greater flexibility of both spouses' work schedules rather than lower income.

Many lawyers rely on extraordinary flexibility and commitment from their child-care providers. Patricia Borden, a government staff attorney who works three days a week, is married to another attorney. She requires an at-home child-care provider who can stretch her own workday to care for her two children. Day-care centers available to her have strict time limits and are not "flexible the way a human can be." She remarked,

> I have . . . a tremendously flexible arrangement, both the after-school for him [her older son], and a sitter [for her toddler] for as long as I need her. She's tremendously flexible. If she has some appointment, she'll clear it with me. And then I'll know that I absolutely have to be home by then. Otherwise it's easy to sort of bleed into 7 o'clock without trying hard. So my days are generally sort of 9:30 to 7.

"Family-Friendly" Work Settings

Some places of legal employment are more desirable than others because of their "family-friendly" atmosphere. A Westchester, New York, manufacturing concern at which we interviewed part-time attorneys has such a reputation. There, breaking away from work to attend a child's soccer game or ballet recital is considered necessary. In this setting, women with small children often are given work assignments with little or no travel. But official organizational friendliness may not solve the interpersonal problems that develop because of different parental statuses of employees. For instance, questions of fairness were raised by two childless women attorneys when they were asked to increase their work travel so that a woman attorney with children could be freed from travel obligations. When one of them balked she was queried by her supervising attorney, "What's the matter? You don't have any kids."

One government agency has a reputation for being a good place for parents to work because of its flexibility toward part-time commitments and a staff with a large percentage of parents with young children. Patricia Brooke, who moved from a lucrative position at a midsize firm, spelled out why she sought employment there:

> It was very interesting work, a three-day-a-week schedule . . . and mostly the head of this department was very supportive of part-time people and did not consider them to be second-class citizens. At my previous firm, while I was part time. . . . I was certainly a second-class citizen.

Negotiating Part-Time Status with a Spouse

Decisions about childbearing, time off, and part-time work were pondered and made by these lawyers within a broad context that incorporated economics, norms of professional commitment, and ideas about gender roles. The decision about which spouse will work part time is generally made against three criteria: a "rational" economic assessment, the couple's response to traditional sex roles, and their agreed-upon ideology. All of these criteria may be seen as ideological concepts that are intertwined and susceptible to challenge and negotiation.

There are economic repercussions on the family when a spouse cuts back work time and income, but because of the income differentials in the various sectors of the profession the impact on family lifestyle may vary. Usually, when a spouse cuts back on work time, family income falls precipitously. Virtually all families decide jointly whether to reduce paid labor from two full-time jobs, and most couples negotiate over how much their work schedules can be reduced and what child-care arrangements can be made. Many husbands initially were reluctant to accept their wives' working a reduced schedule, but others saw this as the wife's decision. Patricia Brooke said her husband, Tom, was skeptical about her working part time, for financial and professional reasons. "He was . . . thinking, 'Gee, we're now gonna be poor,' " she said. Tom is also a lawyer and has doubts about the seriousness and legitimacy of part-time lawyering.

> The fact that we're both lawyers in many ways makes the relationship difficult, because he has . . . standards, and he doesn't think of part-time lawyers as . . . serious. . . . He would never admit any of this, but I think his reluctance about part-time [makes him see] me as less legitimate as a lawyer because I'm only working three days.

The decision about which spouse will work full-time is rarely couched today in the language of traditional roles, but is usually justified in terms of maximizing income over a long time period. Yet studies show that it is common for men to regard themselves as the "breadwinner" no matter how much income a wife brings into the family (Potuchek, 1997). Indeed, we heard from a male government attorney that many of his colleagues had come to the agency because of idealistic motivations to "help people," but found their salaries could not support growing families, home mortgages, and wives who felt they should cut back in their own careers. Moving to legal work that was more lucrative, was, therefore, the "daddy track." Thus we see many decisions are interactive with people's views of appropriate roles and future needs. Couples weigh effort versus return; sacrifices are calculated against potential gains. Many husbands have incomes sufficient to forgo their wives' contributions. When the men are in independent professional practices or are small-business owners, couples usually decide it is more important to invest in his career than hers. Finally, families often use the language of economic rationalization when deciding which spouse should work part time. Karyn Post works four days a week as a senior associate in the corporate department of a prestigious midtown New York firm. She was hired on a part-time basis from a firm where she also had worked a reduced schedule. She has no plans to return to a full-time schedule and does not need to because her husband does very well working in the financial sector. She describes the process through which she and her husband agreed that she should work a reduced schedule:

> We decided that the financial rewards of partnership versus the hours that I would have to work to accomplish that were not worth it, and that it was better for me to go part-time and take on a bigger role at home. . . . I'm happy I was able to do that because I'd rather be at home and be with the kids. It was better to invest more in his career.

As we have seen, women report that they, together with their husbands, often make the decision to work part-time because they accept the idea that men will ultimately make more money than women. This is based on common knowledge that in general, women workers make less money for equal or similar work. Although this is not really the case for *professional* women who work in the same spheres as men and put in the same amount of time, couples still regard it as logical to invest in the husband's career.

Of course, powerful norms setting appropriate gender roles form a backdrop to all of these decisions even when the stated rationales are economic.

But sometimes, traditional sex-role assignments are a clearly stated factor in such decisions. Fiona Scott, a federal attorney, remarked that she was "more maternalistic than [her] husband was paternalistic." Others reported their husbands were uninterested in child rearing. Carrie Little, an associate at a large firm, explained that her husband did not consider reducing his work schedule because "he didn't really want to stay home and take charge. . . . He's more of a male." The traditional gender roles are not necessarily seen as "natural" but many regard them as inevitable. Jeannette Warren, a part-time partner at a prestigious firm, left her first job in the public interest sector in the early 1970s because it did not permit her to take a reduced schedule. She had the major responsibility for child care, a responsibility she desired. As she outlined her thinking:

> Women have . . . family responsibilities . . . that men just don't have. . . . My husband could do anything that I would do with my girls, but there were times when they just wanted me; and the other side of it is . . . maternal instinct, . . . I wanted to take them to the doctor; I didn't want him to take them to the doctor. . . . Women genetically or instinctively [are different].

Several mothers attributed their husbands' relative disinterest in child care to societal norms. "Of course, I wish my husband were more involved, but he's not. Society just doesn't value that for men, and he's just not that different from other men."

As the husband of a part-time lawyer described it, many attitudes come from the general society about the propriety of men and women taking on certain work and family roles. Philip Smith, an associate in a large firm, talked to us about having considered going part-time himself. He and his wife discussed it "jokingly . . . with an edge of seriousness." Sex roles played a major part in his thinking:

> You're brought up and programmed to think you're supposed to be and do [certain things]. . . . And I guess you're brought up to think that well, if someone works part-time, it's going to be the wife. That's just how it is. And how shocking it would be if it was any other way.

Even if the subject is broached, the mechanisms that persuade people to conform to society's norms are sometimes right on the surface. Sharon Winick, a seventh-year associate in a large firm, recounted a discussion with her husband:

> Some of the issues [my husband and I discussed] were: Is it easy for a man to work part time? Is the stigma greater on a man? Can he ever redeem himself if he does that? Is it even possible to do that? He didn't experience the pull to want to be home. He experienced it as wanting to support me.

A part-time attorney whose husband is a lawyer who works at home confronted the cultural view of her husband's decision: "Real men do not work at home."

IDEOLOGICAL RENEGADES

When men chose to work part-time they explained it in ways that seemed a conscious attempt to subvert social norms and to offer themselves as alternative examples. They tended to have a political commitment to a gender-free ideology and a commitment to raising their children with maximum parental involvement. Robert Malcolm worked part-time for two years beginning four months after his first child was born. His father had played a very traditional role as a parent, which made him seek a different role. "I don't understand why men would want it to be any other way in . . . their relationships with their kids," he said. Equality of responsibility in child rearing is also a political issue, as he described it:

> In terms of household responsibilities . . . it's sort of a political issue. I come from the left side of the spectrum, and I'm a fairly strong feminist, and I think it's the proper way to live your life.
>
> • • •
>
> It was important to us that the kids viewed us equally. It was important to us that they didn't view the stereotyped roles for men and women in the household, . . . that the kids basically had parents home with them for most of the time.

His wife, Leila, has worked three days a week in a municipal agency for two years and will continue to do so for the foreseeable future; she supports his decision. She feels that the reward for this political commitment was the way in which their son was socialized. "My son was totally equally bonded to both parents. He didn't have one primary over the other," she said. Their larger political commitment to set themselves as an example was important in this decision:

> We did it [worked part time] for ourselves, but we were really happy [to] set an example. . . . When [only] a few men do it . . . you'll continue to have a situation where women rank behind men. Women will always be doing other things at home, and men will keep advancing their careers. So we both thought that the best thing would be if [we] share child-care responsibility.

In both cases where men worked reduced schedules to be with their children they became dissatisfied, feeling they were missing out on their careers and failing to enjoy their parenting roles. Both male lawyers returned to full-time work, leaving their wives to work part time. One of the men returned to a full-time schedule because he missed the supervisory role that is denied in his department to part-timers; the other, because of a trial that required his full-time participation. As we found in our study of large corporate firms (Epstein *et al.*, 1995), most men find that attempts to adjust their work schedules to accommodate family needs meet extreme resistance from employers, and the costs they face are felt to be too high to pay (Rhode, 1997). It is simply easier for their wives to find accommodation in the workplace.

Furthermore, sometimes knowingly and sometimes quite unconsciously, many women place constraints on their husbands' interest in reducing their workloads and spending more time with their children. Some who have tried it find also that women in the community resist their attempts to participate in parenting that goes beyond the traditional father's role as a soccer or baseball coach. John Spiegel, a government attorney whose wife works for the same agency two days a week on site, two days at home, told us it was clear that his wife "had more of a need" to be with the children. He felt also that if he spent more time at home he would be more isolated because he didn't think he'd be included in the activities arranged by mothers. Several mothers were candid about not encouraging their husbands to reduce their work time, saying they wished to be in charge at home. With a husband whose commitment to child care might be the envy of many working mothers, Sara Atkins found herself feeling quite ambivalent. A woman with two post-graduate degrees from elite schools, she left a full-time, high-demand position in a firm because of health problems and a desire to mother her two children. She intimated that her husband's active involvement with the children threatened her role as "primary parent," and she felt somewhat competitive with him. Her work choice effectively undercut her husband's plan to share the parenting role in an equitable way.

PROFESSIONAL IDEOLOGY

Many factors influence an attorney's choice of part-time work. One of the issues for women in law is the conflict between motherhood and the ideology of professionalism. As noted earlier, many of the profession's leaders regard law as a "calling." It is this sense of vocation that partly differentiates a profession from a craft and sets it above other occupations.

Mothers who choose part-time work must adjust to the perception that they are compromising their calling. Of course, many young lawyers, men and women alike, no longer accept this definition of a professional. (It was only among lawyers in government service that we found a sense of mission to accomplish socially useful objectives. Yet even there the attractions of law were its autonomy, variety of work, and potential for a high income, rather than a grandiose ideal.) Margaret Segrest, a recently laid-off counsel in a multinational corporation's legal department with two boys and an attorney husband, expressed a sentiment that was not uncommon:

> I enjoy practicing law . . . I want to keep my foot in for economic reasons. . . . I like getting dressed and coming to work, and I like thinking, and I did invest a lot in going to law school.

What distinguishes a professional from a nonprofessional, in her view, is the professional's commitment to task without regard to other constraints. In contrast to a job in which one just does the required work within a given time period, a professional is supposed to be dedicated to producing the best she can and to provide service at its highest level.

In balancing physical, emotional, and time demands between lawyering and mothering, the allocation of energies required for mothering becomes less problematic for many part-time attorneys when the practice of law is reduced to "work, money, and prestige" as a lawyer sharing a job put it. The choice between children and career, as one woman expressed it, is a "no-brainer." Or as another joked, "There's a saying that on our deathbed nobody ever says, 'Gee, I wish I'd spent more time at work.' "

THE HOUSEHOLD DIVISION OF LABOR: CONSEQUENCES OF PART-TIME WORK

As Seron (1996) points out, the professions in general and the legal profession in particular depend on a gendered division of labor in the home. Totally dedicated male lawyers depend on their wives to handle household duties whether they stay at home or work full time or part time. As in dual-career families studied by Arlie Hochschild (1989), even an "equal" division of household labor tended to be a division of tasks inside and outside the house with unequal results. Several women reported that their husbands shared equally in household tasks, but when those cases are examined the division of labor follows traditional patterns, with men responsible for being "handy," i.e., caring for the car and yard, making repairs, and filling in with some cooking or household chores. Women will more typically manage recurring household finances, do laundry and household chores, and be responsible for all child-care duties. Moreover, women in this study had a common complaint: Their husbands "just don't notice." Even those men who accepted responsibility for housework and child care had to be supervised, in their wives' view. By doing chores that fit within the definition of being handy or neglecting details of housework, men "do gender," in the words of the sociologists Candace West and Don Zimmerman (1987). The ways in which they divide up household tasks and how they do them allow men to reaffirm their gendered identities. Elsie Marshak works as a part-time associate 35 hours a week, or 70 percent of a 50-hour full-time position, at a large firm in midtown Manhattan. With three daughters ranging in age from two to nine, she and her husband, an executive in the electronics industry, employ a full-time nanny. As she described the division of labor in her household:

> It's hard to pinpoint specific jobs. He helps clean up dinner, he helps prepare dinner sometimes. He helps me with the children in the evening. We have our own division that's hard to put into a two-sentence summary. He does everything outside the house. I do everything inside the house. Like, all the bill paying, the party arrangements, vacations, social planning . . . doctor's appointments, kids. I do everything for the kids, clothing, parties, RSVPs, I mean I delegate some of that to the nanny but, basically, it's my responsibility. Basically, I run my house. I delegate things to him.

Another attorney describes herself as the "hunter-gatherer of the family who does all the shopping, cooking, and arranging of things" while her husband is the handyman. By taking on the lion's share of household duties, women allow their spouses to pursue their careers or develop businesses. Some women work part-time so that they can devote more time to household chores in addition to child-rearing responsibilities. By doing these things on weekdays they free weekends for family social activities.

Not all of the women lawyers in our sample embraced or even fully accepted their role in the gendered division of labor in the household. Charlotte Henry, a government attorney, was deeply resentful that when she went part-time her husband expected her to take on more traditional wifely domestic responsibilities such as cooking, cleaning, and shopping. This was not what she had in mind when she reduced her work schedule. In her view, her husband imposed an old framework—assuming that she would spend her time away from work as his mother did, at household tasks. But Ms. Henry chose to go to the gym and engage in other personal interests when child-care responsibilities did not interfere. "Time for oneself" was an issue for many women.

Men's involvement with their children ranged from the father who worked part-time so that he could be a primary caregiver to those who worked long hours and spent little time with their offspring. Most women think that their husbands spend relatively more time and give more attention to their children than men in previous generations, but they are also aware that the traditional role structure has not changed radically. Caren Petrie, a senior associate at a large firm, said of her husband:

> Actually, he's good. In fact, if I tell him, he'll do [household chores]. I wish sometimes he'd do things without my telling him. He's actually very good with the kids. He'll spend a lot more time than my father did with the kids. And, I think, than what his father did. But he has the *good* time with the kids. He doesn't do the grunt work, which I take care of. All the schools and the insurance stuff.

Cheryl Mobry, who works in a municipal legal department, told how her husband once wanted to work a reduced schedule but changed his mind and instead works long hours. "He loves the kids, and I think he'd certainly like to get home earlier . . . But when he has a day by himself with the kids, he's not all excited about it, which I am." She saw an irony in this situation: Middle- and upper-middle-class women can add to their family income, but it has not significantly changed traditional roles. She expanded on this:

It was actually a joint decision that it made more sense for us for him to work hard, for me to take more of a responsibility at home—I take care of everything; he does very little. And he is spoiled. I think that because of women's lib the men have made out very well, because the women bring in money, but still do what their mothers did, and the husbands, it takes a lot to get them to move.

PART-TIME WORK AS A SOLUTION FOR ROLE STRAIN AND ROLE INEQUITIES

Faced with cross-pressures to meet the norms of intensive mothering, the problems of surrogate child care, the curtailing of professional identity, and the continued strength of traditional gender roles in the family, what keeps women lawyers, who usually can afford to, from leaving the paid work force altogether?

Two issues predominate: the fatigue and isolation of parenting, and the attempt to maintain power in marital relationships.

Most of the women lawyers interviewed saw their work as a needed respite from domestic responsibilities. Elsie Marshak, the associate described earlier as working 35 hours a week in a large firm, considers work a condition for sanity: "I need to work. I would go crazy staying at home full time. But I was also going to go crazy doing everything at once." Using similar language, Laurie Potempkin, another part-time associate, asserted, "I think that I would go crazy staying at home. I need some structure to my life. I need the intellectual stimulation. And kids are great. But they're very demanding; it's very physically demanding and not as intellectually so in the early years." She went on to describe mothering as lonely and isolating:

> When I was on maternity leave, I found it lonely. There wasn't the camaraderie of working with people, the interaction with colleagues; you just sit with other mothers. But I guess maybe I didn't click with the other mothers. They were just always talking about kids and play days and stuff.

The gendered division of labor exists and persists because of differences in power between men and women. Some women respond to this imbalance by asserting their need for independence. Part-time work allows them to keep some control over their financial resources, social networks, and professional identities. In large part, they are defending a space with both real and symbolic territories. Their social networks and professional identities are reminders that they are more than mothers. Although, with a few notable exceptions, women attorneys do not earn enough in part-time positions to maintain their standard of living, their earnings are considerable compared to what they would earn in other occupations. Further, an independent income offers the possibility of autonomy; its absence means dependence. In negotiating conflicting norms, they often use their mothers' experience as a guide, stressing their continued employment as a safety net. Elsie Marshak reflected:

> My parents . . . had a rocky marriage for 30 years, and my mother always pushed me to be financially independent. . . . I'm not truly independent. Our lives are so intertwined with kids, but [it's important] knowing that, if I want independence, I can have it.

Though Deborah Seinfield, in her 40s, removed herself from the partnership track, staying in the labor force as a part-time associate gives her a sense of independence:

> I never thought I'd be able to depend on somebody else . . . for money. . . . One of the things that's always kept me from quitting, other than the fact that my husband says, "No," was I couldn't imagine asking him for money, for an allowance.

Neither of these attorneys believe their incomes make them self-sufficient, but they are grounds for claiming at least symbolic autonomy.

The integration of work roles and family roles is negotiated by husbands and wives on the basis of their philosophies, traditions, and practical concerns. Financial pressures, the number of children and their ages, and access to good child-care providers are all important factors, but all are weighed and interpreted within frameworks that mark the pair's private worlds and reflect the larger society.

Editors' Note: References for this reading can be found in the original source.

■READING 26

The Second Shift: Working Parents and the Revolution at Home

Arlie Hochschild, with Anne Machung

Between 8:05 A.M. and 6:05 P.M., both Nancy and Evan are away from home, working a "first shift" at full-time jobs. The rest of the time they deal with the varied tasks of the second shift: shopping, cooking, paying bills; taking care of the car, the garden, and yard; keeping harmony with Evan's mother who drops over quite a bit, "concerned" about Joey, with neighbors, their voluble baby-sitter, and each other. And Nancy's talk reflects a series of second-shift thoughts: "We're out of barbecue sauce. . . . Joey needs a Halloween costume. . . . The car needs a wash. . . ." and so on. She reflects a certain "second-shift sensibility," a continual attunement to the task of striking and restriking the right emotional balance between child, spouse, home, and outside job.

When I first met the Holts, Nancy was absorbing far more of the second shift than Evan. She said she was doing 80 percent of the housework and 90 percent of the child-care. Evan said she did 60 percent of the housework, 70 percent of the childcare. Joey said, "I vacuum the rug, and fold the dinner napkins," finally concluding, "Mom and I do it all." A neighbor agreed with Joey. Clearly, between Nancy and Evan, there was a "leisure gap": Evan had more than Nancy. I asked both of them, in separate interviews, to explain to me how they had dealt with housework and childcare since their marriage began.

One evening in the fifth year of their marriage, Nancy told me, when Joey was two months old and almost four years before I met the Holts, she first seriously raised the issue with Evan. "I told him: 'Look, Evan, it's not working. I do the housework, I take the major care of Joey, *and* I work a full-time job. I get pissed. This is *your* house too. Joey is *your* child too. It's not all *my* job to care for them.' When I cooled down I put to him, 'Look, how about this: I'll cook Mondays, Wednesdays, and Fridays. You cook Tuesdays, Thursdays, and Saturdays. And we'll share or go out Sundays.' "

According to Nancy, Evan said he didn't like "rigid schedules." He said he didn't necessarily agree with her standards of housekeeping, and didn't like that standard "imposed" on him, especially if she was "sluffing off" tasks on him, which from time to time he felt she was. But he went along with the idea in principle. Nancy said the first week of the new plan went as follows: On Monday, she cooked. For Tuesday, Evan planned a meal that required shopping for a few ingredients, but on his way home he forgot to shop for them. He came home, saw nothing he could use in the refrigerator or in the cupboard, and suggested to Nancy that they go out for Chinese food. On Wednesday, Nancy cooked. On Thursday morning, Nancy reminded Evan, "Tonight it's your turn." That night Evan fixed hamburgers and french fries and Nancy was quick to praise him. On Friday, Nancy cooked. On Saturday, Evan forgot again.

As this pattern continued, Nancy's reminders became sharper. The sharper they became, the more actively Evan forgot—perhaps anticipating even sharper reprimands if he resisted more directly. This cycle of passive refusal followed by disappointment and anger gradually tightened, and before long the struggle had spread to the task of doing the laundry. Nancy said it was only fair that Evan share the laundry. He agreed in principle, but anxious that Evan would not share, Nancy wanted a clear, explicit agreement. "You ought to wash and fold every other load," she had told him. Evan experienced this "plan" as a yoke around his neck. On many weekdays, at this point, a huge pile of laundry sat like a disheveled guest on the living-room couch.

In her frustration, Nancy began to make subtle emotional jabs at Evan. "I don't know *what's* for dinner," she would say with a sigh. Or "I can't cook now, I've got to deal with this pile of laundry." She tensed at the slightest criticism about household disorder; if Evan wouldn't do the housework, he had absolutely *no* right to criticize how she did it. She would burst out angrily at Evan. She recalled telling him: "After work *my* feet are just as tired as *your* feet. I'm just as wound up as you are. I come home. I cook dinner. I wash and I clean. Here we are, planning a second child, and I can't cope with the one we have."

About two years after I first began visiting the Holts, I began to see their problem in a certain light: as a conflict between their two gender ideologies. Nancy wanted to be the sort of woman who was needed and appreciated both at home and at work—like Lacey, she told me, on the television show "Cagney and Lacey." She wanted Evan to appreciate her for being a caring social worker, a committed wife, and a wonderful mother. But she cared just as much that she be able to appreciate *Evan* for what *he* contributed at home, not just for how he supported the family. She would feel proud to explain to women friends that she was married to one of these rare "new men."

A gender ideology is often rooted in early experience, and fueled by motives formed early on and such motives can often be traced to some cautionary tale in early life. So it was for Nancy. Nancy described her mother:

My mom was wonderful, a real aristocrat, but she was also terribly depressed being a housewife. My dad treated her like a doormat. She didn't have any self-confidence. And growing up, I can remember her being really depressed. I grew up bound and determined not to be like her and not to marry a man like my father. As long as Evan doesn't do the housework, I feel it means he's going to be like my father—coming home, putting his feet up, and hollering at my mom to serve him. That's my biggest fear. I've had *bad* dreams about that.

Nancy thought that women friends her age, also in traditional marriages, had come to similarly bad ends. She described a high school friend: "Martha barely made it through City College. She had no interest in learning anything. She spent nine years trailing around behind her husband [a salesman]. It's a miserable marriage. She hand washes all his shirts. The high point of her life was when she was eighteen and the two of us were running around Miami Beach in a Mustang convertible. She's gained seventy pounds and she hates her life." To Nancy, Martha was a younger version of her mother, depressed, lacking in self-esteem, a cautionary tale whose moral was "if you want to be happy, develop a career and get your husband to share at home." Asking Evan to help again and again felt like "hard work" but it was essential to establishing her role as a career woman.

For his own reasons, Evan imagined things very differently. He loved Nancy and if Nancy loved being a social worker, he was happy and proud to support her in it. He knew that because she took her caseload so seriously, it was draining work. But at the same time, he did not see why, just because she chose this demanding career, *he* had to change *his own* life. Why should her personal decision to work outside the home require him to do more inside it? Nancy earned about two-thirds as much as Evan, and her salary was a big help, but as Nancy confided, "If push came to shove, we could do without it." Nancy was a social worker because she loved it. Doing daily chores at home was thankless work, and certainly not something Evan needed her to appreciate about him. Equality in the second shift meant a loss in his standard of living, and despite all the high-flown talk, he felt he hadn't *really* bargained for it. He was happy to help Nancy at home if she needed help; that was fine. That was only decent. But it was too sticky a matter "committing" himself to sharing.

Two other beliefs probably fueled his resistance as well. The first was his suspicion that if he shared the second shift with Nancy, she would "dominate him." Nancy would ask him to do this, ask him to do that. It felt to Evan as if Nancy had won so many small victories that he had to draw the line somewhere. Nancy had a declarative personality; and as Nancy said, "Evan's mother sat me down and told me once that I was too forceful, that Evan needed to take more authority." Both Nancy and Evan agreed that Evan's sense of career and self was in fact shakier than Nancy's. He had been unemployed. She never had. He had had some bouts of drinking in the past. Drinking was foreign to her. Evan thought that sharing housework would upset a certain balance of power that felt culturally "right." He held the purse strings and made the major decisions about large purchases (like their house) because he "knew more about finances" and because he'd chipped in more inheritance than she when they married. His job difficulties had lowered his self-respect, and now as a couple they had achieved some ineffable "balance"— tilted in his favor, she thought—which, if corrected to equalize the burden of chores, would result in his giving in "too much." A certain driving anxiety behind Nancy's strategy of actively renegotiating roles had made Evan see agreement as "giving in." When he wasn't feeling good about work, he dreaded the idea of being under his wife's thumb at home.

Underneath these feelings, Evan perhaps also feared that Nancy was avoiding taking care of *him*. His own mother, a mild-mannered alcoholic, had by imperceptible steps phased herself out of a mother's role, leaving him very much on his own. Perhaps a personal motive to prevent that happening in his marriage—a guess on my part, and unarticulated on his—underlay his strategy of passive resistance. And he wasn't altogether wrong to fear this. Meanwhile, he felt he was "offering" Nancy the chance to stay home, or cut back her hours, and that she was refusing his "gift," while Nancy felt that, given her feelings about work, this offer was hardly a gift.

In the sixth year of her marriage, when Nancy again intensified her pressure on Evan to commit himself to equal sharing, Evan recalled saying, "Nancy, why don't you cut back to half time, that way you can fit everything in." At first Nancy was baffled: "We've been married all this time, and you *still* don't get it. Work is important to me. I worked *hard* to get my MSW. Why *should* I give it up?" Nancy also explained to Evan and later to me, "I think my degree and my job has been my way of reassuring myself that I won't end up like my mother." Yet she'd received little emotional support in getting her degree from either her parents or in-laws. (Her mother had avoided asking about her thesis, and her in-laws, though invited, did not attend her graduation, later claiming they'd never been invited.)

In addition, Nancy was more excited about seeing her elderly clients in tenderloin hotels than Evan was about selling couches to furniture salesmen with greased-back hair. Why shouldn't Evan make as many compromises with his career ambitions and his leisure as she'd made with hers? She couldn't see it Evan's way, and Evan couldn't see it hers.

In years of alternating struggle and compromise, Nancy had seen only fleeting mirages of cooperation, visions that appeared when she got sick or withdrew, and disappeared when she got better or came forward.

After seven years of loving marriage, Nancy and Evan had finally come to a terrible impasse. Their emotional standard of living had drastically declined: they began to snap at each other, to criticize, to carp. Each felt taken advantage of: Evan, because his offering of a good arrangement was deemed unacceptable, and Nancy, because Evan wouldn't do what she deeply felt was "fair."

This struggle made its way into their sexual life—first through Nancy directly, and then through Joey. Nancy had always disdained any form of feminine wiliness or manipulation. Her family saw her as "a flaming feminist" and that was how she saw herself. As such, she felt above the underhanded ways traditional women used to get around men. She mused, "When I was a teen-ager, I vowed I would *never* use sex to get my way with a man. It is not self-respecting; it's demeaning. But when Evan refused to carry his load at home, I did, I used sex, I said, 'Look, Evan, I would not be this exhausted and asexual every night if I didn't have so much to face every morning.'" She felt reduced to an old "strategy," and her modern ideas made her ashamed of it. At the same time, she'd run out of other, modern ways.

The idea of a separation arose, and they became frightened. Nancy looked at the deteriorating marriages and fresh divorces of couples with young children around them. One unhappy husband they knew had become so uninvolved in family life (they didn't know whether his unhappiness made him uninvolved, or whether his lack of involvement had caused his wife to be unhappy) that his wife left him. In another case, Nancy felt the wife had "nagged" her husband so much that he abandoned her for another woman. In both cases, the couple was less happy after the divorce than before, and both wives took the children and struggled desperately to survive financially. Nancy took stock. She asked herself, "Why wreck a marriage over a dirty frying pan?" Is it really worth it?

UPSTAIRS-DOWNSTAIRS: A FAMILY MYTH AS "SOLUTION"

Not long after this crisis in the Holts' marriage, there was a dramatic lessening of tension over the issue of the second shift. It was as if the issue was closed. Evan had won. Nancy would do the second shift. Evan expressed vague guilt but beyond that he had nothing to say. Nancy had wearied of continually raising the topic, wearied of the lack of resolution. Now in the exhaustion of defeat, she wanted the struggle to be over too. Evan was "so good" in *other* ways, why debilitate their marriage by continual quarreling. Besides, she told me, "Women always adjust more, don't they?"

One day, when I asked Nancy to tell me who did which tasks from a long list of household chores, she interrupted me with a broad wave of her hand and said, "I do the upstairs, Evan does the downstairs." What does that mean? I asked. Matter-of-factly, she explained that the upstairs included the living room, the dining room, the kitchen, two bedrooms, and two baths. The downstairs meant the garage, a place for storage and hobbies—Evan's hobbies. She explained this as a "sharing" arrangement, without humor or irony—just as Evan did later. Both said they had agreed it was the best solution to their dispute. Evan would take care of the car, the garage, and Max, the family dog. As Nancy explained, "The dog is all Evan's problem. I don't have to deal with the dog." Nancy took care of the rest.

For purposes of accommodating the second shift, then, the Holts' garage was elevated to the full moral and practical equivalent of the rest of the house. For Nancy and Evan, "upstairs and downstairs," "inside and outside," was vaguely described like "half and half," a fair division of labor based on a natural division of their house.

The Holts presented their upstairs-downstairs agreement as a perfectly equitable solution to a problem they "once had." This belief is what we might call a "family myth," even a modest delusional system. Why did they believe it? I think they believed it because they needed to believe it, because it solved a terrible problem. It allowed Nancy to continue thinking of herself as the sort of woman whose husband didn't abuse her—a self-conception that mattered a great deal to her. And it avoided the hard truth that, in his stolid, passive way, Evan had refused to share. It avoided the truth, too, that in their showdown, Nancy was more afraid of divorce than Evan was. This outer cover to their family life, this family myth, was jointly devised. It was an attempt to agree that there was no conflict over the second shift, no tension between their versions of manhood and womanhood, and that the powerful crisis that had arisen was temporary and minor.

The wish to avoid such a conflict is natural enough. But their avoidance was tacitly supported by the surrounding culture, especially the image of the woman with the flying hair. After all, this admirable woman also proudly does the "upstairs" each day without a husband's help and without conflict.

After Nancy and Evan reached their upstairs-downstairs agreement, their confrontations ended. They were nearly forgotten. Yet, as she described their daily life months after the agreement, Nancy's resentment still seemed alive and well. For example, she said:

> Evan and I eventually divided the labor so that I do the upstairs and Evan does the downstairs and the dog. So the dog is my husband's problem. But when I was getting the dog outside and getting Joey ready for childcare, and cleaning up the mess of feeding the cat, and getting the lunches together, and having my son wipe his nose on my outfit so I would have to change—then I was pissed! I felt that I was doing *everything*. All Evan was doing was getting up, having coffee, reading the paper, and saying, "Well, I have to go now," and often forgetting the lunch I'd bothered to make.

She also mentioned that she had fallen into the habit of putting Joey to bed in a certain way: he asked to be swung around by the arms, dropped on the bed, nuzzled and hugged, whispered to in his ear. Joey waited for her attention. He didn't go to sleep without it. But, increasingly, when Nancy tried it at eight or nine, the ritual didn't put Joey to sleep. On the contrary, it woke him up. It was then that Joey began to say he could only go to sleep in his parents' bed, that he began to sleep in their bed and to encroach on their sexual life.

Near the end of my visits, it struck me that Nancy was putting Joey to bed in an "exciting" way, later and later at night, in order to tell Evan something important: "You win, I'll go on doing all the work at home, but I'm angry about it and I'll make you pay." Evan had won the battle but lost the war. According to the family myth, all was well: the struggle had been resolved by the upstairs-downstairs agreement. But suppressed in one area of their marriage, this struggle lived on in another—as Joey's Problem, and as theirs.

NANCY'S "PROGRAM" TO SUSTAIN THE MYTH

There was a moment, I believe, when Nancy seemed to *decide* to give up on this one. She decided to try not to resent Evan. Whether or not other women face a moment just like this, at the very least they face the need to deal with all the feelings that naturally arise from a clash between a treasured ideal and an incompatible reality. In the age of a stalled revolution, it is a problem a great many women face.

Emotionally, Nancy's compromise from time to time slipped; she would forget and grow resentful again. Her new resolve needed maintenance. Only half aware that she was doing so, Nancy went to extraordinary lengths to maintain it. She could tell me now, a year or so after her "decision," in a matter-of-fact and noncritical way: "Evan likes to come home to a hot meal. He doesn't like to clear the table. He doesn't like to do the dishes. He likes to go watch TV. He likes to play with his son when he feels like it and not feel like he should be with him more." She seemed resigned.

Everything was "fine." But it had taken an extraordinary amount of complex "emotion work"—the work of *trying* to feel the "right" feeling, the feeling she wanted to feel—to make and keep everything "fine." Across the nation at this particular time in history, this emotion work is often all that stands between the stalled revolution on the one hand, and broken marriages on the other.

HOW MANY HOLTS?

In one key way the Holts were typical of the vast majority of two-job couples: their family life had become the shock absorber for a stalled revolution whose origin lay far outside it—in economic and cultural trends that bear very differently on men and women. Nancy was reading books, newspaper articles, and watching TV programs on the changing role of women. Evan wasn't. Nancy felt benefited by these changes; Evan didn't. In her ideals and in reality, Nancy was more different from her mother than Evan was from his father, for the culture and economy were in general pressing change faster upon women like her than upon men like Evan. Nancy had gone to college; her mother hadn't. Nancy had a professional job; her mother never had. Nancy had the idea that she should be equal with her husband; her mother hadn't been much exposed to that idea in her day. Nancy felt she should share the job of earning money, and that Evan should share the work at home; her mother hadn't imagined that was possible. Evan went to college, his father (and the other boys in his family, though not the girls) had gone too. Work was important to Evan's identity as a man as it had been for his father before him. Indeed, Evan felt the same way about family roles as his father had felt in his day. The new job opportunities and the feminist movement of the 1960s and '70s had transformed Nancy but left Evan pretty much the same. And the friction created by this difference between them moved to the issue of second shift as metal to a magnet. By the end, Evan did less housework and childcare than most men married to working women—but not much less. Evan and Nancy were also typical of nearly 40 percent of the marriages I studied in their clash of gender ideologies and their corresponding difference in notion about what constituted a "sacrifice" and what did not. By far the most common form of mismatch was like that between Nancy, an egalitarian, and Evan, a transitional.

But for most couples, the tensions between strategies did not move so quickly and powerfully to issues of housework and childcare. Nancy pushed harder than most women to get her husband to share the work at home, and she also lost more overwhelmingly than the few other women who fought that hard. Evan pursued his strategy of passive resistance with more quiet tenacity than most men, and he allowed himself to become far more marginal to his son's life than most other fathers. The myth of the Holts' "equal" arrangement seemed slightly more odd than other family myths that encapsulated equally powerful conflicts.

Beyond their upstairs-downstairs myth, the Holts tell us a great deal about the subtle ways a couple can encapsulate the tension caused by a struggle over the second shift without resolving the problem or divorcing. Like Nancy Holt, many women struggle to avoid, suppress, obscure, or mystify a frightening conflict over the second shift. They do not struggle like this because they started off wanting to, or because such struggle is inevitable or because women inevitably lose, but because they are forced to choose between equality and marriage. And they choose marriage. When asked about "ideal" relations between men and women in general, about what they want for their daughters, about what "ideally" they'd like in their own marriage, most working mothers "wished" their men would share the work at home.

But many "wish" it instead of "want" it. Other goals—like keeping peace at home— come first. Nancy Holt did some extraordinary behind-the-scenes emotion work to prevent her ideals from clashing with her marriage. In the end, she had confined and miniaturized her ideas of equality successfully enough to do two things she badly wanted to do: feel like a feminist, and live at peace with a man who was not. Her program had "worked." Evan won on the reality of the situation, because Nancy did the second shift. Nancy won on the cover story; they would talk about it as if they shared.

Nancy wore the upstairs-downstairs myth as an ideological cloak to protect her from the contradictions in her marriage and from the cultural and economic forces that press upon it. Nancy and Evan Holt were caught on opposite sides of the gender revolution occurring all around them. Through the 1960s, 1970s, and 1980s masses of women entered the public world of work—but went only so far up the occupational ladder. They tried for "equal" marriages, but got only so far in achieving it. They married men who liked them to work at the office but who wouldn't share the extra month a year at home. When confusion about the identity of the working woman created a cultural vacuum in the 1970s and 1980s, the image of the supermom quietly glided in. She made the "stall" seem normal and happy. But beneath the happy image of the woman with the flying hair are modern marriages like the Holts', reflecting intricate webs of tension, and the huge, hidden emotional cost to women, men, and children of having to "manage" inequality. Yet on the surface, all we might see would be Nancy Holt bounding confidently out the door at 8:30 A.M. briefcase in one hand, Joey in the other. All we might hear would be Nancy's and Evan's talk about their marriage as happy, normal, even "equal"—because equality was so important to Nancy.

10 *Family Diversity*

Mixed Doubles

Roberto Suro

Swarms of young people representing a rainbow of racial and ethnic groups are now a regular feature in advertisements for hip, casual clothes and music, and even some glitzy electronics goods. But where the united colors of America appear next may be determined in large measure by how—or if—marketing managers and advertising executives respond to some of the newest and most perplexing data to emerge from the melting pot: The number of married couples who are of different races or ethnic groups has doubled since 1980. And they tend to be upscale, well-educated, and young.

Just when politicians, advertisers, and social scientists had gotten used to the idea of dividing up the American population into a handful of distinct ethnic or racial groups and addressing each specifically, a new trend threatens to rip up niches and shred the conventional wisdom. An analysis of Census Bureau data conducted for American Demographics shows that the growth in the number of mixed marriages is breaking down—or at least shifting—age-old barriers. These couples emerge from the statistics as pioneers in a demographic landscape that is being transformed by the first great wave of immigrants made up primarily of non-whites. Trying to understand their impact is an exercise in predicting the future at a time when the foreign-born population is growing at a rate that is nearly four times that of the native-born.

That future will be further defined by the results of the 2000 census, with its expanded list of racial and ethnic categories, which will ratify a widespread understanding that "the country is indelibly changed by this convergence of cultures," says Gary Berman, CEO of the Market Segment Group, a Miami-based brand consultancy specializing in the multicultural market. Then, Berman says, "It will just be a matter of time before there is a rush to seek opportunities in that change."

For a preview of what the next census will show about intergroup marriages, American Demographics asked William H. Frey, senior fellow of demographic studies at the Milken Institute in Santa Monica and a professor at the State University of New York—Albany, to conduct a computer analysis of data from the U.S. Census Bureau's 1998 Current Population Survey. Frey's findings—unpublished until now—offer the first detailed glimpse of the scope and characteristics of a phenomena that has the long-term potential to transform the American family and the consumer marketplace.

More than 35 percent of Hispanics with four-year degrees cross group lines when they marry, and the out-marriage rate is one in three for Hispanics in the top income bracket, Frey has found. A fifth of all married Asian women have chosen a spouse of a different race or ethnicity, nearly twice the rate among Asian men overall. Not surprisingly, the Asians most likely to out-marry are those living in areas with relatively small immigrant populations. Meanwhile, Frey's analysis shows that in populous, trend-setting California, nearly one of every 12 non-Hispanic whites who gets hitched is marrying an Asian or a Hispanic. In contrast, out-marriage rates remain low for blacks, roughly a third of the rates for Hispanics and Asians.

Marrying someone of the same race, the same ethnicity, even the same religion, and marrying them forever were enduring social norms in the United States—until recently. Today, although the inhibitions to unions between blacks and whites prevail, attitudes toward marriage have shifted profoundly. That is evident in divorce rates and the prevalence of nontraditional households of all sorts. Intergroup marriage is part of this fundamental change in core social structures, and it is more than just a minor symptom. Today, there are nearly 3 million mixed marriages—about 5 percent of all married couples, compared to 3 percent in 1980. And if the large but incalculable number of mixed couples who are cohabiting but not married were added in, the phenomenon would undoubtedly encompass an even bigger slice of the nation's households.

But the data have a significance that goes far beyond marriage. These intergroup pairings illuminate fundamental trends in relations between whites and minorities. More specifically, these couples illustrate some of the slow, underlying changes in American culture and society that are taking place during an era of large-scale immigration. According to Census Bureau estimates, there are some 17 million foreign-born Asians and Hispanics resident in the United States, comprising the fastest-growing segments of the population. Finally, intermarriage touches on some of the most sensitive—and for a politician or advertiser, some of the most precarious—aspects of racial identity and bias.

"This is the beginning point of a blending of the races," Frey states. "You can expect that in these households racial or ethnic attitudes will soften, that identities will be less distinct, and that there will be an impact on attitudes in the communities surrounding these households. And this trend has real momentum behind it because it is so pronounced among young people."

Frey's data show that fully 30 percent of married Asians between the ages of 15 and 24 have found a spouse of a different group. Out-marriage is also strongly associated with youth among Hispanics, though to a slightly lesser extent, with nearly 16 percent of all married Hispanics between 15 and 24, and 17 percent of those ages 25 to 34, involved in an intergroup marriage. Even among blacks the rate of out-marriage among the young is far higher than average, with about 11 percent of the married 15-to-24-year-olds going outside the group, compared to just 5 percent for blacks overall. "To be able to accept a person of a different race in marriage—to merely be open to the possibility—is very definitely a form of assimilation," says Wanla Cheng, principal and owner of the Asia Link Consulting Group, a New York City-based marketing research and consulting company.

"And it is a very distinct kind of assimilation that we see most clearly among young people, especially well-educated young people who are able to put aside these differences that get so much emphasis in the rest of society."

Defining the assimilation that takes place in these households, understanding which partners are changing and how, and then designing strategies to address the new tastes and appetites loom as important challenges. How many marketers and advertisers are taking up the cause?

"Almost no one," says Cheng.

"Many are still at the beginning, just learning the need to communicate with a Spanish or Asian market," says Berman. "Some others have gone farther and are learning to address different sub-groups according to nationality. But only a relatively small number have drilled down to what you might call the third level, where you are dealing with the very dynamic kind of multiculturalism represented by interracial marriages."

When business executives reach that level, they are often required to perform intellectual acrobatics. "A lot of firms have become reliant on niche marketing that divides up the world very simply into Anglos, Asians, Hispanics, and African Americans," says Shelley Yamane, vice president of strategic services at Muse Cordero Chen & Partners, a multicultural advertising agency based in Los Angeles. "But the high degree of intermarriage among the young means you can't just lump people together into those categories anymore. It means that there is a growing audience out there—a desirable audience that doesn't fit neatly in any niche."

For one thing, that audience is almost always half white and half something else, because out-marriage by Hispanics, Asians, and blacks overwhelmingly involves a white spouse, according to Frey's analysis. And even that audience can be very different, depending on which kind of mix you examine.

Among Hispanics, for example, the rates of intergroup marriage are about the same for men and women, and although the trend is concentrated among the young, there are also significant numbers of older Hispanics in mixed marriages. Among Asians, the trend is much more pronounced among women, while among blacks it is just the opposite: Black men marry women of other races at twice the rate of black females. For Hispanics, the correlation to economic success and education is stronger than for other groups: Hispanics with a college degree and a substantial income are more than five times as likely to out-marry than those who didn't finish high school or who live in poverty. Meanwhile, among both Hispanics and Asians, the native-born are much more likely than immigrants to find a white spouse, with intermarriage rates approaching 30 percent of all native-born married couples. Among immigrants of both groups the prevalence of intermarriage steadily increases with the length of time spent in the United States.

Understanding the geodemographic patterns is no less complicated an endeavor. At first, intergroup marriages appear to be clustered in the obvious places. They are disproportionately concentrated in the states that have disproportionately high Hispanic and Asian populations: California, Texas, Florida, and New York. California, for example, has 11 percent of the nation's married-couple households and 23 percent of the mixed-marriages. But going beyond that rough cut, Frey's data suggest that the geographic patterns are different depending on whether you are looking at the trends among whites or among minorities.

For non-Hispanic whites, the rates of out-marriage as a percentage of the whole are far higher in those states with big Asian and Hispanic populations than in the rest of the country. White-Hispanic marriages, for example, are roughly four to five times as common in California and Texas than in states with relatively smaller Hispanic populations.

To see any significant degree of intermarriage by non-Hispanic whites, says Frey, "It seems there must be a critical mass of a minority population before you get the kind of interaction, especially among young people, that leads to these elevated rates." Frey's data show that in California, for example, 8.5 percent of all married whites are in intergroup couples, versus 2 percent in low-immigration states.

But for Hispanics and Asians, the geographic trend is reversed. The rate of out-marriage by Hispanics is more than twice as high in the low immigration states as in the states where these populations are concentrated: In California, Texas, Florida, and New York combined, Frey's analysis shows that 12.5 percent of the married Hispanics are in intergroup marriages, while in the rest of the country the rate is 26.5 percent. And the trend is similar for Asians—11.5 percent, versus 19.4 percent. (Among blacks there is no distinct geographic pattern to out-marriage.)

"Availability would seem to be one factor: In states where there are fewer fellow Asians and Hispanics, they are more likely to find a white spouse," Frey explains. "But this is such an intimate measure of attitudes toward racial differences that it also suggests an especially powerful form of assimilation is taking place among the Asians and Hispanics who move up and out of the melting pot states."

But very little in this age of immigration moves in a straight line. One has to ask who is doing the assimilating and what is the end result, especially if the goal is to understand attitudes, tastes, and habits. Consider the case of Xijuan Wang, who now answers her office phone "Lauren Greenstein." Greenstein, 42, came to the U.S. from China in 1987 on a scholarship to study English literature. While in a graduate program at Columbia University in New York, she switched to computer science. It was in New York City, at a party in 1995, that she met her future husband, Mark, an attorney.

Now living in the Washington, D.C., area, Greenstein works for a computer network services firm, speaks English fluently, and in many ways might seem entirely assimilated. The conversation around the dinner table is in English, for example. But look at the food and you will find that most of the home-cooked meals are traditional Chinese cuisine. Then follow Mark and Lauren on the many evenings they eat out and you'll see they rarely go to a Chinese restaurant, pursuing eclectic tastes instead. And ask their baby daughter, almost 2 years old, her name, and she'll say "Leah," something perfectly American. But her chatter increasingly includes Chinese words learned from her mother and a Chinese babysitter.

"As people marry out, there is a lifestyle change because English is almost always the dominant language of the household and they are more likely to make purchasing decisions based on English-language media," Yamane says. "But you also often see a boomerang effect because people feel disconnected from their past and so there is a strong pull back to the home country or community."

In the Greenstein household, one of the major monthly expenses and a key purchasing decision is the long-distance carrier. "I have to be able to call home a lot, whenever I want, and that costs money," Greenstein says.

But acculturation works both ways. "When you look at how people dress, the food they eat, and the music they listen to, particularly in places like California and Florida, even New York, you can see that the non-whites are under less pressure to assimilate, because it is cool to be Latin, it is cool to be Asian," Berman says. "Intermarriage is [also] a sign that assimilation by the dominant white culture is under way. And it is more than just a matter of tastes. You see it in the way Americans are embracing the family values that are so basic to Asian and Hispanic societies."

Does this all mean we'll soon see advertisements on prime-time, English-language television or in mainstream publications featuring mixed-race couples walking hand-in-hand to their new car? Multicultural marketing experts are unanimously cautious on this point.

"Portraying mixed marriages is a double-edged sword," says Cheng. "This can be a very dangerous subject to address directly in advertising."

Enough bias persists in the white population that portrayals of interracial couples could cause a backlash. And even in minority communities there are complex issues. "Intermarriage is a very delicate matter in Asian communities because there is a strong underlying resentment among many Asian men over the large number of Asian women who go outside the community to find husbands," says Cheng. Moreover, there are large technical hurdles to overcome before messages can be aimed directly at intergroup couples.

"You have to ask, first, whether this sub-group can be described in enough detail and with enough precision to get an advertiser interested, and then you have to ask whether there are unique media to reach them," says Saul Gitlin, vice president of strategic marketing services at Kang & Lee Advertising, a Young & Rubicam company specializing in the Asian marketplace. "And then you have to show that you have some way to measure results for the effort."

But rather than promote ever-more-specialized advertising aimed at narrowly sliced market niches, the impact of intergroup marriage may be felt in general advertising, according to some marketing executives. "A brand can demonstrate a commitment to multiculturalism in very broad terms," says Berman. And, Gitlin notes, "In the general advertising market, you may be able to have an impact with more diversity at the creative end, such as a greater mix of races in the talent. That might allow you to speak to the different racial groups within a household without explicitly depicting a racially mixed marriage."

Philips Electronics is one brand that has already decided to make a diverse "tribe" of young people an essential part of its advertising identity. "The best advertising holds a mirror up to society and that is what we are doing," says Elissa Moses, director of global consumer and market intelligence for the Netherlands-based company.

Recent Philips television commercials have used multiethnic groupings of twenty-somethings to promote products like flat-screen TVs. "Young people are the leading edge of interest in, comfort with, and adoption of a whole range of technological products," Moses says. Although Philips had some understanding of the growth in intermarriage rates, the trend was only "tangential" to their effort, Moses says. Instead, Philips commercials are meant to be "emblematic of the emergence of a global culture, in which the dominant characteristic is humanism rather than separatism."

Politically, socially, culturally—as well as commercially—the rapid growth of the Hispanic and Asian populations in recent years has heightened attention to group differences. Over time, intermarriage could prove a powerful counterforce to this emphasis on segmentation. As Gregory Rodriguez, research scholar at the Pepperdine Institute for Public Policy, put it recently, "Intermarriage is not only a sign that a person has transcended the ethnic self-segregation of the first years of immigration, it is also the most potent example of how Americans forge a common national experience out of a diverse cultural past."

Diversity within African American Families

Ronald L. Taylor

PERSONAL REFLECTIONS

My interest in African American families as a topic of research was inspired more than two decades ago by my observation and growing dismay over the stereotypical portrayal of these families presented by the media and in much of the social science literature. Most of the African American families I knew in the large southern city in which I grew up were barely represented in the various "authoritative" accounts I read and other scholars frequently referred to in their characterizations and analyses of such families. Few such accounts have acknowledged the regional, ethnic, class, and behavioral diversity within the African American community and among families. As a result, a highly fragmented and distorted public image of African American family life has been perpetuated that encourages perceptions of African American families as a monolith. The 1986 television documentary *A CBS Report: The Vanishing Family: Crisis in Black America*, hosted by Bill Moyers, was fairly typical of this emphasis. It focused almost exclusively on low-income, single-parent households in inner cities, characterized them as "vanishing" non-families, and implied that such families represented the majority of African American families in urban America. It mattered little that poor, single-parent households in the inner cities made up less than a quarter of all African American families at the time the documentary was aired.

As an African American reared in the segregated South, I was keenly aware of the tremendous variety of African American families in composition, lifestyle, and socioeconomic status. Racial segregation ensured that African American families, regardless of means or circumstances, were constrained to live and work in close proximity to one another. Travel outside the South made me aware of important regional differences among African American families as well. For example, African American families in the Northeast appeared far more segregated by socioeconomic status than did families in many parts of the South with which I was familiar. As a graduate student at Boston University during the late 1960s, I recall the shock I experienced upon seeing the level of concentrated poverty among African American families in Roxbury, Massachusetts, an experience duplicated in travels to New York, Philadelphia, and Newark. To be sure, poverty of a similar magnitude was prevalent throughout the South, but was far less concentrated and, from my perception, far less pernicious.

As I became more familiar, with the growing body of research on African American families, it became increasingly clear to me that the source of a major distortion in the portrayal of African American families in the social science literature and the media was the overwhelming concentration on impoverished inner-city communities of the Northeast and Midwest to the near exclusion of the South, where more than half the African American families are found and differences among them in family patterns, lifestyles, and socioeconomic characteristics are more apparent.

In approaching the study of African American families in my work, I have adopted a *holistic* perspective. This perspective, outlined first by DuBois (1898) and more recently by Billingsley (1992) and Hill (1993), emphasizes the influence of historical, cultural, social, economic, and political forces in shaping contemporary patterns of family life among African Americans of all socioeconomic backgrounds. Although the impact of these external forces is routinely taken into account in assessing stability and change among white families, their effects on the structure and functioning of African American families are often minimized. In short, a holistic approach undertakes to study African American families *in context*. My definition of the *family*, akin to the definition offered by Billingsley (1992), views it as an intimate association of two or more persons related to each other by blood, marriage, formal or informal adoption, or appropriation. The latter term refers to the incorporation of persons in the family who are unrelated by blood or marital ties but are treated as though they are family. This definition is broader than other dominant definitions of families that emphasize biological or marital ties as defining characteristics.

This chapter is divided into three parts. The first part reviews the treatment of African American families in the historical and social sciences literatures. It provides a historical overview of African American families, informed by recent historical scholarship, that corrects many of the misconceptions about the nature and quality of family life during and following the experience of slavery. The second part examines contemporary patterns of marriage, family, and household composition among African Americans in response to recent social, economic, and political developments in the larger society. The third part explores some of the long-term implications of current trends in marriage and family behavior for community functioning and individual well-being, together with implications for social policy.

THE TREATMENT OF AFRICAN AMERICAN FAMILIES IN AMERICAN SCHOLARSHIP

As an area of scientific investigation, the study of African American family life is of recent vintage. As recently as 1968, Billingsley, in his classic work *Black Families in White America*, observed that African American family life had been virtually ignored in family studies and studies of race and ethnic relations. He attributed the general lack of interest among white social scientists, in part, to their "ethnocentrism and intellectual commitment to peoples and values transplanted from Europe" (p. 214). Content analyses of key journals in sociology, social work, and family studies during the period supported Billingsley's contention. For example, a content analysis of 10 leading journals in sociology and social work by Johnson (1981) disclosed that articles on African American families constituted only 3% of 3,547 empirical studies of American families published between 1965 and 1975. Moreover, in the two major journals in social work, only one article on African American families was published from 1965 to 1978. In fact, a 1978 special issue of the *Journal of Marriage and the Family* devoted to African American families accounted for 40% of all articles on these families published in the 10 major journals between 1965 and 1978.

Although the past two decades have seen a significant increase in the quantity and quality of research on the family lives of African Americans, certain features and limitations associated with earlier studies in this area persist (Taylor, Chatters, Tucker, & Lewis, 1990). In a review of recent research on African American families, Hill (1993) concluded that many studies continue to treat such families in superficial terms; that is, African American families are not considered to be an important unit of focus and, consequently, are treated peripherally or omitted altogether. The assumption is that African American families are automatically treated in all analyses that focus on African Americans as individuals; thus, they are not treated in their own right. Hill noted that a major impediment to understanding the functioning of African American families has been the failure of most analysts to use a theoretical or conceptual framework that took account of the totality of African American family life. Overall, he found that the preponderance of recent studies of African American families are

> (a) fragmented, in that they exclude the bulk of Black families by focusing on only a subgroup; (b) ad hoc, in that they apply arbitrary explanations that are not derived from systematic theoretical formulations that have been empirically substantiated; (c) negative, in that they focus exclusively on the perceived weaknesses of Black families; and (d) internally oriented, in that they exclude any systematic consideration of the role of forces in the wider society on Black family life. (p. 5)

THEORETICAL APPROACHES

The study of African American families, like the study of American families in general, has evolved through successive theoretical formulations. Using white family structure as the norm, the earliest studies characterized African American families as impoverished versions of white families in which the experiences of slavery, economic deprivation, and racial discrimination had induced pathogenic and dysfunctional features (Billingsley, 1968). The classic statement of this perspective was presented by Frazier, whose study, *The Negro Family in the United States* (1939), was the first comprehensive analysis of African American family life and its transformation under various historical conditions—slavery, emancipation, and urbanization (Edwards, 1968).

It was Frazier's contention that slavery destroyed African familial structures and cultures and gave rise to a host of dysfunctional family features that continued to undermine the stability and well-being of African American families well into the 20th century. Foremost among these features was the supposed emergence of the African American "matriarchal" or maternal family system, which weakened the economic position of African American men and their authority in the family. In his view, this family form was inherently unstable and produced pathological outcomes in the family unit, including high rates of poverty, illegitimacy, crime, delinquency, and other problems associated with the socialization of children. Frazier concluded that the female-headed family had become a common tradition among large segments of lower-class African American migrants to the North during the early 20th century. The two-parent male-headed household represented a second tradition among a minority of African Americans who enjoyed some of the freedoms during slavery, had independent artisan skills, and owned property.

Frazier saw an inextricable connection between economic resources and African American family structure and concluded that as the economic position of African Americans improved, their conformity to normative family patterns would increase. However, his important insight regarding the link between family structure and economic resources was obscured by the inordinate emphasis he placed on the instability and "self-perpetuating pathologies" of lower-class African American families, an emphasis that powerfully contributed to the pejorative tradition of scholarship that emerged in this area. Nonetheless, Frazier recognized the diversity of African American families and in his analyses, "consistently attributed the primary sources of family instability to external forces (such as racism, urbanization, technological changes and recession) and not to internal characteristics of Black families" (Hill, 1993, pp. 7–8).

During the 1960s, Frazier's characterization of African American families gained wider currency with the publication of Moynihan's *The Negro Family: The Case for National Action* (1965), in which weaknesses in family structure were identified as a major source of social problems in African American communities. Moynihan attributed high rates of welfare dependence, out-of-wedlock births, educational failure, and other problems to the "unnatural" dominance of women in African American families. Relying largely on the work of Frazier as a source of reference, Moynihan traced the alleged "tangle of pathology" that characterized urban African American families to the experience of slavery and 300 years of racial oppression, which, he concluded, had caused "deep-seated structural distortions" in the family and community life of African Americans.

Although much of the Moynihan report, as the book was called, largely restated what had become conventional academic wisdom on African American families during the 1960s, its generalized indictment of all African American families ignited a firestorm of criticism and debate and inspired a wealth of new research and writings on the nature and quality of African American family life in the United States (Staples & Mirande, 1980). In fact, the 1970s saw the beginning of the most prolific period of research on African American families, with more than 50 books and 500 articles published during that decade alone, representing a fivefold increase over the literature produced in all the years since the publication of DuBois's (1909) pioneering study of African American family life (Staples & Mirande, 1980). To be sure, some of this work was polemical and defensively apologetic, but much of it sought to replace ideology with research and to provide alternative perspectives for interpreting observed differences in the characteristics of African American and white families (Allen, 1978).

Critics of the deficit or pathology approach to African American family life (Scanzoni, 1977; Staples, 1971) called attention to the tendency in the literature to ignore family patterns among the majority of African Americans and to overemphasize findings derived from studies of low-income and typically problem-ridden families. Such findings were often generalized and accepted as descriptive of the family life of all African American families, with the result that popular but erroneous images of African American family life were perpetuated. Scrutinizing the research literature of the 1960s, Billingsley (1968) concluded that when the majority of African American families was considered, evidence refuted the characterization of African American family life as unstable, dependent on welfare, and matriarchal. In his view, and in the view of a growing number of scholars in the late 1960s and early 1970s, observed differences between white and African American families were largely the result of differences in socioeconomic position and of differential access to economic resources (Allen, 1978; Scanzoni, 1977).

Thus, the 1970s witnessed not only a significant increase in the diversity, breadth, and quantity of research on African American families, but a shift away from a social pathology perspective to one emphasizing the resilience and adaptiveness of African American families under a variety of social and economic conditions. The new emphasis reflected what Allen (1978) referred to as the "cultural variant" perspective, which treats African American families as different but legitimate functional forms. From this perspective, "Black and White family differences [are] taken as given, without the presumption of one family form as normative and the other as deviant." (Farley & Allen, 1987, p. 162). In accounting for observed racial differences in family patterns, some researchers have taken a *structural perspective*, emphasizing poverty and other socioeconomic factors as key processes (Billingsley, 1968). Other scholars have taken a *cultural approach*, stressing elements of the West African cultural heritage, together with distinctive experiences, values, and behavioral modes of adaptation developed in this country, as major determinants (Nobles, 1978; Young, 1970). Still others (Collins, 1990; Sudarkasa, 1988) have pointed to evidence supporting both interpretations and have argued for a more comprehensive approach.

Efforts to demythologize negative images of African American families have continued during the past two decades, marked by the development of the first national sample of adult African Americans, drawn to reflect their distribution throughout the United States (Jackson, 1991), and by the use of a variety of conceptualizations, approaches, and methodologies in the study of African American family life (Collins, 1990; McAdoo, 1997). Moreover, the emphasis in much of the recent work

> has not been the defense of African American family forms, but rather the identification of forces that have altered long-standing traditions. The ideological paradigms identified by Allen (1978) to describe the earlier thrust of Black family research—cultural equivalence, cultural deviance, and cultural variation—do not fully capture the foci of this new genre of work as a whole. (Tucker & Mitchell-Kernan, 1995, p. 17)

Researchers have sought to stress balance in their analyses, that is, to assess the strengths and weaknesses of African American family organizations at various socioeconomic levels, and the need for solution-oriented studies (Hill, 1993). At the same time, recent historical scholarship has shed new light on the relationship of changing historical circumstances to characteristics of African American family organization and has underscored the relevance of historical experiences to contemporary patterns of family life.

AFRICAN AMERICAN FAMILIES
IN HISTORICAL PERSPECTIVE

Until the 1970s, it was conventional academic wisdom that the experience of slavery decimated African American culture and created the foundation for unstable female-dominated households and other familial aberrations that continued into the 20th century. This thesis, advanced by Frazier (1939) and restated by Moynihan (1965), was seriously challenged by the pioneering historical research of Blassingame (1972), Furstenberg, Hershberg, and Modell (1975), and Gutman (1976), among others. These works provide compelling documentation of the centrality of family and kinship among African Americans during the long years of bondage and how African Americans created and sustained a rich cultural and family life despite the brutal reality of slavery.

In his examination of more than two centuries of slave letters, autobiographies, plantation records, and other materials, Blassingame (1972) meticulously documented the nature of community, family organization, and culture among American slaves. He concluded that slavery was not "an all-powerful, monolithic institution which strip[ped] the slave of any meaningful and distinctive culture, family life, religion or manhood" (p. vii). To the contrary, the relative freedom from white control that slaves enjoyed in their quarters enabled them to create and sustain a complex social organization that incorporated "norms of conduct, defined roles and behavioral patterns" and provided for the traditional functions of group solidarity, defense, mutual assistance, and family organization. Although the family had no legal standing in slavery and was frequently disrupted, Blassingame noted its major role as a source of survival for slaves and as a mechanism of social control for slaveholders, many of whom encouraged "monogamous mating arrangements" as insurance against runaways and rebellion. In fashioning familial and community organization, slaves drew upon the many remnants of their African heritage (e.g., courtship rituals, kinship networks, and religious beliefs), merging those elements with American forms to create a distinctive culture, features of which persist in the contemporary social organization of African American family life and community.

Genovese's (1974) analysis of plantation records and slave testimony led him to similar conclusions regarding the nature of family life and community among African Americans under slavery. Genovese noted that, although chattel bondage played havoc with the domestic lives of slaves and imposed severe constraints on their ability to enact and sustain normative family roles and functions, the slaves "created impressive norms of family, including as much of a nuclear family norm as conditions permitted and . . . entered the postwar social system with a remarkably stable base" (p. 452). He attributed this stability to the extraordinary resourcefulness and commitment of slaves to marital relations and to what he called a "paternalistic compromise," or bargain between masters and slaves that recognized certain reciprocal obligations and rights, including recognition of slaves' marital and family ties. Although slavery undermined the role of African American men as husbands and fathers, their function as role models for their children and as providers for their families was considerably greater than has generally been supposed. Nonetheless, the tenuous position of male slaves as husbands and fathers and the more visible and nontraditional roles assumed by female slaves gave rise to legends of matriarchy and emasculated men. However, Genovese contended that the relationship between slave men and women came closer to approximating gender equality than was possible for white families.

Perhaps the most significant historical work that forced revisions in scholarship on African American family life and culture during slavery was Gutman's (1976) landmark study, *The Black Family in Slavery and Freedom.* Inspired by the controversy surrounding the Moynihan report and its thesis that African American family disorganization was a legacy of slavery, Gutman made ingenious use of quantifiable data derived from plantation birth registers and marriage applications to re-create family and kinship structures among African Americans during slavery and after emancipation. Moreover, he marshaled compelling evidence to explain how African Americans developed an autonomous and complex culture that enabled them to cope with the harshness of enslavement, the massive relocation from relatively small economic units in the upper South to vast plantations in the lower South between 1790 and 1860, the experience of legal freedom in the rural and urban South, and the transition to northern urban communities before 1930.

Gutman reasoned that, if family disorganization (fatherless, matrifocal families) among African Americans was a legacy of slavery, then such a condition should have been more common among urban African Americans closer in time to slavery—in 1850 and 1860—than in 1950 and 1960. Through careful examination of census data, marriage licenses, and personal documents for the period after 1860, he found that stable, two-parent households predominated during slavery and after emancipation and that families headed by African American women at the turn of the century were hardly more prevalent than among comparable white families. Thus "[a]t all moments in time between 1860 and 1925 . . . the typical Afro-American family was lower class in status and headed by two parents. That was so in the urban and rural South in 1880 and 1900 and in New York City in 1905 and 1925" (p. 456). Gutman found that the two-parent family was just as common among the poor as among the more advantaged, and as common among southerners as those in the Northeast. For Gutman, the key to understanding the durability of African American families during and after slavery lay in the distinctive African American culture that evolved from the cumulative slave experiences that provided a defense against some of the more destructive and dehumanizing aspects of that system. Among the more enduring and important aspects of that culture are the enlarged kinship network and certain domestic arrangements (e.g., the sharing of family households with nonrelatives and the informal adoption of children) that, during slavery, formed the core of evolving African American communities and the collective sense of interdependence.

Additional support for the conclusion that the two-parent household was the norm among slaves and their descendants was provided by Furstenberg et al. (1975) from their study of the family composition of African Americans, native-born whites, and immigrants to Philadelphia from 1850 to 1880. From their analysis of census data, Furstenberg et al. found that most African American families, like those of other ethnic groups, were headed by two parents (75% for African Americans versus 73% for native whites). Similar results are reported by Pleck (1973) from her study of African American family structure in late 19th-century Boston. As these and other studies (Jones, 1985; White, 1985) have shown, although female-headed households were common among African

Americans during and following slavery, such households were by no means typical. In fact, as late as the 1960s, three fourths of African American households were headed by married couples (Jaynes & Williams, 1989; Moynihan, 1965).

However, more recent historical research would appear to modify, if not challenge, several of the contentions of the revisionist scholars of slavery. Manfra and Dykstra (1985) and Stevenson (1995), among others, found evidence of considerably greater variability in slave family structure and in household composition than was reported in previous works. In her study of Virginia slave families from 1830 to 1860, Stevenson (1995) discovered evidence of widespread matrifocality, as well as other marital and household arrangements, among antebellum slaves. Her analysis of the family histories of slaves in colonial and antebellum Virginia revealed that many slaves did not have a nuclear "core" in their families. Rather, the "most discernible ideal for their principal kinship organization was a malleable extended family that provided its members with nurture, education, socialization, material support, and recreation in the face of the potential social chaos the slavemasters' power imposed" (1995, p. 36).

A variety of conditions affected the family configurations of slaves, including cultural differences among the slaves themselves, the state or territory in which they lived, and the size of the plantation on which they resided. Thus, Stevenson concluded that

> the slave family was not a static, imitative institution that necessarily favored one form of family organization over another. Rather, it was a diverse phenomenon, sometimes assuming several forms even among the slaves of one community. . . .Far from having a negative impact, the diversity of slave marriage and family norms, as a measure of the slave family's enormous adaptive potential, allowed the slave and the slave family to survive. (p. 29)

Hence, "postrevisionist" historiography emphasizes the great diversity of familial arrangements among African Americans during slavery. Although nuclear, matrifocal, and extended families were prevalent, none dominated slave family forms. These postrevisionist amendments notwithstanding, there is compelling historical evidence that African American nuclear families and kin-related households remained relatively intact and survived the experiences of slavery, Reconstruction, the Great Depression, and the transition to northern urban communities. Such evidence underscores the importance of considering recent developments and conditions in accounting for changes in family patterns among African Americans in the contemporary period.

CONTEMPORARY AFRICAN AMERICAN FAMILY PATTERNS

Substantial changes have occurred in patterns of marriage, family, and household composition in the United States during the past three decades, accompanied by significant alterations in the family lives of men, women, and children. During this period, divorce rates have more than doubled, marriage rates have declined, fertility rates have fallen to record levels, the proportion of "traditional" families (nuclear families in which children live with both biological parents) as a percentage of all family groups has declined, and the proportion of children reared in single-parent households has risen dramatically (Taylor, 1997).

Some of the changes in family patterns have been more rapid and dramatic among African Americans than among the population as a whole. For example, while declining rates of marriage and remarriage, high levels of separation and divorce, and higher proportions of children living in single-parent households are trends that have characterized the U.S. population as a whole during the past 30 years, these trends have been more pronounced among African Americans and, in some respects, represent marked departures from earlier African American family patterns. A growing body of research has implicated demographic and economic factors as causes of the divergent marital and family experiences of African Americans and other populations.

In the following section, I examine diverse patterns and evolving trends in family structure and household composition among African Americans, together with those demographic, economic, and social factors that have been identified as sources of change in patterns of family formation.

Diversity of Family Structure

Since 1960, the number of African American households has increased at more than twice the rate of white households. By 1995, African American households numbered 11.6 million, compared with 83.7 million white households. Of these households, 58.4 million white and 8.0 million African American ones were classified as family households by the U.S. Bureau of the Census (1996), which defines a *household* as the person or persons occupying a housing unit and a *family* as consisting of two or more persons who live in the same household and are related by birth, marriage, or adoption. Thus, family households are households maintained by individuals who share their residence with one or more relatives, whereas nonfamily households are maintained by individuals with no relatives in the housing unit. In 1995, 70% of the 11.6 million African American households were family households, the same proportion as among white households (U.S. Bureau of the Census, 1996). However, nonfamily households have been increasing at a faster rate than family households among African Americans because of delayed marriages among young adults, higher rates of family disruption (divorce and separation), and sharp increases in the number of unmarried cohabiting couples (Cherlin, 1995; Glick, 1997).

Family households vary by type and composition. Although the U.S. Bureau of the Census recognizes the wide diversity of families in this country, it differentiates between three broad and basic types of family households: married-couple or husband-wife families, families with female householders (no husband present), and families with male householders (no wife present). Family composition refers to whether the household is *nuclear*; that is, contains parents and children only, or extended, that is, nuclear plus other relatives.

To take account of the diversity in types and composition of African American families, Billingsley (1968; 1992) added to these conventional categories *augmented* families (nuclear plus nonrelated persons), and modified the definition of nuclear family to include *incipient* (a married couple without children), *simple* (a couple with children), and *attenuated* (a single parent with children) families. He also added three combinations of augmented families: *incipient extended augmented* (a couple with relatives and nonrelatives), *nuclear extended augmented* (a couple with children, relatives, and nonrelatives), and *attenuated extended augmented* (a single parent with children, relatives, and nonrelatives). With these modifications, Billingsley identified 32 different kinds of nuclear, extended, and augmented family households among African Americans. His typology has been widely used and modified by other scholars (see, for example, Shimkin, Shimkin, & Frate, 1978; Stack, 1974). For example, on the basis of Billingsley's typology, Dressler, Haworth-Hoeppner, and Pitts (1985) developed a four-way typology with 12 subtypes for their study of household structures in a southern African American community and found a variety of types of female-headed households, less than a fourth of them consisting of a mother and her children or grandchildren.

However, as Staples (1971) pointed out, Billingsley's typology emphasized the household and ignored an important characteristic of such families—their "extendedness." African Americans are significantly more likely than whites to live in extended families that "transcend and link several different households, each containing a separate . . . family" (Farley & Allen, 1987, p. 168). In 1992, approximately 1 in 5 African American families was extended, compared to 1 in 10 white families (Glick, 1997). The greater proportion of extended households among African Americans has been linked to the extended family tradition of West African cultures (Nobles, 1978; Sudarkasa, 1988) and to the economic marginality of many African American families, which has encouraged the sharing and exchange of resources, services, and emotional support among family units spread across a number of households (Stack, 1974).

In comparative research on West African, Caribbean, and African American family patterns some anthropologists (Herskovits, 1958; Sudarkasa, 1997) found evidence of cultural continuities in the significance attached to coresidence, formal kinship relations, and nuclear families among black populations in these areas. Summarizing this work, Hill (1993, pp. 104–105) observed that, with respect to

> co-residence, the African concept of family is not restricted to persons living in the same household, but includes key persons living in separate households. . . . As for defining kin relationships, the African concept of family is not confined to relations between formal kin, but includes networks of unrelated [i.e., "fictive kin"] as well as related persons living in separate households. . . . [According to] Herskovits (1941), the African nuclear family unit is not as central to its family organization as is the case for European nuclear families: "The African immediate family, consisting of a father, his wives, and their children, is but a part of a larger unit. This immediate family is generally recognized by Africanists as belonging to a local relationship group termed the 'extended family.' "

Similarly, Sudarkasa (1988) found that unlike the European extended family, in which primacy is given to the conjugal unit (husband, wife, and children) as the basic building block, the African extended family is organized around blood ties (consanguineous relations).

In their analysis of data from the National Survey of Black Americans (NSBA) on household composition and family structure, Hatchett, Cochran, and Jackson (1991) noted that the extended family perspective, especially kin networks, was valuable in describing the nature and functioning of African American families. They suggested that the "extended family can be viewed both as a family network in the physical-spatial sense and in terms of family relations or contact and exchanges. In this view of extendedness, family structure and function are interdependent concepts" (p. 49). Their examination of the composition of the 2,107 households in the NSBA resulted in the identification of 12 categories, 8 of which roughly captured the "dimensions of household family structure identified in Billingsley's typology of Black families (1968)—the incipient nuclear family, the incipient nuclear extended and/or augmented nuclear family, the simple nuclear family, the simple extended and/or augmented nuclear family, the attenuated nuclear family, and the attenuated extended and/or augmented family, respectively" (p. 51). These households were examined with respect to their *actual kin networks*, defined as subjective feelings of emotional closeness to family members, frequency of contact, and patterns of mutual assistance, and their *potential kin networks*, defined as the availability or proximity of immediate family members and the density or concentration of family members within a given range.

Hatchett et al. (1991) found that approximately 1 in 5 African American households in the NSBA was an extended household (included other relatives—parents and siblings of the household head, grandchildren, grandparents, and nieces and nephews). Nearly 20% of the extended households with children contained minors who were not the head's; most of these children were grandchildren, nieces, and nephews of the head. The authors suggested that "[t]hese are instances of informal fostering or adoption— absorption of minor children by the kin network" (p. 58).

In this sample, female-headed households were as likely to be extended as male-headed households. Hatchett et al. (1991) found little support for the possibility that economic hardship may account for the propensity among African Americans to incorporate other relatives in their households. That is, the inclusion of other relatives in the households did not substantially improve the overall economic situation of the households because the majority of other relatives were minor children, primarily grandchildren of heads who coresided with the household heads' own minor and adult children. Moreover, they stated, "household extendedness at both the household and extra-household levels appears to be a characteristic of black families, regardless of socioeconomic level" (p. 81), and regardless of region of the country or rural or urban residence.

The households in the NSBA were also compared in terms of their potential and actual kin networks. The availability of potential kin networks varied by the age of the respondent, by the region and degree of urban development of the respondent's place of residence, and by the type of household in which the respondent resided (Hatchett et al., 1991). For example, households with older heads and spouses were more isolated from kin than were younger households headed by single mothers, and female-headed households tended to have greater potential kin networks than did individuals in nuclear households. With respect to region and urbanicity, the respondents in the Southern and North Central regions and those in rural areas had a greater concentration of relatives closer at hand than did the respondents in other regions and those in urban areas. However, proximity to relatives and their concentration nearby did not translate directly into actual kin networks or extended family functioning:

> Complex relationships were found across age, income, and type of household. From these data came a picture of the Black elderly with high psychological connectedness to family in the midst of relative geographical and interactional isolation from them. The image of female single-parent households is, on the other hand, the reverse or negative of this picture.

Female heads were geographically closer to kin, had more contact with them, and received more help from family but did not perceive as much family solidarity or psychological connectedness. (Hatchett et al., 1991, p. 81)

The nature and frequency of mutual aid among kin were also assessed in this survey. More than two thirds of the respondents reported receiving some assistance from family members, including financial support, child care, goods and services, and help during sickness and at death. Financial assistance and child care were the two most frequent types of support reported by the younger respondents, whereas goods and services were the major types reported by older family members. The type of support the respondents received from their families was determined, to some extent, by needs defined by the family life cycle.

In sum, the results of the NSBA document the wide variety of family configurations and households in which African Americans reside and suggest, along with other studies, that the diversity of structures represents adaptive responses to the variety of social, economic, and demographic conditions that African Americans have encountered over time (Billingsley, 1968; Farley & Allen, 1987).

Although Hatchett et al. (1991) focused on extended or augmented African American families in their analysis of the NSBA data, only 1 in 5 households in this survey contained persons outside the nuclear family. The majority of households was nuclear, containing one or both parents with their own children.

Between 1970 and 1990, the number of all U.S. married-couple families with children dropped by almost 1 million, and their share of all family households declined from 40% to 26% (U.S. Bureau of the Census, 1995). The proportion of married-couple families with children among African Americans also declined during this period, from 41% to 26% of all African American families. In addition, the percentage of African American families headed by women more than doubled, increasing from 33% in 1970 to 57% in 1990. By 1995, married-couple families with children constituted 36% of all African American families, while single-parent families represented 64% (U.S. Bureau of the Census, 1996). The year 1980 was the first time in history that African American female-headed families with children outnumbered married-couple families. This shift in the distribution of African American families by type is associated with a number of complex, interrelated social and economic developments, including increases in age at first marriage, high rates of separation and divorce, male joblessness, and out-of-wedlock births

Marriage, Divorce, and Separation

In a reversal of a long-time trend, African Americans are now marrying at a much later age than are persons of other races. Thirty years ago, African American men and women were far more likely to have married by ages 20–24 than were white Americans. In 1960, 56% of African American men and 36% of African American women aged 20–24 were never married; by 1993, 90% of all African American men and 81% of African American women in this age cohort were never married (U.S. Bureau of the Census, 1994).

The trend toward later marriages among African Americans has contributed to changes in the distribution of African American families by type. Delayed marriage tends to increase the risk of out-of-wedlock childbearing and single parenting (Hernandez, 1993). In fact, a large proportion of the increase in single-parent households in recent years is accounted for by never-married women maintaining families (U.S. Bureau of the Census, 1990).

The growing proportion of never-married young African American adults is partly a result of a combination of factors, including continuing high rates of unemployment, especially among young men; college attendance; military service; and an extended period of cohabitation prior to marriage (Glick, 1997; Testa & Krogh, 1995; Wilson, 1987). In their investigation of the effect of employment on marriage among African American men in the inner city of Chicago, Testa and Krogh (1995) found that men in stable jobs were twice as likely to marry as were men who were unemployed, not in school, or in the military. Hence, it has been argued that the feasibility of marriage among African Americans in recent decades has decreased because the precarious economic position of African American men has made them less attractive as potential husbands and less interested in becoming husbands, given the difficulties they are likely to encounter in performing the provider role in marriage (Tucker & Mitchell-Kernan, 1995).

However, other research has indicated that economic factors are only part of the story. Using census data from 1940 through the mid-1980s, Mare and Winship (1991) sought to determine the impact of declining employment opportunities on marriage rates among African Americans and found that although men who were employed were more likely to marry, recent declines in employment rates among young African American men were not large enough to account for a substantial part of the declining trend in their marriage rates. Similarly, in their analysis of data from a national survey of young African American adults, Lichter, McLaughlin, Kephart, and Landry (1992) found that lower employment rates among African American men were an important contributing factor to delayed marriage—and perhaps to nonmarriage—among African American women. However, even when marital opportunities were taken into account, the researchers found that the rate of marriage among young African American women in the survey was only 50% to 60% the rate of white women of similar ages.

In addition to recent declines in employment rates, an unbalanced sex ratio has been identified as an important contributing factor to declining marriage rates among African Americans. This shortage of men is due partly to high rates of mortality and incarceration of African American men (Kiecolt & Fossett, 1995; Wilson & Neckerman, 1986). Guttentag and Secord (1983) identified a number of major consequences of the shortage of men over time: higher rates of singlehood, out-of-wedlock births, divorce, and infidelity and less commitment among men to relationships. Among African Americans, they found that in 1980 the ratio of men to women was unusually low; in fact, few populations in the United States had sex ratios as low as those of African Americans. Because African American women outnumber men in each of the age categories 20 to 49, the resulting "marriage squeeze" puts African American women at a significant disadvantage in the marriage market, causing an unusually large proportion of them to remain unmarried. However, Glick (1997) observed a reversal of the marriage squeeze among African Americans in the age categories 18 to 27 during the past decade: In 1995, there were 102 African American men for every 100 African American women in this age range. Thus, "[w]hereas the earlier marriage squeeze made it difficult for Black women to marry, the future marriage squeeze will make it harder for Black men" (Glick, 1997, p. 126). But, as Kiecolt and Fossett (1995) observed, the impact of the sex ratio on marital outcomes for African Americans may vary, depending on the nature of the local marriage market. Indeed, "marriage markets are local, as opposed to national, phenomena which may have different implications for different genders . . . [for example,] men and women residing near a military base face a different sex ratio than their counterparts attending a large university" (Smith, 1995, p. 137).

African American men and women are not only delaying marriage, but are spending fewer years in their first marriages and are slower to remarry than in decades past. Since 1960, a sharp decline has occurred in the number of years African American women spend with their first husbands and a corresponding rise in the interval of separation and divorce between the first and second marriages (Espenshade, 1985; Jaynes & Williams, 1989). Data from the National Fertility Surveys of 1965 and 1970 disclosed that twice as many African American couples as white couples (10% versus 5%) who reached their 5th wedding anniversaries ended their marriages before their 10th anniversaries (Thornton, 1978), and about half the African American and a quarter of the white marriages were dissolved within the first 15 years of marriage (McCarthy, 1978). Similarly, a comparison of the prevalence of marital disruption (defined as separation or divorce) among 13 racial-ethnic groups in the United States based on the 1980 census revealed that of the women who had married for the first time 10 to 14 years before 1980, 53% of the African American women, 48% of the Native American women, and 37% of the non-Hispanic white women were separated or divorced by the 1980 census (Sweet & Bumpass, 1987).

Although African American women have a higher likelihood of separating from their husbands than do non-Hispanic white women, they are slower to obtain legal divorces (Chertin, 1996). According to data from the 1980 census, within three years of separating from their husbands, only 55% of the African American women had obtained divorces, compared to 91% of the non-hispanic white women (Sweet & Bumpass, 1987). Cherlin speculated that, because of their lower expectations of remarrying, African American women may be less motivated to obtain legal divorces. Indeed, given the shortage of African American men in each of the age categories from 20 to 49, it is not surprising that the proportion of divorced women who remarry is lower among African American than among non-Hispanic white women (Glick, 1997). Overall, the remarriage rate among African Americans is about one fourth the rate of whites (Staples & Johnson, 1993).

Cherlin (1996) identified lower educational levels, high rates of unemployment, and low income as importance sources of differences in African American and white rates of marital dissolution. However, as he pointed out, these factors alone are insufficient to account for all the observed difference. At every level of educational attainment, African American women are more likely to be separated or divorced from their husbands than are non-Hispanic white women. Using data from the 1980 census, Jaynes and Williams (1989) compared the actual marital-status distributions of African Americans and whites, controlling for differences in educational attainment for men and women and for income distribution for men. They found that when differences in educational attainment were taken into account, African American women were more likely to be "formerly married than White women and much less likely to be living with a husband" (p. 529). Moreover, income was an important factor in accounting for differences in the marital status of African American and white men. Overall, Jaynes and Williams found that socio-economic differences explained a significant amount of the variance in marital status differences between African Americans and whites, although Bumpass, Sweet, and Martin (1990) noted that such differences rapidly diminish as income increases, especially for men. As Glick (1997) reported, African American men with high income levels are more likely to be in intact first marriages by middle age than are African American women with high earnings. This relationship between income and marital status, he stated, is strongest at the lower end of the income distribution, suggesting that marital permanence for men is less dependent on their being well-to-do than on their having the income to support a family.

As a result of sharp increases in marital disruption and relatively low remarriage rates, less than half (43%) the African American adults aged 18 and older were currently married in 1995, down from 64% in 1970 (U.S. Bureau of the Census, 1996). Moreover, although the vast majority of the 11.6 million African Americans households in 1995 were family households, less than half (47%) were headed by married couples, down from 56% in 1980. Some analysts expect the decline in marriage among African Americans to continue for some time, consistent with the movement away from marriage as a consequence of modernization and urbanization (Espenshade, 1985) and in response to continuing economic marginalization. But African American culture may also play a role. As a number of writers have noted (Billingsley, 1992; Cherlin, 1996), blood ties and extended families have traditionally been given primacy over other types of relationships, including marriage, among African Americans, and this emphasis may have influenced the way many African Americans responded to recent shifts in values in the larger society and the restructuring of the economy that struck the African American community especially hard.

Such is the interpretation of Cherlin (1992, p. 112), who argued that the institution of marriage has been weakened during the past few decades by the increasing economic independence of women and men and by a cultural drift "toward a more individualistic ethos, one which emphasized self-fulfillment in personal relations." In addition, Wilson (1987) and others described structural shifts in the economy (from manufacturing to service industries as a source of the growth in employment) that have benefited African American women more than men, eroding men's earning potential and their ability to support families. According to Cherlin, the way African Americans responded to such broad sociocultural and economic changes was conditioned by their history and culture:

> Faced with difficult times economically, many Blacks responded by drawing upon a model of social support that was in their cultural repertoire. . . .This response relied heavily on extended kinship networks and deemphasized marriage. It is a response that taps a traditional source of strength in African-American society: cooperation and sharing among a large network of kin. (p. 113)

Thus, it seems likely that economic developments and cultural values have contributed independently and jointly to the explanation of declining rates of marriage among African Americans in recent years (Farley & Allen, 1987).

Single-Parent Families

Just as rates of divorce, separation, and out-of-wedlock childbearing have increased over the past few decades, so has the number of children living in single-parent households. For example, between 1970 and 1990, the number and proportion of all U.S. single-parent households increased threefold, from 1 in 10 to 3 in 10. There were 3.8 million single-parent families with children under 18 in 1970, compared to 11.4 million in 1994. The vast majority of single-parent households are maintained by women (86% in 1994), but the number of single-parent households headed by men has more than tripled: from 393,000 in 1970 to 1.5 million in 1994 (U.S. Bureau of the Census, 1995).

Among the 58% of African American families with children at home in 1995, more were one-parent families (34%) than married-couple families (24%). In 1994, single-parent families accounted for 25% of all white family groups with children under age 18, 65% of all African American family groups, and 36% of Hispanic family groups (U.S. Bureau of the Census, 1995).

Single-parent families are created in a number of ways: through divorce, marital separation, out-of-wedlock births, or death of a parent. Among adult African American women aged 25–44, increases in the percentage of never-married women and disrupted marriages are significant contributors to the rise in female-headed households; for white women of the same age group, marital dissolution or divorce is the most important factor (Demo, 1992; Jaynes & Williams, 1989). Moreover, changes in the living arrangements of women who give birth outside marriage or experience marital disruption have also been significant factors in the rise of female-headed households among African American and white women. In the past, women who experienced separation or divorce, or bore children out of wedlock were more likely to move in with their parents or other relatives, creating subfamilies; as a result, they were not classified as female headed. In recent decades, however, more and more of these women have established their own households (Parish, Hao, & Hogan, 1991).

An increasing proportion of female-headed householders are unmarried teenage mothers with young children. In 1990, for example, 96% of all births to African American teenagers occurred outside marriage; for white teenagers, the figure was 55% (National Center for Health Statistics, 1991). Although overall fertility rates among teenage women declined steadily from the 1950s through the end of the 1980s, the share of births to unmarried women has risen sharply over time. In 1970, the proportion of all births to unmarried teenage women aged 15–19 was less than 1 in 3; by 1991, it had increased to 2 in 3.

Differences in fertility and births outside marriage among young African American and white women are accounted for, in part, by differences in sexual activity, use of contraceptives, the selection of adoption as an option, and the proportion of premarital pregnancies that are legitimated by marriage before the children's births (Trusell, 1988). Compared to their white counterparts, African American teenagers are more likely to be sexually active and less likely to use contraceptives, to have abortions when pregnant, and to marry before the babies are born. In consequence, young African American women constitute a larger share of single mothers than they did in past decades. This development has serious social and economic consequences for children and adults because female-headed households have much higher rates of poverty and deprivation than do other families (Taylor, 1991b).

Family Structure and Family Dynamics

As a number of studies have shown, there is a strong correspondence between organization and economic status of families, regardless of race (Farley & Allen, 1987). For both African Americans and whites, the higher the income, the greater the percentage of families headed by married couples. In their analysis of 1980 census data on family income and structure, Farley and Allen (1987) found that "there were near linear decreases in the proportions of households headed by women, households where children reside with a single parent, and extended households with increases in economic status" (p. 185). Yet, socioeconomic factors, they concluded, explained only part of the observed differences in family organization between African Americans and whites. "Cultural factors—that is, family preferences, notions of the appropriate and established habits—also help explain race differences in family organization" (p. 186).

One such difference is the egalitarian mode of family functioning in African American families, characterized by complementarity and flexibility in family roles (Billingsley, 1992; Hill, 1971). Egalitarian modes of family functioning are common even among low-income African American families, where one might expect the more traditional patriarchal pattern of authority to prevail. Until recently, such modes of family functioning were interpreted as signs of weakness or pathology because they were counternormative to the gender-role division of labor in majority families (Collins, 1990). Some scholars have suggested that role reciprocity in African American families is a legacy of slavery, in which the traditional gender division of labor was largely ignored by slaveholders, and Black men and women were "equal in the sense that neither sex wielded economic power over the other" (Jones, 1985, p. 14). As a result of historical experiences and economic conditions, traditional gender distinctions in the homemaker and provider roles have been less rigid in African American families than in white families (Beckett & Smith, 1981). Moreover, since African American women have historically been involved in the paid labor force in greater numbers than have white women and because they have had a more significant economic role in families than their white counterparts, Scott-Jones and Nelson-LeGall (1986, p. 95) argued that African Americans "have not experienced as strong an economic basis for the subordination of women, either in marital roles or in the preparation of girls for schooling, jobs, and careers."

In her analysis of data from the NSBA, Hatchett (1991) found strong support for an egalitarian division of family responsibilities and tasks. With respect to attitudes toward the sharing of familial roles, 88% of the African American adults agreed that women and men should share child care and housework equally, and 73% agreed that both men and women should have jobs to support their families. For African American men, support for an egalitarian division of labor in the family did not differ by education or socioeconomic level, but education was related to attitudes toward the sharing of family responsibilities and roles among African American women. College-educated women were more likely than were women with less education to support the flexibility and interchangeability of family roles and tasks.

Egalitarian attitudes toward familial roles among African Americans are also reflected in child-rearing attitudes and practices (Taylor, 1991a). Studies have indicated that African American families tend to place less emphasis on differential gender-role socialization than do other families (Blau, 1981). In her analysis of gender-role socialization among southern African American families, Lewis (1975) found few patterned differences in parental attitudes toward male and female roles. Rather, age and relative birth order were found to be more important than gender as determinants of differential treatment and behavioral expectations for children. Through their socialization practices, African American parents seek to inculcate in both genders traits of assertiveness, independence, and self-confidence (Boykin & Toms, 1985; Lewis, 1975). However, as children mature, socialization practices are adapted to reflect "more closely the structure of expectations and opportunities provided for Black men and women by the dominant society" (Lewis, 1975, p. 237)—that is, geared to the macrostructural conditions that constrain familial role options for African American men and women.

However, such shifts in emphasis and expectations often lead to complications in the socialization process by inculcating in men and women components of gender-role definitions that are incompatible or noncomplementary, thereby engendering a potential source of conflict in their relationships. Franklin (1986) suggested that young African American men and women are frequently confronted with contradictory messages and dilemmas as a result of familial socialization. On the one hand, men are socialized to embrace an androgynous gender role within the African American community, but, on the other hand, they are expected to perform according to the white masculine gender-role paradigm in some contexts. According to Franklin, this dual orientation tends to foster confusion in some young men and difficulties developing an appropriate gender identity. Likewise, some young African American women may receive two different and contradictory messages: "One message states, 'Because you will be a Black woman, it is imperative that you learn to take care of yourself because it is hard to find a Black man who will take care of you.' A second message . . . that conflicts with the first . . . is 'your ultimate achievement will occur when you have snared a Black man who will take care of you' " (Franklin, 1986, p. 109). Franklin contended that such contradictory expectations and mixed messages frequently lead to incompatible gender-based behaviors among African American men and women and conflicts in their relationships.

Despite the apparently greater acceptance of role flexibility and power sharing in African American families, conflict around these issues figures prominently in marital instability. In their study of marital instability among African American and white couples in early marriages, Hatchett, Veroff, and Douvan (1995) found young African American couples at odds over gender roles in the family. Anxiety over their ability to function in the provider role was found to be an important source of instability in the marriages for African American husbands, but not for white husbands. Hatchett (1991) observed that marital instability tended to be more common among young African American couples if the husbands felt that their wives had equal power in the family and if the wives felt there was not enough sharing of family tasks and responsibilities. Hatchett et al. (1991) suggested that African American men's feelings of economic anxiety and self-doubt may be expressed in conflicts over decisional power and in the men's more tenuous commitment to their marriages vis-à-vis African American women. Although the results of their study relate to African American couples in the early stages of marriage, the findings may be predictive of major marital difficulties in the long term. These and other findings (see, for example, Tucker & Mitchell-Kernan, 1995) indicate that changing attitudes and definitions of familial roles among young African American couples are tied to social and economic trends (such as new and increased employment opportunities for women and new value orientations toward marriage and family) in the larger society.

African American Families, Social Change, and Public Policy

Over the past three decades, no change in the African American community has been more fundamental and dramatic than the restructuring of families and family relationships. Since the 1960s, unprecedented changes have occurred in rates of marriage, divorce, and separation; in the proportion of single and two-parent households and births to unmarried mothers; and in the number of children living in poverty. To be sure, these changes are consistent with trends for the U.S. population as a whole, but they are more pronounced among African Americans, largely because of a conflux of demographic and economic factors that are peculiar to the African American community.

In their summary of findings from a series of empirical studies that investigated the causes and correlates of recent changes in patterns of African American family formation, Tucker and Mitchell-Kernan (1995) came to several conclusions that have implications for future research and social policy. One consistent finding is the critical role that sex ratios–the availability of mates play in the formation of African American families. Analyzing aggregate-level data on African American sex ratios in 171 U.S. cities, Sampson (1995) found that these sex ratios were highly predictive of female headship, the percentage of married couples among families with school-age children, and the percentage of African American women who were single. In assessing the causal effect of sex ratios on the family structure of African Americans and whites, he showed that the effect is five times greater for the former than the latter. Similarly, Kiecolt and Fossett's (1995) analysis of African American sex ratios in Louisiana cities and counties disclosed that they had strong positive effects on the percentage of African American women who were married and had husbands present, the rate of marital births per thousand African American women aged 20–29, the percentage of married-couple families, and the percentage of children living in two-parent households.

Another consistent finding is the substantial and critical impact of economic factors on African American family formation, especially men's employment status. Analyses by Sampson (1995) and Darity and Myers (1995) provided persuasive evidence that economic factors play a major and unique role in the development and maintenance of African American families. Using aggregate data, Sampson found that low employment rates for African American men in cities across the United States were predictive of female headship, the percentage of women who were single, and the percentage of married-couple families among family households with school-age children. Moreover, comparing the effect of men's employment on the family structure of African American and white families, he found that the effect was 20 times greater for African Americans than for whites. Similar results are reported by Darity and Myers, who investigated the effects of sex ratio and economic marriageability—Wilson and Neckerman's (1986) Male Marriageability Pool Index—on African American family structure. They found that, although both measures were independently predictive of female headship among African Americans, a composite measure of economic and demographic factors was a more stable and effective predictor. Moreover, Sampson found that the strongest independent effect of these factors on family structure was observed among African American families in poverty. That is, "the lower the sex ratio and the lower the male employment rate the higher the rate of female-headed families with children and in poverty" (p. 250). It should be noted that neither rates of white men's employment nor white sex ratios was found to have much influence on white family structure in these analyses, lending support to Wilson's (1987) hypothesis regarding the structural sources of family disruption among African Americans.

Although the findings reported here are not definitive, they substantiate the unique and powerful effects of sex ratios and men's employment on the marital behavior and family structure of African Americans and point to other problems related to the economic marginalization of men and family poverty in African American communities. Some analysts have predicted far-reaching consequences for African Americans and for society at large should current trends in marital disruption continue unabated. Darity and Myers (1996) predicted that the majority of African American families will be headed by women by the beginning of the next decade if violent crime, homicide, incarceration, and other problems associated with the economic marginalization of African American men are allowed to rob the next generation of fathers and husbands. Moreover, they contended, a large number of such families are likely to be poor and isolated from the mainstream of American society.

The growing economic marginalization of African American men and their ability to provide economic support to families have contributed to their increasing estrangement from family life (Bowman, 1989; Tucker & Mitchell-Kernan, 1995) and are identified as pivotal factors in the development of other social problems, including drug abuse, crime, homicide, and imprisonment, which further erode their prospects as marriageable mates for African American women.

In addressing the structural sources of the disruption of African American families, researchers have advanced a number of short- and long-term proposals. There is considerable agreement that increasing the rate of marriage alone will not significantly improve the economic prospects of many poor African American families. As Ehrenreich (1986) observed, given the marginal economic position of poor African American men, impoverished African American women would have to be married to three such men—simultaneously—to achieve an average family income! Thus, for many African American women, increasing the prevalence of marriage will not address many of the problems they experience as single parents.

With respect to short-term policies designed to address some of the more deleterious effects of structural forces on African American families, Darity and Myers (1996) proposed three policy initiatives that are likely to produce significant results for African American communities. First, because research has indicated that reductions in welfare benefits have failed to stem the rise in female-headed households, welfare policy should reinstate its earlier objective of lifting the poor out of poverty. In Darity and Myers's view, concerns about the alleged disincentives of transfer payments are "moot in light of the long-term evidence that Black families will sink deeper into a crisis of female headship with or without welfare. Better a world of welfare-dependent, near-poor families than one of welfare-free but desolate and permanently poor families" (p. 288). Second, programs are needed to improve the health care of poor women and their children. One major potential benefit of such a strategy is an improvement in the sex ratio because the quality of prenatal and child care is one of the determinants of sex ratios. "By assuring quality health care now, we may help stem the tide toward further depletion of young Black males in the future" (p. 288). A third strategy involves improvements in the quality of education provided to the poor, which are key to employment gains.

Although these are important initiatives with obvious benefits to African American communities, in the long term, the best strategy for addressing marital disruptions and other family-related issues is an economic-labor market strategy. Because much of current social policy is ideologically driven, rather than formulated on the basis of empirical evidence, it has failed to acknowledge or address the extent to which global and national changes in the economy have conspired to marginalize significant segments of the African American population, both male and female, and deprive them of the resources to form or support families. Although social policy analysts have repeatedly substantiated the link between the decline in marriages among African Americans and fundamental changes in the U.S. postindustrial economy, their insights have yet to be formulated into a meaningful and responsive policy agenda. Until these structural realities are incorporated into governmental policy, it is unlikely that marital disruption and other adverse trends associated with this development will be reversed.

There is no magic bullet for addressing the causes and consequences of marital decline among African Americans, but public policies that are designed to improve the economic and employment prospects of men and women at all socioeconomic levels have the greatest potential for improving the lot of African American families. Key elements of such policies would include raising the level of education and employment training among African American youth, and more vigorous enforcement of antidiscrimination laws, which would raise the level of employment and earnings and contribute to higher rates of marriage among African Americans (Burbridge, 1995). To be sure, many of the federally sponsored employment and training programs that were launched during the 1960s and 1970s were plagued by a variety of administrative and organizational problems, but the effectiveness of some of these programs in improving the long-term employment prospects and life chances of disadvantaged youth and adults has been well documented (Taylor et al., 1990).

African American families, like all families, exist not in a social vacuum but in communities, and programs that are designed to strengthen community institutions and provide social support to families are likely to have a significant impact on family functioning. Although the extended family and community institutions, such as the church, have been important sources of support to African American families in the past, these community support systems have been overwhelmed by widespread joblessness, poverty, and a plethora of other problems that beset many African American communities. Thus, national efforts to rebuild the social and economic infrastructures of inner-city communities would make a major contribution toward improving the overall health and well-being of African American families and could encourage more young people to marry in the future.

Winning support for these and other policy initiatives will not be easy in a political environment that de-emphasizes the role of government in social policy and human welfare. But without such national efforts, it is difficult to see how many of the social conditions that adversely affect the structure and functioning of African American families will be eliminated or how the causes and consequences of marital decline can be ameliorated. If policy makers are serious about addressing conditions that destabilize families, undermine communities, and contribute to a host of other socially undesirable outcomes, new policy initiatives, such as those just outlined, must be given higher priority.

References

Allen, W. (1978). The search for applicable theories of black family life. *Journal of Marriage and the Family, 40,* 117–129.

Beckett, J., & Smith, A. (1981). Work and family roles: Egalitarian marriage in black and white families. *Social Service Review, 55,* 314–326.

Billingsley, A. (1968). *Black families in white America.* Englewood Cliffs, NJ: Prentice Hall.

Billingsley, A. (1992). *Climbing Jacob's ladder: The enduring legacy of African American families.* New York: Simon & Schuster.

Blassingame, J. (1972). *The slave community.* New York: Oxford University Press.

Blau, Zena. (1981). *Black children/white socialization.* New York: Free Press.

Bowman, P. J. (1989). Research perspectives on black men: Role strain and adaptation across the life cycle. In R. L. Jones (Ed.), *Black adult development and aging* (pp. 117–150). Berkeley, CA: Cobb & Henry.

Bowman, P. J. (1995). Commentary. In M. B. Tucker & C. Mitchell-Kernan (Eds.), *The decline in marriage among African Americans* (pp. 309–321). New York: Russell Sage Foundation.

Boykin, A. W., & Toms, F. D. (1985). Black child socialization: A conceptual framework. In H. P. McAdoo & J. L. McAdoo (Eds.), *Black children* (pp. 33–54). Beverly Hills, CA: Sage.

Bumpass, L., Sweet, J., & Martin, T. C. (1990). Changing patterns of remarriage. *Journal of Marriage and the Family, 52,* 747–756.

Burbridge, L. C. (1995). Policy implications of a decline in marriage among African Americans. In M. B. Tucker & C. Mitchell-Kernan (Eds.), *The decline in marriage among African Americans* (pp. 323–344). New York: Russell Sage Foundation.

Cherlin, A. (1992). *Marriage, divorce, remarriage* (rev. ed.). Cambridge, MA: Harvard University Press.

Cherlin, A. (1995). Policy issues of child care. In P. Chase-Lansdale & J. Brooks-Gunn (Eds.), *Escape from poverty* (pp. 121–137). New York: Cambridge University Press.

Cherlin, A. (1996). *Public and private families.* New York: McGraw-Hill.

Collins, P. (1990). *Black feminist thought.* Boston, MA: Unwin Hyman.

Darity, W., & Myers, S. (1995). Family structure and the marginalization of black men: Policy implications. In M. B. Tucker & C. Mitchell-Kernan (Eds.), *The decline in marriage among African Americans* (pp. 263–308). New York: Russell Sage Foundation.

Demo, D. (1992). Parent-child relations: Assessing recent changes. *Journal of Marriage and the Family, 54,* 104–117.

Dressler, W., Haworth-Hoeppner, S., & Pitts, B. (1985). Household structure in a southern black community. *American Anthropologist, 87,* 853–862.

DuBois, W. E. B. (1898). The study of the Negro problem. *Annals, 1,* 1–23.

DuBois, W. E. B. (1909). *The Negro American family.* Atlanta: Atlanta University Press.

Edwards, G. F. (1968). *E. Franklin Frazier on race relations.* Chicago: University of Chicago Press.

Ehrenreich, B. (1986, July-August). Two, three, many husbands. *Mother Jones,* 8–9.

Espenshade, T. (1985). Marriage trends in America: Estimates, implications, and underlying causes. *Population and Development Review, 11,* 193–245.

Farley, R., & Allen, W. (1987). *The color line and the quality of life in America.* New York: Oxford University Press.

Franklin, C. (1986). Black male-Black female conflict: Individually caused and culturally nurtured. In R. Staples (Ed.), *The black family* (3rd ed., pp. 106–113). Belmont, CA: Wadsworth.

Frazier, E. F. (1939). *The Negro family in the United States*. Chicago: University of Chicago Press.

Furstenberg, F., Hershberg, T., & Modell, J. (1975). The origins of the female-headed black family: The impact of the urban experience. *Journal of Interdisciplinary History*, 6, 211–233.

Genovese, E. (1974). *Roll Jordan roll: The world slaves made*. New York: Pantheon.

Glick, P. (1997). Demographic pictures of African American families. In H. McAdoo (Ed.), *Black families* (3rd ed., pp. 118–138). Thousand Oaks, CA: Sage.

Gutman, H. (1976). *The black family in slavery and freedom, 1750–1925*. New York: Pantheon.

Guttentag, M., & Secord, P. F. (1983). *Too many women*. Beverly Hills, CA: Sage.

Hatchett, S. (1991). Women and men. In J. Jackson (Ed.), *Life in black America* (pp. 84–104). Newbury Park, CA: Sage.

Hatchett, S., Cochran, D., & Jackson, J. (1991). In J. Jackson (Ed.), *Life in black America* (pp. 46–83). Newbury Park, CA: Sage.

Hatchett, S., Veroff, J., & Douvan, E. (1995). Marital instability among black and white couples in early marriage. In M. B. Tucker & C. Mitchell-Kernan (Eds.), *The decline in marriage among African Americans* (pp. 177–218). New York: Russell Sage Foundation.

Hernandez, D. J. (1993). *America's children*. New York: Russell Sage.

Herskovits, M. J. (1958). *The myth of the Negro past* (Beacon Paperback No. 69). Boston: Beacon Press.

Hill, R. (1971). *The strengths of black families*. New York: Emerson Hall.

Hill, R. (1993). *Research on the African American family: A holistic perspective*. Westport, CT: Auburn House.

Jackson, J. (Ed.). (1991). *Life in black America*. Newbury Park, CA: Sage.

Jaynes, G., & Williams, R. (1989). *A common destiny: Blacks and American society*. Washington, DC: National Academy Press.

Johnson, L. B. (1981). Perspectives on black family empirical research: 1965–1978. In H. P. McAdoo (Ed.), *Black families* (pp. 252–263). Beverly Hills, CA: Sage.

Jones, J. (1985). *Labor of love, labor of sorrow: Black women, work, and the family from slavery to the present*. New York: Basic Books.

Kiecolt, K., & Fossett, M. (1995). Mate availability and marriage among African Americans: Aggregate- and individual-level analysis. In M. B. Tucker & C. Mitchell-Kernan (Eds.), *The decline in marriage among African Americans* (pp. 121–135). New York: Russell Sage Foundation.

Lewis, D. (1975). The black family: Socialization and sex roles. *Phylon*, 36, 221–237.

Lichter, D. T., McLaughlin, D. K., Kephart, G., & Landry, G. (1992). Race and the retreat from marriage: A shortage of marriageable men? *American Sociological Review*, 57, 781–799.

Manfra, J. A. & Dykstra, R. P. (1985). Serial marriage and the origins of the black stepfamily: The Rowanty evidence. *Journal of American History*, 7, 18–44.

Mare, R., & Winship, C. (1991). Socioeconomic change and the decline of marriage for blacks and whites. In C. Jencks & P. E. Peterson (Eds.), *The urban underclass* (pp. 175–204). Washington, DC: Brookings Institute.

McAdoo, H. P. (Ed.). (1997). *Black families* (3rd ed.). Thousand Oaks, CA: Sage.

McCarthy, J. (1978). A comparison of the probability of the dissolution of first and second marriages. *Demography*, 15, 345–359.

Moynihan, D. P. (1965). *The Negro family: The case for national action*. Washington, DC: U.S. Government Printing Office.

National Center for Health Statistics. (1991). *Monthly Vital Statistics Report* (Vol. 35, No. 4, Suppl.). Washington, DC: U.S. Department of Health and Human Services.

Nobles, W. (1978). Toward an empirical and theoretical framework for defining black families. *Journal of Marriage and the Family*, 40, 679–688.

Parish, W. L., Hao, L., & Hogan, D. P. (1991). Family support networks, welfare, and work among young mothers. *Journal of Marriage and the Family*, 53, 203–215.

Pleck, E. (1973). The two-parent household: Black family structure in late nineteenth-century Boston. In M. Gordon (Ed.), *The American family in socio-historical perspective* (pp. 152–178). New York: St. Martin's Press.

Sampson, R. J. (1995). Unemployment and unbalanced sex ratios: Race-specific consequences for family structure and crime. In M. B. Tucker & C. Mitchell-Keman (Eds.), *The decline in marriage among African Americans* (pp. 229–254). New York: Russell Sage Foundation.

Scanzoni, J. (1977). *The black family in modern society*. Chicago: University of Chicago Press.

Scott-Jones, D., & Nelson-LeGall, S. (1986). Defining black families: Past and present. In E. Seidman & J. Rappaport (Eds.), *Redefining social problems* (pp. 83–100). New York: Plenum.

Shimkin, D., Shimkin, E. M., & Frate, D. A. (Eds.). (1978). *The extended family in black societies.* The Hague, the Netherlands: Mouton.

Smith, A. W. (1995). Commentary. In M. B. Tucker & C. Mitchell-Kernan (Eds.), *The decline in marriage among African Americans* (pp. 136–141). New York: Russell Sage Foundation.

Stack, C. (1974). *All our kin.* New York: Harper & Row.

Staples, R. (1971). Toward a sociology of the black family: A decade of theory and research. *Journal of Marriage and the Family, 33,* 19–38.

Staples, R., & Johnson, L. B. (1993). *Black families at the crossroads.* San Francisco: Jossey-Bass.

Staples, R., & Mirande, A. (1980). Racial and cultural variations among American families: A decennial review of the literature on minority families. *Journal of Marriage and the Family, 42,* 157–173.

Stevenson, B. (1995). Black family structure in colonial and antebellum Virginia: Amending the revisionist perspective. In M. B. Tucker & C. Mitchell-Kernan (Eds.), *The decline in marriage among African Americans* (pp. 27–56). New York: Russell Sage Foundation.

Sudarkasa, N. (1988). Interpreting the African heritage in Afro-American family organization. In H. P. McAdoo (Ed.), *Black families* (pp. 27–42). Newbury Park, CA: Sage.

Sudarkasa, N. (1997). African American families and family values. In H. P. McAdoo (Ed.), *Black families* (pp. 9–40). Thousand Oaks, CA: Sage.

Sweet, J., & Bumpass, L. (1987). *American families and households.* New York: Russell Sage Foundation.

Taylor, R. L. (1991a). Child rearing in African American families. In J. Everett, S. Chipungu, & B. Leashore (Eds.), *Child welfare: An Africentric perspective* (pp. 119–155). New Brunswick, NJ: Rutgers University Press.

Taylor, R. L. (1991b). Poverty and adolescent black males: The subculture of disengagement. In P. Edelman & J. Ladner (Eds.), *Adolescence and poverty: Challenge for the 1990s* (pp. 139–162). Washington, DC: Center for National Policy Press.

Taylor, R. L. (1997). Who's parenting? Trends and Patterns. In T. Arendell (Ed.), *Contemporary parenting: Challenges and issues* (pp. 68–91). Thousand Oaks, CA: Sage.

Taylor, R. J., Chatters, L., Tucker, M. B., & Lewis, E. (1990). Developments in research on black families: A decade review. *Journal of Marriage and the Family, 52,* 993–1014.

Testa, M., & Krogh, M. (1995). The effect of employment on marriage among black males in inner-city Chicago. In M. B. Tucker & C. Mitchell-Kernan (Eds.), *The decline in marriage among African Americans* (pp. 59–95). New York: Russell Sage Foundation.

Thornton, A. (1978). Marital instability differentials and interactions: Insights from multivariate contingency table analysis. *Sociology and Social Research, 62,* 572–595.

Trusell, J. (1988). Teenage pregnancy in the United States. *Family Planning Perspectives, 20,* 262–272.

Tucker, M. B., & Mitchell-Kernan, C. (1995). Trends in African American family formation: A theoretical and statistical overview. In M. B. Tucker & C. Mitchell Kernan (Eds.), *The decline in marriage among African Americans* (pp. 3–26). New York: Russell Sage Foundation.

U.S. Bureau of the Census. (1990). Marital status and living arrangements: March 1989. *Current Population Reports* (Series P-20, No. 445). Washington, DC: U.S. Government Printing Office.

U.S. Bureau of the Census. (1994). Marital status and living arrangements: March 1993. *Current Population Reports* (Series P-20, No. 478). Washington, DC: U.S. Government Printing Office.

U.S. Bureau of the Census. (1995). Household and family characteristics: March 1994. *Current Population Reports* (Series P-20, No. 483). Washington, DC: U.S. Government Printing Office.

U.S. Bureau of the Census. (1996). *Statistical abstract of the United States: 1996.* Washington, DC: U.S. Govemment Printing Office.

White, D. G. (1985). *Ain't I a woman? Female slaves in the plantation South.* New York: W. W. Norton.

Wilson, W. J. (1987). *The truly disadvantaged: The inner city, the underclass and public policy.* Chicago: University of Chicago Press.

Wilson, W. J., & Neckerman K. (1986). Poverty and family structure: The widening gap between evidence and public policy issues. In S. Danziger & D. Weinberg (Eds.), *Fighting poverty: What works and what doesn't* (pp. 232–259). Cambridge, MA: Harvard University Press.

Young, V. H. (1970). Family and childhood in a southern Negro community. *American Anthropologist, 72,* 269–288.

■READING 29

Diversity within Latino Families: New Lessons for Family Social Science

Maxine Baca Zinn and Barbara Wells

Who are Latinos? How will their growing presence in U.S. society affect the family field? These are vital questions for scholars who are seeking to understand the current social and demographic shifts that are reshaping society and its knowledge base. Understanding family diversity is a formidable task, not only because the field is poorly equipped to deal with differences at the theoretical level, but because many decentering efforts are themselves problematic. Even when diverse groups are included, family scholarship can distort and misrepresent by faulty emphasis and false generalizations.

Latinos are a population that can be understood only in terms of increasing heterogeneity. Latino families are unprecedented in terms of their diversity. In this chapter, we examine the ramifications of such diversity on the history, boundaries, and dynamics of family life. We begin with a brief look at the intellectual trends shaping Latino family research. We then place different Latino groups at center stage by providing a framework that situates them in specific and changing political and economic settings. Next, we apply our framework to each national origin group to draw out their different family experiences, especially as they are altered by global restructuring. We turn, then, to examine family structure issues and the interior dynamics of family living as they vary by gender and generation. We conclude with our reflections on studying Latino families and remaking family social science. In this chapter, we use interchangeably terms that are commonly used to describe Latino national-origin groups. For example, the terms Mexican American, Mexican, and Mexican-origin population will be used to refer to the same segment of the Latino population. Mexican-origin people may also be referred to as Chicanos.

INTELLECTUAL TRENDS, CRITIQUES, AND CHALLENGES

Origins

The formal academic study of Latino families originated in the late 19th and early 20th centuries with studies of Mexican immigrant families. As the new social scientists of the times focused their concerns on immigration and social disorganization, Mexican-origin and other ethnic families were the source of great concern. The influential Chicago School of Sociology led scholars to believe that Mexican immigration, settlement, and poverty created problems in developing urban centers. During this period, family study was emerging as a new field that sought to document, as well as ameliorate, social problems in urban settings (Thomas & Wilcox, 1987). Immigrant families became major targets of social reform.

Interwoven themes from race relations and family studies gave rise to the view of Mexicans as particularly disorganized. Furthermore, the family was implicated in their plight. As transplants from traditional societies, the immigrants and their children were thought to be at odds with social requirements in the new settings. Their family arrangements were treated as cultural exceptions to the rule of standard family development. Their slowness to acculturate and take on Western patterns of family development left them behind as other families modernized (Baca Zinn, 1995).

Dominant paradigms of assimilation and modernization guided and shaped research. Notions of "traditional" and "modern" forms of social organization joined the new family social science's preoccupation with a standard family form. Compared to mainstream families, Mexican immigrant families were analyzed as traditional cultural forms. Studies of Mexican immigrants highlighted certain ethnic lifestyles that were said to produce social disorganization. Structural conditions that constrained families in the new society were rarely a concern. Instead, researchers examined (1) the families' foreign patterns and habits, (2) the moral quality of family relationships, and (3) the prospects for their Americanization (Bogardus, 1934).

Cultural Preoccupations

Ideas drawn from early social science produced cultural caricatures of Mexican families that became more exaggerated during the 1950s, when structural functionalist theories took hold in American sociology. Like the previous theories, structural functionalism's strategy for analyzing family life was to posit one family type (by no means the only family form, even then) and define it as "the normal family" (Boss & Thorne, 1989). With an emphasis on fixed family boundaries and a fixed division of roles, structural functionalists focused their attention on the group-specific characteristics that deviated from the normal or standard family and predisposed Mexican-origin families to deficiency. Mexican-origin families were analyzed in isolation from the rest of social life, described in simplistic terms of rigid male dominance and pathological clannishness. Although the earliest works on Mexican immigrant families reflected a concern for their eventual adjustment to American society, the new studies virtually abandoned the social realm. They dealt with families as if they existed in a vacuum of backward Mexican traditionalism. Structural functionalism led scholars along a path of cultural reductionism in which differences became deficiencies.

The Mexican family of social science research (Heller, 1966; Madsen, 1964; Rubel, 1966) presented a stark contrast with the mythical "standard family." Although some studies found that Mexican family traditionalism was fading as Mexicans became acculturated, Mexican families were stereotypically and inaccurately depicted as the chief cause of Mexican subordination in the United States.

New Directions

In the past 25 years, efforts to challenge myths and erroneous assumptions have produced important changes in the view of Mexican-origin families. Beginning with a critique of structural functionalist accounts of Mexican families, new studies have successfully challenged the old notions of family life as deviant, deficient, and disorganized.

The conceptual tools of Latino studies, women's studies, and social history have infused the new scholarship to produce a notable shift away from cultural preoccupations.

Like the family field in general, research on Mexican-origin families has begun to devote greater attention to the "social situations and contexts that affect Mexican families" (Vega, 1990, p. 1015). This "revisionist" strategy has moved much Latino family research to a different plane—one in which racial-ethnic families are understood to be constructed by powerful social forces and as settings in which different family members adapt in a variety of ways to changing social conditions.

Current Challenges

Despite important advances, notable problems and limitations remain in the study of Latino families. A significant portion of scholarship includes only Mexican-origin groups (Massey, Zambrana, & Bell, 1995) and claims to generalize the findings to other Latinos. This practice constructs a false social reality because there is no Latino population in the same sense that there is an African American population. However useful the terms *Latino* and *Hispanic* may be as political and census identifiers, they mask extraordinary diversity. The category Hispanic was created by federal statisticians to provide data on people of Mexican, Cuban, Puerto Rican, and other Hispanic origins in the United States. There is no precise definition of group membership, and Latinos do not agree among themselves on an appropriate group label (Massey, 1993). While many prefer the term *Latino*, they may use it interchangeably with *Hispanic* to identify themselves (Romero, 1996). These terms are certainly useful for charting broad demographic changes in the United States, but when used as panethnic terms, they can contribute to misunderstandings about family life.

The labels Hispanic or Latino conceal variation in the family characteristics of Latino groups whose differences are often greater than the overall differences between Latinos and non-Latinos (Solis, 1995). To date, little comparative research has been conducted on Latino subgroups. The systematic disaggregation of family characteristics by national-origin groups remains a challenge, a necessary next step in the development of Latino family research.

We believe that the lack of a comprehensive knowledge base should not stand in the way of building a framework to analyze family life. We can use the burgeoning research on Latinos in U.S. social life to develop an analytical, rather than just a descriptive, account of families. The very complexity of Latino family arrangements begs for a unified (but not unitary) analysis. We believe that we can make good generalizations about Latino family diversity. In the sections that follow, we use a structural perspective grounded in intergroup differences. We make no pretense that this is an exhaustive review of research. Instead, our intent is to examine how Latino family experiences differ in relation to socially constructed conditions.

CONCEPTUAL FRAMEWORK

Conventional family frameworks, which have never applied well to racial-ethnic families, are even less useful in the current world of diversity and change. Incorporating multiplicity into family studies requires new approaches. A fundamental assumption guiding our analysis is that Latino families are not merely an expression of ethnic differences but, like all families, are the products of social forces.

Family diversity is an outgrowth of distinctive patterns in the way families and their members are embedded in environments with varying opportunities, resources, and rewards. Economic conditions and social inequalities associated with race, ethnicity, class, and gender place families in different "social locations." These differences are the key to understanding family variation. They determine labor market status, education, marital relations, and other factors that are crucial to family formation.

Studying Latino family diversity means exposing the structural forces that impinge differently on families in specific social, material, and historical contexts. In other words, it means unpacking the structural arrangements that produce and often require a range of family configurations. It also requires analyzing the cross-cutting forms of difference that permeate society and penetrate families to produce divergent family experiences. Several macrostructural conditions produce widespread family variations across Latino groups: (1) the sociohistorical context; (2) the structure of economic opportunity; and (3) global reorganization, including economic restructuring and immigration.

The Sociohistorical Context

Mexicans, Puerto Ricans, Cubans, and other Latino groups have varied histories that distinguish them from each other. The timing and conditions of their arrival in the United States produced distinctive patterns of settlement that continue to affect their prospects for success. Cubans arrived largely between 1960 and 1980; a group of Mexicans indigenous to the Southwest was forcibly annexed into the United States in 1848, and another has been migrating continually since around 1890; Puerto Ricans came under U.S. control in 1898 and obtained citizenship in 1917; Salvadorans and Guatemalans began to migrate to the United States in substantial numbers during the past two decades.

The Structure of Economic Opportunity

Various forms of labor are needed to sustain family life. Labor status has always been the key factor in distinguishing the experiences of Latinos. Mexicans, Puerto Ricans, Cubans, and others are located in different regions of the country where particular labor markets and a group's placement within them determine the kind of legal, political, and social supports available to families. Different levels of structural supports affect family life, often producing various domestic and household arrangements. Additional complexity stems from gendered labor markets. In a society in which men are still assumed to be the primary breadwinners, jobs generally held by women pay less than jobs usually held by men. Women's and men's differential labor market placement, rewards, and roles create contradictory work and family experiences.

Global Reorganization, Including Economic Restructuring and Immigration

Economic and demographic upheavals are redefining families throughout the world. Four factors are at work here: new technologies based primarily on the computer chip, global economic interdependence, the flight of capital, and the dominance of the information and service sectors over basic manufacturing industries (Baca Zinn & Eitzen,

1998). Latino families are profoundly affected as the environments in which they live are reshaped and they face economic and social marginalization because of underemployment and unemployment. Included in economic globalization are new demands for immigrant labor and the dramatic demographic transformations that are "Hispanicizing" the United States. Family flexibility has long been an important feature of the immigrant saga. Today, "Latino immigration is adding many varieties to family structure" (Moore & Vigil, 1993, p. 36).

The macrostructural conditions described earlier provide the context within which to examine the family experiences of different Latino groups. They set the foundation for comparing family life across Latino groups. These material and economic forces help explain the different family profiles of Mexicans, Puerto Ricans, Cubans, and others. In other words, they enable sociologists to understand how families are bound up with the unequal distribution of social opportunities and how the various national-origin groups develop broad differences in work opportunities, marital patterns, and household structures. However, they do not explain other important differences in family life that cut across national-origin groups. People of the same national origin may experience family differently, depending on their location in the class structure as unemployed, poor, working class or professional; their location in the gender structure as female or male; and their location in the sexual orientation system as heterosexual, gay, lesbian, or bisexual (Baca Zinn & Dill, 1996). In addition to these differences, family life for Latinos is shaped by age, generation living in the United States, citizenship status, and even skin color. All these differences intersect to influence the shape and character of family and household relations.

While our framework emphasizes the social context and social forces that construct families, we do not conclude that families are molded from the "outside in." What happens on a daily basis in family relations and domestic settings also constructs families. Latinos themselves—women, men, and children—have the ability actively to shape their family and household arrangements. Families should be seen as settings in which people are agents and actors, coping with, adapting to, and changing social structures to meet their needs (Baca Zinn & Eitzen, 1996).

Sociohistorical Context for Family Diversity among Mexicans

Families of Mexican descent have been incorporated into the United States by both conquest and migration. In 1848, at the end of the Mexican War, the United States acquired a large section of Mexico, which is now the southwestern United States. With the signing of the Treaty of Guadalupe Hidalgo, the Mexican population in that region became residents of U.S. territory. Following the U.S. conquest, rapid economic growth in that region resulted in a shortage of labor that was resolved by recruiting workers from Mexico. So began the pattern of Mexican labor migration that continues to the present (Portes & Rumbaut, 1990). Some workers settled permanently in the United States, and others continued in cycles of migration, but migration from Mexico has been continuous since around 1890 (Massey et al., 1995).

Dramatic increases in the Mexican-origin population have been an important part of the trend toward greater racial and ethnic diversity in the United States. The Mexican population tripled in size in 20 years, from an estimated 4.5 million in 1970 to 8.7 million in 1980 to 13.5 million in 1990 (Rumbaut, 1995; Wilkinson, 1993). At present, approximately two thirds of Mexicans are native born, and the remainder are foreign born (Rumbaut, 1995). Important differences are consistently found between the social experiences and economic prospects of the native born and the foreign born (Morales & Ong, 1993; Ortiz, 1996). While some variation exists, the typical Mexican migrant to the United States has low socioeconomic status and rural origins (Ortiz, 1995; Portes & Rumbaut, 1990). Recent immigrants have a distinct disadvantage in the labor market because of a combination of low educational attainment, limited work skills, and limited English language proficiency. Social networks are vital for integrating immigrants into U.S. society and in placing them in the social class system (Fernandez-Kelly & Schauffler, 1994). Mexicans are concentrated in barrios that have social networks in which vital information is shared, contacts are made, and job referrals are given. But the social-class context of these Mexican communities is overwhelmingly poor and working class. Mexicans remain overrepresented in low-wage occupations, especially service, manual labor, and low-end manufacturing. These homogeneous lower-class communities lack the high-quality resources that could facilitate upward mobility for either new immigrants or second- and later-generation Mexicans.

The common assumption that immigrants are assimilated economically by taking entry-level positions and advancing to better jobs has not been supported by the Mexican experience (Morales & Ong, 1993; Ortiz, 1996). Today's Mexican workers are as likely as ever to be trapped in low-wage unstable employment situations (Ortiz, 1996; Sassen, 1993). Studies (Aponte, 1993; Morales & Ong, 1993; Ortiz, 1996) have found that high labor force participation and low wages among Mexicans have created a large group of working poor. Households adapt by holding multiple jobs and pooling wages (Velez-Ibañez & Greenberg, 1992).

Mexicans are the largest Latino group in the United States; 6 of 10 Latinos have Mexican origins. This group has low family incomes, but high labor force participation for men and increasing rates for women. Mexicans have the lowest educational attainments and the largest average household size of all Latino groups (See Table 1 and Figure 1 for between-group comparisons.)

Puerto Ricans

The fortunes of Puerto Rico and the United States were joined in 1899 when Puerto Rico became a U.S. possession in the aftermath of Spain's defeat in the Spanish-American War. Puerto Ricans are U.S. citizens and, as such, have the right to migrate to the mainland without regulation. A small stream of migrants increased dramatically after World War II for three primary reasons: high unemployment in Puerto Rico, the availability of inexpensive air travel between Puerto Rico and the United States, and labor recruitment by U.S. companies (Portes & Rumbaut, 1990). Puerto Ricans were concentrated in or near their arrival point—New York City—although migrant laborers were scattered throughout the Northeast and parts of the Midwest. They engaged in a variety of blue-collar occupations; in New York City, they were particularly drawn into the textile and garment industries (Torres & Bonilla, 1993). The unique status of Puerto Rico as a commonwealth of the United States allows Puerto Ricans to engage in a circulating migration between Puerto Rico and the mainland (Feagin & Feagin, 1996).

TABLE 1 *Social and Economic Population Characteristics*

	Median Income	Poverty	% Female Head of Household	Labor Force Participation		High School Graduate	Average Household
				Male	Female		
Mexican	23,609	29.6	19.9	80.9	51.8	46.5	3.86
Puerto Rican	20,929	33.2	41.2	70.6	47.4	61.3	2.91
Cuban	30,584	13.6	21.3	69.9	50.8	64.7	2.56
Central/South American	28,558	23.9	25.4	79.5	57.5	64.2	3.54
Other Hispanic	28,658	21.4	29.5			68.4	
All Hispanic	24,313	27.8	24	79.1	52.6	53.4	2.99
All U.S.	38,782	11.6	12	75	58.9	81.7	2.65
	1994	1994	1995	1995	1995	1995	1995

Sources: US Bureau of the Census, Statistical Abstract of the United States: 1996 (116th ed.) Washington, D.C.: U.S. Government Printing Office, 1996, Tables 53,68,241,615,622,723,738.

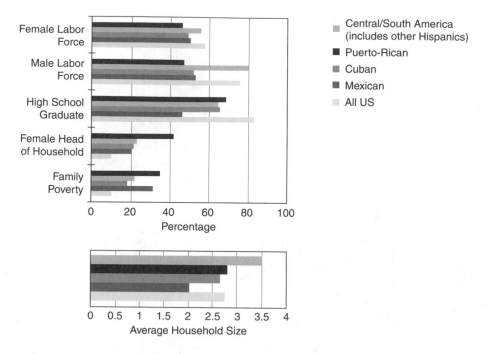

FIGURE 1   Social and Economic Population Characteristics

Puerto Ricans are the most economically disadvantaged of all major Latino groups. The particular context of Puerto Ricans' entry into the U.S. labor market helps explain this group's low economic status. Puerto Ricans with limited education and low occupational skills migrated to the eastern seaboard to fill manufacturing jobs (Ortiz, 1995); their economic well-being was dependent on opportunities for low-skill employment (Aponte, 1993). The region in which Puerto Ricans settled has experienced a major decline in its manufacturing base since the early 1970s. The restructuring of the economy means that, in essence, the jobs that Puerto Ricans came to the mainland to fill have largely disappeared. Latinos who have been displaced from manufacturing have generally been unable to gain access to higher-wage service sector employment (Carnoy, Daly, & Ojeda, 1993).

Compared to Mexicans and Cubans, Puerto Ricans have the lowest median family incomes and the highest unemployment and poverty rates. Puerto Ricans also have a high rate of female-headed households.

Cubans

The primary event that precipitated the migration of hundreds of thousands of Cubans to the United States was the revolution that brought Fidel Castro to power in 1959. This revolution set off several waves of immigration, beginning with the former economic and political elite and working progressively downward through the class structure. Early Cuban immigrants entered the United States in a highly politicized cold-war context as political refugees from communism. The U.S. government sponsored the Cuban Refugee Program, which provided massive supports to Cuban immigrants, including resettlement assistance, job training, small-business loans, welfare payments, and health care (Dominguez, 1992; Perez-Stable & Uriarte, 1993). By the time this program was phased out after the mid-1970s, the United States had invested nearly $1 billion in assistance to Cubans fleeing from communism (Perez-Stable & Uriarte, 1993, p. 155). Between 1960 and 1980, nearly 800,000 Cubans immigrated to the United States (Domiguez, 1992).

The Cuban population is concentrated in south Florida, primarily in the Miami area, where they have established a true ethnic enclave in which they own businesses; provide professional services; and control institutions, such as banks and newspapers (Perez, 1994). The unique circumstances surrounding their immigration help explain the experience of Cubans. U.S. government supports facilitated the economic successes of early Cuban immigrants (Aponte, 1993, Fernandez-Kelley & Schauffler, 1994). High rates of entrepreneurship resulted in the eventual consolidation of an enclave economy (Portes & Truelove, 1987).

Immigrants, women, and minorities have generally supplied the low-wage, flexible labor on which the restructured economy depends (Morales & Bonilla, 1993). However, Cubans "embody a privileged migration" in comparison to other Latino groups (Morales & Bonilla, 1993, p. 17). Their social-class positions, occupational attainments, and public supports have insulated them from the effects of restructuring. Yet Cubans in Miami are not completely protected from the displacements of the new economic order. As Perez-Stable and Uriarte (1993) noted, the Cuban workforce is polarized, with one segment moving into higher-wage work and the other remaining locked in low-wage employment.

Cuban families have higher incomes and far lower poverty rates than do other major Latino groups. Cubans are the most educated major Latino group and have the smallest average household size.

Other Latinos

In each national-origin group discussed earlier, one finds unique socioeconomic, political and historical circumstances. But the diversity of Latinos extends beyond the differences between Mexican Americans, Cuban Americans, and mainland Puerto Ricans. One finds further variation when one considers the experiences of other Latino national-origin groups. Although research on "other Latinos" is less extensive than the literature cited earlier, we consider briefly contexts for diversity in Central American and Dominican families.

Central Americans.   Political repression, civil war, and their accompanying economic dislocations have fueled the immigration of a substantial number of Salvadorans, Guatemalans, and Nicaraguans since the mid-1970s (Hamilton & Chinchilla, 1997). The U.S. population of Central Americans more than doubled between the 1980 and 1990 censuses and now outnumbers Cubans (U.S. Bureau of the Census, 1993). These Latinos migrated under difficult circumstances and face a set of serious challenges in the United

States (Dorrington, 1995). Three factors render this population highly vulnerable: (1) a high percentage are undocumented (an estimated 49% of Salvadorans and 40% of Guatemalans), (2) they have marginal employment and high poverty rates, and (3) the U.S. government does not recognize them as political refugees (Lopez, Popkin, & Telles, 1996).

The two largest groups of Central Americans are Salvadorans and Guatemalans, the majority of whom live in the Los Angeles area. Lopez et al.'s (1996) study of Central Americans in Los Angeles illumined the social and economic contexts in which these Latinos construct their family lives. In general, the women and men have little formal education and know little English, but have high rates of labor force participation. Salvadorans and Guatemalans are overrepresented in low-paying service and blue-collar occupations. Salvadoran and Guatemalan women occupy a low-wage niche in private service (as domestic workers in private homes). Central Americans, especially the undocumented who fear deportation and usually have no access to public support, are desperate enough to accept the poorest-quality, lowest-paying work that Los Angeles has to offer. These immigrants hold the most disadvantageous position in the regional economy (Scott, 1996). Lopez et al. predicted that in the current restructured economy, Central Americans will continue to do the worst of the "dirty work" necessary to support the lifestyles of the high-wage workforce.

Dominicans.   A significant number of Dominicans began migrating to the U.S. in the mid-1960s. What Grasmuck and Pessar (1996) called the "massive displacement" of Dominicans from their homeland began with the end of Trujillo's 30-year dictatorship and the political uncertainties that ensued. Dominican immigrant families did not fit the conventional image of the unskilled, underemployed peasant. They generally had employed breadwinners who were relatively well educated by Dominican standards; the majority described themselves as having urban middle-class origins (Mitchell, 1992).

The Dominican population is heavily concentrated in New York City. They entered a hostile labor market in which their middle class aspirations were to remain largely unfulfilled because the restructured New York economy offers low-wage, marginal, mostly dead-end employment for individuals without advanced education (Torres & Bonilla, 1993). Dominicans lacked the English language competence and educational credentials that might have facilitated their upward mobility (Grasmuck & Pessar, 1996). More than two thirds of the Dominican-origin population in the United States is Dominican born. As a group, Dominicans have high rates of poverty and female-headed families. Approximately 4 in 10 family households are headed by women.

THE STRUCTURE OF ECONOMIC OPPORTUNITY

Latino families remain outside the economic mainstream of U.S. society. Their median family income stands at less than two thirds the median family income of all U.S. families (U.S. Bureau of the Census, 1996). But the broad designation of "Latino" obscures important differences among national-origin groups. In this section, we explore variations in the structure of economic opportunity and consider how particular economic contexts shape the lives of different groups of Latino families.

Class, Work, and Family Life

A number of studies (see, for example, Cardenas, Chapa, & Burek, 1993; Grasmuck & Pessar, 1996; Lopez et al., 1996; Ortiz, 1995; Perez, 1994) have documented that diverse social and economic contexts produce multiple labor market outcomes for Latino families. The quality, availability, and stability of wage labor create a socioeconomic context in which family life is constructed and maintained. Cuban American families have fared far better socioeconomically than have other Latino families. Scholars consistently cite the role of the Cuban enclave in providing a favorable economic context with advantages that other groups have not enjoyed (Morales & Bonilla, 1993; Perez, 1994; Perez-Stable & Uriarte, 1993). Cuban families have the highest incomes, educational attainments, and levels of upper-white-collar employment. Puerto Rican, Mexican, and Central American families cluster below Cubans on these socioeconomic indicators, with Puerto Ricans the most disadvantaged group.

The structure of Mexican American economic opportunity stands in sharp contrast to that of Cubans. Betancur, Cordova, and Torres (1993) documented the systematic exclusion of Mexicans from upward-mobility ladders, tracing the incorporation of Mexican Americans into the Chicago economy to illustrate the historic roots of the concentration of Mexicans in unstable, poor-quality work. Throughout the 20th century Mexican migrants have constituted a transient workforce that has been continually vulnerable to fluctuations in the labor market and cycles of recruitment and deportation. Betancur et al.'s study highlighted the significance of the bracero program of contract labor migration in institutionalizing a segmented market for labor. The bracero program limited Mexican workers to specific low-status jobs and industries that prohibited promotion to skilled occupational categories. Mexicans were not allowed to compete for higher-status jobs, but were contracted to fill only the most undesirable jobs. Although formal bracero-era regulations have ended, similar occupational concentrations continue to be reproduced among Mexican American workers.

The effects of these diverging social-class and employment contexts on families are well illustrated by Fernandez-Kelly's (1990) study of female garment workers—Cubans in Miami and Mexicans in Los Angeles—both of whom placed a high value on marriage and family; however, contextual factors shaped differently their abilities to sustain marital relationships over time. Fernandez-Kelly contended that the conditions necessary for maintaining long-term stable unions were present in middle-class families but were absent in poor families. That is, the marriages of the poor women were threatened by unemployment and underemployment. Among these Mexican women, there was a high rate of poor female-headed households, and among the Cuban women, many were members of upwardly mobile families.

Women's Work

Several studies (Chavira-Prado, 1992; Grasmuck & Pessar, 1991; Lamphere, Zavella, Gonzales & Evans, 1993; Stier & Tienda, 1992; Zavella, 1987) that have explored the intersection of work and family for Latinas have found that Latinas are increasingly likely to be employed. Labor force participation is the highest among Central American women and the lowest among Puerto Rican women, with Mexican and Cuban women equally likely to be employed. Not only do labor force participation rates differ by national origin, but the meaning of women's work varies as well. For example, Fernandez-Kelly's (1990) study demonstrated that for Cuban women, employment was part of a broad family objective to reestablish middle-class status. Many Cuban immigrants initially experienced downward mobility, and the women took temporary jobs to generate income while their husbands cultivated fledgling businesses. These women often withdrew from the workforce when their families' economic positions had been secured. In contrast, Mexican women in Los Angeles worked because of dire economic necessity. They were drawn into employment to augment the earnings of partners who were confined to secondary-sector work that paid less than subsistence wages or worse, to provide the primary support for their households. Thus, whereas the Cuban women expected to work temporarily until their husbands could resume the role of middle-class breadwinner, the Mexican women worked either because their partners could not earn a family wage or because of the breakdown of family relationships by divorce or abandonment.

GLOBAL REORGANIZATION

Economic Restructuring

The economic challenges that Latinos face are enormous. A workforce that has always been vulnerable to exploitation can anticipate the decline of already limited mobility prospects. A recent body of scholarship (see, for example, Lopez et al., 1996; Morales & Bonilla, 1993; Ortiz, 1996) has demonstrated that the restructuring of the U.S. economy has reshaped economic opportunities for Latinos.

Torres and Bonilla's (1993) study of the restructuring of New York City's economy is particularly illustrative because it focused on Puerto Ricans, the Latino group hit hardest by economic transformations. That study found that restructuring in New York City is based on two processes that negatively affect Puerto Ricans. First, stable jobs in both the public and private sectors have eroded since the 1960s because many large corporations that had provided long-term, union jobs for minorities left the New York area and New York City's fiscal difficulties restricted the opportunities for municipal employment. Second, the reorganization of light manufacturing has meant that new jobs offer low wages and poor working conditions; new immigrants who are vulnerable to exploitation by employers generally fill these jobs. The restructuring of the economy has resulted in the exclusion or withdrawal of a substantial proportion of Puerto Ricans from the labor market (Morales & Bonilla, 1993).

Families are not insulated from the effects of social and economic dislocations. Research that has tracked this major social transformation has considered how such changes affect family processes and household composition (Grasmuck & Pessar, 1996; Lopez et al., 1996; Rodriguez & Hagan, 1997). What Sassen (1993) called the "informalization" and "casualization" of urban labor markets will, in the end, shape families in ways that deviate from the nuclear ideal. The marginalization of the Puerto Rican workforce is related not only to high unemployment and poverty rates, but to high rates of nonmarital births and female-headed households (Fernandez-Kelly, 1990; Morrissey, 1987).

Contrasting the experience of Dominicans to that of Puerto Ricans indicates that it is impossible to generalize a unitary "Latino experience" even within a single labor market—New York City. Torres and Bonilla (1993) found that as Puerto Ricans were displaced from manufacturing jobs in the 1970s and 1980s, new Dominican immigrants came into the restructured manufacturing sector to fill low-wage jobs. Dominicans were part of a pool of immigrant labor that entered a depressed economy, was largely ineligible for public assistance, and was willing to accept exploitative employment. Grasmuck and Pessar (1991, 1996) showed how the incorporation of Dominicans into the restructured New York economy has affected families. Although the rate of divorce among early immigrants was high, relationships have become increasingly precarious as employment opportunities have become even more constrained. Currently, rates of poverty and female-headed households for Dominicans approximate those of Puerto Ricans (Rumbaut, 1995).

A Latino Underclass? Rising poverty rates among Latinos, together with the alarmist treatment of female-headed households among "minorities," have led many policy makers and media analysts to conclude that Latinos have joined inner-city African Americans to form part of the "underclass." According to the underclass model, inner-city men's joblessness has encouraged nonmarital childbearing and undermined the economic foundations of the African American family (Wilson, 1987, 1996). Researchers have also been debating for some time whether increases in the incidence of female-headed households and poverty among Puerto Ricans are irreversible (Tienda, 1989). Recent thinking, however, suggests that applying the underclass theory to Latinos obscures more than it reveals and that a different analytical model is needed to understand poverty and family issues in each Latino group (Massey et al., 1995). Not only do the causes of poverty differ across Latino communities, but patterns of social organization at the community and family levels produce a wide range of responses to poverty. According to Moore and Pinderhughes (1993), the dynamics of poverty even in the poorest Latino barrios differ in fundamental ways from the conventional portrait of the under-class. Both African Americans and Puerto Ricans have high rates of female-headed households. However, Sullivan's (1993) research in Brooklyn indicated that Puerto Ricans have high rates of cohabitation and that the family formation processes that lead to these household patterns are different from those of African Americans. Other case studies have underscored the importance of family organization. For example, Velez-Ibañez (1993) described a distinctive family form among poor Mexicans of South Tucson—cross-class household clusters surrounded by kinship networks that stretch beyond neighborhood boundaries and provide resources for coping with poverty.

Immigration

Families migrate for economic reasons, political reasons, or some combination of the two. Immigration offers potential and promise, but one of the costs is the need for families to adapt to their receiving community contexts. A growing body of scholarship has focused on two areas of family change: household composition and gender relations.

Household Composition. Immigration contributes to the proliferation of family forms and a variety of household arrangements among Latinos (Vega, 1995). Numerous studies have highlighted the flexibility of Latino family households. Chavez (1990, 1992) identified transnational families, binational families, extended families, multiple-family households, and other arrangements among Mexican and Central American immigrants. Landale and Fennelly (1992) found informal unions that resemble marriage more than cohabitation among main-land Puerto Ricans, and Guarnizo (1997) found binational households among Dominicans who live and work in both the United States and the Dominican Republic. Two processes are at work as families adapt their household structures. First, family change reflects, for many, desperate economic circumstances (Vega, 1995), which bring some families to the breaking point and leads others to expand their household boundaries. Second, the transnationalization of economies and labor has created new opportunities for successful Latino families; for example, Guarnizo noted that Dominican entrepreneurs sometimes live in binational households and have "de facto binational citizenship" (p. 171).

Immigration and Gender.   Several important studies have considered the relationship between immigration and gender (Boyd, 1989; Grasmuck & Pessar, 1991; Hondagneu-Sotelo, 1994). In her study of undocumented Mexican immigrants, Hondagneu-Sotelo (1994) demonstrated that gender shapes migration and immigration shapes gender relations. She found that family stage migration, in which husbands migrate first and wives and children follow later, does not fit the household-strategy model. Often implied in this model is the assumption that migration reflects the unanimous and rational collective decision of all household members. However, as Hondagneu-Sotelo observed, gender hierarchies determined when and under what circumstances migration occurred; that is, men often decided spontaneously, independently, and unilaterally to migrate north to seek employment. When Mexican couples were finally reunited in the United States, they generally reconstructed more egalitarian gender relations. Variation in the form of gender relations in the United States is partially explained by the circumstances surrounding migration, such as the type and timing of migration, access to social networks, and U.S. immigration policy.

FAMILY DYNAMICS ACROSS LATINO GROUPS

Familism

Collectivist family arrangements are thought to be a defining feature of the Latino population. Presumably, a strong orientation and obligation to the family produces a kinship structure that is qualitatively different from that of all other groups. Latino familism, which is said to emphasize the family as opposed to the individual, "is linked to many of the pejorative images that have beset discussions of the Hispanic family" (Vega, 1990, p. 1018). Although themes of Latino familism figure prominently in the social science literature, this topic remains problematic owing to empirical limitations and conceptual confusion.

Popular and social science writing contain repeated descriptions of what amounts to a generic Latino kinship form. In reality, a Mexican-origin bias pervades the research on this topic. Not only is there a lack of comparative research on extended kinship structures among different national-origin groups, but there is little empirical evidence for all but Mexican-origin families. For Mexican-origin groups, studies are plentiful (for reviews, see Baca Zinn, 1983; Vega, 1990, 1995), although they have yielded inconsistent evidence about the prevalence of familism, the forms it takes, and the kinds of supportive relationships it serves.

Among the difficulties in assessing the evidence on extended family life are the inconsistent uses of terms like *familism* and *extended family system*. Seeking to clarify the multiple meanings of familism, Ramirez and Arce (1981) treated familism as a multidimensional concept comprised of such distinct aspects as structure, behavior, norms and attitudes, and social identity, each of which requires separate measurement and analysis. They proposed that familism contains four key components: (1) demographic familism, which involves such characteristics as family size; (2) structural familism, which measures the incidence of multigenerational (or extended) households; (3) normative families, which taps the value that Mexican-origin people place on family unity and solidarity; and (4) behavioral familism, which has to do with the level of interaction between family and kin networks.

Changes in regional and local economies and the resulting dislocations of Latinos have prompted questions about the ongoing viability of kinship networks. Analyzing a national sample of minority families, Rochelle (1997) argued that extended kinship networks are declining among Chicanos, Puerto Ricans, and African Americans. On the other hand, a large body of research has documented various forms of network participation by Latinos. For three decades, studies have found that kinship networks are an important survival strategy in poor Mexican communities (Alvirez & Bean, 1976; Hoppe & Heller, 1975; Velez-Ibañez, 1996) and that these networks operate as a system of cultural, emotional, and mental support (Keefe, 1984; Mindel, 1980; Ramirez, 1980), as well as a system for coping with socioeconomic marginality (Angel & Tienda, 1982; Lamphere et al., 1993).

Research has suggested, however, that kinship networks are not maintained for socioeconomic reasons alone (Buriel & De Ment, 1997). Familistic orientation among Mexican-origin adults has been associated with high levels of education and income (Griffith & Villavicienco, 1985). Familism has been viewed as a form of social capital that is linked with academic success among Mexican-heritage adolescents (Valenzuela & Dornbusch, 1994).

The research on the involvement of extended families in the migration and settlement of Mexicans discussed earlier (Chavez, 1992; Hondagneu-Sotelo, 1994; Hondagneu-Sotelo & Avila, 1997) is profoundly important. In contrast to the prevailing view that family extension is an artifact of culture, this research helps one understand that the structural flexibility of families is a social construction. Transnational families and their networks of kin are extended in space, time, and across national borders. They are quintessential adaptations—alternative arrangements for solving problems associated with immigration.

Despite the conceptual and empirical ambiguities surrounding the topic of familism, there is evidence that kinship networks are far from monolithic. Studies have revealed that variations are rooted in distinctive social conditions, such as immigrant versus non-immigrant status and generational status. Thus, even though immigrants use kin for assistance, they have smaller social networks than do second-generation Mexican Americans who have broader social networks consisting of multigenerational kin (Vega, 1990). Studies have shown that regardless of class, Mexican extended families in the United States become stronger and more extensive with generational advancement, acculturation, and socio-economic mobility (Velez-Ibañez, 1996). Although an assimilationist perspective suggests that familism fades in succeeding generations, Velez-Ibañez found that highly elaborated second- and third-generation extended family networks are actively maintained through frequent visits, ritual celebrations, and the exchange of goods and services. These networks are differentiated by the functions they perform, depending on the circumstances of the people involved.

Gender

Latino families are commonly viewed as settings of traditional patriarchy and as different from other families because of machismo, the cult of masculinity. In the past two decades, this cultural stereotype has been the impetus for corrective scholarship on Latino families. The flourishing of Latina feminist thought has shifted the focus from the determinism of culture to questions about how gender and power in families are connected with other structures and institutions in society. Although male dominance remains a central theme, it is understood as part of the ubiquitous social ordering of women and men. In the context of other forms of difference, gender exerts a powerful influence on Latino families.

New research is discovering gender dynamics among Latino families that are both similar to and different from those found in other groups. Similarities stem from social changes that are reshaping all families, whereas differences emerge from the varied locations of Latino families and the women and men in them. Like other branches of scholarship on Latino families, most studies have been conducted with Mexican-origin populations. The past two decades of research have shown that family life among all Latino groups is deeply gendered. Yet no simple generalizations sum up the essence of power relations.

Research has examined two interrelated areas: (1) family decision making and (2) the allocation of household labor. Since the first wave of "revisionist works" (Zavella, 1987) conducted in the 1970s and 1980s (Baca Zinn, 1980; Ybarra, 1982), researchers have found variation in these activities, ranging from patriarchal role-segregated patterns to egalitarian patterns, with many combinations in between. Studies have suggested that Latinas' employment patterns, like those of women around the world, provide them with resources and autonomy that alter the balance of family power (Baca Zinn, 1980; Coltrane & Valdez, 1993; Pesquera, 1993; Repack, 1997; Williams, 1990; Ybarra, 1982; Zavella, 1987). But, as we discussed earlier, employment opportunities vary widely, and the variation produces multiple work and family patterns for Latinas. Furthermore, women's employment, by itself, does not eradicate male dominance. This is one of the main lessons of Zavella's (1987) study of Chicana cannery workers in California's Santa Clara Valley. Women's cannery work was circumscribed by inequalities of class, race, and gender. As seasonal, part-time workers, the women gained some leverage in the home, thereby creating temporary shifts in their day-to-day family lives, but this leverage did not alter the balance of family power. Fernandez-Kelly and Garcia's (1990) comparative study of women's work and family patterns among Cubans and Mexican Americans found strikingly different configurations of power. Employed women's newfound rights are often contradictory. As Repack's study (1997) of Central American immigrants revealed, numerous costs and strains accompany women's new roles in a new landscape. Family relations often became contentious when women pressed partners to share domestic responsibilities. Migration produced a situation in which women worked longer and harder than in their countries of origin.

Other conditions associated with varying patterns in the division of domestic labor are women's and men's occupational statuses and relative economic contributions to their families. Studies by Pesquera (1993), Coltrane and Valdez (1993), and Coltrane (1996) found a general "inside/outside" dichotomy (wives doing most housework, husbands doing outside work and sharing some child care), but women in middle-class jobs received more "help" from their husbands than did women with lower earnings.

"Family power" research should not be limited to women's roles, but should study the social relations between women and men. Recent works on Latino men's family lives have made important strides in this regard (Coltrane & Valdez, 1993; Shelton & John, 1993). Still, there is little information about the range and variety of Latino men's family experiences (Mirande, 1997) or of their interplay with larger structural conditions. In a rare study of Mexican immigrant men, Hondagncu-Sotelo and Messner (1994) discussed the diminution of patriarchy that comes with settling in the United States. They showed that the key to gender equality in immigrant families is women's and men's relative positions of power and status in the larger society. Mexican immigrant men's status is low owing to racism, economic marginality, and possible undocumented status. Meanwhile, as immigrant women move into wage labor, they develop autonomy and economic skills. These conditions combine to erode patriarchal authority.

The research discussed earlier suggested some convergences between Latinos and other groups in family power arrangements. But intertwined with the shape of domestic power are strongly held ideals about women's and men's family roles. Ethnic gender identities, values, and beliefs contribute to gender relations and constitute an important but little understood dimension of families. Gender may also be influenced by Latinos' extended family networks. As Lamphere et al. (1993) discovered, Hispanas in Albuquerque were living in a world made up largely of Hispana mothers, sisters, and other relatives. Social scientists have posited a relationship between dense social networks and gender segregation. If this relationship holds, familism could well impede egalitarian relations in Latino families (Coltrane, 1996; Hurtado, 1995).

Compulsory heterosexuality is an important component of both gender and family systems. By enforcing the dichotomy of opposite sexes, it is also a form of inequality in its own right, hence an important marker of social location. A growing literature on lesbian and gay identity among Latinas and Latinos has examined the conflicting challenges involved in negotiating a multiple minority status (Alarcon, Castillo, & Moraga, 1989; Almaguer, 1991; Anzaldúa, 1987; Carrier, 1992; Moraga, 1983; Morales, 1990). Unfortunately, family scholarship on Latinos has not pursued the implications of lesbian and gay identities for understanding family diversity. In fact, there have been no studies in the social sciences in the area of sexual orientation and Latino families (Hurtado, 1995). But although the empirical base is virtually nonexistent and making *families* the unit of analysis no doubt introduces new questions (Demo & Allen, 1996), we can glean useful insights from the discourse on sexual identity. Writing about Chicanos, Almaguer (1991) identified the following obstacles to developing a safe space for forming a gay or lesbian identity: racial and class subordination and a context in which ethnicity remains a primary basis of group identity and survival. "Moreover Chicano *family life* [italics added] requires allegiance to patriarchal gender relations and to a system of sexual meanings that directly mitigate against the emergence of this alternative basis of self identity" (Almaguer, p. 88). Such repeated references to the constraints of ethnicity, gender, and sexual orientation imposed by Chicano families (Almaguer, 1991; Moraga, 1983) raise important questions. How do varied family contexts shape and differentiate the development of gay identities among Latinos? How do they affect the formation of lesbian and gay families among Latinas and Latinos? This area is wide open for research.

Children and Their Parents

Latinos have the highest concentration of children and adolescents of all major racial and ethnic groups. Nearly 40% of Latinos are aged 20 or younger, compared to about 26% of non-Hispanic whites (U.S. Bureau of the Census, 1996). Among Latino subgroups, the highest proportions of children and adolescents are among Mexicans and Puerto Ricans and the lowest among Cubans (Solis, 1995).

Latino socialization patterns have long held the interest of family scholars (Martinez, 1993). Most studies have focused on the child-rearing practices of Mexican families. Researchers have questioned whether Mexican families have permissive or authoritarian styles of child rearing and the relationship of childrearing styles to social class and cultural factors (Martinez, 1993). Patterns of child rearing were expected to reveal the level of acculturation to U.S. norms and the degree of modernization among traditional immigrant families. The results of research spanning the 1970s and 1980s were mixed and sometimes contradictory.

Buriel's (1993) study brought some clarity to the subject of child-rearing practices by situating it in the broad social context in which such practices occur. This study of Mexican families found that child-rearing practices differ by generation. Parents who were born in Mexico had a "responsibility-oriented" style that was compatible with their own life experience as struggling immigrants. U.S.-born Mexican parents had a "concern-oriented" style of parenting that was associated with the higher levels of education and income found among this group and that may also indicate that parents compensate for their children's disadvantaged standing in U.S. schools.

Mainstream theorizing has generally assumed a middle-class European-American model for the socialization of the next generation (Segura & Pierce, 1993). But the diverse contexts in which Latino children are raised suggest that family studies must take into account multiple models of socialization. Latino children are less likely than Anglo children to live in isolated nuclear units in which parents have almost exclusive responsibility for rearing children and the mothers' role is primary. Segura and Pierce contended that the pattern of nonexclusive mothering found in some Latino families shapes the gender identities of Latinos in ways that conventional thinking does not consider. Velez-Ibañez & Greenberg (1992) discussed how the extensive kinship networks of Mexican families influence child rearing and considered the ramifications for educational outcomes. Mexican children are socialized into a context of "thick" social relations. From infancy onward, these children experience far more social interaction than do children who are raised in more isolated contexts. The institution of education—second only to the family as an agent of socialization—is, in the United States, modeled after the dominant society and characterized by competition and individual achievement. Latino students who have been socialized into a more cooperative model of social relations often experience a disjuncture between their upbringing and the expectations of their schools (Velez-Ibañez & Greenberg, 1992).

Social location shapes the range of choices that parents have as they decide how best to provide for their children. Latino parents, who are disproportionately likely to occupy subordinate social locations in U.S. society, encounter severe obstacles to providing adequate material resources for their children. To date, little research has focused on Latino fathers (Powell, 1995). Hondagneu-Sotelo and Avila's (1997) study documented a broad range of mothering arrangements among Latinas. One such arrangement is transnational mothering, in which mothers work in the United States while their children remain in Mexico or Central America; it is accompanied by tremendous costs and undertaken when options are extremely limited. The researchers found that transnational mothering occurred among domestic workers, many of whom were live-in maids or child care providers who could not live with their children, as well as mothers who could better provide for their children in their countries of origin because U.S. dollars stretched further in Central America than in the United States. Other mothering arrangements chosen by Latinas in the study included migrating with their children, migrating alone and later sending for their children, and migrating alone and returning to their children after a period of work.

Intrafamily Diversity

Family scholars have increasingly recognized that family experience is differentiated along the lines of age and gender (Baca Zinn & Eitzen, 1996; Thorne, 1992). Members of particular families—parents and children, women and men—experience family life differently. Scholarship that considers the internal differentiation of Latino families is focused on the conditions surrounding and adaptations following immigration.

While immigration requires tremendous change of all family members, family adaptation to the new context is not a unitary phenomenon. Research has found patterns of differential adjustment as family members adapt unevenly to an unfamiliar social environment (Gold, 1989). Gil and Vega's (1996) study of acculturative stress in Cuban and Nicaraguan families in the Miami area identified significant differences in the adjustment of parents and their children. For example, Nicaraguan adolescents reported more initial language conflicts than did their parents, but their conflicts diminished over time, whereas their parents' language conflicts increased over time. This difference occurred because the adolescents were immediately confronted with their English language deficiency in school, but their parents could initially manage well in the Miami area without a facility with English. The authors concluded that family members experience "the aversive impacts of culture change at different times and at variable levels of intensity" (p. 451).

Differential adjustment creates new contexts for parent-child relations. Immigrant children who are school-aged generally become competent in English more quickly than do their parents. Dorrington (1995) found that Salvadoran and Guatemalan children often assume adult roles as they help their parents negotiate the bureaucratic structure of their new social environment; for example, a young child may accompany her parents to a local utility company to act as their translator.

Immigration may also create formal legal distinctions among members of Latino families. Frequently, family members do not share the same immigration status. That is, undocumented Mexican and Central American couples are likely, over time, to have children born in the United States and hence are U.S. citizens; the presence of these children then renders the "undocumented family" label inaccurate. Chavez (1992, p. 129) used the term *binational family* to refer to a family with both members who are undocumented and those who are citizens or legal residents.

Not only do family members experience family life differently, but age and gender often produce diverging and even conflicting interests among them (Baca Zinn & Eitzen, 1996). Both Hondagneu-Sotelo's (1994) and Grasmuck and Pessar's (1991) studies of family immigration found that Latinas were generally far more interested in settling permanently in the United States than were their husbands. In both studies, the women had enhanced their status by migration, while the men had lost theirs. Hondagneu-Sotelo noted that Mexican women advanced the permanent settlement of their families by taking regular, nonseasonal employment; negotiating the use of public and private assistance; and forging strong community ties. Grasmuck and Pessar observed that Dominican women tried to postpone their families' return to the Dominican Republic by extravagantly spending money that would otherwise be saved for their return and by establishing roots in the United States.

DISCUSSION AND CONCLUSION

The key to understanding diversity in Latino families is the uneven distribution of constraints and opportunities among families, which affects the behaviors of family members and ultimately the forms that family units take (Baca Zinn & Eitzen, 1996). Our goal in this review was to call into question assumptions, beliefs, and false generalizations about the way "Latino families are." We examined Latino families not as if they had some essential characteristics that set them apart from others, but as they are affected by a complex mix of structural features.

Our framework enabled us to see how diverse living arrangements among Latinos are situated and structured in the larger social world. Although this framework embraces the interplay of macro-and microlevels of analysis, we are mindful that this review devoted far too little attention to family experience, resistance, and voice. We do not mean to underestimate the importance of human agency in the social construction of Latino families, but we could not devote as much attention as we would have liked to the various ways in which women, men, and children actively produce their family worlds. Given the sheer size of the literature, the "non-comparability of most contemporary findings" and the lack of a consistent conceptual groundwork" (Vega, 1990, p. 102), we decided that what is most needed is a coherent framework within which to view and interpret diversity. Therefore, we chose to focus on the impact of social forces on family life.

The basic insights of our perspective are sociological. Yet a paradox of family sociology is that the field has tended to misrepresent Latino families and those of other racial-ethnic groups. Sociology has distorted Latino families by generalizing from the experience of dominant groups and ignoring the differences that make a difference. This is a great irony. Family sociology, the specialty whose task it is to describe and understand social diversity, has marginalized diversity, rather than treated it as a central feature of social life (Baca Zinn & Eitzen, 1993).

As sociologists, we wrote this chapter fully aware of the directions in our discipline that hinder the ability to explain diversity. At the same time, we think the core insight of sociology should be applied to challenge conventional thinking about families. Reviewing the literature for this chapter did not diminish our sociological convictions, but it did present us with some unforeseen challenges. We found a vast gulf between mainstream family sociology and the extraordinary amount of high-quality scholarship on Latino families. Our review took us far beyond the boundaries of our discipline, making us "cross disciplinary migrants" (Stacey, 1995). We found the new literature in diverse and unlikely locations, with important breakthroughs emerging in the "borderlands" between social science disciplines. We also found the project to be infinitely more complex than we anticipated. The extensive scholarship on three national-origin groups and "others" was complicated by widely varying analytic snapshots. We were, in short, confronted with a kaleidoscope of family diversity. Our shared perspective served us well in managing the task at hand. Although we have different family specializations and contrasting family experiences, we both seek to understand multiple family and household forms that emanate from structural arrangements.

What are the most important lessons our sociological analysis holds for the family field? Three themes offer new directions for building a better, more inclusive, family social science. First, understanding Latino family diversity does not mean simply appreciating the ways in which families are different; rather, it means analyzing how the formation of diverse families is based on and reproduces social inequalities. At the heart of many of the differences between Latino families and mainstream families and the different aggregate family patterns among Latino groups are structural forces that place families in different social environments. What is not often acknowledged is that the same social structures—race, class, and other hierarchies—affect *all* families, albeit in different ways. Instead of treating family variation as the property of group difference, recent sociological theorizing (Baca Zinn, 1994; Dill, 1994; Glenn, 1992; Hill Collins, 1990, 1997) has conceptualized diverse family arrangements in *relational* terms, that is, mutually dependent and sustained through interaction across racial and class boundaries. The point is not that family differences based on race, class, and gender simply coexist. Instead, many differences in family life involve relationships of domination and subordination and differential access to material resources. Patterns of privilege and subordination characterize the historical relationships between Anglo families and Mexican families in the Southwest (Dill, 1994). Contemporary diversity among Latino families reveals *new* interdependences and inequalities. Emergent middle-class and professional lifestyles among Anglos and even some Latinos are interconnected with a new Latino servant class whose family arrangements, in turn, must accommodate to the demands of their labor.

Second, family diversity plays a part in different economic orders and the shifts that accompany them. Scholars have suggested that the multiplicity of household types is one of the chief props of the world economy (Smith, Wallerstein, & Evers, 1985). The example of U.S.-Mexican cross-border households brings this point into full view. This household arrangement constitutes an important "part of the emerging and dynamic economic and technological transformations in the region" (Velez-Ibañez, 1996, p. 143). The structural reordering required by such families is central to regional economic change.

Finally, the incredible array of immigrant family forms and their enormous capacity for adaptation offer new departures for the study of postmodern families. "Binational," "transnational," and "multinational" families, together with "border balanced households" and "generational hopscotching," are arrangements that remain invisible even in Stacey's (1996) compelling analysis of U.S. family life at the century's end. And yet the experiences of Latino families—flexible and plastic—as far back as the late 1800s (Griswold del Castillo, 1984), give resonance to the image of long-standing family fluidity and of contemporary families lurching backward and forward into the postmodern age (Stacey, 1990). The shift to a postindustrial economy is not the only social transformation affecting families. Demographic and political changes sweeping the world are engendering family configurations that are yet unimagined in family social science.

These trends offer new angles of vision for thinking about family diversity. They pose new opportunities for us to remake family studies as we uncover the mechanisms that construct multiple household and family arrangements.

References

Alarcon, N., Castillo, A., & Moraga, C. (Eds.). (1989). *Third woman: The sexuality of Latinas.* Berkeley, CA: Third Woman.

Almaguer, T. (1991). Chicano men: A cartography of homosexual identity and behavior. *Differences: A Journal of Feminist Cultural Studies, 3,* 75–100.

Alvirez, D., & Bean, F. (1976). The Mexican American family. In C. Mindel & R. Habenstein (Eds.), *Ethnic families in America* (pp. 271–292). New York: Elsevier.

Angel, R., & Tienda, M. (1982). Determinants of extended household structure: Cultural pattern or economic need? *American Journal of Sociology, 87,* 1360–1383,

Anzaldúa, G. (1987). *Borderlands/La Frontera: The new meztiza.* San Francisco: Spinsters, Aunt Lute Press.

Aponte, R. (1993). Hispanic families in poverty: Diversity, context, and interpretation. *Families in Society: The Journal of Contemporary Human Services, 36,* 527–537.

Baca Zinn, M. (1980). Employment and education of Mexican American women: The interplay of modernity and ethnicity in eight families. *Harvard Educational Review, 50,* 47–62.

Baca Zinn, M. (1983). Familism among Chicanos: A theoretical review. *Humboldt Journal of Social Relations, 10,* 224–238.

Baca Zinn, M. (1994). Feminist rethinking from racial-ethnic families. In M. Baca Zinn & B. T. Dill (Eds.), *Women of color in U.S. society* (pp. 303–312). Philadelphia: Temple University Press.

Baca Zinn, M. (1995). Social science theorizing for Latino families in the age of diversity. In R. E. Zambrana (Ed.), *Understanding Latino families* (pp. 177–187). Thousand Oaks, CA: Sage.

Baca Zinn, M., & Dill, B. T. (1996). Theorizing difference from multiracial feminism. *Feminist Studies, 22,* 321–332.

Baca Zinn, M., & Eitzen, D. S. (1993). The demographic transformation and the sociological enterprise. *American Sociologist, 24,* 5–12.

Baca Zinn, M., & Eitzen, D. S. (1996). *Diversity in families* (4th ed.). New York: HarperCollins.

Baca Zinn, M., & Eitzen, D. S. (1998). Economic restructuring and systems in inequality. In M. L. Andersen & P. H. Collins (Eds.), *Race, class and gender* (3rd ed., pp. 233–237). Belmont, CA: Wadsworth.

Betancur, J. J., Cordova, T., & Torres, M. L. A. (1993). Economic restructuring and the process of incorporation of Latinos into the Chicago economy. In R. Morales & F. Bonilla (Eds.), *Latinos in a changing U.S. economy: Comparative perspectives on growing inequality* (pp. 109–132). Newbury Park, CA: Sage.

Bogardus, A. (1934). *The Mexican in the United States.* Los Angeles: University of Southern California Press.

Boss, P., & Thorne, B. (1989). Family sociology and family therapy. In M. McGoldrick, C. M. Anderson, & F. Walsh (Eds.), *Women in families* (pp. 78–96). New York: W. W. Norton.

Boyd, M. (1989). Family and personal networks in international migration: Recent developments and new agendas. *International Migration Review, 23,* 638- 670.

Buriel, R. (1993). Childrearing orientations in Mexican American families: The influence of generation and sociocultural factors. *Journal of Marriage and the Family, 55,* 987–1000.

Buriel, R., & De Ment, T. (1997). Immigration and sociocultural change in Mexican, Chinese, and Vietnamese American families. In A. Booth, A. C. Crouter, & N. Landale (Eds.), *Immigration and the family: Research and policy on U.S. immigrants* (pp. 165–200). Mahway, NJ: Lawrence Erlbaum.

Cardenas, G., Chapa, J., & Burek, S. (1993). The changing economic position of Mexican Americans in San Antonio. In R. Morales & F. Bonilla (Eds.), *Latinos in a changing U.S. economy: Comparative perspectives on growing inequality* (pp. 160–183). Newbury Park, CA: Sage.

Carnoy, M., Daley, H. M., & Ojeda, R. H. (1993). The changing economic position of Latinos in the U.S. labor market since 1939. In R. Morales & F. Bonilla (Eds.), *Latinos in a changing U.S. economy: Comparative perspectives on growing inequality* (pp. 28–54). Newbury Park, CA: Sage.

Carrier, J. (1992). Miguel: Sexual life history of a gay Mexican American. In G. Herdt (Ed.), *Gay culture in America* (pp. 202–224). Boston: Beacon Press.

Chavez, L. R. (1990). Coresidence and resistance: Strategies for survival among undocumented Mexicans and Central Americans in the United States. *Urban Anthropology, 19,* 31–61.

Chavez, L. R. (1992). *Shadowed lives: Undocumented immigrants in American society.* Forth Worth, TX: Holt, Rinehart, & Winston.

Chavira-Prado, A. (1992). Work, health, and the family: Gender structure and women's status in an undocumented migrant population. *Human Organization, 51,* 53–64.

Coltrane, S. (1996). *Family man.* New York: Oxford University Press.

Coltrane, S., & Valdez, E. O. (1993). Reluctant compliance: Work-family role allocation in dual earner Chicano families. In J. Hood (Ed.), *Men, work, and family* (pp. 151–175). Newbury Park, CA: Sage.

Demo, D. H., & Allen, K. R. (1996). Diversity within gay and lesbian families: Challenges and implications for family theory and research. *Journal of Social and Personal Relationships, 13,* 415–434.

Dill, B. T. (1994). Fictive kin, paper sons, and compadrazgo: Women of color and the struggle for survival. In M. Baca Zinn & B. T. Dill (Eds.), *Women of color in U.S. society* (pp. 149–169). Philadelphia: Temple University Press.

Dominguez, J. I. (1992). Cooperating with the enemy? U.S. immigration policies toward Cuba. In C. Mitchell (Ed.), *Western hemisphere immigration and United States foreign policy* (pp. 31–88). University Park, PA: Pennsylvania State University Press.

Dorrington, C. (1995). Central American refugees in Los Angeles: Adjustment of children and families. In R. Zambrana (Ed.), *Understanding Latino families: Scholarship, policy, and practice* (pp. 107–129). Thousand Oaks, CA: Sage.

Feagin, J. R., & Feagin, C. B. (1996). *Racial and ethnic relations.* Upper Saddle River, NJ: Prentice Hall.

Fernandez-Kelly, M. P. (1990). Delicate transactions: Gender, home, and employment among Hispanic women. In F. Ginsberg & A. L. Tsing (Eds.), *Uncertain terms* (pp. 183–195). Boston: Beacon Press.

Fernandez-Kelly, M. P., & Garcia, A. (1990). Power surrendered and power restored: The politics of home and work among Hispanic women in southern California and southern Florida. In L. Tilly & P. Gurin (Eds.), *Women and politics in America* (pp. 130–149). New York: Russell Sage Foundation.

Fernandez-Kelly, M. P., & Schauffler, R. (1994). Divided fates: Immigrant children in a restructured U.S. economy. *International Migration Review, 28,* 662–689.

Gil, A. G., & Vega, W. A. (1996). Two different worlds: Acculturation stress and adaptation among Cuban and Nicaraguan families. *Journal of Social and Personal Relationships, 13,* 435–456.

Glenn, E. N. (1992). From servitude to service work: Historical continuities in the racial division of paid reproductive labor. *Signs: Journal of Women in Culture and Society, 18,* 1–43.

Gold, S. J. (1989). Differential adjustment among new immigrant family members. *Journal of Contemporary Ethnography, 17,* 408–434.

Grasmuck, S., & Pessar, P. R. (1991). *Between two islands: Dominican international migration.* Berkeley: University of California Press.

Grasmuck, S., & Pessar, P. R. (1996). Dominicans in the United States: First- and second-generation settlement, 1960–1990. In S. Pedraza & R. G. Rumbaut (Eds.), *Origins and destinies: Immigration, race, and ethnicity in America* (pp. 280–292). Belmont, CA: Wadsworth.

Griffith, J., & Villavicienco, S. (1985). Relationships among culturation, sociodemographic characteristics, and social supports in Mexican American adults. *Hispanic Journal of Behavioral Science, 7,* 75–92.

Griswold del Castillo, R. (1984). *La familia.* Notre Dame, IN: University of Notre Dame Press.

Guarnizo, L. E. (1997). Los Dominicanyorks: The making of a binational society. In M. Romero, P. Hondagneu-Sotelo, & V. Ortiz (Eds.), *Challenging fronteras: Structuring Latina and Latino lives in the U.S.* (pp. 161–174). New York: Routledge.

Hamilton, N., & Chinchilla, N. S. (1997). Central American migration: A framework for analysis. In M. Romero, P. Hondagneu-Sotelo, & V. Ortiz (Eds.), *Challenging fronteras: Structuring Latina and Latino lives in the U.S.* (pp. 81–100). New York: Routledge.

Heller, C. (1996). *Mexican American youth: Forgotten youth at the crossroads.* New York: Random House.

Hill Collins, P. (1990). *Black feminist thought: Knowledge, consciousness and the politics of empowerment.* Boston: Unwin Hyman.

Hill Collins, P. (1997). African-American women and economic justice: A preliminary analysis of wealth, family, and black social class. Unpublished manuscript, Department of African American Studies. University of Cincinnati.

Hondagneu-Sotelo, P. (1994). *Gendered transitions: Mexican experiences of migration.* Berkeley: University of California Press.

Hondagneu-Sotelo, P., & Avila, E. (1997). "I'm here, but I'm there": The meanings of transnational motherhood. *Gender and Society, 11,* 548–571.

Hondagneu-Sotelo, P., & Messner, M. A. (1994). Gender displays and men's power: The "new man" and the Mexican immigrant man. In H. Brod & M. Kaufman (Eds.), *Theorizing masculinities* (pp. 200–218). Newbury Park, CA: Sage.

Hoppe, S. K., & Heller, P. L. (1975). Alienation, familism and the utilization of health services by Mexican-Americans. *Journal of Health and Social Behavior, 16,* 304–314.

Hurtado, A. (1995). Variations, combinations, and evolutions: Latino families in the United States. In R. E. Zambrana (Ed.), *Understanding Latino families* (pp. 40–61). Thousand Oaks, CA: Sage.

Keefe, S. (1984). Deal and ideal extended familism among Mexican Americans and Anglo Americans: On the meaning of "close" family ties. *Human Organization, 43,* 65–70.

Lamphere, L., Zavella, P., & Gonzales F., with Evans, P. B. (1993). *Sunbelt working mothers: Reconciling family and factory.* Ithaca, NY: Cornell University Press.

Landale, N. S., & Fennelly, K. (1992). Informal unions among mainland Puerto Ricans: Cohabitation or an alternative to legal marriage? *Journal of Marriage and the Family, 54,* 269–280.

Lopez, D. E., Popkin, E., & Telles, E. (1996). Central Americans: At the bottom, struggling to get ahead. In R. Waldinger & M. Bozorgmehr (Eds.), *Ethnic Los Angeles* (pp. 279–304). New York: Russell Sage Foundation.

Madsen, W. (1973). *The Mexican-Americans of south Texas.* New York: Holt, Rinehart & Winston.

Martinez, E. A. (1993). Parenting young children in Mexican American/Chicago families. In H. P. McAdoo (Ed.), *Family ethnicity: Strength in diversity* (pp. 184–194). Newbury Park, CA: Sage.

Massey, D. S. (1993). Latino poverty research: An agenda for the 1990s. Items, *Social Science Research Council Newsletter, 47*(l), 7–11.

Massey, D. S., Zambrana, R. E., & Bell, S. A. (1995). Contemporary issues for Latino families: Future directions for research, policy, and practice. In R. E. Zambrana (Ed.), *Understanding Latino families* (pp. 190–204). Thousand Oaks, CA: Sage.

Mindel, C. H. (1980). Extended familism among urban Mexican-Americans, Anglos and blacks. *Hispanic Journal of Behavioral Sciences, 2,* 21–34.

Mirande, A. (1997). *Hombres y machos: Masculinity and Latino culture.* Boulder, CO: Westview Press.

Mitchell, C. (1992). U.S. foreign policy and Dominican migration to the United States. In C. Mitchell (Ed.), *Western hemisphere immigration and United States foreign policy* (pp. 89–123). University Park: Pennsylvania State University Press.

Moore, J. W., & Pinderhughes, R. (Eds.). (1993). *In the barrios: Latinos and the underclass debate*. New York: Russell Sage Foundation.

Moore, J. W., & Vigil, J. D. (1993). Barrios in transition. In J. W. Moore & R. Pinderhughes (Eds.), *In the barrios: Latinos and the underclass debate* (pp. 27–50). New York: Russell Sage Foundation.

Moraga, C. (1983). *Loving in the war years: Lo que nunca paso por sus labios*. Boston: South End Press.

Morales, E. S. (1990). Ethnic minority families and minority gays and lesbians. In F. W. Bozett & M. B. Sussman (Eds.), *Homosexuality and family relations* (pp. 217–239). New York: Harrington Park Press.

Morales, R., & Ong, P. M. (1993). The illusion of progress: Latinos in Los Angeles. In R. Morales & F. Bonilla (Eds.), *Latinos in a changing U.S. economy: Comparative perspectives on growing inequality* (pp. 55–84). Newbury Park, CA: Sage.

Morales, R., & Bonilla, F. (1993). Restructuring and the new inequality. In R. Morales & F. Bonilla (Eds.), *Latinos in a changing U.S. economy: Comparative perspectives on growing inequality* (pp. 1–27). Newbury Park, CA: Sage.

Morrissey, M. (1987). Female-headed families: Poor women and choice. In N. Gerstel & H. Gross (Eds.), Families and work (pp. 302–314). Philadelphia: Temple University Press.

Ortiz, V. (1995). The diversity of Latino families. In R. Zambrana (Ed.), *Understanding Latino families: Scholarship, policy, and practice* (pp. 18–30). Thousand Oaks, CA: Sage.

Ortiz, V. (1996). The Mexican-origin population: Permanent working class or emerging middle class? In R. Waldinger & M. Bozorgmehr (Eds.), *Ethnic Los Angeles* (pp. 247–277). New York: Russell Sage Foundation.

Perez, L. (1994). Cuban families in the United States. In R. L. Taylor (Ed.), *Minority families in the United States: A multicultural perspective*. Englewood Cliffs, NJ: Prentice Hall.

Perez-Stable, M., & Uriarte, M. (1993). Cubans and the changing economy of Miami. In R. Morales & F. Bonilla (Eds.), *Latinos in a changing U.S. economy: Comparative perspectives on growing inequality* (pp. 133–159). Newbury Park, CA: Sage.

Pesquera, B. M. (1993). In the beginning he wouldn't lift even a spoon: The division of household labor. In A. de la Torre & B. M. Pesquera (Eds.), *Building with our hands* (pp. 181–198). Berkeley: University of California Press.

Portes, A., & Rumbaut, R. G. (1990). *Immigrant America: A portrait*. Berkeley: University of California Press.

Portes, A., & Truelove, C. (1987). Making sense of diversity: Recent research on Hispanic minorities in the United States. *Annual Review of Sociology, 13*, 357–385.

Powell, D. R. (1995). Including Latino fathers in parent education and support programs: Development of a program model. In R. E. Zambrana (Ed.), *Understanding Latino families* (pp. 85–106). Thousand Oaks, CA: Sage.

Ramirez, O. (1980, March). Extended family support and mental health status among Mexicans in Detroit. *Micro, Onda, LaRed, Monthly Newsletter of the National Chicano Research Network*, p. 2.

Ramirez, O., & Arce, C. H. (1981). The contemporary Chicano family: An empirically based review. In A. Baron, Jr. (Ed.), *Explorations in Chicano Psychology* (pp. 3–28). New York: Praeger.

Repack, T. A. (1997). New rules in a new landscape. In M. Romero, P. Hondagneu-Sotelo, & V. Ortiz (Eds.), *Challenging fronteras: Structuring Latina and Latino lives in the U.S.* (pp. 247–257). New York: Routledge.

Rochelle, A. (1997). *No more kin: Exploring race, class, and gender in family networks*. Thousand Oaks, CA: Sage.

Rodriguez, N. P., & Hagan, J. M. (1997). Apartment restructuring and Latino immigrant tenant struggles: A case study of human agency. In M. Romero, P. Hondagneu-Sotelo, & V. Ortiz (Eds.), *Challenging fronteras: Structuring Latina and Latina lives in the U.S.* (pp. 297–309). New York: Routledge.

Romero, M. (1997). Introduction. In M. Romero, P. Hondagneu-Sotelo, & V. Ortiz (Eds.), *Challenging fronteras: Structuring Latina and Latino lives in the U.S.* (pp. xiii–xix). New York: Routledge.

Rubel, A. J. (1966). *Across the tracks: Mexican Americans in a Texas city*. Austin: University of Texas Press.

Rumbaut, R. G. (1995). *Immigrants from Latin America and the Caribbean: A socioeconomic profile* (Statistical Brief No. 6). East Lansing: Julian Samora Research Institute, Michigan State University.

Sassen, S. (1993). Urban transformation and employment. In R. Morales & F. Bonilla (Eds.), *Latinos in a changing U.S. economy: Comparative perspectives on growing inequality* (pp. 194–206). Newbury Park, CA: Sage.

Scott, A. J. (1996). The manufacturing economy: Ethnic and gender divisions of labor. In R. Waldinger & M. Bozorgmehr (Eds.), *Ethnic Los Angeles.* New York: Russell Sage Foundation.

Segura, D. A., & Pierce, J. L. (1993). Chicana/o family structure and gender personality: Chodorow, familism, and psychoanalytic sociology revisited. *Signs, 19,* 62–91.

Shelton, B. A., & John, D. (1993). Ethnicity, race, and difference: A comparison of white, black, and Hispanic men's household labor time. In J. Hood (Ed.), *Men, work, and family* (pp. 1–22). Newbury Park, CA: Sage.

Smith, J., Wallerstein, I., & Evers, H. D. (1985). *The household and the world economy.* Beverly Hills, CA: Sage.

Solis, J. (1995). The status of Latino children and youth: Challenges and prospects. In R. E. Zambrana (Ed.), *Understanding Latino families* (pp. 62–84). Thousand Oaks, CA: Sage.

Stacey, J. (1990). *Brave new families: Stories of domestic upheaval in late twentieth century America.* New York: Basic Books.

Stacey, J. (1995). Disloyal to the disciplines: A feminist trajectory in the border lands. In D. C. Stanton & A. Stewart (Eds.), *Feminisms in the academy* (pp. 311–330). Ann Arbor: University of Michigan Press.

Stacey, J. (1996). *In the name of the family: Rethinking family values in the postmodern age.* Boston: Beacon Press.

Stier, H., & Tienda, M. (1992). Family, work, and women: The labor supply of Hispanic immigrant wives. *International Migration Review, 26,* 1291–1313.

Sullivan, M. L. (1993). Puerto Ricans in Sunset Park, Brooklyn: Poverty amidst ethnic and economic diversity. In J. W. Moore & R. Pinderhughes (Eds.), *In the barrios: Latinos and the underclass debate* (pp. 1–26). New York: Russell Sage Foundation.

Thomas, D., & Wilcox, J. E. (1987). The rise of family theory. In M. B. Sussman & S. Steinmetz (Eds.), *Handbook of marriage and the family* (pp. 81–102). New York: Plenum.

Thorne, B. (1992). Feminism and the family: Two decades of thought. In B. Thorne & M. Yalom (Eds.), *Rethinking the family: Some feminist questions* (pp. 3–30). Boston: Northeastern University Press.

Tienda, M. (1989). Puerto Ricans and the underclass debate. *Annals of the American Association of Political and Social Sciences, 501,* 105–119.

Torres, A., & Bonilla, F. (1993). Decline within decline: The New York perspective. In R. Morales & F. Bonilla (Eds.), *Latinos in a changing U.S. economy: Comparative perspectives on growing inequality* (pp. 85–108). Newbury Park, CA: Sage.

U.S. Bureau of the Census. (1993). *1990 census of the population: Persons of Hispanic origin in the United States.* Washington, DC: U.S. Government Printing Office.

U.S. Bureau of the Census. (1996). *Statistical abstract Of the United States: 1996.* Washington DC: U.S. Government Printing Office.

Valenzuela, A., & Dombusch, S. (1994). Familism and social capital in the academic achievement of Mexican origin and Anglo adolescents. *Social Science Quarterly, 75,* 18–36.

Vega, W. (1990). Hispanic families in the 1980s: A decade of research. *Journal of Marriage and the Family, 52,* 1015–1024.

Vega, W. A. (1995). The study of Latino families: A point of departure. In R. E. Zambrana (Ed.), *Understanding Latino families* (pp. 3–17). Thousand Oaks, CA: Sage.

Velez-Ibañez, C. (1993). U.S. Mexicans in the borderlands: Being poor without the underclass. In J. Moore & R. Pinderhughes (Eds.), *In the barrios: Latinos and the underclass debate* (pp. 195–220). New York: Russell Sage Foundation.

Velez-Ibañez, C. (1996). *Border visions.* Tucson: University of Arizona Press.

Velez-Ibañez, C. G., & Greenberg, J. B. (1992). Formation and transformation of funds of knowledge among U.S.-Mexican households. *Anthropology and Education Quarterly, 23,* 313–335.

Williams, N. (1990). *The Mexican American family: Tradition and change.* Dix Hills, NY: General Hall.

Wilkinson, D. (1993). Family ethnicity in America. In H. P. McAdoo (Ed.), *Family ethnicity: Strength in diversity* (pp. 15–59). Newbury Park, CA: Sage.

Wilson, W. J. (1987). *The truly disadvantaged. The inner city, the underclass, and public policy.* Chicago: University of Chicago Press.

Wilson, W. J. (1996). *When work disappears: The world of the new urban poor.* New York: Alfred A. Knopf.

Ybarra, L. (1982). When wives work: The impact on the Chicano family. *Journal of Marriage and the Family, 44,* 169–178.

Zavella, P. (1987). *Women's work and Chicano families: Cannery workers of the Santa Clara Valley.* Ithaca, NY: Cornell University Press.

■READING 30

Reinventing the Family

Laura Benkov

There is a certain distortion that occurs when we look back at the past through the lens of the present. When what once seemed impossible has become reality, it is easy to forget the groping in the dark along an untrodden and sometimes treacherous path. It was with this in mind that in March 1988 I read the clipping a friend had sent me from the *Hartford Advocate.* Underneath the headline "The Lesbian Baby Boom," it said "Even Geraldo's covered it—but the women who are doing it say it's no big deal." Almost a decade had passed since I first dared to ask myself if I, a lesbian, could choose to have children. Now as I read the words "No big deal" I flashed back to those sleepless nights clouded with confusion, shame, trepidation, grief, and longing.

One's perspective on the lesbian baby boom is clearly a matter of whom you talk to. When I finally broke through my isolation and began to speak to lesbians who had chosen to raise children, some—like the women described in the *Hartford Advocate*—told me they had never viewed their desire for parenthood as incompatible with their lesbianism. Andrea, a mother of two, said, "I always knew that I was going to be a mother, and being a lesbian never felt like I was making a choice not to have children. That probably had a lot to do with the fact that I came out during the seventies, amid a sense of all sorts of opportunities for women." Yet Andrea's ease with her status as lesbian mother was only one story. There were many other lesbians who had come to be mothers only after significant personal struggle. It is no wonder that I found myself drawn to their descriptions of arduous journeys. Susan lived years of ambivalence about her sexuality, not because she was uncertain of whom she loved but because she believed that choosing a woman meant giving up her lifelong dream of being a parent. Esther talked of being suddenly overcome by grief on an otherwise ordinary evening as she watched her lover washing her hair, when she recognized for the first time a yearning she could not imagine would ever come to fruition: to raise a child with this person she loved so deeply.

If we were indeed in the midst of a lesbian baby boom, then it *was* a big deal, for it was a painful and often lonely journey past grief that had brought us here.

Somewhere along the way these lesbians stopped assuming they couldn't be parents and began figuring out how to bring children into their lives. As I listened to their tales of transformation, each marked by a unique moment of revelation, the "boom" seemed the social equivalent of spontaneous combustion. So many lesbians struggled to become parents at precisely the same historical moment, yet each experienced herself as unique and alone. Of course, no one was as alone as she might have felt, and the movement certainly hadn't appeared out of the blue. Many social forces had laid the groundwork for its emergence.

As women influenced by second-wave feminism questioned their roles in the traditional family, they discovered possibility where before there had been only closed doors. Raising children without being married emerged as a potentially positive decision, not an unwanted circumstance. It is no accident that the rise of lesbian parenting has coincided with the burgeoning of single heterosexual women choosing to have children. The idea that women could shape their intimate lives according to their own standards and values rather than conform to constricting social norms was powerful in its own right. But the feminist movement was significant beyond the realm of ideas. On a very practical level, women's fight for control over their reproductive capacities created a context in which the choice to bear a child was as significantly opened up as the choice not to bear one; abortion rights and access to reproductive technology such as donor insemination are flip sides of the same coin.

The gay rights movement also contributed greatly to the parenting boom, enabling people to take a less fearful, more assertive stance toward society and yielding more visible communities, with the support and social dialogue that implies. From that supportive base, many began to define the kinds of lives they wanted to live, and to pursue their wish to be parents.

Perhaps most significant of all to what has become known in some circles as the choosing children movement, were the lesbian and gay parents who'd come out of heterosexual marriages. They had stepped out of the shadows, transforming the notion of lesbian and gay parents from a contradiction in terms to a visible reality that society had to contend with.

The fact that in our society women tend more than men to be intensely involved with raising children was reflected in the choosing children movement, just as it had been in the battles of parents coming out of heterosexual marriages. During the late 1970s, the first signs of lesbians choosing to have children were evident. By the mid-1980s, the trend had expanded from its initial West Coast and urban-center origins to throughout the nation. It was not until the late 1980s that a similar movement, smaller in scope, emerged among gay men. Though gay men's efforts overlap in some ways with lesbian endeavors, they are also distinctive. Often societal taboos against homosexuals more strongly burden gay men. And homosexuality aside, the notion of men as primary nurturing parental figures is ill defined in our culture. Many gay men seeking to become fathers, and perhaps to raise children without significant female input, feel out of place simply by virtue of their gender.

Initially, gay men participated in the lesbian baby boom as fathers sought by lesbians who chose to bear children. The advent of AIDS profoundly curtailed the move toward joint parenting arrangements. But in many communities it also brought gay men and lesbians together; and in more recent years, with growing consciousness about HIV prevention and testing available, joint parenting arrangements seem to be on the rise again.

Taking on secondary parenting roles in families headed by lesbians does suit some gay men, but others want, as do their lesbian counterparts, to have a more intensive, primary parental relationship. Increasingly, gay men are choosing to become parents through adoption, surrogacy, or joint parenting arrangements.

Within a decade, the unimaginable became commonplace. This remarkable shift occurred against a backdrop of skepticism and hostility. Society remained fixed on the question of whether homosexuals should be allowed to raise children, even as they were becoming parents in record numbers. The fierce debates that began in the early 1970s only continued as openly gay men and women chose parenthood. By the mid-1980s, a multitude of new controversies clamored for attention. Lesbian and gay parents had pushed Americans to look more closely than ever before at a deceptively simple question: What is a family? If the family is not defined by heterosexual procreative union, then what indeed is it? Perhaps it was the fear of this very question that underlay the hostility toward lesbian and gay parents to begin with. If the capacity to have and raise children does not distinguish heterosexuals from homosexuals, then what does?

In a recent *New York Times* book review, Margaret O'Brien Steinfels posed the following question: Does a married heterosexual couple's "capacity to have children [represent] a differentiating quality in heterosexual relationships?" According to Steinfels:

> Our legislatures and our religious faiths may come up with new ways to regulate or recognize erotically bound relationships beyond the traditional form of marriage: the state may devise practical solutions to problems like insurance and shared property, and religious bodies may try to encourage lasting and exclusive intimacy in a monogamous setting. Nonetheless society has a legitimate interest in privileging those heterosexual unions that are oriented toward the generation and rearing of children. That, at any rate, is the widely held conviction that remains to be debated. . . .

Steinfels's suggestion that heterosexual unions are uniquely bound to childrearing rings false at this historical moment. Heterosexual procreation is only one of many means of family making. This is underscored not only by the fact that lesbian and gay unions can include childrearing but also because heterosexual unions often do not. Many heterosexual couples choose not to raise children, and many others, despite their heterosexuality, cannot procreate. Divorce, adoption, and reproductive technology mean that children often aren't raised by their birth parents, and likewise many parents aren't genetically connected to their kids. Steinfels's query embodies a myth our society clings to despite its distance from reality: that heterosexual unions, by virtue of their potential link to procreation, are somehow necessary to the survival of the species and therefore morally superior. Lesbians and gay men choosing to parent are not unique in challenging this myth, but they do so most explicitly, often sparking heated backlash.

During his 1992 campaign for reelection, George Bush said that "children should have the benefit of being born into a family with a mother and a father," thus citing the number and gender of parents as a pivotal aspect of optimal family life and implicitly privileging biological connection between parents and children by the phrase "born into." In short, he held up as the ideal the traditional family, characterized by heterosexual procreative unions and legal sanction.

Eight-year-old Danielle, the daughter of lesbian and gay parents, vehemently disagreed. "I have two moms and two dads," she said. "A family is people who all love each other, care for each other, help out and understand each other."

In defining the ideal family, Bush emphasized structural characteristics while Danielle, in contrast, highlighted emotions and relationships. Their disagreement aptly reflects this moment in American society: the tension between idealization of the traditional family and the reality of families that don't fit that mold is strongly emerging as a key issue of our times. As lesbians and gay men choose to raise children, the many different kinds of families they create reveal the inadequacy of a definition of family that rests on one particular structure. Increasingly, our society must heed Danielle's idea that family is defined by the quality of relationships, which can exist in many forms.

DONOR INSEMINATION: A MIMICRY OF PROCREATIVE UNION

In 1884, according to one of the earliest accounts of donor insemination in America, a woman lay unconscious on an examining table while, without her knowledge much less her consent, a doctor inseminated her with sperm from the "handsomest medical student" in his class. It was only after the insemination that the doctor informed the woman's infertile husband, who, pleased by the news, asked that his wife never be told what had occurred. The insemination resulted in the birth of a baby boy, who, presumably along with his mother, wasn't informed of the circumstances of his conception. A little over a century later, though women who are inseminated are neither unconscious nor uninformed, much of this early account remains salient. Donor insemination has evolved as a medically controlled practice, largely restricted to infertile heterosexual couples and shrouded in secrecy. Where then do lesbians fit in?

In the beginning of its use in this country, donor insemination was seen solely as a solution to infertility among married heterosexual couples. As such, donor insemination practices were structured to produce families that mimicked in every way possible the traditional heterosexual family. Both medical practitioners and the law geared donor insemination toward creating families that looked like, and had the legal status of, a family consisting of a married man and woman and their biological offspring.

This attempt to mimic the traditional heterosexual family included an effort to hide the very fact that donor insemination was used. The appearance of a biological connection was painstakingly constructed by matching the donor's physical traits with the husband's. By and large, the fact that a child had been conceived through donor insemination was rarely disclosed within families and was barely discussed in the larger cultural arena. In one major text of the 1960s, a doctor noted that one of the advantages of donor insemination, as compared to adoption, was that its use need never be revealed. He further suggested that screening criteria for couples receiving donor insemination include an assessment of how well they could keep a secret. Now, thirty years later, donor characteristics are still most often matched to that of the husband and secrecy continues.

The effort to hide the use of donor insemination parallels past approaches to adoption. There, too, great pains were taken to match the physical characteristics of children with those of their adoptive parents, and adoption was held as a secret around which much anxiety revolved. More recently, adoption practices have shifted: there is much less emphasis on matching physical characteristics, and experts encourage parents to speak openly about adoption, with the idea that talking to children about their origins from an early age is key to their overall well-being. Unlike earlier practices, this way values honesty in family life over the appearance of a biological family unit. Along with more honesty within adoptive families has come more open discussion of adoption in society. While much thinking about adoption continues to reflect a cultural bias that elevates biological families over all others, adoption practices have begun to move beyond this ideology by coming out of the closet. In contrast, the secrecy surrounding donor insemination points up the continuing emphasis on the appearance of a biological family unit.

The painstaking attention to appearance and the secrecy surrounding donor insemination stem from an insidious ideology: heterosexual procreation is the ideal basis of a family, one which if not achieved in actuality should at least be aspired to in appearance. With this as an undercurrent, donor insemination is characterized by a contradictory view of genetics. On the one hand, the practice distinguishes genetic and social parent roles, relegating genetics to an inconsequential position by severing all ties between donors and their offspring, and by recognizing those who take on the social role of parenthood as fathers of those children. On the other hand, hiding the fact that this process has occurred reveals an almost superstitious belief in the power of genetics. The implication is that biological connection is such a crucial aspect of parenting that its absence is shameful and should be hidden. The social role of a nonbiological parent is not highly valued in its own right, and instead must be bolstered by the illusion of a genetic connection. In this pervasive view, a "real" parent is the biological parent. If you have to, donor insemination is okay to do, but it's not okay to talk about.

THE LEGAL CONSTRUCTIONS OF FAMILY IN DONOR INSEMINATION PRACTICES

As with the secrecy and matching practices, the laws surrounding donor insemination reinforce efforts to make these families look like the standard nuclear model. Children conceived through donor insemination in the context of a heterosexual marriage are deemed the legal children of the recipient and her husband. Donors, on the other hand, waive all parental rights and responsibilities. The complex reality of such families—that there are both a biological and a social father involved—is set aside in favor of a simpler one. Severing the donor tie and sanctioning the husband's parental relationship serve the purpose of delineating one—and only one—father.

As donor insemination was more widely practiced in this country, legal parameters developed that, like the practices themselves, value the traditional family over all others. Among the first legal questions posed about donor insemination was whether it constituted adultery and, along with that, whether the child so conceived was "illegitimate." As the courts decided these initial cases they exhibited a strong conviction that children need to be "legitimate"—that is, to have fathers. From this premise the law constructed the husbands of inseminated women as the legal fathers of the resulting children. Father status thus hinged on marriage— that is, children were considered to be the "issue of the marriage." This was automatic, with no mediating process such as adoption needed to complete the arrangement. Initially these parameters were outlined only when disputes arose, but as the use of donor insemination grew more widespread, legislation was enacted that explicitly delineated what the courts had implicitly held all along: families that, in fact, were not created through the procreative union of a married heterosexual couple were given the legal status of this traditional unit. The state threw a safety net around the families created through donor insemination when, and only when, those families were headed by married heterosexual couples. On a state-by-state basis, the law carved out a distinction between donors and fathers: donors, in surrendering their sperm to doctors, waived parental rights and responsibilities, while the men married to inseminating women took on the legal rights and responsibilities of fatherhood.

Significantly, in many states, the donors' lack of parental status hinges on medical mediation. That is, donors who directly give sperm to women can be, and often are, legally considered parents. Thus, not only is heterosexuality a prerequisite to the legal delineation of families constituted through donor insemination but medical control of the process is built into the law. People creating families through donor insemination do so most safely—that is, with least threat to their integrity as a family unit—if they utilize medical help.

LESBIANS AND SINGLE WOMEN SEEK DONOR INSEMINATION

The extent to which donor insemination practices emphasize the appearance of a procreative heterosexual union has, of course, great implications for lesbians and unmarried heterosexual women—most especially with respect to access to the technology. In conceiving through donor insemination, these women have little possibility of creating "pretend father" relationships that would obscure the fact that donor insemination has occurred. Indeed, when lesbians and single heterosexual women use donor insemination, they bring the practice out of the closet, revealing it to be a way that women can bear children in the absence of any relationship to men. It is no wonder that unmarried women, regardless of their sexual orientation, have been barred from using donor insemination, given the challenge their access poses to deeply held beliefs. To be inseminated as a single straight woman or lesbian is to boldly acknowledge that the resulting child has no father and that women can parent without input from men beyond the single contribution of genetic material. Such inseminations also highlight the separation between social and genetic parenting roles. This last aspect is especially obvious when lesbian couples use donor insemination: a nonbiological mother, clearly not a father, becomes the child's other parent.

For many years, the medical profession would not grant unmarried women access to insemination. A study done in 1979 found that over 90 percent of doctors wouldn't inseminate unmarried women. The doctors gave several reasons for their decision, the most central being their beliefs that lesbians and single women are unfit parents and that all children need fathers. However, some doctors refused to inseminate unmarried women, not out of deep personal conviction, but because they mistakenly believed that it was illegal. Though the statutory language about donor insemination often includes mention of marriage, it does not require it. A number of doctors also feared future wrongful-life suits, assuming that children raised by lesbians or single women would ultimately be unhappy enough to sue those responsible for their existence.

In the late 1970s, into the context of medically controlled, heterosexual-marriage–oriented donor insemination practices, came single heterosexual women and lesbians wanting to have children. The technology was an obvious choice for these women, not only in its most basic sense as a source of sperm, but also as a way of forming families whose integrity would be legally protected. Many want to establish families as couples or individuals without having to negotiate parenting responsibilities with an outside adult. Lesbians choosing to have children are much more vulnerable than married heterosexual couples to disputes about the boundaries of their families. Homophobia in the legal system renders them generally more subject to custody problems. Furthermore, since lesbians are unable to marry, and the female partners of inseminating women by and large can't adopt the resulting children, nonbiological lesbian mothers have no protected legal parent status. In this social context, creating families through known donors poses tremendous legal risks if those donors ever make custody claims. For lesbians, therefore, the legal protection of a family unit created through anonymous donor insemination is crucial.

But since access to the most legally safe source of insemination—that is, medically controlled—was highly restricted in the early days of the lesbian baby boom, many of the first lesbians to have children did so on the margins of mainstream donor insemination practices. Some women created their own alternatives. They inseminated themselves and, in an effort to protect the integrity of their families, created their own systems of anonymity, using go-betweens to conceal the identity of the sperm donors. However, this means of anonymity didn't provide firm protection against the possibility of custody disputes. In practice, the anonymity of donors would often be hard to maintain in small communities, and legally—especially in the absence of medical mediation—an identified donor would have parental rights. Matters became more complicated with the advent of AIDS, which made this way of inseminating a highly risky business. Ultimately, the self-created system gave way to another approach.

Some lesbians moved in a different direction, attempting to change the exclusionary practices themselves. During the late 1970s and early 1980s, as the feminist health-care movement grew and women fought to gain reproductive freedom, unmarried women made headway with demands for access to medically controlled donor insemination. The Sperm Bank of California in Oakland was established in 1982 by women running the Oakland Feminist Women's Health Center in response to the rising number of unmarried women seeking advice about insemination. The Sperm Bank of California led the way in establishing an insemination program that didn't screen out women on the basis of sexual orientation or marital status. Currently there are several such sperm banks throughout the country, and increasingly doctors are willing to inseminate unmarried women. However, access remains restricted in certain areas, and many insurance companies will cover insemination expenses only for married women.

During the last fifteen years, lesbians choosing to be parents have been charting a course through society that began on the margins and has increasingly moved into the mainstream, yielding social changes along the way.

In the realm of donor insemination, the reciprocal influence of heterosexual, nuclear family ideology and lesbian parenthood is strikingly apparent. Lesbians choosing to have children shape their families along parameters stemming from the idealization of the traditional nuclear family, but by the same token they significantly transform many of those parameters. Donor insemination has shifted from a completely medically dominated, heterosexually defined technology to a practice that serves unmarried women, both straight and gay, and thereby yields many different sorts of families. As lesbians and single heterosexual women make more use of donor insemination, the practice itself is changing: by necessity, donor insemination is coming out of the closet. In our culture there are few stories of conception through donor insemination. Despite the fact that approximately a million Americans have been conceived this way, we continue to behave as though conception occurs only through heterosexual union. Ultimately, lesbians will write the stories of donor insemination, as they speak openly to their children about another way that people come into the world.

Choices: Known or Unknown Donors

As the doors to donor insemination opened for lesbians, a new era began. Having access to the technology is not synonymous with wanting to use it. Most lesbian mothers-to-be spend considerable time deciding whether to do so through a known or unknown donor. The complexity of this decision was a theme in many of my talks with lesbian mothers. In December 1991, as I was trying to sort through the many layers of this decision, both for myself and in relation to this book, I decided to visit the sperm bank in Oakland. I was not prepared for the intensity of my response. Barbara Raboy, the director, explained the process of freezing and storing sperm as I stared at hundreds upon hundreds of specimens neatly ordered in dozens of large metal tanks. It was about what I'd expected to see, except for the names scribbled in marker across the outside of the tanks and in smaller letters on the compartments within each tank. In front of me was the Artist tank, with Fuchsia, Chartreuse, and Amber as its subdivisions. Next to it was the Universe tank, with Mars, Pluto, and Jupiter; and behind that, the Landscape tank, with Rocky Mountain, Grand Canyon, and Yellowstone. Barbara noticed my puzzlement and explained: "We thought names would be more fun than a strict number and letter filing system, so the staff take turns naming the tanks and the subdivisions within them—it's how we locate any particular specimen—you know donor number 5003 is in the A row in the Fuschia section of the Artist tank." I was disappointed that the tank names had no more salient correspondence to the sperm inside, but the knowledge freed me from the mind-boggling task of imagining what distinguished a Rocky Mountain sperm specimen from a Jupiter one.

Instead, I began to imagine the people who dreamed up these names: huddled among the slides and test tubes, who had been most pleased by colors, who by mountain vistas or thoughts of intergalactic travel? As the namers became more real to me, so too did the men whose sperm was sequestered in the tiny vials. Several pages listed donor characteristics—no. 2017, Dutch descent, blue eyes, brown wavy hair, 6 feet tall, athletic student of computer technology. If you wanted to know more about a particular donor, there were additional sheets—medical history and some personal information. But when all was said and done, the wish to know would remain just that. To see these vials was to glimpse the unknown. Throughout the country women were waiting—some whose male partners were infertile, some who were single, some who were lesbian. What they had in common was a strong yearning for children. This is what I was thinking as I looked at vial no. 2017. Then my ears rang with the voices of children, and I knew that I was standng in a place of beginnings, surrounded by mystery.

My initial puzzlement about the tank labels was a clue to my state of mind. I'd entered the sperm bank as I would a foreign country, imagining the tank names held some crucial meaning as unintelligible to me as a street sign in China. It struck me as odd that I could feel this way despite the fact that for years I'd thought about becoming a mother through this very process. Donor insemination was potentially a key element of my future, one that would involve my body and my most intimate relationships; yet simultaneously, I experienced it as a strange, foreign, and mystifying process.

I was not alone in this contradictory place. Though donor insemination has been practiced in this country for over a century, as a culture we have barely begun to grapple with the meaning it holds for us. Standing amid the vials of semen at the sperm bank, I could not help but be aware of the unique historical moment in which we are living. The very fact that I, a lesbian, could consider insemination is remarkable. Just ten years earlier I would have been shut out of any insemination program. But choices bring great complexity. Layers of thinking make up the decision about whether to become pregnant through a donor, known or unknown. How do lesbians aspiring to be mothers respond to society's constraints? What ways of forming a family will be safe in a culture that doesn't recognize our primary intimate connections? Because society as yet barely acknowledges donor insemination, an air of mysteriousness pervades the practice. How then do lesbians sort out the meanings donor insemination has for us and may have for our children?

From the language of "illegitimacy" and "bastards" to the tales of adopts searching for their birth parents, we are inundated with ideas that a father's absence is always problematic and knowledge of our genetic roots always essential. What do we accept of these stories? What do we reject? All of this is filtered through our most intensely personal experiences and histories. Ultimately it is from these many layers that lesbians create their families. Self-consciously exploring the meaning of family, each woman writes her own story. But no one writes it alone: each family is shaped by the culture it is embedded in, and in turn, the culture is changed by these emerging families.

The Role of the State

After twelve years together, Jasmine and Barbara agreed they were ready to raise children. Other than the gender of their partners, they envisioned family life in rather traditional terms. Their household would define the boundaries of their family; as a couple, they would jointly share parenting. Jasmine saw their decision to inseminate with an unknown donor as stemming clearly from the surrounding social context.

Jasmine explains: "We were very stuck on the method of conception—a known versus an unknown donor. One of the things that happened around the time we were thinking about this question was the foster-care issue in Massachusetts. We knew women who had adopted young children through foreign adoptions, and I listened to their descriptions of the home-study process. I felt very uncomfortable with the idea that somebody was judging you, and that you in a sense had to give them this little drama that 'I'm the one who's adopting and this woman is my roommate.'

"Not only did we feel angry about the injustice of it, but we also felt frustrated by the fact that as a couple we had so much more to offer in terms of the structure of our lives than this fallacy would indicate. When the foster-care uproar happened, we were very indignant about the idea that we could be judged that way. If we had gone along with the little drama of who we were supposed to be, it wouldn't have barred us from adopting, so it was really our decision that we wanted as few external people as possible out there judging us or making decisions about our lives.

"We didn't want that interference. That spilled over into the issue of the donor. We really needed to feel in control. The thing was, we were the parents and we wanted to make the decisions as the child grew up about other adults in the child's life. It's not that we wanted to shelter the child from other people, but we certainly didn't want an obligation ready-set. So given that we wanted integrity as a family unit, we decided to go with an unknown donor."

The influence of homophobia and heterosexist constructions of the family is apparent in Jasmine's explanation for their decision to use an anonymous donor. Jasmine and Barbara shied away from adoption because they didn't want to be subjected to state scrutiny that would have failed to recognize the value of their relationship. The homophobia unleashed during the Massachusetts foster-care battle was a bitter reminder of their vulnerability. A known donor was also someone who could potentially bring the state to bear on their family life—someone who in the eyes of the law would have parental rights in contrast to the nonbiological mother. Protecting the integrity of their family unit as they defined it meant using an unknown donor.

Though all prospective lesbian parents face the same legal constraint—a definition of family that gives privilege to genetic connection and heterosexual parenting—people see the state's potential role in their lives quite differently. Unlike Jasmine and Barbara, Susan and Dana chose to have a child with a man they knew who would be involved as a parent but in a secondary role. Each had a close relationship with her own father, and they wanted the same for their children. Though concerned about how legally vulnerable the nonbiological mother would be, Susan and Dana proceeded on the assumption that they could work out a trusting relationship with the father, one which would not ultimately bring them face-to-face with the state's ill-fitting definition of family.

Susan, explaining their decision, says: "The legal line obviously is 'don't take risks, therefore don't use a known father who would then have the possibility of having rights.' I agree that that's one way to avoid the particular risk of a custody fight and control issues over the child. But I think it's one of the most personal choices in the world—anything about reproductive issues and how one wants to raise one's children are very intimate and individual, and I think you shouldn't make decisions frankly just on the legal basis.

"You should make them on your whole world view and your values and what you want for your child. Maybe the risk of a custody fight could be minimized by choosing a person carefully and by choosing a gay man rather than a person who would have the gay issue to use against you."

Jasmine and Barbara's thinking diverges from Susan and Dana's along several lines. First, the two couples position themselves very differently in relation to the state. Jasmine and Barbara are acutely focused on the threat the state poses to the integrity of their family unit. Susan and Dana, on the other hand, feel that threat less acutely because they believe that recourse to the state's definition can most likely be avoided through establishing trustworthy relationships. Marie, another lesbian who chose a known donor, explains the position:

I don't have the kind of fears around the legal stuff that some people do. You have to pick really carefully. Obviously there are certainly men out there whom you could enter into this kind of relationship with and it would be a disaster. But I don't think it's impossible to find a situation where you can have some confidence that this guy will do what he says he'll do. I understand legally you leave yourself open. I think it would be dangerous to do this with a man who is conflicted and who's doing this because he wishes he had kids. Then, ten years down the line he might turn around and say, "I want the child."

These women are grappling with the question of whether you can create a family that defies the state's definition and feel safe that its boundaries will remain as you intended them to be. In part, the different choices lesbians make about family structure stem from different perspectives on the state's ultimate power in their lives.

What Makes a Family?

There is another important dimension to the decision of choosing between known and unknown donors: what should constitute the boundaries of a family? Many women, like Marie and her lover, Jana, choose a donor who will be known to the child but won't take on a parental role. Essentially, except for the fact that the child can know the donor, these families closely resemble families like Jasmine and Barbara's, where the women are the child's sole parents. However, often lesbians choosing known donors draw the boundaries around their families a little differently. Though frequently the men aren't primary parents, they do have a parental role. Susan and Dana created this type of family. While they define their family primarily within the bounds of their own household, their arrangement with their children's father is similar to an extended family. Though at first they were most concerned about maintaining their status as primary parents, as the family became securely established, Susan and Dana wanted the father to be more rather than less involved. They encouraged him to develop a strong relationship with the children. Susan says, "You realize that there are so many things to do. There's never enough time in a day. So additional people to help out is wonderful. We should all have bigger extended families, especially when we're all working. We've been lucky that not just our children's biological father but his choice of partners and his family have been a very rich source of additional good people in the kids' lives."

Opening boundaries in this way can be challenging, however. For a while, Dana, who was to be the nonbiological mother struggled with her lack of society-recognized parent status. "I think for a lot of Susan's pregnancy I was obsessed that this child might be born and this father would have more rights than I would. I had this image that he would never be doing the dirty work of everyday parenting. He'd show up as this knight on a white horse and get all this affection and admiration."

Susan and Dana were deeply committed to the idea that Dana was as much a mother as Susan, and Dana's feelings of doubt dissipated soon after their daughter's birth. "Once Danielle was born it was bizarre to think that. Her father is an important part of her life, but there's a whole 'nother ball game in terms of who her parents are who raise her. My fears were so far from reality. Before Danielle and I had this bond I imagined, in the naiveté of someone who's not a parent, that someone who shows up once a week could be an equal parent to someone who's with you twenty-four hours a day."

Deciding who will be part of one's family is, of course, a highly personal endeavor. The decision regarding a known or unknown donor is partly a decision about what kind of intimate relationships to create. Some are comfortable sharing parenting with people outside a romantic relationship, while others find this a complicated and unrewarding situation.

The Ties that Bind?—The Meaning of Genetic Connections

Beyond thinking about the relationships they want for themselves, lesbians choosing between known and unknown donors must consider how their choice will affect their children. As lesbians think about this, beliefs about the importance of genetic connections take center stage. These beliefs come partly from personal history and partly from ideas that dominate our culture. When women consider whether to use a known or unknown donor, complex, intense, and often conflicting feelings arise. Esther, for instance, originally tried to find a man who would be willing to be a sperm donor but maintain a minimal role in the child's life. The men she approached either wanted more involvement or were worried that they would be asked to take on more responsibility than they bargained for. Esther reconciled herself to conceiving with an anonymous donor, but her feelings about her son Ian's origins intensely color her relationship with him. She says, "I'm consumed by the connections. I look at Ian and see my grandmother's hands. He's an incredible dancer and my father was, too. I don't know if there's a dancing gene. That's why I wanted a Jewish donor. I wanted the history and culture. A known donor would have embodied more of that. Ian's relation to the donor has been a presence for me since he was born. It's hard to sort out my own sadness about my father's death and my sadness for Ian in not having that relationship."

It is hard also to separate Esther's personal history from the culture we are immersed in. As a society, we tend to emphasize intergenerational biological connections and pay scant attention to nonbiological relationships. For example, we continually hear stories about adopted children who feel an absence in their lives and need to search for their birth parents. We rarely hear about the adopted children—of whom there are also many—who don't feel a need for this contact. Hearing these stories of searches for genetic roots, many lesbians are uncomfortable with anonymous donor insemination. As Marie put it, "I don't think an anonymous donor is the best thing for a kid. I'm sure that kids conceived that way will manage and will be okay if their parents handle it levelly and matter-of-factly. But we don't really know. We haven't had a generation of kids growing up without knowing anything about half of their genetic material. What we do know about is kids who were adopted and don't have that kind of information. Most of them go through something about it whether they end up searching or not. It just makes sense to me that if you can provide a child with that basic information, then you should."

While many like Marie see children as better off with access to genetic information, even if the donor is uninvolved as a parent, a good case can be made for the opposite decision. Jenny, for instance, chose a sperm bank, in part to protect her child from possibly feeling rejected by a known but uninvolved donor. "I'd rather take responsibility for my choice to have him this way," she said. "He can be angry at me for my decision, rather than feel hurt because there's a man he can identify who doesn't behave as a father."

As important as it is for lesbians to think through their decisions, the reality all ultimately may have to come to terms with is not a singular model. Instead, we must come to recognize and appreciate pluralism: children who are loved and given opportunities to grow can thrive in many different family contexts. Knowing this, we can discard a determination of which family structure is "best" in favor of finding ways to make all the different structures work.

GAY MEN HAVE A DIFFERENT SET OF DECISIONS

Gay men are often in the position of parenting children who are primarily raised by lesbians. This family model fits in a culture in which women are socialized toward primary childrearing and men toward a secondary role. While there are many gay men for whom this arrangement works well, there are also those who, like their lesbian counterparts, want more involvement with their children. But men do not have the same options as lesbians. There is no equivalent of donor insemination. Surrogacy comes the closest, but it is a much more biologically, ethically, legally, financially, and psychologically complex process. Similarly, gay men are considerably less likely to find women willing to be the equivalent of a known donor—that is, to have babies with whom they will be minimally involved (though on occasion people do make such arrangements). For gay men who want to be primary parents, adoption is often a more feasible option than biological parenting. Given all this, the issues faced by gay men who choose to become fathers through biological conception are quite distinct from lesbians' concerns.

Becoming a Father through Surrogacy

Eric and Jeff were college sweethearts who came out together. Though each had imagined they would get married and have children, it was clear early on in their relationship that their futures were bound together. Jeff never gave up the idea of having children, though he didn't actively pursue it until he hit his thirties. At that point, he approached Eric with the idea of advertising for a surrogate mother. Though he thought about adoption, he wanted to have a child who was biologically connected to him. Eric was doubtful that they would find someone willing to be a surrogate. "Everything you read about surrogacy is these women who are married who have several kids, who want to give this to another couple who can't have kids—it's all portrayed in a straight, heterosexual way."

They discussed the possibility of co-parenting with lesbians, but that wasn't an appealing arrangement. Jeff says, "I wanted this to be our child—for this to be a family of three." Eric says, "We've structured a life for ourselves that we feel very comfortable with, that we like a lot, and we set the parameters for that. We don't let others set the parameters, and that's important to us. A co-parenting relationship would just be way too complicated, and too many people who we know don't approach life the way we do." Jeff adds, "Being dependent on someone else would be very frustrating." They placed an ad that specified they were two gay men wanting to raise a child. They got one response, which they pursued.

Paid surrogacy is a complicated social and personal step. It is fundamentally a financial arrangement through which a child comes into the world. The biological parameters, including a woman's efforts to conceive and nine months of carrying a child, are much more extensive than for donor insemination. For these reasons, the social and psychological issues that surround the process are complex.

One of the most troubling aspects of surrogacy is the class imbalance: Eric and Jeff wanted a child and were well off financially; Donna, who responded to their ad, did not want a child, but needed money. Eric and Jeff hoped that they could work out a friendly arrangement, one that would benefit all concerned. At first it seemed they were on their way to doing just that. An agreement was hammered out with lawyers, and the insemination and pregnancy went smoothly. In less than two years since Jeff first proposed parenting, he and Eric had a baby girl, Leah.

Eric, Jeff, and Donna were on friendly terms and had agreed on limited visitation, but this eventually became a source of strife. Jeff and Eric wanted the visits to be supervised and to occur in their home; Donna wanted to take the baby on her own. Communication broke down when Eric and Jeff refused Donna's request. There was a series of exchanges in letters, through which Jeff and Eric tried to establish ground rules for Donna's visitation. Ultimately, Donna didn't respond and contact ceased.

Despite the problems that arose, Eric feels that, "If there wasn't a whole lot of emotional baggage involved on the part of the mother, contact would be preferable. It would be easier for Leah to understand more of her background and her heritage, and who she is as a person if she had that contact, but I could be wrong."

Jeff doesn't quite agree. "I've changed my opinion. Now I feel that other than curiosity, it would be a lot easier for them to have next to no involvement with each other. We have very little in common with her mother . . . . I think those relationships where a gay man helps out two women and stays involved and all are friends are wonderful, but they're unrealistic in these circumstances. Surrogacy is just this bizarre thing where you're dealing with different financial statuses. Because there's such disparity, there's so little in common to base that kind of friendship on."

Like some women who conceive through unknown donors, Jeff is ambivalent about his wish that there be no contact between his child and her biological mother. "I do worry sometimes, like when I see people on television who've been adopted and haven't seen their biological parents, and are freaked out. But I think that doesn't have to happen—that often those people have a lot of other emotional baggage." Eric points out the different positions of gay men and lesbians. "I feel kind of envious of women who go to sperm banks. Once they make that decision, it's over. They may still agonize over not being able to provide that connection for their child, but it's done." In contrast, surrogacy often involves a process of negotiation and the formation of a relationship. As it was for Eric, Jeff, and Donna, surrogacy can be an intense and complex undertaking. What it will ultimately mean to children like Leah is yet to be seen.

As the nonbiological parent, Eric was in a vulnerable position. Like most lesbian and gay couples raising children, Eric and Jeff had to rely on mutual trust. Jeff says, "We can't conceive of ourselves breaking up. If for some unknown reason we ever did, it would have to be amicable—it's just we can't not be that way. We have a relationship where we talk and communicate better than almost anyone we know." Eric adds, "If you can't work out your differences, I believe you have no right to take this kind of adventure. Because we are trailblazing, we take the responsibility very seriously."

Legally, the surrogacy process is not complete until an adoption has occurred. In the case of heterosexual couples, the biological mother terminates her parental rights, and the spouse of the biological father adopts the child, making the couple the child's only legal parents. In their attempt to "close the circle" of the surrogacy arrangement, Jeff and Eric attempted a second-parent adoption. When Donna agreed to terminate her parental rights, it was Eric who would adopt Leah. The legal question revolved around whether he could do that without Jeff giving up his parental rights. If he had not been able to, the couple considered having Eric become the sole legal parent, as a source of balance. However, shortly before Leah's second birthday, Eric and Jeff were successful in their adoption attempt—their particular circumstances making them a first in the country. When Leah was two years old, Jeff and Eric initiated another surrogacy arrangement through which they had a son.

For the most part, access to surrogacy—like access to other alternative modes of bringing children into one's life—is much more available to heterosexual infertile couples than to gay men. However, surrogacy is much like independent adoption, with access strongly related to financial resources. Surrogacy is far less popular among gay men than donor insemination is among lesbians. Its high cost, along with the social complexity it involves, render it a less frequent approach than adoption or joint-family arrangements.

Surrogacy has been practiced since biblical times—in some informal sense, there have always been women bearing children for friends or family members. But formal, paid contracts for surrogacy arrangements first emerged in this country around 1976, and have been on the rise ever since. Though in any given case surrogacy can work well for all involved, it poses major ethical issues not just for its participants but for society as well. It involves much more than a separation between genetic and social parenting roles, since gestation and birth are processes involving not only a woman's body but also her relation to the child she bears. For the most part, these arrangements involve large sums of money, and bring wealthy people who want children together with poor women in need of money. Out of these issues—the psychological ramifications and the financial exchange—arise many crucial questions.

The major societal quandaries about surrogacy fall into two categories: is it baby selling? and is it exploitative of women? These questions came most vividly to public attention in 1987, when Mary Beth Whitehead, having given birth to the child the courts would refer to as Baby M after signing a surrogacy contract for William and Betsy Stem, changed her mind and wanted to keep the baby. Was she bound by the contract she'd signed? Was the contract, in which there was an exchange of money and an exchange of human life, legal? Was it ethical? And, most important, who should get the child? Mary Beth Whitehead argued that the contract was invalid; she captured the complexity of the surrogacy issue in her statement that she'd "signed on an egg, not on a baby." After a much publicized trial, the Stems were awarded full custody of the one-year-old child. However, along with that decision came a ruling that made surrogacy illegal in the state of New Jersey, where the case had occurred.

While there is little legislation explicitly applying to surrogacy, after the Whitehead case, seventeen states enacted some form of applicable legislation. For the most part, these laws make surrogacy contracts unenforceable. The legal reasoning is drawn from several other areas of law. One argument is that a woman cannot consent to adoption before the birth of a child, and hence cannot be bound by a surrogacy contract drawn up at the time of conception. Another is that in every state baby selling is illegal. Here though, much of surrogacy bypasses this idea, treating compensation not as money in exchange for a human life but as payment for the mother's expenses or for her work in gestation—akin to rent. Some of the laws have focused on money as the key issue, strictly forbidding any exchange other than expenses; a few states prohibit mediators (that is, brokers) from accepting fees. Even with the contracts legally unenforceable, many of the problems that arise when mothers change their minds remain unresolved. Since surrogacy arrangements by and large involve men with substantial resources and women in need of money, if a child is born from such an arrangement and the surrogate changes her mind, most often a typical custody battle ensues, with the best-interests-of-the-child standard applied by the courts. Here, surrogate mothers are at a considerable disadvantage, often not well off enough to pursue a court battle. Surrogacy practices contain a major potential for the exploitation of women in desperate financial circumstances. The guidelines that minimize the risk of such exploitation include making contracts unenforceable (that is, permanently decided only after birth, as in adoption) and giving, as only New York does, the woman custody without a court battle in the event that she changes her mind.

Another Kind of Extended Family

Not all surrogacy arrangements involve a financial exchange. At the other end of the spectrum from the tradition of women as primary and men as secondary parents are the more rare arrangements of women who bear children for men to raise. Such was the case with Kevin, John, and Toni. Kevin had always wanted to be a father and had thought seriously about adopting a child, but he was ultimately discouraged by the foster-care debate in Massachusetts. He was a publicly gay man who would neither have nor want the option of passing as straight in order to adopt a child, so he worried that his chances of getting a child were minimal. Over many years, Kevin had become very close friends with Toni, a single bisexual mother. Kevin had been present at the birth of Toni's second child, and he and John were now like uncles to the children. A close-knit extended-family relation was well established by the time Toni shocked Kevin with the offer to bear a child for him and John to raise. Toni felt she could offer a child no better parents than Kevin and John. For his part, Kevin was overwhelmed by Toni's offer. "I would never have asked a woman to have a baby for me—it's way too much to ask. But I was thrilled."

John was skeptical, feeling strongly still that adopting an existing child was a better way to go. But as the foster-care battle raged, "biological parenting began to seem more appealing because of the legal protection it provided." The three carefully hammered out an agreement, one that included a clear commitment on John and Kevin's part not to challenge Toni if she changed her mind and wanted the baby. For her part, however, Toni was far more worried about the opposite occurrence; she did not want to raise another child, and wanted John and Kevin to have primary responsibility. Her involvement with now two-year-old Amber is substantial, and the group does function as an extended family, with Toni's other children clearly Amber's siblings. Though the arrangement thus bears some resemblance to the familiar family, it is also highly unusual, especially because, simultaneously to being Amber's mother, Toni is not her parent; both the power and the responsibility of parenting fall equally on John and Kevin's shoulders.

JOINT PARENTING—LESBIANS AND GAY MEN TOGETHER

Arrangements such as Kevin and John's with Toni, or Susan and Dana's with their children's father, bring lesbians and gay men together to form families. Most commonly these arrangements involve a division into primary and secondary parenting centered in one household, most often the woman or women involved. These setups resemble amicable custody arrangements in cases of divorce, but they are in reality quite different because they are planned this way and from the outset fall outside of the law's definitions.

Lesbians and gay men also come together in a different family form, that of equally shared parenting. Though it has much in common with the arrangement described above, this particular version deserves separate consideration. Joint-parenting arrangements bring lesbians and gay men together in ways that push even further beyond the nuclear family model, creating an altogether new family form. Truly joint-parenting arrangements decenter family life, creating strong bonds between lesbians and gay men established around parenting itself and independent of primary erotic and romantic unions. Such was the family Barry and Adria established.

"I always say this is the longest pregnancy in the world because it took thirteen years of actively trying to become a dad 'til the time Ari was born," Barry said. He had always seen himself as someone who would have children and, though he didn't know how it would happen, that vision didn't change when he came out at age twenty-two. In his late twenties, he began to discuss the possibility of shared parenting with a heterosexual female friend. But over the course of their conversations, it became clear to Barry that the relationship wouldn't work; much as he wanted a child, he decided not to pursue that possibility.

Then he began to look into adoption as a single man, getting as far as the home-study stage. But at that point he backed away from the process. "It was not a time I wanted to invite the state into my home to scrutinize the way I lived. Also I didn't really want to raise a child alone. I really did want to have another parent."

Shortly after that, he was approached by an acquaintance. "She had had a child when she was really young and felt both trapped in her life and not able to figure out how she could get out of the trap in terms of getting more money and some skills. She had seen me interact with her son who was three at the time, and she knew I was trying to become a father and thought it was really unfair that gay men had such a hard time doing it. She offered to be a surrogate mom if I would help her get some kind of training so that she could get a better kind of job. She still wanted to be friends, and thought maybe an appropriate arrangement would be that she would relate to this child like a distant relative. We hadn't worked out the details, but it was '81 and AIDS was happening. There were no tests, and I didn't feel like I could responsibly inseminate so I decided not to do it."

With his third attempt to become a father failing to pan out, and AIDS on the horizon, Barry put the question of children on the back burner for the next four years. Once the HIV test was available and he tested negative, he decided he could continue his quest.

On New Year's Eve, 1986, Barry was introduced by a mutual friend to Adria, a lesbian who was looking for someone with whom to raise a child. In her early adulthood, Adria had assumed she would adopt children. But as she became focused on her work and community, the idea of becoming a parent faded into the background. Unlike Barry,

Adria hadn't spent years engrossed in the pursuit of parenthood. At age forty-two, her world view shifted dramatically when a close friend was diagnosed with AIDS and moved into her home. During the process of caring for him while he was dying, Adria became possessed with an intense desire to be pregnant. What had previously been a source of ambivalence and questioning became definitive. Living through her friend's illness, Adria felt, "If I can do this, I can do anything." The catch was, that Adria had been in a relationship with Marilyn for eight years and Marilyn was not keen on the idea of raising a child. Adria, for her part, wanted her child to have an involved father. This proved to be a good fit, since from Marilyn's perspective it would be more comfortable if Adria had a co-parent other than herself.

Barry describes the tumble of feelings and questions he encountered during their first meetings: "We'd been part of overlapping communities with the same kind of political history, so we knew things about each other and felt very familiar when we actually met, but we had never met before we sat down to ask questions like, 'Would you like to make a commitment for the rest of your life with this stranger and have a very intimate relationship—not sexual, but as close as you can be?' It was very awkward, like going through a series of courting behaviors—checking each other out, putting your best foot forward, and there are these flirtations going on. Our process was that we couldn't say, 'Yes, this is working, let's do it.' It was more like looking for why it wouldn't work until we could find nothing more, then saying, 'Is there any reason why we couldn't do this?' " Adria, on the other hand, immediately impressed by Barry's integrity and level of commitment to parenting, knew at their first encounter that she and Barry would become family.

During the next five months, they let each other into their lives. "It became clear that our sensibility around child-rearing was very similar even though we're very different people," Barry remembers. "Our personalities and backgrounds are very different. Starting this process at an older age, we were both clear about what we wanted and what we didn't want. We wanted to build family with each other. I think we both hoped that ideally that could happen, but if we could find someone close enough, with a similar enough world-view, we knew enough not to expect everything on our list. We introduced each other to our circle of friends, celebrated our birthdays together, gradually doing some of those kinds of family things."

A month after Barry and Adria decided to go ahead with the plan, Barry met Michael. "Here I am, not looking for a relationship, because I'm clear I want kids. You know, if a relationship happens that's fine, that can come later. And then, here's Michael to integrate into this picture. Part of his attraction to me was that I was building a family and he loves children—so we have this dynamic of Michael who is outside wanting in as much as he could, and Marilyn, who is inside wanting to have boundaries as much as she could. And there's Adria and me in the middle, trying to make this happen."

During the next two years, Barry and Adria went through a very intense period that included difficulty conceiving and four miscarriages. The process was particularly discouraging, given Adria's age. One doctor dismissed them completely, chalking up the difficulties to approaching menopause. Adria feared that Barry would abandon the effort to have a baby with her since he so badly wanted a child. But there was never any question in Barry's mind. "We were clear that we really wanted to parent together. That had already been born in this process. We were already really close friends and had this thing that was starting to cross all the traditional lines between gay men and lesbians—building the most physical, intimate relationship you can. Being in the medical part of this process, which was very unpleasant, was really one of the things that pulled us together. Those miscarriages, though I don't recommend this as a strategy, turned out to be a way to find out how you are together. Going through hard times, what we learned is that our instincts pull us together—that's how we deal with hardship. And so that brought us even closer." Barry and Adria supported each other through each episode and were very much partners in the effort. Eventually they saw a fertility specialist, who prescribed Clomid and took over the insemination process. Barry became an expert at assisting the doctor in ultrasound and follicle measuring. At age forty-four, Adria became pregnant and carried to term.

Throughout this process a complicated dynamic developed among the four adults. In many ways Adria and Barry developed a primary intimate relationship, one that had to be balanced with their respective partner relationships. It was the beginning of what was to be their particular sort of family—not a uniform, single entity but more like concentric circles, with four overlapping intimate adult relationships. Though Barry and Adria were at the center of this parenting unit, their approach was inclusive, embracing Michael and Marilyn. This was evident as they moved about the world. Barry remembers the day Adria was late for her first Lamaze class: "So in this room are all these straight couples with very pregnant women, and in walk Barry, Michael, and Marilyn, who is an Olympic athlete, with a very slender toned body—I mean, this woman is not pregnant. It's an awkward threesome. The teacher looks at us and says, "This is the birthing class." And we say, "Great, we're in the right place." Now they're really confused, and we go around the room to introduce ourselves. You have to say your name and the magic due date, so I say 'My name is Barry and I'm the father of this child that Adria, who's not here, is carrying,' and then Michael says, 'My name is Michael and I'm Barry's partner, and I'm going to help parent this child that Adria, who's not here, is carrying,' and then Marilyn, 'I'm Marilyn and I'm Adria's partner.' Their eyes are getting bigger and their mouths are falling open, and finally Adria comes, not having a clue what she was walking into."

Ari was delivered through cesarean section in 1989—Marilyn, Barry, and Michael were all present at his birth. Adria and Barry had agreed to share parenting equally. This is difficult to achieve in the context of two separate households. Each can be with Ari whenever he or she wants and also whenever he is needing one of them. Though they have free access to each other's homes, separation is a key issue in this family. From the very beginning of his life, Ari has gone back and forth between the households almost every other day. Barry and Adria also do a lot of traveling. In the first couple of months, before Ari began to travel back and forth, Barry slept at Adria's house. After that, while Adria was nursing Ari, she would come to Barry's house on the days he wasn't with her. At six months of age, Ari began to take a bottle as well, which somewhat eased the stress.

As they look toward the future, both Barry and Adria have some trepidation about their own feelings regarding separations. They are beginning to feel that Ari, now a preschooler, needs longer stretches in each household. Barry anticipates this. "It's hard for me to imagine him not being home for three days in a row. I just can't—not that I'm not totally comfortable and happy with where he is, because he's at home being loved by his wonderful mother and other parent, and nothing could please me more, but he's not home with me. I find myself wandering into his room a lot when he's not there, looking for him."

Adria has been known to appear at Barry's house in the middle of the night, needing to check in with Ari. Speculating about Ari's responses to the constant comings and goings, Adria says, "I think he suffers as any being would suffer from everything changing all the time. It's the same two houses, it's the same people, and he has everything at both places. He always has his little shopping bag and he carries his blanket with him wherever he goes. I think he'll either grow up to be a person who will only be in one place and will be kind of rigid about it because he's had enough of this, or he'll be someone who any place he hangs his hat will be his home. I think he'll have a certain kind of autonomy and confidence, because he seems to now, but I think he'll also have some issues about being left—people always come back, but they also always leave." One of the issues Barry and Adria are currently trying to address is their desire to have more time together with Ari rather than being on separate shifts.

The complexities of the four-way relationship take a lot of energy to navigate. Though decisions are essentially a matter of consensus, the family's communication about Ari is primarily channeled through Barry and Adria. In a sense, Michael and Marilyn have become the keepers of their respective couple relationships. As Adria sees it, "they watch over the intimacy of the couples—and they help each couple to separate from the other." For Marilyn, Barry's and Michael's involvements with Ari have freed her to be his parent. "The fact that she's not the only other parent besides me, the fact that there's someone else who's fifty percent responsible for him has allowed her a lot of room, to in fact be a very important parent. In our family, because she doesn't want to be a mother, there's not much competition like you'll see in some lesbian couples. And she doesn't want to be his father; there's not competition with Michael and Barry, either. She has her place with Ari. She's the only athlete among us. He's a little talking boy—he's not very athletic. She teaches him how to jump. That's where they live together, in this sort of playful world and he's very close to her."

Michael, unlike Marilyn, has much more interest in a primary parenting role, and has had to grapple with that in the context of a family unit that is clearly centered on Barry and Adria as primary parents. He and Barry think about expanding the family—through having Michael father a child. "When Ari's at our house he's there with both of us and it's fairly equal in terms of day-to-day doing things," Barry says. "Michael has stepped in as the cook. He likes to do it and he cooks for Ari all the time, so he's Ari's best cook and when he's hungry he looks to Michael. I know Michael has felt unseen and unrecognized but not by me or our family. My father, for instance, was watching Michael put Ari to bed one night and he just said 'it's so amazing—he is a father to this child.' But even though Michael gets recognition from our family and community, there's so much in this culture that in basic ways doesn't recognize his role. We try to be especially conscious of it and name it when it's happening."

As with the Lamaze class, as they move about the world this family shakes people's attitudes. Once, Ari closed a car door on his hand. In the emergency room, Barry and Michael met Adria and Ari at the hospital. Barry remembers that day vividly; "So I'm holding Ari and he's telling me the story, saying 'Daddy, I cried a little but it's okay now,' and we go together but they keep trying to separate us all. Then we get to the point of registering, and I'm holding Ari and the clerk is asking me all these questions that I'm answering while Michael and Adria stand behind me. Then the clerk says to me, 'Okay, Michael, so you're the father,' and Michael says 'No, I'm Michael and he's on my plan.' Meanwhile, Ari is pointing to me saying, 'This is the father.' So, okay, this is the father, but Michael learned that in order to get his work to pay these bills—to not raise red flags—he says he's the stepfather. And the clerk must be thinking—well, okay, this is a very friendly divorce—here's the mom, dad, stepfather, and kid. Then he asks Michael for his address. I'd already given him my address as the father and, of course, it's the same address. At this point we're all fidgeting, and Adria says, 'I bet you want to know my address next.' So we have these funny experiences, but we make it work."

Of his family life, Barry says, "It's made us all look at how we do relationships. I think our mode of operating now is basically to act out of the basic goodness that's there in all of these relationships and to let go of a lot of the petty stuff about each other that drives each of us crazy. We pick and choose what we have to deal with. It works incredibly well, and it's also complicated trying to manage these multiple needs." Looking back at his original decision to become a parent in this way, Barry says, "It's important to try to imagine every situation you can before you do something like this, 'cause it gets you thinking, but there's no way to know what the reality will be. No matter how much we talked, there was no way I could be prepared for the instant of Ari's birth, when I went from one primary relationship with Michael to three. And of course it doesn't matter what the adults decide in advance; once the child is born, their needs are going to determine—and should determine—what happens. Sometimes that can bear no relation to all these plans."

Amid all the complexity, Ari seems to thrive. He makes families out of everything, one of his favorites being clothes hangers. The blue one is always himself, and then there is a Mommy, a Daddy, a Marilyn, and a Michael. He wonders why his best friend has no Marilyn or Michael.

THE REINVENTED FAMILY

Lesbian and gay parents essentially reinvent the family as a pluralistic phenomenon. They self-consciously build from the ground up a variety of family types that don't conform to the traditional structure. In so doing, they encourage society to ask, "What is a family?" The question has profound meaning in both the culture at large and the very heart of each of our intimate lives. It is like a tree trunk from which many branches extend: What is a mother, a father, a parent, a sibling? Can a child have two or more mothers or fathers? Is one more "real" by virtue of biological or legal parent status? How does society's recognition (or its absence) foster or impede parent-child relationships? To what extent does the state shape family life? To what extent can nontraditional families alter the state's definition of family?

These questions go well beyond the issue of whether families headed by lesbians and gay men should exist. There emerges a complex reciprocal tension between lesbian and gay family life on the one hand and homophobia and the idealization of the traditional family on the other. Clearly, lesbian and gay parents don't create their families in a vacuum. Their choices are shaped by the institutions that mediate family formation, most notably the legal and medical systems, and adoption agencies. Lesbian and gay parents vary with respect to how they view the state. While some let legal definitions inform their choices, others feel they can probably keep the state out of their lives by relying on trust and goodwill. Sometimes families who've taken this route end up, to their dismay, in the courts, challenging prevailing legal thought.

However they choose to form their families, lesbians and gay men do so in the context of the idealization of the traditional model; their families are inevitably shaped by this fact. Yet at the same time, over the past decade, many changes have been wrought by lesbian and gay family formation itself—ranging from unmarried women's increased access to donor insemination to the particular challenges that lesbian and gay families bring to the law. Though our society is a long way from embracing eight-year-old Danielle's deceptively simple statement that a "family is people who all love each other, care for each other, help out, and understand each other," her words may yet prove to be our most crucial guide to the future.

11 The Age Revolution

■READING 31

The Family in an Aging Society: A Matrix of Latent Relationships

Matilda White Riley

I am going to talk about families and the revolution in longevity. This revolution has produced configurations in kinship structure and in the internal dynamics of family life at every age that have never existed before.

Over two-thirds of the total improvement in longevity from prehistoric times until the present has taken place in the brief period since 1900 (Preston, 1976). In the United States, life expectancy at birth has risen from less than 50 in 1900 to well over 70 today. Whereas at the start of the century most deaths occurred in infancy and young adulthood, today the vast majority of deaths are postponed to old age. Indeed we are approaching the "squared" mortality curve, in which relatively few die before the end of the full life span. For the first time in all history, we are living in a society in which most people live to be old.[1]

Though many facts of life extension are familiar, their meanings for the personal lives of family members are elusive. Just how is increasing longevity transforming the kinship structure? Most problematic of all, how is the impact of longevity affecting those sorely needed close relationships that provide emotional support and socialization for family members (see Parsons and Bales, 1955)? To answer such questions, I must agree with other scholars in the conclusion that we need a whole new way of looking at the family, researching it, living in it, and dealing with it in professional practice and public policy.

Indeed, an exciting new family literature is beginning to map and interpret these unparalleled changes: it is beginning to probe beneath the surface for the subjective implications of the protracted and intricate interplay of family relationships. As the kinship structure is transformed, many studies are beginning to ask new questions about how particular relationships and particular social conditions can foster or inhibit emotional support and socialization—that is, the willingness to learn from one another. They are asking how today's family can fill people's pressing need for close human relationships.

From this developing literature, four topics emerge as particularly thought-provoking: (1) the dramatic extension of the kinship structure; (2) the new opportunities this extension brings for close family relationship; (3) the special approaches needed for understanding these complex relationships; and (4) the still unknown family relationship of older people in the future. I shall touch briefly on each of these topics. From time to time I shall also suggest a few general propositions—principles from the sociology of age (see M. W. Riley, 1976; forthcoming) that seem clearly applicable to changing family relationships. Perhaps they will aid our understanding of increasing longevity and the concomitant changes about us. The propositions may guide us in applying our new understanding in research, policy, and practice.

THE CHANGING CONFIGURATIONS OF THE KINSHIP STRUCTURE

I shall begin with the kinship structure as influenced by longevity. The extent and configurations of this structure have been so altered that we must rethink our traditional view of kinship. As four (even five) generations of many families are now alive at the same time, we can no longer concentrate primary attention on nuclear families of young parents and their children who occasionally visit or provide material assistance to grandparents or other relatives. I have come to think of today's large and complex kinship structure as a matrix of latent relationships—father with son, child with great-grandparent, sister with sister-in-law, ex-husband with ex-wife, and so on—relationships that are latent because they might or might not become close and significant during a lifetime. Thus I am proposing a definition of the kinship structure as a latent web of continually shifting linkages that provide the *potential* for activating and intensifying close family relationships.

The family literature describes two kinds of transformations in this structure that result from increasing longevity: (1) The linkages among family members have been prolonged, and (2) the surviving generations in a family have increased in number and complexity.

Prolongation of Family Relationships

Consider how longevity has prolonged family relationships. For example, in married couples a century ago, one or both partners were likely to have died before the children were reared. Today, though it may seem surprising, couples marrying at the customary ages can anticipate surviving together (apart from divorce) as long as 40 or 50 years on the average (Uhlenberg, 1969, 1980). As Glick and Norton (1977:14) have shown, one out of every five married couples can expect to celebrate their fiftieth wedding anniversary. Because the current intricacy of kinship structures surpasses even the language available to describe it (our step-in-laws might not like to be called "outlaws"), it sometimes helps to do "thought experiments" from one's own life. As marital partners, my husband and I have survived together for over 50 years. What can be said about the form (as distinct from the content) of such a prolonged relationship?

For one thing, we share over half a century of experience. Because we are similar in age, we have shared the experience of aging—biologically, psychologically, and socially—from young adulthood to old age. Because we were born at approximately the same time (and thus belong to the same cohort), we have shared much the same historical experiences—the same fluctuations between economic prosperity and depression, between periods of pacifism and of war, between political liberalism and reactionism, and between low and high rates of fertility. We have also shared our own personal family experiences. We shared the bearing and raising of young children during our first-quarter century together; during our second quarter century we adjusted our couplehood to our added roles as parents-in-law and grandparents. The third quarter-century of our married life, by the laws of probability, should convert us additionally into grandparents-in-law and great-grandparents as well. In sum, prolonged marriages like ours afford extensive common experiences with aging, with historical change, and with changing family relationships.

Such marriages also provide a home—an abiding meeting place for two individuals whose separate lives are engrossed in varied extrafamilial roles. Just as longevity has prolonged the average duration of marriage, it has extended many other roles (such as continuing education, women's years of work outside the home, or retirement). For example, Barbara Torrey (1982) has estimated that people spend at least a quarter of their adult lives in retirement. Married couples, as they move through the role complexes of their individual lives, have many evening or weekend opportunities either to share their respective extrafamilial experiences, to escape from them, or (though certainly not in my own case) to vent their boredom or frustration on one another (see Kelley, 1981).

Thus two features of protracted marriages become apparent. First, these marriages provide increasing opportunity to accumulate shared experiences and meanings and perhaps to build from these a "crescive" relationship, as suggested by Ralph Turner (1970) and Gunhild Hagestad (1981). But second, they also present shifting exigencies and role conflicts that require continual mutual accommodation and recommendation. As Richard Lazarus (DeLongis, et al., 1982) has shown, "daily hassles" can be more destructive of well-being than traumatic family events. And Erving Goffman (1959:132) warns that the home can become a "backstage area" in which "it is safe to lapse into an asociable mood of sullen, silent irritability."

Many marriages, not ended by death, are ended by divorce. The very extension of marriage may increase the likelihood of divorce, as Samuel Preston (1976:176–177) has shown. Returning to my personal experience, I was the only one of four sisters who did not divorce and remarry. But as long as their ex-husbands were alive none of my sisters could ever entirely discount the remaining potential linkages between them. These were not only ceremonial or instrumental linkages, but also affective linkages that could be hostile and vindictive, or (as time passes and need arises) could renew concern for one another's well-being. Whatever the nature of the relationship, latent linkages to ex-spouses persist. Thus, a prolonged marriage (even an ex-marriage) provides a continuing potential for a close relationship that can be activated in manifold ways.

The traditional match-making question—"Will this marriage succeed or fail?"—must be replaced and oft-repeated as the couple grows older by a different question: "Regardless of our past, can we—do we want [to]—make the fresh effort to succeed, or shall we fail in this marriage?"

Here I will state as my first proposition: *Family relationships are never fixed:* they change as the self and the significant other family members grow older, and as the changing society influences their respective lives. Clearly, the longer the relationship endures (because of longevity) the greater the opportunity for relational changes.

If, as lives are prolonged, marital relationships extend far beyond the original nuclear household, parent-offspring relationships also take on entirely new forms. For example, my daughter and I have survived together so far for 45 years of which only 18 were in the traditional relationship of parent and child. Unlike our shorter-lived forebearers, my daughter and I have been able to share many common experiences although at different stages of our respective lives. She shares a major portion of the historical changes that I have experienced. She also shares my earlier experience of sending a daughter off to college, and will perhaps share my experience of having a daughter marry and raise children. Of course, she and I differ in age. (In Alice Rossi's study of biological age differences, 1980, the consequences for parent-offspring relationships of the reciprocal tensions between a pubescent daughter and her older mother who is looking ahead to the menopausal changes of midlife were explored.)[2] Although the relational age between me and my daughter—the 26 years that separate us—remains the same throughout our lives, the implications of this difference change drastically from infancy to my old age.

Number and Stability of Generations

I have dwelt at length on the prolongation of particular relationships to suggest the consequent dramatic changes in the family structure. Longevity has, in addition, increased the stability and the number of generations in a family. A poignant example of this instability (Imhof, 1982) can be found in an eighteenth century parish where a father could spawn twenty-four offspring of whom only three survived to adulthood—a time in which "it took two babies to make one adult." With increased longevity each generation becomes more stable because more of its members survive. For the young nuclear family in the United States, for example, though the number of children born in each family has been declining over this century, increased longevity has produced a new stability in the family structure. In an important quantitative analysis, Peter Uhlenberg (1980) has shown how the probability of losing a parent or a sibling through death before a child reaches age 15 [has] decreased from .51 in 1900 to .09 in 1976. Compared with children born a century ago, children born today are almost entirely protected against death of close family members (except for elderly relatives). To be sure, while mortality has been declining, divorce rates have been increasing but less rapidly. Thus, perhaps surprisingly, Uhlenberg demonstrates that disruptions of marriage up through the completion of child rearing have been declining since 1900. In other words, many marriages have been broken by divorce, but overall more have remained intact because of fewer deaths! Thus the young family as well as each of the older generations becomes more stable through survival.

At the same time, the number of older generations has been increasing. Looking up the generational ladder, increasing numbers of a child's four grandparents survive. Among middle-aged couples, whereas back in 1900 more than half had no surviving elderly parents, today half have two or more parents still alive (Uhlenberg, 1980:318). Conversely looking down the generational ladder, each set of elderly parents has adult children with spouses and children of their own. Meanwhile, the increase in divorce and remarriage (four out of five divorced people remarry) compounds the complexity of this elaborate structure, as Andrew Cherlin (1981) has shown. In my own family, for example, each of our two middle-aged children have their own children, and they also have us as two elderly parents; my daughter's husband also has two parents; and my son (who has married twice) has his ex-wife's parents and his current wife's mother, father, and step-mother in addition to us. A complex array!

Of course, as these surviving generations proliferate and overlap, each generation is continually growing older and moving up the generational ladder to replace its predecessor until ultimately the members of the oldest generation die. Because of longevity, every generation—the oldest as well as the youngest—is increasingly stable and more likely to include its full complement of surviving members.

CHANGING DYNAMICS OF CLOSE FAMILY RELATIONSHIPS

What, then, are the implications of this greatly expanded kinship structure for the dynamics of close family relationships? How does the matrix of latent kinship linkages provide for close ties between particular individual lives, as these lives weave in and out of the intricate and continually shifting kinship network? Under what conditions do some family members provide (or fail to provide) recognition, advice, esteem, love, and tension release for other family members?

The answer, it seems to me, lies in the enlarged kinship structure: It provides many new opportunities for people at different points in their lives to select and activate the relationships they deem most significant. That is, the options for close family bonds have multiplied. Over the century, increased longevity has given flexibility to the kinship structure, relaxing both the temporal and the spatial boundaries of optional relationships.

Temporally, new options have arisen over the course of people's lives because, as we have seen, particular relationships have become more enduring. Particular relationships (even following divorce) are bounded only by the birth and death of members. Now that the experience of losing family members by death is no longer a pervasive aspect of the full life course (and is in fact rare except in old age), people have greater opportunity to plan their family lives. They have time to make mutual adjustments to personal crises or to external threats such as unemployment or the fear of nuclear war. Here we are reminded of my first proposition: Family relationships are never fixed, but are continually in process and subject to change. As family members grow older, they move across time—across history and through their own lives—and they also move upward through the generations in their own families and the age strata of society.[3] As individual family members who each pursue a separate life course, thoughts and feelings for one another are developed; their lives weave together or apart so as to activate, intensify, disregard, or disrupt particular close relationships. Thus the relationship between a mother and daughter can, for example, become close in the daughter's early childhood, her first years of marriage, and again after her children have left home although there may be interim lapses. Or, as current norms permit, couples can try each other out through cohabitation, before deciding whether or not to embark upon marriage.

Just as such new options for close ties have emerged from the prolongation of family relationships, other options have arisen because the number and variety of latent linkages has multiplied across the entire kinship structure. Spatially, close relationships are not bounded by the nuclear households that family members share during their younger lives. Given the intricacy of current kin networks, a wide range of linkages can be activated—between grandchild and grandparent, between distantly related cousins, between the ex-husbands of sisters, or between a child and his or her new step-parent. (Only in Grimm's fairy tales, which reflected the earlier frequency of maternal deaths and successive remarriages, were step-mothers always "wicked.") Aided by modern communication and transportation, affection and interaction can persist even during long periods of separation. On occasion, long-separated relatives or those not closely related may arrange to live together or to join in congregate housing or communes.

Given these options, let me now state a second general proposition: As active agents in directing the course of their own lives, *individuals have a degree of control over their close family relationships.* This control, I submit, has been enhanced because longevity has widened the opportunities for selecting and activating relationships that can provide emotional support and advice when needed.

This part of my discussion suggests a new view of the family. Perhaps we need now to think of a family less as the members of one household with incidental linkages to kin in other households and more as a continuing interplay among intertwined lives within the entire changing kinship structure. The closeness of these intertwined lives and the mutual support they provide depend on many factors (including the predispositions of each individual and the continuing motivation to negotiate and renegotiate their joint lives) but the enlarged kinship structure provides the potential.

NEW APPROACHES TO FAMILY RESEARCH AND PRACTICE

Before considering how the oldest family members—those in the added generation—fit into these intertwined lives, let me pause to ask how we can approach these complex and changing family relationships. If the tidy concept of the nuclear family is no longer sufficient, how can we deal in research and in professional practice with the newly emerging concepts? Clearly, special approaches are required for mapping and understanding the centrifugal and centripetal processes of family relationships within the increasing complexity of the kinship matrix. Such approaches must not only take into account my first two propositions (that relationships continually change, and that family members themselves have some control over this change) but must also consider a third proposition: *The lives of family members are interdependent* such that each person's family life continually interacts with the lives of significant relatives. Though long-recognized by students of the family, this proposition takes on fresh significance in the matrix of prolonged relationships.

As case examples, I shall describe two or three studies that illustrate how we can deal with the family as a system of interdependent lives. These studies are also important as they add to our understanding of emotional support and socialization under current family conditions.

In one study of socialization outcomes, Mavis Hetherington et al. (1977) have shown how parental disruption through divorce has a complex impact on the still-intertwined lives of the spouses and on the socialization of their children. Over a two-year period, detailed investigations were made of nursery school boys and girls and their parents, half of whom were divorced and the other half married. Differences were detected: Divorced parents showed comparatively less affection for their children, had less control over them, and elicited more dependent, disobedient, and aggressive child behavior—particularly in mother-son interactions. But relations between the parents also made a difference in these parent-child relationships: If divorced couples kept conflict low and agreed about child rearing, their ineffectiveness in dealing with children could be somewhat offset. This two-year tracing of the three-way interrelationships among spouses and children in disrupted families yields many insights into the interdependence of life course processes.

As family relationships are prolonged, socialization is more frequently recognized as a reciprocal process that potentially extends throughout the lives of parents and children as well as of marital partners. How can socialization operate across generations that belong to differing periods of historical change? One key mechanism, as Marilyn Johnson (1976) has demonstrated, is normative expectations. Parents can influence offspring by expecting behavior that is appropriate to social change, and can in turn be guided by offspring in formulating these expectations. Such subtleties to intergenerational influence are illustrated in a small study which Johnson and I made of high school students in the early 1960s (see Riley, 1982). Just as women's careers were burgeoning, we found that most girls looked forward to combining a career with marriage, whereas most boys did not anticipate marrying wives who worked. How had these young people been socialized to such sharply conflicting norms? We questioned their mothers and fathers to find out. Indeed we learned that, on the whole, parents wanted self-fulfillment for their daughters both in marriage and in work outside the home, while for their sons they wanted wives who would devote themselves fully to home and children. These slight yet provocative findings did presage the future impact of the women's movement on family lives, but I note them here as another instance of research that fits together the differing perspectives of the several interdependent family members.

Analyzing such studies of close relationships impresses one with the problem of studying families from what is often called the "life course" or "lifespan perspective" (see Dannefer, forthcoming). We are indeed concerned with people moving through life. Yet we are concerned not with a single life or a statistical aggregate of lives, but with the dynamic family systems of interdependent lives. An example I often use in teaching comes from the early work of Cottrell and Burgess in predicting success or failure in marriage. Starting with a case study, Cottrell (1933) saw each partner in a marriage as reenacting his or her childhood roles. He showed how the outcome of the marriage depended upon the mesh between these two different sets of early-life experiences—that is, how nearly they would fit together so that each partner met the role expectations of the other. Unfortunately, however, these researchers subsequently departed from this admirable model by questioning large samples of men and women as individuals and then analyzing the data for separate aggregates of men and women rather than for male-female pairs. Each individual was given a score of likely success in marriage, but without considering the success of a marriage between a particular man and a particular woman! Because the interdependent lives were not examined jointly, the central objective of the project was lost.

This difficulty, which I now call "life-course reductionism," still persists. Although many studies purport to study families as systems, they in fact either aggregate individual lives (as Cottrell and Burgess did) or reason erroneously from the lives of single members about the lives of other family members significant to the relationship. The danger of not considering a key family member is highlighted, for example, in Frank Furstenberg's (1981) review of the literature on kinship relations after divorce. Some studies had suggested that divorce disrupts the relations with parents-in-law (that is, with the parents of the ex-spouse) but these studies failed to include the children of the broken marriage. Only after examining the children's generation was it learned that they, by retaining contact with both sets of their grandparents, could help to link divorced spouses to their former in-laws. Supporting this clue from a small study of his own, Furstenberg found that the ties between grandparents and grandchildren did continue to exist in most cases, even though for the divorced parents (the middle generation) the former in-law relationships were largely attenuated or broken. In reconstituted families, then, grandparents can perhaps serve as "kinkeepers."

Among the studies that pursue close relationships across three generations is a national survey of divorce and remarriage now being conducted by Frank Furstenberg, Andrew Cherlin, Nicholas Zill, and James Peterson. In this era of widespread divorce and remarriage, this study is examining the important hypothesis that new intergenerational ties created by remarriage will balance—or more than balance—the losses incurred as a result of divorce. Step-relationships may replace disrupted natural relationships. The intricacy of interdependent lives within our proliferating kinship structure is dramatized by the design of this study. Starting with a sample of children aged 11 to 16 and their parents (who were originally interviewed five years earlier) the research team will now also question these children's grandparents; note that there can be two sets of grandparents where the parents are in intact first marriages or have been divorced, three sets if one parent has remarried after divorce, and four sets (no less than eight grandparents) if both have remarried. Thus, as surviving generations proliferate, their part in the family system will be explored in this study by questioning the many members of the grandparent generation. Surviving generations cannot be fully understood (as many studies of three generations have attempted) by examining a simple chain of single individuals from each of the generations.

These studies, as models for research, reflect the complex family relationships within which people of all ages today can seek or can give affection, encouragement, companionship, or advice.

OLDER GENERATIONS OF THE FUTURE

About the fourth generation (great-grandparents) that is being contributed by longevity, I want to make three final points.

First, it is too early to tell how an enlarged great-grandparent generation will fit into the kinship structure, or what close family relationships it may form. It is too early because the marked increase in longevity among the old began only in recent decades and are still continuing at a rate far exceeding earlier predictions (Preston, 1976; Manton, 1982; Brody and Brock, n.d.). Will this added generation be regarded as the more familiar generation of grandparents has been regarded—either as a threat to the young adult generation's independence, or as a "social problem" for family and community, requiring care from the mid-generation that is "squeezed" between caring for both young children and aging parents? Or will an added fourth generation mean new coalitions and new forms of personal relationships? And what of five-generation families in which a grandmother can be also a granddaughter (see Hagestad, 1981)? It is still too early to tell what new family norms will develop (see Riley, 1978).

Second, while we do not know how a fourth or even a fifth generation may fit in, we do know that most older family members are not dependent or disabled (some 5 percent of those 65 and over are in nursing homes). For those requiring care or instrumental support, families generally make extraordinary efforts to provide it (see Shanas, 1979). Yet most of the elderly, and especially those who are better educated and more active, are stronger, wiser, more competent, and more independent than is generally supposed. Public stereotypes of old people are far more negative than old people's assessments of themselves (National Council on the Aging, 1981). Healthy members of this generation, like their descendants, must earn their own places in the family and create their own personal ties. They cannot expect obligatory warmth or emotional support.

Third, at the close of their lives, however, old people will need advice and emotional support from kin. This need is not new in the annals of family history. What is new is the fact that terminal illness and death are no longer scattered across all generations but are concentrated in the oldest one. Today two-thirds of all deaths occur after age 65, and 30 percent after age 80 (Brody and Brock, n.d.). And, although most deaths occur outside the home, programs such as the hospice movement are being developed for care of the dying in the home where the family can take part (see J. W. Riley, forthcoming).

In conclusion, I have attempted to trace the impact of the unprecedented increases in longevity on the family and its relationships. In our own time the kinship structure has become more extensive and more complex, the temporal and spatial boundaries of the family have been altered, and the opportunities for close family relationships have proliferated. These relationships are no longer prescribed as strict obligations. They must rather be earned—created and recreated by family members throughout their long lives. Each of us is in continuing need of advice and emotional support from one another, as we contend with personal challenges and troubles, and with the compelling effects of societal changes in the economy, in technology, in culture, and in values. We all must agree with Mary Jo Bane (1976) that the family is here to stay, but in forms that we are beginning to comprehend only now. As members of families and students of the family—whether we are theorists, researchers, counselors, or policy makers—we must begin to realign our thinking and our practice to incorporate the new realities that are being engendered by increasing longevity.

Notes

1. Note that increasing longevity in a society is not necessarily the same as increasing proportions of old people in the population, a proportion influenced in the long-term more by fertility than by mortality. Longevity affects individual lives and family structures, while population composition affects the total society.

2. Gunhild Hagestad (1982) talks even of menopausal grandmothers with pubescent granddaughters.

3. Of course, divisions between generations are only loosely coterminous with age divisions (see the discussion of the difference between "generations" and "cohorts" in the classic piece by Duncan, 1966, and a definitive formulation of this distinction in Kertzer, forthcoming). As Gunhild Hagestad (1981) puts it,

"people do not file into generations by cohorts." There are wide ranges in the ages at which particular individuals marry and have children. In addition to the recognized differences by sex, there are important differences by social class. For example, Graham Spanier (Spanier and Glick, 1980) shows how the later marriage age in upper as compared with lower socioeconomic classes postpones many subsequent events in the lives of family members, thus slowing the proliferation in numbers of surviving generations.

References

Bane, M. J. 1976. *Here to Stay: American Families in the 20th Century.* New York: Basic Books.

Brody, J. A., and D. B. Brock, n.d. "Epidemiologic and statistical characteristics of the United States elderly population." (unpublished)

Cherlin, A. J. 1981. *Marriage, Divorce, Remarriage.* Cambridge, MA: Harvard University Press.

Cottrell, L. S., Jr. 1933. "Roles and marital adjustment." *American Sociological Society*, 27, 107–115.

Dannefer, D. Forthcoming. "The sociology of the life course." *Annual Review of Sociology.*

DeLongis, A., J. C. Coyne, G. Dakof, S. Folkman, and R. S. Lazarus. 1982. "Relationship of daily hassles, uplifts, and major life events to health status." *Health Psychology*, 1, 119–136.

Duncan, O. D. 1966. "Methodological issues in the analysis of social mobility," pp. 51–97 in N. J. Smelser and S. M. Lipsett (eds.), *Social Structure and Mobility in Economic Development.* Chicago, IL: Aldine.

Furstenberg, F. F., Jr. 1981. "Remarriage and intergenerational relations," pp. 115–142 in R. W. Fogel et al. (eds.), *Aging: Stability and Change in the Family.* New York: Academic Press.

Glick, P. C., and A. J. Norton. 1977. "Marrying, divorcing, and living together in the U.S. today." Population Bulletin 32. Washington, D.C. Population Reference Bureau.

Goffman, E. 1959. *The Presentation of Self in Everyday Life.* Garden City, NY: Doubleday.

Hagested, G. O. 1982. "Older women in intergenerational relations." Presented at the Physical and Mental Health of Aged Women Conference, October 21–22, Case Western University, Cleveland, OH.

———. 1981. "Problems and promises in the social psychology of intergenerational relations," pp. 11–46 in R. W. Fogel et al. (eds.), *Aging: Stability and Change in the Family.* New York: Academic Press.

Hetherington, E. M., M. Cox, and R. Cox. 1977. "The aftermath of divorce," in J. H. Stevens, Jr. and M. Matthews (eds.), *Mother-Child, Father-Child Relations.* Washington, D.C.: National Association for the Education of Young Children.

Imhof, A. E. 1982. "Life course patterns of women and their husbands—16th to 20th century." Presented at the International Conference on Life Course Research on Human Development, September 17, Berlin, Germany.

Johnson, M. 1976. "The role of perceived parental models, expectations and socializing behaviors in the self-expectations of adolescents, from the U.S. and West Germany." Dissertation, Rutgers University.

Kelley, H. H. 1981. "Marriage relationships and aging," pp. 275–300 in R. W. Fogel et al. (eds.), *Aging: Stability and Change in the Family.* New York: Academic Press.

Kertzer, D. I. Forthcoming. "Generations as a sociological problem." *Annual Review of Sociology.*

Manton, K. G. 1982. "Changing concepts of morbidity and mortality in the elderly population." Milbank Memorial Fund Q. 60: 183–244.

National Council on the Aging. 1981. *Aging in the Eighties: America in Transition.* Washington, D.C.: Author.

Parsons, T., and R. F. Bales. 1955. *Family, Socialization and Interaction Process.* New York: Free Press.

Preston, S. H. 1976. *Mortality Patterns in National Population: With Special References to Recorded Causes of Death.* New York: Academic Press.

Riley, J. W., Jr. Forthcoming. "Dying and the meanings of death: sociological inquiries." Annual Review of Sociology.

Riley, M. W. 1976. "Age strata in social systems," pp. 189–217 in R. H. Binstock and E. Shanas (eds.), *Handbook of Aging and the Social Sciences.* New York: Van Nostrand Reinhold.

————. 1978. "Aging, social change, and the power of ideas." Daedalus 107, 4: 39–52.

————. 1982. "Implications for the middle and later years," pp. 399–405 in P. W. Berman and E. R. Ramey (eds.), *Women: A Development Perspective NIH Publication* No. 82-2298. Washington, DC: Dept. of Health and Human Services.

————. Forthcoming. "Age strata in social systems," in R. H. Binstock and E. Shanas (eds.), *The New Handbook of Aging and the Social Sciences.*

Rossi, A. S. 1980. "Aging and parenthood in the middle years," in P. B. Baltes and O. G. Brim, Jr. (eds.), *Life-Span Development and Behavior 3.* New York: Academic Press.

Shanas, E. 1979. "Social myth as hypothesis: the case of the family relations of old people." *The Gerontologist* 19: 3–9.

Spanier, G. B., and P. C. Glick. 1980. "The life cycle of American families: an expanded analysis," J. of Family History: 97–111.

Torrey, B. B. 1982. "The lengthening of retirement," pp. 181–196 in M. W. Riley et al. (eds.), *Aging from Birth to Death, vol. II: Sociotemporal Perspectives.* Boulder, CO: Westview.

Turner, R. H. 1970. *Family Interaction.* New York: John Wiley.

Uhlenberg, P. R. 1969. "A study of cohort life cycles: cohorts of native born Massachusetts women. 1830–1920," Population Studies 23, 3: 407–420.

————. 1980. "Death and the family." J. of Family History (Fall): 313–320.

■ R E A D I N G   3 2

The Modernization of Grandparenthood

Andrew J. Cherlin and Frank F. Furstenberg, Jr.

Writing a book about grandparents may seem an exercise in nostalgia, like writing about the family farm. We tend to associate grandparents with old-fashioned families—the rural, extended, multigenerational kind much celebrated in American mythology. Many think that grandparents have become less important as the nation has become more modern. According to this view, the shift to factory and office work meant that grandparents no longer could teach their children and grandchildren the skills needed to make a living: the fall in fertility and the rise in divorce weakened family ties; and the growth of social welfare programs meant that older people and their families were less dependent on each other for support. There is some truth to this perspective, but it ignores a powerful set of historical facts that suggest that grandparenthood—as a distinct and nearly universal stage of family life—is a post–World War II phenomenon.

Consider first the effect of falling rates of death. Much of the decline in mortality from the high preindustrial levels has occurred in this century. According to calculations by demographer Peter Uhlenberg, only about 37 percent of all males and 42 percent of all females born in 1870 survived to age sixty-five; but for those born in 1930 the comparable projections were 63 percent for males and 77 percent for females. The greatest declines in adult mortality have occurred in the last few decades, especially for women. The average number of years that a forty-year-old white woman could expect to live increased by four between 1900 and 1940; but between 1940 and 1980 it increased by seven. For men the increases have been smaller, though still substantial: a two-year increase for forty-year-old whites between 1900 and 1940 and a four-year increase between 1940 and 1980. (The trends for nonwhites are similar.) Consequently, both men and women can expect to live much longer lives than was the case a few decades ago, and more and more women are outliving men. In 1980, the average forty-year-old white woman could expect to live to age eighty, whereas the average forty-year-old white man could expect to live only to age seventy-four. As a result, 60 percent of all the people sixty-five and over in the United States in 1980 were women. Thus, there are many more grandparents around today than just a few decades ago simply because people are living longer—and a majority of them are grandmothers.

This decline in mortality has caused a profound change in the relationship between grandparents and grandchildren. For the first time in history, most adults live long enough to get to know most of their grandchildren, and most children have the opportunity to know most of their grandparents. A child born in 1900, according to Uhlenberg, had a better than nine-out-of-ten chance that two or more of his grandparents would be alive. But by the time that child reached age fifteen, the chances were only about one out of two that two or more of his grandparents would still be alive. Thus, some children were fortunate enough to establish relationships with grandparents, but in many other families the remaining grandparents must have died while the grandchild was quite young. Moreover, it was unusual for grandchildren at the turn of the century to know all their grandparents: only one in four children born in 1900 had four grandparents alive, and a mere one in fifty still had four grandparents alive by the time they were fifteen. In contrast, the typical fifteen-year-old in 1976 had a nearly nine-out-of-ten chance of having two or more grandparents still alive, a better than one-out-of-two chance of having three still alive, and a one-out-of-six chance of having all four still alive. Currently, then, nearly all grandchildren have an extended relationship with two or more grandparents, and substantial minorities have the opportunity for extended relationships with three or even all four.

Indeed, Americans take survival to the grandparental years pretty much for granted. The grandparents we spoke to rarely mentioned longer life when discussing the changes since they were children. *Of course* they were still alive and reasonably healthy; that went without saying. But this taken-for-grantedness is a new phenomenon; before World War II early death was a much greater threat, and far fewer people lived long enough to watch their grandchildren grow up.

Most people are in their forties or fifties when they first become grandparents. Some observers have mistakenly taken this as an indication that grandparents are younger today than in the past. According to one respected textbook:

> Grandparenting has become a phenomenon of middle age rather than old age. Earlier marriage, earlier childbirth, and longer life expectancy are producing grandparents in their forties.

But since the end of the nineteenth century (the earliest period for which we have reliable statistics) there has been little change in the average age at marriage. The only exception was in the 1950s, when ages at marriage and first birth did decline markedly but only temporarily. With the exception of the unusual 1950s, then, it is likely that the age when people become grandparents has stayed relatively constant over the past century. What has changed is the amount of time a person spends as a grandparent: increases in adult life expectancy mean that grandparenthood extends into old age much more often. In our national sample of the grandparents of teenagers, six out of ten had become grandparents while in their forties. When we interviewed them, however, their average age was sixty-six. Grandparenting has been a phenomenon of middle age for at least the past one hundred years. The difference today is that it is now a phenomenon of middle age *and* old age for a greater proportion of the population. To be sure, our notions of what constitutes old age also may have changed, as one woman in our study implied when discussing her grandmother:

> She stayed home more, you know. And I get out into everything I can. That's the difference. That is, I think I'm younger than she was at my age.

Moreover, earlier in the century some middle-aged women may have been too busy raising the last of their own children to think of themselves as grandmothers. Nevertheless, in biological terms, the average grandparent alive today is older, not younger, than the average grandparent at the turn of the century.

Consider also the effects of falling birth rates on grandparenthood. As recently as the late 1800s, American women gave birth to more than four children, on average. Many parents still were raising their younger children after their older children had left home and married. Under these conditions, being a grandparent often overlapped with being a parent. One would imagine that grandparenthood took a back seat to the day-to-day tasks of raising the children who were still at home. Today, in contrast, the birth rate is much lower; and parents are much more likely to be finished raising their children before any of their grandchildren are born. In 1900, about half of all fifty-year-old women still had children under eighteen; but by 1980 the proportion had dropped to one-fourth. When a person becomes a grandparent now, there are fewer family roles competing for his or her time and attention. Grandparenthood is more of a separate stage of family life, unfettered by child care obligations—one that carries its own distinct identification. It was not always so.

The fall of fertility and the rise of life expectancy have thus greatly increased the supply of older persons for whom grandparenthood is a primary intergenerational role. To be sure, there always have been enough grandparents alive so that everyone in American society (and nearly all other societies, for that matter) was familiar with the role. But until quite recently, an individual faced a considerable risk of dying before, or soon after, becoming a grandparent. And even if one was fortunate enough to become a grandparent, lingering parental obligations often took precedence. In past times, when birth and death rates were high, grandparents were in relatively short supply. Today, as any number of impatient older parents will attest, grandchildren are in short supply. Census data bear this out: in 1900 there were only twenty-seven persons aged fifty-five and over for every one hundred children fourteen and under; but by 1984 the ratio had risen to nearly one-to-one. In fact, the Bureau of the Census projects that by the year 2000, for the first time in our nation's history, there will be more persons aged fifty-five and over than children fourteen and under.

Moreover, technological advances in travel and long-distance communication have made it easier for grandparents and grandchildren to *see* or talk to each other. . . . [T]he grandparents at one senior citizen center had to remind us that there was a time within their memories when telephone service was not universal. We tend to forget that only fifty years ago the *Literary Digest* predicted a Landon victory over Roosevelt on the basis of responses from people listed in telephone directories—ignoring the crucial fact that telephones were to be found disproportionately in wealthier, and therefore more often Republican, homes. As late as the end of World War II, only half the homes in the United States had a telephone. The proportion rose quickly to two-thirds by the early 1950s and three-fourths by the late 1950s. Today, more than 97 percent of all homes have telephones. About one-third of the grandparents in our survey reported that they had spoken to the study child on the telephone once a week or more during the previous year.

Nor did most families own automobiles until after World War II, as several grandparents reminded us:

> I could be wrong, but I don't feel grandparents felt as close to grandchildren during that time as they do now. . . . Really back there, let's say during the twenties, transportation was not as good, so many people did not have cars. Fortunately, I can say that as far back as I remember my father always had a car, but there were many other people who did not. They traveled by horse and buggy and some even by wagons. And going a distance, it did take quite some time. . . .

Only about half of all families owned automobiles at the end of the war. Even if a family owned an automobile, long trips still could take quite some time:

> Well, I didn't see my grandmother that often. They just lived one hundred miles from us, but back then one hundred miles was like four hundred now, it's the truth. It just seemed like clear across the country. It'd take us five hours to get there, it's the truth. It was an all-day trip.

But in the 1950s, the Federal government began to construct the interstate highway system, which cut distances and increased the speed of travel. The total number of miles driven by passenger vehicles increased from about 200 million miles in the mid-1930s to about 500 million miles in the mid-1950s to over a billion miles in the 1980s. Not all of this increase represents trips to Grandma's house, of course; but with more cars and better highways, it became much easier to visit relatives in the next county or state.

But weren't grandparents and grandchildren more likely to be living in the same household at the turn of the century? After all, we do have a nostalgic image of the three-generation family of the past, sharing a household and solving their problems together. Surprisingly, the difference between then and now is much less than this image would lead us to believe. To be sure, there has been a drastic decline since 1900 in the proportion of older persons who live with their adult children. In 1900 the proportion was more than three out of five, according to historian Daniel Scott Smith; in 1962 it was one out of four; and by 1975 it had dropped to one in seven. What has occurred is a great increase in the proportion of older people who live alone or only with their spouses. Yet the high rates of co-residence in 1900 do not imply that most grandparents were living with their grandchildren—much less that most grandchildren were living with their grandparents. As Smith's data show, older persons who were married tended to live with unmarried children only; children usually moved out when they married. It was mainly widows unable to maintain their own households who moved in with married children. Consequently, according to Smith's estimates, only about three in ten persons sixty-five and over in 1900 lived with a grandchild, despite the great amount of co-residence between older parents and their adult children. What is more, because of the relative shortage of grandparents, an even lower percentage of grandchildren lived with their grandparents. Smith estimates that about one in six children under age ten in 1900 lived in the same household with someone aged fifty-five or over. Even this figure overestimates the number of children living with their grandparents, because some of these elderly residents were more distant kin, boarders, or servants.

There were just too many grandchildren and too few grandparents for co-residence to be more common. In the absence of more detailed analyses of historical censuses, however, the exact amount of change since 1900 cannot be assessed. Nor was our study designed to provide precise estimates of changes in co-residence. But it is still worth nothing that just 30 percent of the grandparents in our sample reported that at least one of their grandparents ever lived with them while they were growing up. And 19 percent reported that the teenaged grandchild in the study had lived with them for at least three months. Undoubtedly, some of the grandparents in our study had shared a household with some of their own grandchildren, although we unfortunately did not obtain this information. Thus, although our study provides only imperfect and incomplete data on this topic, the responses are consistent with our claim that the change in the proportion of grandparents and grandchildren who share a household has been more modest than the change in the proportion of elderly persons who share a household with an adult child.

Grandparents also have more leisure time today, although the trend is more pronounced for men than for women. The average male can now expect to spend fifteen years of his adult life out of the labor force, most of it during retirement. (The labor force comprises all persons who are working for pay or looking for work.) The comparable expected time was ten years in 1970, seven years in 1940, and only four years in 1900. Clearly, a long retirement was rare early in this century and still relatively rare just before World War II. But since the 1960s, workers have begun to leave the labor force at younger ages. In 1961, Congress lowered the age of eligibility for Social Security benefits from sixty-five to sixty-two. Now more than half of all persons applying for Social Security benefits are under sixty-five. Granted, some of the early retirees are suffering from poor health, and other retirees may have difficulty adjusting to their new status. Still, when earlier retirement is combined with a longer life span, the result is a greatly extended period during which one can, among other things, get to know and enjoy one's grandchildren.

The changes in leisure time for women are not as clear because women have always had lower levels of labor force participation than men. To be sure, women workers also are retiring earlier and, as has been noted, living much longer. And most women in their fifties and sixties are neither employed nor raising children. But young grandmothers are much more likely to be employed today than was the case a generation ago; they are also more likely to have aged parents to care for. Young working grandmothers, a growing minority, may have less time to devote to their grandchildren.

Most employed grandparents, however, work no more than forty hours per week. This, too, is a recent development. The forty-hour work week did not become the norm in the United States until after World War II. At the turn of the century, production workers in manufacturing jobs worked an average of fifty hours per week. Average hours dropped below forty during the depression, rose above forty during the war, and then settled at forty after the war. Moreover, at the turn of the century, 38 percent of the civilian labor force worked on farms, where long hours were commonplace. Even in 1940, about 17 percent of the civilian labor force worked on farms; but currently only about 3 percent work on farms. So even if they are employed, grandparents have more leisure time during the work week than was the case a few decades ago.

They also have more money. Living standards have risen in general since World War II, and the rise has been sharpest for the elderly. As recently as 1960, older Americans were an economically deprived group; now they are on the verge of becoming an economically advantaged group. The reason is the Social Security system. Since the 1950s and 1960s, Congress has expanded Social Security coverage, so that by 1970 nearly all nongovernment workers, except those in nonprofit organizations, were covered. And since the 1960s, Congress has increased Social Security benefits far faster than the increase in the cost of living. As a result, the average monthly benefit (in constant 1980 dollars, adjusted for changes in consumer prices) rose from $167 in 1960, to $214 in 1970, to $297 in 1980. Because of the broader coverage and higher benefits, the proportion of the elderly who are poor has plummeted. In 1959, 35 percent of persons sixty-five and over had incomes below the official poverty line, compared to 22 percent of the total population. By 1982 the disparity had disappeared: 15 percent of those sixty-five and over were poor, as were 15 percent of the total population. The elderly no longer were disproportionately poor, although many of them have incomes not too far above the poverty line. Grandparents, then, have benefitted from the general rise in economic welfare and, as they reach retirement, from the improvement in the economic welfare of the elderly.

Because of the postwar prosperity and the rise of social welfare institutions, older parents and their adult children are less dependent on each other economically. Family life in the early decades of the century was precarious; lower wages, the absence of social welfare programs, and crises of unemployment, illness, and death forced people to rely on their kin for support to a much greater extent than is true today. There were no welfare checks, unemployment compensation, food stamps, Medicare payments, Social Security benefits, or government loans to students. Often there was only one's family. Some older people provided assistance to their kin, such as finding a job for a relative, caring for the sick, or tending to the grandchildren while the parents worked. Sometimes grandparents, their children, and their grandchildren pooled their resources into a single family fund so that all could subsist. Exactly how common these three-generational economic units were we do not know; it would be a mistake to assume that all older adults were cooperating with their children and grandchildren at all times. In fact, studies of turn-of-the-century working-class families suggest that widowed older men—past their peak earning capacity and unfamiliar with domestic tasks as they were—could be a burden to the households of their children, while older women—who could help out domestically—were a potential source of household assistance. Nevertheless, these historical accounts suggest that intensive intergenerational cooperation and assistance was more common than it is today. Tamara Hareven, for example, studied the families of workers at the

Amoskeag Mills in Manchester, New Hampshire, at the turn of the century. She found that the day-to-day cooperation of kin was necessary to secure a job at the mill, find housing, and accumulate enough money to get by. Cooperation has declined because it is not needed as often: social welfare programs now provide services that only the family formerly provided; declining rates of illness, death, and unemployment have reduced the frequency of family crises; and the rising standard of living—particularly of the elderly—has reduced the need for financial assistance.

The structure of the Social Security system also has lessened the feelings of obligation older parents and their adult children have toward each other. Social Security is an income transfer system in which some of the earnings of workers are transferred to the elderly. But we have constructed a fiction about Social Security, a myth that the recipients are only drawing out money that they put into the fund earlier in their lives. This myth allows both the younger contributors and the older recipients to ignore the economic dependency of the latter. The elderly are free to believe that they are just receiving that to which they are entitled by virtue of their own hard work. The tenacity of this myth—it is only now breaking down under the tremendous payment burden of our older age structure—demonstrates its importance. It allows the elderly to accept financial assistance without compromising their independence, and it allows children to support their parents without either generation openly acknowledging as much.

All of these trends taken together—changes in mortality, fertility, transportation, communications, the work day, retirement, Social Security, and standards of living—have transformed grandparenthood from its pre–World War II state. More people are living long enough to become grandparents and to enjoy a lengthy period of life as grandparents. They can keep in touch more easily with their grandchildren; they have more time to devote to them; they have more money to spend on them; and they are less likely still to be raising their own children.

12 *Trouble in the Family*

Why Do They Do It?

Kristin Luker

It's difficult to be the mother of a very young child. It's more difficult still when the mother is a teenager. And if she's not only a teen but unmarried, her life can he even grimmer than the most outspoken opponents of early childbearing can imagine. Many young mothers, when asked about their situation, readily describe how hard it is to raise a child. For some of them, having a baby was a serious mistake.

> I'm not living with my family. I'm living with a friend. It's really bleak and confusing. I miss everything I left behind. (Christina, seventeen, white, Colorado)

> If I thought I didn't have freedom before the baby, I didn't know what freedom was. My parents watch every step I take. After all, they are paying for me and my baby. (Holly, sixteen, white, Colorado)

> After they cut Marquis's umbilical cord, they just put him up on me and I told 'em, "Get that ugly baby off of me!" He was all covered with blood. It upset me. They took him, washed him off, put him back in my arms. I was just so tired. All I could say was, "He look just like William." And I turned my head to the other side. It took me a long time to get use to Marquis. I didn't want to accept at fifteen I have a baby. It took me about two months to get use, to get really use to Marquis. (Sherita, fifteen, black, Washington, D.C.)

> I was going to have an abortion since I was only fifteen, but my family talked me out of it because of their religion, I love my baby now, but I'm only sixteen. I feel like I'm still a child—and here I have a child. It's completely changed my life. I look at other sixteen-year-olds and know that I can never be like them again. I sometimes wonder if an abortion wouldn't have been better. (Angela, sixteen, white, Colorado)

> It's hard to be a parent by yourself. If I had it to do over again, I'd do things really different. When people tell you it's going to be difficult, believe them. My child is with me all

the time . . . shopping, school, wherever I go. It's even harder than they say it is. I knew it would be hard, but not this hard.

Why is it that young people have babies, despite these depressing stories in which teens frankly admit how difficult it is for them to be mothers, and despite the national consensus that it's a very bad idea? No one in the United States is in favor of early child-bearing: elected officials campaign against it, the public disapproves of it, and professionals warn that it is costly for everyone concerned. Even the group thought to be most accepting of unwed teenage mothers—the African American community—is far more disapproving than most people think. Acceptance of a teenage mother or father is not the same as approval: young mothers, both black and white, often report widespread censure from those around them. Their own mothers, many of whom were once teenage mothers themselves and were hoping for a better life for their daughters, sometimes express a disappointment bordering on rage.

So why do they do it? Why do approximately one million young women get pregnant each year? More than half a million carry their babies to term, and about two-thirds of them will be unmarried when they give birth. Certainly, adolescents live in a world very different from that of adults, but the evidence suggests that age is not the only factor leading teenagers to reject the path those older and wiser would choose for them. Through their actions, teens are trying to come to terms, sometimes ineptly, with the immense social and economic challenges they face in today's world: a shrinking job market, an indifferent community network, and public skepticism about the worth of minorities. Early pregnancy and childbearing are not an isolated problem restricted to a small but growing number of poor, young, and minority women; they are the result of an array of problems in American society—problems that have no easy solutions. Unwed teenage mothers are pioneers on a frontier where increasing numbers of Americans are now settling.

DREAMS AND REALITIES

Today, half of all marriages end in divorce, only half of divorced fathers make their full court-ordered child support payments, and unwed fathers visit their children more often than divorced fathers who have remarried. Even as the cultural meanings of "husband" and "wife" are shifting, men and women are expected to work in the paid labor force for much of their adult lives. Although there are still "men's jobs" and "women's jobs," one can no longer automatically assume that the former are better paid and more secure than the latter. In the tidy world of the 1950s, society expected that women would be virgins when they married (or at least when they got engaged); would remain married throughout their lives to the same man; would stay home, take care of the housework, and raise the children while their husband worked at a stable, well-paid job that he would keep until he decided to retire. This predictable scenario no longer exists for today's teenagers, although many of its cultural ideals live on in their dreams.

What it means to be an adult man or woman is now in constant flux, and we do not yet live in a world of perfect gender equality. Indeed, the sexual revolution seems to have stalled: women have taken on many of the responsibilities of men, but men have yet to assume their fair share of the nurturing and caretaking roles traditionally assigned to

women. On the one hard, a young woman can no longer expect that she will have a husband on whom she can be totally dependent, both economically and emotionally. On the
other hand, she can't expect a husband to share the burdens of child rearing and homemaking equally. Such changes in gender roles intersect with new uncertainties surrounding the meanings of race and class in American society. Between World War II and
1973, when wages were steadily rising, minorities and blue-collar workers could hope for
the same job mobility and financial stability that white professionals enjoyed. But today's
young people must compete intensely for jobs that are increasingly scarce, and must
strive to meet meritocratic criteria that punish the less advantaged. They confront the
future with far less assurance.

Young women in particular are finding life extremely complex. The rules that applied in their mothers' day were simple, at least in theory: do what it takes to get a good
man, and keep him happy. Now women are aware of what this formula can lead to: displaced homemakers, divorcees and widows who are unprepared to support themselves,
women who think they have no value unless they have a male partner. But dreams die
hard. Today's young women say that they want a career in addition to, not instead of, a
family life. No teenager hopes to end up as an unmarried mother on welfare. Although
many disadvantaged teens do dream of motherhood, they dream of white-picket-fence
motherhood, or at least the version of it to which girls from poor neighborhoods can realistically aspire.

> I want to have an average American life, not the average Puerto Rican life with a break-
> up here and a fight there. (Diane, Hispanic, New Jersey)

> [I see myself] mainly being a housewife, a mother, and probably going to school, trying to
> get my trade or something like that. I want me a job too, but jobs is so hard to find. I want
> one through the University. My sister told me, she said, "You can't be picky and choosy."
> So I told her, "Okay, I guess I just want me a job so bad." (Roberta, eighteen, black,
> Florida)

> I don't want to be dependent on my parents for the rest of my life. I want to help out, even
> though my parents aren't putting any pressure on me. (Woman from rural New England,
> eighteen, white)

> I want to live in a two-bedroom apartment with a TV and carpeting. Nice and clean. If
> I'm older I have a car. I'd rather work at night and have somebody be there or early in the
> morning and come home by two or three. Other than that I be satisfied. Once I do what
> I want to do, I don't go back, I keep going. That's what I want to do. Get on my own with
> my baby and get situated. You know, I be having a good job. (Young woman living in an
> East Coast city)

> I want to be a good mother, giving my kid all, everythin', and makin' my kids go to school,
> college, somethin' that I can't get.

Unfortunately, the odds against achieving even these modest dreams are getting
longer. Young women with limited educational and labor market skills face many more
obstacles to a stable relationship and a secure job than they used to, especially when they

are members of minority groups and come from poor homes. And the young men in their lives have bleaker employment prospects than ever, making them a slender reed for young women to rely upon. Roberta's sister is right: when it comes to men and jobs, these young women can't be "picky and choosy." But even their willingness to be adaptable may not ensure that they get what they want.

It is hard for young people who have grown up in poverty to figure out how to make their dreams come true, how to negotiate the small steps that get them from one point to another. Moreover, young women of all classes must find a way to balance investments in their own future with commitment to a partner. Women have always had to decide whether and when to make such "selfish" investments, as opposed to devoting their energies to meeting the needs of a partner and children. Today they have to make decisions whose outcomes cannot be known. And teens of both sexes are on radically new terrain when it comes to making choices about sexual activity, marriage, family, and work. The sexual revolution has transformed Americans' values, attitudes, and behavior in ways that are unlikely to be reversed. How do teens—should teens—think and act in this new world, and reconcile its alluring promises with its hard realities? How can they manage the consequences of their sexual freedom?

Many people of all political persuasions think that teenagers should simply stop having sex. Liberals argue that public campaigns have induced teenagers to curtail their drug use and that such campaigns could likewise induce them to abstain from sex; conservatives plead for "a little virginity." Unfortunately both groups are working against the historical tide. Premarital sexual activity has become steadily more common in the twentieth century, throughout the industrialized world. But the sexual revolution has not been fully integrated into people's lives, especially the lives of teenagers. The American public is still unsure whether the tide can or should be turned back. Given society's deep ambivalence about sexual activity among teenagers, young women often find themselves in a state of confusion—a state that is often apparent in the ethnographic accounts. They tell researchers about their decisions concerning sex, conception, and pregnancy. But when we say that teens "decide" on a course of action in such matters, we may be using much too active a verb. On the one hand, young people are told to "just say no"; on the other, their friends, the media, and society at large foster the idea that sexual activity among teenagers is widespread and increasingly commonplace. If a young woman doesn't want to have sex, she has little in the way of support, since sexual activity has come to be expected.

> They looked at a virgin as being something shameful. They were the type of people who would always tell what happened if they made out with a boy or a boy made out with them. I was the only one they never heard from. They would say. "You don't know what you're missing." The more they talked the more curious I got. (Theresa, eighteen, black, Washington, D.C.)

> All of my friends were having sex and I was curious to see what it was all about. I didn't even know the guy very well and I don't even want to know him. It wasn't like it is shown on TV or in the movies. I didn't even enjoy it. (Young woman from Colorado)

> All my friends were doing it and they dared me. After all, I was seventeen and had never had sex. I thought maybe I really was missing something. (I wasn't.)

Some girls will have sex to get guys to like them. Some girls do it thinking. "Well, I'm going to keep this boyfriend." If I could, I would tell them. "Don't, until you feel they respect and love you. You're too good to be chasing and trying to make someone stay with you." (Robyn, black, Colorado)

The sexuality that young women express in such ethnographic accounts is often curiously passive. Although a few young women brag about their sexual conquests and skills, many simply make themselves available, in part because it seems that everyone else is doing it.

Even as they feel pressure to be sexually active, teens are urged to abstain, or at least to "be careful" and use contraceptives. Thus, in their accounts they describe their first sexual intercourse as an experience remarkably devoid of pleasure. They are anxious, in a hurry to get it over with, eager to cross the Rubicon in a leap before courage fails; or they see it as something that "just happened," without anyone's having made an active decision.

Then he asked me to have sex. I was scared and everything, and it was like, "What am I gonna do?" The first time I told him no and he understood. We watched TV. And he brought me home. Then a couple of days after that he asked me again, I said okay. I guess I said so because I just wanted to show him I wasn't scared to have sex. I was scared. And he kinda knew I was scared. But I guess I was playing a role. I wanted to show him that I'm not scared. So we had sex . . . and now it's like we don't get along. (Young black woman from Oakland, California)

We was going together for two years and we didn't do anything. I was like "no" and he was scared also. Finally we just—hurry up and get it over with. We just took off our clothes real quick. Just hurry up and get it over with and we both shaking and crying. (High school student in a midwestern city)

I didn't talk to my boyfriend about sex, and he didn't talk to me. One day we were together and started hugging and kissing, then we just did it. (Latisha, fifteen, black, Chicago)

And I used to go home and he would call me on the phone and then we were like that for about a month or so and then we just started to get involved. I don't know, he just asked me and I said sure, if that was what you want to do . . . We just did it to do it and then I just got pregnant. (Sally, fifteen, white)

He was someone to lean on. When I was depressed, I figured, I'll lean on him. Next thing you know, I figured I started to listen to him. Then I saw him as more of a friend. Then why not kiss him? Why not touch him? It seemed that one thing led to another. Afterward we never made a big deal out of it like, "Wow, wasn't that great last night." We never even talked much about it . . . We said we shouldn't have let that happen. It won't happen again. And then it did happen again. (Ivy, seventeen, black, Boston)

Not only are many young women confused and indecisive when it comes to their first sexual encounters, but they often know few adults whom they can comfortably ask for guidance. According to their own accounts, even their mothers offer little or no help:

Only thing she said was, "Don't be out there messing with no boys." And that was it. (Sherita, twelve, black, Washington, D.C.)

I love my mother, but she never really talked to me, and I don't feel like I can talk to her about private matters. She acts like we shouldn't talk about sex. She only told me after my period, that I shouldn't go with boys. (Latisha, fifteen, black, Chicago)

She didn't want me to know nothing about sex but "just don't do it." But I was like—I was like, gosh, but everybody is doing this and I wanted to try it, too. (Fourteen-year-old, attending high school in a midwestern city)

The little information available on young men shows that they, too, see themselves as failures if they have not had sex. For them, sexual activity is an indication of maturity and masculinity.

If they haven't [had intercourse] then they are like outcasts. Like, "Man, you never made love to a girl!" Some of them get teased a lot. It's like on the baseball team and they start talking about that and you have got the younger guys out there and you could tell because they are all quiet and stuff and they won't talk. Some of the other people start laughing at them and start getting on them and get them kind of upset. (Male high school student in a midwestern city)

Premarital sexual activity has become increasingly common in the twentieth century. This is partly due to the fact that people are getting married later, but it is also a function of America's transition from a rural, kinship based society to a modern industrial one that tends to disconnect sex from marriage. Some experts argue that the real sexual revolution in the United States occurred in the 1880s and was largely over by 1915. Others maintain that there were two sexual revolutions, one between 1915 and 1925 and the other between 1965 and 1975. All agree, however, that sexual activity among teenagers is not peculiar to the late twentieth century; rather, it is the result of long-term trends shaped by social and economic forces that are probably irreversible. Furthermore, whatever it is about modernity that makes sex independent from marriage, it is present in most of the industrialized nations. Teens all over the developed world are engaging in sex before marriage. When in 1984 the United Nations undertook a survey of adolescent sexual and reproductive behavior, it concluded that "without doubt, the proportion of teenagers who have experienced sex by age nineteen has been increasing steadily over the years among all adolescents." Even conservative Japan—a communitarian society with strongly internalized social controls—has reported increases in sexual activity among its teenagers, as well as a rise in out-of-wedlock childbearing. Surveys conducted by the Japanese government in 1981 found that in Japan about 28 percent of young women and 37 percent of young men were sexually active by the end of their teenage years—figures that were less than half of those for the United States but that, compared with the proportions in 1974, represented an increase of 40 percent for young men and an amazing 150 percent for young women.

According to conservatives, the fact that contraception was made available to teenagers in the late 1960s was the fuel that ignited the explosion of early sex. Prior to 1964 contraceptives were nominally illegal in many jurisdictions, were never mentioned in public (much less advertised), and were difficult to obtain. In pharmacies, condoms were typically kept behind the counter and some pharmacists in small towns refused to sell them to young men they knew to be unmarried. Since out-of-wedlock pregnancy was stigmatized and likely to lead to a clandestine abortion or a hasty marriage, there is a certain logic to the notion that the stunning reversal in the status of contraception—from illegal and unmentionable to widely available at public expense—fostered the spectacular increase in sexual activity among teenagers. And since this increase in activity and the proliferation of low-cost birth control clinics both occurred in the late 1960s and early 1970s, there is at least a temporal connection between the two.

This commonsensical and comforting notion (comforting because it implies that one way to curtail sexual activity among teens is to limit the availability of contraception) has several things wrong with it. First, a great many aspects of American society were changing in the sixties and seventies. Public attitudes shifted radically on issues such as contraception, premarital sex, abortion, and illegitimacy; family planning clinics were only one part of the context surrounding teenagers' behavior. Second, as we have seen, young people throughout the industrialized world have increased their premarital sexual activity, despite the fact that policies regarding contraception vary widely from country to country. Finally, and perhaps most tellingly, in the 1980s federal funding of family planning services dropped sharply—from $400 million in 1980 to $250 million in 1990—but sexual activity among teens continued to increase. The states compensated in some measure for the cutbacks, but they by no means filled the gap entirely. Though it is disappointing not to be able to pinpoint a cause for the increase in sexual activity among the young, historical and international evidence suggests that it is probably the result of a blend of factors. What *is* extremely clear is that the welter of societal changes and conflicting messages surrounding sexual activity has left many young people confused, misinformed, and adrift.

THE PATH TO PREGNANCY

Some teenagers get pregnant for exactly the same reason that older women do: they are married and they want a child. It is true that in the United States marriage rates among teens have declined dramatically and the median age at first marriage is higher than it has ever been. Still, in 1990 about 7 percent of all American teens (about 10 percent of all eighteen- and nineteen-year olds) were married, and about one out of every three babies born to a teen was born to a married mother. It is important to keep in mind that discussions of early pregnancy and childbearing include these married teenagers, whom the public usually does not think of as part of the constellation of problems associated with "teenage pregnancy."

Other teens are unmarried but are using contraception to avoid pregnancy. Stereotypes to the contrary, teenagers are using more contraception, and using it more effectively, than ever before. In 1982 about half of all American teenagers used a contraceptive method the first time they had sex; in 1988 about 70 percent of them did. Of all the sexually active teenage women surveyed in the 1988 National Survey of Family Growth who were currently having sex, who were neither pregnant nor seeking pregnancy, and who had not been sterilized, about 80 percent were using some method of contraception. Among poor teens, those whose family income was less than twice the poverty level, the rate was a little lower (72.5 percent), and among affluent teens it was a little higher. But if teens are using contraception to such an extent, why aren't their pregnancy rates plummeting?

One major reason is statistical. Teens today actually do have a lower risk of getting pregnant: in 1972 the odds that a sexually involved teen would become pregnant were about one in four; by 1990 they had decreased to one in five. (These figures include married teens, who accounted for approximately 26 percent of all sexually experienced teens in 1972, but only about 15 percent in 1984.) Unfortunately, however, the decline in the odds that an individual teen would get pregnant did not lead to a decline in the pregnancy rate for all teenagers: the increase in effective contraceptive use was offset by the fact that so many more unmarried teenagers became sexually involved during this period. In 1972, in a population of approximately 10 million teenage women, about 2.5 million were sexually active—a rate of roughly 25 percent. By 1984 the total number of teenagers had decreased slightly to 9 million, but the number of sexually active teens had grown to 4 million—a rate of about 50 percent. Thus, although an individual teen had a smaller chance of getting pregnant, the fact that there were twice as many teens at risk meant that there were more pregnancies. Still, the two trends balanced each other so that the pregnancy rate among all teenage women remained roughly stable: in 1972 it was 95 per thousand; in 1984 it was 108 per thousand; and in 1988 it was 117 per thousand. This may be even better news than it seems: some observers think that teenagers' rates of premarital sexual activity are leveling off, and since there is no evidence that the propensity to use contraception is declining, some of the incidence of pregnancy among teens may be a lag effect that will persist only while they are learning how to use contraception well. But the pregnancy rates among American teenagers are worrisome, especially when about half of the pregnancies end in abortion. Despite more than two decades' worth of research on the matter, there are no clear answers as to why the rates remain so high in the United States, compared to those in other countries.

Within a general pattern of increased contraceptive use, there are a number of factors that enable one to predict which teenagers will use contraception more consistently and effectively than others. For example, the higher a teen's socioeconomic status and educational aspirations, the more likely he or she is to use contraception. Older teens are more consistent users than younger ones, for two reasons: sexually active teens get better at it over time; and teens who are older when they have their first sexual experience are more careful than those who start at an earlier age. Contraceptive use also tends to be relationship specific. That is, young men and women are not users or nonusers, but change their practice with individual partners. We know that older women (that is women whose teen years are behind them) are likely to get pregnant after the breakup of a relationship: about one-fourth of all babies born out of wedlock are born to women who have left one marriage but have not entered into another. This suggests that when experienced users move out of a stable relationship, the meaning and practice of contraception change. Thus, young women are even more at risk, since their sexual relationships tend to be more short-lived and sporadic. Studies have shown that sexually active teens in fact go through long periods during which they have no sex at all because they are not involved in a relationship and often have relatively low rates of sex even when they are. And when sexual activity is unpredictable, using contraceptives becomes more difficult.

Contraceptive use may also change over the course of a relationship. When young people have sex for the first time, they tend to rely on male protection methods, notably condoms. In 1982, 23 percent of teenage women reported using condoms the first time they had intercourse, and an additional 13 percent said they used withdrawal; in 1988 about

65 percent used condoms and virtually none used withdrawal. After their first sexual encounter, unmarried adolescents tend increasingly to use female contraceptives (diaphragms and the Pill) instead of male methods. In 1982 about 43 percent of sexually active teenage women were on the Pill, 15 percent were using condoms, and almost 30 percent were using no contraception at all. Similarly, in 1988 about 47 percent were on the Pill, 27 percent were using condoms, and 20 percent were using no contraception. Contrary to stereotype, young black women are *more* likely than young white women to use highly effective contraception, mostly because they are much more likely to be Pill users; but they also tend to begin using contraception at a later age, so their overall risk of pregnancy is higher. Poor teens and affluent teens are almost equally likely to be Pill users.

So why do teens get pregnant if so many of them are using contraception? The short answer is that some get pregnant the first time they have sex, because they use no contraception, use relatively ineffective methods, or use methods inadequately. Others get pregnant during transitions—either within a relationship, as they move from male methods to female methods, or between relationships, when they stop using a certain method. (About 70 percent of all sexually active teenage women have had more than one partner by the time they reach their twenties.) Still others get pregnant because they use no contraception: either they have never used it, or they are not presently using a method they used earlier. Finally, a small number get pregnant even though they are using contraception faithfully.

One troubling and rarely acknowledged fact is that teenagers' sexual involvements are not always consensual, particularly in the case of young women. The younger the woman, the more likely this is to be a problem. In one national survey of American teens, about 7 percent answered yes when they were asked, "Was there ever a time when you were forced to have sex against your will, or were raped?" Thirteen percent of the white women and 8 percent of the black women reported having coercive sex before they were twenty; among young men, the figures were 1.9 percent for whites and 6.1 percent for blacks. An astonishing 74 percent of all women who had had sex before the age of fourteen reported that they had had coerced sex; among those who had had sex before the age of fifteen, the figure was 60 percent. Since most experts think that the respondents in such interviews underreport coercive sex, these numbers are probably conservative. And the question used in the survey defined coercive sex rather narrowly: as the national debate on rape and date rape makes clear, it is difficult to draw the exact boundaries of sexual consent.

In the days when premarital sex was considered wrong, young men and women typically negotiated the meaning of each step (the first kiss, the first caress, "petting") and where it fit into the relationship; the woman permitted increasing sexual intimacy in return for greater commitment from the man. Young women today have no such clear-cut rules. Society has become more tolerant of the notion that an unmarried couple may be sexually involved if they are emotionally committed to each other, but the emotional and social context within which sexual encounters take place has become quite fluid.

When sexual activity is coerced, as it is for a small but important subset of American teens, it is extremely unlikely that the victim will have planned ahead to use contraception. But even in consensual situations, young people—especially young women—still face obstacles to effective contraception use. Social pressures concerning gender roles and sexual activity exert some real constraints on the ability to use contraception effectively—constraints that are similar in effect, if not in degree or kind to those of coercive sex.

During the past thirty years, for example, contraceptive use has become increasingly feminized: both men and women tend to think that contraception is the responsibility of the woman and that it's the woman's fault when something goes wrong. This represents a revolution—one so subtle that most Americans have scarcely noticed it. Until 1965 condoms were the most frequently used form of contraception in America, at least among married couples. There was a time when a young man would carry a lone, crumbling condom with him wherever he went, and carry it so long that it would wear its oulines into his wallet. But with the development of the Pill and the IUD, contraception came to be considered something for which women were responsible and accountable. Interestingly, concerns about sexually transmitted diseases (especially AIDS) and the health effects of the Pill have made condoms popular once again, only today they are marketed to both men and women. What this means in practice is that couples often must negotiate which contraceptives to use and when to use them, with little in the way of clear social rules.

In such negotiations, women tend to be culturally handicapped by society's expectations of appropriate female sexual behavior. The first time a woman has intercourse, she is considered to be "giving away" something valuable: her virginity. If she is young and unmarried, she is culturally enjoined from looking too "ready." (This may explain the increasing popularity of the condom, which the man usually provides and which became popular among teens prior to the recent concern with AIDS and other sexually transmitted diseases.) An unmarried woman who is in the early stages of getting involved in a relationship and who must not look too "ready" for sex is therefore forced to rely on the goodwill and motivation of her partner, who may not be as committed to the relationship as she is and who will suffer fewer consequences if something goes wrong. The first time the couple has sex, he is the one who typically takes the contraceptive precautions, yet he has a very different set of incentives and faces a very different set of risks. Many of these pressures at first intercourse recur every time a woman has a new sexual partner. (Most adolescent women are still having sex in serially monogamous relationships.)

The prevalence of premarital sex means that a "nice girl" is no longer defined as a young woman who has never had sex. Rather, it means a young woman who has had sex but not too much of it, or who is sexually active but not promiscuous. Alas, one simple way of showing that one is a "nice girl" is to be unprepared for sex—to have given no prior thought to contraception. Both at first sex and with each new partner, a young woman is thus subject to powerful cultural pressures that penalize her for taking responsibility. To use contraception, a woman has to anticipate sexual activity by locating the impetus within herself, rather than in the man who has overcome her hesitancy. She must plan for sex, must be prepared to speak about contraception frankly with someone she may not know very well (at the time when, according to cultural expectations, her emotions rather than her intellect are supposed to hold sway), and must put her own long-term welfare before the short-term pleasure of the couple, especially of the man.

When young women talk about the obstacles to using contraception, they frequently describe the way in which conflicting social pressures intersect with their own ambivalent and contradictory feelings:

> I went to Planned Parenthood and I had my aunt help me get the diaphragm. I didn't like it, it didn't feel comfortable and I was embarrassed, You know, jump up [during sex] and say, "Um, wait a minute."

Many American teenagers receive at least some information about contraception (often in sex education classes), but this information must be assessed in terms of a complex set of parameters concerning the way in which a teenager views sexual activity and why he or she is using contraception. Young people often report misunderstandings about contraception—misunderstandings that are shared by those around them.

> I think I was thirteen when I first started having sex. My best friend thought I was crazy 'cause I went to my mother and said, "Well, Mom, I like this boy and I might be doing something with him and would you take me to get birth control?" And she said, "No, because once you start taking these pills, you'll become sterile." See, I love kids, I love 'em and I want 'em. So it scared me . . . but she knew I was going to do something. (Sixteen-year-old)

> I wish I had taken the pill. I waited too long. I just kept telling myself, "Well, I can wait a little bit longer." And then I found out it was too late. I wasn't afraid to take it—I just kept putting it off and putting it off, and I put it off too long. (Kimberly, white, Colorado)

In short, the skills a young woman needs in order to use contraception effectively are precisely the skills that society discourages in "nice girls," who are expected to be passive, modest, shy, sexually inexperienced (or at least less experienced than their partners), and dedicated to the comfort of others. A woman who obtains contraception in anticipation of sexual activity is thought to be "looking for sex" (as teens say) and is culturally devalued. More to the point, she risks being devalued within the relationship. When it comes to contraception, she is caught in a net of double binds. She is the one who is supposed to "take care of it," the one at whom most contraceptive programs are aimed, and the one for whose body the most effective methods have been developed. Yet she is expected to be diffident about sex, and interested in it only because love and erotic arousal have spontaneously led her to be "carried away." And if she seems too interested in sex for its own sake, as evidenced by her use of contraception, she is in a weak position to trade sex for commitment and intimacy from the man involved. These pressures are often exacerbated because the woman's partner is older than she is, and presumably more experienced and sophisticated. Scattered data suggest that the partners of teenage mothers are typically older, sometimes significantly older: in 1988, although about 80 percent of teenage mothers had a partner who was within a few years of their own age, 29 percent had a partner who was six or more years older than they were; for very young mothers (fifteen-year-olds), the figure climbed to 30 percent.

A couple may go through a period in which they use no contraception, while they try to work out the meaning of the relationship and how contraception fits into it. Young women who seek contraceptive services sometimes say that they are doing so because their relationship is becoming more serious—meaning they have used no contraception up to that point. Of course, their statistical risk of getting pregnant is just as high in the early months of their relationship as it is later, and may in fact be higher: one study showed that most young women who got pregnant did so in the early, perilous part of their relationship. This suggests that what has changed are not the statistical odds of getting pregnant, but the social cost. Once a relationship is defined as getting serious, it's easier for the young woman to make the commitment to contraception without risking her commitment to her boyfriend. And it may be easier for him to argue for contraception without seeming as if he's "leading her on."

So commitment to and by a partner may counteract some of the pressures that serve as obstacles to contraception. Some young women say that they put off seeking contraceptive services because they are afraid of being found out, particularly by their parents. Yet once their relationship is defined as serious and the young man has demonstrated his commitment, the young woman's sexual desire is transformed from potentially promiscuous into true love, and she is equipped to take the public step of obtaining contraception. Young women whose significant others (parents, partners, and best friends) urge them to get contraception are more likely to obtain it before becoming sexually active and more likely to use it effectively.

Teenagers from different classes and racial groups tend to have different patterns of contraceptive use, both at first intercourse and subsequently. Although there are few studies of the way in which class and race affect the meanings attached to specific contraceptives and to contraception in general, one can make two broad observations. First, when sexual partners come from different social or ethnic groups (as they increasingly do these days), they may have additional problems communicating about contraception. Second, researchers who study sexual and contraceptive decisions in contexts where AIDS is a factor tell us that young women who have a sense of power and efficacy in their lives are more able to protect themselves in their sexual relationships than women who feel weak. Since many poor and minority women lack sources of esteem and power in their lives, they may be more vulnerable in their relationships.

Of course, the desire or lack of desire for a baby plays an important role in the decisions that people make about contraception. The American public often assumes that teenagers have babies simply because they know little about, or ignore, birth control practices. But in many cases this is untrue. In 1984 a sixteen-year-old urban black woman named Tauscha Vaughan made the following comment to *Washington Post* reporter Leon Dash: "Will you please stop asking me about birth control? Girls out here know all about birth control. There's too much birth control out here. All of them know about it. Even when they twelve, they know what birth control is. Girls out here get pregnant because they want to have babies!" This young woman highlights an important fact: that decisions about contraception are intimately related to whether or not one wants a child. But the situation is more complex than this simple statement would make it appear.

When young women talk about their lives, it is clear that their feelings about childbearing exist in a context of numerous shifting assessments. For example, they often describe a partner who does not use contraception or who stops using a contraceptive.

> It [the condom] didn't feel comfortable, and I didn't enjoy it either, so I kept taking my chances on withdrawal. (Reggie, black, Washington, D.C.; father of Tauscha Vaughan's baby)

> We had sex for about a year before I got pregnant. I wasn't using birth control, not at first. Then he said, we'll use something. We didn't really talk about it. The condoms he used hurt him and they irritated me, you know, real bad. I didn't enjoy it and I said, "No, I don't think we'll have it, if it's gonna bother me so bad."

> I knew that it could happen; I just thought I would be lucky and not get caught. We used condoms sometimes, but he said it feels better without them. But when I knew I was pregnant I kept acting like it wasn't real. (Young woman in a Teen Parenting program with black, white, and Hispanic participants)

For many adults, quotes such as these are just one more example of teenagers' fecklessness, of their inability to plan ahead or to see the consequences of their own actions. But when such accounts are read more carefully, many of them reveal that behind the seeming aimlessness are some serious, complex, and often hidden negotiations about the meaning of the relationship—negotiations that teens, like adults, are often reluctant to conduct straightforwardly. In many cases, for example, a young woman thinks that if she and her boyfriend use no contraception, there is a tacit assumption that they are sharing the risk: he must love her so much that he wants to have a child with her and is willing to stand by her if she does:

> I expected the father to be helpful; to take care of the baby. All three of us to go places and have fun. Live together as a family. (Shana, black, Oakland, California)

> I expected commitment of just being a father. Of being there saying "I'm going to help you. I'll be there to take care of Jimmy when you want, when you need to do other things." I expected his support emotionally, financially as much as he could, I expected him to be there for me . . . I expected him to love me because I was the woman who had his baby. But he loves everyone else who didn't. (Diane, black, Oakland, California)

Cynics may ascribe such expectations to wishful thinking; but caught up in a relationship, boys sometimes do make promises—promises that are difficult to keep.

> We were going to be married in April. We didn't want to have a baby right away, but neither of us wanted to use birth control, so when I asked J. if he was ready for the consequences he said yes. He said if I got pregnant he'd want to be with me and the baby always, which is what he said when he found out I was pregnant. Then he changed his mind and split. (Seventeen-year-old, white, rural New England)

> I dated John for about a year. He always told me that if anything happened he would take care of me. When I told him I was pregnant he said that it wasn't his baby. He dropped me and started dating my best friend. It was hard for me to accept that he didn't care as much as he said he did before I got pregnant. (Robyn, black, Colorado)

Although some teenagers try to prevent pregnancy and fail, others get pregnant because they believe pregnancy is not such a bad thing. Young unmarried women, like young married ones, may become pregnant because they want to or at least because they are not sufficiently motivated to avoid it. Experts have long debated whether teenagers want their pregnancies and births. A recent study by the Alan Guttmacher Institute estimated that only 7 percent of all such pregnancies were intended. Does this fully capture what we know about teens and their plans?

It seems at first glance that most young women would prefer not to have a baby. About half of all pregnant teens have abortions, and about 87 percent of those who carried their babies to term in 1988 described their pregnancies as unintended. These findings come from the National Survey of Family Growth (conducted in four cycles: 1973, 1976, 1982, and 1988), which asked a national sample of women the following question: "Was the reason you (had stopped / were not) using any contraceptive method because you yourself wanted to become pregnant?" If a woman answered no, she was asked another question: "It is sometimes difficult to recall these things; but just before that pregnancy began, would you say you probably wanted a(nother) baby at some time or probably not?" This is a rather inflexible way to investigate a fluid, complex, and constantly reexamined decision. The National Center for Health Statistics is revising its methods for the next round of the survey, but we must keep in mind the language of the questions as they were posed if we are to understand the responses fully. Until the 1970s, the typical woman in need of family planning was a woman who had already had all the children she wanted and who was at risk of having additional children she did not want, and the language of the questions reflected the situation of such women. Teens fit into this group awkwardly, if at all. Since teens are just starting to build their families, the questions posed by the survey do not reveal their plans or preferences very well. Few teens have babies that are unwanted in this traditional sense; mostly they say that their babies came earlier than planned. Thus far, the wording of survey questions has not allowed researchers to assess the effects (if any) that early childbearing may have on women's life plans.

The concept of wantedness has been subject to a good deal of criticism. A woman may find it very difficult to tell interviewers that she did not want her baby. Moreover, an unwanted pregnancy may well result in a wanted child. And there is a deeper and more philosophical problem with efforts to measure wantedness by means of questionnaires, particularly in the case of teenagers. Surveys assume that people perceive clear choices and that they feel empowered to act on them. Such certainty and confidence can, of course, be deduced in some instances. If a woman and her partner say that they consistently and effectively used birth control up to the date of conception, and then terminate the pregnancy, we can be fairly confident that they did not want the child. Likewise, if a woman tells an interviewer that she deliberately stopped using contraception because she wanted to become pregnant, we can be reasonably certain that she wanted her baby. But for most teenage mothers, these two extremes rarely capture the lived experience. Contraception, particularly among unmarried people and particularly among the young, may be a casualty of unspoken dynamics in the relationship. Say, for instance, a young man complains about using condoms and finally decides not to use one, and his girlfriend interprets this to mean that he will marry her if she gets pregnant. Is her subsequent pregnancy a wanted pregnancy? What complicated negotiations between a woman and a man determine whether a baby is wanted or unwanted?

Still, the information that interviewers glean from women is interesting, especially when it changes over time. In 1973 the National Survey of Family Growth revealed that of all the children that had been born to American wives in the previous five years, 14 percent had been unwanted at the time of conception. In 1982, when the survey included both married and unmarried mothers, it found that only 7.7 percent of the children born in the previous five years had been unwanted. By 1988, the figure had risen again, to 10.3 percent. And the survey revealed significant differences according to age, race, and socioeconomic status: black women, poor women, and older women were all more likely (again, because of the way the question was worded) to tell interviewers that their children had been unwanted.

But the data are most troubling and most opaque in the case of teenagers. Since the survey asked women if they wanted a baby or another baby at some time, it presumably succeeded in reaching teenagers who had definitely not wanted a baby. Prior to 1982 unmarried women were not interviewed unless they had a child living with them, so we have comparative data only from 1982 and 1988. But in 1988, about 15 percent of white teens and about 30 percent of black teens said that they had not wanted their baby at the time of conception. Thus, although many young mothers did find themselves with babies they had not wanted, 85 percent of white teens and 70 percent of black teens told researchers that they had indeed wanted their children. Most, however, were unhappy about the timing of the birth: more than eight out of ten teenagers who said that they had wanted their babies also asserted that they had become pregnant sooner than planned.

In 1988 analysts took a new approach to the data. Previously the survey had made a distinction only between babies that had been wanted at the time of conception and those that had not; and this made sense, given that the women of interest were older and had nearly completed building their families. Wanted babies were then subdivided into those wanted at the time of conception and those wanted later. In 1988, however, the number of unwanted children was combined with the number of wanted children who had arrived sooner than expected. The resulting new category of "unintended" births was probably designed to accommodate the new demographic reality that teens represented. But the concept of unintendedness is just as slippery as the notion of wantedness. From the available data, we just cannot tell when a young woman would have preferred to have the baby that came too soon. In view of the way the survey questions were worded, a teen who was eager to be a mother but who would have preferred to wait a few months cannot be distinguished from a teen who planned eventually to become a mother but who viewed her recent pregnancy as a serious disruption in her life plans.

According to other studies. poor teenagers are more likely than affluent ones to report that a pregnancy was intended, and are more likely to continue their pregnancies to term. Furthermore, those who deliberately become pregnant and who do not seek abortions tend to be less advantaged teenagers. The entire issue of wantedness must thus be considered in the context of teenagers' available choices, which are often highly constrained.

■ READING 34

Family Values against the Odds

Katherine S. Newman

Rosa Lee Cunningham, the subject of Leon Dash's Pulitzer Prize–winning series in the *Washington Post*, is an epitome of poverty for the end of the twentieth century.[1] Born the eldest girl in a Washington, D.C., family that had been liberated from the privations of southern sharecropping only in the 1930s, Rosa Lee quickly spiraled down into oblivion.

Rosa Lee's first child was born when she was a mere fourteen years old. By the time she was twenty-four, Rosa Lee's children numbered eight and their six fathers were nowhere to be seen. She raised her kids on her own by waitressing in nightclubs, selling drugs, and shoplifting. In the wake of her own disillusionment and the overwhelming burden of taking care of her children, Rosa Lee was drawn to heroin. When stealing to support her family and her habit proved unreliable, she sold herself on the street and then turned her own daughter into a hooker to maintain the needed cash flow.

Responses to Dash's series, and the book that followed, have taken a predictable path: reviewers have been as worried as they have been disgusted by the cultural disintegration Rosa Lee and her ilk represent. Rosa Lee, who could not stay away from men of questionable character, and then did disastrously poorly by the children that resulted, takes center stage as the prototypical underclass mother, the prime mover in her own despair. And the crime and degradation that follow are depicted as the inevitable result of a culture of poverty so deep that it defies remedy. No jobs program, no drug program, no heavenly social worker, can rescue someone like Rosa Lee Cunningham. She is a lost soul, with children condemned to repeat her mistakes,[2] while the rest of society suffers the consequences of predatory criminals in its midst.

Powerful portraits of this kind have shaped public impressions of inner-city families. They present implicit explanations for how poor people fall to the bottom of society's heap: by failing to control their impulses. American culture is predisposed to find such an explanation appealing, since it rests upon the view that people are masters of their own destinies, that they can, by dint of individual effort, control the circumstances of their lives. Those that fail fall to the ground where they belong, not because they have been denied opportunity, or are victims of forces larger than anyone could control, but because they have succumbed to temptation or lack the brains to do any better—the story told by Herrnstein and Murray's book *The Bell Curve*. It is a story as old as the Puritans and as resonant today as it was in the seventeenth century.

The inner city does indeed have more than its share of families like the Cunninghams. Their problems reflect the crushing personal costs of living in parts of our country where good jobs have gone the way of the dinosaurs, where schools can be hard to distinguish from penitentiaries, and where holding families together has become women's work, while the means to do so have become the object of a fierce competition. More than a few in central Harlem have found themselves in Rosa Lee's situation.

But they are a minority, and a despised one at that. They are so far from the accepted, approved personification of motherhood and family life that they do not even belong in the same world with the families of Latoya or Carmen. Journalists and scholars who write about the Rosa Lees of this world have focused their energies on those inner-city residents who are the most troubled and who inflict the greatest damage on their neighbors. Their passions are understandable, for in keeping with the spirit that animated the original War on Poverty, they want to reawaken America's conscience and persuade us that we have a cancer growing in the midst of our prosperity. That message worked effectively in the 1960s, when the country was bursting with economic growth, the middle class was secure in its comforts, and faith in the capacity of government to eradicate social ills had not yet been eviscerated.

The same message delivered in the 1990s has had the opposite impact. Focusing on the deviant cases, on the whoring mothers, the criminal fathers, the wilding teenagers, and the abandoned toddlers, merely confirms a knowing hopelessness or worse: a Darwinian conviction that perhaps we should just "let it burn," sacrificing the present generation in the hope of rehabilitating future ghetto dwellers. Attitudes have hardened in part as the litany of broken lives dominates the only "news" in print from the inner city.

It would be absurd to suggest that the downbeat reports are untrue. The "underclass" story is a persistent, intractable, and most of all depressing reality for those who cannot escape it. But there is a war for the soul of the ghetto, and it has two sides. On the other side of deviance lie the families who embrace mainstream values, even if they don't look like Ozzie and Harriet, who push their children to do better, even when they have not progressed far in life themselves. Indeed, these families—the working poor and many a "welfare family" as well—are the first to condemn Rosa Lees of their own neighborhood, to point to them as examples of what they don't want to be.

Who is winning this culture war? What are the *dominant* values of inner-city residents? The sociological emphasis on separated subcultures in the inner city has ignored the power of mainstream models and institutions like schools, the influence of the media, the convictions of poor parents, and the power of negative examples to shape the moral world of the ghetto poor. We must not confuse the irregular social structures of families—which do indeed depart from the canonical forms of middle-class society—with a separate set of values. Structure and culture can diverge in ghetto society as they do elsewhere in this country.

FAMILY VALUES

Latoya has a complicated family tree. Her mother, Ilene, who is on disability because of her diabetes, lives in the Bronx, far enough away to be in another world. Latoya's father, Alvin, has had many jobs in the course of his adult life—working mainly as a truck driver—and has only recently, in his later years, become once again a constant presence in Latoya's life. His problems with alcohol have made him a nuisance at times, but he has been welcomed back into the extended family fold because "he's blood" and has, for now at least, made a sincere effort to leave the booze behind.

Many years ago, Latoya's father began living with Elizabeth, then a recent migrant from rural Georgia, from a sleepy little town where there was nothing much to do and nowhere to go. First chance she got, Lizzie had boarded a bus for New York and begun her lifelong career cleaning houses for wealthy whites on New York's Upper East Side. She has been doing domestic work now for about twenty-five years, during which she gave birth to two daughters, Natasha and Stephanie, Latoya's half sisters through the father they share.

Though Alvin has been only sporadically in the picture, Latoya, Natasha, and Stephanie became a devoted band of sisters who look to Lizzie as the spiritual and practical head of the family. Together they form an extended family of long standing. They live within a few blocks of one another; they attend church together, especially on the important holidays.

Latoya was the first of the sisters to land a job at Burger Barn, but she was able to get Natasha on the crew not long thereafter. The two half sisters have worked together, covering for one another, blowing off the steam generated by confrontational customers, and supporting one another in the face of problem-seeking managers for nearly five years now. Little sister Stephanie, a junior in high school who has also had a summer stint at the Barn, makes it possible for Latoya to maintain a steady presence at work. It falls to Stephanie to retrieve Latoya's children from their city-funded day care center and after-school programs on those days when Latoya has to work late. Stephanie is often the one who stays with her nieces and nephews when Latoya has to work the night shift. Natasha used to do the same for Latoya.

Without the support that Natasha and Stephanie provide, Latoya would have a very hard time holding on to her job. But if we reduced the role these sisters play in Latoya's life to the instrumental need for emergency child care, we would miss the true depth of their interdependence. This is really one family, spread over several physical households in a pattern that will be familiar to readers of Carol Stack's classic book *All Our Kin*. Stack describes the complex exchange relations that characterize the families of the "Flats," a poor community in southern Illinois where goods and people circulate in a never-ending swap system. Reciprocal relations provide mothers with an insurance system against scarcity, unpredictable landlords, jobs that come and go, AFDC checks that get cut off without warning, and men who give what they can but much of the time find they have little to contribute.

FAMILY CIRCLES—SUPPORT STRUCTURES AMONG THE WORKING POOR

No one in Latoya's extended family network is on welfare; the adults are working, even Alvin, drinking problem and all. The children are in school. Yet because they are poor as well, these folk live in clusters of households that are perpetually intertwined. Although Latoya and Lizzie are separate "heads of households" as the Census Bureau might define them, in a very real sense they are one social system with moving parts that cannot stand alone. The older sisters, Natasha and Latoya, go out to clubs together when they can get Stephanie to baby-sit; together they hatch surprise birthday celebrations for Lizzie. Joining forces with their cousins, aunts, and uncles, they haul turkeys and cranberries up the stairs to whichever apartment can hold the largest number of people when it is time to host the Thanksgiving feast. And when Christmas comes, Latoya's children, sisters, and cousins and Lizzie and Alvin dress up in their Sunday best and lay claim to nearly a whole pew in the Baptist church several blocks away. Lizzie complains that her children don't attend church in the regular way she does, a habit born of her southern origins. But like many American families, Latoya and her sisters honor their mother's attachment to the church and participate in this family ritual.

Latoya, Natasha, Stephanie, and Lizzie have deliberately stayed close to one another not only because they need one another for practical support but because they value family above all else. "Family are your best friends," Natasha explains. Latoya is Natasha's closest friend, the person she socializes with, the person she confides in, her defender at work, the woman she goes shopping with when they want to look their best after hours. Danielle, cousin to them both, is part of the same inner circle, and together with her children they all form a tightly knit extended family.

Indeed, Latoya's three children look upon their aunts, Natasha and Stephanie, as permanent members of their household, people they can depend on to braid their hair

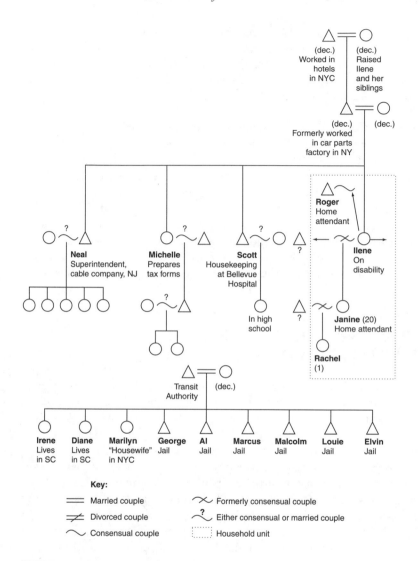

FIGURE 1A

for church, answer the occasional homework question, and bring them home an illicit burger or two. It was rare to find Latoya and her children at home without one of her half sisters as well.

Public perceptions of America center around middle-class nuclear families as the norm, the goal toward which others should be striving. Yet in those suburban households, it would be rare to find the intensity of relations that knits these sisters and cousins together, keeping them in daily contact with one another. Middle-class Americans value autonomy, including autonomous relations between generations and siblings once they reach adulthood. And, of course, if they have a stable hold on a decent income, there is

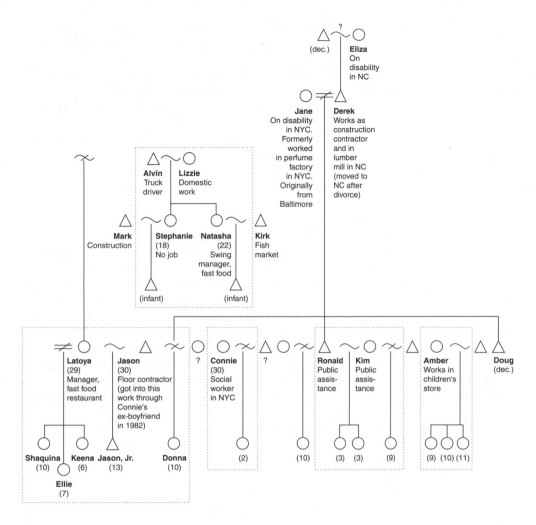

FIGURE 1B

Katherine S. Newman/Catherine Ellis

little forcing them together into the sort of private safety net that Latoya and her relatives maintain.

The same could be said, and then some, for the immigrant families who make up a significant part of Harlem's low-wage workforce. Dominicans, Haitians, Jamaicans, West Africans, and South Americans from various countries have settled in Harlem's outer pockets. Immigrant workers in the low-wage economy depend upon extensive family networks—composed of seasoned migrants who have lived in New York for some time and those newly arrived—to organize their housing, child care, and a pool of income that they can tap when the need arises. Streaming into New York in an age-old pattern of chain migration, immigrants are often faced with the need to support family members back home while they attempt to meet the far higher costs of living they encounter in their adopted city. Families that are ineligible for government benefits routinely provided to the native-born must work long hours, pack a large number of people into small apartments, and recruit as many wage earners into the network as possible.

Immigrants cluster into apartment buildings in much the same fashion as the African-American poor do, both because relatives have been instrumental in helping their family members find housing and because proximity makes it that much easier to organize collective child-minding or communal meals. In Carmen's building there are five households linked together by kinship connections. Their members move freely between them, opening the refrigerator door in one to see whether there's anything good to eat, watching television in another because it has a cable hookup, using the one phone that hasn't been cut off for nonpayment. Carmen's grandmother watches her grandchildren, a half-dozen in all now, so that their parents can go to work.

Yet to really understand the meaning of family in Carmen's life, one has to look back to the Dominican Republic, where her mother and one of her sisters still live. Carmen had to leave her mother behind to join her father and his kin, a transition necessitated both by her ambitions and by the declining purchasing power of her mother's paycheck. Carmen sends back money whenever she can, usually once a month, and that remittance spells the difference between a decent standard of living in *La Republica* and a slide into poverty.[3] For Carmen, though, this is a poor substitute for the intimacy she longs for, the daily love and affection of her mother. What she really wants, more than anything in this world, is to obtain a green card so that she can sponsor her mother and younger sister in New York. Now that she is a young parent herself, she wants her own mother close by so that she does not have to depend exclusively on her paternal relatives. That prospect is far off, though, and Carmen has to be content with the occasional trip back to her homeland, something she manages once every two or three years.

For immigrants, then, the meaning of family stretches over the seas and persists through long absences. It is organized into daisy chains of people who have followed each other, one by one, and then settled into pockets that turn into ethnic enclaves dense with interlocking ties. Families that lived next door to one another in Haiti land on adjacent blocks in Harlem. The same pattern organizes the native migrants from America's rural South, who also put down roots in Harlem neighborhoods. One can still find blocks dominated by people from particular towns in Georgia or the Carolinas and their descendants. In this respect, the native-born and the international migrant share common settlement patterns, which, in turn, provide the social structure that is so vital to the survival of the working poor.

Well-heeled families can buy the services they need to manage the demands of work and family. They can purchase child care, borrow from banks when they need to, pay their bills out of their salaries, and lean on health insurance when a doctor is needed. Affluence loosens the ties that remain tight, even oppressive at times, in poor communities. Yet there is an enduring uneasiness in our culture about the degree of independence generations and members of nuclear families maintain from one another, a sense that something has been lost. We look back with nostalgia at the close-knit family ties that were characteristic of the "immigrant generations" of the past and that still bind together newcomers to our shores, for the same reasons immigrants clung together at the turn of the century.[4]

What we fail to recognize is that many inner-city families, especially the majority who work to support themselves, maintain these close links with one another, preserving a form of social capital that has all but disappeared in many an American suburb.[5] These strong ties are the center of social life for the likes of Latoya and Natasha. It is true that these family values compete with other ambitions: the desire for a nice house and a picket fence in a suburb where graffiti doesn't mar the scenery and mothers needn't worry constantly about street violence. They dream about the prospect of owning a home and garden somewhere far away from Harlem. Yet if that miracle day arrived, they would be faced with a serious dilemma: unless they could afford to take everyone near and dear to them along on the adventure, they would find it very hard to live with the distance such a move would put between them and their relatives.

Why do we assume that family values of this kind are a thing of the past in the ghetto? While the answer lies in part on the emphasis that writers have given to people like Rosa Lee, it is just as much an artifact of the way we confuse kinship structures with the moral culture of family life in the inner city. Very few of the people who work for Burger Barn live in households that resemble the Bill Cosby model. Most are adult children in single-parent households, and some are single parents themselves. Latoya, for example, divorced her first husband when he turned to drugs, and has for a number of years now had a common-law relationship with Jason, the father of her son, the youngest child (at age two) in her household. Jason has lived with Latoya's family most of this time, taking on much of the financial responsibility for Latoya's children, since his earnings as a skilled craftsman are much higher than her Burger Barn wages. Still, their relationship has had its ups and downs; they have broken up and reconciled more than once.

Family patterns of this kind certainly do not sound like suburban America, or at least not the middle-class culture we would like to believe defines mainstream life.[6] The instability of family organization in America's ghettos has been the source of much hand-wringing. There can be little doubt that children born out of wedlock face an uphill battle, as they are more likely to be raised in poverty,[7] and that children of divorce, no matter what segment of society they come from, are similarly disadvantaged.[8]

However, we should not assume that "irregular" household structures suggest a diminished regard for the importance of family life, for the closeness of kin. Even though Latoya anguishes over Jason during their rough spots, she is no less attached to or attentive to her children. She draws the rest of her kin, especially her female kin, closer to her and builds a nest of loving relatives who sustain the familial bond and help her create a stable environment for her children. Latoya's values place family, particularly the well-being of her children, at the top of her priorities. Were we to look at the structure of her household and focus only on the ways it deviates from the nuclear family norm, we would miss what is most important about it: the quality of the relationships inside and the links between them and the web of kin who live in nearby apartments. Without them, it is true, Latoya would have a difficult time sustaining order or protecting her children in the dicey neighborhood where they live. But her story is a success in part because it is a story of a family that has pulled together against considerable adversity.

Patty began her career ten years ago at Burger Barn. She worked fulltime for the entire nine months of her first pregnancy and didn't leave work until the baby was born. She continued working and finished high school even though her second child was on the way. Her attachment to the job, through the thick-and-thin of a failed marriage and a stint on welfare, reflects the values her mother instilled. Patty's mother has worked all her life as a home attendant, first with mothers recently home from the hospital with their new babies in tow and then with homebound elderly. Working as a home aide was something of an upward step in the family, for Patty's maternal grandmother spent her whole life as a housekeeper.

> My grandmother, who just passed [away], was my idol all during the time I was growing up. She bought a house in Queens off scrubbing floors. She bought that house and mortgaged it two or three times, so she had to start all over paying it off. But she did it.

Hence Patty and her sister, who also is in home health care, taking care of AIDS patients, have come from a long line of women who have shouldered the burdens of earning a living and raising their children. None of them would have been able to manage these responsibilities were it not for the fact that each in turn has made the extended family the core of her life. Patty's mother lives on the sixth floor of her building and still has her son, Patty's brother, under her wing. Patty's sister lives just a few blocks away. Their proximity has made a big difference in Patty's life, for with their collective help, she has been able to go to work knowing that there are other adults in her family who can help watch her children.

This web of kinship does not supersede the individual household or substitute collective child-rearing for that of the mother-in-charge. Patty remains the main figure around whom her kids' lives revolve. She is the one who feeds and clothes them, watches over their homework, and puts the Band-Aids on when they skin their knees. She keeps them safe from the pitfalls of the streets that surround her apartment in a Harlem public housing complex. She has gone without things she needs for herself so she could afford air-conditioning and a Nintendo machine, items that sound like luxuries but turn out to be the key—or at least one key—to keeping her kids indoors and safe through the hot summer months. They must have something to play with and somewhere to cool off if she is to leave the teenagers to their own devices while she is working. At least equally important, however, is Patty's reliance upon her siblings and her mother as substitute supervisors of her kids, her adjunct eyes and ears, when she is at work. Without them, she would be faced with some unhappy choices.

While family support is critical for working parents, it is no less important in the lives of working youth. Teenagers at Burger Barn are often on the receiving end of the same kind of care from older relatives or "friends of the family" who are so close they constitute what anthropologists call "fictive kin," honorary aunts and uncles. Shaquena, who began working in a gym for little kids sponsored by a local church when she was just eleven, has had a difficult life. Her mother has been in and out of jail on drug convictions; one of her brothers was convicted of murder. Had her grandmother not been willing to take her in, Shaquena might have joined the thousands of New York City children shuffled into foster care.

As it is, she lives with her grandmother, who has raised her since she was ten years old. And Shaquena isn't the only one in the family who has sheltered under Grandma's wing. The household includes Shaquena's aunt, her aunt's two children, a cousin, two unmarried uncles, and an aunt and uncle who have a child as well. The grandmother has taken in her adult children and grandchildren, so that the household is a three-generation affair, albeit with several missing links (like Shaquena's own mother). Together the generations share the burden of supporting this extended household, relying on a combination of earned income and state aid: SSI for the grandmother, unemployment insurance for one of the aunts, the wages brought in by one of the uncles who works in a police station, the underground earnings of another who washes cars, and Shaquena's Burger Barn salary.

The Harlem neighborhood Shaquena calls home is jam-packed with people—kin and friends—who visit one another, eat together, and borrow from one another when the need arises.

> My aunt . . . lives right across the street from us. She, like last night, my grandmother ran out of sugar. My grandmother called my aunt and my aunt bought her the sugar. The guy down the hall, he real cool with us, he give us stuff, and my grandmother's cool with a lot of elderly on our floor. She will ask her daughter, my aunt, for things before she asks a friend, but she's got friends [to ask]. If I need something, I go right upstairs, because my best friend lives right upstairs. Her grandmother and my grandmother are friends and they keep a kitchen full of food.

Shaquena can depend upon this circle of friends and relatives to take care of her basic needs, so she can reserve her own earnings for the necessities of teenage life. But she is conscious of the dry periods when funds are tight and often uses her savings to buy toothpaste, soap, and little things for the baby in the house or for her godson who lives across the street with her aunt. It is important to her to pull her own weight and to contribute to the collective well-being of her family whenever she knows it's needed.

The practical side of this arrangement is important. Yet so too is the emotional value of having a big family, especially since Shaquena has had such a rocky relationship with her mother. With her grandmother, aunts, uncles, and cousins, she has a secure place in a situation that is as real and important to her as any nuclear family, suburban-style.

"ABSENT" MEN

Popular accounts of the ghetto world often lament the declining presence of men—especially fathers—in the life of the family. Men are in jail in record numbers; they have no interest in marrying the mothers of their children; they "hit" and run. That men cause grief to the women and children who need them is hardly news. As the divorce statistics remind us, this is a sad story repeated in every class. All over America there are children who need fathers but don't have them. We have developed a culture, both in the ghetto and outside it, that assigns to women the responsibility for raising children, leaving men peripheral to the task.

This is not to minimize the difference between a jailed father and a divorced father, a poor father who has never married the mother of his children and a more affluent father who fails to pay child support. There are differences, and they have consequences. Survey research tells us, for example, that single-parent children of never-married mothers are more likely than those of divorced parents to drop out of high school, and that daughters of never-married mothers are more likely than those of divorced parents to become teen mothers—though, it should be added, the differences are not as large as some pundits might claim.[9]

Yet it would be drawing too broad a brush stroke to suggest that men have absented themselves wholesale from the inner city. Uncles, fathers, brothers, sons, boyfriends—and husbands—are very much in evidence in the daily comings-and-goings of working poor families in Harlem. They help to support the households they live in and often provide regular infusions of cash, food, and time to the mothers of their children with whom they do not live.[10] The Bureau of the Census or a sociologist looking at a survey could easily miss the presence of men in Harlem households where they do not officially live, but to which they are nonetheless important as providers. Juan, father of Kyesha's son, is a case in point. He regularly gives part of his paycheck to his mother, who has several younger children and has been on AFDC for as long as he can remember. Juan also gives money to Kyesha to help take care of their son. Little of this check is left by the time he takes care of everyone who depends on him.

> It is a struggle to make ends meet. Like if I plan on buying something that week, then I got to hold back on that. 'Cause we got cable and you got to help out, you know. Or say the lights got to be paid. So I give a hundred dollars this week, fifty the next week. My mother has a bad habit sometimes. She doesn't think reasonably. So sometimes a lot of money has to come out of my pocket—I pay whole bills so I can get that off my back.

When the welfare authorities discovered that Juan was giving his mother money, they moved to take away some of her grant. He countered by finding a couch to sleep on in a friend's apartment so that his mother could report that he no longer lives in her home.

Reynaldo, whose mother is Puerto Rican and father from Ecuador, is a jack-of-all-trades who worked for a brief time at Burger Barn in between various hustles as a nonunion electrician, car repairman, carpenter, and cellular phone dealer for fellow Latinos in his Dominican neighborhood. A tall, stocky young man with a love of baggy pants and gold chains, Rey is a classic entrepreneur. He mixes and matches his job opportunities, picking up anything he can get on the side. For a time he had a job stocking shelves in a drugstore, but during his off-hours he made money fixing up broken-down cars for neighbors and rewiring a vacant apartment for his landlord. Rey works all the hours that are not consumed by school, his girlfriend, and hanging out with his younger brother.

No doubt he is influenced in his own brand of workaholism by the example of his father, Ernie, who taught him much of what he knows about electrical and machine repair. Ernie has never met a mechanical device he couldn't tear down to the foundation and rebuild just like new. Outside on the street curb sit the broken-down Fords, Dodges, and GM cars that await his attention. His auto repair shop is just the sidewalk in front of their apartment building, but everyone in the neighborhood knows that this is a business venue. Ernie is forever walking around with a cloth in his hands, wiping away the grease and oil from an old car he has torn apart and made whole again. The shelves of the family's back room are crammed with blowtorches, pliers, hammers, wrenches, reels of plastic-coated wiring—all the equipment needed to fix the long line of radios and TV sets that friends and friends of friends have left behind for repair.

As if he weren't busy enough, Ernie has a lively sideline as an off-the-books contractor; renovating apartments destined for immigrant families just like his own. Old apartment buildings in the Dominican neighborhoods have bad plumbing, plaster weeping off the walls, tiles missing, caulking cracked and flaking, windows shattered and taped. Landlords claim to have little money for keeping apartments up to code and in any case prefer to use local workers and avoid union labor. Their preferences keep Ernie in work as the apartments turn over. In turn, Ernie has kept Rey at his side and taught him everything he knows so he can turn over some of the work he has no time for, maintaining the opportunity "in the family."

Rey's mother is a student, working toward an Associate in Arts degree that will, she hopes, make it possible for her to work in computer administration someday. Most of her days are spent going to a community college that is a long subway ride from home. Until Mayor Giuliani canceled the policy, her education was subsidized by the city welfare system (in an effort to further the long-term career prospects of women on AFDC). After many years of working in a bra factory, she has come to understand the importance of credentials and is determined to accumulate them so that she can get a good job with decent pay.

Rey's younger brother, now sixteen, has staked his future on the prospect of going to college, for he seems to have the academic gifts. Where Rey coasts through school and sees little purpose in it, his brother would visit me at Columbia University and look eagerly at the college as heaven. He works during the summers and on the weekends for a print shop that is owned by a friend of the family.

In contrast to the households discussed earlier, whose earnings come mainly from the hard work of women, Rey's family relies largely on the income of the menfolk. While his mother has worked odd factory jobs now and again and hopes to find a real job when she finishes her studies, it is the entrepreneurial spirit of the men in the household that keeps the family going. Between them, father and sons earn enough in the (nontaxed) underground economy and the formal (wage-labor) system to keep the family at a lower-working-class standard of living. They have nothing to spare, they cannot do without any of these sources of income, but they are not starving. They can even hope that the youngest child will be able to get through high school and make it into a public college, something that will require heavy doses of financial aid, but is not an unthinkable goal.

It is tempting to look at Rey's family as an inner-city exception, an icon of middle-class virtue. The two-parent family, the loving brothers, and the entrepreneurial energy all add up to an admirable portrait of a stable, supportive circle of kin pulling together. And there is much truth to the view. Yet, Rey's parents are actually divorced. They broke up years ago in order to qualify the household for welfare. Rey's father maintains an official address elsewhere.

If we were to look at an official government census of Rey's household, we would find that the adults within it are classified as out of the labor force. Indeed, it would be deemed a single-parent household supported by the welfare system. Harlem is populated by thousands of families whose official profiles look just like this. Yet there is a steady income stream coming into Rey's home, because most of the adults are indeed working, often in the mostly unregulated economy of small-scale services and self-employment, including home-based seamstresses, food vendors, gypsy cab drivers, and carpenters.[11] Most of this income never sees the tax man.

Much of what has been written about this underground system focuses on the drug world. But for thousands of poor people in New York who cannot afford a unionized plumber or electrician, unlicensed craftsmen and informal service workers (who provide child care or personal services) are more important exemplars of the shadow economy.

Men like Rey and his father provide reasonably priced services and products, making it possible for people who would otherwise have to do without to get their cars fixed, their leaking roofs patched, or their children looked after. Immigrants who lack legal papers find employment in this shadow world, and those who are legal take second jobs in the underground economy.

It has proved extremely hard to estimate the size of this alternative system,[12] but it is so widespread in poor communities that it often rivals the formal economy. The multipurpose shop Rey's father runs from the living room and the street corner is the mainstay of the family's income, and in this they are hardly alone. The thoroughfares of Harlem have, for many years, had an active sidewalk market trade that is largely invisible to the Internal Revenue Service.[13]

Whether we look at employment or "family structure," Rey's household departs from the normative model of the nuclear family. The statistical observer or census-taker might lump this family together with others as dissolved, or as one whose adult members have been out of the labor force for many years. But anyone who is paying closer attention will see that this makes no sense. These people do make up an actively functioning family, and in fact kinship means everything to them. Their values place work and family at the center of their own culture in a form that would be embraced even by conservative forces in American society. And the men of the family are at least as committed to these norms as the women.

Jamal is the only income-earner in his tiny household. His commonlaw wife, Kathy, once received SSA, a government support provided to her because her father died when she was just a child. But once she ran away to live with Jamal, these funds were appropriated by her mother. Nowadays Jamal spends hours on the bus to reach his job sweeping floors and cleaning toilets in a Burger Barn in another borough. In Jamal's opinion, a real man earns a living and supports his family, and he puts his dictum into practice daily in a job that most Americans wouldn't waste their time on. In this, he follows a path, a cultural definition of manhood, that continues to emphasize responsibility to family, responsibility that is sometimes expressed from a distance (as in Juan's case), while other times defined by coresidence (as is true for Ernie or Jamal).

Black men have been blanketed with negative publicity, excoriated as no good, irresponsible, swaggering in their masculinity, trapped in a swamp of "ghetto-related behavior."[14] Is this simply the force of stereotypes at work on a national psyche predisposed to believe the worst? Of course not. There are men in Harlem who have turned their backs on their mothers, wives, girlfriends, and children. Yet while we deplore the damage these males cause, we may overlook people like Jamal or Juan, or fifteen-year-old James, who brings his paycheck home to his parents to help with the rent, or Salvador, who works two jobs so that his wife, Carmen, and daughter will have a roof over their heads. We will not see the contributions that Latoya's common-law husband has made to the support of her children. And if we are to truly understand the role that men play in sustaining family values, we have to credit the existence of these honorable examples, while recognizing that many of their brethren have failed to follow through.

Some of those "failures" are young blacks who have irregular connections to family, who have no real place to live, whose seasonal labor is so poorly paid that there isn't much they can do to provide for their girlfriends even when they are so inclined.[15] Ron's mother died when he was a teenager. He now lives somewhat uneasily on the sufferance of his girlfriend while working at Burger Barn off and on. Since this relationship also is off and on, his living arrangements are precarious.

> You could say I work and pay my rent. I pay for where I stay at with my girl. My girl is my landlord, but nobody knows that. She does want money. I don't like to say this is my own bread, 'cause I don't like to be caught up in that "I'm gonna kick you out." So I always stay in contact with my family. That way, if something happens between me and her, my sister lives in Brooklyn and she always has the door open for me until I make me another power move. My sister's household is secure, but me, I'm on the edge when it comes to financial things. 'Cause if Burger Barn falls off, then I'm off.

Ron is so close to the edge that he cannot do anything more than contribute some of his wages to whatever household he lands in for the time being. People in his situation have nothing left over for anyone else, which is one of the reasons they don't behave like people with commitments. This is no excuse for siring children they can't support, but it does point to the importance of steady, reasonably paid employment in encouraging responsibility, a point William Julius Wilson has brought to national attention in *When Work Disappears*. Men who lack the wherewithal to be good fathers, often aren't.

FAMILY FLAWS

In pointing to the continuous importance of family as a set of values expressed in practice, I do not mean to paint the households of the working poor as indistinguishable from the "mainstream model." Seen through middle-class eyes, there is much to worry about. Parents who work at the bottom of the income pyramid are stressed, tired, and stretched to the limit of their ability to cope. The irregularity of the income they receive, whether from low-wage jobs, undependable partners, or both, subjects families like Latoya's to unpredictable shortages, gnawing insecurities. Welfare reform is blowing like an ill wind through many of these kin networks, and because the working poor and the AFDC recipients are interleaved, policy directives aimed at the latter are derailing many of the former. Lacking vacations, having little left over to pamper themselves with after a long day flipping burgers, and seeing so little advancement ahead of them, Burger Barn workers are often short-tempered at home. Economic pressures cannot descend upon families without showing their effects, especially on young kids.

Kyesha's two-year-old son, Anthony, spends much of his day in front of a television set tuned perpetually to soap operas and game shows. Sesame Street crosses the screen on occasion, but the purpose of the tube is not to educate little Anthony but to entertain his grandmother, stuck at home with him and several children of her own. Grandma Dana is not particularly attentive to Anthony's emotional needs, even though she keeps him fed and safe. He is never left alone, he does not run into the street, and his clothes are clean. But the focus stops there, and Anthony's behavior reflects the absence of sustained adult attention.

When Kyesha comes home, she wants to flop down on her bed and skim through movie star magazines. She lacks the energy to play with an active child.[16] She spends a lot of time figuring out how she is going to get to see her boyfriend and works on Dana in the hope that she will babysit Anthony for yet another evening so she can go out. The little boy is given to wandering into the tiny room they share and sounding off in an attempt to get Kyesha's attention. More often than not, she shoos him away so she can relax. If, like any normal two-year-old, he fails to obey, he is likely to be swatted.

Anthony will not start kindergarten knowing his colors and numbers, or the daily drill of communal "circle time" that is thoroughly familiar to any child who has spent time in a quality day care center. He will head down the road with a lack of basic experience that will weigh heavily when his teachers begin to assess his reading readiness or language fluency. There are consequences to growing up poor in a household of people who are pedaling hard just to stay afloat and have no time or reserve capacity left to provide the kind of enrichment that middle-class families can offer in abundance.

Shaquena has a rich array of people to turn to when she needs help. She has a web of kin and family friends living all around her, people who feed her and give her a place to hang out when all is not well at home. Yet her mother is a drug addict and her family broke up long ago under the strain. Had it not been for her grandmother, she would have found herself in foster care, her mother declared unfit. Hanging out with her girlfriends in the public housing project near her apartment in her younger years, she was known for getting into trouble. Fights, retaliation for insults, conflicts over boys—all have escalated to the point of serious violence. Shaquena's attachment to the work world is impressive because of this unlikely background, but the traces of her upbringing are visible enough in her temper, in the difficulty she has getting along with people at work from time to time. Her family cares about her, but to say that they are just as loving and stable in their irregular configuration as any Bill Cosby family in the suburbs would be pure romanticism.

Latoya and her common-law husband have had an on-again-off-again relationship that has caused her no end of grief. He messes up and she kicks him out. Left behind is his ten-year-old daughter by a previous relationship, not to mention the son they have in common. Latoya dreams of having a house in the suburbs, something she could afford if she could get her man to settle down, for he has a well-paid job as a carpenter, a unionized position that gives him benefits and upward of $15 an hour. Together they could make a break for it, but the instability of their relationship renders this fantasy almost unattainable. Latoya's heart bears the scars of his irresponsibility, and her children miss their dad when he is not around. Latoya's salary from Burger Barn barely stretches to meet the mounting expenses of a family of five, even with Jason's contributions. When they are together, though, their joint income puts them well above the poverty line, straight into the blue-collar working class. Hence family stability and standard of living go hand in hand in Latoya's household: when the family is together, everything looks rosy, and when things fall apart, the struggle is monumental.

Middle-class families have their ups and downs too, of course. Television is a babysitter in many families. Suburban marriages break up, leaving children in serious economic straits, with divorced mothers facing a job market that will not allow them to keep a secure hold on their lives their children are accustomed to.[17] The poor have no lock on the pitfalls of modern family life. Yet the consequences of family instability in poor neighborhoods are clearly more devastating because the whole institutional structure that surrounds folks at the bottom—the schools, the low-wage work place, the overcrowded labor market, the potholed streets, the unsavory crack dealers on the front stoop—creates more vulnerability in families that have to deal with internal troubles. Support is more problematic, more likely to depend upon the resources of relatives and friends who are, in turn, also poor and troubled.

Editor's Note: *Notes for this reading can be found in the original source.*

■READING 35

Anatomy of a Violent Relationship

Neil S. Jacobson and John M. Gottman

BASIC FACTS ABOUT BATTERING: MYTHS VS. REALITIES

During and following the O. J. Simpson trials the media were full of information about domestic violence. One of the few positive outcomes of the O. J. Simpson murder trial was that the public consciousness about domestic violence greatly increased. Unfortunately, this increased consciousness was a double-edged sword, as misinformation competed with facts, and misinformed opinions often substituted for reality.

Domestic violence is a problem of immense proportions. Unfortunately, there is much that is still not understood about the nature of battering, despite the plethora of opinions and speculative theories. In our presentation of basic information about battering, we hope to begin the process of separating fact from fiction and myth from reality.

Myth #1: Both Men and Women Batter

There has been a backlash against the advocacy movement on behalf of battered women, a backlash that says, "Wait a minute! It is not just women who get battered. It is men too." O. J. Simpson referred to himself repeatedly as a battered husband. There are even those who claim that a huge underground movement of battered husbands refuse to tell their stories because they are reluctant to be identified as "wimps."

In support of these claims, some people cite statistics from two national surveys conducted by sociologists Murray Straus, Richard Gelles, and their colleagues.[1] These statistics show that the *frequency* of violent acts is about the same in men and women. However, these statistics do not take into account two aspects of violence that are crucial to understanding battering: the impact of the violence and its function. According to statistics from the national surveys of domestic violence conducted by the New Hampshire Family Violence Research Center[2] as well as research reported by Dr. Dina Vivian and her colleagues at the State University of New York at Stony Brook,[3] male violence does much more damage than female violence: women are much more likely to be injured, much more likely to enter the hospital after being assaulted by their partner, and much more likely to be in need of medical care. Wives are much more likely to be killed by their husbands than the reverse; in fact, women in general are more likely to be killed by their male partners than by all other types of perpetrators combined.[4]

Because men are generally physically stronger than women, and because they are often socialized to use violence as a method of control, it is hard to find women who are even *capable* of battering their husbands. However, battering is not just physical aggression: it is physical aggression with a purpose. The purpose of battering is to control, intimidate, and subjugate one's intimate partner through the use or the threat of physical aggression. Battering often involves injury, and in our sample, it was usually accompanied by fear on the part of the victim. As we shall show more conclusively in chapter 3, fear is the force that provides battering with its power. Injuries help sustain the fear. The vast majority of physical assaults reported in the national surveys were pushes, shoves, and other relatively minor acts of violence. They were not the kinds of battering episodes that typically end up in the criminal justice system.

All indications are that in heterosexual relationships, battering is primarily something that men do to women, rather than the reverse. However, as we will show, there are many battered women who are violent, mostly, but not always, in self-defense. Battered women are living in a culture of violence, and they are part of that culture. Some battered women defend themselves: they hit back, and might even hit or push as often as their husbands do. But they are the ones who are beaten up. On a survey that simply totals the frequency of violent acts, they might look equally violent. But there is no question that in most relationships the man is the batterer, and the woman is the one who is being battered.

Myth #2: All Batterers Are Alike

Although there is still a tendency for professionals to talk about batterers as if they were all alike, there is growing recognition that there are different types of batterers. There are at least two distinguishable types that have practical consequences for battered women, and perhaps more. Each type seems to have its unique characteristics, its own family history, and perhaps different outcomes when punished by the courts or educated by groups for batterers. Based on our findings of a distinction between the Cobras and the Pit Bulls, and the work of Dr. Amy Holtzworth-Munroe and Gregory Stuart,[5] we think a compelling case can be made for at least two subtypes, roughly corresponding to our distinction between the Cobras and the Pit Bulls.

Cobras.   Cobras appear to be criminal types who have engaged in antisocial behavior since adolescence. They are hedonistic and impulsive. They beat their wives and abuse them emotionally, to stop them from interfering with the Cobras' need to get what they want when they want it. Although they may say that they are sorry after a beating, and beg their wives' forgiveness, they are usually not sorry. They feel entitled to whatever they want whenever they want it, and try to get it by whatever means necessary. Some of them are "psychopaths," which means they lack a conscience and are incapable of feeling remorse. In fact, true psychopaths have diminished capacity for experiencing a wide range of emotions and an inability to understand the emotions of others: they lack the ability to sympathize with the plight of others, they do not experience empathy, and even apparent acts of altruism are actually thinly veiled attempts at selfishness. They do not experience soft emotions such as sadness, and rarely experience fear unless it has to do with the perception that something bad is about to happen to *them*.

But not all Cobras are psychopaths. Whether psychopathic or merely antisocial, they are incapable of forming truly intimate relationships with others, and to the extent that they marry, they do so on their terms. Their wives are convenient stepping-stones to gratification: sex, social status, economic benefits, for example. But their commitments are superficial, and their stance in the relationship is a "withdrawing" one. They attempt to keep intimacy to a minimum, and are most likely to be dangerous when their wives attempt to get *more* from them. They do not fear abandonment, but they will not be controlled. Their own family histories are often chaotic, with neither parent providing love or security, and they were often abused themselves as children.

As adults, they can be recognized by their history of antisocial behavior, their high likelihood of drug *and* alcohol abuse, and the severity of their physical and emotional abuse. Their wives fear them, and are often quite depressed. But fear and depression do not completely explain why the women are unlikely to leave the relationship. Nor is it simply that they lack economic and other resources: indeed, Cobras are often economically dependent on their wives. Despite the fact that they are being severely abused, it is often the women rather than the men who continue to fight for the continuance of the relationship. It is these couples where the men exude macabre charisma.

Pit Bulls.   The Pit Bulls are more likely to confine their violence to family members, especially their wives. Their fathers were likely to have battered their mothers, and they have learned that battering is an acceptable way to treat women. But they are not as likely as the Cobras to have criminal records, or to have been delinquent adolescents. Moreover, even though they batter their wives and abuse them emotionally, unlike the Cobras, the Pit Bulls are emotionally dependent on their wives. What they fear most is abandonment. Their fear of abandonment and the desperate need they have *not* to be abandoned produce jealous rages and attempts to deprive their partners of an independent life. They can be jealous to the point of paranoia, imagining that their wives are having affairs based on clues that most of us would find ridiculous.

The Pit Bulls dominate their wives in any way they can, and need control as much as the Cobras do, but for different reasons. The Pit Bulls are motivated by fear of being left, while the Cobras are motivated by a desire to get as much immediate gratification as possible. The Pit Bulls, although somewhat less violent in general than the Cobras, are also capable of severe assault and murder, just as the Cobras are. Although one is safer trying to leave a Pit Bull in the short run, Pit Bulls may actually be more dangerous to leave in the long run. Cobras strike swiftly and with great lethality when they feel threatened, but they are also easily distracted after those initial strikes and move on to other targets. In contrast, Pit Bulls sink their teeth into their targets; once they sink their teeth into you, it is hard to get them to let go!

It is not clear how Cobras and Pit Bulls are apportioned within the battering population. In our sample, 20 percent of the batterers were Cobras. Interestingly, Dr. Robert Hare, an internationally renowned expert on psychopaths, estimates that 20 percent of batterers are psychopaths.[6] This correspondence is provocative. However, our guess is that Cobras constitute a larger percentage of the clinical or criminal population of batterers than the 20 percent found in our study. The Cobras fit the profile of the type of batterer who comes into contact with the criminal justice system much more than the Pit Bulls do. The profile of the Cobra also describes those referred by judges to treatment groups much better than the profile of the Pit Bull.

Myth #3: Battering Is Never Caused by Drugs and Alcohol

Dr. Kenneth E. Leonard reviewed a body of literature in 1993 suggesting a strong relationship between alcohol use and battering.[7] However, there was at that time a great deal of ambiguity about the extent to which drug and alcohol abuse causes men who would otherwise not be batterers to beat their wives. In 1996, Dr. Leonard conducted the most definitive study to date on the role of alcohol in physical aggression by husbands toward wives.[8] In this study of newlyweds, Dr. Leonard reported that alcohol use was one of the strongest indicators that men would be physically aggressive during their first year of marriage. Although the research on drug abuse has been less extensive, it is clear that batterers are a great deal more likely to be drug abusers than are men who do not batter.

None of this research proves that alcohol or drugs "cause" battering. It simply suggests that batterers tend to have drug and alcohol problems. Because of this connection, battered women who haven't given up the dream often see treatment for drugs and alcohol abuse as the ray of hope: "If only he would stop drinking [or shooting up, or snorting coke], everything would be fine." It is easy to understand how it is that battered women develop this belief. Indeed, it may be true that for some batterers, stopping the substance abuse *will* lead to an end to battering.

However, the relationship between substance abuse and battering is an extremely complicated one. First, a substantial portion of batterers are not alcohol or drug abusers. Although battered women married to batterers without drug and alcohol problems would not be inclined to see treatment for substance abuse as relevant, the point is worth making because many people assume that the substance abuse is more connected to battering than it really is. Some batterers use alcohol; some don't. Some batterers abuse illegal substances; others don't.

Second, just because batterers abuse drugs or alcohol doesn't mean that they batter only when they are intoxicated. A battered woman may be just as likely to be beaten when a substance abuser is sober as she is when the batterer is under the influence of these substances.

Third, even when battering episodes typically occur while the batterer is high on drugs, it is not always the intoxication itself that increases the likelihood of battering. The majority of men with drug and alcohol problems do not batter their wives. Alcohol and drug intoxication may lower inhibitions, but they also make for handy rationalizations. Some batterers in our sample got high in order to provide a way of justifying the beating that they had planned before getting high. Many men we talked to attributed their violence to drugs and alcohol: when they did so, it was an attempt to minimize the significance of the battering per se to deny that violence was a problem beyond the other problem of drug abuse, and to distort the cause of the violence, which was the need for control.

Too much focus on drug and alcohol abuse leads us away from the central issue: battering is fundamentally perpetuated by its success in controlling, intimidating, and subjugating the battered woman. The types of men who abuse their partners are also the types of men who abuse drugs and alcohol. Alcohol and drug abuse are part of the lifestyle of the batterer. But it would be a mistake to assume that the drug use causes the violence.

However, it is also true that substance abuse can be one of the causes of violence, and to see it as nothing but an excuse is to oversimplify a complex relationship. We believe that in rejecting alcohol and drug abuse as causal explanations for battering, many theorists in the field of domestic violence have thrown the baby out with the bathwater: in fact, some batterers *do* only batter while intoxicated *because* the state of intoxication transforms them. But these men should not be allowed to use the substance abuse as a justification for the violence. The fact that the batterer was intoxicated should not be grounds for legal exoneration, or a "diminished capacity" defense if the batterer is charged with a battering-related crime. The batterer's accountability should not be affected by whether or not he is sober while battering: a batterer should *always* be held accountable for battering. Nevertheless, any insistence on separating substance abuse from domestic violence results in lost opportunities for combining what we know about stopping substance abuse with what we know about stopping violence.

As things currently stand, the substance abuse and domestic violence experts typically study one or the other but not both. Rarely do experts from the different fields communicate with one another. If leading figures in the field of substance abuse worked together with leaders in the prevention of domestic violence, it might be possible to develop more effective ways of reducing both problems. And it is entirely possible that if men can be successfully treated for substance abuse, some of them *will* stop battering. It is perfectly consistent to hold the position that drug and alcohol abuse can be one of many causes of battering on the one hand, and continue to hold the batterer responsible for the violence on the other hand.

Myth #4: Batterers Can't Control Their Anger

This is a complicated issue, because there is a sense in which all behavior, even behavior that we think of as voluntary, is actually caused by past and current events in our environment. We are all products of our own unique history, and that history helps to explain how we respond in particular situations.

But voluntary behavior involves a choice, and depending on the outcome one seeks, different choices will be made. Battering is usually voluntary. There are some people with temporal lobe epilepsy whose brains literally trigger violent outbursts that bear no relationship to anything that is going on in the environment. There are some batterers (a small minority) whose battering rampages are truly impulsive and uncontrollable, at least in the early stages of each incident. But in the vast majority of cases, battering is a choice in the same sense that all other voluntary actions are. With Cobras, their physiological responses to conflict are consistent with increased concentration and focused attention. Their lowered heart rates during arguments probably function to focus their attention, to maximize the impact of their aggression. We suspect that Cobras are not only in control, but that they use their control over their own physiology to strike more effectively. But even Pit Bulls, who are highly aroused when they strike, still choose to strike.

Psychologist Donald Dutton and others have written of the "dissociation" often associated with violent episodes.[9] Dutton is talking about the type of batterer whom we would classify as a Pit Bull, and provides some anecdotal evidence that some of them experience an altered state of consciousness during battering episodes. In extreme cases they do not even remember the episodes afterward. Although dissociative states are consistent with the interpretation that they are "out of control" when they batter, few of the batterers in our sample described their episodes of violence in a manner that suggested dissociation. They remembered the episodes but either minimized their significance or denied responsibility for them. Occasionally, they would deny that the violence had occurred. Our interpretation of this denial is that these batterers are lying, using another method of extending their control over their battered wives. The relationship between voluntarily lying and dissociation (truly not remembering) remains an unresolved issue, to be determined by future research. But in the vast majority of violent episodes that occurred among our sample, although the batterers may have been behaving impulsively, they were not out of control.

Myth #5: Battering Often Stops on Its Own

We found in our research that while many men decrease their level of violence over time, few of them stop completely. And when they do stop, the emotional abuse usually continues.

This is quite important, because most research considers only physical abuse. But emotional abuse can be at least as effective a method of maintaining control, if the physical violence was once there. Once a batterer has achieved dominance through violence and the threat of more violence, emotional abuse often keeps the battered woman in a state of subjugation without the batterer having to use physical force. Since the violence is used in order to obtain control, it is more convenient for the batterer to restrict himself to emotional abuse. That abuse reminds her that the threat of violence is always present, and this threat is often sufficient to retain control. Any intervention which defines success without taking emotional abuse into account will inflate its effectiveness. In our sample, although many batterers *decreased* the frequency and severity of their violence over time, almost none of them stopped completely *and* also ended the emotional abuse.

Frank stopped being violent for eighteen months, and Jane, his wife, was quite happy about it. If we hadn't also studied emotional abuse, they might have looked like a couple whose problems had been solved. But, if anything, we found that Frank was even more emotionally abusive two years later than he had been initially, despite ceasing the physical violence. He was more insulting, more verbally threatening, drove more recklessly when angry, and humiliated Jane at every opportunity. All of these emotionally abusive acts were extremely hurtful and degrading to her. But they served an additional function: they reminded her of the violence, and the tightrope she had to walk to avoid recurrences of that violence. These reminders were all she needed. Frank maintained his control without having to risk breaking the law. Emotional abuse, as destructive as it is, is not against the law.

Myth #6: Psychotherapy Is a More Effective "Treatment" Than Prison

Our prisons are overcrowded and judges are constantly looking for alternatives to prison when given discretion in sentencing. Because psychotherapy is available for batterers, judges often find some referrals for court-mandated treatment irresistible as alternatives to imprisonment, especially since domestic assault charges are often misdemeanors rather than felonies.

Unfortunately, what appears at first glance to be an enlightened alternative to imprisonment is often a mistake. There is very little evidence that currently existing treatment programs for batterers are effective, and much reason to be concerned that in their present form, they are unlikely to stop the violence and even less likely to end the emotional abuse.[10] Yet people in our culture believe in psychotherapy, and battered women are no exception. Therefore, when their husbands are "sentenced" to psychotherapy they may be lulled into a false sense of security, thus leading them to return home from a shelter falsely convinced that they are now safe.[11]

As a matter of fact, Roy had been to therapy once, and Helen received glowing reports from the anger-management therapist. Roy received sixteen weeks of group therapy, and his therapist wrote the following during an evaluation at the conclusion of these sixteen weeks:

"In my professional opinion, Roy no longer constitutes a danger to his wife, Helen. He has been a model patient. He has accepted responsibility for being a batterer, has shown no inclination to repeat the violence from the past, and even stands a chance of qualifying for work as a therapist himself, working with batterers who have not yet developed the insight that has changed Roy's life."

Naturally, Helen was quite excited to make things work with the new Roy. But Roy's therapist had been conned. And Roy's therapist had inadvertently misled Helen. Less than two months after the group treatment had ended, Roy came at Helen with a knife, nearly killing her.

Violent criminals who assault strangers are seldom offered psychotherapy as an alternative to prison, in contrast to perpetrators of wife battering. What does this tell us about the criminal justice system and how it views "family violence"? Family violence is still regarded as less serious than violence against strangers, even though most women who are murdered are not killed by strangers but by boyfriends, husbands, ex-husbands, and ex-boyfriends.[12] But accountability is a prerequisite to decreased violence. We believe that referrals to psychotherapy, in the absence of legal sanctions, send the wrong message to batterers: they have gotten away with a violent crime with nothing but a slap on the wrist. O. J. Simpson is an excellent example. In 1989, he pleaded "no contest" to the charge of misdemeanor assault, after beating his wife Nicole Brown Simpson on New Year's Eve. He received a small fine and was ordered to seek treatment. The treatment ended up being nothing more than a few sessions, some of which were conducted by telephone. We now know just how ineffective this "punishment" and the treatment that was required of him were.

We have no illusions about the rehabilitative power of prison, but at least prison stops the violence temporarily and gives the battered woman time to make plans. It also sends a powerful message to the batterer.

Consider also the ability of the most violent batterers—like Roy and George, both Cobras—to con judges, police, probation officers, and therapists. The Cobra will figure out what the therapist wants him to say, sound contrite, be counted as a success, and yet all that has been accomplished is that the system has been exploited by the Cobra. We believe that some form of treatment, either education or group therapy, should be offered to all convicted batterers on a voluntary basis, but it should never be mandated and it should never be offered as an alternative to the appropriate legal sanctions. We also believe that after the first offense, domestic assault should automatically be a felony. There is no reason to give up on education and treatment. But there is even less reason to allow batterers to use them as additional methods of control: control of the criminal justice system as well as the partner. The message has to be clear and unambiguous: violent crime will not be tolerated, whether the victim *is* a stranger or a family member.

Myth #7: Women Often Provoke Men into Battering Them

This myth is held by most batterers, many members of the general public, and even by some professionals. But men initiate violence independently of what their wives do or say. One husband came home from work after being criticized by his boss, and as his wife came to greet him at the door, he punched her in the face, knocking her unconscious. Drs. Lenore Walker and Donald Dutton have both described the internal build-up of tension that seems to occur in many batterers, regardless of what the battered woman is doing or saying.[13] Ultimately, this tension leads to an explosion of violent rage.

One of the couples in our sample had been in treatment with a family therapist. The husband and wife both quoted the therapist as saying to the wife: "If you would stop using that language, perhaps he wouldn't get so out of control." The husband wore this therapist's comment as a badge of honor and even referred to her use of profanity as "violence." In his view, she started the violence whenever she swore at him. The therapist appeared to be supporting this view. The wife never felt understood by the therapist, but the outcome of treatment was that she blamed herself for the battering and thought that the solution was "to be a better wife."

Holding the husband accountable for using violence, regardless of what the wife does or says, is a necessary step for the violence to stop, but it is not sufficient. The batterer has to "feel" accountable in order for the violence to stop. Feeling the accountability means that in addition to the batterer being punished, he must feel that his punishment is justified. It is the rare batterer who feels this way, which helps to explain why battering infrequently stops on its own. Instead of holding themselves accountable, batterers minimize the severity of their violent actions, deny that they are responsible for them, and distort them to the point where they become trivial, as George did when he said after beating up Vicky, "I didn't think nothing of it because it wasn't important."

In those rare instances where the husband feels accountable, the violence as well as the emotional abuse might stop. One of the few batterers in our sample to stop the abuse entirely told us from the beginning that, "I never felt right about it. Even while I was doing it. When I was arrested I deserved it. No man has the right to hit a woman unless she's trying to kill him."

Thus, even if the husband's violence *is* a response to remarks made by the wife, it is a mistake to think of these remarks as "provocations." Provocation implies that "she got what she deserved." George believed he was justified in beating Vicky because she had an "attitude" about his being late for dinner. Batterers make choices when they beat their wives. There is no remark or behavior that justifies a violent response unless it is in self-defense.

In our sample, men were rarely if ever defending themselves when they started battering. Nothing a woman says to a man gives him the right to hit her. Therefore, women couldn't possibly precipitate male battering unless they initiated the violence, which they rarely did in our sample. And even if they do initiate physical aggression by pushing their husbands, punching them in the arm out of frustration, or throwing something at them, they haven't provoked a beating. Husbands have a right to defend themselves: when they are punched, they can deflect the blow; when they are pushed, they can hold their wives so that they stop; and when something is thrown at them, they can duck and yell at their wives to stop. None of these physically aggressive behaviors constitute battering. However, they are commonly used by batterers as excuses for battering that would have occurred anyway.

Sam gave Marie a black eye when she shook him in the middle of the night, waking him up. She couldn't sleep because he had been flirting with another woman at a party, and in fact had been dancing with her in a way that was blatantly sexual. He got angry when she woke him up, refused to discuss it with her, and when she hit him with a pillow out of frustration, he punched her in the face.

There is a philosophy of marriage inherent in the view that women provoke men to be violent. It says that the man is the head of the household, the boss. In the old days, being the boss meant having the right to beat and even kill your wife, the way masters had the right to kill their slaves. Now, it means viewing the wife as someone who deserves to be beaten under certain conditions. Wives never deserve to be beaten by their husbands. Battering is a criminal act, and verbal challenges from the wife do not constitute mitigating circumstances.

Harry, one of the husbands in our sample, almost choked his wife Beth to death after she taunted him: "You're probably a fag, just like your father." What she said was wrong, but she didn't deserve to be choked for it. Harry should have been charged with attempted murder.

Myth #8: Women Who Stay in Abusive Relationships Must Be Crazy

This myth actually assumes a fact, namely, that most battered women *do* stay in abusive relationships. In our sample, within two years of their first contact with us, 38 percent of the women had left their husbands. When you consider that about 50 percent of couples divorce over the course of their lives,[14] 38 percent in two years is very high indeed! Many battered women *are* getting out of abusive relationships. Abused women ought not to be blamed for not leaving. In fact, they do leave at high rates. And their leaving is often an act of courage because it means having to cope with enormous fear as well as financial insecurity.

But what about those who haven't left yet? Does this mean that there is something wrong or odd about them? The answer is no. It is much easier to get into an abusive relationship than it is to get out of one.[15] Women are often afraid to leave, and with good reason. Their chances of getting seriously hurt or killed increase dramatically for the first two years after they separate from their husbands.[16] Leaving is risky, and often staying is the lesser of two evils. Tracy Thurman went all the way across the country to escape from her abusive husband. But he tracked her down in rural Connecticut, and came after her with a knife, disabling her for life and almost killing her. Police and neighbors watched the slaughter. Her case was a watershed in the quest of advocates for mandatory arrest laws, laws which require that arrests are made when the police find probable cause for a domestic dispute.

Second, women often can't afford to leave, especially if they have children. They are economically dependent on their husbands, and that economic leverage is part of the control exerted by the batterer. Vicky had to wait a long time after she had decided to leave George until she was financially able. So did Clara, who was a homemaker married to a university professor. He controlled all the finances, and whenever he thought she might be contemplating leaving, he would remind her of his resources to hire the best divorce lawyer in town. He assured her that he would settle for nothing less than full custody of the children, and that she would get nothing. Clara was trapped by economic dependency.

Third, after being subjected to physical and emotional abuse for a period of time, women are systematically stripped of their self-esteem, to the point where they falsely believe that they need their husbands in order to survive, despite the violence. This lowering of self-esteem is often part of a constellation of symptoms that are common to survivors of trauma.

Battered women experience trauma similar to that of soldiers in combat, abused children, and rape victims (many battered women *are* also raped by their husbands). These symptoms include depression, anxiety, a sense of being detached from their bodies and numb to the physical world, nightmares, and flashbacks of violent episodes. The syndrome characterized by these symptoms is "post-traumatic stress disorder" (PTSD).[17]

Many battered women suffer from mild to severe versions of PTSD, and as a result are not functioning well. Their parenting is affected, their problem-solving abilities are impaired, and their ability to plan for the future is disrupted. Given this common experience of trauma, it is amazing that battered women manage to be as resourceful and resilient as they are, especially since their lives and the lives of their children are often at stake. The corrosive and cumulative effects of battering go a long way toward explaining how hard it is to get out of an abusive relationship.

Erin had long ago stopped loving her husband, Jack. But Jack had convinced her that she lacked the ability to survive without him. He was constantly telling her that she was stupid, disorganized, ugly, and needed him around in order to get through the day. After years of public insults, severe beatings, and successful attempts at isolating her from the rest of the world, Erin began to believe him. She stayed.

Another thing that keeps some women in violent relationships is that they are holding on to a dream that they have about what life could be like with these men. They love their husbands and they have developed a sympathy for them and their plight in life. They hope that they can help their men become normal husbands and fathers. These dreams can be powerful and are very hard to give up.

Some Cobras exude an inexplicable type of charisma for their partners. Battered women stay in these relationships because they are quite attached to and love their husbands, not because of the violence, but in spite of it. They are afraid of their husbands and want the violence to stop. But to them, violence is not a sufficient reason to leave the relationship. In fact, the wives of Cobras are often *more* committed to maintaining the relationship than their husbands are, despite the severe beatings.

Although as outsiders, it is hard for us to understand this attachment, it helps to remember that violence is normal in many subcultures within North America. When violence is all around you, it tends to be accepted as a fact of life. As hard as it might be to imagine, many battered women assume that violence is part of marriage. They don't like it. They continue to try to change it. But they don't view it as a reason for getting out. They have accepted the culture of violence.

Cobras seem to choose women who are especially vulnerable to their macabre charisma. They also figure out quite quickly where the woman's particular vulnerabilities lie. George, for example, figured out quite quickly that Vicky had a dream, and he altered his presentation of himself so that it would be in accord with that dream. He also happened to meet Vicky at a unique time in her life: she was vulnerable not just because of her dream, but because her self-esteem was at an all-time low, and her life was in shambles. Vicky is no longer vulnerable to the Georges of the world. She has become streetwise. In fact, she would have probably resisted his "charms" at an earlier time. But George met her when she was uniquely available to join with him in the relationship that was to become her worst nightmare.

Another couple with a similar dynamic was Roy and Helen. They had met in prison, where he was serving time for armed robbery, and she was visiting her boyfriend, who bad been locked up for sexually abusing Helen's daughter. Helen was one of the most severely battered women in our sample. When they first came into contact with us, Roy and Helen were homeless, although she held a job as a hotel receptionist. He had broken her neck and her back on separate occasions, caused eight miscarriages by beating her whenever he got her pregnant (he refused to use birth control), and he had even stabbed her once or twice, "not to kill her, just to scare her." He was an alcoholic and a heroin addict, and refused to enter treatment for either. He also engaged in frequent extramarital affairs. Yet even though she had made it to a shelter on one occasion, she didn't stay because they "tried to talk me into leaving him." As she put it, "I don't want to leave him; I just want him to stop beating me." She loved him and was committed to him not *because of* the violence, but *in spite of* it. What Vicky once told us about George's mother was probably applicable to Helen: "She never knew that there was anything different; where she was brought up, men beat women. They don't know that they deserve better. They don't even know that there is anything better."

A small percentage of the battered women in our study married to Cobras were themselves antisocial before getting involved in their current abusive relationships, just like their husbands. These women were themselves impulsive and often had criminal records going back to childhood. Helen was one of these women. She and Roy hit it off, immediately decided to live together, and soon after that they were married. Their marriage was both volatile and violent.

Some women in our sample expressed a preference for romance "on the edge," unpredictable and potentially both dangerous and adventurous. They would have it no other way. Even though they did not want to be battered, they found their husbands charismatic and attractive, and had no interest in leaving them. Often they stay against their family's advice and the advice of their friends. By their own account, they had no interest in relationships with boring nice guys.

Myth #9: Battered Women Could Stop the Battering by Changing Their Own Behavior

By now, it should be clear that battering cannot be changed through actions on the part of the victim. Battering has little to do with what the women do or don't do, what they say or don't say. It is the batterer's responsibility—and his alone—to stop being abusive. We collected and analyzed data on violent incidents as they unfolded at home, and examined sequences of actions that led up to the violence. We discovered that there were no triggers of the violence on the part of the men, nor were there any switches available for turning it off once it got started.

Countless women from our sample still believed that it was their job to stop the husbands' violence. Helen was a perfect example. She would defend Roy when given the opportunity, usually by blaming herself. "He is a good man who is easily stressed out. I work hard to make it easier for him, but not hard enough. Like when he wants to have sex. I should be there for him more because I know a lot of this has to do with sexual tension. And I like to drink. If there wasn't alcohol around, he probably wouldn't hit me as much."

Because battering has a life of its own, and seems to be unrelated to actions on the part of the woman, couples therapy makes little sense as a first-line treatment. One would not expect couples therapy to stop the violence, since the violence is not about things that the women are doing or saying. Couples therapy has other disadvantages. First, it can increase the risk of violence by forcing couples to deal with conflict on a weekly basis, leaving the batterer in a constant state of readiness to batter. Second, when the couple is seen together, the therapist implies that they are mutually responsible for the violence. This implication is handy for the batterer, since it supports his point of view: "If she would just change her behavior, the violence would stop." The victim ends up being blamed for her own victimization.

Couples therapy can work for couples where there is low-level physical aggression without battering. It might also work in relationships where the husband has demonstrated the ability to stop being abusive for one or two years. But we would never recommend couples therapy as the initial treatment strategy for batterers, even in those instances where psychotherapy of some sort might be appropriate.

Myth #10: There Is One Answer to the Question "Why Do Men Batter Women?"

There are many competing theories among social scientists, legal experts, and advocates about what causes battering. The theories are often pitted against one another as if one is correct and another incorrect. In fact, no one knows what causes battering, and there is in all likelihood no one cause. We are not attempting to answer that question in this book. Instead, we are describing what we have learned about the dynamics of battering by looking intensively at the relationships between batterers and battered women, and we recognize that any complete understanding of battering has to include analyses that are beyond the scope of this book.

Most important, any complete understanding of battering has to take into account the historical, political, and broad socioeconomic conditions that make battering so common. The subordination of women to men throughout the history of our civilization, and the resulting oppression, is pivotal in this analysis. Our culture has been patriarchal as far back as we can trace it. Patriarchy has sanctioned battering historically and continues to operate to perpetuate battering today: the continued oppression of women provides a context that makes efforts to end violence against women difficult if not impossible.

Battering also is intimately related to social class. It is much more common in lower socioeconomic classes than it is in middle and upper classes. Where violence in general is common, so is violence against women. All of the economic forces which operate to perpetuate class differences, racism, and poverty contribute to high rates of battering. The fact that our book is not about these class differences does not mean that they are not important. They are.

Finally, it should be noted that our sample was 90 percent Caucasian. Although the couples in our sample were predominantly working class and lower class, there were few African American, Latino, and Native American couples in our sample. Therefore, we are unable to discuss potentially important cross-cultural differences in battering, and are forced to discuss battering without taking into account possibly unique dynamics among ethnic and sexual (gay and lesbian) minorities. This is a crucial area for future research.

In short, battering occurs within a patriarchal culture, and is made possible because such a culture dominates American society. It is further fueled by poverty, racism, and heterosexism. Our focus is on individual differences within the broader society. Not all men are batterers, despite the culture. Therefore, we think our intensive focus on the dynamics of relationships is one crucial area where understanding is needed. But it is only one of many foci that are necessary for a complete understanding of battering.

Although not all or even most men are batterers, most batterers in heterosexual relationships are men. Batterers come in different shapes and sizes. Drug and alcohol abuse are often important components of violent episodes. However, most batterers do not commit their beatings in a state of uncontrollable rage.

Battering can and often does decrease over time, but it seldom completely stops on its own. Until batterers are consistently punished by the criminal justice system in a way that is commensurate with the crime committed, the rates of domestic violence are likely to remain staggeringly high. Women do not, cannot, and should not be implicated, either directly or indirectly, as contributors to the problem of battering, even when they challenge their husbands verbally or stay in abusive relationships. In fact, there is little women *can* do to change the course of a violent episode, or affect its onset.

However, we have personally witnessed many heroic and resourceful steps taken by battered women that have ultimately freed them from their violent relationships, or in other cases turned the relationships in a positive direction. Even though stopping the abuse is the husband's responsibility, these heroic initiatives taken by women despite dangerous and traumatic circumstances inspired us to write this book.

For now, having laid to rest some common misconceptions about domestic violence, we want to put the dynamics of battering episodes under a microscope.

Editors' Note: *Notes for this reading can be found in the original source.*

Monster Moms: On the Art of Misdirection

Barry Glassner

Another frightening thing about America's children: they have children of their own. Or so politicians and the media would have us believe.

The most talked about pregnant person in the world in early 1996 was a ten-year-old runaway. "With heavy makeup framing her exotic almond-shaped eyes and her long, dark hair piled high, Cindy Garcia looked at least 14," began an Associated Press story. "It wasn't until two weeks ago that the shocking truth came out. Cindy—8½ months pregnant—had innocently handed welfare workers her birth certificate to qualify for food stamps and child support. Cindy, her belly bulging, was only 10."[1]

Throughout a four-day period during which the Texas police hunted for her the media ran stories about how, as Britain's Daily Telegraph put it, "police and doctors are in a race against time," knowing that "with a 10-year-old body, she is going to require a Caesarean section and a lot of medical attention." Talk radio show hosts had a field day with the story as listeners and legislators discoursed on how sick our society has become.[2]

Only grudgingly did the news media eventually take note of the fact, revealed after the girl's capture, that she was actually fourteen and had said as much from the start. Never mind that neighbors had told reporters that Cindy was a pregnant teenager, or that social workers said her reading and math skills were those of a ninth or tenth grader. In the story's brief heyday reporters casually dismissed these observations. "The truth is, she's a 4th-grade dropout. She hasn't been to school for more than a year," the Associated Press had avowed.[3]

As it turns out the girl's name wasn't even Cindy Garcia, it was Adella Quintana. Her mother, Francesca Quintana, had gotten a phony birth certificate for her daughter when she moved from Mexico to Houston to enroll the girl in American schools.[4]

NOW YOU SEE IT, NOW YOU DON'T

The real story here is not about "babies having babies," as commentators put it, but the plight of a mother and her teenage daughter who, like millions of families before them, fled their homeland for what they hoped would be a better life in the United States only to experience a sea of new troubles. In the latter part of the twentieth century, however, this story was scarcely being told. It had been nearly obliterated from American public discourse, partly by intense fear mongering about Spanish-speaking immigrants and partly by what magicians call the art of *misdirection*.

To make an object seem to vanish, a magician directs the audience's attention away from where he hides it. Stories such as the one about Cindy-Adella likewise misdirected, focusing public attention away from real and enduring struggles of women trying to care for their children in an uncaring world.

During the early and mid-1990s teen mothers were portrayed as much more ominous and plentiful than they actually were. Although only about one-third of teen mothers were younger than eighteen, and fewer than one in fifty was fourteen or younger, you would not have known it from the media. An edition of the *Ricki Lake* Show in 1996 titled "I'm Only 13 But I'm Gonna Make a Baby" began with the popular TV talk show personality asking her studio audience, "Is it possible for a thirteen-year-old to be ready to be a mother?" The audience yelled "No-o-o!" as Lake introduced Kassie and Angela, thirteen-year-olds who looked even younger than their age. For close to an hour the two girls had insults and allegations hurled at them by members of the audience, by their own mothers, by Ricki Lake, and by a regretful sixteen-year-old mother of two.[5]

Kassie and Angela proved themselves remarkably composed and articulate. Accused of having no experience raising children, they pointed to skills they had gained from bringing up their younger siblings. Asked who would take care of their babies when they were at school, the girls nominated relatives who could help out and said they knew of schools that provided day care. Told by a member of the audience that her boyfriend would abandon her once the baby arrived, one of the girls calmly replied, "I know he's not going to be around."[6]

All in all they came off as more thoughtful potential parents than some I have known who are twice or three times their age, but no matter. Neither of these girls was actually "gonna make a baby" anytime soon. Kassie's mother let it be known that she had had her daughter injected with a birth control drug that would make her infertile for several months, and Kassie herself blurted out at one point that she knew she wasn't ready yet. Angela, meanwhile, made it clear that she had no intention of getting pregnant, though she did hope to convince her mother to adopt a child whom she would help raise. In other words, Ricki Lake's producers had come up with a pregnant topic but no pregnant thirteen-year-olds.

More high-minded programs also promulgated the fiction of an epidemic of pregnancy among very young teens. In an interview on National Public Radio's "Morning Edition" in 1995 Gary Bauer of the conservative Family Research Council intoned: "It was not many years ago in this country when it was not common for thirteen-year-olds and fourteen-year-olds to be having children out of wedlock. I'm enough of an optimist to believe that we can re-create that kind of a culture." The interviewer, NPR's Bob Edwards, failed to correct this patently misleading statement. Nowhere in the segment did he indicate that it remains extremely uncommon for thirteen- and fourteen-year-olds to have children.[7]

Nor did Edwards note that, until relatively recently, most thirteen- and fourteen-year-olds were *unable* to bear children. Considering the tendency of American journalists to overemphasize studies that show biochemical causes for a range of other social problems, such as hyperactivity in children, depression in adults, and crime in the streets, they have done little to call the public's attention to a fundamental statistic about teen pregnancy. As recently as a century ago the average age for menarche was sixteen or older, whereas today girls typically have their first menstrual period by age thirteen, and some as early as age nine. Some scientists blame high-calorie diets and sedentary lifestyles for the early biological maturity of contemporary girls, but whatever the reason, the implications of early menarche are plain. Only lately have girls been called on by society to wait so long from the onset of sexual maturity before having children.[8]

Reporters, politicians, and social scientists all give intricate explanations for why adolescents get pregnant. But why not account for teen pregnancies the same way we do other pregnancies? As the British sociologists Sally Macintyre and Sarah Cunningham-Burley noted in an essay, "Ignorance about contraception, psychopathology, desire to prove adulthood, lack of family restraint, cultural patterns, desire to obtain welfare benefits, immorality, getting out of school—a host of reasons are given for childbirth in women under 20, while 'maternal instinct' is thought to suffice for those over 20."[9]

AMERICA'S WORST SOCIAL PROBLEM

The causes of teen motherhood *must* be treated as distinct and powerful. Otherwise, it would make no sense to treat teen moms themselves as distinct and powerful—America's "most serious social problem," as Bill Clinton called them in his 1995 State of the Union address. Nor would it have seemed rational when legislators included in the 1996 Federal Welfare law $250 million for states to use to persuade young people to practice premarital abstinence.

In what may well qualify as the most sweeping, bipartisan, multimedia, multidisciplinary scapegoating operation of the late twentieth century, at various times over the past decade prominent liberals including Jesse Jackson, Joycelyn Elders, and Daniel Patrick Moynihan and conservatives such as Dan Quayle and Bill Bennett all accused teen moms of destroying civilization. Journalists, joining the chorus, referred to adolescent motherhood as a "cancer," warned that they "breed criminals faster than society can jail them," and estimated their cost to taxpayers at $21 billion a year. Members of my own profession, social science, had alarming things to say as well. "The lower education levels of mothers who began childbearing as teenagers translates into lower work force productivity and diminished wages, resulting in a weaker, less competitive economy," Stephen Caldas, a policy analyst, wrote in an educational research journal. (Translation: You can thank teen moms for America's declining position in the world economy.)[10]

These claims are absurd on their face. An agglomeration of impoverished young women, whose collective wealth and influence would not add up to that of a single Fortune 100 company, do not have the capacity to destroy America. What these pundits did was to reverse the causal order. Teen pregnancy was largely a response to the nation's educational and economic decline, not the other way around. Girls who attend rotten schools and face rotten job prospects have little incentive to delay sex or practice contraception. In 1994 at least 80 percent of teenage moms were already poor before they became pregnant.[11]

Early motherhood in itself does not condemn a girl to failure and dependency. Journalists put up astounding statistics such as "on average, only 5 percent of teen mothers get college degrees, compared with 47 percent of those who have children at twenty-five or older" (*People*, in an article bleakly title "The Baby Trap"). Yet the difference is attributable almost entirely to preexisting circumstances—particularly poverty and poor educational opportunities and abilities. Studies that compare teen moms with other girls from similar economic and educational backgrounds find only modest differences in education and income between the two populations over the long term. Some experts report that young women tend to become *more* motivated to finish school and find jobs once they have offspring to support. Data indicate too that teen moms are less likely than their peers to engage in other self-destructive behaviors, such as drug abuse, participation in gangs, and suicide. Motherhood can bring about what sociologist Joan Moore of the University of Wisconsin, an expert on delinquent girls, calls "a conversion to conventionality."[12]

The failure of greater public awareness of conventional teenage mothers results in part because studies about them receive relatively little media attention and in part because adults in positions of power actively strive to make their achievements invisible. In 1998 two seventeen-year-old mothers in Kentucky filed suit against their school board after they were denied membership in the National Honor Society. Exemplary students with grade-point averages of 3.9 and 3.7 on a scale of 4.0, the girls were told they did not meet the "character" requirement. The admissions committee announced they did not want the girls to be seen as role models for other students.[13]

Another stereotype of adolescent mothers envisions them as invariably incapable of rearing healthy children. This one too has been conclusively refuted. Researchers document that teenagers having recently cared for younger siblings are sometimes more realistic in their expectations about parenthood than older parents, and more devoted to parenting as a primary endeavor. They tend to have more help than most of the public realizes because as a rule they live with parents or other relatives. At the height of the teen motherhood scare fewer than 22,000 teen moms throughout the entire United States lived without supervision, according to a report from the Congressional Budget Office.[14]

Evidence of adolescent mothers' own competence turns up in a variety of studies but usually goes unnoticed. An ironic case in point is a famous set of experiments conducted by the psychologist René Spitz in the 1940s. Spitz compared two groups of babies, the first housed in a nursery where their mothers cared for them, the other in a foundling home where they were cared for by nurses. The babies tended by their mothers flourished, while those cared for by strangers cried and screamed excessively, became depressed, and lost weight. Within two years more than a third of the second group died, and much has been made of their sad fate by those who advocate the importance of early bonding between mothers and their children. Largely neglected in the debates over Spitz's studies is the fact that the nursery where he observed mothers taking care of their babies was a penal institution for delinquent girls. The mothers of the children who developed normally in Spitz's experiments were adolescent moms.[15]

Over the longer haul and out in the real world children or teenage mothers do appear to fare poorly compared with other children, thereby providing politicians and reporters with the oft-cited finding that 70 percent of men in prison were born to teenage mothers. The implication, however, that their mothers' age when they were born was the single or most important variable that caused them to end up in jail is iffy at best. When the children of teenage mothers are compared to the children of older mothers from similar socioeconomic circumstances there is little difference between the two groups in outcomes such as criminality, substance abuse, or dropping out of school. The age at which a woman gives birth appears to be far less consequential for how her child turns out than are factors such as her level of income and education, and whether she suffered physical and emotional abuse in her own youth.[16]

BEARERS OF ILLEGITIMATE CHILDREN

In addition to all the contemporary evidence contradicting their position, those who would blame teen moms for the nation's social ills confront an awkward historical reality. The teenage birth rate reached its highest level in the 1950s, not the current era. Indeed, between 1991 and 1996 the rate declined by nearly 12 percent.[17]

Demonizers of today's young mothers either ignore such facts, or when they cannot, direct the audience's attention away from them. Jean Bethke Elshtain, a professor of ethics at the University of Chicago and contributing editor of *The New Republic*, began a book review in that magazine with the words "I was a teenage mother." Considering that she would go on to condemn the book under consideration (Kristin Luker's *Dubious Conceptions*) for being too accepting of teen moms, this was a provocative confession on Elshtain's part. Yet Elshtain quickly clarified that she, like most other teen mothers of the 1950s, was *married* when she had her child. The "prevalent concern" of the American public today, Elshtain declared, is "the growing rate of out-of-wedlock births, with all their attendant difficulties." The real problem, Elshtain argued, is "illegitimacy."[18]

It is a measure of how clouded our public discourse has become that *illegitimacy*, having largely disappeared from the lexicon, would make a comeback in an era when nearly one in three children was born to an unwed mother. But what a powerful comeback. The U.S. Senate, following the election of large numbers of conservative Republicans in 1994, seriously considered applying an "illegitimacy ratio" to determine how much money states were eligible to receive in federal block grants. States with high rates of unwed motherhood or abortion would have lost funds. Although the proposal lacked sufficient support from Democrats to succeed, a couple of years later a bonus system did pass Congress. States with the lowest out-of-wedlock birth rates were eligible for $20 million each in 1998. Even liberals joined in the panic mongering about illegitimacy. "I don't think anyone in public life today ought to condone children born out of wedlock . . . even if the family is financially able," Health and Human Services Secretary Donna Shalala told reporters.[19]

Newspaper and magazine columnists called illegitimacy "the smoking gun in a sickening array of pathologies—crime, drug abuse, mental and physical illness, welfare dependency" (Joe Klein in *Newsweek*) and "an unprecedented national catastrophe" (David Broder in the *Washington Post*). Richard Cohen, also of the *Post*, asserted that "before we can have crime control, we need to have birth control" and deemed illegitimacy "a national security issue."[20]

A national security issue? Images come to mind of children of single moms selling state secrets to Saddam Hussein. Again, when pondering the effects of single motherhood it is important to compare apples to apples. Studies that compare single-parent households and two-parent households with similar levels of income, education, and family harmony find few differences in how the children turn out. The great majority of children of single mothers don't become criminals, drug addicts, mentally ill, or security threats. A study that looked at 23,000 adult men found that those raised by single mothers had income and education levels roughly equal to those raised by two parents. Research shows that as a group, children of single moms tend to fare better emotionally and socially than do offspring from high-conflict marriages or from those in which the father is emotionally absent or abusive.[21]

Scare campaigns can become self-fulfilling, producing precisely the negative outcomes that the doomsayers warn about. Exaggerations about the effects of unwed motherhood on children stigmatize those children and provoke teachers and police, among others, to treat them with suspicion. Why do so many children from single-parent families end up behind bars? Partly, studies find, because they are more likely to be arrested than are children from two-parent households who commit similar offenses. Why do children from single-parent families do less well in school? One factor came out in experiments where teachers were shown videotapes and told that particular children came from one-parent families and others from two-parent families. The teachers tended to rate the "illegitimate" children less favorably.[22]

PAY NO ATTENTION TO THE MAN BEHIND THE CURTAIN

Fear mongering about mothers directs attention away from fully half of America's parent population—the fathers. Warnings parallel to those about mothers are nowhere to be found. Rarely do politicians and journalists warn about unwed dads, and seldom does the National Honor Society refuse admission to them. On the contrary, wifeless fathers are practically revered. A headline in *USA Today* in 1997 proclaimed, "Unwed fathers, increasingly unencumbered by social stigma, are raising kids in greater numbers than ever before."[23]

There *was* one noteworthy scare about dads, and political leaders and social scientists issued warnings seemingly as dire as those about monster moms. "The single biggest social problem in our society may be the growing absence of fathers from their children's homes, because it contributes to so many other social problems," President Clinton declared in a speech at the University of Texas in 1995. "Father absence is the engine driving our biggest social problems," echoed David Blankenhorn, author of *Fatherless America*, in an "Eye on America" segment on CBS's "Evening News." "Our national crime problem," he said, "is not driven by young black males. It is driven by boys who are growing up with no fathers." Blankenhorn went so far as to suggest that violence against women is attributable to boys who grow up without dads and become resentful.[24]

A front-page story in the *New York Times* posed the fatherlessness menace no less sweepingly: "Over all, children in homes without fathers are more likely to be poor, to drop out of high school and to end up in foster care or juvenile-justice programs than are those living with their fathers."[25]

But notice the logic here. Unlike mothers, who are deemed deficient on account of what they do or what they believe, dads are judged on whether or not they're around. Men's mere *presence* is apparently adequate to save their children and the nation from ruin.

In truth, the crusade against fatherlessness is but another surreptitious attack on single mothers. Most advocates are too sophisticated to offer sound bites such as that given by Wade Horn, president of the National Fatherhood Initiative, to the *Washington Post*: "Growing up without a father is like being in a car with a drunk driver." However one phrases it, to insist that children are intrinsically better off with fathers regardless of who the fathers are or how they behave is to suggest that no single mother can adequately raise a child. About boys Blakenhorn made this claim explicitly. A mother cannot raise a healthy son on her own, Blankenhorn decreed, because "the best mother in the world can't tell her son what it means to be a man."[26]

Scares about missing dads also impugned lesbian mothers, whose children Blankenhorn disparaged as "radically fatherless," though in fact studies find that kids reared by lesbians have no greater academic, emotional, or behavioral difficulties than other children—aside from those caused by discrimination against homosexuals.[27]

Several bodies of research—mostly missing from media accounts about the fatherlessness menace—reveal the spuriousness of the evidence behind the scare. Literature on divorce shows that the main negative impacts on children are conflicts between the parents before the divorce and loss of the father's income afterward, rather than absence of the father per se. Research on how children fare following divorce also disputes the alleged power of poppa's presence. Studies of children who live with their divorced or separated mothers find, for instance, no improvement in school performance or delinquency when the children's fathers visit more often.[28]

A large national study was conducted by Kaiser Permanente and Children Now of troubled children in *two-parent* families. Asked to whom they turn for help, only 10 percent selected their fathers, while 45 percent chose their mothers, and 26 percent chose their friends.[29]

One category of children, invisible in the brouhaha over fatherlessness, clearly benefits by *not* having their fathers around. Studies of child abuse often focus on mothers, but in fact fathers commit about half of all parental child abuse. In some surveys more than half of divorced women say that their former husbands struck them or their children. Blanket statements about the dangers of fathers' absence conveniently ignore the existence of such men. They overlook the unfortunate fact that, apart from the extra money and "respectability" fathers might provide, many have little they are willing or able to contribute to their children's well-being, and some do considerable harm. If as a group kids from fatherless homes fare less well, this is partly because women have difficulty supporting themselves and their children on what they are paid, and more than half of divorced dads get away with underpayment of child support. Such a result is also attributable to the factor mentioned earlier: the continuing stigma of growing up in a single-parent household, a stigma further reinforced through fear mongering about fatherlessness.[30]

WICKED WITCHES

Of the innumerable myths told about single mothers the most elemental is single status itself. In reality, many are single only temporarily or only in the legal sense. Two out of five women who are unmarried when their first child is born marry before the child's fifth birthday. One in four unwed mothers lives with a man, often with the child's father.[31]

On occasion mothers portrayed as single do not qualify even on temporary or legal grounds. In its coverage of Awilda Lopez, the New York woman who brutally murdered her young daughter, Elisa Izquierdo, the *New York Post* spoke of the man in Lopez's life as her "boyfriend." In fact, Lopez was married. As Richard Goldstein of the *Village Voice* suggested in a critique of the coverage, an intact family might have confused the issue of who was to blame for the horrific treatment of Elisa, especially since the husband apparently participated in the little girl's abuse, and neighbors said he beat and stabbed Lopez, sometimes in front of her children. Yet the *Post* depicted him as a man who would "cook, clean, and take the children out to a nearby playground."[32]

Much of the media framed the Elisa Izquierdo tragedy literally as a fairy tale. *Time*, in a five-page cover story, reported that Elisa, like the princesses in fairy tales, was "born humble" but "had a special enchanted aura" and liked to dance. "And," the article went on, "unlikely as it may seem, there was even a prince in Elisa's life: a real scion of Greece's old royalty named Prince Michael, who was a patron of the little girl's preschool." But in this real-life fairy tale, the story went, neither the prince nor any government agency could rescue the princess from the wicked witch, Elisa's "single" mother. "Some Mothers Are Simply Evil," read a headline in the *New York Post*. "A monster like this should have stopped living long ago," proclaimed a writer for the *New York Daily News*.[33]

Time, in its cover article, relayed police reports from neighbors, of little Elisa pleading, "Mommy, Mommy, please stop! No more! No more!" as Lopez sexually molested her with a toothbrush and a hairbrush. When her screams grew too loud, *Time* said, Lopez turned up the radio.[31]

That these sordid details made their way into the pages of a family newsmagazine that repeatedly decries graphic depictions of depravity in print, on television, and in cyberspace is telling in itself. There must be something terribly compelling about gruesome tales of sadistic moms. Katha Pollitt of *The Nation* captured part of their appeal when she commented that "lurid replays of Awilda Lopez's many acts of sadism, while officially intended to spur outrage, also pander to the readers' sadomasochism." An observation by Bruno Bettelheim in an essay on children's fairy tales also helps to explain the allure of what are essentially fairy tales for adult readers. "The fairy tale suggests how the child may manage the contradictory feelings which would otherwise overwhelm him," Bettelheim wrote. "The fantasy of the wicked stepmother not only preserves the good mother intact, it also prevents having to feel guilty about one's angry thoughts and wishes about her."[35]

Media tales about monster moms serve a parallel purpose for adults. They say that we—or our wives, sisters, daughters, or friends—are good mothers by comparison. They invite us to redirect (more accurately, misdirect) our self-doubts. When we lose our temper or strike out at our children we may secretly worry about our potential for child abuse. But at least we know we could never do the things Awilda Lopez did.

How can we be so certain? Reporters spelled out for us precisely how Lopez differed from us. "Drugs, drugs, drugs—that's all she was interested in," *Time* quoted a neighbor saying of Lopez, and not just any drugs, not the sort that subscribers to *Time* might use. Lopez was "dominated by crack," a drug that, according to the *New York Times*, "can overwhelm one of the strongest forces in nature, the parental instinct." Crack "chemically impairs" mothers, the *Times* quoted one psychologist as saying, to the point where they "can't take responsibility for paying the rent or seeing that there is food on the table for their children."[36]

Infanticidal mothers are routinely depicted by the media as depraved beyond what any of us can imagine about ourselves or our friends and relatives. The year before Awilda Lopez, the media-anointed monster mother was a South Carolinian named Susan Smith, who drowned her two little boys in a lake. She too was portrayed as severely degenerate. She had been having an affair with her boss's son and planned to dump her husband and marry the boyfriend. After her lover wrote her a note saying he wasn't ready for the responsibilities of fatherhood, the story went, she decided to kill her kids. As if all of this weren't perverse enough, she had been having consensual sex with her stepfather, reporters revealed.

It took some doing, though, for the news media to portray Smith as the personification of depravity. They had to invalidate everything they themselves had been saying about her. Throughout the first week after the death of her children the press depicted her as a loving, heroic, small-town mom. They even bought in to Smith's weepy tale about a black man carjacking her kids, a story that should have made reporters wary, considering their embarrassment five years earlier after Charles Stewart, a Boston man, hoodwinked them with exactly the same racist ruse following the murder of his pregnant wife in an insurance scam.[37]

When the truth came out that Susan Smith had strapped her kids in car seats and let the car roll into the lake, reporters recast her faster than you can say "baby-killing bitch" (a neighbor's description quoted the following week in *Newsweek*). All of the glowing descriptions that journalists had been printing about Smith suddenly evaporated. There was no more discussion of her classmates having voted her "friendliest senior" of the class of 1989, or her teachers describing her as "a good kid," or the neighbor who said of Smith and her husband, "I saw the love that they had for these children."[38]

Reporters also had to ignore reports that Smith's stepfather, a six-foot-four, 300-pound man, admitted to sexually abusing Smith ever since she was fifteen, when he allegedly began fondling her breasts and forcing her to rub his genitals. Presumably journalists felt justified in referring to this man's sexual assaults as an "affair" because Smith herself had called them that. Most failed to point out that she had done so when she was neither legally nor psychologically capable of giving consent: Smith had made the statement at age seventeen, during an interview with therapists at a hospital after she had swallowed thirty aspirin in a suicide attempt.[39]

As much as we might like to settle on some fatal character or behavior flaw to explain why a woman killed her children, the truth is seldom so clear-cut. The women's own pathologies are invariably more complex, and other parties usually are involved. Even extreme cases like Awilda Lopez are not as simple as they may seem. To attribute her actions to her crack addiction is to disregard the obvious fact that most crack abusers do *not* kill their kids. Nor do they lose their maternal instincts, as the article in the *Times* suggested. "These women are not monsters. They do not hate their kids, they do not hit their kids any more than their counterparts who do not use crack," Sheigla Murphy and Marsha Rosenbaum of the Institute for Scientific Analysis in San Francisco, who have studied crack-using mothers extensively, report. No one denies that a mother's use of crack injures her children, or that children are ignored or abused when their mothers go on crack binges. But many of the crack users Murphy and Rosenbaum followed took great pride in their children's achievements and worked to steer them away from drugs. During periods when their own drug use got out of hand they placed their children with relatives.[40]

It may have provided a handy way for the American public to differentiate themselves from her, but Awilda Lopez's use of crack defines neither what kind of mother she is nor the cause of Elisa's death. Numerous other parties besides Elisa's mother and her crack dealer—from Lopez's husband to the entire New York City child welfare administration—also were at fault.[41]

THE WOMAN NEXT DOOR

Like the elephant that vanishes behind clouds of smoke on the magician's stage, the larger cast of characters that give rise to child mistreatment are obscured amid melodramatic reporting about evil mothers. The coverage can leave the impression that it is not so much social policies or collective irresponsibility that endanger many children in this country but rather an overabundance of infanticidal women.

Making a fairly small number of women appear massive is an impressive feat of legerdemain, and several features of the media's coverage of child abuse intersect to create the illusion. Coupled with the relentless attention paid to notorious baby killers such as Smith and Lopez, there is an *underplaying* of stories about a much larger and more important group of deficient parents. Michael Shapiro, a professor of journalism at Columbia University, calls these parents "the screwups."

> There have always been parents who kill their children, and there always will be psychotic and evil parents who do. The true story of child welfare—the more than half a million children in the care of the state, the twenty state child welfare agencies across the nation in such disarray that they are under court-ordered supervision, the seeming inability of the state to help the children it feels it must take from their homes—is about "the screwups."

Screwup parents, Shapiro goes on to explain, love their children and neither torture nor murder them. They simply have trouble providing for them in a consistent and competent manner. Critical of journalists' infatuation with infanticidal parents, Shapiro observes, "When the death of a child becomes the context in which all subsequent child welfare stories get reported and written, then all the failing parents become the homicidal parent and all their children are in grave peril."[42]

Local newspapers and TV news programs pick up where the national media leave off in creating the false impression that a large proportion of failing parents are homicidal. Local media run story upon story about deadly mothers who never make it to national infamy. Around the time of the Smith and Lopez chronicles, for example, the New York City media ran hundreds of news stories about a woman named Sherain Bryant, who tortured and beat her four-year-old daughter to death in 1994. A focus of media attention for the following two years, Bryant was finally sentenced to twenty-five years to life in prison.

Following her conviction in 1996 the *New York Daily News* ran an editorial that concluded with a leading question: "She has now been removed. But how many more Bryants are out there?" As if to answer the question, around this same time the *Daily News*—along with most of the rest of the New York City media—relayed hideous particulars about several other local moms as well. Two notable examples are the Brooklyn woman who scratched and burned her seven-year-old daughter while smoking crack cocaine in front of her, and the Queens mother who, despondent after an argument with her husband, shot her two-year-old and six-year-old in the head, killing them both.[43]

The *New York Times* article about the Queens woman includes another common journalistic gambit: implying that behind any door may reside a would-be murderous mom. A neighbor is quoted, saying what neighbors are so often quoted as saying after a woman has killed her child. "She seemed like such a nice lady. She was a friendly person, and she had nice little kids. I'm shocked," the manager of a nearby laundromat says, suggesting ipso facto that other nice, friendly moms might someday slaughter their children too.[44]

Stories that blithely pass along frightening statistics on child abuse likewise promote the mythic impression of a nation teeming with potentially lethal women. Donna Shalala announced in 1996 that the number of children abused and neglected by their parents had doubled during a recent seven-year period, from 1.4 million to 2.8 million, and the number of seriously abused children had quadrupled from about 143,000 to nearly 570,000. She did not specify how much of the abuse was committed by mothers, but since the vast majority of single parents are women (and Shalala emphasized that children of single parents are almost twice as likely to be harmed), she implicitly singled out mothers.[45]

By and large reporters took the numbers at face value and labeled them "alarming," and crusaders for various causes used them to argue for everything from greater spending on welfare programs to a ban on abortion—the latter from the author of an op-ed piece in the *Minneapolis Star Tribune*, who argued that "abortion on demand has had a polluting effect, which is at least partially responsible for the dramatic rise in child abuse and neglect."[46]

Absent from almost all of the coverage was readily available evidence suggesting that rates of child abuse had not increased as drastically as Shalala indicated. For instance, statistics from the National Committee to Prevent Child Abuse showed that the annual number of fatalities resulting from child abuse had increased by only about 200 during the period in question, from 1,014 in 1986 to 1,216 in 1993. If the number of kids seriously abused and neglected quadrupled, as Shalala avows, should not then the number of deaths have increased by a large number as well?[47]

A closer look at Shalala's study reveals that much of what is described as a "skyrocketing" increase in child abuse is really a growth in *expectations* of abuse. According to Douglas Besharov, a former director of the National Center on Child Abuse and Neglect who helped design the study and lately has been on the staff of the American Enterprise Institute, more than half of the additional 1.4 million children were not actually said to be abused or neglected but rather "endangered." That is to say, these children were deemed by social services professionals to be at risk of future harm."[48]

SHE BEATS HER OLD MAN TOO

Another ill-reported set of statistics further buttresses the illusion of an epidemic of savage mothers. Their interest sparked initially by Lorena Bobbitt, who severed her husband's penis in 1993, and by O. J. Simpson, who claimed in 1994 that his murdered wife had battered him, journalists set out to inform the public about the prevalence of "husband abuse."

"It's Far More Widespread Than People Think" read a headline in the *Washington Post* in 1993 in a lengthy story revealing the existence of battered husbands, about whom the mental health community and general public "have been in deep denial," according to the reporter. How common is husband battering? According to a headline in *USA*

Today in 1994, "Husbands Are Battered as Often as Wives." In an article the following year a writer for the *National Review* cited a study showing that "54 per cent of all severe domestic violence is committed by women." In 1996, in one of several columns he has published on this issue, John Leo of *U.S. News & World Report* revealed that "children are now more likely to see mommy hit daddy" than the other way around. Not only that, the whole thing has been covered up by "feminist scholars," according to Dennis Byrne of the *Chicago Sun-Times*. "Researchers have known for years that women are as, if not more, likely to report violently abusing their husbands or partners," Byrne revealed in 1998.[49]

A major source of statistical information behind these stories is research conducted by a colleague of mine, the sociologist Richard Gelles, director of the Family Violence Research Program at the University of Rhode Island. The writers accurately identified Gelles's research as the best available studies, but they wrongly reported the findings. Gelles does not hold that millions of men get beaten by their wives, as a casual reader of newspapers and magazines might be led to believe. On the contrary, he maintains that 100,000 to 200,000 men are battered in the United States—a number that pales in comparison to the 2 million battered women. Supporting Gelles's findings, FBI data show that one in four female murder victims is killed by a husband or boyfriend, compared to just 3 percent of murdered men slain by wives or girlfriends.[50]

By overlooking or downplaying what Gelles considers vital, writers make his assertions seem like evidence of an epidemic of moms beating up dads. "The statement that men and women hit one another in roughly equal numbers is true," Gelles admits. "But it cannot be made in a vacuum without the qualifiers I always include in my writing: number one, women are seriously injured at seven times the rate of men; and number two, women are killed by partners at more than two times the rate of men." When women do kill their husbands, he adds, they are often reacting to years of brutal assaults or to a current attack. In reality, when mommies hit daddies most of the time they don't hurt them very much, but unfortunately the same cannot be said the other way around. As Gelles puts it, "The most brutal, terrorizing, and continuing pattern of harmful intimate violence is carried out primarily by men."[51]

Husband abuse never became a predominant scare on a par with, say, teenage motherhood. Yet the fact that several respectable publications helped to promote it evinces how intense the moral panic over motherhood became in the 1990s. That conservative columnists and talk show hosts continue to promote the scare in the late 1990s—half a decade after Gelles began publicly condemning it as misogynistic—also demonstrates something. Fear mongers do not have to stop performing their hocus-pocus just because their secrets have been revealed.[52]

Editors' Note: *Notes for this reading can be found in the original source.*

Credits

13. Furstenberg, Jr., Frank F. "The Future of Marriage" is from *American Demographics*, Vol. 18, No. 6, pp. 34–40. Copyright © 1996 by Frank F. Furstenberg, Jr. Reprinted by permission of the author.

14. Edin, Kathryn. "Few Good Men: Why Poor Mothers Stay Single" is reprinted with permission from *The American Prospect*, Vol. 11, No. 4, January 3. Copyright © 2000 The American Prospect, P.O. Box 772, Boston, MA 02102–0772. All rights reserved.

15. Schwartz, Pepper. "Peer Marriage: What Does It Take to Create a Truly Egalitarian Relationship?" is from *Family Therapy Networker*, Vol. 18, No. 5, pp. 57–61. This article first appeared in the *Family Therapy Networker* and is copied here with permission.

16. Hackstaff, Karla B. "Divorce Culture: A Quest for Relational Equality in Marriage" is from *Marriage in a Culture of Divorce* by Karla B. Hackstaff. Copyright © 1999 by Temple University Press. Reprinted by permission of Temple University Press.

17. Bernstein, Anne C. "Women in Stepfamilies: The Fairy Godmother, the Wicked Witch, and Cinderella Reconstructed" is from *Women in Context: Toward a Feminist Reconstruction of Psychotherapy* edited by Marcia Pravder Mirkin. Copyright © 1994 by The Guilford Press. Reprinted by permission of The Guilford Press.

18. Hetherington, E. Mavis, Tracy C. Law, and Thomas G. O'Connor. "Divorce: Challenges, Changes, and New Chances" is from *Normal Family Processes* edited by Froma Walsh. Copyright © 1993 by The Guilford Press. Reprinted by permission of The Guilford Press.

19. Cowan, Carolyn P., and Phillip A. Cowan. "Becoming a Parent" is from *When Partners Become Parents* by Carolyn Pape Cowan and Phillip A. Cowan. Copyright © 2000 by Lawrence Erlbaum Associates. Reprinted by permission of Lawrence Erlbaum Associates and the authors.

20. Hertz, Rosanna. "A Typology of Approaches to Child Care: The Centerpiece of Organizing Family Life for Dual-Earner Couples" is from *Journal of Family Issues*, Vol. 18, No. 4, pp. 355–385. Copyright © 1997 by Sage Publications, Inc. Reprinted by permission of Sage Publications, Inc.

21. Ragoné, Helena. "Chasing the Blood Tie: Surrogate Mothers, Adoptive Mothers, and Fathers" is from *Situated Lives* edited by Louise Lamphere, Helena Ragoné, and Patricia Zavella. Copyright © 1997. Reproduced by permission of Taylor & Francis, Inc./Routledge, Inc., http://www.routledge-ny.com.

22. Hernandez, Donald, with David E. Myers. "Revolutions in Children's Lives" is reprinted from *America's Children* by Donald Hernandez. Copyright © 1993 Russell Sage Foundation, New York, New York.

23. Galinsky, Ellen. "What Children Think about Their Working Parents" is from pp. 58–95 from *Ask the Children* by Ellen Galinsky. Copyright © 1999 by Ellen Galinsky. Reprinted by permission of HarperCollins Publishers, Inc.

24. Rubin, Lillian B. "Families on the Fault Line" is from the book *Families on the Fault Line* published by HarperCollins. Copyright © 1994 by Lillian B. Rubin. Permission granted by The Rhoda Weyr Agency, New York.

25. Epstein, Cynthia Fuchs, Carroll Seron, Bonnie Oglensky, and Robert Sauté. "The Family and Part-Time Work" is from *The Part-Time Paradox* edited by Cynthia Fuchs Epstein, Carroll Seron, Bonnie Oglensky, and Robert Sauté. Copyright © 1998. Reproduced by permission of Taylor & Francis, Inc./Routledge, Inc., http://www.routledge-ny.com.

26. Hochschild, Arlie, with Anne Machung. "The Second Shift: Working Parents and the Revolution at Home," originally titled "Joey's Problem: Nancy and Evan Holt," is from *The Second Shift* by Arlie Hochschild and Anne Machung. Copyright © 1989 by Arlie Hochschild. Used by permission of Viking Penguin, a division of Penguin Putnam Inc.